CLIMATE CHANGE LITIGATION IN THE ASIA PACIFIC

This is the first scholarly examination of climate change litigation in the Asia Pacific region. Bringing legal academics and lawyers from the Global South and Global North together, this book provides rich insights into how litigation can galvanize climate action in countries including Pakistan, Indonesia, Malaysia and China. Written in clear and accessible language, the fourteen chapters in this book shed light on the important question of how litigation may unfold as a potential regulatory pathway towards decarbonization in the world's most populous region.

JOLENE LIN is Associate Professor at the Faculty of Law, National University of Singapore and Director of the Asia Pacific Centre for Environmental Law. She has published in leading journals including the American Journal of International Law and the European Yearbook of International Law, and is author of Governing Climate Change: Global Cities and Transnational Lawmaking (2018). She is on the editorial boards of Journal of Environmental Law, Climate Law and the Chinese Journal of Environmental Law.

DOUGLAS A. KYSAR is Deputy Dean and Joseph M. Field '55 Professor of Law at Yale Law School. He publishes in the areas of torts, environmental law, climate change, animal law, products liability, and risk regulation. In addition to his articles and chapters, he is the author of Regulating from Nowhere: Environmental Law and the Search for Objectivity (2010). He has taught climate change law as a visiting professor at the National University of Singapore and the University of Hong Kong.

CLIMATE CHANGE LITIGATION IN THE ASIA PACIFIC

Edited by

JOLENE LIN

National University of Singapore

DOUGLAS A. KYSAR

Yale University

CAMBRIDGE
UNIVERSITY PRESS

CAMBRIDGE
UNIVERSITY PRESS

University Printing House, Cambridge CB2 8BS, United Kingdom

One Liberty Plaza, 20th Floor, New York, NY 10006, USA

477 Williamstown Road, Port Melbourne, VIC 3207, Australia

314–321, 3rd Floor, Plot 3, Splendor Forum, Jasola District Centre, New Delhi – 110025, India

79 Anson Road, #06–04/06, Singapore 079906

Cambridge University Press is part of the University of Cambridge.

It furthers the University's mission by disseminating knowledge in the pursuit of education, learning, and research at the highest international levels of excellence.

www.cambridge.org
Information on this title: www.cambridge.org/9781108478465
DOI: 10.1017/9781108777810

First published 2020

A catalogue record for this publication is available from the British Library.

ISBN 978-1-108-47846-5 Hardback

CONTENTS

FIGURES

TABLES

CONTRIBUTORS

CONRADO M. CORNELIUS is a corporate lawyer and environmental law researcher in Indonesia.

ANITA FOERSTER is Senior Lecturer at Monash University Business School.

JOSHUA ULAN GALPERIN is Visiting Associate Professor of Law at the University of Pittsburgh School of Law.

JACQUES HARTMANN is Reader in Law at the School of Law, University of Dundee.

DANIEL HORNUNG is a JD candidate at Yale Law School.

KETAN JHA is a final-year PhD candidate at Sussex Law School.

DOUGLAS A. KYSAR is Deputy Dean and Joseph M. Field '55 Professor of Law at Yale Law School.

JIANGFENG LI is a JSD candidate at Yale Law School.

JOLENE LIN is Associate Professor at the Faculty of Law, National University of Singapore, and Director of the Asia-Pacific Centre for Environmental Law.

WEI LIU is a postgraduate student at the School of Law, Sichuan University of China.

SHUANG LYU is a postgraduate student at the School of Law, Sichuan University of China.

MILLICENT MCCREATH is a Scientia PhD Scholar at University of New South Wales, Sydney, Australia.

WAQQAS AHMAD MIR is Partner at Axis Law Chambers in Pakistan.

MAIZATUN MUSTAFA is Associate Professor at Ahmad Ibrahim Faculty of Laws, International Islamic University Malaysia.

HARI M. OSOFSKY is Dean of Penn State Law and the Penn State School of International Affairs, and Distinguished Professor of Law, Professor of International Affairs, and Professor of Geography.

HUI PANG is a PhD candidate at University of New South Wales, Sydney, Australia.

JACQUELINE PEEL is Professor at Melbourne Law School.

ANNALISA SAVARESI is Lecturer in Environmental Law at the University of Stirling.

MARGARETHA WEWERINKE-SINGH is Assistant Professor of Public International Law at Leiden University.

ANDRI G. WIBISANA is Vice-Dean and Senior Lecturer in Environmental Law and Economic Analysis of Law at the Faculty of Law, University of Indonesia.

ZHU YAN is Professor of Law at the Law School of Renmin University of China.

YUE ZHAO is Researcher Associate at the School of Law, Sichuan University of China.

FOREWORD

The impacts of climate change will intensify over the course of the twenty-first century. There remains a substantial gap between what governments have promised to do and the actions they have undertaken to date. The Climate Action Tracker predicts a 1.5°C warming by 2035, a 2°C warming by 2053 and a 3.2°C warming by 2100. Climate change is a critical existential issue that threatens all life forms on this planet. It is, therefore, larger than human rights and will require all hands on deck across all sectors.

Courts are sworn to impartiality, justice, protection of human rights and upholding the rule of law. As governments fail to meet their climate targets, people increasingly are turning to courts to referee the adequacy of governments' responses to and inaction regarding climate change. In recent cases, courts have played a significant role by holding governments accountable for their inadequate climate action; mitigating carbon emissions; helping evolve adaptation solutions, including compensation; promoting sustainable development goals; influencing climate policymakers; safeguarding human rights and ensuring sustainable development and climate justice. Judges and courts are no longer bystanders and are being hailed for their judicial stewardship in some countries.

In *Climate Change Litigation in the Asia Pacific*, Jolene Lin and Douglas A. Kysar have initiated a conversation that is long overdue. It is a collection of scholarship that carefully examines the purpose, trends, impact and future of climate change litigation in the Asia Pacific, raising the question of what role litigation and judicial action can play in the world of climate change. This book brings together diverse judicial approaches and ideas from different countries to explore the common judicial theme of climate change litigation across the Asia Pacific, while being aware of their political, social, economic and cultural diversity. The book tries to find a more holistic and sustainable definition for climate change litigation in order to build collegiality of judicial thought across these countries to promote and advance climate change efforts. The various chapters chronicle that judicial approaches in different countries vary according to the constitutional and legal frameworks, responsiveness of the courts and robustness of the civil society. Some countries, therefore, play a more significant role in climate change litigation compared to others. The authors share evolving ideas, approaches and techniques applied in climate change litigation across the Asia Pacific, which is a treasure trove for judges, litigators, climate activists and policymakers. The conversation that *Climate Change Litigation in the Asia Pacific* starts will help cross-fertilize ideas and approaches in various jurisdictions, leading to awareness, dialogue and the possibility of a powerful coalition.

Setting the stage for the current state of climate change litigation, some countries[1] in the Asia Pacific have had a strong historical tradition of dealing with public interest environmental litigation based on their democratic and fundamental rights-based constitutional schemes. These courts have a rich jurisprudence of safeguarding nature, ecosystems, biodiversity and the quality of life of their citizens. These judges have intelligently carved international environmental principles of sustainable development, precautionary principles, environmental impact assessments, public trust doctrines and so forth into their constitutional values of political, economic and social justice, along with fundamental constitutional rights like right to life and dignity. Environmental public interest litigation has not been adversarial but more inquisitorial, informed by a good understanding of environmental science and other life sciences.

In environmental litigation, it is often the case that the polluter largely falls in the local jurisdiction – the courts hold the polluter accountable and impose penalties. The issues are limited to air, water or land pollution. However, climate change brings a totally new set of challenges to litigation in the Global South. Countries that contribute insignificantly toward greenhouse gas (GHG) emissions but suffer at the hands of climate change need to learn to adapt. Adaptation climate change litigation is a new paradigm and very different from mitigation climate change litigation. For instance, countries faced with extreme weather, floods, droughts, erratic monsoon rains, melting of glaciers, siltation of dams, low agricultural productivity, reduction in forest cover, natural migration of adversely affected plant species, damage to coastal areas, natural

[1] South Asian countries like Pakistan, India, Bangladesh and Sri Lanka, and the Philippines in Southeast Asia.

disasters and reduction of freshwater reserves need to deal with issues regarding water, food and energy security. This climatic imbalance strikes hard at the most vulnerable in the society – that is, children, women and the poor. These countries generally have inadequate infrastructure and weak resilience in the face of natural disasters. For this, pro-adaptation climate change litigation primarily focuses on strengthening institutions, in almost all sectors, to increase their resilience and capacity to adapt to climate change. In the *Leghari* case,[2] this was made possible through the collaborative and participatory tool of a commission[3] comprising the main stakeholders, including the government, working together to collaborate and find solutions. The court monitored and regulated the commission. State policies (e.g., agriculture, irrigation, water or energy or infrastructure development) are being challenged before the courts to ensure that they are climate resilient.

Climate Change Litigation in the Asia Pacific can spark an impetus for change, as it starts a dialogue and questions the importance of and need for climate change litigation in the Asia Pacific. This scholarly work regarding climate change litigation can help convert judges into climate judges with a common goal. The book will connect countries on a singular platform of human rights, rule of law and climate justice, overcoming the political, geographical and cultural divide. To enhance climate change litigation, judges need to come together and exchange ideas via helpful forums such as the Asian Judges Network (AJNE) and the Roundtable of Judges on Environment/Climate, regularly organized by the Asian Development Bank (ADB). Social mobilization, public awareness, understanding of climate science and better judicial coordination can go a long way to promote climate change litigation. This book makes a step in the right direction. It is a new beginning and one full of hope.

Syed Mansoor Ali Shah

Judge

Supreme Court of Pakistan
Islamabad
25 October 2019

2 *Asghar Leghari* v. *Federation of Pakistan and Others* (PLD 2018 Lahore 364).
3 Dr. Parvez Hassan, *Resolving Environmental Disputes in Pakistan: The Role of Judicial Commissions* (1st ed., Pakistan Law House 2018).

ABBREVIATIONS

1MDB	1Malaysia Development Berhad
ACCC	Australian Competition and Consumer Commission
ACF	Australian Conservation Foundation
ADB	Asian Development Bank
APEC	Asia-Pacific Economic Cooperation
ASEAN	Association of Southeast Asian Nations
BBC	British Broadcasting Corporation
CCC	Committee on Climate Change
CCL	climate change litigation
CCP/CPC	Chinese Communist Party
CCSBT	Convention on the Conservation of Southern Bluefin Tuna
CDM	Clean Development Mechanism
CEDAW	Convention on the Elimination of All Forms of Discrimination against Women
CER	certified emission reduction
CETA	Canada-EU Trade Agreement
CIEL	Center for International Environmental Law
CJ	chief justice
CJEU	Court of Justice of the European Union
CLS	critical legal studies
CNOOC	China National Offshore Oil Corporation
CO_2	carbon dioxide
CPL	civil procedure law
CRC	Convention on the Rights of the Child
CRPD	Convention on the Rights of Persons with Disabilities
DENR-EMB	Department of Energy and Natural Resources' Environmental Management Bureau
DOE	Department of Environment
ECT	Energy Charter Treaty
ECtHR	European Court of Human Rights
EDO	Environmental Defender Office
EE	energy efficiency
EIA	environmental impact assessment

EIS	environmental impact statement
ENGO	environmental non-governmental organization
EPA	Environmental Protection Agency
EPB	Environmental Protection Bureau
EPI	environmental public interest
EPIL	environmental public interest litigation
EPL	Environmental Protection Law
EPMA	Environmental Protection and Management Act
EQA	Environmental Quality Act 1974
ERF	Emissions Reduction Fund
ESD	ecologically sustainable development
EU	European Union
FYP	Five-Year Plan
GDP	gross domestic product
GHG	greenhouse gas
GLAN	Global Legal Action Network
HRC	Human Rights Council
ICCPR	International Covenant on Civil and Political Rights
ICERD	International Convention on the Elimination of All Forms of Racial Discrimination
ICESCR	International Covenant on Economic, Social and Cultural Rights
ICJ	International Court of Justice
IDR	Indonesian rupiah
IEA	International Energy Agency
IIA	international investment agreement
IMCC	Inter-ministerial Committee on Climate Change
IPCC	Intergovernmental Panel on Climate Change
ISDS	investor-state dispute settlement
ITLOS	International Tribunal for the Law of the Sea
IUCN	International Union of Conservation of Natural Resources
LBT	'Lahore Bachao Tehrik' (Save Lahore Movement)
LDA	Lahore Development Authority
LGBTQ	lesbian, gay, bisexual, transgender and queer or questioning
LHC	Lahore High Court
MEE	Ministry of Ecology and Environment
MEP	Ministry of Environmental Protection
MoEF	Ministry of Environment and Forestry
NAACP	National Association for the Advancement of Colored People
NAFTA	North American Free Trade Agreement
NDC	nationally determined contribution
NDRC	National Development and Reform Commission
NEPA	National Environmental Policy Act

Introduction

DANIEL HORNUNG, DOUGLAS A. KYSAR,
AND JOLENE LIN

Any plausible solution to the world's growing climate crisis will need to take root in the Asia Pacific region. With Asia holding 54 per cent of the world's projected 2050 population[1] and 41 per cent of its projected 2040 energy use,[2] a policy response to climate change that does not include a major role for Asia and does not give voice to the region's governments and citizens would be wholly incapable of achieving the kind of decarbonization that scientists agree is necessary to avert climate catastrophe.

As the urgency and difficulty of achieving adequate progress on climate policy continue to mount, a salient question becomes what role (if any) litigation and judicial action could play. That question has already been debated in several countries – including, for example, in the United States and the United Kingdom,[3] where climate change litigation has spread and has even begun to affect the way policymakers think about climate policy outside of the courts.[4] The idea of climate change litigation, however, has received far less attention in the Asia Pacific region, with perhaps the exception of Australia, where climate change litigation has had a relatively long history.[5]

1 United Nations, 'World Population Prospect Key Findings and Advanced Tables' (UN Population Division, 2017), www.population.un.org/wpp/, accessed 29 August 2019.

2 Linda Capuano, 'International Energy Outlook 2018 for Center for Strategic and International Studies' (US Energy Information Administration, 24 July 2018), 4, www.eia.gov/pressroom/presentations/capuano_07242018.pdf, accessed 29 August 2019.

3 See Douglas A Kysar, 'What Climate Change Can Do about Tort Law' (2010) 41(1) *Environmental Law* 1; Jacqueline Peel and Hari M Osofsky, *Climate Change Litigation: Regulatory Pathways to Cleaner Energy* (Cambridge University Press, 2015).

4 See, e.g., Umair Irfan, 'Exxon Is Lobbying for a Carbon Tax. There Is, Obviously, a Catch' (Vox, 18 October 2018), www.vox.com/2018/10/18/17983866/climate-change-exxon-carbon-tax-lawsuit, accessed 29 August 2019 ('In exchange for a [carbon] tax, [Exxon] wants immunity from all climate lawsuits in the future.').

5 See Chapter 7.

Commentators have correctly identified several legal, social, and institutional variables that, as a general matter, make the role of litigation likely to be less significant in many Asia Pacific jurisdictions versus countries where climate change litigation has already begun to emerge.[6] But the question demands further academic attention in light of the profound stakes at issue. As the Asia Pacific becomes an increasingly important actor in global affairs, as the world becomes increasingly interdependent, and as the climate crisis deepens, *Climate Change Litigation in the Asia Pacific* offers a novel perspective on whether climate litigation has a meaningful future in the Asia Pacific, what such litigation could look like, and the implications it would hold for the future of international climate change law and policy.

Naturally, given the political, economic, social, and cultural diversity of the Asia Pacific region, this book cannot and does not offer readers tidy, uniform answers that comprehensively characterize climate change litigation in the entire region. Rather, the book aims to explore common themes and critical differences within emerging and future climate change litigation. And it aims to do so in countries that, although diverse and divergent in countless ways, are nevertheless geographically proximate and firmly recognized as a coherent group by international institutions like the Asia-Pacific Economic Cooperation, the Asian Development Bank, and the ASEAN Regional Forum. Even for countries in the region that have historically shared little beyond geographic proximity and political affiliation, the impacts of climate change may force a greater collective self-awareness. Distinctive regional impacts of climate change – such as shifts in the Asian monsoon cycle or the particularly pronounced threat of sea-level rise to Asian megacities – will bind Asia Pacific countries together in important ways such that a regional analysis is appropriate, notwithstanding critical differences among them.

I.1 What Is Climate Change Litigation?

Beyond the diversity of the countries in the region, another reason this book cannot offer tidy, uniform answers that comprehensively characterize climate change litigation in the entire region is that scholars differ on what

6 See, e.g., Jolene Lin, 'Litigating Climate Change in Asia' (2014) 4 *Climate Law* 140, 142 ('In many Asian jurisdictions, litigation is not an option. It is prohibitively expensive; cases can get caught up for years in a tangle of bureaucratic channels; there are few, if any, well-trained environmental lawyers who are able and willing to litigate test cases. In some jurisdictions, the judiciary is simply not independent.').

constitutes climate change litigation generally. More specifically, scholars also differ on whether such litigation should be defined or theorized differently in different regions, such as the Global South or the Asia Pacific. As one of us wrote in a recent article with Jacqueline Peel, 'there is a danger that [the] seemingly universal definitions of climate change litigation' that have been put forward to date 'will fail to capture adequately developments occurring outside the Global North'.[7] As a result, this book – which deals with many countries that are part of the Global South – includes chapters that explore several definitions of climate change litigation and does not limit this analysis to previously provided definitions. As a starting point, however, it is useful to understand some of the definitions that scholars have previously put forward, and how the definitions most frequently used in this volume might differ from those definitions.

To begin, Columbia University's Sabin Center for Climate Change Law relies on a definition of 'climate litigation' as 'any piece of federal, state, tribal, or local administrative or judicial litigation in which the ... tribunal decisions directly and expressly raise an issue of fact or law regarding the substance or policy of climate change causes and impacts'.[8] This approach, however, excludes cases that do not explicitly raise an issue of fact or law related to climate change, but involve environmental harms that to some degree can be traced to the impacts of climate change. As a result, Chris Hilson has relied on a broader definition of climate change litigation: 'to count as climate change litigation, cases must be framed as such' and 'this framing may not always appear on the face of the legal judgment itself.'[9] Finally, Jacqueline Peel and Hari M. Osofsky have identified a range of cases that might be considered climate change litigation, beginning with 'core' cases where climate change is 'a central issue in the litigation'.[10] But beyond these cases, according to Peel and Osofsky, climate change litigation also includes 'cases where (1) climate change is raised but as a peripheral issue in the litigation, and (2) lawsuits motivated at least in part by

[7] Jacqueline Peel and Jolene Lin, 'Transnational Climate Litigation: The Contribution of the Global South' (2019) 113(4) *American Journal of International Law* 679–726.

[8] Columbia Law School Sabin Center for Climate Change Law and Arnold & Porter Kaye Scholer LLP, 'US Climate Change Litigation (Climate Change Litigation Databases)' http://climatecasechart.com/us-climate-change-litigation, accessed 29 August 2019.

[9] Chris Hilson, 'Climate Change Litigation in the UK: An Explanatory Approach (or Bringing Grievance Back In)', in Fabrizio Fracchia and Massimo Occhiena (eds), *Climate Change: La Risposta del Diritto* (Editoriale Scientifica 2010).

[10] Jacqueline Peel and Hari M. Osofsky, *Climate Change Litigation: Regulatory Pathways to Cleaner Energy* (Cambridge University Press 2015), 8.

concerns over climate change but brought and decided on other grounds'.[11] Peel and Osofsky also acknowledge that '[a]t the outer limits of the boundaries of climate change litigation lie cases that are not explicitly tied to specific climate change arguments but which have clear implications for climate change mitigation or adaptation'.[12]

While chapter authors in this volume have taken somewhat differing views of what constitutes climate change litigation, many have taken the view that an analysis of climate change litigation should include cases that are outside of what Peel and Osofsky refer to as the 'core' of climate change litigation – litigation that, as Kim Bouwer has written, is 'in the context of climate change, as well as litigation about climate change'.[13] This view has allowed many of our chapter authors to analyse a growing body of case law that would be missed under a narrower definition of climate change litigation, given the lack of 'core' climate change litigation in many Asia Pacific jurisdictions to date. Moreover, this view has allowed many of our chapter authors to begin a conversation about climate change litigation in countries, where such a conversation is only just beginning – a central goal of this book.

I.2 The Conceptual Approach

The question of if and how climate change litigation could develop in the Asia Pacific has been foremost in the minds of many of the contributors to this book since well before the formal work on this book commenced. Motivated by these questions and the limited discussion of them to date, we decided to convene an exceptional group of scholars and practitioners in the fields of environmental, climate change, and international law for a first-of-its-kind conference on climate change litigation in the Asia Pacific. The conference took place in Singapore during June 2018. The Singapore convening – hosted jointly by the Asia-Pacific Centre for Environmental Law at the National University of Singapore (NUS) and Yale Law School (YLS) – featured paper presentations and commentaries by scholars working in Australia, China, Indonesia, Malaysia, Pakistan, the Philippines, Singapore, the United Kingdom, the United States, and Vanuatu.

[11] Peel and Osofsky, *Climate Change Litigation*, 9.

[12] ibid.

[13] Kim Bouwer, 'The Unsexy Future of Climate Change Litigation' (2018) 30(3) *Journal of Environmental Law* 483.

The goals of the conference were multifold. Most obviously, we aimed to generate a significant collection of original research on the vital topic of climate change litigation in the Asia Pacific. By encouraging scholars to think and write about the topic, including in their home countries, and providing a forum for them to share their ideas, we believed even a short conference could spur a conversation about climate change litigation in the region. Second, we hoped to inspire academics in the region to take on the kind of theoretical, normative, and empirical scholarship that provides the standard of excellence for legal academia in many leading jurisdictions around the world. Third, we aimed to assemble a group that was diverse along many dimensions, including seniority in the academic profession. In particular, we aimed to use our convening power to recruit and bolster several promising young scholars and to expose them to more senior scholars who could potentially serve as role models and mentors. Fourth, we hoped to create the beginnings of a transnational network of scholars and practitioners who could continue to engage and collaborate in years to come, with the Asia-Pacific Centre for Environmental Law serving as a hub for their endeavours.

Unsurprisingly, the conference did not lead to a definitive conclusion on whether climate change litigation in the Asia Pacific will or should play a major role in global climate change mitigation. As noted above, a single such answer does not and should not exist across such a diverse region. Yet, the papers that were presented, critiqued, and discussed reinforced our view that there are many questions related to climate change litigation in the Asia Pacific that merit further academic inquiry and debate. Furthermore, we believe the conference succeeded in spurring a serious academic conversation around these issues to a point where the insights of the scholars in attendance needed to be shared beyond the conference itself – which, of course, became the purpose of this book.

In particular, the conference and the papers presented raised a number of questions about climate change litigation in the Asia Pacific that we believe should be explored in more depth. For example, are there particular private or public law avenues to domestic climate change litigation in the Asia Pacific that may offer success in achieving mitigation outcomes? What kind of contributions would climate change litigation in the Asia Pacific make to domestic political organizing efforts surrounding climate change? What is the likelihood of climate change litigation emerging in specific countries throughout the region? How is China different or similar to the rest of the region on these issues? And from a normative standpoint, is climate change litigation in the region something scholars and advocates should actively push for?

These questions, among others, are the focus of this collection. And while we believe this book addresses many questions of importance related to climate change litigation in the Asia Pacific, it does not answer all of them. In particular, we do not take a comprehensive handbook-style approach to climate change litigation in the Asia Pacific, in which each country within the region is given a comprehensive examination of past and potential climate change litigation. The approach we adopt instead is driven by our desire to encourage authors to examine and innovate in the area of climate litigation scholarship. While the literature on climate litigation is well developed in Europe and the United States, it is comparatively sparse in the Asia Pacific. By affording our chapter authors a degree of scholarly autonomy and encouragement, we sought to catalyse an academic discourse that is currently at an embryonic stage. Moreover, given the nascent state of climate change litigation in many of the region's jurisdictions, asking each author to write a section on a predetermined list of elements in each country would have likely yielded empty sections throughout.

Climate Change Litigation in the Asia Pacific instead offers scholarly analyses in four key thematic areas: the theoretical underpinnings and implications of climate change litigation; the use of international law and international tribunals for climate change litigation in the Asia Pacific; case studies of the potential for climate change litigation to take root in several specific Asia Pacific jurisdictions; and an extended focus on the possibility of China, the world's largest greenhouse-gas emitter, to embrace climate change litigation as part of its comprehensive climate change policy.

I.3 Overview of the Book

The book's first of four sections begins with a simple yet important question: what role should judges play in the pronouncement of norms of responsibility regarding the causes and consequences of climate change? In the first chapter, Joshua Galperin and Douglas Kysar show that the answer is complex. After reviewing academic literature on the institutional strengths and weaknesses of courts as environmental lawmakers, Galperin and Kysar argue that most commentators overlook the role of courts as prods or instigators of governmental action. In the context of climate change – an intractable commons dilemma of existential proportions – the authors argue that the judicial capacity to catalyse the hydraulics of governance is of utmost significance.

Through its analysis, this chapter also introduces a thematic question that several of the book's other contributors attempt to tackle: what are the principal purposes and goals of climate change litigation? Some of the potential answers are to vindicate science, to spur public mobilization, to alter behaviour toward regulatory goals, to compensate for loss and damage, and to condemn tortious or wrongful actors.

In the next chapter 'Networked Public Interest Litigation: A Novel Framework for Climate Claims?', Ketan Jha takes a deeper dive into one of those possibilities: litigation as a spur to public mobilization. Drawing on a sophisticated co-constitutive understanding of law and social movements, Jha argues that climate change litigation has led citizens to undertake a significant and unique role in law-making. This, he argues, will be among the great lasting legacies of climate change litigation, not just for climate policy but for citizen engagement and 'cause lawyering' more generally.

The collection then moves in its second section to a more applied analysis of what climate litigation could look like within international fora or by using international law. This section begins with a chapter by Annalisa Savaresi and Jacques Hartmann that analyses the Carbon Majors Petition before the Human Rights Commission of the Philippines. In particular, the chapter considers the role of international human rights law in attributing responsibility for climate change damages. The authors argue that the Petition is far from a mere symbolic gesture and has the potential to engender significant domino effects, including the ultimate provision of compensation to climate victims. Savaresi and Hartmann conclude by addressing how significant issues like causality, retrospectivity, and apportionment – as well as the provision of an adequate remedy – can be addressed in the context of human rights law.

The next chapter, by Margaretha Wewerinke-Singh, analyses the significant international litigation options for a group of countries that have arguably contributed the least to anthropogenic climate change but are suffering its impacts the most: the Pacific Small Island Developing States. The author considers government actions in domestic courts or human rights bodies against fossil fuel companies, regional cooperation between Pacific Island nations, and government action before international human rights bodies against major fossil fuel companies or foreign States.

The third chapter of the section, by Millicent McCreath, analyses whether climate change claims could be brought by states through the binding dispute resolution mechanism of the United Nations Convention on Law of the Sea (UNCLOS). In the absence of such a binding dispute mechanism in the Paris Agreement, the author asks whether UNCLOS could be the best forum for holding underperforming states accountable or whether this approach could have an adverse effect on global mitigation efforts. Her analysis shows that, as a legal matter, the UNCLOS tribunal could be available as a valid forum for adjudicating the contours of state responsibility for climate change, particularly in relation to ocean-specific adverse climate impacts like acidification. Whether such adjudication is politically advisable remains a separate and complicated question, however.

The second section concludes with a chapter by Hui Pang, examining the climate policy effects of investor-state arbitration proceedings. Specifically, Pang examines the case of foreign investors utilizing dispute resolution procedures under international investment agreements in response to state revocation of renewable energy incentives. Pang hypothesizes that deeming revocation of the incentives a breach of obligation by host countries could encourage states to uphold their renewable energy incentive commitments. On the other hand, the author argues, such decisions could also exert a 'policy chill' that discourages states from offering these renewable energy supports in the first place. Through a careful review of existing arbitral tribunal decisions that have examined renewable energy incentive schemes, Pang seeks to present a comprehensive view of the potential impact of investor-state dispute resolution on climate change policy.

The book's third section continues with a more applied analysis of climate change litigation in the Asia Pacific but shifts focus to domestic law and litigation in several key countries. The section's first chapter, by Jacqueline Peel, Hari Osofsky, and Anita Foerster, examines the well-developed climate change case law in Australia and asks what a 'new generation' of climate change litigation might look like for that jurisdiction. Specifically, the authors consider whether conditions in Australia might be ripe for the kind of litigation pioneered in the Netherlands and Pakistan that has sought to hold governments accountable for inadequate ambition in their climate change policies.

In the next chapter 'Climate Change Litigation: A Possibility for Malaysia?', Maizatun Mustafa takes a deeper dive into potential litigation in Malaysia, a country where, to date, there has been no climate change litigation. She identifies the major barriers to Malaysian climate change litigation to include the state of the judiciary, limited access to courts, limited environmental awareness, and limited recognition of environmental rights. As a result, she argues that climate change liability in Malaysia would be best addressed through a nationally consistent, clear regulatory framework, instead of through courts.

The section's third chapter, by Andri Wibisana and Conrado Cornelius, engages in a discussion that is similar to Mustafa's for another Southeast Asian jurisdiction: Indonesia. Unlike Mustafa's analysis, the authors point to existing case law that could pave the way for future climate change litigation: forest and peatland fire cases in Indonesia where courts have held plantation companies liable and ordered the companies to pay damages, including amounts assessed for the emission of greenhouse gases associated with the fires. They argue that these cases may provide a model in Indonesia and elsewhere for how the goals of climate mitigation may be met through tort law – specifically by addressing greenhouse gas emissions as secondary claims under the heading of other, more firmly established nuisance and negligence tort claims.

In the chapter 'From Shehla Zia till Ashar Leghari: Pronouncing Unwritten Rights Is More Complex than a Celebratory Tale', Waqqas Ahmad Mir casts his critical gaze on the landmark case of *Leghari* and evaluates its significance within the broader context of Pakistani constitutional law. His chapter argues that *Leghari* is the result of the Pakistani constitutional courts' growing receptiveness to the adjudication of environmental issues. While this is often lauded as a positive development, Waqqas Ahmad Mir points to the danger that judicial activity can have stultifying effects on the role of the executive in developing, implementing and enforcing environmental laws. As such, while there is good reason to celebrate *Leghari*, there is also a need to be cautious. His chapter also raises questions about the long-term practical value of cases like *Leghari* and environmental public interest litigation more broadly.

The section's final chapter, by Jacqueline Peel and Jolene Lin, seeks to shed light on the potential for climate change litigation in three key Southeast Asian jurisdictions where there has been little case law to date: the Philippines, Malaysia, and Singapore. The authors focus specifically on the relationship between climate change litigation and adaptation planning, using Australia's climate litigation experience as a lens for understanding preconditions for the emergence of adaptation litigation. They explore how the conventional understanding of climate change litigation may need to be refashioned to appropriately capture cases arising in the Global South context. And they highlight likely barriers to climate change litigation in Southeast Asia, including inadequate planning law frameworks, access to justice constraints, corruption, and limitations on judicial capacity, such as caseload backlogs.

The book's final section focuses on China – the country that will arguably play the greatest role in global climate policy over the next several decades. Analysts predict that China's economic growth will outpace that of the OECD's through 2040 by nearly three times.[14] As a result, the US Energy Information Administration projects that China will represent between 35 and 41 per cent of global energy-intensive goods production in 2040.[15] Despite this growth, recent Chinese policy and a shift in the US international climate posture has led some to argue that China has become a global leader in climate policy and diplomacy.[16] What role, if any, will litigation play in China as the nation struggles to contain its emissions while continuing to offer growth and opportunity to its massive population? This section offers three different perspectives from leading Chinese legal scholars.

First, Jiangfeng Li argues that, while China has not to date relied on climate change litigation as a significant part of its climate efforts, the Chinese government is beginning to open the door to climate change litigation. However, Li argues that, moving forward, China should take further steps to overcome the economic, cultural, legal, and historical barriers to climate change litigation. She maintains this is critical because climate change litigation can serve as a driving force in developing the regulatory landscape in China.

In the second chapter of this section, Zhu Yan sees less of a role for the development of climate change litigation in China. He highlights the dominance of criminal over civil, environmental litigation in China. He also emphasizes the importance of the executive – with the judiciary playing only a 'secondary supportive role' – in Chinese environmental policy. And while the chapter discusses the establishment of special environmental resources tribunals within Chinese courts and takes an in-depth look at environmental public interest litigation, the author concludes that neither provides robust tools for environmental policy making in Chinese governance.

14 Asa Johansson et al., 'Looking to 2060: Long-Term Global Growth Prospects' (*OECD Economic Policy Papers*, No. 3, November 2012), 22.

15 Capuano (n 2) 13.

16 See, e.g., Edward Wong, 'China Is a Climate Leader but Still Isn't Doing Enough on Emissions, Report *Says*' (*New York Times*, 19 July 2018), www.nytimes.com/2018/07/19/world/asia/china-climate-change-report.html, accessed 29 August 2019.

Finally, Yue Zhao, Wei Liu, and Shuang Lyu offer an empirical analysis of existing litigation related to climate change. The vast majority of these cases they find to be contract disputes relevant to energy enterprises, leading the authors to conclude that true climate change litigation has not emerged in China due to various legal, administrative, and institutional barriers. The authors hypothesize, however, that climate change litigation may emerge as an important force in Chinese climate policy. Specifically, they foresee increased litigation against sources of traditional air pollutants serving as an indirect channel to achieve the goals of climate change litigation.

Moving beyond the specific chapters, we share the view that our approach – focused on four specific questions or methods of analysis of climate change in the Asia Pacific – presents some of the region's most promising scholars in this area, with a practical opportunity to make a significant contribution to this area of scholarship. We opted for this approach over a broader handbook style approach, given the state of climate change litigation in the region and the nature of our specific project. And we believe that, as a result, the chapter authors have made a scholarly contribution that they and other scholars can build on for years to come. Our hope is that through our conference in Singapore and this book, the scholarly conversation on this topic has taken an important step forward and will only continue to grow and evolve.

That is not to say, however, that the approach we have taken to analysing climate change litigation in the Asia Pacific in this book will be the appropriate methodology in the years and decades to come. We believe that both the case law and the legal academic scholarship in the Asia Pacific will likely develop over the medium term to the point where a more comprehensive and all-encompassing handbook-style examination of climate change litigation in the Asia Pacific will become appropriate and necessary. That future volume would aim to answer additional questions and discuss additional topics beyond this one. For example, it might consider in more depth the future of climate change litigation in South Asia, including India, Pakistan, and Bangladesh. In addition to considering the Australian experience, it might analyse the potential role of climate change litigation in New Zealand. And it might analyse a set of substantive issues that cut across jurisdictions, including a more in-depth discussion of corruption and its impact on law and legal institutions in countries across the region, in addition to a broader discussion of legal issues surrounding emerging low-carbon or carbon sequestration technologies.

NGO	non-governmental organization
NHRI	National Human Rights Institution
NPC	National People's Congress
NSW	New South Wales
NSWLEC	New South Wales Land and Environment Court
NUS	National University of Singapore
OECD	Organization for Economic Cooperation and Development
OHCHR	Office of the High Commissioner of Human Rights
PCC	Punjab Coal Company
PCIJ	Permanent Court of International Justice
PCS	Pollution Control Study
PEPA	Pakistan Environmental Protection Act 1997
PIL	public interest litigation
PRC	People's Republic of China
RE	renewable energy
RMB	Chinese renminbi
SEC	Securities and Exchange Commission
SIDS	Small Island Developing States
SITA	Suppression of Immoral Traffic Act
SME	small- and medium-sized enterprise
SPC	Supreme People's Court
TAN	transnational advocacy network
TCFD	Task Force on Climate-Related Financial Disclosures
UN	United Nations
UNCLOS	United Nations Convention on Law of the Sea
UNCTAD	United Nations Conference on Trade and Development
UNFCCC	United Nations Framework Convention on Climate Change
UPR	Universal Period Review
USD	US dollars
VCAT	Victorian Civil Administrative Tribunal
WAPDA	Water and Power Development Authority
WTO	World Trade Organization
XR	Extinction Rebellion
YLS	Yale Law School

Until such a project is possible, however, we hope this book serves as an important scholarly starting point for the conversation about climate change litigation in the Asia Pacific. And we hope its pages encourage scholars, policymakers, litigators, government regulators, and those interested in climate policy and legal development in Asia to further engage in this important conversation.

This book would not have been possible without the support of many individuals along the way. We would like to express our heartfelt gratitude to Melinda Tan for her meticulous and thoughtful organization of the conference that took place in June 2018; the contributors to this book for their enthusiastic intellectual engagement; Carol Yuen, Vanessa Yung, Eden Teoh, Daniel Ling, and Sean Rafferty Thenadi for their superb research assistance; Joe Ng at Cambridge University Press for his support and helpful guidance for this project; the Asia Pacific Centre for Environmental Law at the National University of Singapore and the Oscar M. Ruebhausen Fund at Yale Law School for financial support; and Justice Syed Mansoor Ali Shah for bestowing us the honour of including his voice in this project through his Foreword.

PART I

Theoretical Underpinnings and Implications of Climate Change Litigation

1

Uncommon Law: Judging in the Anthropocene

JOSHUA ULAN GALPERIN AND DOUGLAS A. KYSAR

In the beginning, there was only common law, and it was good. Man toiled on great expanses of the land, and only rarely did swine wander or did waste and water overrun their banks. When such offenses did befall man's neighbor, the pillars of earthly judgment – pillars with names like nuisance, trespass, and public trust – did work to make the neighbor whole. Then lo, a dark flood of industrialization began to rise. Air darkened, food spoilt, water ran foul. Man's neighbors moved too close, and he toiled no longer in the field but in the factory. Children were sickened, and the most brave of men were bowed. For years, such wickedness burdened mankind. The pillars began to crumble. There was only common law, but it was not good; it did not defend against the mounting flood. The law made by judges was defeated by capital and complexity. But then great men came together to still the tide, to fight back against the rising waters. They erected dikes built from science, administrative management, and public accountability. They commanded that the air and water shall be free of poisons to a most practicable extent. The old pillars were abandoned, and it was good. The new pillars were erected. In the end only legislatures and agencies, statutes and regulations mattered, and it was good.

The preceding origin story of modern environmental law in the United States – written only partly tongue-in-cheek – paints a picture of the country's judges struggling to protect people and the environment from the offenses of growing human density, development, and industrialization.[1] Judge-made law, the story goes, proved insufficient to the task of environmental protection, and thus an age of statutes, agencies, and regulations eventually emerged to more effectively take up the burden.[2]

[1] See, e.g., Robert V. Percival et al., *Environmental Regulation: Law, Science, and Policy* (7th ed., Wolters Kluwer 2013) 63. ("Prior to the explosion of environmental legislation in the 1970s, the common law was the legal system's primary vehicle for responding to environmental problems.")

[2] See, e.g., Percival (n 1) 63 ("After centuries of wrestling with environmental conflicts, the common law now has been supplemented, and in some cases supplanted, by regulatory statues."); Richard A. Epstein, "From Common Law to Environmental Protection: How

Though not without some truth, this origin story of modern environmental law is too simplistic. Careful historical examination reveals that common law courts in the United States displayed far more scientific sophistication, remedial ingenuity, and political sensitivity than they have been given credit for.[3] Indeed, important features of the US environmental regulatory scheme that historically have been most successful at combating air and water pollution actually appeared first in little-remembered but highly significant tort suits.[4]

In addition to being too simplistic, the origin story of US environmental law also carries little rhetorical persuasiveness in an age when legislatures and agencies struggle to address the magnitude of the climate change crisis. Whether or not they are well equipped to address contemporary environmental issues, courts cannot stand aside in the coming decades. The current age is one in which a new origin story is being written. Courts demur from participating in the formation of that new story at their – and our – peril.[5]

Accordingly, this chapter provides a more nuanced review of the role of adjudication – with a special focus on the common law of tort – as a tool for environmental protection. It does so with the express purpose of considering the role of courts and litigation in an altogether unholy age, the Anthropocene.[6] Around the world, governments are grappling with the challenge of addressing climate change – the greatest threat to collective survival that humanity has ever generated. Without radical and rapid transformation in energy, food, transport, manufacturing, and

the Modern Environmental Movement Has Lost Its Way" (2015) 23 *Supreme Court Economic Review* 141, 143 (The author asserted that "most people" believe strong state and federal administrative agencies are necessary for environmental protection, "even though these were not in evidence in the United States until the 1970s."); Kenneth S. Abraham, "The Relation between Civil Liability and Environmental Regulation: An Analytical Overview" (2001–2002) 41(3) *Washburn Law Journal* 379.

3 See Douglas A. Kysar, "The Public Life of Private Law: Tort Law as a Risk Regulation Mechanism" (2018) 9(1) *European Journal of Risk Regulation* 48.

4 See Conor Reynolds, *Independent Together* (forthcoming).

5 See Benjamin Ewing and Douglas A. Kysar, "Prods and Pleas: Limited Government in an Era of Unlimited Harm" (2011) 121(2) *Yale Law Journal* 350.

6 The term "Anthropocene" has both a scientific usage, denoting the proposed geological epoch in which human activity has become a major driving influence of planetary systems as evidenced via technical stratigraphic criteria, and a less formal usage, referring to the perceived dominance over, and threat to, the Earth's climate, oceans, and environments posed by post–Industrial Revolution humanity. For an insightful collection of essays exploring the implications of the term for environmental law and policy, see Louis J. Kotzé, *Environmental Law and Governance for the Anthropocene* (Bloomsbury Publishing 2017).

other major systems supporting human development, the world will soon enough hit greenhouse gas concentration levels in the atmosphere not seen since previous great extinction events, tens of millions of years ago, in which nearly all life on the planet was destroyed. What will be the role of courts in navigating this apocalyptic moment?

This chapter addresses the three most significant themes in the Anglo-American academic literature addressing tort law's role in environmental protection: purpose, effectiveness, and integration with modern statutory and regulatory schemes. It begins with a description of two competing explanations of the fundamental purpose of tort law. Understanding these alternate theories of tort law is helpful for appreciating why a society might retain both a tort and a regulatory system, despite their apparent overlap. The next part considers practical considerations pertaining to the use of tort law to protect the environment. It does so by surveying the academic literature on the effectiveness of the common law as a source of environmental protection.

Although focused on the common law, many of the considerations reviewed also apply when judges are asked to utilize constitutional or public law sources to devise and apply notions of environmental protection. That context includes such examples as the now famous Dutch judicial rulings that the national government of the Netherlands failed its duty of care to its citizens by not taking adequate steps to reduce greenhouse gas emissions,[7] along with the equally expansive ruling by the Lahore High Court Green Bench which found that the government of Pakistan violated constitutional rights to life and dignity through its inadequate implementation of climate change policy.[8] In both private and public law contexts, the juris-generative role of the judge and the institutional capacities of courts are brought into sharp relief when confronted by climate change and other grave environmental concerns.

[7] *Urgenda Foundation* v. *State of the Netherlands* ECLI:NL:RBDHA:2015:7196 C/09/456689 / HA ZA 13-1396 (English translation), affd *State of the Netherlands* v. *Urgenda Foundation* ECLI:NL:GHDHA:2018:2610. For discussion, see Jonathan Verschuuren, "The *State of the Netherlands* v. *Urgenda Foundation*: The Hague Court of Appeal Upholds Judgment Requiring the Netherlands to Further Reduce Its Greenhouse Gas Emissions" (2019) 28(1) *Review of European, Comparative & International Environmental Law Special Issue* 94; Josephine van Zeben, "Establishing a Governmental Duty of Care for Climate Change Mitigation: Will Urgenda Turn the Tide?" (2015) 4(2) *Transnational Environmental Law* 339; Jaap Spier, "There Is No Future without Addressing Climate Change" (2019) 37(2) *Journal of Energy & National Resources Law Special* 181.

[8] *Leghari* v. *Federation of Pakistan* W.P. No. 25501/2015 Orders of September 4, 2015 and September 14, 2015.

Whether shaping common law duties or giving content to abstract constitutional principles, in either case judges are asked to develop norms of responsibility, not merely apply them.

This chapter concludes by reconsidering the task of judging in the age of the Anthropocene. It argues that the judicial role must be seen as part of a complex field of risk regulation in which we must be willing to grasp every available lever in the strive for sustainability. No matter how appealing in the abstract, the construction of judges and courts as merely passive, apolitical implementers of the rule of law has always been contentious.[9] Today that construction has also become dangerous – for the price of judicial passivity in the Anthropocene may literally be extinction. Instead, courts must heed the call of those who are laying out pathways for constructive judicial engagement.[10]

It bears stressing that the account presented in this chapter is relevant to legal systems in the Asia Pacific and elsewhere. Whether courts act in a private or public law guise, or in a common or civil law context, the experience of the US courts before and during the emergence of modern environmental law is likely to be instructive. As noted above, many of the institutional strengths and weaknesses of courts identified in the academic literature on environmental protection generalize beyond the common law tort context. Likewise, the argument that courts and judges have a significant role to play within a complex assemblage of risk-regulation institutions in the age of the Anthropocene is not one that is limited to the common law of tort. The gap between "is" and "ought" in the climate change realm is so profound that no potential source of normative authority can be ignored in the search for sustainability.

1.1 Two Philosophical Views of Tort Law

To evaluate the role of tort law as a tool for environmental protection, it is important to consider the underlying purpose of tort. Unfortunately, there is little academic agreement on this point, and debate endures about whether tort fundamentally serves an end aimed at private justice or public policy.[11] Proponents of the latter view assert that tort is

[9] See, e.g., Duncan Kennedy, "The Structure of Blackstone's Commentaries" (1979) 28 *Buffalo Law Review* 209.

[10] See Jaap Spier, "The Oslo Principles and the Enterprises Principles: Legal Strategies to Come to Grips with Climate Change" (2017) 8(2) *Journal of European Tort Law* 218, 218ff.

[11] Christopher H. Schroeder, "Lost in Translation: What Environmental Regulation Does That Tort Cannot Duplicate" (2002) 41(3) *Washburn Law Journal* 583, 587 ("The

a public-ordering mechanism in which private conflict resolutions aggregate into economic signals that help actors manage their risk taking.[12] In contrast to this public instrumentalist approach is a private law, justice-oriented view, which holds that tort law creates and protects private rights and duties, assuring that when actors wrongfully cause harm, they also are required to atone or answer for that harm.[13]

Whether described as law and economics, a deterrence scheme, or judicial risk regulation, the public-policy approach to tort law has dominated over the past half century within US legal academic scholarship.[14] This view centers on the idea that the common law should "prevent those harms whose costs of precaution are less than the anticipated cost of the harm."[15] This view imbues the common law with an "economic meaning,"[16] in which tort law arranges rights, duties, and remedies in a way that optimizes societies' limited resources.[17] Although conflicts between private actors trigger common law analysis, when courts resolve those conflicts by contemplating a resolution's effects on widespread social welfare, they imply a purpose that goes beyond private conflict resolution into the realm of public policy. The nature of that policy remains somewhat abstract. Unlike environmental statutes, which are, by and large, normatively committed to environmental protection, the public-policy view of torts is ostensibly neutral, striving for welfare maximization without

objectives of tort are the subject of a long-running debate that shows no signs of resolving itself any time soon."); Peter Cane, "Using Tort Law to Enforce Environmental Regulation?" (2002) 41(3) *Washburn Law Journal* 427, 428, 430; Daniel A. Farber, "The Story of *Boomer*: Pollution and the Common Law" in Richard J. Lazarus and Oliver A. Hauk (eds.), *Environmental Law Stories* (Foundation Press 2005) 37; Abraham (n 2) 387.

12 Guido Calabresi, *The Costs of Accidents: A Legal and Economic Analysis* (Yale University Press 1970); Keith N. Hylton, "The Economic Theory of Nuisance Law and Implications for Environmental Regulation" (2008) 58(3) *Case Western Reserve Law Review* 673.

13 Cane (n 11) 429.

14 See Adam D. K. Abelkop, "Tort Law as an Environmental Policy Instrument" (2014) 92 (2) *Oregon Law Review* 382, 392 ("The dominant position, however, seems to be the instrumentalist view, which emphasizes the general deterrent effects of liability as a public law.") See also Guido Calebresi and A. Douglas Melamed, "Property Rules, Liability Rules, and Inalienability: One View of the Cathedral" (1972) 85(6) *Harvard Law Review* 1089; Steven Shavell, "Liability for Harm Versus Regulation of Safety" (1984) 13 *Journal of Legal Studies* 357; Keith N. Hylton, "The Economics of Public Nuisance Law and the New Enforcement Actions" (2010) 18 *Supreme Court Economic Review* 43.

15 Schroeder (n 11) 583, 587.

16 Richard A. Posner, "A Theory of Negligence" (1972) 1(1) *Journal of Legal Studies* 29, 32.

17 Calebresi and Melamed (n 14) 1096–1097; Farber, *The Story of Boomer* (n 11) 37.

any special regard for or commitment to reducing environmental harms.[18]

The instrumentalist view is a modern idea that took shape in parallel to the proliferation of statutory environmental law.[19] In hindsight, by describing tort as an implicit form of regulation, the instrumentalist reinvention might be seen as a response to criticisms of statutory environmental law as inappropriate or over-burdensome government interference.[20] In the late 1960s and early 1970s, a clear public consensus may have held that the government needed to address environmental problems,[21] but that consensus evaporated as environmentalism came to be seen as a politically partisan issue in the United States. For those scholars who see the proliferation of statues and administrative regulation as unnecessarily blunt and overreaching tools, it is understandable that they might prefer reliance on tort as a bureaucratically leaner and superficially neutral public policy instrument.[22] In this model, tort regards environmental harms not as inherently wrong but as natural consequences of industrialized life that should be discouraged only when their benefits fail to outweigh their costs.

The instrumentalist perspective is a fundamental departure from the view of tort that predates the age of environmental statues and the rise of law and economics. The more traditional view of tort is one that centers on tort as a private law system of justice aimed at rectifying one person's injuries when those injuries result from the fault of another, even if providing justice to the injured individual has no direct bearing on broader public policy.[23] Tort, according to this thinking, is comfortable identifying a wrongdoer and a victim based on societal norms rather than

[18] See, e.g., Richard A. Epstein, "Too Pragmatic by Half" (2000) 109(7) *Yale Law Journal* 1639, 1643, which argued that that statutory law is a form of special pleading for the environment because statutes explicitly elevate environmental protection over competing societal interests while the common law is neutral, as among various social values.

[19] See, e.g., Calabresi (n 12), which may have given birth to this way of thinking. The book was published in 1970, the same year that the Clean Air Act (42 US Code § 7401 [2017]) and the National Environmental Policy Act (42 U.S.C. § 4321 et seq. [2017]) took effect. Posner's article (n 16) was published in 1972, the same year as the Clean Water Act (33 US Code §§ 1251–1387 [2017]).

[20] James L. Huffman, "The Past and Future of Environmental Law" (2000) 30(1) *Environmental Law* 23, 28–30.

[21] Daniel A. Farber, *Eco-pragmatism: Making Sensible Environmental Decisions in an Uncertain World* (University of Chicago Press 1999).

[22] Richard Epstein, however, reminds us an expectation of tort as neutral only arose with the law and economics model of tort. See Epstein, *Too Pragmatic by Half* (n 18) 1649.

[23] Schroeder (n 11) 583, 587.

on economic costs and benefits.[24] Tort is therefore "a responsibility based mechanism for repairing harm."[25]

On this account, "repair" is achieved primarily through compensation,[26] although injunctive relief also may be available in appropriate circumstances. For scholars who view tort through the lens of corrective justice, the payment of damages for harm aims to make the plaintiff whole or to return the plaintiff to the same place she would have been had the harm never occurred. Recognizing that restoration in the context of harm to life and limb is not perfectly achievable through monetary payment, "civil recourse" scholars argue that the goal of the tort system is not corrective justice but "satisfaction."[27] That is, the tort system offers an official stage upon which parties may demand an accounting from their wrongdoers and a restoration of the equal dignity that each holds before the law and their shared community. The judgment awarded does not annul or erase the harm caused, as corrective justice proponents would have it, but it does serve to restore a status of equal standing within the political body.[28]

As with private law approaches, compensation is also central to the public policy model of tort law, but in the public model, compensation's perceived significance comes from the possibility that court-mandated compensation will serve as a deterrent to wrongful risk taking in the future. With compensation at the center of both perspectives, the primary element that distinguishes a corrective justice or civil recourse frame of tort from a public policy frame is the concept of *duty*. By asking courts to focus their analysis on individual "rights and obligations . . ., the function of tort law is to protect rights and to enforce obligations."[29] While deterrence and other consequences relevant to public policy may occur as a *secondary* effect of tort law, the corrective justice and civil recourse views hold that tort is first and foremost a "mechanism for imposing obligations of repair on the basis of ideas of personal responsibility."[30]

Despite their vast theoretical differences, the public policy and the private law views of tort share a common feature that is of significance to

24 Epstein (n 18) 1649.
25 Cane (n 11) 429.
26 ibid.
27 Benjamin C. Zipursky, "Civil Recourse, Not Corrective Justice" (2003) 91 *Georgetown Law Journal* 695.
28 John C. P. Goldberg and Benjamin C. Zipursky, "Accidents of the Great Society" (2005) 64(1) *Maryland Law Review* 364.
29 Cane (n 11) 430.
30 ibid 465, 466.

this chapter: neither view treats the environment as a *distinctive* area of concern. On the public policy view, environmentally harmful behavior only becomes problematic if it fails to maximize public welfare. Even then, welfare-decreasing behavior is not strictly an environmental problem because on the public policy view all problems are simply ones of welfare maximization; their particular qualitative substance is of no import. The private law view, in contrast, recognizes the environment at least as a medium through which harm may be caused, most obviously through the strong protections traditionally given to the use, enjoyment, and possession of land. However, the private law view only *sees* the environment to the extent that it is used by duty-bearing actors to harm rights-bearing persons. Thus, the environment as such is not a significant category on either framing of tort law. To the extent that tort is being positioned as a flexible body of law to address environmental ills, this basic omission must be borne in mind.

1.2 Fifteen Practical Views of Tort Law and the Challenge of Environmental Protection

First principles of tort aside,[31] there are practical aspects of tort as an institution that argue for and against the common law as an effective tool for environmental protection. Although scholars do recognize that the common law has some advantages over statutory environmental law,[32] the general consensus is that a common law system alone could never be adequate to ensure environmental protection.[33] It is noteworthy that the

[31] See Kenneth S. Abraham, *The Liability Century* (Harvard University Press 2008) 9, 10. According to Abraham, putting first principles aside is perhaps the best course given that tort "probably is not terribly good at achieving any of its possible goals." Damages are not effective for risk regulation, he argues, and justice notions are, at best, "only partially successful." Pragmatists urge the same disregard for first principals, arguing that such a priori reasoning is unjustified as it fails to give sufficient attention to measurable progress. See, e.g., Joshua Ulan Galperin, "Trust Me, I'm A Pragmatist: A Partially Pragmatic Critique of Pragmatic Activism" (2017) 42(2) *Columbia Journal of Environmental Law* 425.

[32] See, e.g., Hylton, "The Economic Theory of Nuisance Law and Implications for Environmental Regulation" (n 12) 673, 676; Roger E. Meiners and Andrew P. Morriss (eds.), *The Common Law and the Environment* (Rowman & Littlefield Publishers 2000) 17; Thomas O. McGarity, "Regulation and Litigation: Complementary Tools for Environmental Protection" (2005) 30 *Columbia Journal of Environmental Law* 371; Michael Anderson, "Transnational Corporations and Environmental Damage: Is Tort the Answer?" (2002) 41 *Washburn Law Journal* 399, 408; Abelkop (n 14) 381, 393.

[33] Susan Rose-Ackerman, "Public Law versus Private Law in Environmental Regulation: European Union Proposals in the Light of United States Experience" (1995) 4(4) *Review of European, Comparative and International Environmental Law* 312, 317.

literature addressing courts and the common law almost exclusively measures their effectiveness according to a public policy lens, without considering the private law theorists' argument that tort serves distinctive purposes that are not captured by the metrics of public policy analysis. Some of the perceived weaknesses of tort from a public policy lens become strengths when seen through a private law lens and vice versa. Additionally, as noted at the outset,[34] conventional wisdom regarding tort law's institutional weaknesses overlooks important historical counterexamples that may be of special significance in the climate change era.

Such complications notwithstanding, this part summarizes conventional wisdom regarding the effectiveness of tort law as a tool for environmental protection. The scholarship in this area is sprawling and diverse. However, the following claims tend to recur with prominence in the literature:

1. ***The long-term nature of environmental problems is incompatible with the largely retrospective vantage point of the common law system.*** Many environmental harms may not manifest until long after the act or acts that eventually lead to the harm.[35] Likewise, while a harm may begin at the same time as a causal act, a plaintiff may not notice the harm or connect the harm with the act for months, years, or even decades.[36] A paradigmatic example is that of latent diseases that only manifest many years after exposure to an environmental contaminant.[37] Or, a contaminant may need to build up for many years in the environment to reach a point where it will have an identifiable health impact.[38]

   Lengthy lag-times between act and consequence present two problems for common law courts, which are generally oriented toward ex-post evaluation of wrongdoing rather than ex-ante prevention of harm.

> First, because the burden of proof generally rests with plaintiffs, gathering the necessary evidence to prove acts that occurred in years past may prove too difficult.[39] Second, statues of limitations may prohibit common law suits when

[34] See text accompanying n 14.
[35] Abraham (n 2) 380.
[36] ibid.
[37] ibid.
[38] Abelkop (n 14) 400.
[39] Abraham (n 2) 380.

the plaintiff only discovers environmental harms many years after a defendant's causal act.[40] Even if the statute is tolled by a discovery rule or other equitable mechanism, the necessary evidence to link the plaintiff's harm, once manifested, to the defendant's act may no longer be available. Likewise, where an injured party does recognize an environmental injury, she may feel compelled to bring a common law suit and recover damages without the full extent of her injuries having emerged.[41] In such a case, her recovery will not fully compensate for the harms of the injury or provide the proper deterrence signals to other actors.

In the climate change context, an additional complication is posed by the considerable longevity of greenhouse gas emissions in the atmosphere. Depending on the particular greenhouse gas at issue, emissions can exert a warming effect decades or even centuries after their initial release. Likewise, greenhouse gases disperse and accumulate into a single atmospheric phenomenon. Sorting out causation within this lagged and latticed context is an epistemological problem of the highest order.[42]

2. ***The diffuse nature of environmental offenses makes defendants hard to identify.*** For many environmental problems, the acts of multiple actors aggregate to cause harm, or many potential defendants act similarly, making it difficult to determine which individual actor caused the harm in question.[43] In these cases, it may be impossible for a common law plaintiff to sufficiently prove which actor is the cause of her suffering.[44] In the case of a car accident or a medical mistake, for example, an injured person usually can point to the responsible actor without difficulty. In the case of toxic water pollution or ambient air pollution, on the other hand, it may simply be impossible to pinpoint any individual, or even group of actors, who directly cause or substantially cause the harm.

40 Abelkop (n 14) 401.

41 ibid 401, 402.

42 See Douglas A. Kysar, "What Climate Change Can Do About Tort Law" (2010) 41(1) *Environmental Law* 1.

43 Abraham (n 2) 386; Abelkop (n 14) 405.

44 Abraham (n 2) 386; Andrew Jackson Heimert, "Keeping Pigs Out of Parlors: Using Nuisance Law to Affect the Location of Pollution" (1997) 27(2) *Environmental Law* 403.

Climate change is a paradigmatic example of this multiple-defendant problem, given the huge array of greenhouse gas emitters: "[E]ven if a plaintiff establishes general causation by showing that she suffered an injury directly from the CO_2 emissions, it would be nigh impossible for her to establish specific causation by showing that it was the *defendant's* CO_2 emissions that caused the harm."[45] In an effort to overcome this difficulty, plaintiffs in a recent wave of climate change lawsuits in the United States have offered historical emissions data in an attempt to characterize major fossil fuel companies as especially significant nodes within the complex network of human institutions and activities that give rise to emissions.[46] The Philippines Human Rights Commission "Carbon Majors" inquiry – discussed in Chapter 3 of this volume – similarly marshals evidence of cumulative company-specific emissions in an effort to assess the responsibility of global corporations for contributing to climate-related human rights violations. Despite the impressive empirical basis of these claims, the success of the characterizations will ultimately depend on contestable normative arguments about where to place responsibility within the chain of actors connected to any given emitting activity.

3. ***The technical complexity of environmental harms makes causation difficult to demonstrate.*** Just as it is difficult, if not impossible, to pinpoint specific defendants in many environmental cases, it is equally difficult to link harms to specific acts, even if the defendants are identifiable.[47] Complex processes such as groundwater migration, atmospheric mixing, and aquatic dilution tend to intervene between the point at which a pollutant enters the environment and reaches a plaintiff.[48] Likewise, the unique health considerations of each individual, and the myriad other substances to which they are exposed, can pose challenges to demonstrating that any given emission has directly caused their specific harm.[49]

45 Abelkop (n 14) 407 (emphasis in original).
46 See, e.g., Complaint for Public Nuisance, *People ex rel Herrera* v. *BP PLC*, Case No. CGC-17-561370 (Superior Court of the State of California, September 19 2017), www.sfcityattorney.org/wp-content/uploads/2017/09/2017-09-19-File-Stamped-Complaint-for-Public-Nuisance.pdf, accessed August 1, 2019.
47 Schroeder (n 11) 592.
48 Abelkop (n 14) 405; Abraham (n 2) 382.
49 Abraham (n 2) 382.

In the climate change context, a field of "attribution science" has arisen to enable researchers to estimate an adverse event's increased likelihood of occurrence due to human contributions to atmospheric greenhouse gas levels.[50]

> Still, in many instances, the link between anthropogenic greenhouse gas emissions and a particular harmful event may be difficult to establish.

4. ***There is too little incentive to bring a common law suit for environmental offenses with primarily public rather than private damages.*** If the common law is to be an effective tool for environmental protection, it must be suitable to address the full array of environmental harms. Unfortunately, many environmental problems create relatively minor individual harms to a very large group of victims.[51] Under such circumstances, any potential plaintiff may have too little incentive to bring a suit because, despite suffering real harm, the potential recovery may be too small.[52] Likewise, individuals may rationally decide to free ride by letting another plaintiff expend the time and money to bring a suit.[53] Repeated instances of free riding or unwillingness to bring claims because of low per-victim harm undermines the effectiveness of common law to address many environmental damages.[54]
5. ***The transaction costs associated with bringing a claim may limit the ability of the common law to effectively combat environmental problems.*** Related to the previous critique, the costs of common law litigation can be significant.[55] In addition to typical litigation expenses such as court and attorney fees, plaintiffs in environmental suits may need to expend time and money on data gathering, technical analysis, epidemiological studies, expert fees, and more.[56] The

[50] Michael Burger, Radley Horton, and Jessica Wentz, "The Law and Science of Climate Change Attribution" *Columbia Journal of Environmental Law* (forthcoming 2020), https://ssrn.com/abstract=3051178, accessed August 1, 2019.

[51] David Schoenbrod, "Unsettled Expectations: Reflections on Four Views of the Common Law and the Environment Symposium: Common Law and Environmental Protection" (2008) (2008) 58(3) *Case Western Reserve Law Review* 863, 875.

[52] ibid.

[53] Heimert (n 44) 414; Hylton, "The Economic Theory of Nuisance Law and Implications for Environmental Regulation" (n 12) 694, 695.

[54] Schroeder (n 11) 592.

[55] Anderson (n 32) 409.

[56] Edward Brunet, "Debunking Wholesale Private Enforcement of Environmental Rights" (1992) 15(2) *Harvard Journal of Law & Public Policy* 311, 314.

high cost of bringing a successful environmental suit will discourage some potential plaintiffs, thereby leaving environmental harms unaddressed.[57]

6. ***Judges may not be qualified, scientifically and politically, to make judgments about complex environmental problems.*** Many commentators assume that judges and juries lack the expertise necessary to understand the technical nuances of toxicological, epidemiological, geological, or ecological processes.[58] Likewise, many argue that courts lack an institutional mandate from the public to make "far-reaching value judgments that . . . extend well beyond the participants in the immediate litigation."[59] Without the ability to resolve scientific and technical aspects of environmental conflicts, and with an unwillingness to shoulder the public policy components of environmental harms, common law may be an inappropriate vehicle for pursuing environmental protection.[60] Although these twin views regarding judges' scientific and political competence should be seriously questioned,[61] they nevertheless persist as widely held beliefs in the literature.
7. ***The common law is not cognizant of all the values that environmental damage may affect.*** The common law system resolves disputes between parties before the court and in so doing is capable of remedying economically measurable damages.[62] For many people, however, environmental concerns extend well beyond the measurable and monetizable harms that are suffered by human individuals. Broadly speaking, for these people, environmental concerns emerge from "non-anthropocentric ethical systems such as those positing that animals and even ecosystems are entitled to respect in their own right."[63] The common law system ignores these concerns and arguably exacerbates them by focusing almost exclusively on private transactional facets of environmental problems.[64]

[57] Brunet (n 56) 314.
[58] Heimert (n 44) 415.
[59] ibid.
[60] See, e.g., *Boomer* v. *Atlantic Cement Co.*, 257 N.E.2d 870, 871 (1970), which asserted that "the judicial establishment is neither equipped . . . nor prepared to lay down and implement an effective policy for the elimination of air pollution."
[61] See Kysar, *The Public Life of Private Law* (n 3).
[62] Schroeder (n 11) 586.
[63] ibid.
[64] ibid.

8. ***The nature of common law environmental defendants could underproduce compensation and deterrence.*** When corporate actors, rather than individuals, are the source of environmental harms, several institutional features can cabin the usefulness of common law remedies, particularly as a tool for deterrence.[65] Christopher Schroeder identifies a number of specific factors. Actors underestimate the levels of harm that their actions might cause and thereby take greater risks than they would if they could more accurately evaluate the consequences of their acts.[66] This problem is compounded by the short-term nature of corporate decision-making. Individual managers, for instance, may only consider the short-term harms of their risk taking because their tenure with a company will likely end before any environmental harms manifest and because short-term profitability is generally weighted more heavily than the long-term risk of tort liability.[67] Similarly, most corporate structures limit individual liability. With limited liability, even if the common law system otherwise sends a very high deterrent signal, that signal is truncated when in practice there is an effective liability cap.[68] Put slightly differently, sometimes defendants cannot pay the judgments against them.[69] When this happens, an environmental suit fails to fulfill its promise of offering the plaintiff compensatory justice. If the defendant knows that it is judgment proof at the time of its action, then the potential judgment is also not an effective deterrent.
9. ***The ad hoc and fragmented nature of common law suits undercuts consistent environmental protection.*** Perhaps the most basic problem identified with the common law's role in environmental protection is that, if the common law serves any broad environmental policy goals, it does so only as an accidental consequence of other more fundamental goals – as described in the first part of this chapter. Whether the common law is conceived as a public risk regulation system or a private justice-serving forum, any environmental benefits the common law provides are incidental. As such, any environmental policy outcomes are unlikely to accumulate into a coherent overall approach, coming as they do from inconsistent facts highlighted in case-by-case litigation.[70] In other words, the common law may offer environmental

[65] ibid 592.
[66] ibid.
[67] ibid.
[68] ibid.
[69] Rose-Ackerman (n 33) 313.
[70] Anderson (n 32) 409.

benefits, but those benefits will be merely fortuitous and will not reflect "the rationality of a consistent regulatory framework."[71]

Despite this laundry list of problems, the academic literature does identify a series of benefits to using the common law for environmental protection:

1. ***Common law can avoid the inefficiencies and economic costs of administrative regulation.*** Keith Hylton collects many of the inefficiencies of administrative regulation under the heading, "agency cost problem."[72] The agency cost problem underscores very generally the potential that administrative processes may operate with skewed incentives.[73] For instance, because of possible malfeasance such as corruption, or lack of interest or information, administrators may have incentives that differ from the interests of the intended beneficiaries of a policy.[74] This discrepancy can produce regulations that impose societal costs without solving the problems at which they are aimed, leaving a remainder of costs that would not exist in a common law system which effectively empowers beneficiaries of legal protections to bring suit.[75]
2. ***Common law enforces social norms in a decentralized bottom-up fashion rather than through top-down administrative fiat.*** Theorists have long argued that public satisfaction with a policy will make the policy more effective because satisfaction begets cooperation and compliance.[76] The common law may produce more satisfying results

[71] Anderson (n 32) 409.
[72] Hylton, "The Economic Theory of Nuisance Law and Implications for Environmental Regulation" (n 12) 676.
[73] ibid.
[74] ibid.
[75] ibid. In addition to the cost of misaligned incentives in administrative rule making, statutory commands often explicitly prohibit administrators from fully considering economic costs. Most environmental statutes circumscribe the way regulators factor in the economic costs of environmental regulations, focusing the regulators primarily on environmental benefits and technical solutions. By and large, the common law will consider costs in resolving an environmental dispute. For those scholars who endorse an economic perspective on environmental law, balancing costs and benefits will enable better use of societal resources and perhaps conserve those resources for additional environmental protection. See Meiners and Morriss (n 32).
[76] See, e.g., John Dewey, *The Public and Its Problems: An Essay in Political Inquiry*, ed. Melvin L. Rogers (Penn State University Press 2012) 69; Farber, *Eco-Pragmatism* (n 21) 113.

insofar as common law courts enforce and slowly adapts to social norms.[77] Administrative regulations, on the other hand, impose top-down requirements that may undermine or oppose social norms, reducing satisfaction, limiting compliance, and undermining effective environmental protection.[78]

3. ***Common law corrects for politics, wealth disparity, and agency capture.*** The "agency cost problem" targets the politics of administrative rule making as plagued by inefficiencies that may lead to "suboptimal outcomes."[79] Thomas McGarity argues, outside of welfarist reasoning, that the common law can also provide more fairness and accountability than regulatory processes.[80] McGarity writes that "[t]ort law corrects for a regulatory system that is too easily controlled by the very interests that it is supposed to be controlling."[81] Regulated parties are powerful political forces that intentionally seek to influence regulatory agencies to take favorable actions.[82] The disparity between these powerful players and the diffuse public interest in environmental protection sets up an unequal system. The common law system, while still tainted by unequal wealth and power,[83] may be less amenable to capture.[84] Thus, "the practical impact of the resource disparity may not be as large" in the context of common law litigation as compared to administrative regulation.[85] Because the common law system can at least partially account for the limited political power of environmental interests, it can better promote environmental protection.
4. ***The public has direct access to justice under the common law.*** While the regulatory system effectively demands threshold considerations of cost-benefit analysis and data availability that can slow or stop regulatory relief,[86] an injured party can always commence, on his or her own initiative, common law proceedings.[87] Injured parties may have

77 Meiners and Morriss (n 32).
78 ibid.
79 Hylton, "The Economic Theory of Nuisance Law and Implications for Environmental Regulation" (n 12) 676.
80 McGarity (n 80).
81 ibid.
82 ibid. 381.
83 Marc Galanter, *Why the Haves Come Out Ahead* (Quid Pro Books 2014).
84 McGarity (n 80) 382.
85 ibid.
86 ibid 390; *Michigan* v. *Environmental Protection Agency* 135 S Ct 2699.
87 Anderson (n 32) 409.

more information that can lead to better environmental results, and they may be able to force action where regulatory processes stall (or never commence).[88] That is, the private individual can contribute to broad environmental protection policy simply by enforcing his or her private rights.[89]

Even when a regulatory process is ongoing, the opportunity for regulators to hear individual voices is often truncated. Environmental interest groups, for instance, do speak for individuals and (potentially) nonhuman interests in the regulatory process.[90]

> But victims of environmental offenses "cannot rely exclusively upon special interest groups to ensure that regulatory agencies reduce long-term environmental risk through the regulatory process. Even when they are invited to participate, nonprofit public interest groups are always spread very thin."[91] The common law court is open directly to an injured party to speak for herself.

5. ***The common law system enables decentralized, divergent responses to fraught societal decisions.*** Because individual common law decisions only purport to resolve the specific social conflict presented in a particular case, judges and juries need not bear the burden of pronouncing specific behavioral rules to govern all manner of social interactions. Likewise, common law judges typically do not operate in a context in which they will bind an entire nation or other political body to a particular resolution of an environmental conflict. As such, they can render their decisions without fear of unduly stifling outcomes in other social situations. Through the decentralized, organic process of common law decision-making, candidate rules for resolving social conflicts can be tried and tested before uniform adoption across an entire society.

88 Anderson (n 32) 409.

89 ibid. In the United States and elsewhere, administrative law often provides vast opportunities for direct public engagement in the form of administrative petitioning, submission of data and views, or even legal challenges to administrative action and inaction. See, e.g., 5 US C § 500 et seq, which provide for administrative petitions, notice and comment opportunities, and judicial review of agency actions and inactions. These tools are remarkable and perhaps essential to good governance, but they differ from the common law system because the administrative system requires voluntary action and associated costs without the expectation of individual recovery while the common law "incentivizes" action with the promise of damage awards.

90 McGarity (n 80) 389.

91 ibid.

6. ***The common law discovery process can uncover valuable information and expose agency failings.*** Private actors often have relevant environmental information that is not available to regulators.[92] Discovery is a critical part of the adjudicatory process because it uncovers information necessary to fully argue claims; accordingly, information gathered in discovery can provide details that may only become available to environmental regulators through litigation.[93] Where appropriate, judges can shift burdens of proof and adopt other procedural mechanisms to encourage the development and production of information that might not otherwise be revealed through agency procedures. Additionally, because agency procedures often do not permit cross-examination or other means of direct adversarial scrutiny, adjudication can expose instances in which agencies have been presented with false or misleading information by regulated actors. Whether information uncovered through adjudication induces regulatory action by shining light on industry malfeasance, identifies risks that environmental regulators had not recognized, or simply facilitates additional common law litigation, it can have environmental benefits that far exceed what would have ensued in a system without the availability of adjudication.

1.3 One Integrated View of the Governance Ecosystem

In light of the strengths and weaknesses summarized in the preceding section, it may surprise the reader to know that many scholars treat the common law and statutory environmental law as competing tools for environmental protection.[94] As the review above demonstrates, however, common and statutory law have complementary features that fill gaps in the opposing institution and create emergent benefits when both tools are simultaneously available.[95] The question facing environmental law therefore should not be which system is *the* tool for environmental protection. Rather, the question should be how to "coordinate the common law and modern regulatory regimes"[96] so that they function together as overlapping protective mechanisms within a risk regulation ecosystem.

[92] Anderson (n 32) 409.
[93] McGarity (n 80) 391, 396; Abelkop (n 14) 393.
[94] Abelkop (n 14) 386. See also, e.g., Epstein, *From Common Law to Environmental Protection* (n 2).
[95] See, e.g., Shavell (n 14).
[96] Farber, *The Story of Boomer* (n 11).

The primary reason that neither the common law nor the regulatory system should work to the exclusion of the other is that each system has its respective focus, procedures, and institutional characteristics. The common law, as described above, focuses on interpersonal relationships and therefore on reparation rather than prevention.[97] Statutes, to the contrary, focus on preventing environmental harms in the first place and do so on a broad societal level.[98] The common law determines responsibility based on the actual occurrence of harm and the reasonableness of the underlying activity, while statutory law looks to risks of harm from a given activity regardless of common law notions of wrongfulness.[99] These are not strengths and weaknesses; they are distinctions that allow the institutions to work concurrently.[100]

Common and statutory law already work together in a number of important ways. The environmental regulatory universe does not, for instance, address every known or potential environmental problem.[101] Therefore, in addition to providing direct compensation, sending deterrent signals, and providing procedural justice, the common law also can address environmental problems not considered by the regulatory system. In the same vein, statutes address environmental problems by reducing risk, but not by eliminating it. In these cases, the statutory system serves as a protective baseline that sets a standard, but where particular harms arise despite that standard, common law may still perform all of its various functions including compensation and deterrence where appropriate.[102] Conversely, statutes buttress the common law. Statutes set standards and establish enforcement in their own right, but they also offer guidance to common law judges, informing

[97] Cane (n 11) 442. Except to those who see only a blinkered view of the common law as public policy tool used to send aggregate price signals that prevent inefficiently risky behavior, as described by Cane.

[98] ibid.

[99] ibid 443.

[100] H. Marlow Green, "Can the Common Law Survive in the Modern Regulatory Environment" (1998) 8(1) *Cornell Journal of Law and Public Policy* 89, 107. To temper the notion that statutes have occupied the environmental field, leaving no room for the common law, Marlow Green notes that since the passage of the key US environmental statutes in the early 1970s, the number of common law environmental claims in the country has actually *increased*. This could suggest that not only do statutes and common law work cooperatively in their legal application; statutes may also popularize environmental considerations, stimulating more use of both tools.

[101] Rose-Ackerman (n 33) 314; Heimert (n 44) 406.

[102] Rose-Ackerman (n 33) 315 .

application of the common law to environmental problems.[103] In rarer cases, statutes integrate common law analysis and standards, as in the case of the US Resource Conservation and Recovery Act's imminent and substantial endangerment provisions[104] and the Comprehensive Environmental Response, Compensation, and Liability Act's joint liability provisions.[105]

The case for complementarity grows even stronger in the age of the Anthropocene. To begin with, the common law has an important, unacknowledged advantage over statutory law when considering the challenge of environmental governance *after nature*.[106] Historically, many statutory environmental laws have been premised on the idea of protecting "nature" from human influence by setting portions of land aside as parks or wilderness. Likewise, many pollution laws have been framed around trying to restore air, water, and other natural resources to an imagined quality that existed before human interference.

In the age of the Anthropocene, such prehuman or nonhuman constructs of nature offer only illusory guidance. Through anthropogenic climate change, no natural system anywhere on the planet will be free of significant human influence for at least many centuries, even if all greenhouse gas emissions ceased tomorrow. Traditional statutory environmental laws will soon seem ill-fit for this reality. Protected lands will lose their intended significance as they no longer prove hospitable to the flora and fauna for which they were set aside. Agencies will feel compelled to save endangered species by relocating them to more suitable climes, but will also have to grapple with the fact that those species are exotic in relation to the new habitats. All of nature will be seen as needing management – after all, it is being "managed" by human influence whether intentionally or unintentionally – but an important strand of environmental law historically has been aimed at preserving or restoring nature apart from human influence.

One unique benefit of the common law is that it is not built on "managerial" environmentalism like many of its statutory counterparts. The common law has always been explicitly focused on human-to-human relations; the environment is merely a medium within which

103 Farber, *The Story of Boomer* (n 11) 38.
104 42 US Code § 6972.
105 42 US Code § 9607.
106 Jedediah Purdy, *After Nature: A Politics for the Anthropocene* (Harvard University Press 2015).

those relations occur.[107] Thus, when courts are asked to situate a phenomenon like climate change within a common law framework like tort, they are not required to fundamentally alter the normative underpinnings of the framework. Although vast in scale and complexity, climate change and the greenhouse gas emissions that cause it can be analyzed through traditional doctrines like trespass and nuisance, without those doctrines breaking down into conceptual confusion. Many environmental statutes, by contrast, will become unworkable or even nonsensical in the coming decades. In the United States, this possibility has already played out dramatically as the Environmental Protection Agency has been forced to try to apply the Clean Air Act to the problem of greenhouse gas emissions, despite the statute's imperfect fit for that purpose.[108] As a result, the agency has been forced to choose between adopting impractical regulations that accord with statutory mandates or adopting practical ones that may exceed agency authority. Such a dilemma would not confront judges operating under a framework like nuisance or public trust, in which normative principles are stated with a level of generality adequate to evolve with changing needs and circumstances.

In addition to the flexibility and capaciousness it offers, judge-made law also should be prized within the Anthropocene simply because it represents a potential source of normative guidance in the strive toward sustainability. *All* such potential sources must be on the table as humanity faces the climate change crisis. Legal systems are generally oriented toward securing order and stability, thus resisting radical change. Yet radical change is precisely what is required to address the climate crisis. At present, one cannot predict where the normative pressures needed to achieve that dramatic transformation will come from within governments. Thus, there is a need to envision ecosystems of governance, in which virtues such as redundancy, diversity, and resilience are prized over a single-minded quest for optimal allocation of decision-making authority. It is no coincidence that powerful business interests expend great sums advocating the view that climate change should not be addressed by judges on their own substantive accord.[109] Business

[107] Joshua Ulan Galperin, "No Farms, No Food? A Response to Baylen Linnekin" 45(4) *Fordham Urban Law Journal* 1141, 1143–1144.

[108] Carbon Pollution Emission Guidelines for Existing Stationary Sources: Electric Utility Generating Units (Final Rule), 40 CFR Part 60, 80 Fed Reg 64661 (October 23, 2015).

[109] Laurence H. Tribe, Joshua D. Branson, and Tristan L. Duncan, "Too Hot for Courts to Handle: Fuel Temperatures, Global Warming, and the Political Question Doctrine" (2010) Washington Legal Foundation Critical Legal Issues Working Paper Series Number 169, January 2010, www.wlf.org/2010/01/29/publishing/too-hot-for-courts-to-handle-fuel-temperatures-global-warming-and-the-political-question-doctrine, accessed August 1, 2019.

interests prefer to only require capturing one branch of government in order to forestall climate action; thus, they promote doctrines such as preemption, displacement, political question, and other justiciability notions that limit judicial engagement with the causes and consequences of climate change.

The common law and administrative systems provide additional complementarity in the search for meaningful public participation. Each framework invites individual visions of how we will shape the future. The common law system may provide the most powerful opportunities, inviting, as it does, each person to express his or her own arguments for what we owe to each other and what we recognize as a legal harm.[110] But the common law system likewise translates individual expression into public choices in only small bursts, and the choices are always first based in individual notions of harm. The regulatory system may provide less individual power, but what power it provides is widespread and relatively accessible. In the United States, administrative law allows individuals the chance to petition the government for action, to submit views and data on the nature of regulatory action and inaction, and to seek judicial review of inadequate administrative behavior.[111] Administrative managers and judges need not accept such entreaties, but even in rejection, officials must give reasons and demonstrate deliberation,[112] thus contributing to a collective process of reasoning about how we face the world. Together, common law and regulatory participation help foster a polity more robust and inclusive, more capable of advancing public discussion than either majoritarian vote counting or dismissive assurances that the right course of action is merely a matter of information gathering and technical management (such assurances having long been part of environmental statutory law).[113]

Seen from this perspective, the tort system plays a significant role in the governance of risk simply by holding open a forum for the adjudication of grievances and the declaration of norms of right and responsibility. The direct regulatory effects of this traditional role of tort law can be significant, notwithstanding an apparent scholarly consensus that "[m]odern statutory-based environmental liability developed . . . largely in response to the inadequacies of the traditional common law rules."[114] Moreover, among

[110] Joshua Ulan Galperin, "Value Hypocrisy and Policy Sincerity: A Food Law Case Study" (2018) 42 *Vermont Law Review* 345, 370–373.

[111] 5 US Code § 500 et seq.

[112] *Motor Vehicle Manufacturers Ass'n of the United States Inc* v. *State Farm Mutual Automobile Insurance Co.* 463 U.S. 29, 103 S. Ct. 2856.

[113] Joshua Ulan Galperin, *The Death of Administrative Democracy* (forthcoming).

[114] Abraham, *The Liability Century* (n 31) 149.

the many side effects of tort law's core function is the possibility that common law adjudication can shine a light on threats of individual suffering that are under-attended to by the more recognizably political branches of government. Put differently, the larger hydraulics of governance may be catalyzed simply by virtue of the common law judges' task of forthrightly addressing the merits of claims before them. With that understanding, it becomes all the more critical that judges avoid the temptation to shy from tort claims that involve significant, complex, or politically sensitive issues like climate change. Fraught though they may seem, such moments are precisely when judicial engagement may be needed most.

Although this chapter has focused on the Anglo-American tort law tradition, its lessons regarding the catalytic potential of civil litigation in relation to other departments of government are not limited to the common law context. Indeed, civil law jurisdictions might offer even greater catalytic potential insomuch as they sometimes afford litigants wide latitude to assert claims on behalf of the public interest and subject government to broad-sweeping affirmative duties of care.[115] Whatever the legal system, climate change demands of all government actors, judges included, a willingness to use their limited domains of authority creatively, ethically, and bravely to help effectuate the transition to carbon-free economies. A new origin story for environmental law will be written from the choices that they make. Will the story be one in which the climate is stabilized and the life it supports saved? If so, what will be the role of judges in bringing about that salvation?

> *It was once written that the common law lay beneath the statute, that the great judge was not great, but a captive of the past, that the administrator was a pure accountant and the politician a faithful servant to the people. But when the sky filled with gas and the seas were filled with acid, all was rewritten. We saw the trembling pillars not only of the law but of the earth itself, of all life, and all life chose to tell a new story. Only then were leaders forced to reckon with their choices, to confess their flawed accounting and their faithless service. The judges wrote of the warming sky and the sinking land, they wrote of perseverance and reclamation, they wrote of the need to forge a new path. And the uncommon was made common.*

[115] See, e.g., David R. Hodas, "Private Actions for Public Nuisance: Common Law Citizen Suits for Environmental Harms" (1989) 16(4) *Ecology Law Quarterly* 883; Christopher Serkin, "Passive Takings: The State's Affirmative Duty to Protect Property" (2014) 113(3) *Michigan Law Review* 345.

2

Networked Public Interest Litigation: A Novel Framework for Climate Claims?

KETAN JHA

Implicitly, legal scholarship has asked what public interest litigation can do about the wicked problem of global anthropogenic climate change. In this chapter, I focus on the converse question: what can climate change do about public interest litigation? I propose that the *globalisation* of public interest litigation throughout the latter half of the twentieth century has set the stage for novel forms of collaboration between advocacy groups, lawyers, and members of the public. This chapter argues that ordinary citizens, despite their nominal remoteness from international decision-making processes, are undertaking a significant role in climate governance in and outside of courts. Using Guinier and Torres' conception of demosprudence, this chapter asks whether citizens mobilised towards climate justice are engaged in new forms of democratic law-making, finding that though many of the barriers to change remain the same, emergent properties of recent legal actions warrant a reappraisal of how climate activism and legal activism interact.

The structure of this chapter is as follows. Section 1 reviews the vast literature addressing the relationship between courts and social change, extracting key arguments from legal activists and critics. Section 2 introduces the recent turn towards social movements in this scholarship and focuses on demosprudence. Section 3 examines the international spread of public interest litigation and offers a brief example of how demosprudence reconfigures this process and proceeds to frame contemporary climate change activism in the context of social science scholarship on transnational networks. Section 4 links that scholarship to transnational law and climate change. Section 5 sets out the tentative characteristics of a new framework to synthesise insights from transnational scholarship and demosprudence, using crowdfunding and crowdsourcing as case studies. Section 6 concludes.

2.1 Cause Lawyering and Its Discontents

'There is a parallel here with the situation in the 1950s in the United States. It was the courts that decided that segregation in schools was not constitutional. It wasn't a big issue in society and it wasn't political but it was a few people fighting and the courts following up that created a huge change in American society.'[1]

Roger Cox's comment to *The Guardian*, provided shortly before judgment was handed down in the landmark Dutch climate case *Urgenda*, explicitly linked climate lawyers to the American public interest law movement, framing climate litigation as a way of using the courts as a space of resistance against social and political inaction. Rather than racial minorities, Cox contemplates that climate litigators are advancing the underrepresented interests of environmentalists, those who stand to lose the most from climate change, and indeed the planet itself. This sharp focus on courts blurs the better part of a deeply complex historical picture, but the scale of social and legal mobilisation around climate change makes Cox's comparison ripe for analysis.

The field of public interest law includes organisations with a large number of political commitments, budgetary constraints, and countries of operation. While the term eludes easy classification, there is good reason to adopt a broad approach. Scholars have raised questions about who determines the nature of the 'public interest'.[2] This chapter considers that 'traditional' public interest law organisations are non-profit tax-exempt groups that attempt to use law to achieve social objectives,[3] but seeks to situate the contemporary situation more broadly to include a wider range of actors who occupy the rapidly expanding space intersecting social movements and the law.[4]

Historically, the term *public interest law* is associated with the proliferation of identity-based social movements in the latter half of the

[1] Roger Cox, quoted in Emma Howard, 'Dutch Government Facing Legal Action over Failure to Reduce Carbon Emissions' *The Guardian* (London, 14 April 2015) www.theguardian.com/environment/2015/apr/14/dutch-government-facing-legal-action-over-failure-to-reduce-carbon-emissions.

[2] Anne Southworth, 'Conservative Lawyers and the Contest over the Meaning of Public Interest Law' (2005) 52 *UCLA Law Review* 1223; Edgar S. Cahn and Jean Camper Cahn, 'Power to the People or the Profession? – The Public Interest in Public Interest Law' (1970) 79(2) *Yale Law Journal* 1005, 1008.

[3] This definition is adopted from Deborah L. Rhode, 'Public Interest Law: The Movement at Midlife' (2008) 60(6) *Stanford Law Review* 2027, 2029.

[4] Scott L. Cummings, 'The Puzzle of Social Movements in American Legal Theory' (2017) 64 (1) *UCLA Law Review* 1554.

twentieth century. These movements were a response to the myriad ways in which the law of the day oppressed minority groups, whether through immigration restrictions, discrimination in public services, or employment exclusion.

Differential legal treatment at once concretised both minority groups and the multitude of barriers they sought to overcome: a better defined forum exists for challenging insidious laws than for combating insidious social ills. If 'it is easier . . . to smash an atom than a prejudice', it may be easier still to smash a statute.[5] Whether their political commitments focused on public morality,[6] redistribution of private wealth, or recognition of minority rights, such movements engaged with the law, placing a particular faith in the ability of courts to produce social change. If there was an accepted 'canon' of public interest litigation, it would likely begin with activist American lawyers at the NAACP Legal Defense and Educational Fund who sought to harness the norm-articulating function of courts to achieve social, economic, and political rights for African Americans.[7] Visions of societal change centred on the success of legal battles that proliferated in the 1960s and 1970s, underpinning the development of early public interest law organisations and the resultant interest of the legal academy. This juriscentric approach to change attracted investment in organisations relying on the test case litigation strategy.[8] The 'core' of the movement, as one early study recounted, consisted of about eighty-six organisations.[9]

In addition to the civil rights project, movements to secure rights for the lesbian, gay, bisexual, transgender, and queer or questioning (LGBTQ) community; women; and persons with disabilities all allied lawyers with social mobilisation to catalyse change. Of course, these histories are not identical in terms of the form of legal mobilisation: disability rights advocates in the United States balanced strategic litigation with administrative and legislative victories, and landmark

[5] Gordon W. Allport, *The Nature of Prejudice* (1st ed., Addison Wesley 1954) xv.

[6] Owen M. Fiss, 'Foreword: The Forms of Justice' (1979) 93(1) *Harvard Law Review* 1, 9.

[7] Mark Tushnet, *The NACCP's Legal Strategy against Segregated Education, 1925–1950* (University of North Carolina Press 1987).

[8] Joel F. Handler, Ellen Jane Hollingworth, and Howard S. Erlanger, *Lawyers and the Pursuit of Legal Rights* (Academic Press 1978) 41–2; Joel F. Handler, *Social Movements and the Legal System: A Theory of Law Reform and Social Change* (Academic Press 1979).

[9] Joel F. Handler, Betsy Ginsberg, and Arthur Snow, 'The Public Interest Law Industry' in Burton A. Weisbrod, Joel F. Handler, and Neil K. Komesar (eds.), *Public Interest Law: An Economic and Institutional Analysis* (University of California Press 1978).

law reform occurred largely in the absence of a mass movement.[10] The gay rights movement pursued incremental changes in local law and policy alongside national efforts, while racial equality efforts broadly favoured top-down tactics.[11] Despite these differences, three major characteristics are inherent to these movements, with different movements exhibiting them more or less precisely. First, these movements framed their goals – whether in public rhetoric or substantive legal argument – through the language of rights. Rights, in this framing, served to counter the creep of both state and private power.[12] The second characteristic emerges from the first: the judiciary was tasked with the recognition and preservation of these rights once articulated. By necessity, judicial ratification of individual rights could contradict majority will. As different movement strategies show, courts were not the sole forum for articulating these rights but remained an important site of resistance. Finally, these movements relied, implicitly or explicitly, on recourse to moral justifications for the recognition of rights.

This nascent movement of 'legal liberalism' placed faith in courts as a constraint on uncomfortable outcomes of pluralism, relied on lawyers as the guardians of distributive justice through strategic litigation, and would attempt to achieve its aims by enforcing individual rights for the benefit of minorities.[13] Legal liberalism thus leveraged on 'an alliance of activist courts and activist lawyers in the pursuit of progressive reform'.[14] So what of the courts' relationship to social movements? At the very least, the Supreme Court of the United States nurtured legal and social spaces for the seeds of activism to germinate and flourish.[15] The familiar account of the judicial role reads key decisions as reducing the costs of participation in collective action – oppressed individuals are more likely to participate in organising if their activism is not sanctionable by the state.

[10] Richard K. Scotch, *From Good Will to Civil Rights* (2nd ed., Temple University Press 2001) 140. Scotch argues that embedding equality in disability rights legislation was not 'the product of some broadly based movement for political change' but of a few legislative staff members.

[11] William N. Eskridge, 'Channeling: Identity-Based Social Movements and Public Law' (2001) 150 *University of Pennsylvania Law Review* 419.

[12] Whether public or private power was the biggest threat to an ideal society divided scholars. See Robin L. West, 'Constitutional Scepticism' (1992) 72 *Boston University Law Review* 765, 774.

[13] Laura Kalman, *The Strange Career of Legal Liberalism* (Yale University Press 1996).

[14] Scott L. Cummings, 'The Social Movement Turn in Law' (2018) 43(2) *Law and Social Inquiry* 360, 362.

[15] Eskridge (n 11) 452, arguing that a 'speech-protective' body of law developed from 1963 to 1972 facilitated mass mobilisation.

2.1.1 *Critiques of Public Interest Litigation*

However, these progressive movements faced powerful critics. From the outset, public interest lawyers would have to confront the counter-majoritarian problem inherent to expansive judicial review.[16] Activist lawyers and academics would participate in a timeless dance about whether courts could at once curb the excesses of the majority and maintain democratic legitimacy. Scholarship also contested the ability of tactical litigation to produce meaningful and sustainable policy outcomes: even successful legal claims deferred the implementation of desired outcomes to administrative agencies with a wide margin of appreciation.[17] This implementation hurdle is particularly pronounced where substantial state action is required – as with climate change. Gerald Rosenberg argues that the prospect of victory in the courtroom invites social change advocates to put all their cards in the judiciary, spearheading an institutionally impossible brand of transformative politics.[18] Resources poured into litigation, on this view, would attract significant opportunity costs in terms of political mobilisation. This criticism seems to hold water in the context of climate change. If the seed of climate inaction is the abject failure of international environmental law, does climate litigation divert our attention from achieving greater ambition through UNFCCC mechanisms and domestic legislatures, ultimately channelling the energy of a movement into improper fora?[19] Relatedly, the 'myth of rights'[20] vindicated in court exhausted movement energy in mobilisation around legal claims, occasionally resulting in a movement whose lifetime is no longer than the court cases to which it is hewn.[21]

[16] Alexander Bickel, *The Least Dangerous Branch: The Supreme Court at the Bar of Politics* (Yale University Press 1962); Barry Friedman, 'The Birth of an Academic Obsession: The History of the Countermajoritarian Difficulty, Part Five' (2002) 112(1) *Yale Law Journal* 153.

[17] Joel F. Handler, *Social Movements and the Legal System: A Theory of Law Reform and Social Change* (n 8) 18–22. (Finding that administrative discretion to implement victories in court creates an insurmountable 'bureaucratic contingency' for public interest law.)

[18] Gerald N. Rosenberg, *The Hollow Hope: Can Courts Bring about Social Change?* (University of Chicago Press 1991).

[19] Eskridge (n 11) 470.

[20] Stuart A. Scheingold, *The Politics of Rights: Lawyers, Public Policy, and Political Change* (University of Michigan Press 2004) 3–10.

[21] This diagnosis of illusory rights talk may be replicated in some post-*Urgenda* litigation. See Jacqueline Peel and Hari M. Osofsky, 'A Rights Turn in Climate Litigation?' (2018) 7(1) *Transnational Environmental Law* 37.

In response, a vision of law 'subordinated to other modes of activism and other disciplines' began to form.[22] This shift is plainly visible in contemporary scholarship on the civil rights movement, where the focus has shifted from landmark court cases towards community organising.[23] Still more criticism emerged from the left through the Critical Legal Studies (CLS) movement, whose proponents 'trashed' the view that collective problems could be resolved through the existing legal order, especially through individual rights.[24] Broadly speaking, this critique focusses on the failure of lawyers to understand that 'instruments of the state are merely the reflections of the political and economic ideology of the dominant group'.[25] On this view, not only can rights do little to counter private sources of oppression; they are a symptom of fundamental deficiencies in the modern state, where the terrain of individual rights impedes structural reform.[26]

Even the result of these criticisms, a body of work that seeks to put lawyers and the social change proponents they represent on equal footing, is vulnerable to the 'extralegal cooptation' critique. This critique holds that the response to the undue primacy of law in mid-century social movements is so overdrawn as to stifle the social change that litigation can produce.[27]

Perhaps the most contentious criticism is the backlash hypothesis, wherein momentous decisions such as *Brown* v. *Board of Education*[28] and *Roe* v. *Wade*[29] served as the flashpoint for the resurgence of political conservatism, requiring social movements to fill the space vacated by legal activism after ephemeral court victories.[30] This backlash could be violent, as with the groundswell of white supremacy in the southern

22 Richard L. Abel, 'Lawyers and the Power to Change' (1985) 7(1) *Law and Policy* 5, 9.

23 Risa L. Goluboff, 'Lawyers, Law, and the New Civil Rights History' (2013) 126 *Harvard Law Review* 2312.

24 Mark Kelman, 'Trashing' (1984) 36(1) *Stanford Law Review* 293.

25 Ralph J. Bunche, 'A Critical Analysis of the Tactics and Program of Minority Groups' (1935) 4(3) *Journal of Negro Education* 308, 315.

26 Duncan Kennedy, 'Form and Substance in Private Law Adjudication' (1976) 89(8) *Harvard Law Review* 1685.

27 Orly Lobel, 'The Paradox of Extralegal Activism: Critical Legal Consciousness and Transformative Politics' (2007) 120(2) *Harvard Law Review* 937.

28 347 US 483 (1954).

29 410 US 113 (1973).

30 Michael J. Klarman, 'How Brown Changed Race Relations: The Backlash Thesis' (1994) 81(1) *Journal of American History* 81; see also Derrick Bell, 'Serving Two Masters: Integration Ideals and Client Interests in School Desegregation Litigation' (1976) 85(4) *Yale Law Journal* 470.

United States after *Brown*[31], or generate political polarisation and vigorous counter-movements in civil society and the halls of the legislature, as with the abortion debate.[32]

The backlash narrative is particularly interesting because both its proponents and detractors strive to prove the power of the courts in determining the contours of social norms and policy. Where the aforementioned critiques of public interest law undermine a causal or determinate relationship between law and society, both sides of the backlash debate bolster it. So seasoned scholars declare that *Brown* 'inspired southern whites to try to destroy the NAACP';[33] a US Supreme Court Justice opines that *Roe* 'stopped the momentum on the side of change';[34] and if it was not for a state court decision invalidating sex-based marriage requirements under local law, a federal statute limiting marriage to different-sex couples would not exist.[35] Refuting these theories, detractors mine historical sources for indications that political and social conditions required for counter-mobilisation already existed – legislative proceedings, contemporary newspapers, and opinion polls become heuristics for whether popular consensus was in step with activist courts.[36]

The American discourse on the efficacy of public interest litigation provides pressing questions for climate change governance during a critical period of growth. If historical reappraisals serve a similar role in the future, will tomorrow's lawyers and legal scholars reckon with characterisations of imminent climate catastrophe and the rise of climate denial in the United States? Will they ruffle through Gallup polls to discover whether percentages predicted precedent, perhaps paying heed

[31] Klarman, 'How Brown Changed Race Relations' (n 31), 141–9; David J. Garrow, *Bearing the Cross: Martin Luther King Jr. and the Southern Christian Leadership Conference* (William Morrow 1986) 83–6; Michael J. Klarman, *From Jim Crow to Civil Rights: The Supreme Court and the Struggle for Racial Equality* (Oxford University Press 2007).

[32] Robin West, 'From Free Choice to Reproductive Justice: Deconstitutionalizing Abortion Rights' (2009) 118 *Yale Law Journal* 1394; cf. Robert C. Post and Reva B. Siegel 'Roe Rage: Democratic Constitutionalism and Backlash' (2007) 42 *Harvard Civil Rights - Civil Liberties Law Review* 373.

[33] Klarman, 'From Jim Crow to Civil Rights' (n 31) 468.

[34] Emily Bazelon, 'Backlash Whiplash' (*Slate*, 14 May 2013), www.slate.com/articles/news_and_politics/jurisprudence/2013/05/justice_ginsburg_and_roe_v_wade_caution_for_gay_marriage.html.

[35] Michael J. Klarman, *From the Closet to the Altar: Courts, Backlash, and the Struggle for Same-Sex Marriage* (Oxford University Press 2012) 212.

[36] See Linda Greenhouse and Reva B. Siegel, 'Before (and After) *Roe* v. *Wade*: New Questions about Backlash' (2011) 120 *Yale Law Journal* 2028; Mary Ziegler, 'Beyond Backlash: Legal History, Polarization, and Roe v. Wade Roe at 40' (2014) 71(2) *Washington & Lee Law Review* 969.

to the literature indicating that the attitudes of political elites are a strong determinant of public opinion on climate change?[37]

2.2 Movement Lawyering and Demosprudence

The trajectory of debates about the place of law in producing social change may at times seem circular. Court-centred approaches are criticised as ineffective or even counterproductive; advocates reply that they do not place undue reliance on litigation, and the myopia of historical memory is impugned by both sides for coupling our understanding of change with mythologized accounts of crucial moments and actors.[38] The most recent development in this scholarship can crudely be summarised in two parts. First, there is a descriptive account of the ways in which contemporary public interest lawyers have responded to the alleged deficiencies of earlier strategies. This turn, termed *movement lawyering*,[39] draws on social scientific scholarship about courts and the legal profession[40] to avoid some critiques of the liberal legal order by harnessing the power of grassroots organisation. The underlying logic is that law must not outpace social change or displace movement activists: the problem of trade-offs between social/political and legal mobilisation[41] and the overemphasis on adjudication is cured by balancing ambitious lawsuits with more holistic strategies. Movement lawyering crucially involves seeking remedies outside of courts, a keen awareness of the relationship between law and politics, and an attunement to wider movement goals. When deployed, these characteristics generate a model of 'integrated advocacy' whereby movement resources are used flexibly across political and legal spaces without privileging one over the other.[42]

[37] Jason T. Carmichael and Robert J. Brulle, 'Elite Cues, Media Coverage, and Public Concern: An Integrated Path Analysis of Public Opinion on Climate Change' (2001–2013) 26 *Environmental Politics* 232.
[38] Post and Siegel (n 32) 376.
[39] Scott L. Cummings, 'Movement Lawyering' (2017) 5 *University of Illinois Law Review* 1645.
[40] See, for example, Robin Stryker, 'Half Empty, Half Full or Neither? Law, Inequality, and Social Change in Capitalist Democracies' (2007) 3(1) *Annual Review of Law & Social Science* 69.
[41] Lester Mazor, 'The Crisis of Liberal Legalism' (1972) 81(5) *Yale Law Journal* 1032.
[42] But cf. Susan D. Carle, 'Ethics and the History of Social Movement Lawyering' (2018) *Wisconsin Law Review Online*. Using historical sources, Carle argues that the first generation of public interest lawyers exhibited the same characteristics.

This descriptive model is paired with an aspirational theoretical counterpart that Guinier and Torres call 'demosprudence'.[43] Demosprudence situates law and social movements as mutually constituted, proposing that social movements can be a source of law.[44] Rather than analysing the role of law made solely in the courts or in the halls of legislatures, demosprudence examines how groups committed to a particular vision of change, or 'constituencies of accountability', use contentious politics to articulate alternative understandings of the law's content. Demosprudence takes as its principle question: 'how do courts and social movements influence each other to interpret the meaning of law?'[45] Demosprudence departs from legal liberalism and shares with CLS critiques a skepticism of individual rights, instead emphasizing the historic chasm between the mere judicial recognition of minority rights and the realisation of effective remedies. However, this wariness of rights consciousness does not mean lawyers and litigation are excluded from demosprudential analysis; it shares with movement lawyering an understanding of law-making as the product of 'mobilised citizens in conjunction with, not separate from, legal professionals'.[46] Indeed, the first example of demosprudence emerged out of Guinier's analysis of oral dissents in the US Supreme Court.[47] Though scholarly use of demosprudence focusses on constitutional claims in the United States and India,[48] I argue that aspects of climate change governance illustrate how demosprudence applies at a transnational scale.[49]

From a scholarly perspective, demosprudence and movement lawyering are borne out of the cross fertilization of previously isolated strands of legal and sociological scholarship.[50] Where early legal scholars made

[43] Lani Guinier and Gerald Torres, 'Changing the Wind: Notes toward a Demosprudence of Law and Social Movements' (2014) 123(8) *Yale Law Journal* 2740.

[44] ibid 2740.

[45] ibid 2756–7. Social movements, for the purpose of demosprudence, are distinct from interest groups. Social movements consist of '(1) collective challenges, based on (2) common purposes and (3) social solidarity in (4) sustained interaction with elites, opponents, and authorities'.

[46] ibid.

[47] Lani Guinier, 'Foreword: Demosprudence through Dissent' (2008) 122(1) *Harvard Law Review* 4.

[48] Upendra Baxi, 'Demosprudence versus Jurisprudence: The Indian Judicial Experience in the Context of Comparative Constitutional Studies' (2014) 14 *Macquarie Law Journal* 3, cf. Nick O'Brien, 'Administrative Justice in the Wake of I, Daniel Blake' (2017) 89(1) *Political Quarterly* 82.

[49] Guinier and Torres (n 43) 2754.

[50] Mazor (n 41).

lawyers and courts central to the analysis of social change, adherents to Parsonian frameworks[51] often rendered law a marginal consideration in the sociological scholarship.[52] Much of the literature has since coalesced, with scholars of both disciplines according more weight to the other.

We might find one example – and particularly one that is suitable for discussing climate change – in tobacco litigation, which successfully galvanised a broad base of both political and scientific support. Tobacco litigation eventually achieved many of its proposed outcomes: stricter regulation and a set of astronomically high payouts to local governments.[53] Yet winning the substantial legal arguments is not the only way to achieve a 'victory', especially in planning cases where sufficient delays can render projects financially unfeasible.[54] As the originators of demosprudence note, process-based considerations – concerning how change happens – are crucial to the relationship between rule-shifting and culture-shifting.[55] Put differently, when citizens, NGOs, and lawyer-activists use courts, supranational adjudicative bodies, and other policy fora as pressure points, they seek to 'expose the conflict between the aspirations of law and its grim reality'.[56] Even a negative ruling on the merits can expose where failures occurred, vindicate salient facts, and place the onus for future action on another branch of government. Within the context of demosprudence, *law-making* refers both to the informal aspects of the legal process that might be regarded as soft law, as well as to the articulation of alternative legal meanings.[57] Where a social movement contests the content of the law, offering their aspirational approach, they too are engaged in a kind of law-making.

This chapter argues that climate litigation is increasingly taking on demosprudential characteristics by engaging with a diverse set of actors – especially the public– across a growing number of jurisdictions. This builds chiefly on two interdisciplinary strands of scholarship. First, academic work on public interest litigation, movement lawyering, and law as

[51] Talcott Parsons, *Politics and Social Structure* (Free Press 1969) ix.

[52] See Jean L. Cohen, 'Strategy or Identity: New Theoretical Paradigms and Contemporary Social Movements' (1985) 52(4) *Social Research* 663, 671.

[53] Lynn Mather, 'Theorizing about Trial Courts: Lawyers, Policymaking, and Tobacco Litigation' (1998) 23(4) *Law and Social Inquiry* 897.

[54] Douglas NeJaime, 'Winning through Losing' (2011) 96(2) *Iowa Law Review* 941.

[55] Thomas B. Stoddard, 'Bleeding Heart: Reflections on Using the Law to Make Social Change' (1997) 72(5) *NYU Law Review* 967.

[56] Jules Lobel, 'Courts as Forums for Protest' (2004) 52 *UCLA Law Review* 477, 479.

[57] Janet Koven Levit, 'Bottom-Up International Lawmaking: Reflections on the New Haven School of International Law' (2007) 32(2) *Yale Journal of International Law* 393, 409.

a form of social change underpin the present inquiry and are particularly relevant in light of the number of NGOs involved in climate litigation.[58] Second, transnational law scholarship born out of the international and comparative law traditions provides a frame through which to understand climate litigation across multiple jurisdictions. Recent transnational law scholarship has embraced social scientific approaches to studying the role of non-state actors in global governance; this chapter uses demosprudence to extend this body of scholarship to social movements and citizen engagement. In so doing, this chapter proposes that emergent properties in climate litigation amount to a novel development termed *networked public interest litigation*.

The next section sets out one precondition of climate law's interaction with scholarship on law and social change: the internationalisation of public interest litigation and the integration of 'indirect' or diffuse ways of making law in the public interest.

2.2.1 Internationalising Public Interest Law

US public interest law in the pre-*Brown* era was not insulated from the development of international human rights. Indeed, for some time, public interest lawyers sought to use the spirit and letter of the United Nations Charter to challenge racial discrimination in the administration of public services[59] and in property law.[60] However, vociferous anti-communism spurred by the Cold War served to shut out internationalist critiques of domestic civil rights and therefore constrained the role of public interest law firmly within the American sphere; change from *within* the contours of American democracy became the politically salient route for cause lawyers to pursue.[61]

Global market integration spurred a variety of public interest strategies chiefly in response to transnational immigration flows and the associated human rights complications both at home and abroad.[62] Legal

[58] As I explain below, the framework I propose considers that state actors may bring public interest suits.

[59] Bert B. Lockwood, 'The United Nations Charter and United Nations Civil Rights Litigation: 1946-1955' (1984) 69 *Iowa Law Review* 901, 938.

[60] Paul L. Sayre, '*Shelley v Kraemer* and United Nations Law' (1948) 34(1) *Iowa Law Review* 1.

[61] Mary L. Dudziak, *Cold War Civil Rights: Race and the Image of American Democracy* (Princeton University Press 2000).

[62] A detailed analysis is offered in Scott L. Cummings, 'The Internationalisation of Public Interest Law' (2006) 57(4) *Duke Law Journal* 891.

developments such as the reinterpretation of the Alien Tort Statute in the *Filartiga* v. *Pena-Irala* case[63] allowed non-citizens and NGOs such as Earthrights to contest alleged human rights violations of corporate actors in US courts.[64] In relation to the environment, a number of organisations tried to curb transboundary pollution by using the side agreement to the North American Free Trade Agreement (NAFTA), which allowed NGO challenges to violations of environmental laws by member states.[65]

Although these initiatives did not necessarily achieve fundamental objectives, the international aspect of claims filed outside traditional courts is illuminating.[66] The use of these venues, above and beyond innovative interpretations of the law, speaks to the first central criticism of 'traditional' public interest litigation: advocates incorrectly attribute a transformative capacity to litigation and thus inefficiently allocate limited resources available to achieve political and social change.[67] But, as the literature shows, cause lawyers are simply not under this illusion. They instead view lawsuits as part of a wider toolbox to influence domestic and international policy.

Environmental organisations are a prominent example of this measured view of litigation's reach. The president of the Natural Resources Defence Council noted that at its inception in the 1970s, the organisation's role was 'black and white' in that their purview was to 'identify polluters and make them stop.' Similarly, though the Sierra Club's original posture focused on 'shutting down' big polluters, their modern purpose is 'to shape, design, and accelerate the arrival of a new, sustainable economic order'.[68] As Deborah Rhode summed up a thorough study of public interest lawyers, 'the picture that emerged was of a diverse, self-critical community, proud of its achievements but conscious of its challenges and the diverse strategies necessary to address

63 630 F. 2d 876 (2d Cir. 1980).

64 Hari M. Osofsky, 'Environmental Human Rights under the Alien Tort Statute: Redress for Indigenous Victims of Multinational Corporations' (1997) 20(2) *Suffolk Transnational Law Review* 335; EarthRights and other organisations did not succeed in staking claims purely based on environmental damage under the Alien Tort Statute – environmental torts continued to be contingent on human rights considerations; *Jesner* v. *Arab Bank PLC* No. 16–499, 584 US ___ (2018) (holding that foreign corporations cannot be liable under Alien Tort Statute).

65 Commission for Environmental Cooperation, *Determination of Public Submission No. SEM/95-001* (1995). Available at www.cec.org/files/pdf/sem/95-1-DET-E2.pdf.

66 John H. Knox, 'The Neglected Lessons of the NAFTA Environmental Regime' (2010) 45 (2) *Wake Forest Law Review* 391.

67 Scheingold (n 20) 3–10.

68 Rhode (n 3) 2035.

them'.[69] Reflecting this change, Rhode found that the organisations surveyed slightly decreased the amount of resources devoted to litigation in courts while increasing spending in legislative work, research, reports, education, and media.[70] This shift in the outlook of US-based organisations is mirrored on the international stage.

2.2.2 Development and the Rule of Law Movement

The Ford Foundation and the US Agency of International Development enhanced public interest advocacy in the 1980s and 1990s by investing financial resources into international human rights work. This work served two relevant purposes. First, these funding activities exported the American form of strategic litigation, which underpins the later analysis of climate litigation, to countries in the Global South. Second, work on the rule of law became intertwined with efforts to create constitutions containing environmental rights used in strategic climate litigation, as in Dejusticia's successful suit against the Colombian government.[71]

Streams of charitable funding available for the burgeoning legal NGO sector were accompanied by capacity building and training within legal education. In the 1960s, early programmes in law and development targeted legal education around the world, training law professors in American legal methodologies.[72] The decision of the United States not to ratify or thoroughly implement important human rights treaties prompted funders like the Ford Foundation – pivotal to the invigoration of domestic public interest law – to invest in indigenous human rights organisations rather than exclusively funding the expansion of US influence.[73]

International human rights activists drew upon but also departed from the US public interest law model. Domestic activists in the Global South would try to find recourse in the United Nations, the European Court of

[69] Rhode (n 3) 2035.

[70] ibid.

[71] *Demanda Generaciones Futuras* v. *Minambiente*, Case 11001220300020180031900 (Superior Court of Bogota), Case 11001-22-03-000-2018-00319-01 (Supreme Court of Colombia).

[72] James A. Gardner, *Legal Imperialism: American Lawyers and Foreign Aid in Latin America* (University of Wisconsin Press, 1980).

[73] Hugo Frühling, 'From Dictatorship to Democracy: Law and Social Change in the Andean Region and the Southern Cone of South America'; Stephen Golub, 'Battling Apartheid, Building a New South Africa', both in Mary McClymont and Stephen Golub (eds.), *Many Roads to Justice: The Law Related Work of the Ford Foundation* (Ford Foundation 2000).

Human Rights, and the Inter-American Commission on Human Rights, but also through transnational networks of funders, activists, and lawyers. These resources would allow human rights abuses – sounding through any variety of legal or moral logic – to reverberate in an international space.[74] Finally, the Rule of Law movement in the 1990s tried to inject the logic of accountability into marketisation to remedy its perceived excesses through the expansion of 'good governance'.[75] Rule of Law reform aspired to create a hospitable environment for international investment while entrenching political and civil rights facilitated by access to justice in independent courts, now seen by funders as the institution responsible for ensuring probity and transparency in government.[76] Investments in clinical legal education and pro-bono programmes in the Global South allowed the familiar language of public interest law to bubble up in states with distinct traditions.[77] The Rule of Law movement thus paved the way for some convergence between public interest law, international development, and human rights.

With its mission to export democracy, the Rule of Law movement sought to rebrand human rights lawyers practicing under authoritarian regimes as the purveyors of public interest law in nascent democracies.[78] These transitional phases fostered the creation of a variety of legal rights and administrative structures. In Brazil, the Rule of Law movement helped form the *Ministerio Publico*, a collection of agency lawyers tasked with protecting vulnerable groups.[79] Elsewhere in South America, the movement undergirded the development of 'world constitutionalism', in which new constitutions were passed in, inter alia, Brazil (1988), Colombia (1991), and Peru (1993).[80] These constitutions variously

[74] Margaret E. Keck and Kathryn Sikkink, *Activists beyond Borders: Advocacy Networks in International Politics* (University of Michigan 1998).

[75] Bryant G. Garth, 'Building Strong and Independent Judiciaries through the New Law and Development: Behind the Paradox of Consensus Programs and Perpetually Disappointing Results' (2002) 52(2) *Depaul Law Review* 383, 388.

[76] Frühling (n 74) 69.

[77] These came primarily from USAID, the United Nations, and the World Bank. See Cummings, 'The Internationalization of Public Interest Law' (n 63).

[78] Edwin Rekosh, 'Constructing Public Interest Law: Transnational Collaboration and Exchange in Central and Eastern Europe' (2008) 13(1) *UCLA Journal of International Law and Foreign Affairs* 55. Rekosh recounts how activists turned to public interest law to enforce new social and environmental rights.

[79] Oscar Vilhena Vieira, 'Public Interest Law: A Brazilian Perspective' (2008) 13(1) *UCLA Journal of International Law and Foreign Affairs* 219, 231–4.

[80] César A. Rodriguez-Garavito and Luis Carlos Arenas, 'Indigenous Rights, Transnational Activism, and Legal Mobilization: The Struggle of the U'Wa People in Colombia' in

include provisions for the rights of indigenous peoples, the environment itself, and ethnic identity, while also creating causes of action and procedural reforms granting direct access to courts to allege infringements of new rights.[81]

2.2.3 *Non-Western Approaches to Public Interest Litigation*

A cautionary note is necessary. Framing the political contingencies of public interest litigation as values exported by the United States[82] is rife with historical difficulty. That framing simultaneously minimises the role of local legal actors, relegating them to passive recipients of Western bounties, while also neglecting the interactions that occurred *between* non-Western countries.[83] Ordinary citizens in India, for example, brought claims far before the Rule of Law movement, and such claims often articulated legal interpretations that radically departed from orthodoxy. The case of Husna Bai is worth briefly recounting, not least because it is ripe for analysis through the framework of demosprudence.

On 1 May 1958, a twenty-four-year-old Muslim prostitute filed a writ petition in the Allahabad High Court contesting the constitutionality of the Suppression of Immoral Traffic Act (SITA), which had come into force that day.[84] Her claim alleged that the statute, which gave force to Article 23 of the Indian Constitution's prohibition of forced labour and human trafficking by criminalising the running of brothels and public solicitation, unlawfully infringed on her right – drawn from Article 19 of the Indian Constitution – to carry out her ancient profession. Crucially, the act was passed as a result of sustained lobbying by relatively elite women ensured that the new republican welfare state could protect vulnerable people. An early female lawyer and politician recounted in correspondence with Prime Minister Nehru that it was 'painful . . . to

Boaventura de Sousa Santos and César A. Rodriguez-Garavito (eds.), *Law and Globalization from Below: Towards a Cosmopolitan Legal Identity* (Cambridge University Press 2003).

[81] Frühling (n 74) 70; Patrick Reinsborough, 'How the Uwa and People's Globalisation Beat Big Oil' in David Solnit (ed.), *Globalise Liberation: How to Uproot the System and Build a Better World* (City Lights 2004).

[82] See, generally, Teemu Ruskola, *Legal Orientalism: China, the United States, and Modern Law* (Harvard University Press 2013).

[83] Meredith Teretta, 'Anti-colonial Lawyering, Postwar Human Rights, and Decolonization across Imperial Boundaries in Africa' (2017) 52(3) *Canadian Journal of History* 448.

[84] This account is adopted from Rohit De, *A People's Constitution: The Everyday Life of Law in the Indian Republic* (Princeton University Press 2018) 169–209.

hear an attempt made to invoke fundamental rights in an argument to uphold the right to carry on prostitution'.[85] Husna Bai's petition evinced an understanding of constitutional meaning entirely at odds with the political and legal elites of the day, upturning the expectations of leaders who purported to speak for the marginalised.[86] But this attempted subversion of the orthodox legislative and judicial understanding was not simply about the judicial vindication of individual rights. On the same day the petition was filed, more than four hundred 'singers, dancing girls, and women of ill fame' formed the Allahabad Dancing Girls Union. The organisation committed to direct action in response to the law, claiming that '[SITA] was a clear encroachment on the right to carry on any profession guaranteed by the Constitution'.

Rather than an organised effort by those with power and resources, Husna Bai's case represents the ability of grassroots organisations to create alternate interpretations of the law and proliferate those interpretations through the public sphere. Nearly 800 kilometres away in Calcutta, prostitutes threatened to go on hunger strike if the state could not provide another career for them.[87] Their peers raised money from members of the public (and perhaps customers) in Delhi's red light district, and seventy-five women demonstrated outside parliament, warning that the statute would simply push sex workers into different areas. Across India's diverse physical geography, sex workers articulated their own understanding of constitutional meaning through protest.

A glance at how sex workers in a newly independent state turned the rift between citizen and legislative interpretations of the constitution into a site of resistance is instructive for two reasons. First, it demonstrates that the internationalisation of public interest lawyering – especially the sort closely aligned with social movements contemplated by demosprudence – was not simply a Western export.[88] Second, if we are to understand the emergence of climate change litigation as part of a networked global movement, the Indian example demonstrates the need for sensitivity to the sociolegal context of different states and legal cultures. In the

[85] De (n 84) 170.

[86] Guinier and Torres (n 43) 2754 (noting that representatives are not engaging in demosprudence when they substitute their own view for their constituents).

[87] De (n 84) 181. The merits of this public grievance were also recognised by the Allahabad High Court: *Shama Bai and Ors* v. *State of Uttar Pradesh and Ors* AIR 1959 All 57, 60 ('the Government owe[s] a duty to rehabilitate the prostitutes if they are by law being forced to give up their profession', at paragraph 2).

[88] Balakrishnan Rajagopal, *International Law from Below: Development, Social Movements and Third World Resistance* (Cambridge University Press 2003).

most general terms, the absence of a politically independent judiciary and the judicial policy-making endemic to the common law tradition changes the balance of power in cause lawyering. Comparing civil and common law institutions in France and the United States, Bourdieu observed that civil law traditions endow different legal actors with the symbolic power of law, sometimes favouring judges and legal scholars as purveyors of legal entrepreneurship over lawyers.[89] In the context of demosprudence, which examines how lawyer-citizens and social activists co-produce 'new meanings for law-making',[90] a still wider cast of legal actors emerges. As Frank Munger asked, writing in relation to the effect of the Rule of Law movement on activist litigation in developing countries, 'Who is the "cause lawyer" in a non-common law system – a solicitor, barrister, judge, notary, prosecutor, administrator, mediator, journalist, village elder, or ordinary citizen?'[91] We might ask instead, in the emerging demosprudence of climate change, outside of the treaty-making process, who can wield the symbolic power of law?

2.3 Climate Change and Transnational Advocacy

By combining external change through 'naming and shaming' with an exported public interest model for piecemeal internal change, new public interest lawyers and human rights activists adjusted to the demands of trying to change policy in the age of globalisation.[92] These new alliances can be usefully framed, in the rhetoric of comparative politics, as 'transnational advocacy networks' (TANs). TANs 'promote causes, principled ideas, and norms, and they often involve individuals advocating policy changes that cannot be easily linked to a rationalist understanding of their interests'.[93] Advocacy networks bring together state actors and civil society to provide resources to domestic actors, influence policy, and monitor implementation. Information, personnel, and sometimes

[89] See, generally, Pierre Bourdieu, 'The Force of Law: Towards a Sociology of the Juridical Field' (1987) 38(2) *Hastings Law Journal* 814.

[90] Guinier and Torres (n 43) 2750.

[91] Frank Munger, 'Constructing Law from Development: Cause Lawyers, Generational Narratives, and the Rule of Law in Thailand' in John Gillespie and Pip Nicholson (eds.) *Law and Development and the Global Discourses of Legal Transfers* (Cambridge University Press 2012) 242.

[92] Martha Minow, 'Instituting Universal Human Rights Law: The Invention of Tradition in the Twentieth Century' in Austin Sarat, Bryant Garth, and Robert A. Kagan (eds.) *Looking Back at Law's Century* (Cornell University Press 2002) 62–3.

[93] Keck and Sikkink (n 75) 11.

financial resources move fluidly between actors in these networks. Their success is measured by changes in how debates are framed, commitments from state actors, or concrete policy reforms. Environmental organisations have been operating in ways that resemble transnational advocacy networks for decades.[94] Early examples include the global coalitions that mobilised in protests against the World Trade Organisation and the creation of an alternative in the form of the World Social Forum. Alongside the coordinated grassroots activism, a coalition lead by Environmental Defense and the Center for International Environmental Law (CIEL) contributed to the creation of the World Bank Inspection Panel by lobbying the US legislature to withdraw funding if reforms were not pursued.[95] US organisations challenged the development of extractive industries in the Global South through the Inspection Panel, which was tasked with remedying non-enforcement of Bank policies.[96] Similarly, CIEL succeeded in its mission to force the WTO Appellate Body to allow the submission of amicus briefs in state disputes.[97] Though the results of these advocacy efforts varied, the translation of societal concerns about international economic development into the legal lexicon points to the internationalisation of public interest law.

TANs and the individuals who practise contentious politics within them ought to be included as legal actors within public interest law.[98] Sometimes the role of such actors is apparent. Recent quantitative research shows that Article 19, an NGO dedicated to enhancing freedom of information, effectively influenced the strength of domestic freedom of information statutes in twenty countries by publishing draft legislation.[99]

94 Keck and Sikkink (n 75) 11.

95 Jonathan A. Fox and L. David Brown, 'Introduction', in Jonathan A. Fox and L. David Brown (eds.), *The Struggle for Accountability: The World Bank, NGOs, and Grassroots Movements* (MIT Press 1998) 7.

96 Kay Treakle, Jonathan Fox, and Dana Clark, 'Lessons Learned', in Kay Treakle, Jonathan Fox, and Dana Clark (eds.), *Demanding Accountability: Civil-Society Claims and the World Bank Inspection Panel* (Rowman & Littlefeld 2003) 248–50.

97 See Center for International Environmental Law and Others, *Amicus Brief to the Appellate Body on United States – Import Prohibition of Certain Shrimp and Shrimp Products* (Center for International Environmental Law 1999), http://ciel.org/Publications/shrimpturtlebrief.pdf.

98 In the absence of this categorisation, there would be nothing *new* about public interest law. See Gerald Torres, 'Legal Change' (2007) 55(2) *Cleveland State Law Review* 135, 142. ('Cause lawyering may try to shift the rules, which ultimately may change the culture, but the problem with cause lawyering is that decisions about which rules are being shifted and how those rule shifts are being enforced is ultimately made by elites.')

99 Daniel Berliner, 'Transnational Advocacy and Domestic Law: International NGOs and the Design of Freedom of Information Laws' (2016) 11(1) *Review of International*

However, most scholarship on TANs linked to climate change focusses on minority group representation within the treaty process.[100] If the growth of climate litigation partially results from domestic lawyers' loss of faith in the treaty system, the work of TANs on domestic climate policy serves as an important point of comparison. Where TANs successfully advocate for legislative change outside of the courts, they are an important node in a network of *legal* actors. One important example comes from the United Kingdom: the origin of that jurisdiction's climate change statute is attributed to a coordinated campaign initiated by Friends of the Earth. [101,102]

Perhaps the most intriguing emergent direction in this kind of transnational climate change action comes from the protest group Extinction Rebellion (XR). Though the group consisted of about six organisers in early 2018, they successfully shut down major bridges in London, attracting more than six thousand protestors, through non-violent direct action. Their protest is framed in terms of a collective right to life in the face of catastrophe, and they demand three commitments from the government: (1) recognition of a state of climate emergency, (2) creation of a comprehensive and binding national climate change policy to achieve net zero carbon emissions by 2025, and (3) institution of a national citizen's assembly to oversee those policies.[103] The demands, then, are a resistance to quiet 'annihilation by the elites and politicians'. Though often framed as a UK-based group, XR also supported intergovernmental organisations in the global south at the Katowice Climate Change Conference.[104]

In parallel and with XR's support,[105] school climate strikes coordinated across 128 countries saw more than one million youth protestors

Organisations 121; Article 19 is also a founding member of the International Freedom of Expression Exchange, an advocacy network consisting of NGOs around the world.

[100] David Ciplet, 'Contesting Climate Injustice: Transnational Advocacy Network Struggles for Rights in UN Climate Politics' (2014) 14(4) *Global Environmental Politics* 75.

[101] Neil Carter and Mike Childs, 'Friends of the Earth as a Policy Entrepreneur: "The Big Ask" Campaign for a UK Climate Change Act' (2018) 27(6) *Environmental Politics* 994.

[102] Charles Tilly and Sidney G. Tarrow, *Contentious Politics* (2nd ed., Oxford University Press 2015).

[103] Matthew Taylor, 'Dozens Arrested after Climate Protest Blocks Five London Bridges', *The Guardian* (London, 11 November 2018), www.theguardian.com/environment/2018/nov/17/thousands-gather-to-block-london-bridges-in-climate-rebellion.

[104] Farhana Yamin, 'Die, Survive, or Thrive?' in Clare Farrell and others (eds.), *This Is Not a Drill: An Extinction Rebellion Handbook* (Penguin 2019) 26.

[105] ibid. Constituents of TANs use protest tactics more frequently if adjacent organisations do the same. See Jennifer Hadden and Lorien Jasny, 'The Power of Peers: How Transnational Advocacy Networks Shape NGO Strategy on Climate Change' (2019) 49(2) *British Journal of Political Science* 637.

demonstrate, urging national governments to cut carbon emissions by up to 15 per cent per year. In the absence of a central coordinating body, the youth strikes grew autonomously out of the lone protest of Swedish teenager Greta Thunberg, who urged politicians to treat climate change as a crisis by heavily curbing national emissions.[106]

Both movements exhibit the multiscalar characteristics of a TAN: they consist of actors across borders advancing transnational normative claims about climate policy in local settings. They each reframe climate change in terms of global catastrophe, thereby placing particularities of local law and policy – and even climate vulnerability – peripherally. This geographical scale-shifting is contingent on a normative claim: it is the appeal to superior moral norms displaces the centrality of the legal and political.[107] Parliament's unprecedented declaration of a climate emergency points to the capacity of these reframing efforts to achieve a discursive outcome.

Extinction Rebellion's other demands neatly map onto the typology of outcomes sought by TANs. The second demand seeks a legislative outcome while the third corresponds to a related democratic outcome. In the context of demosprudence, these climate activists are part of a 'constituency of accountability' committed to visions of a sustainable society. Those visions do not unfold in the arena of domestic constitutional law or regional human rights regimes, but in a transnational public sphere.

These movement actors are significant for climate change because of their particular mix of contentious strategies. By operating transnationally, using the rhetoric of catastrophe, and relying on mass mobilisation, these networks seek to change the environment in which formal legal rules are made. As the next section shows, however, existing frameworks in international law do not fully account for role of the citizen.

2.4 Climate Litigation, Legal Dialogue, and Transnational Networks

Climate litigation is particularly well suited to analysis from the perspective of demosprudence and transnational advocacy networks for at least two reasons: (1) climate change is by nature a multiscalar problem that

[106] Greta Thunberg, *No One Is Too Small to Make a Difference* (Penguin 2019) 8.

[107] Brian Doherty, Joost de Moor, and Graeme Hayes, 'The "New" Climate Politics of Extinction Rebellion?' *Open Democracy* (27 November 2018), www.opendemocracy.net/en/new-climate-politics-of-extinction-rebellion/.

requires multiscalar solutions and (2) a form of transnational public interest litigation or law-making can effectively operate at those scales. Still, some theoretical intervention is required in order to legitimate as legally relevant important actions taken by citizens and NGOs.

More than a decade ago, Hari Osofsky saw the value of examining climate litigation as a *pluralist* legal dialogue that stretched beyond the courts.[108] Central to that inquiry was whether local legal efforts, such as state-level climate litigation in California, and petitions to supranational bodies such as the Inter-American Commission on Human Rights, could properly constitute a form of international law-making. Responding affirmatively, Professor Osofsky noted that 'when California litigates on climate change, it arguably aims to influence the international legal discourse in many ways beyond merely forcing US policy in a regulatory direction'.[109] Participants in this legal dialogue have an important law-making role not as legislators or adjudicators, but as actors who contribute to shifting state and international practice. She explains further that the question of whether a Westphalian approach to international law-making, centred ultimately on state consent to international obligations, is blind to the role of local actors may be insoluble. Thus the point of moving away from state-centred approaches to international law is more about gleaning insights than circumscribing rigid boundaries.

A similar waiver applies here, where the semantic boundaries between demosprudence and an expansive view legal pluralism, as they apply to a wider appreciation of the actors involved in 'climate law-making', might be a road to nowhere. What remains, however, is the utility of decentring our approach to climate law-making from the courts themselves. In other words, if pluralist legal dialogue can include the linkages between state courts and climate law on the international stage, then it ought to incorporate the significant contribution of non-state actors to climate policy.[110] If state level litigation and policy-making form part of a legal dialogue about climate change, a demosprudential perspective

[108] Hari M. Osofsky, 'Climate Change Litigation as Pluralist Legal Dialogue' (2007) 26(1) *Stanford Journal of International Law* 181, 194–5 ('Simply put, pluralism questions whether we have drawn the boundaries of what constitutes lawmaking inclusively enough.')

[109] ibid 227.

[110] Earlier models do not typically account for the role of non-state actors. See Hari M. Osofsky, 'The Geography of Climate Change Litigation: Implications for Transnational Regulatory Governance' (2005) 83(6) *Washington University Law Quarterly* 1789.

hones in on the role of citizens and social movements within that dialogue, situating them as potential law-makers. That focus departs from pluralist scholarship on climate change law, which sees the citizen only through their legal representatives.[111]

2.4.1 *Transnational Legal Process*

When climate change is viewed through the narrow lens of Westphalian international law-making,[112] an issue solely in domestic courts or the treaty making process, we can extract only a fragmentary picture of the issues involved, consigning ourselves to a spatially and temporally limited vision of how events caused or exacerbated by climate change interface with the law. Climate law constrained as such runs the risk of missing the forest for the trees. The prospect of climate migration, for example, just grazes up against the law through the preambular text of the Paris Agreement. Moreover, some of the mitigation strategies covered below could not count as law-making under a Westphalian view.[113] Similarly, the work of activist lawyers and financial professionals in reforming reporting and disclosure standards would fall outside the realm of law-making, despite the potential effects on how sustainable and unsustainable projects are financed. In other words, an approach that is too 'zoomed in' to one legal lens will likely miss relevant outputs of climate governance. Westphalian international law-making is not, however, the only analytical lens through which we might see climate change.

Harold Koh's transnational legal process framework accommodates these interactions to a significant degree – it breaks down the boundaries between domestic/international and public/private, dynamically shifts between those categories, accounts for the role of non-state actors, and

[111] Osofsky, 'Climate Change Litigation as Pluralist Legal Dialogue' (n 109) 234. On whether citizens contribute to law-making, Osofsky considers that analysis should focus 'on the actors who participate directly by formally filing or adjudicating'.

[112] A Westphalian model, premised on the actions of sovereign states, would not see most forms of climate law contemplated here as law-making. See, for example, James Crawford, *Brownlie's Principles of Public International Law* (Oxford University Press, 2012).

[113] UNFCCC, Conference of the Parties, Twenty-first Session (Paris, 30 November–11 December 2015), Adoption of the Paris Agreement under the United Nations Framework Convention on Climate Change, Document FCCC/CP/2015/L.9/Rev.1, 12 December 2015, 50 https://unfccc.int/resource/docs/2015/cop21/eng/l09r01.pdf. The agreement recommends that two of its committees and relevant experts 'develop recommendations for integrated approaches to avert, minimize and address displacement related to the adverse impacts of climate change' 7–8.

posits that law can shape these interactions as much as the interactions shape law.[114] This analysis accounts for public-private and state-corporate dialogue that characterise suits that target local or national regulations as well as those aimed at private actors, whether brought by states or NGOs. Within this framework, scholarship has addressed the interactions between state judicial systems[115] and government agencies,[116] categorising both as important sites of governance or pluralist law-making. Transnational networks within the legal profession have recently contributed significantly to climate governance through drafting of the Oslo Principles on Global Climate Change Obligations[117] and the Principles on Climate Obligations of Enterprises,[118] which set out the legal rationales for states and private enterprise, respectively, to be required to pursue mitigation and adaptation strategies.

However, it is more difficult to see how *citizens* are non-state actors with policy influence in this analytic space, even if they can be theoretically brought under the umbrella of the NGOs who represent their interests. In such circumstances, citizens remain passive objects of power.[119] That is where demosprudence may intervene, as it crucially tries to account for the critiques of models of representation that 'do not reflect the dynamic equilibrium of power that organized constituencies bring to the representational connection'.[120] In other words, the transnational legal process model is blind to the 'participatory, power-sharing process' that demosprudence finds possible in the lawyer-client relationship. More to the point, demosprudence allows us to see how mobilised individuals have 'power with' their representatives, whether the latter are NGOs, subnational entities, or private firms.

[114] Harold Hongju Koh, 'Transnational Legal Process' (1996) 75(1) *Nebraska Law Review* 181.

[115] Michael Kirby, 'Transnational Judicial Dialogue, Internationalisation of Law, and Australian Judges' (2008) 9(1) *Melbourne Journal of International Law* 171.

[116] Anne-Marie Slaughter, 'Global Government Networks, Global Information Agencies, and Disaggregated Democracy' (2003) 24(4) *Michigan Journal of International Law* 1041.

[117] Expert Group on Global Climate Change Obligations, 'Oslo Principles on Global Climate Change Obligations' (1 March 2015) https://globaljustice.yale.edu/sites/default/files/files/OsloPrinciples.pdf.

[118] Expert Group on Climate Obligations of Enterprises, *Principles on Climate Obligations of Enterprises* (Eleven International Publishing 2018).

[119] William H. Simon, 'Visions of Practice in Legal Thought' (1984) 36(1) *Stanford Law Review* 469.

[120] Guinier and Torres (n 43) 2774.

Osofsky uses geographical conceptions of networks to complement the transnational legal process analysis in the context of both local climate policy[121] and municipal lawsuits.[122] Broadly speaking, the nexus of spaces of dependence (spaces we depend on for material well-being) and spaces of engagement (where 'the politics of securing a space of dependence unfolds') are best represented by interactions occurring across formal and informal networks in place of a single level of governance. Applied to climate change litigation, 'the dynamics among interested actors at multiple levels in the disputes shape spaces that help to determine emissions choices at multiple scales'.[123] These networks frame the relationships between local climate initiatives and the national and international bodies with which they interact. Where American cities file public nuisance suits against major emitters, they may cooperate or conflict with the state and federal government, while at the same time working with informal coalitions to realise treaty goals. Similarly, NGOs may reach out formally to coordinate advocacy tactics with 'adjacent' organisations through working groups, as where Oxfam America planned climate lobbying efforts jointly with religious and development groups.[124] These NGOs, in turn, also interact with intergovernmental organisations across scales.[125] Unifying the variegated strands of literature across transnational law, network analysis, and public interest litigation allows for a more complete map of climate governance actors.

The remainder of this chapter examines how recent trends in climate litigation – in addition to being multiscalar and in novel ways – possess some of the characteristics of demosprudence in that they aim to engage the public in climate law-making. The jurisdictions, types of actors involved, and degrees of success vary, but each example speaks to forms of actual or attempted engagement between the law and citizens concerned about climate change.

[121] Hari M. Osofsky, 'Rethinking the Geography of Local Climate Action: Multilevel Network Participation in Metropolitan Regions' (2015) 1 *Utah Law Review* 173.

[122] Hari M. Osofsky, 'Is Climate Change International – Litigation's Diagonal Regulatory Role' (2009) 49(3) *Virginia Journal of International Law* 585.

[123] ibid 642.

[124] Jennifer Hadden, 'The Relational Sources of Advocacy Strategies: Comparative Evidence from the European and U.S. Climate Change Sectors' (2018) 46(2) *Policy Studies Journal* 248.

[125] Tana Johnson, 'Cooperation, Co-optation, Competition, Conflict: International Bureaucracies and Non-governmental organizations in an Interdependent World' (2016) 23(5) *Review of International Political Economy* 737.

2.5 Networked Public Interest Litigation: Crowdsourcing and Crowdfunding Claims

As transnational social movement actors gain momentum, their tactics increasingly interact with strategic litigation. Where governance frameworks downplay the role of social movements and social movement scholarship tends to minimise the role of law, how can the complexity of climate change actors be captured? This framework must embrace the features of TANs while adding substate actors and due consideration of domestic law. Drawing on demosprudence, it must also emphasise the role of mobilised citizens. But to fulfil the herculean task of learning from public interest litigation's messy history, we must also carefully apply historical lessons to the complexities of climate change. It has been suggested that the vast economic and political reforms required by climate change and a history of mixed success cut in favour of a shift towards small-scale litigation rather than 'holy grail' cases.[126] Domains such as planning law and private energy efficiency standards may generate significant consequences for climate change governance, and a preoccupation with high-profile rights-related litigation might be blind to their significance.[127] Even if high-profile litigation is successful, the American experience indicates that ambitious programmes will face implementation hurdles.[128]

The central nodes of *networked public interest litigation* may be characterised by (1) increased citizen engagement, either as parties to litigation or members of TANs; (2) distributed financing of lawsuits and transactions with significant mitigation potential; (3) media presence focusing on particular claimants or affected citizens; and (4) framing of climate change harm through the lens of human rights and catastrophe. Finally, the peripheral nodes of the network embrace 'mundane' cases and initiatives without these characteristics.[129] Crowdfunding mitigation efforts and crowdsourcing claimants are particularly innovative avenues that demonstrate the demosprudential characteristics of contemporary climate litigation.

[126] Kim Bouwer, 'The Unsexy Future of Climate Litigation' (2018) 30(3) *Journal of Environmental Law* 483.

[127] Bouwer (n 126) 499.

[128] Scheingold (n 20) 3–10.

[129] Or, for example, cases dealing with subsequent implementation of judgments. The position of these nodes may shift towards the core in the future.

2.5.1 *Demosprudence through Crowdfunded Green Transactions*

Crowdfunding allows large groups of interested parties to invest relatively small amounts of capital into goods or services on a prospective basis and essentially without the intervention of financial institutions as intermediaries.[130] In 2015, Greenpeace Nordic planned to crowdfund the capital necessary to acquire two coal-fired power plants and the German lignite operations of Vattenfall, a company owned wholly by the Swedish government, for the sole purpose of phasing out those operations and replacing them with clean energy through the establishment of a transitional German charity.[131] Portions of their statement of interest read, in Osofsky's sense, as a pluralist legal dialogue. Here, the dialogue is between Greenpeace (as a TAN), a power company operating in Germany, the Swedish state as their shareholders, and – most crucially – the citizens from around the world who would co-finance the purchase.

Greenpeace's statement of interest contests Vattenfall's asset valuation, projecting that new emissions regulations and clean-up costs would reduce the value of the operations to roughly a fourth of what the energy conglomerate had projected based on new emissions regulations, as well as the cost of decommissioning and reclamation.[132] In part, this would serve to hold the Swedish government to account on its promise to decarbonise. A section of the statement entitled 'Vision for structural change' reads in pertinent part:

> Our recent past has been dominated by fossil fuels, but our future will be different. . . . In order to avoid catastrophic climate change, coal power plants throughout the world need to be closed and replaced by renewable power generation. . . . [I]n a situation in which the operators of these industries fail to live up to their social and environmental responsibility to lead this transformation, the process needs to be accelerated by civil society. Therefore it is Greenpeace Nordic's vision to turn Lusatia into an iconic region for a successful energy transition.[133]

The planned acquisition capitalised on the financial costs of climate change – which insurers and actuaries have been integrating into

[130] Ethan Mollick, 'The Dynamics of Crowdfunding: An Exploratory Study' (2014) 29(1) *Journal of Business Venturing* 1, 1.

[131] Greenpeace Nordic, 'Statement of Interest for the Acquisition of Vattenfall's German Lignite Activities' (20 October 2015), www.greenpeace.org/sweden/Global/sweden/klimat/dokument/2015/Vattenfall_Statement_of_Interest.pdf ('Statement of Interest').

[132] International Energy Agency, *Redrawing the Energy-Climate Map: World Energy Outlook Special Report* (International Energy Agency, 2013) 98.

[133] 'Statement of Interest' (n 131) 8.

assessments for at least a decade – to pressure Vattenfall and by proxy the Swedish state to decarbonise rapidly. The apparent purpose is to produce a tangible reduction in emissions based on the opportunity cost of a typical sale, where an acquirer might continue to run the power plants for years. Yet the choice of language, referencing the catastrophic risks of climate change, and the social and environmental responsibilities of Vattenfall, reproduce the same moral imperative found in appeals to supranational bodies as well as in rights-based public interest litigation.[134] Cutting across spatial and jurisdictional scales, Greenpeace's attempted acquisition is illustrative of a broader approach to public interest law and advocacy.

Financial approaches to decarbonisation – and environmental lawyering more broadly[135] – are not new. By arguing that Vattenfall's assessments did not internalise non-physical 'carbon risks' that would depreciate the value of their operations, Greenpeace replicated a strategy employed by activist environmental lawyers: pressuring companies to take climate action through corporate law.[136] Though the extent of climate risk regulation is typically confined to disclosure requirements, better understanding of the economic loss associated with climate change has prompted the possibility that fiduciary duties require analysis of such risks.[137] By engaging a wide variety of actors in climate risk discourse, climate activists pull marginal approaches to corporate governance into the mainstream.[138]

[134] Osofsky, 'Climate Change Litigation as Pluralist Legal Dialogue' (n 109) 194.

[135] Frühling (n 74) 70.

[136] See, for example, ClientEarth, 'Climate Risk: ClientEarth Lawyer Urges Two-Year Deadline' (6 February 2018) www.clientearth.org/climate-risk-clientearth-lawyer-urges-two-year-deadline/.

[137] Alexia Staker and Alice Garton, 'Directors' Liability and Climate Risk: United Kingdom – Country Paper' (Commonwealth Climate and Law Initiative 2018), www.smithschool.ox.ac.uk/research/sustainable-finance/publications/CCLI-UK-Paper-Final.pdf ; Anita Foerster and others, 'Keeping Good Company in the Transition to a Low Carbon Economy? An Evaluation of Climate Risk Disclosure Practices in Australia' (2017) 35(3) *Company and Securities Law Journal* 154. Furthermore, a coalition of environmental charities in the United Kingdom are pressuring the relevant regulator to issue guidance or seek declaratory judgment in relation to whether charitable investments are constrained by their objects. See Bates Wells, 'Call for New Landmark Judgment on Responsible Investment' (4 March 2019) https://bateswells.co.uk/2019/03/call-for-new-landmark-judgment-on-responsible-investment-join-the-coalition-and-sign-up/.

[138] Sarah Baker and Jay Youngdahl, 'From Ethical Fringe to Investment Mainstream: Governance, Law and Climate Change Risk Management' (2015) 67(9) *Governance Directions* 525.

Greenpeace's acquisition model uses the logic and language of capital markets to encourage mitigation efforts, but it is unique in how it seeks to engage the citizenry as participants in climate change law. Raising capital this way requires a strong network of funders, meaning effectiveness is linked to a TANs ability to engage mobilised citizens. Greenpeace's statement of interest was summarily rejected by the bank responsible for managing the sale – they did not provide reasons for refusal. Their strategy nonetheless provides an important model for democratising climate mitigation efforts.

2.5.2 *Crowdsourcing Claimants and Crowdfunding Claims*

Much has been written about the Urgenda Foundation's groundbreaking lawsuit against the Dutch government, including the importance of the first instance court's endorsement of scientific consensus about the disastrous effects of climate change.[139] However, the optics of Urgenda's lawsuit have received comparatively less attention. Urgenda crowdsourced more than eight hundred claimants through its website. This served several purposes: (1) suing on behalf of concerned citizens allowed Urgenda to allege violations of human rights law, (2) the unusually large number of claimants arguably helped attract press coverage, and (3) the Court was pressured to livestream proceedings, allowing members of the public to engage with a historic case.[140] Adjacent to Urgenda in this climate law network is the NGO Klimaatzaak, who filed a claim alleging a similar theory in Belgium; the organisation's website allows for prospective claimants to join the suit online, advertising that the process can be finished within two minutes. Klimaatzaak advertised that more than 61,161 claimants had registered for the case, which had been stalled on choice of language proceedings since September 2015.[141] A claim filed by 450 Swiss women represented by a foundation called KlimaSeniorinnen in 2016, all at least 65 years of age, is currently pending.[142] As in

[139] R. Henry Weaver and Douglas A. Kysar, 'Courting Disaster: Climate Change and the Adjudication of Catastrophe' (2017) 93(1) *Notre Dame Law Review* 295.

[140] Howard (n 1).

[141] See Klimaatzaak, 'Aperçu du déroulement de notre action en justice', https://affaire-climat.be/fr/the-case#you_are_here.

[142] Letter of Petition in the matter *Swiss Senior Women for Climate Protection and Others v. Swiss Federal Council and Others*, filed 25 October 2016, https://klimaseniorinnen.ch/wp-content/uploads/2016/10/161024_summary_swiss-climate-case_def.pdf.

Urgenda, the claimants argue that existing legal targets are insufficient to safeguard their rights under both the European Convention on Human Rights and Swiss constitutional law. These cases use a client-centred media strategy where the rights rhetoric of citizens is just like the substantive legal arguments used – both seek to capitalise on the indirect effects that climate litigation can have on governments and corporate actors.[143]

Equally, there is an element of 'legal transfer' in cases modelled on Urgenda. KlimaSeniorinnen, which was asked by Greenpeace to investigate options for suing the Swiss government after Urgenda, published an analysis of its suit, arguing that shared environmental principles and international law constituted 'strong legal grounds to bring human rights based climate lawsuits against governments'.[144] Most recently, seven organisations including the Dutch operations of Greenpeace and Friends of the Earth have threatened to sue Royal Dutch Shell if the company does not take significant steps to decarbonise, and they have already recruited more than 13,000 citizens as co-claimants.[145]

Of course, financial implications mean that not all jurisdictions are as favourable for mass claimant litigation as Switzerland, the Netherlands, or Belgium. In the United Kingdom, a mass claimant suit could proceed via a Group Litigation Order,[146] but each claimant could be forced to pay up to £10,000, depending on judicial discretion around cost protection.[147] Where there is uncertainty around cost liability or local civil procedure is not conducive to mass claimant suits, crowdfunding provides a way for citizens to meaningfully participate in litigation. Crowdfunding can be usefully be separated into two categories: (1) equity crowdfunding or litigation finance, where investors receive a financial

[143] Jacqueline Peel and Hari M. Osofsky, *Climate Change Litigation: Regulatory Pathways to Cleaner Energy* (Cambridge University Press 2015) 47–51.

[144] Cordelia Christiane Bähr and others, '*KlimaSeniorinnen*: Lessons from the Swiss Senior Women's Case for Future Climate Litigation' (2018) 9(2) *Journal of Human Rights and the Environment* 194, 221. Pre-publication version available online at https://klimaseniorinnen.ch/wp-content/uploads/2018/03/JHRE-9-2-FINAL-180307.pdf.

[145] Friends of The Earth International, 'Climate litigation against Shell' (28 July 2018), www.foei.org/civicrm?page=CiviCRM&q=civicrm/petition/sign&sid=19&reset=1.

[146] CPR 19.11.

[147] A GLO in respect of a 500-claimant private nuisance claim was at issue in *Austin & Others* v. *Miller Argent (South Wales) Ltd* [2011] EWCA Civ 928. The court did not find it necessary to issue judgment in relation to whether a claim in private nuisance could in theory proceed through a GLO, although this and the question of whether such a suit would be amenable to cost capping were left open.

return on the proceeds of litigation,[148] and (2) donor crowdfunding, where citizens finance causes they believe in without any monetary recompense.[149] Donor crowdfunding, which is open to unaccredited investors, is a promising pathway for democratic engagement. Through the lens of demosprudence, crowdfunding may be capable of expanding the 'quotient of democratic legitimacy'.[150]

A UK-based NGO called CrowdJustice is at the forefront of donor crowdfunding of process costs for lawsuits, including climate lawsuits. The Global Legal Action Network (GLAN), with six Portuguese children between the ages of five and fourteen as claimants, will attempt to file suit against forty-seven countries simultaneously in the European Court of Human Rights.[151] In less than a month, GLAN raised £27,496.

In the United Kingdom, Plan B Earth filed papers for judicial review in December 2017, alleging that the ongoing failure to revise carbon reduction targets promulgated under a domestic climate change statute was unlawful.[152] Plan B was joined by eleven claimants representing various aspects of climate vulnerability. University students and a minor represent the interest in intergenerational equity; a Rabbi speaks to the theological imperatives to act urgently; a lawyer from an island nation represents the risk to life and property posed by rising sea levels.[153] Through CrowdJustice, 831 individuals donated a total of £54,225. Though Plan B did not succeed on the merits, the UK's clean growth minister announced at a meeting of the heads of government of the Commonwealth that domestic carbon targets would be reviewed with the expert body in charge of setting targets, the Committee on Climate Change (CCC).[154] Through lobbying efforts and direct action, Plan

[148] See David S. Abrams and Daniel L. Chen, 'A Market for Justice: a First Empirical Look at Third Party Litigation Funding' (2013) 15(4) *University of Pennsylvania Journal of Business Law* 1075.

[149] Ronen Perry, 'Crowdfunding Civil Justice' (2018) 59(4) *Boston College Law Review* 1357.

[150] Guinier and Torres (n 43) 2751.

[151] Global Legal Action Network, 'Children -v- Governments of Europe & Climate Change', www.crowdjustice.com/case/climate-change-echr/, accessed 10 June 2020.

[152] *R. (Plan B Earth and others)* v. *Secretary of State for Business, Energy and Industrial Strategy* (2018) EWHC 1892 (Admin).

[153] Statement of Grounds filed in *Plan B Earth and Others* v. *The Secretary of State for Business, Energy, and Industrial Strategy*, Claim No. CO/16/2018, http://blogs2.law.columbia.edu/climate-change-litigation/wp-content/uploads/sites/16/non-us-case-documents/2017/20171207_Claim-No.-CO162018-_points-of-claim-1.pdf.

[154] Jillian Ambrose, 'UK on Path to "Zero Carbon" Economy' *The Telegraph* (London, 17 April 2018), www.telegraph.co.uk/business/2018/04/17/uk-path-zero-carbon-economy/; Roger Harrabin, 'Climate Change: Ministers Should Be 'Sued' over targets'

B also contributed to the minister's decision to ask the CCC for advice on the setting of a net zero emissions target.[155] The suit is therefore typical of networked public interest litigation: conventional arguments about statutory interpretation are amplified by a human rights framing.

2.6 Conclusion

Amid new calls for citizens to flood the courts with climate change lawsuits are familiar problems. The uneasy historical relationship between the law and social change demonstrates several limitations. Lawsuits may sap movement energy, even successful claims may not be adequately implemented, and a narrow focus on rights may not be compatible with systemic change. However, where public-interest lawyers operate alongside mobilised social movements, traditional legal actions and other forms of contentious politics are complementary.

When youth climate strikers in Sydney implore the state to protect their future, they invoke and invigorate the *legal* concept of intergenerational equity and the attendant principles connecting climate change and human rights.[156] They need not enumerate the analytic substance of environmental rights to effectively pressure the legislature, which may embed principles into decision-making. This reciprocity is even stronger where movement tactics amplify the effect of lawsuits. In New Zealand, a recent statutory claim sought to compel amendments to domestic climate change targets. The regulatory targets were held to be reviewable, but the electoral victory of a government committed to eliminating emissions by 2050 rendered the substantial issue academic.[157] Following the introduction of a bill to implement that political commitment, youth strikers demanded that the net-zero target be brought forward; they also argued for the removal of any provision limiting the judicial remedy for breach to declaratory relief. Though such claims concern formal rights as either a second-order issue (in New Zealand)

BBC (London, 27 September 2017), www.bbc.co.uk/news/uk-41401656, accessed 10 June 2020.

155 'UK Climate Targets: Request for Advice from the Committee on Climate Change' (15 October 2018), www.gov.uk/government/publications/uk-climate-targets-request-for-advice-from-the-committee-on-climate-change, accessed 10 June 2020.

156 See Edith Brown Weiss, *In Fairness to Future Generations: International Law, Common Patrimony, and Intergenerational Equity* (Transnational Publishing 1989).

157 *Thomson* v. *Minister for Climate Change Issues* (2017) NZHC 733.

or only nominally (in Sydney), these social movement actors frame rights as part of a long-term collective strategy.

Today's climate activists operate in a networked world. The map of climate governance involves actors ranging from cities to coalitions of private companies. These levels of governance interact in non-linear ways, and transnational advocacy networks seek to influence climate policy across all of them. The momentous work of two groups in particular point to a shift in how these movements interact with domestic climate policy. Extinction Rebellion disrupted the streets of more than eighty cities over the course of eleven days, asking for specific legislative action from governments. In the United Kingdom, their demands for a parliamentary declaration of emergency and a citizens' assembly to feed in to climate change policy have been met.[158] This autonomous group, along with youth strikers in New Zealand, built on and implemented the goals of public law litigation, arguing for similar legal outcomes through different means. But the language of 'advocacy' does not fully capture what these movements have done. When protestors disrupting urban life force governments to consider the catastrophic effects of climate change, they are engaging in law-making.

Mobilised citizens may also participate in innovative green financing mechanisms, fund lawsuits, or become claimants. In all of these capacities, they should remind us of the scales at which climate change operates; focusing on narrow frames of rights or governance will exclude important dynamics.

Whether through formal litigation or other mechanisms of climate governance, movement actors – both legal and lay – articulate alternate visions of the law. Like coalitions of Indian sex workers asserting constitutional employment rights, climate change activists are articulating alternative visions of what the law must protect. As they get closer to realising these visions, perhaps an addendum to Munger's list is in order. Greta Thunberg, the school strikers she inspired in the Global South, and the eighty-three-year-old XR activist who chained himself to a train in London's financial district are all cause lawyers, but their power is far from symbolic.

[158] Damian Carrington, 'UK Citizens Assembly on Climate Emergency Announced', *The Guardian* (London, 20 June 2019), www.theguardian.com/environment/2019/jun/20/uk-citizens-assembly-on-climate-emergency-announced.

PART II

International Law and International Adjudication

3

Using Human Rights Law to Address the Impacts of Climate Change: Early Reflections on the Carbon Majors Inquiry

ANNALISA SAVARESI AND JACQUES HARTMANN

Introduction

With increasingly strong storms, droughts and wildfires, harm to persons, property and the environment associated with climate change has started to manifest all around the world. The 2015 Paris Agreement acknowledges the need to tackle the so-called loss and damage- encompassing various forms of permanent and irreversible impacts of human-induced climate change[1] – but has not delivered any concrete means to address this enormous problem, so far.[2] Yet, climate change is predicted to cause unprecedented damage, which is not adequately covered by extant liability and insurance schemes.

In 2007, Faure and Nollkaemper noted how it was unlikely that litigation would lead to decisions 'whereby plaintiffs would be directly compensated for climate change damage suffered'.[3] More than a decade later, no court has found that particular emissions relate causally to adverse climate change impacts for the purpose of establishing liability. Still, recent years have witnessed a surge in

[1] Paris Agreement under the United Nations Framework Convention on Climate Change (adopted 12 December 2015, entered into force 4 November 2016) (2016) 55 *International Legal Materials* 740, Art. 8 ('Paris Agreement').

[2] M. J. Mace and Roda Verheyen, 'Loss, Damage and Responsibility after COP21: All Options open for the Paris Agreement' (2016) 25 *Review of European, Comparative and International Environmental Law* 197, 205–7.

[3] Michael G. Faure and Andre Nollkaemper, 'International Liability as an Instrument to Prevent and Compensate for Climate Change' (2007) *26A Stanford Journal of International Law* 123, 179.

climate change litigation all over the world,[4] including requests for compensation for harm associated with the impacts of climate change.[5] Through these test cases, litigants are pushing the boundaries of private, public and administrative law to obtain redress for damage to persons, property and/or the environment associated with climate change. So far, only a few such cases have been argued on the basis of human rights law.[6] Nevertheless, this chapter maintains that human rights may be used as a 'gap filler' until other areas of law satisfactorily address the harm associated with the adverse impacts of climate change.

The use of human rights law as a gap filler to provide remedies where other areas of the law do not is nothing new, especially in the environmental context.[7] Human rights remedies are not designed to redress environmental damage. They have, nevertheless, historically been used as an avenue to redress personal and property damage associated with pollution, especially where no other remedies are available. The issue is, therefore, to establish when and how they can be used in relation to the impacts of climate change.

These questions are at the core of the so-called Carbon Majors inquiry by the Human Rights Commission of the Philippines. The inquiry was initiated at the request of a group of Filipino citizens and non-governmental organisations. The petitioners asked the Commission to investigate for the first time the responsibility of global corporations for human rights violations, or threats thereof, resulting from the impacts of

[4] See the litigation database curated by the Sabin Center for Climate Change Law at Columbia Law School; Sabin Center for Climate Change Law, 'Climate Change Litigation Databases', http://climatecasechart.com, accessed 15 June 2019.

[5] See, for example, *Saúl Luciano Lliuya v RWE AG* (2015), Case No. 2 0285/15 of the Essen Regional Court, pending in Germany. Lawsuits against the Carbon Majors have been lodged in the United States, France and the Netherlands. See the reportage in *Climate Liability News*, www.climateliabilitynews.org, accessed 15 June 2019.

[6] See the analysis in Annalisa Savaresi and Juan Auz, 'Climate Change Litigation and Human Rights: Pushing the Boundaries' (2019) 9 *Climate Law* 3.

[7] The practice in this area has been the subject of much scholarly interest. See, for example, Alan E. Boyle and Michael R. Anderson, *Human Rights Approaches to Environmental Protection* (Oxford University Press 1998); Alan E. Boyle, 'Human Rights or Environmental Rights? A Reassessment' (2007) 18 *Fordham Environmental Law Review* 471; Dinah L. Shelton, *Human Rights and the Environment* (Edward Elgar 2011); Alan E. Boyle, 'Human Rights and the Environment: Where Next?' (2012) 23 *European Journal of International Law* 613; Donald K. Anton and Dinah L. Shelton, *Environmental Protection and Human Rights* (Cambridge University Press 2012).

climate change in the Philippines.[8] The petitioners lamented widespread human rights violations associated with the increasingly violent typhoons striking the Philippines and drew on recent climate change attribution studies[9] to single out forty-seven corporations – dubbed the 'Carbon Majors' and including the likes of BP, Chevron, Exxon and Shell – none of which are headquartered in the Philippines.

The inquiry differs from other climate change litigation against corporate actors for two main reasons. First, it is conducted by a national human rights commission – a quasi-judicial body normally tasked to look into domestic, rather than transnational, breaches of human rights. Second, the remedies that the Commission can offer to the petitioners are constrained by its limited ability to affect the behaviour of the Carbon Majors.

The fact that the Commission has decided to proceed with the inquiry is in and of itself ground-breaking, and has already demonstrated the potential to use human rights remedies available at the national level to give a voice and address the grievances of those affected by the impacts of climate change.[10] This chapter (written in 2019 before the Commission issued its recommendations) poses that the acknowledgement of the responsibility of the Carbon Majors for the impacts of climate change will be a primer and could potentially engender domino effects, including, eventually, the provision of compensation by domestic courts.

This chapter thus looks at the Carbon Majors inquiry to critically appraise the role of human rights law in solving complex questions associated with a responsibility for the impacts of climate change. Building on the authors' experience providing expert advice to the

[8] Republic of the Philippines Commission on Human Rights, Case No: CHR-NI-2016-0001, 'Petition Requesting for Investigation of the Responsibility of the Carbon Majors for Human Rights Violations or Threats of Violations Resulting from the Impacts of Climate Change' (2015), www.greenpeace.org/seasia/ph/PageFiles/735291/Petitioners-and-Annexes/CC-HR-Petition.pdf, accessed 15 June 2019.

[9] The Carbon Majors petition relies on Richard Heede, 'Tracing Anthropogenic Carbon Dioxide and Methane Emissions to Fossil Fuel and Cement Producers, 1854–2010' (2014) 122 *Climatic Change* 229. Subsequent studies have furthered Heede's research. See Peter C. Frumhoff, Richard Heede and Naomi Oreskes, 'The Climate Responsibilities of Industrial Carbon Producers' (2015) 132 *Climatic Change* 157; and Brenda Ekwurzel and others, 'The Rise in Global Atmospheric CO2, Surface Temperature, and Sea Level from Emissions Traced to Major Carbon Producers' (2017) 144 *Climatic Change* 579.

[10] As argued in Annalisa Savaresi, Ioana Cismas and Jacques Hartmann, 'The Philippines Human Rights Commission and the "Carbon Majors" Petition' (*EJIL: Talk!*, 22 December 2017), www.ejiltalk.org/the-philippines-human-rights-commission-and-the-carbon-majors-petition/, accessed 15 June 2019.

Philippines Human Rights Commission,[11] this chapter uses the inquiry as a point of departure to unpack the questions concerning jurisdiction, causality, retrospectivity, attribution and the provision of an adequate remedy. The conclusion provides some reflections on the potential of and limits to the use of human rights remedies as a means to address the harm associated with the impacts of climate change.

3.1 Translating Harm Associated with the Impacts of Climate Change into Human Rights Grievances

In the last decade, the special relationship between climate change and human rights obligations has increasingly been recognised in the literature,[12] by both the parties to the climate regime[13] and human rights bodies. A series of Human Rights Council (HRC) resolutions have stressed the potential of human rights obligations to 'inform and strengthen' climate change law and policy-making by 'promoting policy coherence, legitimacy and sustainable outcomes'.[14] John Knox, who served as the first UN Special Rapporteur on human rights and the environment between 2012 and

[11] See Annalisa Savaresi, Ioana Cismas and Jacques Hartmann, 'Amicus Brief – Human Rights and Climate Change' (2017), Asia Pacific Forum of National Human Rights Institutions and the Global Alliance of National Human Rights Institutions, www.asiapacificforum.net/media/resource_file/APF_Paper_Amicus_Brief_HR_Climate_Change.pdf, accessed 15 June 2019.

[12] See, for example, Stephen Humphreys (ed.), *Human Rights and Climate Change* (Cambridge University Press 2009); Daniel Bodansky, 'Symposium: International Human Rights and Climate Change' (2010) 38 *Georgia Journal of International and Comparative Law* 511; Lavanya Rajamani, 'The Increasing Currency and Relevance of Rights-Based Perspectives in the International Negotiations on Climate Change' (2010) 22 *Journal of Environmental Law* 391; Siobhan McInerney-Lankford, Mac Darrow and Lavanya Rajamani, *Human Rights and Climate Change: A Review of the International Legal Dimensions* (World Bank 2011); Ottavio Quirico and Mouloud Boumghar (eds.), *Climate Change and Human Rights: An International and Comparative Law Perspective* (Routledge 2015); Sebastien Duyck, Sebastien Jodoin and Alyssa Johl (eds.), *Routledge Handbook of Human Rights and Climate Governance* (Routledge 2018).

[13] UNFCCC Decision 1/CP.16, 'The Cancun Agreements: Outcome of the Work of the Ad Hoc Working Group on Long-Term Cooperative Action under the Convention' (15 March 2011) UN Doc FCCC/CP/2010/7/Add.1, Appendix I, para 2(a); and Paris Agreement (n 1) Preamble.

[14] UNHRC Res 7/23 'Human Rights and Climate Change' (28 March 2008) UN Doc A/HRC/7/78; UNHRC Res 10/4 'Human Rights and Climate Change' (25 March 2009) UN Doc A/HRC/Res/10/4; UNHRC Res 18/22 'Human Rights and Climate Change' (30 September 2011) UN Doc A/HRC/RES/18/22; UNHRC Res 26/27 'Human Rights and Climate Change' (27 June 2014) UN Doc A/HRC/Res/26/27 (2014); UNHRC Res 29/15 'Human Rights and Climate Change' (2 July 2015) UN Doc A/HRC/Res/29/15; UNHRC Res 32/33 'Human Rights and Climate Change' (1 July 2016) UN Doc A/

2018,[15] prepared a dedicated report on climate change, which clarified the framework of human rights obligation relating to climate change, mapping existing state practice.[16]

These developments clearly show that states and international mechanisms acknowledge the relevance of human rights law in the fight against climate change and in the implementation of climate change response measures,[17] and increasingly practice systemic integration in the interpretation of obligations under international climate change and human rights treaties.[18]

Human rights arguments have been successfully made in litigation concerning states' failure to mitigate climate change.[19] The scope to make human rights complaints in relation to the impacts of climate change, however, largely remains to be tested.

A 2009 report by the Office of the High Commissioner of Human Rights (OHCHR) cautioned that qualifying the effects of climate change as human rights violations poses a series of technical obstacles, concerning the jurisdiction to adjudicate human rights complaints associated with the impacts of climate change; how to attribute responsibility in terms of causality, retrospectivity and apportionment; and what may be regarded as adequate remedies for human rights violations associated with the impacts of climate

HRC/RES/32/33; Res. 35/20, 'Human Rights and Climate Change' A/HRC/35/20 (2017); and Res. 38/4 'Human Rights and Climate Change' A/HRC/38/4 (2018).

[15] John Knox was initially appointed to serve as the Independent Expert (2012–2015) and subsequently as Special Rapporteur (2015–2018).

[16] UNHRC 'Report of the Independent Expert on the Issue of Human Rights Obligations Relating to the Enjoyment of a Safe, Clean, Healthy and Sustainable Environment, John H. Knox: Mapping Report' (30 December 2013) UN Doc A/HRC/25/53; and UNHRC 'Report of the Special Rapporteur on the Issue of Human Rights Obligations Relating to the Enjoyment of a Safe, Clean, Healthy and Sustainable Environment' (1 February 2016) UN Doc A/HRC/31/52.

[17] For arguments concerning a rights-based approach to the implementation of the climate treaties, see Sebastien Duyck and others, 'Human Rights and the Paris Agreement's Implementation Guidelines: Opportunities to Develop a Rights-Based Approach' (2018) 12 *Carbon and Climate Law Review* 191.

[18] As argued also in Annalisa Savaresi, 'Climate Change and Human Rights: Fragmentation, Interplay and Institutional Linkages' in Sebastien Duyck, Sebastien Jodoin and Alyssa Johl (eds.), *Routledge Handbook of Human Rights and Climate Governance* (Routledge 2018), 42; and Annalisa Savaresi, 'Human Rights and Climate Change' in Tuula Honkonen and Seita Romppanen (eds.), *International Environmental Law-Making and Diplomacy Review 2018* (United Nations Environment Programme and University of Eastern Finland, 2019).

[19] See Savaresi and Auz (n 6).

change.[20] Yet, recent litigation seemingly indicates that these obstacles may not be insurmountable. The historical contribution of state and non-state actors to greenhouse gas emissions causing climate change is increasingly well documented, and advances in scientific knowledge are making it easier to trace causal connections between particular emissions and the resulting harms.[21]

Even though conventionally greenhouse emissions are attributed to states, it is non-state actors that are largely responsible for causing emissions. Recent studies suggest that a group of global corporations are historically responsible for the lion's share of global greenhouse gas emissions.[22] These studies have prompted a surge in climate litigation against corporate actors, within and outside the United States.[23] The responsibility of corporations for human rights breaches associated with climate change has also increasingly come under the spotlight, as a result.

As the grim judicial saga associated with the Bhopal disaster well exemplifies, however, it is often difficult to obtain redress for damage to persons, property or the environment caused by foreign corporate actors.[24] This is in spite of the fact that the 'polluter pays' principle is widely accepted in both international and national law,[25] and that the law of several countries provides joint and several liability regimes, a reduced standard of proof,[26] and even regimes of strict liability for

[20] UNHRC 'Report of the Office of the United Nations High Commissioner for Human Rights on the Relationship between Climate Change and Human Rights' (15 January 2009) UN Doc A/HRC/10/61 (2009), paras. 69–70.

[21] As argued also in UNHRC, 'Report of the Special Rapporteur on the Issue of Human Rights Obligations Relating to the Enjoyment of a Safe, Clean, Healthy and Sustainable Environment' (1 February 2016) UN Doc A/HRC/31/52, paras. 36–7.

[22] See Heede (n 9); Frumhoff, Heede and Oreske (n 9); and B. Ekwurzel and others (n 9).

[23] In May 2019, the database of Sabin Centre database listed twenty-two such cases outside the United States, but does not systematically report information concerning lawsuits within the United States, which are instead widely reported in the press. See, for example, Karen Savage, '*Judge Rejects Exxon Challenges to New York's Climate Fraud Suit*' (*Climate Liability News*, 12 June 2019) www.climateliabilitynews.org/category/exxon-climate-investigation/, accessed 15 June 2019.

[24] See Upendra Baxi, 'Mass Torts, Multinational Enterprise Liability and Private International Law' (1999) 276 *Recueil Des Cours* 297, 354–5.

[25] Julie Adshead, 'The Application and Development of the Polluter-Pays Principle across Jurisdictions in Liability for Marine Oil Pollution: The Tales of the "Erika" and the "Prestige"' 30 *Journal of Environmental Law* 425.

[26] Eberhard Feess, Gerd Muehlheusser and Ansgar Wohlschlegel, 'Environmental Liability under Uncertain Causation' (2009) *European Journal of Law and Economics* 133, 137.

professional activities, and of absolute liability for ultra-hazardous activities.[27]

In all events, existing liability schemes scarcely seem fit to address harm associated with the impacts of climate change. As a matter of scale, climate change is predicted to cause unprecedented damage to property, persons and the environment.[28] This damage is predictable, but only to the extent that we know it will happen – not where and when. Thus, extant liability and insurance schemes need to be adapted in order to address the complex restorative and distributive justice considerations associated with the impacts of climate change.[29] Before this happens, human rights arguments may be used on an interim basis to fill in the gap.

In general, human rights are helpful in dealing with environmental matters because they are widely recognised in both international and national law as a set of basic rights and freedoms that belong to every person.[30] The obligations associated with the protection of human rights may be enforced both nationally and internationally against states and – to some extent – non-state actors,[31] and, in certain circumstances, in an

[27] Council Directive 2004/35/CE of 21 April 2004 on environmental liability with regard to the prevention and remedying of environmental damage (2004) OJ L143/56.

[28] Ove Hoegh-Guldberg and others, 'Impacts of 1.5°C Global Warming on Natural and Human Systems' in Valerie Masson-Delotte and others (eds.), *Special Report: Global Warming of 1.5°C* (Intergovernmental Panel on Climate Change, 2018).

[29] As argued, for example, in Simon Caney, 'Cosmopolitan Justice, Responsibility, and Global Climate Change' (2005) 18 *Leiden Journal of International Law* 747; Maria Lee, 'Climate Change Tort' (2015), https://papers.ssrn.com/abstract=2695107, accessed 15 June 2019.

[30] The core international instruments include Universal Declaration of Human Rights (adopted 10 December 1948) UNGA Res 217 A(III); International Covenant on Civil and Political Rights (adopted 16 December 1966, entered into force 23 March 1976) 999 UNTS 171; International Covenant on Economic, Social and Cultural Rights (adopted 16 December 1966, entered into force 3 January 1976) 993 UNTS 3. Additional specialised international instruments include International Convention on the Elimination of All Forms of Racial Discrimination (Adopted 21 December 1965, entered into force 4 January 1969) 660 UNTS 195; Convention on the Elimination of All Forms of Discrimination against Women (adopted 18 December 1979, entered into force 3 September 1981) 1249 UNTS 13; Convention on the Rights of the Child (adopted 20 November 1989, entered into force 022 September 1990) 1577 UNTS 3; Convention on the Rights of Persons with Disabilities (adopted 13 December 2006, entered into force 3 May 2008). Finally, there are regional human rights treaties: African Charter on Human and Peoples' Rights (adopted 27 June 1981, entered into force 21 October 1986) (1982) 21 ILM 58; American Convention on Human Rights (22 November 1969, entered into force 18 July 1978) 1144 UNTS 123; European Convention for the Protection of Human Rights and Fundamental Freedoms (4 November 1950, entered into force 3 September 1953) 2889 UNTS 221.

[31] See, for example, the arguments put forward in Andrew Clapham, *Human Rights Obligations of Non-State Actors* (Oxford University Press 2006). See also

extraterritorial context.[32] Some states and companies have resisted this understanding of the reach of human rights law, maintaining that states are the *sole* bearers of human rights obligations, which only protect those within a state's territory, or in another territory under its effective control.[33]

Recent developments in international,[34] regional[35] and national[36] law, however, clearly show that states are starting to hold companies accountable for human rights violations.[37] National and international judges are increasingly interpreting the law in a way to impose at least some human right obligations upon corporate actors.[38] Ongoing negotiations

Andrew Clapham, 'Human Rights Obligations for Non-State-Actors: Where Are We Now?' in Fannie Lafontaine and Francois Larocque (eds.), *Doing Peace the Rights Way: Essays in International Law and Relations in Honour of Louise Arbour*, (1st ed., Intersentia 2019), https://ssrn.com/abstract=2641390, accessed 15 June 2019.

[32] See, for example, Marko Milanovic, *Extraterritorial Application of Human Rights Treaties: Law, Principles, and Policy* (Oxford University Press 2011); Karen da Costa, *The Extraterritorial Application of Selected Human Rights Treaties* (Martinus Nijhoff 2013); Malcolm Langford and others (eds.), *Global Justice, State Duties: The Extraterritorial Scope of Economic, Social, and Cultural Rights in International Law* (Cambridge University Press 2013).

[33] See, for example, Supplemental Amicus Briefs in Support of Neither Party (Kiobel II) in *Kiobel* v. *Royal Dutch Shell Petroleum Co.*, 621 F.3d 111 (2d Cir. 2010) 12.

[34] See UNHRC Res 26/9 'Elaboration of an International Legally Binding Instrument on Transnational Corporations and Other Business Enterprises with Respect to Human Rights' (14 July 2014) UN Doc A/HRC/RES/26/9, establishing the mandate of the open-ended intergovernmental working group on transnational corporations and other business enterprises with respect to human rights. See also UNHRC 'Report of the Special Representative of the Secretary-General on the Issue of Human Rights and Transnational Corporations and Other Business Enterprises, John Ruggie – Guiding Principles on Business and Human Rights: Implementing the United Nations "Protect, Respect and Remedy" Framework' (21 March 2011) UN Doc A/HRC/17/31 ('UN Guiding Principles on Business and Human Rights').

[35] Parliament and Council Directive 2014/95/EU of 22 October 2014 amending Directive 2013/34/EU as regards disclosure of non-financial and diversity information by certain large undertakings and groups Text with EEA relevance [2014] OJ L330/1. See also Protocol on Amendments to the Protocol on the Statute of the African Court of Justice and Human Rights (Malabo Protocol; adopted 27 June 2014, not yet entered into force), art 46.

[36] See, for example, Décret n° 2012-557 du 24 avril 2012 relatif aux obligations de transparence des entreprises en matière sociale et environnementale. See the review of this and similar national laws in: Claire Methven O'Brien and Sumithra Dhanarajan, 'The Corporate Responsibility to Respect Human Rights: A Status Review' (2015) NUS Law Working Paper 2015/005, https://papers.ssrn.com/abstract=2607888, accessed 15 June 2019

[37] Clapham (n 32).

[38] See, for example, *Urbaser S.A. and Consorcio de Aguas Bilbao Bizkaia, Bilbao Biskaia Ur Partzuergoa* v. *The Argentine Republic*, ICSID Case No ARB/07/26, Award (2016); *Vedanta Resources PLC and another* v. *Lungowe and others* (2019) UKSC 20.

concerning transnational corporations and other business enterprises with respect to human rights may furthermore soon deliver the first international treaty explicitly recognising corporate obligations in this connection.[39]

The Carbon Majors inquiry provides an opportunity to see whether this evolving understanding of corporate human rights responsibility extends to the impacts of climate change. As a quasi-judicial body, the Philippines Human Rights Commission has no power to provide compensation to victims of human rights violations. Its inquiry is nevertheless faced with the same key questions concerning liability for the impacts of climate change – namely, causality, retrospectivity, attribution, as well as the provision of an adequate remedy. The next sections, therefore, look at how these matters have been addressed in the context of the Carbon Majors inquiry, thereby translating the complex liability questions associated with the impacts of climate change into human rights language.

3.2 Overcoming the Hurdles

The suitability of human rights law to address the harm caused by climate change depends upon whether a victim can substantiate a claim that a duty bearer has contributed to climate change, in such a way as to amount to a human rights violation. In the Carbon Majors inquiry, the petitioners must prove that they have suffered human rights violations, which are imputable to the Carbon Majors.

3.2.1 Attributing Responsibility

Determining a prima facie human rights violation associated with the impacts of climate change in the Philippines is relatively straightforward. Citing damage to property and persons associated with increasingly frequent mega-typhoons, the petitioners maintain that they have suffered violations of a range of human rights – most saliently, the rights to life, the highest attainable standard of physical and mental health, food, water, sanitation, adequate housing and self-determination.[40] Their

[39] 'Legally Binding Instrument to Regulate, in International Human Rights Law, the Activities of Transnational Corporations and Other Business Enterprises: Zero Draft, 16 July 2018', www.ohchr.org/Documents/HRBodies/HRCouncil/WGTransCorp/Session3/DraftLBI.pdf, accessed 2 November 2018.

[40] Petition (n 9), p 7.

contention that there is a link between the impacts of climate change and violations of these human rights is supported by numerous HRC resolutions and can be regarded as fairly uncontroversial.[41]

Determining *who* is to be held responsible for these human rights violations, however, is much more complex. Human rights law hinges on the obligations of states, as primary duty holders. While a body of human rights obligations relating to the environment certainly exists,[42] the obligation to protect human rights does not require states to prohibit all activities that may cause all instances of environmental degradation. Instead, states have the discretion to strike a balance between environmental protection and other legitimate societal interests. As noted by Knox, however, states 'must not strike an unjustifiable or unreasonable balance between environmental protection and other social goals'.[43] In assessing whether a balance is reasonable, national and international health standards may be particularly relevant, with a strong presumption against retrogressive measures. In addition to a general non-discrimination requirement, states owe specific obligations to members of groups particularly vulnerable to harm.[44]

States' obligation to address environmental harm that interferes with the full enjoyment of human rights arguably extends to human rights violations caused by climate change impacts.[45] As not all states have ratified the same human rights treaties, their obligations may vary to a certain extent. Yet, the work of the UN Special Rapporteur has demonstrated that states have a set of core obligations in this

41 See UNHRC Res 7/23 'Human Rights and Climate Change' (28 March 2008) UN Doc A/HRC/7/78; UNHRC Res 10/4 'Human Rights and Climate Change' (25 March 2009) UN Doc A/HRC/RES/10/4; UNHRC Res 18/22 'Human Rights and Climate Change' (30 September 2011) UN Doc A/HRC/RES/18/22; and UNHRC Res 26/27 'Human Rights and Climate Change' (27 June 2014) UN Doc A/HRC/RES/26/27.

42 These obligations were recently compiled by the UN Special Rapporteur JH Knox in UNHRC 'Report of the Special Rapporteur on the Issue of Human Rights Obligations Relating to the Enjoyment of a Safe, Clean, Healthy and Sustainable Environment' (24 January 2018) UN Doc A/HRC/37/59, http://legal.un.org/docs/?symbol=A/HRC/37/59, accessed 15 June 2019, Annex (Framework principles on human rights and the environment), para 33(c).

43 Ibid. Annex para 33(e).

44 UNHRC 'Report of the Independent Expert on the Issue of Human Rights Obligations Relating to the Enjoyment of a Safe, Clean, Healthy and Sustainable Environment, John H. Knox: Mapping Report' (30 December 2013) UN Doc A/HRC/25/53, paras 53, 80.

45 UNHRC 'Report of the Special Rapporteur on the Issue of Human Rights Obligations Relating to the Enjoyment of a Safe, Clean, Healthy and Sustainable Environment' (1 February 2016) UN Doc A/HRC/31/52, paras. 50–4, 72–3.

connection. First, states have *procedural obligations* to assess environmental impacts on human rights and to make environmental information public, to facilitate participation in environmental decision-making, and to provide access to remedies.[46] Second, states have *substantive obligations* to adopt legal and institutional frameworks that protect against environmental harm interfering with the enjoyment of human rights.[47] Most saliently for the present purposes, states must take measures to 'prevent, punish, investigate or redress the harm caused ... by private persons or entities'.[48] This state duty to protect the human rights of individuals and groups from corporate violations is well established in the interpretative work of UN treaty bodies and UN special procedures, and in international case law.[49] Indeed, states ordinarily prevent, stop, obtain redress for or punish third-party interference through state regulation of private party

[46] UNHRC 'Report of the Independent Expert on the Issue of Human Rights Obligations Relating to the Enjoyment of a Safe, Clean, Healthy and Sustainable Environment, John H. Knox' (24 December 2012) UN Doc A/HRC/22/43, paras. 29–43.

[47] Ibid. paras. 44–68.

[48] Ibid. paras 58–61. See also 'Report of the Special Rapporteur on the Issue of Human Rights Obligations Relating to the Enjoyment of a Safe, Clean, Healthy and Sustainable Environment' (n. 43) para. 3; and UNHRC 'General Comment No. 31 [80]: The Nature of the General Legal Obligation Imposed on States Parties to the Covenant' (26 May 2004) UN Doc CCPR/C/21/Rev.1/Add.13, para 8.

[49] For an overview of positive obligations in the case law of the European Court of Human Rights, see Jean-François Akandji-Kombe, *Positive Obligations under the European Convention on Human Rights* (*Council of Europe Human Rights Handbooks Series*, no. 7, 2007). In the Inter-American system, the stage for the development of positive obligations was set in the case *Velasquez Rodriguez* v. *Honduras*, Judgment of July 29, 1988, Inter-AmCtHR (Ser C) No 4 (1988). In the African system, African Commission on Human and Peoples' Rights, *The Social and Economic Rights Action Center and the Center for Economic and Social Rights* v. *Nigeria* (2001) Communication No 155/96 (African Commission on Human and People's Rights) is particularly relevant. Relevant concluding observations of UN treaty bodies include: UNHRC 'Concluding observations on the sixth periodic report of Germany, adopted by the Committee at its 106th session (15 October–2 November 2012)' (12 November 2012) UN Doc CCPR/C/DEU/CO/6, para 16; UN Committee on the Elimination of Racial Discrimination, 'Consideration of reports submitted by States parties under article 9 of the Convention –Concluding observations of the Committee on the Elimination of Racial Discrimination: United Kingdom of Great Britain and Northern Ireland' (14 September 2011) UN Doc CERD/C/GBR/CO/18-20, para 29, and 'Consideration of reports submitted by States parties under article 9 of the Convention – Concluding observations of the Committee on the Elimination of Racial Discrimination: Australia' (13 September 2010) UN Doc CERD/C/AUS/CO/15-17. See also Ineta Ziemele, 'Human Rights Violations by Private Persons and Entities: The Case-Law of International Human Rights Courts and Monitoring Bodies' (2009) EUI Working Paper 2009/8, http://hdl.handle.net/1814/11409, accessed 15 June 2019.

conduct, inspection and monitoring of compliance, or administrative and judicial sanctions.[50]

Furthermore, the so-called business and human rights regime[51] consists of hard and soft rules under international and domestic law that regulate the relationship between the state, corporate entities and individuals. The regime hinges on the state duty to protect, the corporate responsibility to respect and access to remedy – which form the three pillars of the UN Guiding Principles on Business and Human Rights,[52] unanimously endorsed by the Human Rights Council in 2011. Subordinate to the state's binding obligation to protect and enforce, the Guiding Principles entail a 'moral responsibility and societal expectation'[53] that corporations respect human rights, 'understood, at a minimum, as those expressed in the International Bill of Human Rights and the principles concerning fundamental rights set out in the International Labour Organization's Declaration on Fundamental Principles and Rights at Work'.[54]

Although they do not expressly stipulate corporate obligations, newer human rights treaties entail provisions that explicitly mention 'private entities' and the state duty to protect peoples from abuse by such entities.[55] These treaty provisions tie into the requirements of the business and human rights regime, with corporations acknowledging their corporate responsibilities and states ensuring compliance.[56]

50 See *International Commission of Jurists, Courts and the Legal Enforcement of Economic, Social and Cultural Rights: Comparative Experiences of Justiciability* (*Human Rights and Rule of Law Series* 2, 2008), 45.

51 This section of the paper draws on the reflections, in A. Savaresi, I. Cismas and J. Hartmann, 'Amicus Curiae Brief' (n 11).

52 UN Guiding Principles on Business and Human Rights (n 35).

53 International Law Association, 'Committee on Non-State Actors, Washington Conference Report' (Washington Conference, Washington, 2014), www.ila-hq.org/en/committees/index.cfm/cid/1023, accessed 2 November 2018, 12.

54 UN Guiding Principles on Business and Human Rights (n 35), Principle 12.

55 Convention on the Rights of Persons with Disabilities (adopted 13 December 2006, entered into force 3 May 2008) 2515 UNTS 3, arts 4.e, 9.2.b, 20.d, 21.c; Convention on the Elimination of all Forms of Discrimination against Women (adopted 18 December 1979, entered into force 3 September 1981) 1249 UNTS 13, art 2.e.

56 M. Sornarajah, 'Linking State Responsibility for Certain Harms Caused by Corporate Nationals Abroad to Civil Recourse in the Legal Systems of Home States' in Craig Scott (ed.), *Torture as Tort: Comparative Perspectives on the Development of Transnational Tort Litigation* (Hart 2001).

This understanding is confirmed by the recent interpretative work of treaty bodies and international jurisprudence.[57] For example, in General Comment No. 16, the Committee on the Rights of the Child addresses corporate bodies directly, seemingly as duty bearers under the Convention on the Rights of the Child.[58] Equally, the 2016 arbitral award in *Urbaser* v. *Argentina*[59] concluded, 'At this juncture, it is therefore to be admitted that the human right for everyone's dignity and its right for adequate housing and living conditions are complemented by *an obligation on all parts, public and private parties, not to engage in activity aimed at destroying such rights.*'[60]

Other international courts have relied on the UN Guiding Principles to establish that businesses '*must* respect and protect human rights, as well as prevent, mitigate, and accept responsibility for the adverse human rights impacts directly linked to their activities'.[61]

Building on this basis, in the Carbon Majors petition the applicants asked the Philippines National Human Rights Commission to find that corporate actors are responsible for human rights violations associated with the impacts of climate change in the Philippines. In particular, the petitioners argued that the Carbon Majors have breached their responsibilities to respect the rights of Filipinos 'by directly or indirectly contributing to current or future adverse human rights impacts through the extraction and sale of fossil fuels and activities undermining climate action'.[62]

57 See discussion in Ioana Cismas and Sarah Macrory, 'The Business and Human Rights Regime under International Law: Remedy without Law?' in James Summers and Alex Gough (eds.), *Non-State Actors and International Obligations: Creation, Evolution and Enforcement* (Brill 2018) 224–60.

58 Committee on the Rights of the Child 'General Comment No. 16 (2013) on State Obligations Regarding the Impact of the Business Sector on Children's Rights' (17 April 2013) UN Doc CRC/C/GC/16, para 8.

59 The company Urbaser was a shareholder in a concession for water and sewage services in the Province of the Greater Buenos Aires. The claimants alleged that Argentina's emergency measures at the time of the 2001–2002 economic crisis caused the concession financial loss and ultimately insolvency. Urbaser started arbitration proceedings claiming breaches of the 1991 Bilateral Investment Treaty between Argentina and Spain. Argentina raised a counter-claim based on the claimants' 'alleged failure to provide the necessary investment into the Concession, thus violating its commitments and its obligations under international law based on the human right to water.' *Urbaser S.A. and Consorcio de Aguas Bilbao Bizkaia, Bilbao Biskaia Ur Partzuergoa* v. *The Argentine Republic*, ICSID Case No ARB/07/26, Award (2016) [36].

60 Ibid., *Urbaser* v. *Argentina*, para. 1199.

61 Case of the *Kaliña and Lokono Peoples* v. *Suriname*, Inter-AmCtHR, Judgment, 25 November 2015 (Merits, Reparations and Costs), (224) (emphasis added).

62 Carbon Majors Petition (n 8) 21.

3.2.2 Causation and Retrospectivity

Under human rights law, victims are saddled with a less stringent burden of proof, when compared, for example, with tort law.[63] In this regard, the UN High Commissioner for Human Rights has specifically recommended that all States strike an appropriate balance between 'evidential burdens of proof between the claimant and the defendant company'.[64] Similarly, the Committee on Economic, Social and Cultural Rights has noted how 'shifting the burden of proof may be justified where the facts and events relevant for resolving a claim lie wholly or in part within the exclusive knowledge of the corporate defendant'.[65]

At the operational level, the corporate responsibility to respect translates into a duty of due diligence, which requires corporations 'to identify, prevent, mitigate and account for how they address their adverse human rights impacts'.[66] Corporate human rights violations can result from environmental impacts, for example, related to health, including such impacts that have a 'delayed effect'.[67] Corporations should in this connection rely on 'established and quite precise international as well as national standards' in undertaking due diligence in relation to these environmental impacts.[68]

When applied to the Carbon Majors, the corporate obligation of due diligence has two crucial elements. First, a growing body of research attributes the lion's share of global emissions to the Carbon Majors.[69] Second, recent studies suggest that these corporations have long known that the production and use of their products contribute substantially to

[63] Juliane Kokott, *The Burden of Proof in Comparative and International Human Rights Law: Civil and Common Law Approaches with Special Reference to the American and German Legal Systems* (Martinus Nijhoff 1998) 182. See, for example, *Tătar* v. *Romania*, App No 67021/01 (ECtHR 5 July 2007) (107)–(124).

[64] UNHRC 'Improving Accountability and Access to Remedy for Victims of Business-Related Human Rights Abuse: Report of the United Nations High Commissioner for Human Rights' (10 May 2016), UN Doc. A/HRC/32/19, policy objective 12.5. See also the Opinion from the European Union Agency for Fundamental Rights at 'More Justice for Victims of Business-Related Human Rights Abuses' (*European Union Agency for Fundamental Rights*, 10 April 2017), http://fra.europa.eu/en/news/2017/more-justice-victims-business-related-human-rights-abuses, accessed 15 June 2019.

[65] Committee on Economic, Social and Cultural Rights, 'General Comment No. 24 (2017) on State Obligations under the International Covenant on Economic, Social and Cultural Rights in the Context of Business Activities' (10 August 2017) UN Doc E/C.12/GC/24.

[66] Ibid. principle 17.

[67] UN Guiding Principles on Business and Human Rights (n 35) 8, 53.

[68] Ibid.

[69] See above (n 9).

climate change, and to the related impacts.[70] Indeed, these studies allege that corporations knowingly advanced or deliberately promoted misleading information, casting doubt on the connection between fossil fuels and climate change.[71] It is therefore possible to argue, as the petitioners did, that, on the one hand, corporate actors had an obligation of due diligence, and, on the other, they did not attend to this obligation, thus contributing to climate-related human rights violations in the Philippines and beyond.[72]

The issue of so-called retrospectivity does not seem to pose particular challenges in this connection. The fact that emissions took place, or at least started, at a time when corporations were unaware of their impacts is not in and of itself an obstacle to liability arguments.[73] In principle, it is possible to argue for responsibility for climate change ever since widespread scientific consensus emerged, and certainly since the establishment of the Intergovernmental Panel on Climate Change and the adoption of the United Nations Framework Convention on Climate Change.[74] Similar to the tobacco industry, the Carbon Majors have long been aware of the risks associated with their actions, failed to inform the public of these risks and to adopt measures to stop further harm and remedy harm already caused.[75] The applicants in the Carbon Majors petition have asked the Philippines National Human Rights Commission to regard these elements as an indicator of reprehensibility and to establish responsibility.[76] Similar arguments are being made against an ongoing investigation for fraud in the United States against Exxon.[77]

[70] Ibid.

[71] This matter is currently being investigated in the United States, in the context of the so-called Exxon climate investigation: Exxon Climate Investigation (*Climate Liability News*), www.climateliabilitynews.org/category/exxon-climate-investigation/, accessed 15 June 2019.

[72] '*Joint Summary of the Amicus Curiae Briefs to the Philippines Commission on Human Rights*' (Philippines Commission on Human Rights 2018) 59–60, www.ciel.org/reports/philippines-joint-amicus, accessed 15 June 2019.

[73] Faure and Nollkaemper (n 3) 172.

[74] See, for example, Richard S. J. Tol and Roda Verheyen, 'State Responsibility and Compensation for Climate Change Damages – A Legal and Economic Assessment' (2004) 32 *Energy Policy* 1109; Faure and Nollkaemper (n 3) 174.

[75] See also Martin Olszynski, Sharon Mascher and Meinhard Doelle, 'From Smokes to Smokestacks: Lessons from Tobacco for the Future of Climate Change Liability' (2017) SSRN Scholarly Paper, https://papers.ssrn.com/abstract=2957921, accessed 15 June 2019.

[76] Carbon Majors Petition (n 8) 23. 'Joint Summary of the Amicus Curiae Briefs' (n 73) paras. 59–60.

[77] As reported in Ucilia Wang, 'New York Attorney General Files Suit against Exxon for Climate Fraud' (*Climate Liability News*, 24 October 2018), www.climateliabilitynews.org/2018/10/24/new-york-attorney-general-exxon-climate-fraud/, accessed 15 June 2019.

3.2.3 *Extraterritoriality*

The Carbon Majors inquiry was initiated to 'help establish processes for hearing human rights victims especially with regard to trans-boundary harm, clarifying standards for corporate reporting and helping to identify basic rights and duties relative to climate change'.[78] The decision to investigate human rights violations allegedly perpetrated by actors headquartered outside the Philippines, however, was not uncontroversial.

Some of the respondents challenged the Commission's jurisdiction to hear the petition, arguing that 'the jurisdiction of a state is limited only to the confines of its physical boundaries'.[79] They further suggested that the exercise of jurisdiction over foreign corporations is an 'act of interference' or 'usurpation' of other states' sovereignty,[80] and 'tantamount to an undue encroachment on the territorial jurisdiction and sovereignty of such other states where Respondents are domiciled and operate'.[81]

The petitioners tried to brush these objections aside, asserting that, since the Commission is not a court of law, the term jurisdiction 'should not be construed and applied in the current inquiry'.[82] In practice, however, the use of the term 'jurisdiction' is not limited to courts of law but is commonly applied to any body that exercises governmental powers, such as a court or administrative authority,[83] or indeed, as in the case of the inquiry, a quasi-judicial body, like the Commission.

When announcing its decision to go ahead with the inquiry, the Commission was careful to specify that it is within 'its constitutional

[78] Roberto Eugenio T. Cadiz, 'New Approaches to Climate Justice: Framing Climate Change as a Human Rights Issue in a Global Dialogue' (*Environmental Science for Social Change*, 13 September 2018), http://essc.org.ph/content/new-approaches-to-climate-justice-framing-climate-change-as-a-human-rights-issue-in-a-global-dialogue, accessed 15 June 2019.

[79] See for the motion to dismiss filed by CEMEX in www.greenpeace.org/seasia/ph/PageFiles/735291/Corporate_Responses_and_Comments/Cemex_Response.pdf, accessed 15 June 2019, 11.

[80] Ibid. 16.

[81] See, for example, the motion to dismiss filed by Shell in 2016, available at www.greenpeace.org/seasia/ph/PageFiles/735291/Corporate_Responses_and_Comments/Shell_Response.pdf, accessed 15 June 2019, 1.

[82] Petitioners' consolidated reply to the respondent Carbon Majors in the National Public Inquiry being conducted by Commission on Human Rights of the Philippines, para 2.5, available at https://secured-static.greenpeace.org/seasia/ph/PageFiles/735291/Human_Rights_and_Climate_Change_Consolidated_Reply_2_10_17.pdf, accessed 15 June 2019.

[83] See, for example, Michael Akehurst, 'Jurisdiction in International Law' (1975) 46 *British Yearbook of International Law* 145, 178.

mandate to investigate allegations of violations of human rights of the Filipino people'.[84] The arguments concerning the Commission's powers to look into the Carbon Majors' responsibility for human rights violations in the Philippines merit further consideration.

States exercise jurisdiction over persons or events outside their territory as a matter of course.[85] The exercise of jurisdiction is generally accepted, as long as there is a clear connecting factor between the state exercising jurisdiction and the person or conduct that it seeks to regulate.[86] More specifically, neither prescriptive jurisdiction (i.e., the power to create, amend or repeal legislation) nor adjudicative jurisdiction (i.e., the ability of national courts, tribunals or other bodies exercising judicial functions to hear and decide on matters) is territorially limited to acts occurring within a state, whereas enforcement jurisdiction (i.e., the state's right to enforce legislation, for example, by using powers of arrest and investigation) is.[87]

The Carbon Majors inquiry needs to fall within one of the established principles of jurisdiction, to be in accordance with international law. As we argued elsewhere, the most relevant principles in this connection are the territorial and protective principles.[88]

[84] Ibid.

[85] This section of the paper draws on the arguments made in Savaresi, Cismas and Hartmann (n 11) paras 9–22.

[86] See, for example, R. Y. Jennings, 'Extraterritorial Jurisdiction and the United States Antitrust Laws' (1957) 33 *British Year Book of International Law* 146, 146; F. A. Mann, *The Doctrine of Jurisdiction in International Law*, vol. 111 (Recueil des Cours 1964); Akehurst (n 84); D. W. Bowett, 'Jurisdiction: Changing Patterns of Authority over Activities and Resources' (1983) 53 *British Yearbook of International Law* 1; F. A. Mann, *The Doctrine of International Jurisdiction Revisited after Twenty Years*, vol. 186 (Recueil des Cours 1984); L. Oppenheim, *Oppenheim's International Law*, vol. 1, R. Y. Jennings and Arthur Watts (eds.) 9th ed. (Longman 1996) 456 ff.; Rosalyn Higgins, *Problems and Process: International Law and How We Use It* (Clarendon Press 1995) ch. 4; Hélène Ruiz Fabri and Jean-Marc Sorel (eds.), *La Saisine Des Juridictions Internationales* (Pedone 2006); James Crawford, *Brownlie's Principles of Public International Law* 8th ed. (Oxford University Press 2012) ch. 7; Malcolm N. Shaw, *International Law* 7th ed. (Cambridge University Press 2014) ch. 12; and Christopher Staker, 'Jurisdiction' in Malcolm Evans (ed.), *International Law* 4th ed. (Oxford University Press 2014). See also *Restatement of the Law (Third), The Foreign Relations Law of the United States* (1987) vol. 1, part 4.

[87] At times, states will nonetheless exercise enforcement jurisdiction extraterritorially; this is especially true during military operations. See, for example, Jacques Hartmann, 'Detention in International Military Operations: Problems and Process' (2013) 52 *Military Law and the Law of War Review* 304.

[88] See Savaresi, Cismas and Hartmann (n 11), 17–25.

The authority of states to exercise legislative or adjudicative jurisdiction over acts that take place in their own territory – also known as the *territorial principle* – is generally uncontested. In particular, the subjective territorial principle allows states to exercise jurisdiction over activities committed within that state, even if completed abroad. Conversely, the objective territorial principle allows a state to exercise jurisdiction over activities that are completed within its territory, even if initiated abroad. Both principles therefore allow states to regulate conduct with an extra-territorial element.

The territorial principle also allows states to exercise prescriptive and adjudicative jurisdiction whenever the effects of the relevant conduct occurred in their territory. The so-called effects doctrine gives states 'leeway to unilaterally stretch the arm of their domestic laws in order to clamp down on harmful acts arising beyond their borders'.[89]

Already in 1945, in the *Alcoa* case, Judge Learned Hand noted: 'It is settled law . . . that any state may impose liabilities, even upon persons not within its allegiance, for conduct outside its borders that has consequences within its borders, which the state reprehends.'[90]The effects doctrine has been acknowledged by international tribunals in the *Lotus*[91] and in the *Arrest Warrant* case.[92] Currently, it finds wide application especially in relation to antitrust, tort, bribery and corruption, security, insolvency and criminal law.[93] Accordingly, and contrary to what was suggested by some of the Carbon Majors, the territorial principle does not preclude states from regulating conduct or adjudicating in relation to actors outside their territory. Quite the opposite is true. The territorial principle provides ample scope for the Philippines authorities to exercise jurisdiction over conduct outside the territory of the Philippines. On this basis, the Commission could legitimately investigate complaints regarding human rights violations carried out by the Carbon Majors, as long as it is satisfied that the relevant conduct is initiated, completed or has effects in the Philippines.

[89] Cedric Ryngaert, 'Jurisdiction: Towards a Reasonableness Test' in Malcolm Langford (ed.), *Global Justice, State Duties: The Extraterritorial Scope of Economic, Social, and Cultural Rights in International Law* (Cambridge University Press 2013) 194.

[90] *United States* v. *Aluminium Co. of America*, 148 F 2d 416, 443 (2d Cir 1945), (118).

[91] The Case of the S.S. "Lotus" (*France* v. *Turkey*) (1927) PCIJ (ser a) No 10, 23.

[92] Case Concerning the Arrest Warrant of 11 April 2000 (*Democratic Republic of the Congo* v. *Belgium*), Judgment [2002] ICJ Rep 3, [63], joint separate opinion of Higgins, Kooijmans and Buergenthal.

[93] See International Bar Association, 'Report of the Task Force on Extraterritorial Jurisdiction' (2009).

Finally, the *protective principle* (also known as '*competence réelle*') authorizes states to protect themselves by regulating and adjudicating in relation to conduct carried out abroad that may damage their essential security interests.[94] The principle applies regardless of the place of the conduct or the nationality of the alleged offender or victim. It was initially applied only in the context of criminal law, but since the 1980s, numerous states have applied it more broadly.[95] It is generally accepted that the application of the protective principle can only be justified by the need to protect the essential or vital interests of the state, but there is little consensus on how these should be defined. States have relied on the protective principle on several occasions to ensure environmental protection. Both the United States and Canada have, for example, relied on the protective principle to exercise their prescriptive jurisdiction over instances of pollution in the high seas, through the 1970 Arctic Water Pollution Prevention Act and the 1990 Oil Pollution Act, respectively.[96] Accordingly, the protective principle provides scope for the exercise of jurisdiction over conduct outside its territory, and for the Commission to assert its jurisdiction to consider complaints related to human rights violations carried out by foreign corporations, as long as it is necessary to protect essential or vital interests of the Philippines.

In sum, even though the Commission did not elaborate on which jurisdiction principles it relied on – and indeed did not need to, as, in accordance with the well-established doctrine of *compétence de la compétence*, it is for the Commission to determine the scope of its own mandate[97] – its decision to investigate the Carbon Majors implicitly relied on one or the other. In this connection, the very fact that the inquiry is taking place has already marked an important milestone, by demonstrating that national human rights institutions may look at the

[94] Iain Cameron, *The Protective Principle of International Criminal Jurisdiction* (Dartmouth 1994).

[95] See, for example, Eckhard Rehbinder, 'Extra-territoriality of Pollution Control Laws from a European Perspective' in Gunther Handl, Joachim Zekoll and Peer Zumbansen (eds.), *Beyond Territoriality: Transnational Legal Authority in an Age of Globalization* (Martinus Nijhoff 2012) 127–35 and Jonathan Remy Nash, 'The Curious Legal Landscape of the Extra-Territoriality of US Environmental Laws' in Gunther Handl, Joachim Zekoll and Peer Zumbansen (eds.), Beyond Territoriality: Transnational Legal Authority in an Age of Globalization (Martinus Nijhofff 2012) 163.

[96] Richard B. Bilder, 'The Canadian Arctic Waters Pollution Prevention Act: New Stresses on the Law of the Sea' (1970) 69 *Mich. L. Rev.* 1; Maria Gavouneli, *Functional Jurisdiction in the Law of the Sea* (Martinus Nijhoff 2007) 32.

[97] As argued also in Savaresi, Cismas and Hartmann (n 11) 4.

responsibilities of corporations, even when these are not headquartered in the territory of the state where the investigation takes place, as long as the exercise of their powers can be justified under one of the principles of jurisdiction.[98]

3.3 Conclusion

The Paris Agreement set out to address the matter of loss and damage caused by climate change, although at least for the time being, its parties have excluded using it as a means to establish liability for climate change impacts.[99] Even though no inter-state litigation in this connection has taken place, or is likely to take place in the foreseeable future, there has been a marked intensification of litigation concerning the impacts of climate change at the domestic and at the transnational level.

This chapter has shown that human rights law arguments are playing a small but not insignificant role in this litigation, and potentially lend themselves to holding corporations accountable for the impacts of climate change. Historically human rights law has been repeatedly used as a gap filler to supply remedies where none are available. Human rights remedies may be used to supplement regulatory action to change behaviour, and to help address restorative and distributive justice questions associated with climate change impacts.

Should the Philippines Human Rights Commission acknowledge that the Carbon Majors are responsible for the impacts of climate change, this would mark a milestone in the history of climate change litigation worldwide. The Commission's findings may furthermore help to set the contours of corporate due diligence obligations in relation to climate change, including in the extraterritorial context.

This is, however, an area where human rights law also presents clear limitations. Human rights law typically provides declaratory relief to name and shame human rights abusers but offers limited, if any, compensatory relief, or means to deter further harm. The Philippines Human Rights Commission is a case in point. Its powers are largely limited to declaratory relief and rest with the domestic authorities' limited capability to affect the future behaviour of the Carbon Majors.

[98] Savaresi, Cismas and Hartmann (n 11) 4.
[99] ibid., para. 51.

In conclusion, human rights law remedies are no replacement for a dedicated form of liability for climate change impacts. Yet, past experience shows that successful human rights complaints can help to bring about a change in attitude by courts and law-makers.[100] In this connection, the use of human rights law remedies can contribute to engendering a shift in legal culture to deal with one of the most intractable challenges facing humankind. The fact that this has not happened yet does not mean that it cannot happen in the future. In this (as was the case in many other such instances before), where there is a will, there is a way.

[100] As suggested, for example, in Boyle, 'Human Rights and the Environment' (n 7) 642.

4

Litigating Human Rights Violations Related to the Adverse Effects of Climate Change in the Pacific Islands

MARGARETHA WEWERINKE-SINGH

Introduction

In June 2015, forty community leaders from across the Pacific Island nations of Vanuatu, Kiribati, Tuvalu, Fiji, the Solomon Islands and the Philippines gathered on board Greenpeace's flagship vessel the *Rainbow Warrior*, anchored at the harbor of Port Vila, Vanuatu. The *Rainbow Warrior* had come to Vanuatu to assist with the delivery of relief to Vanuatu's outlying islands following category five cyclone Pam, which had struck the island nation in March that year and left thousands of Ni-Vanuatu in need of emergency shelter and goods.[1] On board the *Rainbow Warrior*, community leaders discussed potential legal actions to hold polluters to account for alleged human rights violations associated with the adverse effects of climate change. The meeting, which included activists and lawyers involved in the landmark *Greenpeace South Asia* v. *Chevron et al.* case[2] before the Commission on Human Rights of the Philippines, culminated in a declaration committing to bring a case to 'investigate the human rights implications of climate change and hold the big carbon polluters accountable to appropriate international bodies or processes'.[3] The initiative was notably supported by then Vanuatu

[1] Greenpeace International, 'Greenpeace Ship *Rainbow Warrior* Brings Relief to Vanuatu's Stranded Islands' (Press Release, 17 May 2015) www.greenpeace.org/international/press-release/7625/greenpeace-ship-rainbow-warrior-brings-relief-to-vanuatus-stranded-islands/, accessed 13 August 2018.

[2] Case no CHR-NI-2016-0001 (9 May 2016), Philippines Commission on Human Rights.

[3] Peoples' Declaration for Climate Justice, adopted in Port Vila, Vanuatu on 8 June 2015, www.greenpeace.org/international/Global/international/briefings/climate/2015/People's%20Declaration%20for%20Climate%20Justice.pdf, accessed 2 August 2018.

president Baldwin Lonsdale, who attended the meeting and received the declaration.[4]

While no actual rights-based climate litigation has, as yet, materialised in Vanuatu or elsewhere in the Pacific Islands region,[5] there are compelling reasons for Pacific Island individuals, communities or indeed States to use human rights litigation to confront climate change. First of all, the adverse effects of climate change experienced in the Pacific Islands region already have distinct human rights consequences.[6] Among the most conspicuous of those relate to the loss of habitable territory. The increasingly hostile environment created by cyclones, sea-level rise and other impacts of climate change poses a direct threat to Pacific Islanders' cultures and identities, which are often intertwined with their land.[7] Rising sea levels, higher king tides and storm surges, saltwater intrusion and changing weather patterns are already forcing a growing number of communities and individuals to leave their traditional homelands.[8] The Pacific Island peoples' wholesale rejection of the 'climate refugee' label underscores the importance of preserving the habitability of their islands – and thus respecting their rights to self-determination and culture – through more ambitious mitigation and adaptation measures.[9] At the same time, the actual loss, damage and migration

[4] Ed King, 'Vanuatu Backs Plan to Sue Major Carbon Polluters for Climate Damage' (*Climate Home News*, 9 June 2015), www.climatechangenews.com/2015/06/09/vanuatu-to-sue-major-carbon-polluters-for-climate-damage, accessed 16 August 2018.

[5] There is, however, a growing number of cases involving Pacific Island citizens seeking refuge or asylum in foreign States on environmental grounds. See, for example, 0907346 [2009] RRTA 1168; *AD (Tuvalu)* [2014] NZIPT 501370-371; *Teitiota* v. *Chief Executive of the Ministry of Business, Innovation and Employment* [2015] NZSC 107.

[6] See, generally, Margaretha Wewerinke-Singh and Wesley Morgan, 'Human Rights and Climate Change in the Pacific Islands: An Overview of the Issues' (Office of the UN High Commissioner for Human Rights 2018).

[7] See, for example, Karen McNamara and Chris Gibson, '"We Do Not Want to Leave Our Land": Pacific Ambassadors at the United Nations Resist the Category of "Climate Refugees"' (2009) 40(3) *Geoforum* 475, and Nikita Perumal, 'The Place Where I Live Is Where I Belong: Community Perspectives on Climate Change and Climate-Related Migration in the Pacific Island Nation of Vanuatu' (2018) 13(1) *Island Studies Journal* 45.

[8] See, for example, Megan Rowling, 'Solomons Town First in Pacific to Relocate Due to Climate Change' (*Reuters*, 15 August 2014), www.reuters.com/article/us-foundation-climatechange-solomons-idUSKBN0GF1AB20140815, accessed 15 August 2018; Ella Rubeli, 'Escaping the Waves: a Fijian Village Relocates' *Sydney Morning Herald* (Sydney, 3 October 2015); Ropate Valemei, 'More Villages Set to Face Relocation' *Fiji Times* (Fiji, 23 June 2016), and Ana Ravulo, '64 Villages to be Relocated Due to Climate Change' *Fiji Village* (Fiji, 1 August 2016).

[9] See further Rebecca Hingley, 'Climate Refugees: An Oceanic Perspective' (2017) 4 *Asia and thePacific Policy Studies* 158.

that are already occurring as a result of climate change signal a need for remedies tailored to *restoring* the enjoyment of human rights affected by climate change to the greatest possible extent, including in situations where people have been forced to flee their homes.[10] The right to a remedy – a central premise of human rights law – could remain an empty promise to Pacific Islanders who are affected by the adverse effects of climate change if no legal action is taken to enforce it.[11]

A pragmatic reason why Pacific Islanders may resort to human rights as a cause of action in climate litigation is the increasing global recognition of the relationship between climate change and human rights: among other things, the UN Human Rights Council has adopted eight resolutions on human rights and climate change,[12] and the Paris Climate Agreement adopted in December 2015 recognises the necessity for States to take into account their human rights obligations when taking climate action.[13] Pacific Island States have been at the forefront of forging this connection between climate change and human rights at the international level: they were among the first to raise concerns about climate change at international human rights forums[14] and helped ensure that climate change was placed on the agenda of the UN Human Rights Council.[15] At the regional level, Pacific Island leaders adopted the Suva Declaration on Climate Change in 2015, which expresses grave distress about climate change creating 'existential

[10] See also Margaretha Wewerinke-Singh, 'Climate Migrants' Right to Culture' in Avidan Kent and Simon Behrman (eds.), *Climate Refugees: Beyond the Legal Impasse?* (Routledge 2018).

[11] This is particularly so in light of the exclusion of liability and compensation from the scope of the Loss and Damage provision of the Paris Agreement. See UNFCCC, Decision 1/CP.21, *Report of the Conference of the Parties on Its Twenty-First Session, Held in Paris from 30 November to 13 December 2015*, FCCC/CP/2015/10/Add.1 (2016) ('*Paris Agreement*'), para 51. See further Margaretha Wewerinke-Singh and Curtis Doebbler, 'The Paris Agreement: Some Critical Reflections on Process and Substance' (2016) 39(4) *University of New South Wales Law Journal* 1486, 1505–6.

[12] UN Human Rights Council Resolutions 7/23 (2008) UN Doc A/HRC/Res/7/23, 10/4 (2009) UN Doc A/HRC/Res/10/4, 18/22 (2011) UN Doc A/HRC/Res/18/22, 26/27 (2014) UN Doc A/HRC/Res/26/27, 29/15 (2015) UN Doc A/HRC/Res/29/15, 32/33 (2016) UN Doc A/HRC/Res/32/33, 35/20 (2017) UN Doc A/HRC/Res/35/20 and 38/4 (2018) UN Doc A/HRC/Res/38/4.

[13] *Paris Agreement* (n 11), preamble para 7.

[14] See, for example, 'Initial Report of Kiribati to the Committee on the Rights of the Child' (7 December 2005) UN Doc CRC/C/KIR/1.

[15] See Small Island Conference, Malé, Maldives, 13–14 November 2007, Malé Declaration on the Human Dimension of Global Climate Change (14 November 2007).

threats to our very survival and other violations of human rights to entire Pacific Small Island Developing States'[16] and highlights that climate change 'is already resulting in forced displacement of island populations and the loss of land and territorial integrity and . . . results in breaches of social and economic rights'.[17] These human rights concerns are cited almost verbatim in a model 'Pacific Climate Treaty' that is currently being discussed under the auspices of the Pacific Islands Development Forum (PIDF) as a possible regional response to the Paris Agreement.[18]

Against the backdrop of a growing number of rights-based climate cases litigated in courts around the world,[19] but (as noted previously) none so far in the Pacific, this paper provides an overview of options available to Pacific Island individuals, communities and states to seek redress for human rights violations related to climate change. The focus is on actions against States and private actors who have contributed most to the atmospheric greenhouse gas emissions that are causing climate change, in light of the fact that the Pacific Islands region as a whole contributes no more than 0.03 per cent to global greenhouse gas emissions.[20] Two levels of action are explored: first, action by individuals, communities or governments before domestic courts or human rights bodies in Pacific Islands against major fossil fuel companies; second, action by Pacific Island individuals, communities or States before international human rights bodies against major fossil fuel companies or foreign States. More specifically, the paper discusses potential actions through the Special Procedure mechanisms of the UN Human Rights Council and the individual or inter-State complaint procedures of human rights treaty bodies. The paper sheds light on the benefits and drawbacks

[16] Pacific Islands Development Forum, 'Suva Declaration on Climate Change', adopted on 4 September 2015 in Suva, Fiji, preamble.

[17] ibid para 7.

[18] See Pacific Islands Development Forum & Pacific Climate Action Network, 'Thinking Globally, Acting Regionally: The Case for a Pacific Climate Treaty' (2016), http://pacificidf.org/wp-content/uploads/2013/07/Pacific-Climate-Treaty.pdf, accessed 15 August 2016 (preamble).

[19] See Jacqueline Peel and Hari M Osofsky, 'A Rights Turn in Climate Change Litigation?' (2018) 7 *Transnational Environmental Law* 37.

[20] *Paris 2015: Save Oceania!*, 3rd Oceania 21 Summit, Lifou, Loyalty Islands, New Caledonia (30 April 2015) ('Lifou Declaration'), www.sprep.org/attachments/VirLib/New_Caledonia/Lifou_Declaration_2015.pdf, accessed 1 August 2018.

of each type of action, taking into account legal hurdles facing Pacific Island plaintiffs as well as extra-legal factors relating to process and remedies. Potential actions against foreign States *not* discussed in this paper include actions before foreign courts[21] or regional human rights bodies such as the European Court of Human Rights (ECtHR).[22] The focus here is on international bodies because of their potential to simultaneously consider the relative contributions of States from different regions to the alleged human rights violations of climate change, and because the Pacific Islands region does not have its own human rights body or regional court.[23] Potential litigation before the International Court of Justice (ICJ) is discussed briefly in relation to the Convention on the Elimination of all Forms of Discrimination against Women (CEDAW), adding to existing scholarship on the ICJ's potential to address climate change.[24] Although some of the options discussed could be explored in relation to all Pacific Island countries and territories, the focus is on Pacific Island States that are members of the United Nations and

[21] Notably, there is a precedent for climate litigation on behalf of Pacific Island people before domestic courts in third States: in March 2011, the Federated States of Micronesia (FSM) requested a Transboundary Environmental Impact Assessment to examine the proposed expansion and life-extension of a brown coal-fired power plant in the Czech Republic. See Greenpeace International, 'Threatened Pacific Island Nation Makes Legal History by Challenging European Carbon Emitter' (Press Release, 23 May 2011), www.greenpeace.org/archive-international/en/press/releases/2011/Threatened-Pacific-Island-Nation-makes-legal-history-by-challenging-European-carbon-emitter, accessed 3 August 2018.

[22] Although not a human rights court, the Court of Justice of the European Union has become the first (and so far only) regional court to be confronted with a rights-based climate case involving Pacific Island plaintiffs. See *Armando Ferrao Carvalho and others* v. *the European Parliament and the Council*, Application for annulment pursuant to Article 263 TFEU, Application/claim for non-contractual liability pursuant to article 268 and 340 TFEU and Application for Measures of Inquiry pursuant to articles 88 and 91 of the Rules of Procedure of the General Court (2018), available at www.peoplesclimatecase.caneurope.org/wp-content/uploads/2018/05/application-delivered-to-european-general-court-1.pdf, accessed 16 August 2018.

[23] The notion of a regional human rights body for the Asia Pacific region has been on the agenda of civil society groups for more than thirty years, but a mechanism has never materialised. Debate about a Pacific regional human rights mechanism resurfaced a few years ago but seems to have stagnated. See, for example, 'Strategies for the Future: Protecting Rights in the Pacific' Conference in Apia, Samoa, from 27 to 29 April 2008, where the topic was on the agenda.

[24] See, for example, Daniel Bodansky, 'The Role of the International Court of Justice in Addressing Climate Change: Some Preliminary Reflections' (2017) 49 *Arizona State Law Journal* 689; Tracey Skillington, 'Climate Change and the Human Rights Challenge: Extending Justice beyond the Borders of the Nation State' (2012) 16 *The International Journal of Human Rights* 1196.

therefore able to take legal action against another State or States under international law.[25]

4.1 Legal Action before Domestic Courts or National Human Rights Institutions in Pacific Island States

4.1.1 Domestic Courts

All Pacific Island States have domestic legal systems that appear to be, in principle, amenable to rights-based climate litigation. They are premised on written constitutions that entrench a range of civil and political rights, including the right to life and in many cases also the right to property. The constitution of Vanuatu, for example, provides that 'all persons' are entitled to protection of their right to life.[26] Tuvalu's constitution protects the right to property against wrongful deprivation, including 'its destruction; and . . . the making of it useless or valueless for the purposes for which it was used'.[27] Fiji's constitution also enshrines a wide range of economic, social and cultural rights such as the rights to adequate food and water, housing, sanitation and health, as well as a right to a clean and healthy environment.[28] In interpreting constitutional rights and other provisions of domestic law, Pacific Island judges may also draw on the provisions of international human rights instruments and customary international law.[29] Senior judges from the region have recognised the universality, interdependence and interrelatedness of all human rights,[30] which indicates potential for

[25] Of the twenty-two Pacific Island countries and territories, the following twelve are Members of the United Nations: Fiji, Kiribati, the Marshall Islands, the Federated States of Micronesia, Nauru, Palau, Papua New Guinea, Samoa, the Solomon Islands, Tuvalu, Vanuatu and Tonga. The Cook Islands and Niue do not have UN membership, but their freely associated state status with New Zealand has been recognised by UN organisations as equivalent to independence for international law purposes. The eight dependent Pacific island territories are American Samoa, French Polynesia, Guam, New Caledonia, Commonwealth of the Northern Mariana Islands, Pitcairn Islands, Tokelau, and Wallis and Futuna Islands.

[26] Constitution of the Republic of Vanuatu [1980] art 5(1).

[27] Constitution of Tuvalu [1986] ss 20(1)(c)–(d).

[28] Constitution of the Republic of Fiji [2013] arts 8–42.

[29] See, for example, the Pacific Island Judges Declaration on Gender Equality in the Courts (Denarau, Fiji, 4 July 1997). See also *Naduaniwai* v. *Commander, Republic of Fiji Military Forces* [2004] FJHC 8 (in which the court considered human rights protections derived from customary international law to interpret domestic law).

[30] Conclusions and Recommendations of the Colloquium and Workshop for Judges and Lawyers on the Justiciability of Economic, Social and Cultural Rights in the Pacific region (Suva, Fiji 1–3 June 2006).

invoking legal arguments that reflect the international consensus that climate change has 'a range of implications for the effective enjoyment of human rights including, inter alia, the right to life, the right to adequate food, the right to the highest attainable standard of health, the right to adequate housing, the right to self-determination and the right to safe drinking water and sanitation',[31] even if those rights are not expressly enshrined in a Pacific Island nation's constitution. The threats posed by climate change to human lives and livelihoods have already become so evident in the Pacific Islands that claimants are unlikely to face an uphill battle in convincing judges who are themselves based in the region of the applicability of human rights law to climate change impacts.[32] While climate change cases will confront Pacific Island courts with complex legal and evidential questions that are absent from 'traditional' human rights cases, courts could draw upon a growing body of jurisprudence from around the world that has grappled with the link between climate change and human rights. Moreover, regional and international organisations have begun to train chief justices and senior judges from the region in adjudicating disputes with climate change components in their respective jurisdictions.[33]

The rights protected in Pacific Island constitutions are generally coupled with the right to a remedy for their violation, available through the courts. As noted previously, a pressing question in the context of human rights harm associated with climate change is who is responsible for ensuring this right. In light of the negligible contributions of Pacific Island States to the accumulated atmospheric greenhouse gases that have caused climate change, it would not only seem futile but also contrary to 'climate justice'[34] to bring a claim against Pacific Island States for human rights violations associated with the adverse effects of climate change. Some foreign States are responsible for much larger shares of global

[31] UNHRC Res 18/22 (2011) UN Doc A/HRC/Res/18/22.

[32] See, for example, Rory A. Walshe and others, 'Perceptions of Adaptation, Resilience and Climate Knowledge in the Pacific: The Cases of Samoa, Fiji and Vanuatu' (2017) 10(2) *International Journal of Climate Change Strategies and Management* 303 (showing significant concern about climate change among school teachers, rural communities and media personnel in Samoa, Fiji and Vanuatu).

[33] See, for example, Asian Development Bank, 'Regional: Developing Judicial Capacity for Adjudicating Climate Change and Sustainable Development Issues' (December 2016) www.adb.org/projects/50177-001/main, accessed 13 October 2018.

[34] 'Climate justice' is understood here as requiring not only that every effort is made to address climate change but also that its uneven burdens are corrected.

emissions and also have greater capacities to decarbonise their economies.[35] However, claims before Pacific Island courts against foreign States are likely barred by legal doctrines of State immunity. An attractive alternative option for Pacific Island plaintiffs seeking to address the root causes of climate change through litigation is therefore to target 'carbon majors' – the ninety oil, gas, coal and cement companies that have contributed most to anthropogenic climate change and its adverse effects.[36] The number of cases against carbon majors is on the rise globally, with a range of actions brought by coastal communities, cities, counties and states before different courts in the United States seeking damages and other relief,[37] and the Philippines Human Rights Commission currently investigating the responsibility of carbon majors for human rights violations resulting from the impacts of climate change following a petition from Greenpeace Southeast Asia.[38]

In most Pacific Island States, there appears to be no principled restrictions on seeking remedies, including compensation, for human rights violations committed by private actors. For example, Vanuatu's Constitution provides that '[a]nyone who considers that any of the rights guaranteed to him by the Constitution has been, is being or is likely to be infringed may, independently of any other possible legal remedy, apply to the Supreme Court to enforce that right'.[39] The Supreme Court is in turn mandated to 'make such orders, issue such writs and give such directions, including the payment of compensation, as it considers appropriate to enforce the right'.[40] The broad phrasing of both provisions

[35] For precise figures on historical responsibility of States and a proposal for the equitable division of the remaining carbon budget, see Tim Crosland, Aubrey Meyer and Margaretha Wewerinke-Singh, 'The Paris AgreementImplementation Blueprint: a Practical Guide to Bridging the Gap between Actions and Goal and Closing the Accountability Deficit (Part 1)' (2017) 25(2) *Environmental Liability* 114.

[36] Brenda Ekwurzel and others, 'The Rise in Global Athmospheric CO2, Surface Temperature, and Sea Level from Emissions traced to Major Carbon Producers' (2017) 144(4) *Climatic Change* 579.

[37] Office of Richmond Mayor Tom Butt, 'City of Richmond Becomes Ninth Community Seeking to Hold Fossil Fuel Companies Accountable and Protect *Its* Taxpayers from Costs and Consequences of Climate Change' (Press Release, 22 January 2018), www.sheredling.com/wp-content/uploads/2018/01/1.22.18-NEWS-RELEASE-City-Sues-Fossil-Fuel-Companies-for-Climate-Change-Damages.pdf, accessed 1 August 2018.

[38] *Greenpeace South Asia* v. *Chevron et al.* (n 2).

[39] Constitution of the Republic of Vanuatu art 6. See also Constitution of Fiji art 44(1) (stating that anyone who 'considers that any of the provisions of this Chapter has been or is likely to be contravened in relation to him or her' may apply to the High Court for redress').

[40] Constitution of the Republic of Vanuatu, art 6.

suggests that individuals could enforce their rights even if the infringement is committed by non-State actors – an interpretation that appears to be supported by case law.[41] The situation is similar in the Solomon Islands, Western Samoa and Tonga, where the constitution leaves open the possibility that fundamental rights have a horizontal as well as a vertical effect, with case law confirming that there may be a horizontal effect in some cases.[42] In Tuvalu, the section of its constitution relating to the scope of fundamental rights states expressly that it applies 'between individuals as well as between governmental bodies and individuals' and 'to and in relation to corporations and associations (other than governmental bodies) in the same way as it applies to and in relation to individuals, except where, or to the extent that, the context requires otherwise'.[43]

The implied or express right to claim a remedy from private actors appears to extend to private actors based in third countries. Fiji's Constitution states explicitly that 'to the extent that it is capable of doing so, [the chapter that contains human rights] extends to things done or actions taken outside Fiji'.[44] This suggests that domestic courts in Fiji may assume jurisdiction over claims against carbon majors based on alleged violations of human rights in Fiji, even where these violations are caused by action taken elsewhere. In other words, the lack of a significant physical presence of carbon majors in Fiji does not form a barrier to the enforcement of rights allegedly violated by their contributions to climate change. The situation may be similar in other Pacific Island States: while other Pacific Island constitutions do not expressly provide for remedies for human rights violations caused by action elsewhere, they do not prohibit such remedies either. Interpreting these constitutions as if restricting remedies for violations committed within their territories would unnecessarily deprive entire populations of adequate and effective remedies for human rights harm resulting from climate change and thus appears contrary to the constitutional and international law provisions that protect the right to a remedy.

[41] In re *the Constitution of the Republic of Vanuatu, Infant P* [1984] VUCA 2; In re the *Nagol Jump, Assal & Vatu* v. *Council of Chiefs of Santo* [1992] VUSC 5; *Public Prosecutor* v. *Walter Kota and Ten Others* [1993] VUSC 8. Cf. *Family Kalontano* v. *Duruaki Council of Chiefs* [2002] VUSC 32. See also Sue Farran, *Human Rights in the South Pacific: Challenges and Changes* (Routledge 2009) 73.

[42] *Loumia* v. *DPP* [1985–86] SILR 158 (Solomon Islands); *Tuivaiti* v. *Sila* [1980–93] WSLR 181 (Western Samoa); *Pale* v. *Pohiva* [2006] TOSC 16 (Tonga).

[43] Constitution of Tuvalu, ss 12(1)(a) and (b).

[44] Constitution of the Republic of Fiji, art 6.

This brings us to the question of potential plaintiffs in rights-based climate lawsuits before Pacific Island courts. In light of the vast scale of the loss and damage resulting from climate change, lawsuits by local or national governments on behalf of those whose rights are implicated by this loss and damage appear to be the most efficient way of seeking redress for the human rights implications of climate change. At the same time, individuals and communities may want to seek recourse to justice for climate change–related human rights violations where their governments are unwilling or unable to act on their behalf. Most Pacific Island States' legal systems include a notion of standing derived from common law, requiring that a plaintiff must show some direct interest in the matter at dispute in order to bring a case.[45] Based on this notion, potential plaintiffs in a constitutional case against carbon majors could include individuals or communities whose constitutional rights are affected, as well as national or local governments representing those who have suffered damage to their legal rights. Where the plaintiff seeking standing is a Pacific Island government, inspiration could be drawn from the reasoning of the US Supreme Court in *Massachusetts* v. *EPA*,[46] where standing was granted to several states based on their sovereign capacity 'to have the last word as to whether its mountains shall be stripped of their forests and its inhabitants shall breathe pure air'.[47] In a case based on human rights, however, the emphasis would be on the State's right and obligation to protect the constitutional rights of its people against infringements by private actors. These obligations were recognised in broad terms by the Hague Court of Appeal in *Urgenda* v. *the Netherlands*,[48] where the court stated that the existence of 'a real threat of dangerous climate change, resulting in the serious risk that the current generation of citizens will be confronted with loss of life and/or a disruption of family life' triggered an obligation on the State 'to protect against this real threat'.[49] It can be argued that litigation against carbon majors is among the most appropriate and effective measures Pacific Island States could take to protect the rights of *their* citizens and seek

[45] Jennifer Corrin and David Newton Bamford, *Courts and Civil Procedure in the South Pacific*, 2nd ed. (Intersentia 2016) 53.

[46] *Massachusetts* v. *EPA* 549 US SC 497 (2007).

[47] *Massachusetts* v. *EPA* 549 US SC 497 (2007) [14] (quoting from *Georgia* v. *Tennessee Copper Co.* 206 US SC 230 [1907]).

[48] *The Urgenda Foundation* v. *Kingdom of the Netherlands* C/09/456689/HA ZA 13–1396, The Hague Court of Appeal, Civil-Law Division, 9 October 2018, para 45.

[49] *The Urgenda Foundation* v. *Kingdom of the Netherlands* C/09/456689/HA ZA 13–1396, The Hague Court of Appeal, Civil-Law Division, 9 October 2018, para 4.74.

redress for harm that has already occurred as a result of climate change, given Pacific Island States' lack of regulatory control over carbon majors and the apparent unwillingness of industrialised States to ensure that carbon majors are held liable for the damages caused by their products.

If a Pacific Island court would be prepared to consider the merits of a constitutional case against carbon majors, another hurdle facing the plaintiffs is the need to establish a link between the conduct of carbon majors, on the one hand, and infringements with constitutional rights, on the other. It remains an open-ended question what kind of test the courts would apply on this point. Notably, international and regional human rights bodies have highlighted that human rights violations can be established even in the absence of scientific probability regarding a causal link.[50] This approach is based on the positive obligations of States to protect human rights, which essentially shifts part of the burden of uncertainty about environmental impacts to the State, in line with the precautionary principle.[51] Importantly, this approach allows plaintiffs to hold States responsible for human rights violations associated with climate change, even in situations where the harm has not yet materialised. However, despite widespread recognition that corporations have a responsibility to avoid causing or contributing to human rights harm,[52] businesses are not the primary duty bearers under human rights law, and therefore shifting the burden of uncertainty to corporations is not as straightforward as it is in cases against public authorities. Indeed, it is conceivable that Pacific courts would require plaintiffs to establish a causal link between defendants' conduct and actual harm suffered, along the lines of a tortious causation test rather than a public or international law test. In relation to this point, defendants often argue that the emissions for which they are responsible are only a fraction of the global total and hence cannot be found to have caused a particular harm.[53] In a case against carbon majors, however, plaintiffs could draw on a growing body of 'attribution research', including recent research that calculates the contribution of each major fossil fuel company to particular climate

[50] See, for example, *Tatar C. v. Roumanie*, EctHR Appl. No. 67021/01, Judgment of 5 July 2007, paras 107–24.

[51] See also Dinah Shelton, *Remedies in International Human Rights Law*, 2nd ed. (Oxford University Press 2010) 50, 317.

[52] UN OHCHR, *Guiding Principles on Business and Human Rights: Implementing the United Nations 'Protect, Respect and Remedy' Framework* (New York and Geneva 2011).

[53] See also Jacqueline Peel, 'Issues in Climate Change Litigation' (2011) 5(1) *Carbon and Climate Law Review* 15, 16.

impacts.[54] This evidence, coupled with evidence about the specific impacts of climate change already experienced in the Pacific Islands, might be sufficient to establish causation, especially if the court in question takes due account of victims' right to a remedy for human rights violations.

If successful, the litigation would result in a binding judgment that could include an order for equitable relief to prevent future harm as well as compensatory damages, including the means for as full rehabilitation as possible.[55] The litigation could thus bring significant fiscal benefit to a Pacific Island State in case of a court victory. However, a legal hurdle facing plaintiffs in this type of litigation is the enforcement of the judgment. Given the insignificant presence of carbon majors in most Pacific Island jurisdictions, plaintiffs would likely rely on foreign courts to enforce any damages award obtained in a Pacific Island court. Whether and how this could happen depends on the laws on the enforcement of foreign judgments and the collection of international debts in the relevant foreign jurisdiction.[56] While not all jurisdictions would allow for this type of enforcement orders, many jurisdictions do, and the presence of carbon majors in multiple countries means that a certain amount of 'forum shopping' is available to Pacific Island plaintiffs seeking to enforce a judgment against carbon majors obtained from a court in their home jurisdiction.[57]

Besides the opportunity to access tangible redress for the human rights implications of climate change, another significant benefit of litigating a case of this nature before a domestic court in a Pacific Island State is that it offers tremendous opportunities for involving civil society, the private sector, academia and the local media in the legal action. Those whose rights are affected by climate harm could relatively easily serve as

[54] See Ekwurzel and others (n 36). According to the study, the carbon majors are responsible for 50 per cent of global surface temperature rise, 57 per cent of the increase in carbon dioxide in the atmosphere and between 26 and 32 per cent of global sea-level rise.

[55] The right to rehabilitation as part of redress is found in several international instruments, with perhaps the strongest formulation in the Convention against Torture and Other Cruel, Inhuman or Degrading Treatment or Punishment (adopted 10 December 1984, entered into force 26 June 1987) 1465 UNTS 85, art 14.

[56] Ralf Michaels, 'Recognition and Enforcement of Foreign Judgments' in Rüdiger Wolfrum (ed.), *Max Planck Encyclopedia of Public International Law* (Oxford University Press 2009), https://scholarship.law.duke.edu/faculty_scholarship/2076, accessed 5 May 2018.

[57] See also Andrew Gage and Margaretha Wewerinke, *Taking Climate Justice into Our Own Hands: A Model Climate Compensation Act* (West Coast Environmental Law and Vanuatu Environmental Law Association 2015) 20.

witnesses, which would likely be more cumbersome and expensive in international-level litigation. The bottom-up nature of this litigation strategy also allows for important legal capacity building within Pacific Island States, creating an opportunity for Pacific Island lawyers and members of the judiciary to become crucial players in the global climate law movement.

4.1.2 Ombudsman and National Human Rights Institutions

Ombudsman and National Human Rights Institutions have similar advantages as domestic courts in terms of their accessibility to Pacific Island plaintiffs, witnesses, local media and the general public; proximity to the experienced impacts of climate change; and capacity-building opportunities. Several but not all Pacific Island States have Ombudsman institutions. Fiji, Papua New Guinea, the Solomon Islands and Vanuatu[58] provide for an Ombudsman in their constitutions, while Pacific Island States such as Tuvalu,[59] the Cook Islands, Samoa and Western Samoa have established the institution by statute. However, the mandates of these institutions are generally limited to investigating and resolving complaints about the actions or omissions of national government ministries and agencies. Further limitations follow from the fact that most Ombudsman institutions in Pacific Island States are often under-resourced and over-burdened.[60] Perhaps the one exception is the Ombudsman of Samoa, which also functions as the country's National Human Rights Institution (NHRI).[61] This institution has a broad mandate that includes a function 'to inquire into, and report on, alleged violations of human rights'.[62] The Ombudsman can initiate an inquiry if it 'becomes aware of widespread, systemic or entrenched situations or practices that violate human rights'.[63] There are no qualifications as to the alleged perpetrator of the violation, which suggests that Samoa's Ombudsman could, at least in principle, launch an inquiry about the responsibility of carbon majors for human rights violations resulting from climate change. However, the Ombudsman considers itself an option of second resort when it comes to redress for human rights

[58] Constitution of the Republic of Vanuatu, art 6.
[59] Tuvalu Leadership Code Act 2008, s 38.
[60] See, generally, the annual reports of the Pacific Ombudsman Alliance, www.pacificombudsman.org/publications-and-resources/annual-reports, accessed 5 August 2018.
[61] Komesina O Sulufaiga Act 2013 parts 4–6.
[62] Komesina O Sulufaiga Act 2013, ss 33(b).
[63] Komesina O Sulufaiga Act 2013, s 34.

violations. It states on its website that individuals who have a right to review by a Court or Tribunal of the merits of a complaint should resort to that avenue of redress rather than to the Ombudsman.[64]

Fiji is currently the only other Pacific Island State with its own NHRI. Fiji's NHRI, the Human Rights and Anti-Discrimination Commission, has a broad mandate that includes monitoring, investigating and reporting on the observance of human rights; receiving and investigating complaints about alleged abuses of human rights; taking steps to secure appropriate redress if human rights have been violated, including making applications to court for redress or for other forms of relief or remedies; investigating or researching, on its own initiative or on the basis of a complaint, any matter in respect of human rights; and making recommendations to improve the functioning of public or private entities.[65] The constitution states that 'anyone' can lodge complaints about alleged human rights violations in Fiji with the Commission, which suggests that the mechanism can be used not only by individuals or communities whose rights are allegedly violated as a result of the adverse effects of climate change but also by public authorities on their behalf. Moreover, complaints can concern situations where rights have already been violated, as well as situations that constitute a threat to human rights.[66]

It is worth noting that the Commission on Human Rights of the Philippines appears to have assumed jurisdiction over the carbon majors petition based on its constitutional mandate 'to investigate and monitor all matters concerning the human rights of the Filipino people'.[67] The mandate of Fiji's Human Rights and Anti-Discrimination Commission is similarly broad, and thus likewise seems to allow for an approach where jurisdiction is based on the location of those whose human rights are infringed upon. When it comes to legal causation and attribution, the plaintiffs could presumably draw on much of the same evidence concerning carbon majors' responsibility for climate change as put forward by the plaintiffs in the Philippines case, coupled with evidence about specific climate change impacts in Fiji. Should a case be successful, the

64 Website of the Ombudsman of Samoa, www.ombudsman.gov.ws/index.php?option=com_content&view=article&id=81&Itemid=73, accessed 4 August 2018.

65 Constitution of the Republic of Fiji, arts 45(4)(c), (e) and (f). See also Human Rights Commission Decree 2009/11 art 12(1).

66 Constitution of the Republic of Fiji, art 45(4)(f).

67 Republic of the Philippines Commission on Human Rights, 'Press Release: National Inquiry on the Impact of Climate Change on the Human Rights of the Filipino People' (27 March 2018), http://chr.gov.ph/wp-content/uploads/2018/03/Press-Release_CHR-to-hold-1st-NICC-hearing-26-March-18.pdf, accessed 3 August 2018.

Human Rights and Anti-Discrimination Commission could make an application to a court for redress, which could be either a domestic court in Fiji or, conceivably, a foreign court in a jurisdiction where one or more carbon majors have significant assets or presence.

Further options for rights-based climate cases may emerge as more Pacific Island States are establishing NHRIs. Tuvalu has passed a National Human Rights Institution Act that will give its Ombudsman a mandate similar to that of Samoa's NHRI,[68] while Nauru, the Federated States of Micronesia, the Cook Islands and the Marshall Islands recently hosted scoping missions on the establishment of an NHRI.[69] Vanuatu has established a National Human Rights Committee that is supposed to coordinate the process of establishing a NHRI,[70] and Papua New Guinea has been in the process of establishing a NHRI for several years now.[71] More Pacific Island States can be expected to follow suit, either by extending the mandate and strengthening the infrastructure of existing Ombudsman institutions or by creating entirely new institutions. The broad understanding of human rights within the region means that there will likely be significant potential to engage meaningfully with NHRIs on climate justice issues once these institutions are established and operational.

4.2 Action before International Human Rights Bodies to Address the Human Rights Implications of Climate Change in the Pacific Islands

4.2.1 The United Nations Human Rights Council

The Human Rights Council (HRC) is the primary intergovernmental human rights body of the United Nations (UN) and mandated to promote the effective coordination and mainstreaming of human rights within the UN system.[72] Members of the HRC are elected directly and

68 National Human Rights Institution Act 2017.

69 Pacific Community, 'Pacific Leaders Can Celebrate Impressive Human Rights Achievements over Past Year' (24 January 2018), www.spc.int/blog/pacific-leaders-can-celebrate-impressive-human-rights-achievements-over-past-year/, accessed 12 August 2018.

70 Vanuatu Council of Ministers Decision 96 of 2013.

71 See 'National Report Submitted by Papua New Guinea in Accordance with Paragraph 5 of the Annex to Human Rights Council Resolution 16/21' (3 May 2016) UN Doc A/HRC/WG.6/25/PNG/1 para 18.

72 UNGA Res 60/251 (3 April 2006) A/RES/60/251 para 3.

individually by a majority of the members of the General Assembly to three-year terms.[73] Climate change has featured on the agenda of the HRC since 2008, when the HRC adopted its first resolution on human rights and climate change at the initiative of Small Island Developing States (SIDS) led by the Maldives.[74] Since then, the Council has adopted an additional seven resolutions, requested and received four analytical reports from the Office of the United Nations High Commissioner for Human Rights (OHCHR), and held four panel discussions as well as three seminars on different aspects of the relationship between climate change and human rights.[75] Climate change has also been discussed as part of the Universal Period Review (UPR) process, and Pacific Island States have used the process to raise concerns about the adverse effects of climate change on the enjoyment of human rights within their own territories[76] and to recommend that industrialised States cut their emissions in order to comply with their human rights obligations.[77] This in itself signals a shift away from the paradigm of States being exclusively responsible for the realisation of human rights within their own territories. Instead, States would be internationally responsible for the consequences of their acts or omissions on human rights irrespective of the location of the rights holders.[78]

Although the Council itself is an intergovernmental body premised on international collaboration, it has a number of Special Procedures – including Special Rapporteurs, Independent Experts and Working Groups – with quasi-judicial mandates to report and advise on human rights issues. Among other things, Special Procedures undertake country visits, conduct studies, convene expert consultations, contribute to the development of international human rights standards, engage in advocacy and advise governments.[79] Many existing Special Procedure mandate holders

[73] UNGA Res 60/251 (3 April 2006) A/RES/60/251 paras 7 and 14. No Pacific Island State is currently a member of the Human Rights Council.

[74] UNHRC Res 7/23 (2008) A/HRC/7/23.

[75] See UN OHCHR, 'Human Rights and Climate Change', www.ohchr.org/EN/Issues/HRAndClimateChange/Pages/HRClimateChangeIndex.aspx, accessed 7 August 2018.

[76] See, for example, the documentation on the reviews of Tuvalu, Kiribati, Vanuatu, Nauru, Micronesia, Palau, Papua New Guinea, Solomon Islands and Fiji, accessible via www.upr-info.org/database, accessed 7 August 2018.

[77] See, for example, the documentation on the reviews of Australia and the United States (noted previously).

[78] See also Inter-American Court of Human Rights, 'Advisory Opinion on the Environment and Human Rights' (15 November 2017) [95], [101]–[102].

[79] See the UN OHCHR website, www.ohchr.org/EN/HRBodies/SP/Pages/Welcomepage.aspx, accessed 7 August 2018.

have already considered climate change under their respective mandates through reports, country visits, statements and press releases and contributions to HRC debates, seminars and panel discussions.[80] Many Special Procedures also have a mandate to consider individual cases of alleged human rights violations,[81] which have so far not been used to address climate change. These complaint procedures are among the most flexible of all human rights complaint procedures: victims' abilities to complain do not depend on the ratification of human rights treaties by their own State; there are usually no jurisdictional restrictions on the scope of complaints; complaints could refer to past, ongoing, as well as potential future violations; and victims may identify any State or non-State actor as the alleged perpetrators of the violation. There is no requirement that domestic remedies be exhausted. These features make the Special Procedures particularly suitable for filing innovative human rights complaints relating to climate change, including complaints against foreign States or carbon majors brought by Pacific Island communities. Essentially, all it takes to use the procedure is filling out a two-page questionnaire available on the OHCHR website and sending it to a dedicated email address. Although the questionnaire asks for 'identification of the person(s) or organization(s) submitting the communication, if different from the victim', the flexible and discretionary nature of the procedure makes it unlikely that information would not be considered if it were to be submitted by a Pacific Island State. Indeed, Pacific Island States could generate global attention even by attempting to use the procedure to hold foreign States or carbon majors to account for the human rights implications of climate change.

There are two significant limitations of the Special Procedures: first, the mandate holder's response to a complaint is discretionary; a complaint submitted by Pacific Islanders affected by climate change can therefore be simply ignored. Second, the powers of mandate holders do not go beyond diplomacy and 'naming and shaming'; if a mandate holder does decide to act upon a complaint, the most likely intervention

[80] For Pacific Island States, the most notable has been a visit of the Special Rapporteur on the Right to Water and Sanitation, Catarina de Albuquerque, to Kiribati and Tuvalu in July 2012. The visit involved consultations with communities and resulted in reports highlighting the adverse effects of climate change on the enjoyment of rights related to water and sanitation. See UNHRC, 'Report of the Special Rapporteur on the Human Right to Safe Drinking Water and Sanitation, Catarina de Albuquerque: Mission to Kiribati (23–26 July 2012)' UN Doc A/HRC/24/44/Add.1, and UNHRC 'Report of the Special Rapporteur on the Human Right to Safe Drinking Water and Sanitation, Catarina de Albuquerque: Mission to Tuvalu (17–19 July 2012)' UN Doc A/HRC/24/44/Add.2.

[81] See the website of UN OHCHR (n 79).

is a letter to the allegedly responsible States or carbon majors identifying 'the facts of the allegation, applicable international human rights norms and standards, the concerns and questions of the mandate-holder(s), and a request for follow-up action'.[82] The text of the communications sent by mandate holders and any replies received would be reported to the Human Rights Council and made publicly available.[83] If the purpose of the action is to achieve tangible redress for the human rights implications of climate change, perhaps the most sensible strategy would be to combine legal action before a domestic court with political pressure that could be generated through the existing Special Procedures. Special Procedures could even provide targeted support in litigation, as the Special Rapporteur on Human Rights and the Environment, David Boyd, demonstrated when submitting a statement in support of a rights-based climate case brought before the High Court of Ireland.[84]

At the same time, Pacific Island communities and governments could continue to advocate for a dedicated Special Procedure on Human Rights and Climate Justice,[85] which could be created at any session of the Council through the adoption of a resolution. A dedicated Climate Justice mandate could contribute to norm-development on human rights and climate change, including on complex legal questions such as the status of those who lose their traditional land as a result of climate change, and support ongoing advocacy for systemic change to safeguard human rights in the face of climate change.

4.2.2 United Nations Human Rights Treaty Bodies

There are a number of UN human rights treaties that provide avenues for reporting, expert discussion and quasi-judicial litigation in relation to

[82] See UN OHCHR, 'Communications', www.ohchr.org/EN/HRBodies/SP/Pages/Communications.aspx, accessed 7 May 2018.

[83] See website of UN OHCHR, 'Communications Reports of Special Procedures', www.ohchr.org/EN/HRBodies/SP/Pages/CommunicationsreportsSP.aspx, accessed 7 August 2018.

[84] David R. Boyd, UN Special Rapporteur on Human Rights and Environment, 'Statement on the Human Rights Obligations Related to Climate Change, with Particular Focus on the Right to Life' (25 October 2018), www.iucn.org/sites/dev/files/content/documents/2019/friendsirishenvironment25oct2018.pdf, accessed 4 May 2019.

[85] Statement by Penelisa Alofa, National Coordinator for the Kiribati Climate Action Network, at the full-day panel discussion of the UN Human Rights Council (March 2015), http://webtv.un.org/watch/general-segment-10th-meeting-28th-regular-session-human-rights-council/4095103978001# (at 1:40:56), accessed 1 August 2018.

climate change. The most prominent treaties are the two International Covenants adopted in 1966, which form, together with the Universal Declaration of Human Rights, the International Bill of Human Rights. Both treaties contain rights that are implicated by the adverse effects of climate change. Most notably, article 1 common to the two treaties protects the right of self-determination, while the International Covenant on Civil and Political Rights (ICCPR)[86] also protects the rights to life and culture and the International Covenant on Economic, Social and Cultural Rights (ICESCR)[87] protects the rights to health, an adequate standard of living and education. Both treaties could therefore potentially serve as bases for action regarding the adverse effects of climate change on human lives, livelihoods and cultural identities in the Pacific Islands. The ICCPR has 167 State parties, including all high-income States listed in Annex I to the UN Framework Convention on Climate Change. The vast majority of States have also ratified ICESCR with 160 State parties.[88] There are many other widely ratified international human rights treaties, including conventions that protect rights of particular categories of people. The number of ratification of these treaties has risen rapidly in recent years, with all UN Member States having ratified at least one core human rights treaty and 80 per cent having ratified four or more.[89] However, ratification rates of human rights treaties in the Pacific Islands region are notoriously low. Of all Pacific Island States, only Papua New Guinea and the Marshall Islands have ratified both the ICCPR and the ICESCR. Samoa and Vanuatu have both ratified the ICCPR, while the Solomon Islands has ratified the ICESCR.[90]

Treaties that protect the rights of specific groups and aim to eradicate discrimination enjoy a higher rate of ratification in the region.[91] The

[86] International Covenant on Civil and Political Rights (adopted 16 December 1966, entered into force 23 March 1976) 999 UNTS 171 (ICCPR).

[87] International Covenant on Economic, Social and Cultural Rights (adopted 16 December 1966, entered into force 3 January 1976) 993 UNTS 3 (ICESCR).

[88] For ratification status, see United Nations Treaty Collection (UNTC), 'Multilateral Treaties Deposited with the Secretary-General', http://treaties.un.org/Pages/Treaties.aspx?id=4&subid=A&lang=en, accessed 4 August 2018.

[89] See UN OHCHR, 'Monitoring the Core International Human Rights Treaties', www.ohchr.org/EN/HRBodies/Pages/TreatyBodies.aspx, accessed 2 August 2018.

[90] See UNTC (n 88).

[91] The Convention on the Rights of the Child (CRC) is ratified by all Pacific Island States; the Convention on the Elimination of All Forms of Discrimination (CEDAW) is ratified by all Pacific Island States except Niue, Palau and Tonga; the International Convention on the Elimination of All Forms of Discrimination (ICERD) is ratified by Fiji, Papua New Guinea, the Solomon Islands and Tonga; and the Convention on the Rights of Persons

Convention on the Rights of the Child (CRC)[92] – ratified by all Pacific Island States – is particularly promising as a basis for actions related to climate change, as it contains a comprehensive set of civil, political, social, economic and cultural rights, many of which are affected by climate change, while its focus on children provides a natural basis for litigating concerns about the impacts of climate change on future generations. Moreover, the Committee on the Rights of the Child (which monitors compliance with the CRC) has consistently emphasised States' extraterritorial human rights obligations in its jurisprudence.[93] It has also recently adopted a comprehensive General Comment on State obligations regarding the impact of the business sector on children's rights which, among other things, highlights States' obligations to respect, protect and fulfil children's rights in the context of businesses' extraterritorial activities and operations.[94] The scope of the CEDAW,[95] the International Convention on the Elimination of All Forms of Racial Discrimination (ICERD)[96] and the Convention on the Rights of Persons with Disabilities (CRPD)[97] is more limited than that of the ICCPR, ICESCR or CRC, as the focus of these treaties is squarely on eliminating discrimination based on particular characteristics (namely, gender in case of CEDAW; race, colour, descent, or national or ethnic origin in case of CERD; and disability status in case of CRPD). Possible claims would therefore need to focus on the ways in which particular groups are disproportionately affected by the impacts of climate change. For example, evidence suggests that the increasingly severe impacts of climate change affect Pacific women disproportionately, with reduced access to key decision-making processes, increased

with Disabilities (CRPD) is ratified by Kiribati, the Marshall Islands, Nauru, Palau, Papua New Guinea, Tuvalu and Vanuatu. See UNTC (n 88).

92 Convention on the Rights of the Child (adopted 20 November 1989, entered into force 2 September 1990) 1577 UNTS 3 (CRC).

93 See, for example, CRC, 'Concluding Observations on Switzerland' (26 February 2015) UN Doc CRC/C/CHE/CO/2-4 paras 22–23; 'Concluding Observations on Australia' (28 August 2012) UN Doc CRC/C/AUS/CO/4 paras 27–28); 'Concluding Observations on Canada' (6 December 2012) UN Doc CRC/C/CAN/CO/3-4 paras 28–29.

94 CRC, General Comment No 16 on State obligations regarding the impact of the business sector on children's rights, (2013) UN Doc CRC/C/GC/16.

95 Convention on the Elimination of All Forms of Discrimination against Women (adopted 1 March 1980, entered into force 3 September 1981) 1249 UNTS 13.

96 International Convention on the Elimination of All Forms of Racial Discrimination (adopted 20 November 1963, entered into force 4 January 1969) 660 UNTS 195.

97 Convention on the Rights of Persons with Disabilities (adopted 30 March 2007, entered into force 3 May 2008) 2515 UNTS 3.

rates of sexual and gender-based violence and a fourteen-fold increased likelihood of death or injury to women or children during a disaster compared to men.[98] Claims could also focus on de facto discriminatory impacts of climate change on Pacific Island ethnicities or nationalities, or the disproportionate impacts of climate change on persons with disabilities. State responsibility could arise from a State's failure to take affirmative measures to correct these uneven burdens of climate change.[99] However, positive obligations to take affirmative action to address discrimination are less clearly established in international law than positive obligations to protect human rights generally, especially in a global context. Therefore, the ICCPR, ICESCR and CRC appear to provide the most robust substantive basis for State responsibility claims relating to the adverse effects of climate change.

The international human rights system has several quasi-judicial procedures that allow individuals (and, in some cases, groups of individuals) to submit complaints about alleged human rights violations to human rights treaty bodies. Most of these individual complaint procedures are established under Optional Protocols to the core human rights treaties. Very few Pacific Island States have ratified these Protocols,[100] which means that the possibilities for submitting complaints before human rights treaty bodies about human rights violations allegedly committed by Pacific Island States are limited. However, Pacific Island individuals or communities could submit communications about human rights violations allegedly attributable to third party States based on their respective contributions to climate change. Indeed, most high-income States that are responsible for a significant portion of greenhouse gasses stocked in the global atmosphere have recognised the competency of at least some human rights treaty bodies to consider complaints from individuals or groups of individuals.

[98] Kristina Peterson, *Reaching Out to Women When Disaster Strikes* (Soroptimist White Paper, 2007), www.soroptimist.org, accessed 11 August 2018. See also UN Women, 'Why Is Climate Change a Gender Issue?' (UN Women Multi-Country Office Series on the Links between Climate Change, Gender and Development, date unknown), www.uncclearn.org/sites/default/files/inventory/unwomen704.pdf, accessed 5 August 2018.

[99] See Curtis Doebbler, *The Principle of Non-Discrimination in International Law* (CD Publishing 2007) 13.

[100] No Pacific Island State has ratified the Optional Protocol to the ICESCR, and of all Pacific Island States, only Vanuatu has ratified the First Optional Protocol to the ICCPR; only Samoa has ratified the Third Optional Protocol to the CRC; only Vanuatu and the Solomon Islands have ratified the Optional Protocol to CEDAW; only Palau has ratified the Optional Protocol to the CRPD. See UNTC (n 88).

States confronted with such a complaint from alleged victims of climate change-related human rights violations in Pacific Island States would almost certainly refer to jurisdictional clauses contained in most human rights treaties and Optional Protocols, which arguably limit the territorial scope of States' human rights obligations, and/or bar treaty bodies from considering complaints from individuals or groups of individuals outside a State's territory. However, the practice of human rights treaty bodies generally emphasises individuals' rights to adequate and effective remedies for human rights violations, which in turn leads to a broad interpretation of the scope of States' human rights obligations and treaty bodies' own mandates to consider alleged breaches of those obligations. For example, claims about the extraterritorial human rights implications of climate change could build on the reasoning of the UN Human Rights Committee that a State should not be allowed 'to perpetrate violations of the Covenant on the territory of another State, which violations it could not perpetrate on its own territory'.[101] The extent to which this reasoning also applies in climate change cases where the infringement of human rights may be characterised as an unintended and indirect consequence of the omission of a State to take measures to protect the enjoyment of the rights of individuals abroad remains to be determined by case law.

Another hurdle facing individuals or groups of individuals submitting the complaint is the requirement to demonstrate that they are 'victims' of the alleged violation or that they are acting on behalf of an alleged victim.[102] Meeting this requirement in a climate change case would probably involve providing proof of a link between State conduct relating to climate change on the one hand and the specific impacts of climate change on the alleged victims on the other. As noted previously in relation to litigation at the national level, victims or those acting on their behalf could rely on a growing body of evidence about the attribution of specific impacts to global climate change. To establish the other end of the causal chain, they could refer to evidence of States' respective contributions to accumulated global emissions.[103] Whether or not the evidence will be sufficient to establish

[101] *Sergio Euben Lopez Burgos* v. *Uruguay* (Communication no R12/52) para 12.3.

[102] See, for example, Optional Protocol to the International Covenant on Economic, Social and Cultural Rights (adopted 10 December 2008, entered into force 5 May 2013) 14531 UNTS (OP-ICESCR), art 2.

[103] Tim Crosland, Margaretha Wewerinke-Singh and Aubrey Meyer, 'The Paris AgreementImplementation Blueprint: A Practical Guide to Bridging the Gap between Actions and Goal and Closing the Accountability Deficit (Part 1)' (2017) 25(2) *Environmental Liability* 114.

'victim' status would depend mostly on the extent to which the particular impacts in question can be attributed to factors other than climate change. Finally, using the individual complaint procedures is only possible where domestic remedies are exhausted, unreasonably prolonged or unlikely to bring effective relief.[104] Arguably this requirement will be met in most cases originating from Pacific Island States, given the negligible contributions of Pacific Island States to global emissions and the doctrine of State immunity barring claims against foreign States responsible for the lion's share of global emissions before domestic courts in Pacific Islands. Taking all these factors into account, the chances of success for Pacific Island individuals or communities in an innovative case against a foreign State or States before an international human rights body are uncertain but certainly not insignificant.

As an alternative to action by individuals or groups of individuals, Pacific Island States could bring a complaint about the human rights implications of climate change before a human rights treaty body on behalf of their people. The ICCPR and ICERD both have established inter-State complaint procedures, while a complaint procedure for the ICESCR is established as part of its Optional Protocol and CEDAW allows State parties to submit a dispute with another party concerning the interpretation or application of the treaty to arbitration or – when the parties are unable to agree on the organisation of the arbitration within six months – referral of the dispute to the ICJ.[105] None of these procedures would require a State to represent or even identify 'victims' of human rights violations: the focus is on alleged non-compliance with treaty obligations or (in case of CEDAW) the interpretation or application of the treaty, which presumably makes it easier to complain about a State's alleged failure to prevent future impacts of climate change. However, the ICCPR's complaint procedure applies only to State parties who have made a declaration recognising the competence of the Committee to consider inter-State complaints, which no Pacific Island State has, as yet, done. This seems like a missed opportunity, as making the declaration would allow Pacific Island State parties to bring a claim before an international body against some of the major historical polluters that have refused to recognise the jurisdiction of most other international

[104] See, for example, Optional Protocol to the Convention on the Elimination of All Forms of Discrimination against Women (adopted 6 October 1999, entered into force 22 December 2000) 20378 UNTS (OP-CEDAW) art 4(1); OP-ICESCR, art 3.

[105] CEDAW, art 29. Although State Parties to CEDAW can opt out of this possibility, neither Pacific Island States nor Annex I States that have ratified CEDAW have done so.

bodies.[106] The inter-State complaint procedure under the ICESCR is currently not accessible to Pacific Island States due to a lack of ratifications of the Optional Protocol. The only inter-State complaint procedure that is readily available to Pacific Island States wishing to raise a complaint about alleged human rights violations resulting from climate change is that established under ICERD, which appears to allow Pacific Island States that have ratified ICERD to claim that another State party has breached its obligations under the treaty by failing to take measures to correct the disproportionate impacts of climate change on Pacific Island peoples. The promises and pitfalls of this course of action remain somewhat uncertain, as the inter-State complaint procedures of international human rights bodies have remained unused until very recently (when Palestine filed an inter-State complaint against Israel for alleged breaches of its obligations under ICERD), and this recent attempt has not yet produced an outcome.[107]

What is clear in any event, however, is that treaty bodies do not have the power to make binding judgments that would provide tangible remedies to victims of climate change in case of a victory. This is true irrespective of whether it is an individual, a community or a State that files the complaint. The only opportunity for a binding judgment consists in the dispute settlement provisions of CEDAW, which provide a rare opportunity to bring climate change before the ICJ.[108] However, the scope of the procedure seems somewhat limited, both in terms of substance (requiring a narrow focus on the allegedly discriminatory impacts of climate change on women) and in terms of procedure (focussing on disputes concerning the interpretation or application of CEDAW rather than on alleged non-compliance with treaty obligations). Even if a Pacific Island State would succeed in getting the dispute to the ICJ, it remains to

106 The most prominent example is the United States, which made the declaration upon ratification in 1992.

107 Oliver Holmes, 'Palestine Files Complaint against Israel under Anti-racism Treaty' (*The Guardian*, 23 April 2018), www.theguardian.com/world/2018/apr/23/palestinians-file-complaint-against-israel-under-anti-racism-treaty, accessed 5 August 2018.

108 Although Tuvalu has at various occasions expressed an interest in bringing a contentious case concerning climate change harm against the United States and Australia, it has so far not taken any steps to actually pursue such a case (or even to declare that it recognises the jurisdiction of the Court as compulsory ipso facto, which would allow Tuvalu to file a case against other States accepting the same obligation). See further Rebecca Elizabeth Jacobs, 'Treading Deep Waters: Substantive Law Issues in Tuvalu's Threat to Sue the United States in the International Court of Justice' (2005) 14 *Pacific Rim Law and Policy Journal* 103.

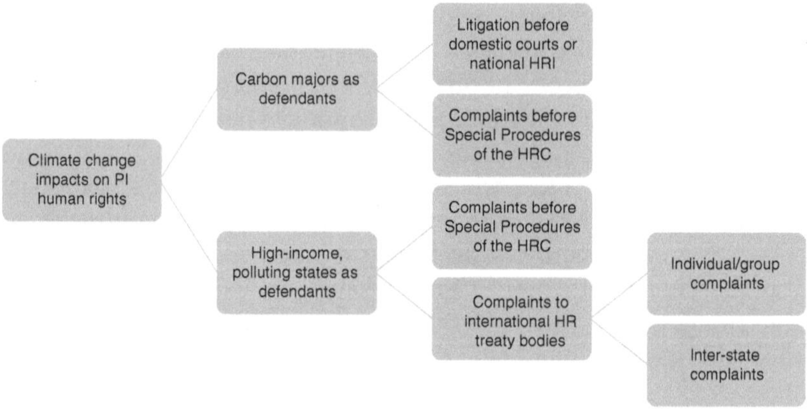

Figure 4.1 Overview of human rights litigation avenues for Pacific Islanders (with thanks to Jacqueline Peel)

be seen whether the Court would be amenable to accepting an invitation to interpret CEDAW in a way that would probably be mind-boggling to its original drafters. Finally, an important extra-legal consideration in inter-State cases is the risk of undermining relationships with the State or States in question (which may well be important donors of foreign aid). In light of all this, perhaps the most promising options for Pacific plaintiffs are the individual complaint procedures under the ICCPR, ICESCR and CRC, which – despite their non-binding nature – could result in some form of redress for specific human rights violations related to climate change without significant geopolitical consequences.

4.3 Concluding Remarks

This contribution has analysed several litigation options that could be pursued by Pacific Island States, individuals or groups against those most responsible for anthropogenic climate change. Some of these options appear to be mutually exclusive – for example, the requirement that domestic remedies must be exhausted before individuals or communities can bring a case before a human rights treaty body seems to prescribe a sequential approach to litigation, starting at the domestic level. However, if the aim of the litigation is to target major historical emitters of greenhouse gases, there is unlikely to be a clash of potential litigation initiatives: the doctrine of State immunity bars claims against foreign States before Pacific courts, which makes international human rights bodies an appropriate forum for such claims. In contrast, claims against 'carbon majors' could be entertained by Pacific Island courts and Special Procedure mandate holders, but not by human rights treaty bodies. Special Procedure mandate holders will not require that the alleged victim has exhausted domestic remedies in order to consider a communication, which opens the door to simultaneous action at the national and international levels.

The options for rights-based climate litigation to seek redress for the adverse effects of climate change on human life, livelihoods and cultures in the Pacific Islands are ultimately innumerable. Individuals, communities and governments across the region could pursue litigation jointly or in parallel. Bottom-up, community-led action is particularly appropriate for cases seeking to highlight the impacts of climate change on people's lives, livelihoods and cultural identities through the lens of human rights. The apparent interest of Pacific Island leaders in creating an optimal regulatory environment for innovative climate litigation is therefore commendable and promising.[109] And while enhancing the chances that victims of climate change will be able to access redress at the domestic level, Pacific Island leaders could at the same time initiate action against 'carbon majors' or even foreign States, using either their domestic courts or international human rights bodies. No one option can guarantee even incremental progress towards climate justice. However, a 'let a thousand flowers bloom' approach to litigating human rights violations resulting from the impacts of climate change on Pacific Island nations is likely to have significant impact in terms of both increased awareness and greater chances of obtaining actual remedies for the victims.

[109] See Pacific Islands Development Forum and Pacific Climate Action Network (n 18) art 9.

5

The Potential for UNCLOS Climate Change Litigation to Achieve Effective Mitigation Outcomes

MILLICENT MCCREATH

Introduction

As the effects of anthropogenic climate change are increasingly felt, and the global community continues to fail to take effective mitigation action, individuals and organisations are turning to courts and tribunals in an attempt to enforce climate change legal obligations against states and corporations. Climate change litigation comes in many forms and forums, perhaps because the causes and effects of climate change are so disparate. With a few notable exceptions, to date this litigation has largely been limited to the domestic legal sphere, as although states are bound by climate change obligations on an international level, climate change treaties and agreements rarely include binding dispute settlement procedures.[1] It is also arguable that diplomacy and international politics would prevent the widespread use of international litigation under the climate change treaties, even if it was legally feasible.

It is the oft-stated and unfortunate reality that the states that have contributed the least to the causes of climate change are often those that are already and will continue to feel its effects most harshly. The most developed states, being those that are responsible for most of the world's historic greenhouse gas (GHG) emissions, naturally also have the greatest political power on the global scale. Small island developing states (SIDS) and states with large low-lying coastal populations, have not been able to trigger sufficiently effective international mitigation action, despite exhaustive efforts. Despite years of negotiations, there has been limited

[1] See Hari M. Osofsky, 'Climate Change and Dispute Resolution Processes' in Rosemary Rayfuse and Shirley Scott (eds.), *International Law in the Era of Climate Change* (Edward Elgar 2012) 350–2.

success in delivering a binding regime for the meaningful reduction of GHG emissions.

On 12 December 2015, the Paris Agreement[2] was adopted under the auspices of the United Nations Framework Convention on Climate Change (UNFCCC)[3]. It entered into force on 4 November 2016 and currently has 180 states parties. In some ways, the Paris Agreement is a significant achievement, securing ratifications at a level the Kyoto Protocol was not able to and by its inclusion of certain binding obligations. However, a great deal of compromise was required to secure such widespread ratification. Therefore, although the 2°C (aiming for 1.5°C) temperature rise limit objective is enacted as the objective of the Agreement, each state may work to achieve the objective in its own way. Unlike the Kyoto Protocol, parties do not have binding emissions reduction targets, but must prepare, communicate and maintain 'nationally determined contributions' (NDCs) that they 'intend[s] to achieve'.[4] The currently announced NDCs are considered to be insufficient to achieve the 1.5–2°C objective,[5] and there is no effective enforcement mechanism under the Agreement. The success of the Paris Agreement will depend on the willingness of states to adopt and implement rigorous NDCs amounting to substantial reductions in GHG emissions[6] – a willingness that has been lacking throughout the history of climate change negotiations.

Against this backdrop, the dispute settlement system under the United Nations Convention on the Law of the Sea (UNCLOS)[7] may present an alternative approach for disproportionately affected states to achieve effective global mitigation outcomes. While climate change may not instinctively be considered a law of the sea issue, UNCLOS regulates all forms of pollution that harm the marine environment, and therefore encompasses climate change causes and effects. Unlike the UNFCCC or the Paris Agreement, UNCLOS contains compulsory binding third party dispute settlement procedures. A contentious case alleging a breach of the UNCLOS climate change mitigation obligations

[2] Paris Agreement (adopted 12 December 2015, entered into force 4 November 2016).
[3] United Nations Framework Convention on Climate Change (adopted 9 May 1992, entered into force 21 March 1994) 1771 UNTS 107.
[4] Paris Agreement art 4(2).
[5] See Climate Action Tracker, '2100 Warming Projections' https://climateactiontracker.org/global/temperatures/ accessed 16 June 2019.
[6] James Harrison, *Saving the Oceans Through Law* (Oxford University Press 2017) 252–3.
[7] United Nations Convention on the Law of the Sea (adopted 10 December 1982, entered into force 16 November 1994) 1833 UNTS 396 (UNCLOS).

brought against a major polluter could lead to both direct and indirect outcomes that may trigger effective global climate change mitigation action.

5.1 Climate Change and UNCLOS

Although UNCLOS was negotiated (1973–1982) before climate change was a pressing global concern, the drafters were careful to include a comprehensive and flexible regime for the protection of the marine environment. Many of the obligations in Part XII of UNCLOS on the Protection and Preservation of the Marine Environment relate to the prevention, reduction and control of marine pollution from a range of sources. Part XII also contains general obligations to protect the marine environment,[8] including rare or fragile ecosystems and the habitat of depleted, threatened or endangered species and other forms of marine life.[9]

5.1.1 Climate Change as Pollution of the Marine Environment

As most of the Part XII obligations relate to 'pollution of the marine environment', the utility of the UNCLOS dispute settlement system in the climate change context is highly dependent on defining climate change as marine pollution. 'Pollution of the marine environment' is defined in article 1(4) of UNCLOS as follows:

For the purposes of this Convention:

. . .

> (4) 'pollution of the marine environment' means the introduction by man, directly or indirectly, of substances or energy into the marine environment, including estuaries, which results or is likely to result in such deleterious effects as harm to living resources and marine life, hazards to human health, hindrance to marine activities, including fishing and other legitimate uses of the sea, impairment of quality for use of sea water and reduction of amenities;

At the time of negotiating UNCLOS, the most significant forms of marine pollution came from ships,[10] and the provisions in Part XII on vessel-source

[8] UNCLOS arts 192, 194.

[9] UNCLOS art 194(5).

[10] Doris König, 'Marine Environment, International Protection' in Rudiger Wolfrum (ed.), *The Max Planck Encyclopedia of Public International Law* (Oxford University Press 2012) 1018–19.

pollution are the most detailed.[11] However, in drafting the definition of marine pollution, the negotiators clearly intended that it would be able to encompass new forms or sources of marine pollution not contemplated at the time.[12] Like all parts of UNCLOS, the drafters were determined to produce a text that would 'stand the test of time'.[13]

The definition contains several cumulative elements. Substances or energy must be introduced into the marine environment by humans either directly or indirectly. This introduction must result or be likely to result in deleterious effects such as harm to living resources and marine life, or hazards to human health, or hindrance to marine activities, or impairment of quality for use of sea water, or reduction of amenities. It is now generally accepted that several of the causes and effects of climate change can be considered pollution of the marine environment.[14] Some of the causes are as follows. First, the release of carbon dioxide into the atmosphere leads to introduction of carbon dioxide into the oceans, which causes ocean acidification.[15] According to the Intergovernmental Panel on Climate Change (IPCC), 30 per cent of anthropogenic GHG emissions have been absorbed by the oceans.[16] Ocean acidification undoubtedly has deleterious effects on the marine environment, including on living resources and marine life, such as through the dissolving of carbonate structures, including coral.[17] Second, the increased concentration of GHGs in the atmosphere is leading to an increase in global temperatures, including the temperature of the oceans.[18] This can be described as the indirect introduction of energy (heat) into the marine environment. Increased ocean temperatures are already resulting in numerous deleterious effects, including

[11] See UNCLOS arts 211, 217–21, 234. Section 7 'Safeguards' of Part XII is also largely focussed on vessel-source pollution.

[12] König (n 10) 1021.

[13] Tommy T. B. Koh, 'A Constitution for the Oceans' in Myron Nordquist (ed.), *United Nations Convention on the Law of the Sea 1982: A Commentary, Volume 1* (Brill Nijhoff 1985) 11.

[14] Alan Boyle, 'Law of the Sea Perspectives on Climate Change' (2012) 27(4) *International Journal of Marine and Coastal Law* 831, 832; Harrison (n 6) 255.

[15] Secretariat of the Convention on Biological Diversity, *An Updated Synthesis of the Impacts of Ocean Acidification on Marine Biodiversity*, CBD Technical Series No. 75 (Montreal, 2014) 11.

[16] Intergovernmental Panel on Climate Change (IPCC), Climate Change 2014: Synthesis Report. Contribution of Groups I, II and III to the Fifth Assessment Report of the Intergovernmental Panel on Climate Change (IPCC, Geneva, 2014) 2–5.

[17] Secretariat of the Convention on Biological Diversity (n 15) 7–10.

[18] IPCC (n 16) 2–5.

deoxygenation, coral bleaching and increased stratification, resulting in reduced food supply to the deep sea. Warmer water also causes species to move towards the cooler water near the Earth's poles, and deoxygenation forces species closer to the surface where they are vulnerable to overfishing. Third, increased global surface temperatures caused by anthropogenic GHG emissions is causing the melting of the polar ice caps.[19] An argument could also be made that the melting of the polar ice caps, to the extent they are located on land (e.g., the Antarctic and Greenlandic ice sheets), resulting in melted fresh water flowing into the ocean, is also the introduction of a substance into the marine environment. The melting of the ice caps is causing sea level rise, which is already and will increasingly result in deleterious effects to both humans and marine life in a range of different ways.[20]

5.1.2 UNCLOS Climate Change Obligations

With climate change recognised as pollution of the marine environment, the majority of the obligations in Part XII come into operation. While the general obligation to protect and preserve the marine environment in article 192 extends beyond pollution prevention, reduction and control,[21] most other Part XII obligations focus on pollution.

The Part XII obligations relevant in the climate change context include both general obligations and obligations targeting specific sources or forms of pollution. A state bringing proceedings for a breach of UNCLOS climate change obligations could find numerous obligations on which to base their claim – namely, article 117, which imposes a duty on states to take measures to conserve the living resources of the high seas, the general obligations in articles 192 and 194, and the specific obligations in article 207 (pollution from land-based sources) and article 212 (pollution from or through the atmosphere). The obligation in article 192 'to protect and preserve the marine environment' was interpreted in the *South China Sea Arbitration* as 'entail[ing] the positive obligation to take active measures to protect and preserve the marine environment'.[22] Expanding on the general obligation, article 194(1) provides:

[19] ibid 4.
[20] ibid 13–16.
[21] Art 192 provides that 'states have the obligation to protect and preserve the marine environment'.
[22] See Art 192.

> States shall take, individually or jointly as appropriate, all measures consistent with this Convention that are necessary to prevent, reduce and control pollution of the marine environment from any source, using for this purpose the best practicable means at their disposal and in accordance with their capabilities, and they shall endeavour to harmonize their policies in this connection.

Pursuant to article 194(2) states must take all measures necessary to ensure that activities under their jurisdiction or control do not cause damage by pollution outside their maritime zones. Paragraph (3) of article 194 specifically highlights that measures taken to prevent, reduce and control pollution shall include 'those designed to minimize to the fullest possible extent ... the release of toxic, harmful or noxious substances ... from or through the atmosphere'. These measures must also 'include those necessary to protect and preserve rare or fragile ecosystems as well as the habitat of depleted, threatened or endangered species and other forms of marine life'.[23]

Both articles 207 (land-based sources) and 212 (from or through the atmosphere) provide that states must adopt laws and regulations to prevent, reduce and control pollution from the relevant source, 'taking into account internationally agreed rules, standards and recommended practices and procedures'.[24] States must also 'take other measures as may be necessary to prevent, reduce and control such pollution', as well as endeavour to establish through the competent international organisation or diplomatic conference global rules and standards.[25] They must also enforce their laws adopted accordingly, and must adopt laws and take other measures necessary to implement international rules adopted by the competent international organisation or diplomatic conference.[26]

However, UNCLOS environmental obligations have been recognised by courts and tribunals to be obligations of due diligence,[27] meaning that states are not obliged to eliminate all forms of pollution absolutely. Further, article 193 provides that 'states have the sovereign right to exploit their natural resources pursuant to their environmental policies and in accordance with their duty to protect and preserve the marine

[23] UNCLOS art 194(5).
[24] UNCLOS art 207(1), 212(1).
[25] UNCLOS art 207(2), 207(4), 212(2), 212(3).
[26] UNCLOS art 213, 222.
[27] South China Sea Arbitration, Merits, Award of 12 July 2016, paras 956, 959, 964, 971; Request for an Advisory Opinion submitted by the Sub-Regional Fisheries Commission, Advisory Opinion, 2 April 2015, ITLOS Reports 2015, 4, 63.

environment'. UNCLOS therefore specifically provides for a balancing between a state's right to exploit its natural resources, and its duty to protect and preserve the marine environment. In determining what action is required to satisfy the UNCLOS Part XII obligations in the context of climate change, science and particularly the work of the IPCC will be crucial.

5.1.3 Interpreting UNCLOS in Light of the UNFCCC Regime and the Paris Agreement

Many of the Part XII obligations are broad and vague, perhaps because they were written in order to be able to adapt to future circumstances and new sources of pollution.[28] Courts and tribunals have therefore found that the content of these obligations is informed by other applicable rules of international law, including principles of international environmental law such as the precautionary approach and the no-harm rule[29] The provisions of UNCLOS are to be interpreted in good faith in accordance with their ordinary meaning in their context and in light of the object and purpose.[30] To be taken into account are 'any relevant rules of international law applicable in the relations between the parties'.[31] In interpreting the UNCLOS provisions in the climate change mitigation context, the UNFCCC and Paris Agreement would be the most relevant rules of international law. With 197 and 189 parties, respectively,[32] the memberships of the UNFCCC and the Paris Agreement encompass essentially all parties to UNCLOS.[33]

When considering whether a treaty should be interpreted in an evolutionary or static manner, the intentions of the parties are relevant.[34] By

[28] König (n 10) 1018, 1021.

[29] See, for example, *South China Sea Arbitration* (n 27) para 941.

[30] Vienna Convention on the Law of Treaties (adopted 23 May 1969, entered into force 27 January 1980) 1155 UNTS 331 art 31(1).

[31] Vienna Convention on the Law of Treaties (adopted 23 May 1969, entered into force 27 January 1980) 1155 UNTS 331 art 31(3)(c).

[32] For the list of Parties to the UNFCCC, see https://unfccc.int/process/parties-non-party-stakeholders/parties-convention-and-observer-states. For the list of Parties to the Paris Agreement, see https://unfccc.int/process/the-paris-agreement/status-of-ratification.

[33] Notably the United States is party to the UNFCCC, but not UNCLOS. It has notified of its withdrawal from the Paris Agreement, which will not take effect until November 2020 due to the rules in article 28 of the Agreement.

[34] Panos Merkouris, Article 31(3)(c) VCLT and the Principle of Systemic Integration: Normative Shadows in Plato's Cave (Brill Nijhoff 2015) 161.

defining 'pollution of the marine environment' so that it would be able to encompass future forms of pollution, and by including frequent references to other international rules and standards, it would seem clear that the parties intended that Part XII of UNCLOS would be interpreted in an evolutionary manner.[35] As stated previously, the parties intended to conclude a treaty that would stand the test of time.[36] Further, the ICJ found in the *Dispute Regarding Navigational and Related Rights* that

> where the parties have used generic terms in a treaty, the parties necessarily having been aware that the meaning of the terms was likely to evolve over time, and where the treaty has been entered into for a very long period or is "of continuing duration", the parties must be presumed, as a general rule, to have intended those terms to have an evolving meaning.[37]

Most of the terms in the relevant Part XII provisions are highly general. Particularly in the environmental context, the ICJ in the *Gabčikovo-Nagymaros Case* found that new norms of international environmental law are relevant in the interpretation of general environmental provisions in treaties.[38] Pursuant to article 293 of UNCLOS, an UNCLOS court or tribunal may apply other rules of international law that are not incompatible with it, and it would seem that the parties expected other rules of international law to be relevant when interpreting UNCLOS.

Therefore, in determining where the balance between resource exploitation and environmental protection is to be found, reference can be had, alongside scientific research and the conclusions of the IPCC, to the UNFCCC system including the Paris Agreement,[39] which represents a legal consensus by a vast majority of states on the action necessary to mitigate climate change. Where the obligations discussed above refer to rules and standards adopted by the competent international organisation

[35] König (n 10) 1021.

[36] Koh (n 13); see Seokwoo Lee and Lowell Bautista, 'Part XII of the United Nations Convention on the Law of the Sea and the Duty to Mitigate against Climate Change: Making Out a Claim, Causation, and Related Issues' (2018) 45 *Ecology Law Quarterly* 129, 138.

[37] Dispute regarding Navigational and Related Rights (*Costa Rica* v. *Nicaragua*), Judgment, ICJ Reports 2009, 213, para 66.

[38] Gabčikovo-Nagymaros Project (Hungary/Slovakia), Judgment, ICJ Reports 1997, 7, para 112.

[39] Alan Boyle and Navraj Singh Ghaleigh, 'Climate Change and International Law beyond the UNFCCC' in Kevin R Gray, Richard Tarasofsky and Cinnamon Carlarne (eds.), *The Oxford Handbook of International Climate Change Law* (Oxford University Press 2015) 26, 47; Harrison (n 6) 256.

or diplomatic conference, they can be taken to refer to the UNFCCC and the Paris Agreement, to the extent that they are relevant to the protection of the ocean.[40] The content of these agreements can inform the interpretation of the UNCLOS due diligence ocean protection obligations.

Authors have previously concluded that breach of the UNCLOS Part XII climate change obligations could be found by reference to non-compliance with the Kyoto Protocol.[41] According to Tim Stephens, because the Kyoto Protocol's emission reduction targets were not adequate to prevent serious and irreversible damage to the marine environment, 'it is difficult to see how States can meet their overriding obligation under Article 192 . . . by satisfying the modest requirements of the Kyoto Protocol'.[42] Despite this, he concluded that due to the difficulty of identifying emission reduction requirements without such a global agreement, ultimately the UNFCC and its implementing agreements 'remain the primary means to drive mitigation policy that will protect the oceans'.[43]

The Paris Agreement, the successor to the Kyoto Protocol, operates underneath the UNFCCC and has as one of its stated aims the enhanced implementation of the UNFCCC. The objective of the UNFCCC is the

> stabilisation of greenhouse gas concentrations in the atmosphere at a level that would prevent dangerous anthropogenic interference with the climate system. Such a level should be achieved within a time frame sufficient to allow ecosystems to adapt naturally to climate change, to ensure that food production is not threatened and to enable economic development to proceed in a sustainable manner.[44]

Relevantly in the oceans context, under article 4 of the UNFCCC, parties commit to 'promote and cooperate in the conservation and enhancement, as appropriate, of sinks and reservoirs of all greenhouse gases not controlled by the Montreal Protocol, including biomass, forests and oceans as well as other terrestrial, coastal and marine ecosystems'.[45]

[40] Boyle (n 14) 834–5.
[41] ibid 834; William C. G. Burns 'Potential Causes of Action for Climate Change Damages in International Fora: The Law of the Sea Convention' (2006) 2(1) *McGill International Journal of Sustainable Development Law and Policy* 27, 47; Harrison (n 6) 256; Tim Stephens, 'Warming Waters and Souring Sea: Climate Change and Ocean Acidification' in D. Rothwell and others (eds.) *The Oxford Handbook of the Law of the Sea* (Oxford University Press 2015) 777, 783.
[42] Stephens (n 41).
[43] ibid.
[44] UNFCCC art 2.
[45] UNFCCC art 4(1)(d).

The Paris Agreement does not specifically refer to the ocean, except in the preamble. Unlike the Kyoto Protocol, which set binding emission reductions targets, the Paris Agreement takes has a bottom-up approach, with state parties free to decide on their own NDCs towards the overall temperature goal of the Agreement. This means that finding a 'breach' of the Paris Agreement, unless a state has not adopted an NDC at all, is not as clear as it would have been under the Kyoto Protocol. Under article 4(2) of the Paris Agreement, parties have individual and binding obligations to prepare, communicate and maintain NDCs, as well as to take domestic measures in furtherance of their NDC. While states have discretion to determine their own contribution, an NDC must be 'ambitious'.[46] However, these obligations are obligations of conduct, not of result, and while there is a good faith expectation that parties will achieve their NDC, the Agreement does not go so far as to require them to do so.[47]

Further, by not specifying which GHG emissions must be reduced, a state may choose to meet its targets by reducing GHGs other than CO_2. CO_2 emissions are the cause of ocean acidification, which, as discussed earlier in this chapter, is one of the primary climate change–related threats facing the ocean.[48] In theory, though perhaps unlikely in practice, a state can therefore be in compliance with the Paris Agreement while taking no steps to prevent ocean acidification. The UNCLOS provisions clearly require at least some action to be taken to prevent, reduce and control marine pollution from all sources,[49] and therefore they cannot be read exclusively through the prism of the Paris Agreement. It is also important to note that the Paris Agreement is guided by an overall temperature goal; however, scientific knowledge is lacking on how global surface temperatures affect the oceans.[50] The IPCC is currently in the process of producing a special report on climate change and the oceans and cryosphere to fill the numerous knowledge gaps related to climate change and the oceans.[51] Without scientific research, it is therefore

46 Paris Agreement art 3.

47 Lavanya Rajamani, 'Ambition and Differentiation in the 2015 Paris Agreement: Interpretative Possibilities and Underlying Politics' (2016) 65 *International and Comparative Law Quarterly* 493, 497–8.

48 Stephens (n 41).

49 UNCLOS art 194.

50 Nilufer Oral, 'Ocean Acidification: Falling between the Legal Cracks of UNCLOS and the UNFCCC?' (2018) 45 *Ecology Law Quarterly* 9, 21–2.

51 See IPCC, 'The Ocean and Cryosphere in a Changing Climate', www.ipcc.ch/report/srocc/, accessed 16 June 2019.

difficult to determine just how relevant the Paris Agreement is to the protection of the oceans. The Paris Agreement is undoubtedly a significant international climate change instrument; however, it almost completely ignores the oceans. When it comes to the ocean, the Paris Agreement clearly does not 'cover the field' on climate change mitigation.

Applying the Paris Agreement in the interpretation of UNCLOS, considering the minimal attention it pays to the protection and preservation of the ocean, it is clear that the mere adoption of an NDC will not constitute 'all necessary measures' under article 194 of UNCLOS, unless the NDC includes ambitious measures targeted at mitigating the effects of climate change on the ocean. To find that the UNCLOS climate change mitigation obligations are met merely by the adoption of an NDC, no matter whether or not it is achieved, and whether or not it targets the ocean, would remove all substance from the Part XII obligations.

Although the Paris Agreement is relevant when interpreting the Part XII obligations, it does not erase them. Article 311(3) of UNCLOS provides that state parties may conclude subsequent agreements modifying the operation of UNCLOS as between themselves, provided that the subsequent agreement does not affect the application of the basic principles of the convention. The protection and preservation of the marine environment is an essential part of UNCLOS, as recognised in the preamble. It can arguably be considered one of its 'basic principle[s]'. If so, the Paris Agreement may only modify the operation of the Part XII obligations relevant to climate change mitigation to the extent that the overall goal of preservation and protection of the marine environment is maintained. The lack of attention paid to the ocean in the negotiation of the Paris Agreement demonstrates that, in any case, the parties did not intend that it would modify the operation of UNCLOS.

5.2 Making the Case

Causation has been a major hurdle in other forms of climate change litigation due to the difficulties of linking the activities of one state with the harm resulting from climate change being such a global and multidimensional problem.[52] A major advantage of an UNCLOS climate change case is that the applicant does not need to prove causation in

[52] For discussion, see, e.g., Christian Tomuschat, 'Global Warming and State Responsibility' in Holger Hestermeyer and others (eds.), *Law of the Sea in Dialogue* (Springer, 2011) 3, 25–6.

order to succeed. As an 'injured state', the applicant would be entitled to claim compensation from the respondent if a breach is found to have occurred. In such cases, the applicant would need to prove the causal link between the respondent's conduct and the damage caused to the applicant itself.[53] However, if a state alleges a breach of an UNCLOS climate change obligation and seeks only a declaration from the court or tribunal as to the respondent state's wrongful conduct, as well as cessation, assurances and guarantees of non-reparation, it would not be necessary to prove a causal link with the harm resulting from climate change and the wrongful acts of the respondent. As will be discussed below in Section 5.4, a finding from an international court or tribunal that the respondent state is in breach of its international obligations may be sufficient to trigger effective mitigation action on the part of that state.

5.2.1 Who Should Bring the Case

Under the International Law Commission's Articles on the Responsibility of States for Internationally Wrongful Acts, a state may either invoke the responsibility of another state as an 'injured state' or as a 'state other than an injured state'.[54] The UNCLOS climate change obligations can be considered as being owed to all states parties ('a group of states'), and therefore to be an injured state, the applicant

[53] *Gabcikovo-Nagymaros* para 152; Draft Articles on Responsibility of States for Internationally Wrongful Acts, adopted by the Commission at its fifty-third session in 2001 (Final Outcome) (International Law Commission [ILC]) UN Doc A/56/10 (ILC Articles) arts 46 and 47; International Law Commission, Commentary to the Articles on State Responsibility, art 46(4).

[54] Arts 42, 48. The status of these articles is not entirely settled; however, they have been relied on generally by the International Tribunal for the Law of the Sea in its 2015 Advisory Opinion (n 26) 144. Article 48 represents progressive development of international law, rather than the codification of custom, and has not been examined extensively by an international court or tribunal. However, it is reflective of a general trend in international law towards the recognition of multilateral disputes and 'community interests'. See Yoshifumi Tanaka, 'Protection of Community Interests in International Law: The Case of the Law of the Sea' in Armin von Bogdandy and Rüdiger Wolfrum (eds.), *Max Planck Yearbook of United Nations Law*, vol. 15 (Koninklijke Brill NV 2011) 311, 329; Bruno Simma, 'Bilateralism and Community Interest in the Law of State Responsibility' in Yoram Dinstein (ed.), *International Law at a Time of Perplexity: Essays in Honour of Shabtai Rosenne* (Martinus Nijhoff 1989) 821, 823; James Crawford, 'Responsibility for Breaches of Communitarian Norms: An Appraisal of Article 48 of the ILC Articles on Responsibility of States for Internationally Wrongful Acts' in Ulrich Fastenrath and others (eds.), *From Bilateralism to Community Interest: Essays in Honour of Judge Bruno Simma* (Oxford University Press 2011) 224.

must be 'specially affected' by the breach of the obligation.[55] A state other than an injured state can bring proceedings if 'the obligation breached is owed to a group of states including that state, and is established for the protection of a collective interest of the group'.[56] An injured state, as opposed to a non-injured state, is able to claim the full range of remedies available under international law including compensation and restitution. An injured state is only able to claim cessation of the internationally wrongful act, and assurances and guarantees of non-repetition, and performance of the obligation of reparation in the interest of the injured state or the beneficiaries of the obligation breached.[57] However, considering, as discussed above, the evidential difficulties in making a claim for compensation, the applicant would be advised to seek only a declaration, cessation and assurances and guarantees of non-repetition. This means that in practice it does not matter whether the applicant is specially affected by the breach of the UNCLOS climate change obligations.[58]

On the other hand, in order to strengthen the case and perhaps make the court or tribunal more willing to exercise jurisdiction, it would seem advantageous that the applicant be a specially affected state, such as a small island developing state or a state with a low-lying coastal population. The applicant should also be one that has made only a minor or insignificant contribution to climate change itself, thus avoiding an inadmissibility finding based on the 'clean hands' principle. Although the status of this principle is unclear in international law,[59] it has been applied by the ICJ in the *Gabčikovo-Nagymaros Case*[60] and by the PCIJ in the 1937 case of *The Diversion of Water from the Meuse* between the Netherlands and Belgium.[61] The ideal applicant would also be one that is experiencing the detrimental effects of climate change in ways particularly related to the oceans, such as sea-level rise or loss of seafood for subsistence and economy. By showing that it experiences the effects of climate change most

[55] ILC Articles art 42(b)(i).

[56] ILC Articles art 48(1)(a).

[57] ILC Articles art 48(2).

[58] International Law Commission, Commentary to the Articles on State Responsibility, art 48, para (4). See, for a discussion of standing in the context of domestic rights-based litigation, Chapter 4 in this volume.

[59] Stephen M. Schwebel, 'Clean Hands, Principle' in Rüdiger Wolfrum (ed.), *Max Planck Encyclopedia of Public International Law* (Oxford University Press 2013).

[60] Schwebel (n 38).

[61] The Diversion of Water from the Meuse (*Netherlands* v. *Belgium*), Judgment of 28 June 1937, PCIJ Series A/B, No. 70, 3, 25.

acutely in ways affecting the ocean, the applicant would be more likely to satisfy the court or tribunal that this is, in fact, an UNCLOS case and not a UNFCCC or Paris Agreement case.

5.2.2 *Whom to Bring the Case Against*

The respondent state for an UNCLOS climate change case must first be a party to UNCLOS, which immediately eliminates the United States. Considering the references in article 194 of UNCLOS to states' 'capabilities' and 'the best practicable means at their disposal', it would seem that a higher standard of due diligence would be applied to a wealthy developed state with the resources to take effective mitigation action. The ideal respondent state would be one that, despite having the resources and capabilities to take effective mitigation actions, has historically and is currently making a significant contribution to climate change. In order to make out the case, the respondent state must be in breach of their UNCLOS climate change obligations, measured partly by reference to their non-compliance with the UNFCCC and Paris Agreement. The fact that many states may be in breach of their UNCLOS climate change obligations does not prevent an applicant from invoking the responsibility of only one.[62]

5.2.3 *Jurisdiction*

5.2.3.1 A Dispute Exists

An UNCLOS court or tribunal has jurisdiction over 'any dispute concerning the interpretation or application' of UNCLOS.[63] The first jurisdictional requirement, therefore, is that a dispute exists. The definition of a 'dispute' that has been applied by UNCLOS courts and tribunals is 'a disagreement on a point of law or fact, a conflict of legal views or of interests between two persons'.[64] This question is decided objectively, and the dispute must have existed prior to the submission of the dispute to the court or tribunal.[65]

[62] ILC Articles art 47.
[63] UNCLOS art 286.
[64] *Mavrommatis Palestine Concessions*, Jurisdiction, Judgment of 30 August 1924, PCIJ Series A, No. 2, 6, 11; *South China Sea Arbitration*, Jurisdiction and Admissibility, Award of 29 October 2015, para 149.
[65] South China Sea Arbitration, para 149.

The threshold of establishing that a dispute exists was previously considered to be a low one.[66] However, following the 2016 decisions of the International Court of Justice (ICJ) in the *Marshall Islands* cases,[67] establishing that a dispute exists may present a significant barrier for a prospective applicant in an UNCLOS climate change case. In the three *Marshall Islands* cases (against India, Pakistan and the United Kingdom), the ICJ found that no dispute existed and therefore that it did not have jurisdiction. Applying a new 'objective awareness' test, the ICJ stated that for a dispute to exist, the applicant must demonstrate on the evidence that the respondent was aware or could not have been unaware that its views were 'positively opposed' to the applicant.[68] The ICJ found that the applicant had failed to sufficiently formulate its case against the respondents prior to filing the cases.[69] The *Marshall Islands* cases concerned the issue of nuclear weapons and alleged breaches of the Nuclear Non-proliferation Treaty. To the extent that they both arise out of a multilateral treaty and have a public interest dimension, there are similarities between the *Marshall Islands* cases and a potential UNCLOS climate change case. Despite criticism of the judgments for their emphasis on form rather than substance,[70] a prospective applicant would be wise to take steps to ensure that all elements of the 'dispute' test in the *Marshall Islands* cases are met. In the case of climate change, this may mean that it would not be sufficient for the applicant to make public and diplomatic statements opposing inaction on climate mitigation, but

[66] *Marshall Islands* cases, Dissenting Opinion of Judge Crawford, para 2; James Harrison, 'Defining Disputes and Characterizing Claims: Subject-Matter Jurisdiction in Law of the Sea Convention Litigation' (2017) 48(3–4) *Ocean Development and International Law* 269, 270.

[67] Obligations Concerning Negotiations Relating to Cessation of the Nuclear Arms Race and to Nuclear Disarmament (*Marshall Islands* v. *India*), Jurisdiction and Admissibility, Judgment of 5 October 2016; Obligations Concerning Negotiations Relating to Cessation of the Nuclear Arms Race and to Nuclear Disarmament (*Marshall Islands* v. *Pakistan*), Jurisdiction and Admissibility, Judgment of 5 October 2016; Obligations Concerning Negotiations Relating to Cessation of the Nuclear Arms Race and to Nuclear Disarmament (*Marshall Islands* v. *UK*), Preliminary Objections, Judgment of 5 October 2016.

[68] *Marshall Islands* v. *UK*, para 41; *Marshall Islands* v. *India*, para 38; *Marshall Islands* v. *Pakistan*, para 38; see criticism in the dissenting opinion of Judge Crawford.

[69] *Marshall Islands* v. *UK*, para 57; *Marshall Islands* v. *India*, para 52; *Marshall Islands* v. *Pakistan*, para 52; Vincent-Joël Proulx, 'The World Court's Jurisdictional Formalism and Its Lost Market Share: The *Marshall Islands* Decisions and the Quest for a Suitable Dispute Settlement Forum for Multilateral Disputes' (2017) 30 *Leiden Journal of International Law* 926, 932.

[70] Proulx (n 69).

rather that those statements should be targeted at the respondent in particular. In the UNCLOS context, however, this requirement is less likely to be an issue considering that, as discussed below, an exchange of views is required to take place before proceedings may be commenced. Therefore, had a dispute not crystallised prior to the exchange of views, it most likely would have after an exchange of opposing views or if the respondent state fails to reply.

5.2.3.2 The Dispute Concerns the Interpretation or Application of UNCLOS

Not only must a dispute exist between the parties; the dispute must concern the interpretation or application of UNCLOS.[71] UNCLOS was drafted with the intention of settling 'all issues relating to the law of the sea'.[72] With such wide subject matter, it is inevitable that some elements of UNCLOS are also regulated under other instruments, leading to 'parallelism of treaties'.[73] It is likely that the respondent state to an UNCLOS climate change case would argue that the case is in reality a UNFCCC/Paris Agreement case, with the UNCLOS element only incidental. However, courts and tribunals have found on several occasions that a case arising under UNCLOS may simultaneously arise under another instrument, and that this does not prevent their exercise of jurisdiction over the UNCLOS dispute.[74]

Article 288(1) of UNCLOS provides that an UNCLOS court or tribunal 'shall have jurisdiction concerning the interpretation or application of this Convention'.[75] Once satisfied that the dispute presented to it concerns the interpretation or application of UNCLOS, the court or tribunal may go on to apply UNCLOS and 'other rules of international law not incompatible with [UNCLOS]'.[76] The distinction between subject matter jurisdiction (article 288(1)) and applicable law (article 293(1)) has not always been clearly made by UNCLOS courts and tribunals.[77] Certain tribunals have made findings on questions of obligations not arising

[71] UNCLOS art 288(1).
[72] UNCLOS preamble.
[73] Harrison (n 66), 376.
[74] ibid.
[75] UNCLOS art288(1).
[76] Art 293(1).
[77] See Kate Parlett, 'Beyond the Four Corners of the Convention: Expanding the Scope of Jurisdiction of Law of the Sea Tribunals' (2017) 48(3–4) *Ocean Development and International Law* 284; Peter Tzeng, 'Jurisdiction and Applicable Law under UNCLOS' (2016) 126 *Yale Law Journal* 242.

under UNCLOS.[78] However, there would indeed appear to be a clear distinction between subject matter jurisdiction and applicable law under UNCLOS, and the preferred view is that an UNCLOS court or tribunal 'does not have jurisdiction to determine breaches of obligations not having their source in the Convention'.[79] Although pleaded under UNCLOS, the UNFCCC and Paris Agreement will be clearly relevant to an UNCLOS climate change case. However, an UNCLOS court or tribunal would not have jurisdiction to make a formal finding on a breach of the UNFCCC or Paris Agreement in the dispositif.[80]

It is important to emphasise that the drafters of UNCLOS intended that Part XII would regulate pollution of the marine environment from any source, including those not recognised at that time.[81] Therefore, to state that UNCLOS imposes climate change mitigation obligations to the extent that it can be defined as marine pollution is not seeking to expand the jurisdiction of an UNCLOS court or tribunal. A UNCLOS climate change case should properly be pleaded as a case concerning the interpretation or application of UNCLOS, particularly the relevant provisions of Part XII. That these obligations may be interpreted in light of the Paris Agreement and UNFCCC does not change the fact that these obligations 'hav[e] their source' in UNCLOS.[82]

5.2.3.3 Part XV Is Not Excluded by the Existence of Other Applicable Procedures

Despite containing compulsory binding procedures, the UNCLOS dispute settlement system is deferential, applying only when the parties have failed to resolve their dispute by other agreed means. If the parties to an UNCLOS dispute come to an ad hoc agreement to resolve their dispute by other peaceful means, the UNCLOS procedures will only become applicable if no settlement is reached and the agreement does not exclude any further procedure.[83] If the parties to an UNCLOS dispute are also party to a standing agreement that provides for a compulsory binding dispute settlement procedure, that procedure will apply in lieu of the

[78] See, for example, M/V 'Saiga' (No. 2) (*Saint Vincent and the Grenadines* v. *Guinea*), Judgment, ITLOS Reports 1999, p. 10, 72; In the Matter of an Arbitration between Guyana and Suriname, Award of the Arbitral Tribunal, 17 September 2007, 165; M/V 'Virginia G' Case (Panama/Guinea-Bissau), Judgment, ITLOS Reports 2014, 4, 125.

[79] *Duzgit Integrity Arbitration,* Award, 5 September 2016, paras 207–10.

[80] *Arctic Sunrise Arbitration,* Award on Merits, 14 August 2015, paras 192, 198.

[81] König (n 10) 1021.

[82] *Duzgit Integrity Arbitration* (n 79) para 207.

[83] UNCLOS art 281.

UNCLOS procedures unless the parties otherwise agree.[84] The respondent state to an UNCLOS climate change case would likely argue the case is more properly characterised as a UNFCCC case and thus that the dispute settlement procedures in the UNFCCC take precedence.

However, as just discussed, even though the UNCLOS environmental obligations can be interpreted by reference to the obligations in the Paris Agreement, this does not mean that it is a Paris Agreement or UNFCCC case. If the applicant pleads the case based on a breach of the UNCLOS climate change obligations, interpreted by reference to the Paris Agreement, the court or tribunal should find that it is an UNCLOS dispute, to be resolved by the Part XV compulsory binding procedures. In any case, neither the Paris Agreement nor the UNFCCC includes compulsory binding dispute settlement procedures so they would not 'trump' the UNCLOS procedures, even if the court or tribunal considered that the case is more properly a UNFCCC case.

In the 2000 *Southern Bluefin Tuna* case, an ad hoc arbitral tribunal under UNCLOS came to the opposite conclusion in a case brought by Australia and New Zealand against Japan concerning the conservation and sustainable use of Southern Bluefin Tuna. The case was pleaded as an UNCLOS case; however, the *Convention on the Conservation of Southern Bluefin Tuna* (CCSBT) concluded between the three parties was also relevant. The tribunal relied on article 281 of UNCLOS to find that it did not have jurisdiction to hear the case, as the CCSBT implicitly excluded further procedures. This case is widely considered to have been decided incorrectly, as article 281 applies in the case of an ad hoc agreement between the parties to a particular dispute, not in the case of a standing regional treaty such as the CCSBT.[85] The relevant article, article 282, would not have served to exclude jurisdiction as the CCSBT does not include compulsory binding dispute procedures.[86]

5.2.3.4 An Exchange of Views Has Taken Place

The prospective applicant in an UNCLOS climate change case must prior to submitting the dispute 'exchange views' with the intended respondent. Pursuant to article 283, when a dispute arises between UNCLOS states

[84] UNCLOS art 282; David Anderson, 'Peaceful Settlement of Disputes under UNCLOS' in Jill Barrett and Richard Barnes (eds.), *Law of the Sea: UNCLOS as a Living Treaty* (BIICL 2016) 385, 403.

[85] Anderson (n 84) 385, 403; Alan Boyle, 'The Southern Bluefin Tuna Arbitration' (2001) 50 (2) *International and Comparative Law Quarterly* 447, 449.

[86] Boyle (n 85) 447, 449.

parties concerning the interpretation or application of the convention, they must 'proceed expeditiously to an exchange of views regarding its settlement by negotiation or other peaceful means'.[87] It has been emphasised by courts and tribunals that the correct interpretation of this provision is that the exchange of views must relate to the means of resolving the dispute, not the subject matter of the dispute.[88] This requirement is not particularly strenuous, and a prospective applicant is 'not obliged to continue with an exchange of views when it concludes that the possibilities of reaching agreement have been exhausted'.[89] The requirement may be satisfied even if the other side fails to reply.[90] The UNCLOS requirement of exchanging views would likely trigger the crystallisation of a dispute, if it had not crystallised prior. A prospective applicant would in any case be advised to exchange views, as by doing so, a negotiated outcome may be achieved and the need to commence litigation can be avoided.

5.2.4 *Admissibility*

Various admissibility issues may arise in an UNCLOS climate change case, and it is likely to be highly controversial. In the case decided in 2016 between the Marshall Islands and the United Kingdom, the United Kingdom raised several preliminary objections and was successful on its first objection that a dispute did not exist between the parties. The United Kingdom also raised an objection that was not finally decided by the ICJ that the case was not admissible due to the absence of other nuclear weapon states from the proceedings, whose essential interests were said to be engaged in the proceedings.[91] Such an objection could be raised in an UNCLOS climate change case, as there are many states that make major contributions to climate change and who would not be

[87] UNCLOS article 283(1).

[88] South China Sea Arbitration, Award on Jurisdiction and Admissibility, para 333–4; Chagos Marine Protected Area (*Mauritius* v. *United Kingdom*), Award of 18 March 2015, paras 382–3; Arctic Sunrise (*Kingdom of the Netherlands* v. *Russian Federation*), Merits, Award of 14 August 2015, para 151.

[89] Land Reclamation by Singapore in and around the Straits of Johor (*Malaysia* v. *Singapore*), Provisional Measures, Order of 8 October 2003, ITLOS Reports 2003, p. 10, para 47; MOX Plant (*Ireland* v. *United Kingdom*), Provisional Measures, Order of 3 December 2001, ITLOS Reports 2001, p. 95, para 60.

[90] M/V 'NORSTAR' Case (*Panama* v. *Italy*), Preliminary Objections, Judgment, ITLOS Reports 2016, para 215.

[91] *Marshall Islands* v. *UK* (n 67) para 23.

included in the proceedings. However, as the ICJ found in the *Certain Phosphate Lands in Nauru* case, the fact that other states are also in breach of their UNCLOS climate change obligations does not mean that a claim against only one or a number of states is inadmissible.[92] On the other hand, the case will not be admissible if the principal issue to be decided 'requires the Court to pass on the legal position of a third State which is not a party to the proceedings'.[93] This objection is unlikely to be successful in an UNCLOS climate change case, as although the actions or policies of other states, as GHG emitters, may be indirectly condemned, the court or tribunal would not be required to rule on the lawfulness of the conduct of another state in order to find one respondent in breach.[94] As stated previously regarding the framing of the dispute, the applicant would be advised in any case to target their pre-litigation statements and demonstrations regarding breaches of UNCLOS climate change obligations to the particular anticipated respondent. Doing so would help to avoid the 'element of artifice' that might arise if there appears to be no obvious connection or relationship between the applicant and respondent.[95]

5.2.5 *Choosing the Forum for the Dispute*

UNCLOS permits state parties to declare in writing at any time their preferred 'choice of procedure' (or, more accurately, dispute settlement body) out of either the International Tribunal for the Law of the Sea (ITLOS), the ICJ, ad hoc arbitration or 'special' arbitration.[96] If no choice is made, or the parties to a dispute have not made the same choice, the default option is ad hoc arbitration.[97] The majority of developing states, and the likely applicants for an UNCLOS climate change case, have made no choice, and therefore ad hoc arbitration would be the only option to resolve the dispute. The costs and practical difficulties of ad hoc

92 Certain Phosphate Lands in Nauru (*Nauru* v. *Australia*), Preliminary Objections, Judgment, ICJ Reports 1992, 240, para 48.

93 Case of the Monetary Gold removed from Rome in 1943 (Preliminary Question), Judgment of 15 June 1954, ICJ Reports 1954, 19; Shabtai Rosenne, The Law and Practice of the International Court, 1920–2005, Volume I, The Court and the United Nations, 539.

94 East Timor (*Portugal* v. *Australia*), Judgment, ICJ Reports 1995, 90, paras 32–5.

95 Philippe Sands, 'Climate Change and the Rule of Law: Adjudicating the Future in International Law' (2016) 28 *Journal of International Law* 19, 28.

96 UNCLOS art 287.

97 UNCLOS art 287(5).

arbitration in the climate change context mean that the default to ad hoc arbitration could be seen as a problem facing UNCLOS climate change litigation. In contrast to ad hoc arbitration, parties to cases before standing bodies such as the ICJ or ITLOS do not have to pay arbitrator or registry fees, and can take advantage of the existing procedural framework and the registry facilities already in place.[98] For developing states particularly this is a major advantage. Although many developing states currently have the default ad hoc arbitration option recorded, several of the biggest GHG emitters have made a declaration for the ICJ, ITLOS or both.[99] Prior to commencing a dispute, there is no reason why the prospective applicant could not change its declaration to match the standing body identified in the respondent's declaration, thereby avoiding the cost of ad hoc arbitration. It is reasonable to suggest that any state sufficiently sophisticated to commence an UNCLOS climate change case would also be sufficiently sophisticated to make or alter their choice of forum declaration.

For prospective applicant states attracted by the flexibility afforded by ad hoc arbitration, and the ability to select the arbitrators, the possibility of forming an ad hoc special chamber of ITLOS could present the best of both worlds.[100]

5.3 Potential Outcomes

An UNCLOS climate change case has the potential to lead directly and indirectly to effective mitigation outcomes. Effective mitigation outcomes may be triggered directly by the remedies awarded by the court or tribunal in a successful case, or indirectly, for example due to the attention drawn by the case to the actions of non-compliant states. UNCLOS climate change litigation, by reason of its wide jurisdiction and compulsory binding procedures, presents significant advantages over other forms of international climate change litigation. As discussed previously, by not seeking damages, but merely a declaration, cessation and assurances and guarantees of non-repetition, it is not necessary for

[98] See Millicent McCreath and Zoe Scanlon, 'Prospects for the Future Use of ITLOS ad hoc Special Chambers after the Ghana/Cote d'Ivoire Case' (2018) 17(2) *The Law and Practice of International Courts and Tribunals* 309–34.

[99] See United Nations Division for Ocean Affairs and the Law of the Sea, 'Settlement of Disputes Mechanism' (20 June 2017), www.un.org/depts/los/settlement_of_disputes/choice_procedure.htm, accessed 16 June 2019.

[100] McCreath and Scanlon (n 98).

the applicant to prove the causal link between the respondent's actions and a particular harm resulting from climate change. Although a monetary remedy would present advantages, particularly to a developing state applicant, the difficulty of identifying the necessary causal link means that an applicant would be ill-advised in pursuing a monetary remedy. The applicant in an UNCLOS climate change case would instead be advised to seek a declaration that the respondent has breached its UNCLOS climate change obligations and an order that the respondent complies with its obligations.

At the most basic level, it can be said that states in general comply with their international obligations, including the judgments of international courts and tribunals.[101] High-profile cases of non-compliance such as that of China and its non-recognition and to some extent non-compliance with the award in the *South China Sea Arbitration* could potentially contribute to ensuring compliance of states wishing to be seen as responsible international actors. States such as Australia that made strong public statements condemning China's actions regarding that case may be less likely to reject or ignore the judgment in an UNCLOS climate change case.[102] The difficulty is, however, that even if the UNCLOS court or tribunal is able to find a breach of an UNCLOS climate change obligation, it may not decide or may not be able to decide what mitigation action those obligations require.[103] A finding that a state is not meeting its UNCLOS climate change obligations would require that state to do more to mitigate climate change, but it is unlikely that the court or tribunal would prescribe the precise action to be taken. Nonetheless, by clarifying to some extent the climate change mitigation action required by UNCLOS, or even what action is deemed inadequate, the judgment may encourage other states to amend their climate change policies to comply with its findings.

Although a finding from an UNCLOS court or tribunal on the responsibility of states parties to mitigate climate change has the potential to advance the climate change mitigation agenda, it also comes with risks. Even if the court or tribunal was able to make a finding specifically

[101] See Harold Koh, 'Why Do Nations Obey International Law?' (1997) 106 *The Yale Law Journal* 2599.

[102] See, for example, Minister for Foreign Affairs, The Hon Julie Bishop MP's media release issued on the date of the Final Award in the *South China Sea Arbitration*, www.foreignminister.gov.au/minister/julie-bishop/media-release/australia-supports-peaceful-dispute-resolution-south-china-sea, accessed 10 June 2020.

[103] Harrison (n 6) 257.

describing the respondent state's obligations to mitigate climate change under UNCLOS, there is a risk that the obligation defined by the court may be weaker than anticipated. It may be a more prudent strategy to ask the court or tribunal to find that the respondent has breached its obligations under UNCLOS to mitigate climate change, but not to request a finding on the specific action that is required.

The indirect outcomes of an UNCLOS climate change case may also be effective in triggering global mitigation efforts. The potential for climate change litigation in general to put pressure on key emitters and governments and to draw attention to the need for climate change mitigation is recognised.[104] Many of the states most affected by climate change are developing states without a great deal of international political power. Interstate litigation, particularly in the case of compulsory binding proceedings, can equalise the power imbalance between a politically weak applicant and a politically strong respondent. Interstate cases such as those under UNCLOS are often high profile and receive a great deal of media attention, particularly if they relate to a controversial issue such as climate change. The *South China Sea Arbitration* between the Philippines and China continues to feature heavily in the global media over two years after the award on the merits was delivered.[105] An UNCLOS climate change case could give a voice and a platform to a small developing island state or a state with a large low-lying coastal population. It could also help increase the global demand for climate change action and could contribute to the strengthening of states' climate change policies and NDCs. The threat of international litigation could also force states to increase their mitigation action so as to avoid having to defend an UNCLOS case

[104] Osofsky (n 1).

[105] See, for example, Panos Mourdoukoutas, 'Duterte's South China Sea Flip-Flops Will Put the Philippines in a Place It Doesn't Want to Be' (*Forbes*, 30 May 2018), www.forbes.com/sites/panosmourdoukoutas/2018/05/30/dutertes-south-china-sea-flip-flops-will-put-the-philippines-in-a-place-it-doesnt-want-to-be/#3a307f6f4877; 'Philippines' Top Judge Says Beijing's South China Sea Claims Pose "Gravest Threat to Nation Since World War II"' (*Japan Times*, 25 November 2018), www.japantimes.co.jp/news/2018/11/25/asia-pacific/philippines-top-judge-says-beijings-south-china-sea-claims-pose-gravest-threat-nation-since-world-war-ii/#.XEWiAFwzaUk; Richard Heydarian, 'Major Hurdles – and Rewards – as China and Philippines Try to Forge Deal to Share South China Sea Resources' (*South China Morning Post*, 22 September 2018), www.scmp.com/news/china/diplomacy/article/2165237/major-hurdles-and-rewards-china-and-philippines-try-forge-deal; Bill Hayton, 'Two Years On, South China Sea Ruling Remains a Battleground for the Rules-Based Order' (*Chatham House: The Royal Institute of International Affairs*, 11 July 2018), www.chathamhouse.org/expert/comment/two-years-south-china-sea-ruling-remains-battleground-rules-based-order, all accessed 18 June 2019.

of their own. As stated by Burns, 'the spectre of litigation may help to deepen the commitment of States to confront the most pressing environmental issue of our generation'.[106]

5.4 Conclusions

Climate change is having increasingly severe impacts on the marine environment in a variety of different ways. UNCLOS regulates all forms of pollution of the marine environment, including causes and effects of climate change. The 168 parties to UNCLOS are subject to binding obligations to take all measures necessary to prevent, reduce and control such pollution from climate change. What sets UNCLOS apart in the context of global climate change treaties is its compulsory binding dispute settlement procedure. This presents an opportunity for a disproportionately affected state to bring interstate proceedings against a major polluter to enforce its compliance with its UNCLOS climate change obligations. There are several procedural and substantive hurdles that will have to be crossed in order to achieve a successful and useful outcome; however, they would not appear to be insurmountable. Although an UNCLOS climate change case has the potential to trigger effective mitigation outcomes, it will not on its own be able to keep global temperatures below a 1.5–2°C rise. While a court or tribunal may find the respondent in breach of its obligations, due to the due diligence nature of the UNCLOS environmental obligations, and the difficulty of applying the bottom-up Paris Agreement obligations in the UNCLOS context, it is difficult to imagine the judgment prescribing the exact standard of required conduct.

However, a finding from an international court or tribunal that a certain major polluter is in breach of its international obligations due to its failure to take sufficient climate change mitigation action could lead to beneficial direct and indirect outcomes. Considering that states generally comply with their international obligations, a state subject to an adverse judgment may be likely to amend its policies to comply with its obligations as described by the court or tribunal. Indirectly, the case would generate a great deal of media attention, increasing public awareness of the need to take climate change action. It may also encourage other states to improve their policies in order to avoid defending a case of their own.

[106] Burns (n 41) 50–1.

6

Investor-State Dispute Settlement in Renewable Energy: Friend or Foe to Climate Change?

HUI PANG

Introduction

There is international consensus that decarbonization is essential for preventing climate change. The parties to the Paris Agreement recognized that rapid decarbonization is needed to avoid climate disaster in the Marrakesh Conference in 2016, the first conference of the parties to implement the Paris Agreement.[1] The recent decision to fully implement the Paris Agreement also placed emphasis on the need to accelerate decarbonization before 2050. The development of renewable energy is an important tool to limit greenhouse gas (GHG) emissions, and how the investor-state arbitration tribunals are dealing with renewable energy investment cases can influence the future growth of the renewable energy sector, creating an impact on our efforts to tackle climate change. Although these disputes have not yet appeared in the Asia Pacific region, valuable experiences can be drawn from these cases, especially from a policy perspective. The current cases in renewable energy investment demonstrate a dilemma in states' policies regarding renewable energy. On one hand, as a capital-sensitive and relatively new industry, renewable energy needs government subsidies to compete with traditional fossil fuel. On the other hand, the renewable energy sector changes swiftly due to the advancement of technology, and states have found it difficult to calculate the precise subsidies that give renewable energy the same level of competitiveness without making it reliant on state subsidies to earn a profit. The balance between supporting renewable energy while allowing it to integrate into the market so that it can be self-sufficient has

[1] United Nations Climate Change, 'Rapid Decarbonization Needed to Prevent Climate Disaster' (UNCC, 12 October 2016), https://unfccc.int/news/rapid-decarbonization-needed-to-prevent-climate-disaster, accessed 10 June 2020.

been difficult to establish. Through analyzing renewable energy investment cases that have arisen in Europe and North America, this chapter hopes to provide guidance for Asia Pacific countries that intend to promote renewable energy through policy incentives.

Supportive national policies for renewable energy played a critical role in promoting clean energy investments and the growth of the renewable energy industry in general.[2] Many states have established regulatory frameworks to provide tax deductions, feed-in tariffs, and other subsidies to investments in renewable energy. For instance, the United States spent US$11 billion on subsidizing renewable energy in 2016 at the federal level,[3] while its most progressive state – California – implemented legislation to require 50 per cent of the state's electricity to come from renewable energy by 2030.[4] The European Union (EU) issued the Renewable Energy Directive in 2009, requiring the EU to fulfil at least 20 per cent of its total energy needs with renewables by 2020.[5] This directive was recently amended, changing that requirement, to achieve at least 32 per cent of its total energy needs via renewables by 2030.[6] The EU has recently decided to gradually phase out feed-in tariff subsidies and substitute it with tax reductions and other means that will assist the renewable energy sector to adjust to market-based mechanism.[7] Through these supportive measures, renewable energy has become more affordable to consumers,[8] allowing renewable energy to grow under the competition from fossil fuels.

[2] Marcella Nicolini, Simona Porcheri, and Massimo Tavonic, 'Are Renewable Energy Subsidies Effective? Evidence from Europe', (2017) 74 *Renewable and Sustainable Energy Reviews* 412; LSE Grantham Research Institute on Climate Change and the Environment, 'Do Renewable Energy Technologies Need Government Subsidies' (14 May 2018), www.lse.ac.uk/GranthamInstitute/faqs/do-renewable-energy-technologies-need-government-subsidies/.

[3] University of Huston Energy Fellows, 'Renewable Energy Subsidies – Yes or No?' (*Forbes*, 23 March 2018), www.forbes.com/sites/uhenergy/2018/03/23/renewable-energy-subsidies-yes-or-no/#288e7a3b6e23, accessed 30 December 2018.

[4] Renewable Energy Programs of California Energy Commission, www.energy.ca.gov/renewables/renewable_links.html, accessed 30 December 2018.

[5] Directive 2009/28/EC of the European Parliament and of the Council of 23 April 2009 on the promotion of the use of energy from renewable sources and amending and subsequently repealing Directives 2001/77/EC and 2003/30/EC, [2009] OJ L140/16.

[6] 'Factsheet: The Revised Renewable Energy Directive' (December 2018), https://ec.europa.eu/energy/sites/ener/files/documents/directive_renewable_factsheet.pdf, accessed 10 January 2018.

[7] Guidelines on State Aid for Environmental Protection and Energy 2014–2020 [2004] OJ C200/23.

[8] International Renewable Energy Agency, 'Global Levelised Cost of Electricity from Utility-Scale Renewable Generation Technologies 2010-2017', http://resourceirena.irena.org/gateway/dashboard/?topic=3&subTopic=1065, accessed 10 January 2018.

However, state subsidies for renewable energy have proven to be susceptible to changes. In some cases, the government chooses to withdraw subsidies when the state's economy weakens or when the production of renewable energy has been more successful than anticipated. Under such circumstances, the investor in question may feel that the state has backed down from its previous commitment and that the investment was induced under false pretences. For domestic investors, they may choose to bring a suit against the authority that enacts such a change in a local court under domestic laws. The foreign investor has the option of avoiding national courts and initiating arbitration at an independent international arbitration institution if two conditions are met. First, the investor's home state must have an international investment agreement (IIA) with the country in which the investment is situated (the host state). And, second, that agreement must contain an investor-state dispute settlement (ISDS) provision that allows the investor to bring the claim against the host state through international arbitration.

As of April 2019, there are 2,659 IIAs in force,[9] and most contain an ISDS provision, allowing foreign investors to seek adjudication under a neutral forum unaffected by the political environments of the host states. Under the IIA, the host state is subjected to obligations to provide a series of investment protection treatments, among which are non-expropriation, national treatment, most-favoured-nation treatment, and fair and equitable treatment. In the scenario where the host state withdraws or substantially alters its incentive framework for renewable energy, the arguments most often invoked are the breach of non-expropriation and fair and equitable treatment obligations.[10] The wording of the non-expropriation provisions differs from agreement to agreement. However, the basic notion remains the same – expropriation of foreign investment is deemed a breach of the IIA, unless it is for a public purpose, done under due process, non-discriminatory in nature, and accompanied by the payment of prompt, adequate, and effective compensation.[11] If changes in the incentive framework deplete the investment of its substantive value, the

[9] Figures gathered from the United Nations UNCTAD Investment Policy Hub, http://investmentpolicyhub.unctad.org/IIA.

[10] Figures gathered from the United Nations UNCTAD Investment Policy Hub. According to accessible data, out of 522 alleges of breach of treaty obligations, 380 were indirect expropriation and 433 were breach of fair and equitable treatment. For claims vastly exceeding others under IIAs, see 'Breaches of IIA Provisions Alleged and Found', https://investmentpolicyhub.unctad.org/ISDS/FilterByBreaches.

[11] Energy Charter Treaty, (1995) 2080 UNTS 95, 34 ILM 360, Art 13(1); see also Tarcisio Gazzini, 'Beyond Antagonism: Legal Protection of Foreign Investment in the

investor could argue that the host state had breached the IIA subject to the aforementioned exception.

Furthermore, the investor could also claim the breach of fair and equitable treatment obligation when incentives have been retracted. Under the fair and equitable treatment obligation, 'an investor has the legitimate expectation that, when modifying the regulation under which it made the investment, the State will not act unreasonably, contrary to the public interest, or in a disproportionate manner'.[12] Even though legitimate expectations cannot offer the investor 'immutable economic rights that could not be altered by changes in the regulatory regime',[13] several cases have found that such expectations may grant the investor the right to expect 'stable and equitable conditions of the legal and business framework'.[14]

In such disputes, the host state would usually claim that it is within its sovereignty to enact regulatory measures that benefit the public interest and rebut the investor's claim by stating that the change of law is a risk that an investor should have foreseen. Thus, if an investor decides to invest and enjoy the incentives, it should also bear the burden of the risk when such incentives change. The outcomes of such disputes have

Natural Resources Sector' in Marc Bungenberg and others (eds.), *European Yearbook of International Economic Law* 2018 (Springer 2019).

12 *Charanne B.V. and Construction Investments S.a.r.l.* v. *Kingdom of Spain*, SCC Case No 062/2012, Award, 21 January 2016, Unofficial English Translation by Mena Chambers (hereinafter *Charanne* v. *Spain*) para 232.

13 *Eiser Infrastructure Limited and Energia Solar Luxembourg S.à r.I.* v. *Kingdom of Spain*, ICSID Case No ARB/13/36, Award, 4 May 2017 (hereinafter *Eiser* v. *Spain*) para 363.

14 In *Occidental Exploration and Production Company* v. *The Republic of Ecuador*, LCIA Case No UN 3467, Final Award, 1 July 2004 (hereinafter *Occidental* v. *Ecuador*) para 183, the tribunal concluded that 'the stability of the legal and business framework is . . . an essential element of fair and equitable treatment'. And this 'stability element' of fair and equitable treatment has been reaffirmed by several subsequent cases. In *Plama Consortium Limited* v. *Republic of Bulgaria*, ICSID Case No ARB/03/24, Award, 27 August 2008, (hereinafter *Plama* v. *Bulgaria*) para 173, the tribunal stated that 'stable and equitable conditions are clearly part of the fair and equitable treatment standard under the ECT'. In *CMS Gas Transmission Company* v. *The Argentine Republic*, ICSID Case No ARB/01/8, Award, 12 May 2005 (hereinafter *CMS* v. *Argentina*) para 274, the tribunal stated that 'one principle objective of the protection envisaged is that fair and equitable treatment is desirable to maintain a stable framework for investments and maximum effective use of economic resources. There can be no doubt, therefore, that a stable legal and business environment is an essential element of fair and equitable treatment'. Also see *LG&E Energy Corp., LG&E Capital Corp., and LG&E International Inc.* v. *Argentine Republic*, ICSID Case No ARB/02/1, Decision on Liability, 3 October 2006 (hereinafter *LG&E* v. *Argentina*) para 125, and *BG Group Plc.* v. *The Republic of Argentina*, Award, 24 December 2007, para 307.

significant repercussions for foreign investment in the renewable energy sector. This is a capital sensitive sector where foreign investment is a significant contributor. Further, tribunal decisions offer lessons to other states that intend to implement similar regulatory measures. On the one hand, deeming the substantial changes or revocation of the incentives as a breach of an IIA's obligations would encourage the states to uphold its commitments to the investors and create a favourable environment for renewable energy, thus motivating the private sector to participate in eliminating greenhouse emissions and help reduce climate change.

On the other hand, if the tribunals conclude that the states' changes of incentive frameworks were breaches of obligations under the IIAs, other states may be discouraged from implementing similar incentive frameworks, due to the fear that those incentives could not be retracted without a large amount of compensation. In the end, potentially renewable energy–friendly states may decide to backtrack from their plans and not subsidize foreign investments in renewable energy at all, leaving the renewable energy sector in an even worse economic environment. Furthermore, the decisions of the tribunals have a wider overarching significance. If a state's new legal framework regarding renewable energy promotion can be challenged successfully, potentially any state regulations that exceed the boundaries delineated in the IIAs can also be challenged. If such rights are interpreted too broadly or wrongly abused, it could target regulations that serve the general public interests, as demonstrated in the *Philip Morris* v. *Australia* case where the investor intended to use the international arbitration system to challenge Australia on its newly enacted regulation of plain-tobacco packaging.[15]

Similarly, investors could also challenge any regulations implemented for environmental protection if they believe the regulation has breached their right under an IIA. With the risk of high compensation at hand, states may find themselves bound to the present environmental standards and may be less willing to burden the investors with higher environmental obligations. This could act as a policy chill for states that intend to be heralds in promoting the synergy of environmental protection and economic development. Therefore, the ISDS mechanism holds several facets of implications for climate change. In the past few years, the arbitral tribunals have been presented with cases concerning renewable energy investments in European countries and Canada, where the host

[15] *Philip Morris Asia Limited* v. *The Commonwealth of Australia*, PCA Case No 2012-12.

state retracted their previous incentive frameworks. The decisions of the tribunals have varied, despite similarities in legal claims and facts. Thus, one cannot help but wonder, what are the criteria used by the tribunal to determine whether the state has expropriated the investment or breached its fair and equitable treatment obligation under the relevant IIA? Are these criteria reasonable, and what are the bases for the tribunals to reach these different decisions? What policy implications do these cases render to the host states on renewable energy, and what effects would they have on the rule of law and global governance of climate change? This chapter intends to explore these issues in the hopes of presenting a perspective on the overarching question of the impact of ISDS on climate change.

6.1 Does the Change of Incentive Framework for Renewable Energy Investment Constitute a Breach of Obligation under IIAs?

This section has several goals in mind. First, it intends to critique the factors that the tribunals rely on when deciding the legality and legitimacy of the regulatory actions of the host states. It will also explore the limitations of these criteria to illustrate the uncertainties in deeming the boundaries of legitimate regulatory acts. Furthermore, the policy implications of investor-state arbitration regarding renewable energy and climate change will be discussed.

Changes in renewable energy investment incentive regimes have currently only resulted in arbitration across Europe and North America. In Europe, Spain has been the target of investor-state arbitration in the past several years due to its energy reforms, which include imposing a 7 per cent tax on renewable energy power plants, in addition to the reduction of subsidies. Up until April 2019, there are presently forty-three cases filed against Spain as a result of its dramatic policy reversal.[16] Most of these cases arise under the Energy Charter Treaty (ECT).[17] Only

[16] Figures gathered from the UNCTAD Investment Policy Hub, 'Spain as Respondent State', http://investmentpolicyhub.unctad.org/ISDS/CountryCases/197?partyRole=2; and the Energy Charter Treaty Website with Spain as the respondent in advanced search, available at www.energychartertreaty.org/cases/list-of-cases/. Please note that these are the known cases filed with the International Center for Settlement of Investment Disputes under the World Bank Group. There are forty-four cases filed against Spain concerning the retraction of the subsidies. However, *Solarpark Management GmbH & Co Atum I KG* v. *Kingdom of Spain*, SCC Case No 2015/163 was discontinued; thus, at the time of this writing (April 2019), there are forty-three cases filed against Spain regarding the retraction of subsidies for renewable energy investments.

[17] Energy Charter Treaty (n 12).

seven of these cases have been decided, out of which five were decided in favour of the investor and the other two in favour of the state.[18] The basic facts of these cases are similar, with the investor claiming that Spain violated the ECT by amending its previously promised incentive framework, subsequently causing substantial damage to the investment. In *Charanne* v. *Spain* and *Eiser* v. *Spain*, despite the similarities in facts and the alleged breach of the same investment agreement, the tribunals of these two cases reached different outcomes. The tribunal ruled in favour of the state in *Charanne* v. *Spain*, but the second tribunal ruled in favour of the investor in *Eiser* v. *Spain*. It can be argued that the tribunals in these two cases reached different conclusions because they applied different criteria to evaluate the scope of the state's right to regulate. In *Eiser* v. *Spain*, the tribunal decided that it was a breach of treaty obligations to revoke the support schemes completely through a new regulatory measure adopted in 2010, whereas in *Charanne* v. *Spain*, the state mainly amended the previous support scheme, not completely depriving the investor of its previously promised support.

Similarly, other EU members, such as Italy and the Czech Republic, have also retracted or substantially diminished their supportive framework for renewable energy investments. As of April 2019, seven cases have been filed against the Czech Republic for the amendments of the pre-existing incentive regime on photovoltaic electricity generators, including imposing a levy on electricity generate from solar power plants.[19] Only two of these seven cases have been decided, and in both

[18] The five cases decided in favour of the investors are (1) *Eiser* v. *Spain* (n 14); (2) *Novenergia II – Energy & Environment (SCA) (Grand Duchy of Luxembourg), SICAR* v. *The Kingdom of Spain*, SCC Case No 2015/063, Final Award, 15 February 2018 (hereinafter *Novenergia II* v. *Spain*); (3) *Antin Infrastructure Services Luxembourg S.à.r.l and Antin Energia Termosolar B.V* v. *The Kingdom of Spain*, ICSID Case No ARB/13/31, Award, 15 June 2018 (hereinafter *Antin* v. *Spain*); (4) *Masdar Solar & Wind Cooperatief U.A* v. *Kingdom of Spain*, ICSID Case No ARB/14/1, Award, 16 May 2018 (hereinafter *Masdar* v. *Spain*); and (5) *Foresight Luxembourg Solar 1 S.à.r.l and Others* v. *The Kingdom of Spain*, SCC Case No 2015/150, Award, 14 November 2018 (hereinafter *Foresight* v. *Spain*). The two cases decided in favour of the state are *Charanne* v. *Spain* (n 13) and *Isolux Netherlands, BV* v. *Kingdom of Spain*, SCC Case No V2013/153, Final Award, 17 July 2016 (hereinafter *Isolux* v. *Spain*).

[19] The seven cases are (1) *Antaris Solar GmbH and Dr Michael Göde* v. *The Czech Republic*, PCA Case No 2014-01, Award 2 May 2018 (hereinafter *Antaris and Göde* v. *Czech Republic*); (2) *JSW Solar GmbH & Co. KG, Gisela Wirtgen, Jürgen Wirtgen, and Stefan Wirtgen* v. *The Czech Republic*, PCA Case No 2014-03, Final Award, 11 October 2017 (hereinafter *JSW Solar and Wirtgen* v. *Czech Republic*); (3) *WA Investments-Europa Nova* v. *The Czech Republic*, UNCITRAL, pending; (4) *I.C.W. Europe Investment Limited* v. *The Czech Republic*, UNCITRAL, pending; (5) *Natland Group Limited and others* v. *The Czech*

cases, the arbitral tribunals ruled in favour of the state, relying mainly on the grounds that the legitimate expectations of the investors were not breached, since there was no guarantee that the specific regulatory framework will remain unchanged.[20]

Italy has nine cases pending regarding a series of governmental decrees to cut tariff incentives for solar power projects, causing the bankruptcy of several solar power energy companies.[21] Two cases have been decided out of the nine cases. One of the cases was *Blusun* v. *Italy*, where the arbitral tribunal recognized that Article 10(1) of the ECT incorporates the fair and equitable treatment under customary international law,[22] thus granting the minimum standard of protection to foreign investors. The tribunal generally agreed that such a provision is not merely preambular or hortatory,[23] but carries the requirement that the host state shall provide fundamental stability in the essential characteristics of the legal regime relied on by investors when making long-term investments.[24] It does not suggest that the regulatory regime cannot be altered, since any reasonable legitimate expectations of the investor should include the possibility of change, but not so radically as to cause

Republic, PCA Case No 2013-35, pending; (6) *Photovoltaik Knopf Betriebs-GmbH* v. *The Czech Republic*, UNCITRAL, pending; (7) *Voltaic Network GmbH* v. *The Czech Republic*, UNCITRAL, pending.

20 See *JSW Solar and Wirtgen* v. *Czech Republic* (n 19) 109–19, and *Antaris and Göde* v. *Czech Republic* (n 19) paras 339–446.

21 These cases are (1) *Blusun S.A., Jean-Pierre Lecorcier and Michael Stein* v. *Italian Republic*, ICSID Case No ARB/14/3, Award, 27 December 2016 (hereinafter *Blusun* v. *Italy*); (Greentech Energy Systems A/S, NovEnergia II Energy & Environment (SCA) SICAR, and NovEnergia II Italian Portfolio SA v. *The Italian Republic*, SCC Case No 2015/095, Final Award, 23 December 2018 (hereinafter *Greentech and NovEnergia* v. *Italy*); (3) *CIC Renewable and others* v. *Italian Republic*, ICSID Case No ARB/16/39; (4) *ESPF Beteiligungs GmbH, ESPF Nr. 2 Austria Beteiligungs GmbH, and InfraClass Energie 5 GmbH & Co. KG* v. *Italian Republic*, ICSID Case No ARB/16/5; (5) *Sun Reserve Luxco Holdings SRL* v. *Italy*, SCC Case No 132/2016; (6) *Belenergia S.A.* v. *Italian Republic*, ICSID Case No ARB/15/40; (7) *CEF Energia BV* v. *Italian Republic*, SCC Case No 158/2015; (8) Eskosol S.p.A. in *Liquidazione* v. *Italian Republic*, ICSID Case No ARB/15/50; and (9) *Silver Ridge Power BV* v. *Italian Republic*, ICSID Case No ARB/15/37. There is also another case pending under ECT concerning the renewable energy sector – *Veolia Propreté SAS* v. *Italian Republic*, ICSID Case No ARB/18/20. However, further information about this case has not been released. Therefore, it remains to be seen if this case concerns the retraction of support schemes for renewable energy.

22 The was first recognized in *Electrabel S.A.* v. *Republic of Hungary*, ICSID Case No ARB/07/19, Decision on Jurisdiction, Applicable Law and Liability, 30 November 2012 (hereinafter *Electrabel* v. *Hungary*) para 7.158.

23 *Blusun* v. *Italy* (n 22) para 319(1).

24 *Eiser* v. *Spain* (n 14) para 382.

substantial deprivation to the investment.[25] After finding that the value of the investment was not completely destructed, the tribunal dismissed the claimant's position that these regulatory acts constitute indirect expropriation and subsequently ruled in favour of the state. In *Greentech Energy Systems A/S and others* v. *Italy*, where 134 solar plants were influenced, the tribunal also decided that the state did not breach its IIA obligations on the grounds that there was no guarantee that the laws and regulations would not be changed.[26]

Outside the EU, two cases concerning the change of the feed-in-tariff on renewable energy by Ontario, Canada, have also led to different rulings by the tribunals. In *Mesa Power* v. *Canada*, the investor brought arbitration proceedings to challenge governmental measures that are allegedly arbitrary and discriminatory, violating the minimum standard of treatment under North America Free Trade Agreement (NAFTA). Despite noting that 'at least some criticism may be levelled at Ontario's decision',[27] the tribunal found the government's change of the incentive framework consistent with its international obligations.[28] In *Windstream* v. *Canada*, the investor entered into a feed-in-tariff contract with the Ontario government regarding offshore wind development; later on, however, the government decided to defer such renewable energy experiments due to the need to conduct further research on environmental impacts, causing loss of investment to the investor.[29] The government never provided the results of the research, and the investor claimed that the decision was not for a public purpose but for political considerations. The tribunal sided with the investor on this claim and decided that the decision to defer the offshore wind development itself was not a violation of the minimum standard of treatment; however, the arbitrary decision of not actually conducting the scientific research to address this regulatory uncertainty amounts to a breach of obligation under NAFTA.[30]

Out of all the protective standards that the investors often invoke in arbitrations, indirect expropriation and fair and equitable treatment have

[25] *Eiser* v. *Spain* (n 14) para 382.

[26] *Greentech and NovEnergia* v. *Italy* (n 22) paras 500–6.

[27] *Mesa Power Group, LLC* v. *Government of Canada*, PCA Case No 2012-17, Award, 24 March 2016, para 682.

[28] ibid. paras 669, 682.

[29] *Windstream Energy LLC* v. *Government of Canada*, PCA Case No 2013-22, Award, 27 September 2016, para 103.

[30] ibid. paras 377–82.

gained the tribunals' favour much more than other claims.[31] The following discussion will focus on these two standards, as they have generated the most debate in legal scholarship of what constitutes an acceptable regulatory measure that is in alignment with international obligations and is non-compensatory.[32]

6.1.1 *Indirect Expropriation*

Indirect expropriation is not a concept generated by the IIAs; rather, it is a known concept in international law imported to international investment law through scholarly writings and international cases. The history of the concept predates the proliferation of IIAs and the ISDS mechanism. For present purposes, indirect expropriation may be defined in the following terms: 'even though a State may not purport to interfere with rights to property, it may, by its actions, render those rights so useless that it will be deemed to have expropriated them'.[33] In *Harza Engineering Company* v. *Iran*, the tribunal concluded that 'a taking of property may occur under international law, even in the absence of formal nationalization or expropriation, if a government has interfered unreasonably with the use of property'.[34]

The focus on the deprivation of ownership has resulted in the longstanding 'sole effect doctrine', whereby tribunals determine expropriation

[31] Figures come from United Nations UNCTAD Investment Policy Hub. As of April 2019, according to accessible data from 553 alleged breaches, 189 were decided that the state actions indeed breached the investment treaty. Breach of fair and equitable treatment accounted for 121, while indirect expropriation accounted for 57; these two exceed other deemed breaches by a wide margin. 'Breaches of IIA Provisions Alleged and Found', https://investmentpolicyhub.unctad.org/ISDS/FilterByBreaches.

[32] See, for example, R. Dolzer, 'Indirect Expropriations: New Developments?' (2003) 11 *N.Y. U. Envtl. L.J.* 64; W. Michael Reisman and R. D. Sloane, 'Indirect Expropriation and Its Valuation in the BIT Generation' (2004) 74 *BYIL* 115; J. Paulsson and Z. Douglas, 'Indirect Expropriation in Investment Treaty Arbitration' in N. Hom and S. Krill (eds.), *Arbitrating Foreign Investment Disputes* (Kluwer 2004) 145; L. Yves Fortier and Stephen L. Drymer, 'Indirect Expropriation in the Law of International Investment: I Know It When I See It, or Caveat Investor' (2005) 13 *Asia Pac. L. Rev.* 79, 110.

[33] G. C. Christie, 'What Constitutes a Taking Under International Law' (1962) 38 *BYBIL* 307, 310–11. The cases that Christie referred to were Certain German Interests in Polish Upper Silesia (*Germany* v. *Poland*), 1926 PCIJ Rep Series A No 7 (May 25), and Norwegian Shipowners Claims (*Norway* v. *US*) (1922) I RIAA 307. For more detailed explanation of Christie's definition, see Reisman and Sloane (n 32) 119.

[34] *Harza Engineering Company* v. *Iran*, Award No 19-98-2 (30 December 1982), reprinted in 1 Iran–US Cl Trib Rep 499. Also see *Tippetts, Abbett, McCarthy, Stratton* v. *TAMS-AFFA Consulting Engineers*, Award No 141-7-2 (29 June 1984), reprinted in 6 Iran–US Cl Trib Rep 219, 225-26.

mainly by relying on whether the value of the investment has been completely destroyed. The determination of deprivation is affected by the nature of the regulatory action (final or in progress) and the loss of value attributable to the regulatory action. Specifically regarding a renewable energy incentive framework, expropriation claims are hard to succeed due to the fact that the value of the investment cannot be considered as 'destroyed' simply because of retraction of the state's incentives. For instance, in *Charanne* v. *Spain*, the tribunal dismissed the expropriation claim because the investment remained in place with a lower rate of return instead of being completely deprived of value. Furthermore, the *Charanne* v. *Spain* tribunal looked into the domestic regulation and found that because the changes were only amendments of the incentive program, rather than the abolition of the entire regulatory system, the claim that the investment suffered substantial deprivation cannot be sustained. This line of reasoning took reference from a series of previous awards that had adopted the sole effect doctrine, including *Nykomb* v. *Latvia*, *Metalclad* v. *Mexico*, *Pope & Talbot* v. *Canada*, and *CMS* v. *Argentina*.[35]

The proliferation of IIAs and the emergence of different types of expropriation have prompted international arbitration tribunals to look beyond the sole effect doctrine and explore other approaches to determine whether expropriation has taken place. The principle of proportionality and the margin of appreciation, derived from the jurisprudence of the European Court of Human Rights concerning expropriation of personal property,[36] are now often applied by tribunals to determine if the state's action is a non-compensable regulatory action or an act of indirect expropriation. For instance, in *LG&E* v. *Argentina*, the tribunal held that indirect expropriation occurs when 'the State's action is obviously disproportionate to the need being addressed'.[37] However,

[35] In *Nykomb Synergetics Technology Holding AB (Sweden)* v. *The Republic of Latvia*, SCC Case No 118/2001, Arbitral Award, 16 December 2003 (hereinafter *Nykomb* v. *Latvia*), the tribunal rejected the investor's claim that Latvia's withdraw previously agreed tariff rate constituted 'indirect expropriation' on the ground that Latvia did not take possession of the investment, thereby construing 'indirect expropriation' in narrow terms. This application of the 'sole effect doctrine' was subsequently reinforced in *Metalclad Corporation* v. *The United Mexican States*, ICSID Case No ARB(AF)/97/1, Award, 30 August 2000 (hereinafter *Metalclad* v. *Mexico*); *Pope & Talbot Incorporated* v. *The Government of Canada*, Interim Award, 26 June 2000 (hereinafter *Pope & Talbot* v. *Canada*); and CMS v. Argentina (n 15).

[36] See *James and Others* v. *United Kingdom* (1986) 8 EHRR 123, App 8793/79 (ECHR, 21 February 1986) para 50. The proportionality test is also incorporated in the Charter of Fundamental Right of the European Union (2000) OJ C364/01, Art 17.

[37] *LG&E* v. *Argentina* (n 15) para 195.

the tribunal did not elaborate on what constitutes 'disproportionate' actions, and as some legal scholars intuitively point out, the introduction of an unclear concept of proportionality may lead to a rudimentary and inaccurate application of the test and result in inconsistent outcomes.[38] In *Tecmed* v. *Mexico*, the tribunal tried to give a more detailed explanation of the principle of proportionality by stating that the public purpose of the state's action ought to be balanced against the burden on the foreign investor.[39] These approaches are attempts to balance the state right to regulate with investment protection under the IIAs and the collaborative ISDS mechanism.

However, it is often difficult to draw the line between lawful regulation and indirect expropriation. As the tribunal in *Saluka* v. *Czech Republic* concluded, 'international law has yet to draw a bright and easily distinguishable line between non-compensable regulations on the one hand and, on the other, measures that have the effect of depriving foreign investors of their investment and are thus unlawful and compensable in international law'.[40] This lack of systemic articulation has generated abundant discussion in legal literature, all intending to delineate this foggy line.[41] Despite all the criteria that the tribunals applied to distinguish between lawful regulation and indirect expropriation,[42]one criteria

38 Tarcisio Gazzini, 'Drawing the Line between Non-Compensable Regulatory Powers and Indirect Expropriation of Foreign Investment-An Economic Analysis of Law Perspective' (2010) 7 *Manchester J. Int'l Econ. L.* 36, 43.

39 *Técnicas Medioambientales Tecmed, S.A.* v. *The United Mexican States*, ICSID Case No ARB (AF)/00/2, Award, 29 May 2003 (hereinafter *Tecmed* v. *Mexico*) para 122. See also *Azurix Corp* v. *The Argentine Republic*, ICSID Case No ARB/01/12, Award, 14 July 2006, para 311; *Continental Casualty Company* v. *Argentina*, ICSID Case No ARB/03/9, Award, 5 September 2008, para 276.

40 *Saluka Investments BV* v. *Czech Republic*, Partial Award, 17 March 2006, para 263.

41 See Dolzer (n 33); A. Reinisch, 'Expropriation', report submitted to the ILA, www.ilahq.org/pdf/Foreign%20Investment/ILA%20paper%20Reinisch.pdf; Reisman and Solane (n 33); Paulsson and Douglas (n 33) 145; Fortier and Drymer (n 33) 110; Andrew Newcombe, 'The Boundaries of Regulatory Expropriation in International Law' (2005) 20(1) *ICSID Rev. for Inv. L.J.* 1; Organization for Economic Co-operation and Development (OECD), '"Indirect Expropriation" and the "Right to Regulate" in International Investment Law' (2004), OECD Working Papers on International Investment 2004/04, http://dx.doi.org/10.1787/780155872321; Ursula Kriebaum, 'Regulatory Takings: Balancing the Interests of the Investor and the State' (2007) 8 *J. World Investment & Trade* 717, 744; A. K. Hoffmann, 'Indirect Expropriation' in A. Reinisch (ed.), *Standards of Investment Protection* (Oxford University Press 2008) 151; S. Montt, *State Liability in Investment Treaty Arbitration* (Hart 2009), chapter 5.

42 The Organization for Economic Co-operation and Development (OECD) conceded in a working paper that the tribunal should undertake a case-by-case examination and pay careful consideration of the specific wording of the treaty. In the working paper, the

remains the dominating factor – substantial deprivation. In *PSEG* v. *Turkey*, the tribunal held that 'while indirect expropriation can take many forms there must be some form of deprivation of the investor in the control of the investment . . . or depriving the company of its property or control in total or in part', which the tribunal characterized as the 'extreme forms of interference'.[43] This emphasis on the sole effect doctrine places the requirement of substantial deprivation in a hierarchy above any other elements when determining whether indirect expropriation took place and deems 'substantial deprivation' to be the same as complete deprivation of the value of investment. A classic example is *Tecmed* v. *Mexico*, where the tribunal found that a measure equivalent to an expropriation should have 'radically deprived of the economical use and enjoyment of its investments, as if the rights related thereto had ceased to exist'.[44]

Similarly, the line of reasoning that over-emphasizes the sole effect doctrine in determining expropriation has also been frequently applied in cases concerning the ECT, from which most renewable energy disputes arise. It has led the tribunal to construe substantial deprivation in a narrow way: it is often equated with the total destruction of investment value. Apart from *Nykomb* v. *Latvia*, other cases under the ECT that explicitly address the determination of what constitutes indirect expropriation have all taken the view that total or near-total deprivation of value is needed to establish expropriation. In *Plama* v. *Bulgaria*, the tribunal clarified the decisive element in determining indirect expropriation, and 'substantially complete deprivation of the economic use and enjoyment of the rights to the investment, or of identifiable, distinct parts thereof (i.e., approaching total impairment)' was put forward as the first and foremost element.[45] In *Electrabel* v. *Hungary*, the tribunal stated that through examining tribunal jurisprudence and legal literature, it has found that for indirect expropriation to be concluded there has to be 'substantial, radical, severe, devastating or fundamental deprivation of its

OECD also stated that 'a close examination of the relevant jurisprudence reveals that, in broad terms, there are some criteria that tribunals have used to distinguish these concepts: i) the degree of interference with the property right, ii) the character of governmental measures, i.e. the purpose and the context of the governmental measure, and iii) the interference of the measure with reasonable and investment-backed expectations'. See OECD (n 41).

[43] *PSEG Global Inc. and Konya Ilgin Elektrik Üretim ve Ticaret Limited Şirketi* v. *Republic of Turkey*, ICSID Case No ARB/02/5, Award, 19 January 2007, paras 278–9.

[44] *Tecmed* v. *Mexico* (n 40) para 115.

[45] *Plama* v. *Bulgaria* (n 15) para 193.

rights or virtual annihilation, effective neutralization or factual destruction of its investment, its value or enjoyment'.[46]

However, this narrow construction of 'substantial deprivation' is questionable from a treaty interpretation standpoint. The tribunals in the aforementioned cases based their narrow construction of 'substantial deprivation' on the reasoning of the interim award of *Pope & Talbot* v. *Canada*. However, the *Pope & Talbot* v. *Canada* case itself did not deem 'substantial deprivation' as complete destruction of value. In *Pope & Talbot* v. *Canada*, the tribunal understood 'substantial deprivation' as 'interference sufficiently restrictive to support a conclusion that the property has been "taken" from the owner', and then proceeded to interpret 'the taking of property' with reference to the *Harvard Draft Convention* and the *Restatement*.[47] Neither the *Harvard Draft Convention* nor the *Restatement* construe 'substantial deprivation' so narrowly as to deem it to be complete deprivation. The *Harvard Draft Convention* defines 'a taking of property' as including 'any such unreasonable interference with the use, enjoyment, or disposal of property as to justify an inference that the owner thereof will not be able to use, enjoy, or dispose of the property within a reasonable period of time after the inception of such interference'.[48] The wording of 'unreasonable interference' demonstrates that this term is not to be narrowly construed in the sense that only complete deprivation of the investment value can be deemed as 'taking'. Similarly, when addressing the question of whether regulation may be considered as expropriation, the *Restatement* also seems to take a broader view, stating that 'action that is confiscatory, or that prevents, unreasonable interferes with, or unduly delays, effective enjoyment of an alien property' is expropriation.[49] Together with the definition stated in the *Restatement*, it seems reasonable to suggest that 'substantial deprivation' is not equal to the complete deprivation of the value of the investment. Instead, it should refer to a gross level of interference that renders the investment unprofitable or to a level that, if the investor is to evaluate the investment opportunity now, it will not

[46] *Electrabel* v. *Hungary* (n 23) para 6.62.

[47] *Pope & Talbot* v. *Canada* (n 36) para 102; L. Sohn and B. Baxter, 'Draft Convention on the International Responsibility of States for Injuries to Aliens' (1961) 55 *Am. J. Int'l L.* 548 (hereinafter, Harvard Draft Convention); and Restatement (Third) of the Foreign Relations Law of the United States vol 1 (American Law Institute Publishers 1987) (hereinafter, the Restatement).

[48] Harvard Draft Convention (n 47) Art 10.3.

[49] Restatement (n 48), Section 712 Comment g.

make the investment. Furthermore, it should also be noted that the *Harvard Draft Convention* and the *Restatement* were produced by private bodies and should be regarded as 'the teachings of the most highly qualified publicists of various nations' that function as 'subsidiary means for the determination of rules of law'.[50] It does raise a question, however, is referring to the *Harvard Draft Convention* and the *Restatement* a reasonable approach to determine the definition of indirect expropriation globally? Or is it simply the proliferation of the United States' interpretation of expropriation in international investment law? The *Restatement* reflects the United States perspective on expropriation, but if neither party is from the United States, then the tribunal should mainly rely on the IIA in question and relevant international law. When none could provide guidance, it should refer to the parties' interpretation of 'expropriation'. Only when none exists could a third party's interpretation (such as the *Restatement*) be used a guidance, but with supporting justifications.[51]

Equating 'substantial deprivation' with total deprivation makes it very difficult for renewable energy investors to establish indirect expropriation due to regulation changes. Out of the seven cases that have reached a decision regarding Spain's retraction of its renewable energy incentives, both tribunals in *Charanne* v. *Spain* and *Isolux* v. *Spain* have decided that indirect expropriation requires the 'destruction of its value', thus ruling against the investor's claim.[52] Even in the *Eiser* v. *Spain* case, where the tribunal decided in favour of the investor and where the change of regulatory system resulted in a considerable loss of the value of the investment, the tribunal decided that there was no indirect expropriation. Many of the criteria used to determine if there was an indirect expropriation are also the criteria for the fair and equitable treatment standard. Despite sharing many criteria, the tribunal in *Eiser* v. *Spain* decided against finding the alleged indirect expropriation but held in favour of the investor for the breach of fair and equitable treatment standard by the host state. The tribunal deciding on the Czech Republic's change of the pre-existing incentive regime regulation on photovoltaic electricity generators also dismissed the investor's claim of indirect expropriation on the grounds that no destruction of value occurred.[53] This overly narrow construction of 'substantial deprivation' fails to recognize the

[50] Statute of the International Court of Justice (1945) United States Treaty Series 993, Art 38.
[51] Vienna Convention on the Law of Treaties (1969) 1155 UNTS 331, Art 31 and Art 32.
[52] *Isolux* v. *Spain* (n 19) para 868.
[53] *JSW Solar and Wirtgen* v. *Czech Republic* (n 20) paras 354–7.

characteristics and form of indirect expropriation, where total destruction of value rarely occurs but substantial interference of the state to the point where the investment is no longer economically operable can happen through the changes of regulations.

As an emerging industry that relies heavily on the support of state incentives to survive and develop, it seems unsustainable to expect renewable energy investors to bear the burden of the risk of the retraction of these incentives alone. A specific tax deficit due to the incentives granted to the investors per se seems insufficient to completely abolish state support for renewable energy. When deciding the amount and structure of the support system, it is the state's obligation to calculate the appropriate incentive amount. It should act with due diligence and bear the responsibility to the general public to make sure that these incentive goals are achievable and sustainable. The information that a foreign investor could acquire is incomparable to that of the state, making it difficult for the investor to calculate what amount of support would render the state tax deficit and thus expect a retraction. However, it would also be wrong and impractical for the investors to assume that the state cannot change its regulatory framework for renewable energy subsidies when its previous calculations created severe burden for the state. The principle of proportionality in international law offers a method to balance the situation. Under the principle of proportionality, the state should adopt the approach that would create the least harm to the renewable energy industry when aiming to resolve its tax deficits. For instance, the state may lower the cost of financing for renewable energy investments through banking regulations, gradually reduce the subsidies over a lengthy period, or allow a certain grace period for the investors to respond. Furthermore, introducing public participation into the process is also important. In the case of retracting renewable energy subsidies, the state is making a policy choice of favouring one domestic public good (tax stability) over a global common (climate change). When the state is exercising its regulatory power, it seems only fair that the public should have a say in deciding whether one public interest can override the other, particularly when the concept of 'public purpose' in the IIAs is not clearly defined. As IIAs are negotiated behind closed doors, it is hard to say if the 'public purpose' concept in the IIAs reflects the constitutional public values of the contracting states. Without public participation, imploring the public purpose exception clause of the IIAs as a defence against the protection of another public interest seems rather arbitrary.

6.1.2 *Fair and Equitable Treatment*

Fair and equitable treatment is frequently invoked in ISDS due to the broad and, at times, vague content that the concept entails. According to the most recent special update on investor-state disputes, the claimants alleged breaches of fair and equitable treatment in about 80 per cent of cases (for which information on alleged breaches was available) – that is, 401 out of 530 cases concluded.[54] The standard has been expressed in treaties and interpreted by the tribunal in many different ways, and they range from the customary international minimum standard to standards of procedural justice such as transparency and due process. Some tribunals have even declared that there is no precise concept of fair and equitable treatment; instead, the function of the standard is more important than its term.[55] Despite some variations on the exact definition of the term, certain elements are repeatedly discussed and are of vital importance to renewable energy arbitrations. This section will focus on these elements and the impact they have on the investors' claims against the states for retracting incentive frameworks.

6.1.2.1 Does the Incentive Framework Constitute a Specific Commitment?

There is a general consensus that when specific commitments have been made by the host state to the investor, the host state is under an obligation to uphold the specific commitment and the circumstances it relies on when making that commitment, subject to the fair and equitable treatment standard in IIAs. Thus specific commitment is an important concept in IIAs, as it serves as an exception to the rule that the host state is not liable for enacting general regulations for a public purpose that may negatively impact the investor's rights.[56] However, the concept of specific commitment has been

[54] UNCTAD, Special Update on Investor-State Dispute Settlement: Facts and Figures (IIA Issues Note 3, 2017) 5-6, http://unctad.org/en/PublicationsLibrary/diaepcb2017d7_en.pdf.

[55] *Spyridon Roussalis* v. *Romania*, ICSID Case No ARB/06/1, Award, 1 December 2011, para 318. (The tribunal found that the scope of the fair and equitable treatment is not precisely defined beyond general principles [i.e., transparency, good faith].) *Inversión y Gestión de Bienes, IGB, S.L. and IGB18 Las Rozas, S.L.* v. *Kingdom of Spain*, ICSID Case No ARB/12/17, Award (Excerpts), 14 August 2015, paras 204-05. (The tribunal notes that there is no precise definition of fair and equitable treatment, and whether the host state has breached the fair and equitable treatment should be examined on a case-by-case basis.)

[56] Lise Johnson and Oleksandr Volkov, 'Investor-State Contracts, Host-State "Commitments" and the Myth of Stability in International Law' (2013) 4 *Am. Rev. Int'l Arb.* 361, 370.

rather elusive. Whether specific commitments simply refer to commercial contracts entered into between the host state and the investor – such as permits, licenses, and leases – has been controversial. When deciding if certain regulations or policies that were targeted at a specific group of investors constitute specific commitments, tribunals have leaned towards declining such a claim. In *Charanne* v. *Spain*, for instance, the first of many 'green energy' investment cases to be decided on the merits, the tribunal ruled that Royal Decrees that offered subsidies and feed-in tariffs to renewable energy investors could not be deemed specific commitments, despite being 'directed to a limited group of investors'.[57] The tribunal believed that allowing any regulatory standard to be deemed as a specific commitment 'would constitute an excessive limitation on the power of states to regulate the economy in accordance with the public interest'.[58] This line of reasoning deserves further discussion for three reasons.

First, a host state's regulatory action is not exempt from international obligations. The goal of forming IIAs is to ensure that the host state upholds its international responsibility to provide the investor with the minimum standard of protection and not act arbitrarily. The proliferation of IIAs has created a global governance regime for foreign investments, and the standards incorporated serve as the baseline of the host state's actions. To allow regulatory actions to be exempted from the scrutiny of international law just because of their regulatory nature is to reject the concept of international law and global governance altogether. International law in essence is the rule of law that limits and regulates the power of states.

Second, different public interests may conflict, and when the state chooses to place one over the other, specific reasons should be provided, and the actions undertaken should be proportional and follow due process. In *Charanne* v. *Spain*, the ultimate aim of the regulations targeted at inducing investment in renewable energy was to promote clean energy and eliminate pollution. Overcoming tax deficits to ensure a stable financial system was the other public purpose, and since the government is the one in charge of designing the incentive regime for inducing foreign investment in renewable energy, it should also have shouldered the due diligence responsibility to ensure that the regime would not result in a tax deficit in the first place. For investors to bear the entire burden of the cost of the government's miscalculations is

[57] *Charanne* v. *Spain* (n 13) para 493.
[58] ibid.

a questionable approach – especially with the investors that rely heavily on the governmental support to overturn a previously heavily polluted market into one that would result in sustainable development. Furthermore, it seems that the citizens of the host state have no say in what constitutes public purpose stated in the IIAs, nor does the public get to decide which public interest should be prioritized when conflicts arise.

Third, the government can render contractual offers through regulatory regimes. The incentive framework that takes the form of a regulation or policy is closely assimilated to offers in contract law; similarly, when the investor registers with the administrative branch to be verified as a qualified renewable energy investor, it should be viewed as accepting the offer to invest/contract, thus forming a contractual relationship with the government. Ignoring the contractual nature of the incentive framework and only emphasizing the power of the state is contrary to the aim of IIAs and an arbitrary use of state power itself.

6.1.2.2 Alternatively, Is an Incentive Regulatory Framework a Sufficient Basis for Forming Legitimate Expectations?

As we can see from above cases, tribunals are unwilling to hold an incentive regulatory framework as a specific commitment, for fear that it would result in a regulatory freeze and encroach the state's right to regulate. However, it does not answer the question: can an incentive regulatory framework per se be the basis of an investor's legitimate expectation, and therefore its change is a breach of the fair and equitable treatment standard? This issue can be divided into two sub-questions: (a) 'Can an incentive regulatory framework be considered as a binding unilateral declaration that creates legal obligations for the state under international law?' and (b) 'Can an incentive regulatory framework targeted at a specific group of investors be the basis of legitimate expectation per se, or does it need to be supplemented by other provisions in the IIA?'

6.1.2.2.1 Can an Incentive Regulatory Framework Be Considered as a Binding Unilateral Declaration That Creates Legal Obligations for the State under International Law? It is a violation of customary international law for a state to act against a unilateral binding declaration or a specific obligation entered into between the states and the relevant party. Of course, not every unilateral declaration by the state is legally binding. According to the International Court of Justice in the *Nuclear*

Test cases and *Frontier Dispute* case,[59] unilateral declarations made by states that concern legal or factual situations may create legal obligations when '(i) interpretation establishes that the intention of the state was to bind itself with respect to a legal or factual situation; (ii) the declaration is given publicly and repeatedly, so that it cannot be dismissed as a random statement or a "trial balloon"; and (iii) those to whom the statements were directed could reasonably rely upon them'.[60] Out of these three, the first is often difficult to determine. Whether a state intends to bind itself rests very much on the content of the declaration. However, if the state has issued regulations to carry out the goal established in the declaration with the hope of inducing benefit for the state, then it is seemingly reasonable to infer that the state intends to be bound by such declaration. It is against the principle of good faith for a state to expect the benefit of an action while rejecting the obligation that comes with it, unless it is for a necessary public purpose conducted proportionately and with respect to due process. Estoppel is another doctrine that sheds light on the definition of fair and equitable treatment in customary international law. As the International Court of Justice puts it in the *Territorial Dispute* case, 'it is reasonable to expect that any legal system should possess a rule designed to prevent a person who makes or concurs in a statement upon which another person in privity with him relies to the extent of changing his position, from later asserting a state of different affairs'.[61]

The second prerequisite places the unilateral declaration within the entire context of the state's actions, including the laws of the host state and its general policies. The declaration per se is not enough to result in binding legal obligations. The declaration needs to be paired with other policies and regulations that enforce the legal obligations or the legal facts stated within the declaration. For instance, the presentation and prospectus released by the Ministry of Industry, Energy and Tourism of Spain, titled 'the sun can be yours', which included several examples of the percentage of profit for renewable energy investors, could not stand

[59] Case Concerning Frontier Dispute (*Burkina Faso* v. *Republic of Mali*), Judgment of 22 December 1986, ICJ Reports 1986, 554, 574, para 40; and Nuclear Tests Case (*Australia* v. *France*), Judgment of December 20, 1974, ICJ Reports 1974, 253.

[60] W. Michael Reisman and Mahnoush H. Arsanjani, 'The Question of Unilateral Governmental Statements as Applicable Law in Investment Disputes' (2004) 19 *ICSID Rev.* 328, 336.

[61] Case Concerning Territorial Dispute (*Libyan Arab Jamahiriya* v. *Chad*), Separate Opinion of Judge Ajibola, ICJ Reports 1994, 51, 78, para 98.

by itself as a binding unilateral declaration that stabilized the profit percentage. It had to be taken into account with the Royal Decrees released subsequently and should be allowed to change within a fair and equitable margin.[62]

The last prerequisite is that the investor should have relied on the declaration when making the investment. The problematic issue is the degree of due diligence required of the investor. Should the investor be expected to foresee the possibility of a change in the incentive framework that would drastically decline its profit at the time the investment was made? And, therefore, should they have not relied upon the declaration and refrained from making a high-risk investment? And if they did make such an investment accordingly, is it fair to expect the investors to bear the risk alone when the host state has enthusiastically tried to entice the investor in order to promote investment in a specific industry? It is common sense for the investor to acknowledge that regulations are not immobile and therefore it should have calculated the risk of regulatory change when making the investment. However, there is a limitation to the amount of change that is foreseeable for the investor due to the asymmetry of information. While it can be reasonably expected that the investor would predict and calculate the risk of reduced incentives, foreseeing a complete overturn of the incentive framework due to tax deficit would require a much more in-depth knowledge of the host state's tax regime, which is rather difficult for a foreign investor to do considering the information asymmetry. Therefore, the last prerequisite is, in fact, requiring investors to undertake due diligence as a reasonable person when relying on the declaration.

6.1.2.2.2 Can the Incentive Regulatory Framework Targeted at a Specific Group of Investors Per Se Be the Basis of Legitimate Expectation, or Does It Need to Be Supplemented by Other Requirements? Whether the regulatory incentive framework per se constitutes a sufficient basis for the investor's legitimate expectations is a controversial question. Through analyzing the decisions of tribunals, the *UNCTAD Report on Fair and Equitable Treatment* concluded:

> [A]n investor may derive legitimate expectations either from (a) specific commitments addressed to it personally, for example, in the form of

[62] See the tribunal's discussion on the legal nature of 'the sun can be yours' presentation and prospectus at *Charanne* v. *Spain* (n 13) paras 495–504.

> a stabilization clause, or (b) rules that are not specifically addressed to a particular investor but which are put in place with a specific aim to induce foreign investments and on which the foreign investor relied in making his investment.[63]

This was referred to in the dissenting opinion of the *Isolux* v. *Spain* case, where Professor Tawil reasoned that the legal framework in place at the time of investing, which is directed at a specific category of investors to attract investment to a specific sector of the economy (generating renewable energy), creates legitimate expectations.[64] Professor Tawil further argued that such expectations do not have the effect of freezing the host state's regulatory regime. In fact, a state can always modify its current incentive regulatory regime due to public purposes, but compensation must be paid to the investors for the loss they sustain due to the violation of their legitimate expectation.[65] In the Decision on Liability in *Lemire* v. *Ukraine*, the tribunal also held that the investor could derive legitimate expectations that a regulatory system would be 'consistent, transparent, fair, reasonable, and enforced without arbitrary or discriminatory decisions'.[66] The tribunal in *Enron* v. *Argentina* also deemed that domestic regulations gave rise to a promise to foreign investors as a class and were sufficient to create legitimate expectations,[67] subject to exception clause where maintenance of public order is necessary and the principle of necessity under customary international law.[68]

Conversely, several tribunals have deemed that the legislation per se is not a sufficient basis for legitimate expectations; other elements such as the host state law, the nature of the investment, and the inclusion of stability or umbrella clause in the relevant IIA should also be taken into consideration. For instance, in *National Grid* v. *Argentina*, the tribunal held that 'the host state law is relevant for the purpose of measuring the investor's expectations under the Regulatory Framework governing the

[63] UNCTAD, Fair and Equitable Treatment, UNCTAD Series on Issues in International Investment Agreements II (UNCTAD 2012) 69, http://unctad.org/en/Docs/unctaddiaeia2011d5_en.pdf.

[64] *Isolux Netherlands, BV* v. *Kingdom of Spain*, SCC Case No V2013/153, Dissenting Opinion of Arbitrator Prof Dr Guido Santiago Tawil, 6 July 2016, para 4.

[65] ibid. paras 9–11.

[66] *Joseph C. Lemire* v. *Ukraine*, ICSID Case No ARB/06/18, Decision on Jurisdiction and Liability, 21 January 2010, para 267.

[67] *Enron Corporation and Ponderosa Assets, L.P.* v. *Argentine Republic*, ICSID Case No. ARB/01/3, Award, 22 May 2007, paras 262, 264, 265.

[68] *Enron Corporation and Ponderosa Assets, L.P.* v. *Argentine Republic*, ICSID Case No. ARB/01/3, Decision on the Application for Annulment of the Argentine Republic, 30 July 2010, 147–65.

newly privatized electricity transmission services'.[69] In the Decision on Liability in *Total* v. *Argentina*, the tribunal concluded that 'absent specific commitments, changes to the regulatory framework applicable to capital intensive long-term investments and the operation of utilities can be considered as a breach of fair and equitable treatment if they are contrary to commonly recognized financial and economic principles of "regulatory fairness" or "regulatory certainty" applied to investments of that type (be they domestic or foreign)'.[70] The tribunal's emphasis on the intended audience of the legislative regime suggests that if the economic policy was targeted at a specific group of investors, the investors thus enjoy a legitimate expectation that if changes were to happen to the regulatory framework, they must not be arbitrary nor unforeseeable. Furthermore, the changes should allow the investor to 'recover its operations costs, amortize its investments and make a reasonable return over time'.[71] In other cases, tribunals dismissed the claim based on the violation of the legitimate expectation of the investors unless there is a stability clause or umbrella clause within the relevant IIA. In *JSW Solar and Wirtgen* v. *Czech Republic*, the tribunal dismissed the relevance of alleged representations invoked as a source of legitimate expectations where investors specifically referred to a specific regulatory regime as the basis of such alleged expectations. The tribunal further stated that the legitimate expectation of the investors that the legal regime remain unchanged must derive from a stabilization commitment or a specific assurance, of which the content, clarity, and form shall all be taken into account.[72] In the cases concerning the fair and equitable treatment provision of the ECT,[73] while the tribunals acknowledge the legal requirement of maintaining a stable legal environment for the investors, they also reject the idea of curtailing the state's right to change its own laws, subject to the requirement of not substantially depriving the investment value.[74] For instance, in *Novenergia II* v. *Spain*, the tribunal held that while the fair and equitable treatment standard has an objective core, its application will depend on the expectations that were cultivated and fostered by local

[69] *National Grid p.l.c.* v. *Argentina Republic*, UNCITRAL, Award, 3 November 2008, para 84.
[70] *Total S.A* v. *Argentine Republic*, ICSID Case No ARB/04/01, Decision on Liability, 27 December 2010, para 309(f).
[71] ibid. para 122.
[72] *JSW Solar and Wirtgen* v. *Czech Republic* (n 20) para 409.
[73] Energy Charter Treaty (n 12) Art 10(1).
[74] See *Electrabel* v. *Hungary* (n 23) para 7.158; and *Blusun* v. *Italy* (n 22) para 319(1).

laws and regulations as they were specifically at the time of the investment.[75]

Through cases concerning the regulatory change of renewable energy incentives in Spain, the Czech Republic, and Italy, it seems that under the fair and equitable standard in IIAs and Article 10(1) of the ECT, the pre-existing regulatory incentive regime is sufficient to give rise to a legitimate expectation of the investor that the host state would refrain from fundamental changes that would result in substantial deprivation of the investment, regardless of the existence of a stabilization clause or umbrella clause in the IIA. The host state domestic laws, the nature of the investment (whether it is long term or capital sensitive), the public purpose of the change, and the principle of proportionality are all considered in the process of determining whether the investor enjoys the legitimate expectation to demand the incentive regimes to remain as they are.

6.2 The Implications of Renewable Energy Investor-State Arbitration for Climate Change

While the fossil fuel industry received around $300 billion in 2017,[76] it seems unreasonable for governments not to provide adequate support to facilitate the transition to clean energy to help tackle climate change. Greening the energy sector is an important tool to eliminate GHG emissions and renewable energy is a rapidly growing market. For states that have implemented incentive frameworks to promote investments in renewable energy, the ISDS mechanism provides a platform for investors to request the states to honour previous commitments, regardless of political changes or economic preferences, or else risk compensation. With the combination of international treaty obligations and investor-state arbitration, there is a higher chance that states will uphold their previous commitments to support renewable energy, which in turn will help us transit to cleaner energy consumption. This hybrid mode of private enforcement of public goods might not assimilate typical climate change litigation; however, it shares the same effect – pressing the government to support actions that mitigate GHG emissions. Furthermore, renewable energy investor-state disputes bring another

[75] *Novenergia II* v. *Spain* (n 19) paras 534–5.

[76] Figures from the International Energy Agency, 'Fossil Fuel Subsidies', www.iea.org/weo/energysubsidies/. The newest figures for 2018 are not yet available.

facet to climate change litigation globally, allowing scholars and activists to explore a wider-range of dispute settlement/litigation strategies to promote state commitments to tackle climate change.

Currently, this model of the private enforcement of public goods faces three challenges. Due to the regulatory form of many incentives granted to renewable energy investors, in investor-state arbitration, tribunals seem to be very cautious when adjudicating the legal nature and the relationship between domestic regulations and treaty obligations, for fear that if wrongly generalized, the decision would impair the state's right to regulate and cause a regulatory freeze that would prevent the state from elevating its environmental standards in general. Therefore, tribunals shoulder the difficult task of finding an optimum level of balance between state sovereignty and investor protection, and this has not yet reached an outcome. This challenge could be addressed by certain reforms within the ISDS system to ensure that both the state and the investors can protect and promote public interests. One example is allowing states to bring counter-claims within the ISDS when environmental damage is caused by foreign investors.[77] Another measure is to insert specific carve-out provisions regarding the protection of environment, for instance, deeming new legislations requiring a lower-carbon emission standard beyond the scope of ISDS. These measures allow the state to safeguard its public interest from the invasion of irresponsible investors, while permitting adequate protection to foreign investors that do not intend to derogate the public policies of the host state.

Second, regional interference with IIAs is another challenge. Out of all the cases filed against Spain for retracting its renewable energy incentives to investors, five were decided in favour of the investor. However, compensation rendered to investors through these awards are on halt due to the European Commission's intervention. The European Commission deemed Spain's reformed subsidy scheme illegal and any compensation to the investor due to the previous regime would constitute state aid that requires the approval of the European Commission. Similarly, it also intervened in *Micula* v. *Romania*[78] and characterized

[77] See *Burlington Resources Inc* v. *Republic of Ecuador*, ICSID Case No ARB/08/5, Decision on Ecuador's Counterclaims, 7 February 2016, para 6. The tribunal awarded Ecuador US$2.8 billion due to the damages caused by the investor in violation of Ecuador's domestic environmental rules.

[78] Commission Decision (EU) 2015/1470 of 30 March 2015 on state aid SA.38517 (2014/C) (ex 2014/NN) implemented by Romania – Arbitral award *Micula* v. *Romania* of 11 December 2013 (2015) OJ L232/43.

any payouts to be illegal. The intervention of the European Commission on investor-state arbitration concerning government's retraction of renewable energy incentives makes the development of the green energy market difficult and could also block an effective tool to tackling climate change in the private sector. With the new *Achmea* case deeming intra-EU investment agreements incompatible with EU law[79] and the establishment of a permanent investment court within the EU to substitute ad hoc investor-state arbitral tribunals in certain treaties it has most recently signed,[80] renewable energy investment disputes and contributions to tackling climate change may undergo some dramatic changes in the future. Even the EU seems undecided in this matter. In January 2019, the Advocate General of the Court of Justice of the European Union (CJEU) issued a non-binding opinion holding that the Investment Court System under the Canada-EU Trade Agreement (CETA) is compatible with EU law.[81] Therefore, it remains to be seen if CJEU will agree with the Advocate General's opinion when it issues its binding decision on the matter. It's interesting to note, however, the CJEU disagreed with the Advocate General's opinion in the *Achmea* case. Despite deciding that the ISDS system in the intra-EU bilateral investment agreement is inconsistent with EU law, the CJEU had not specifically ruled on the compatibility of the ISDS system under the ECT. Similarly, this issue also remains undecided within the investor-state arbitration. Although several tribunals have rejected the relevance of the *Achmea* ruling in the recent awards rendered concerning the Energy Charter Treaty,[82] dissenting opinion exists among the tribunals.[83] It seems that the EU is quite determined to reform the ISDS under international investment law; however, it needs to determine what should happen to the pending cases that already exists under intra-EU bilateral investment treaties and under the ECT. The EU's plan of establishing a permanent court for foreign investments to replace the current ISDS could resolve the conflict of legal regimes and contribute to the defragmentation of

[79] Case C-284/16 *Slowakische Republik (Slovak Republic)* v. *Achmea BV* (ECJ, 6 March 2018) para 59.
[80] Comprehensive and Economic Trade Agreement, (2017) OJ L11/23, Art 8.29.
[81] Opinion 1/17 Request for an Opinion by the Kingdom of Belgium, (2017) OJ C369/2, Opinion of Advocate General Bot, para 94.
[82] *Antin* v. *Spain* (n 19) paras 56–8; *Masdar* v. *Spain* (n 19) para 678; *Foresight* v. *Spain* (n 19) paras 220–1.
[83] *Foresight Luxembourg Solar 1 S.à.r.l and others* v. *The Kingdom of Spain*, SCC Case No 2015/150, Partial Dissenting Opinion of Co-Arbitrator Raúl E. Vinuesa, 14 November 2018, para 22.

international law, especially in trade and investment issues concerning international environmental law. However, it is important to consider the pending cases regarding renewable energy under the current ISDS, so that renewable energy investments would not be the sacrificial lamb on the EU's way to deeper integration of dispute settlement.

Lastly, it has not been determined if the renewable energy investors could invoke international environmental agreements to support to their argument that the state cannot abolish the support scheme completely. In other words, when the investor's interest is in alignment with the protection of a global public good, is the state bound to obligations beyond the international investment treaty? In a previous case where the investor invoked an international environmental agreement, claiming that the state's lack of compliance caused loss to its investment, the tribunal did a thorough analysis of the loss incurred and rejected the investor's claim.[84] Despite the negative outcome, however, the tribunal did not, however, rule out the possibility of investors applying international environmental agreements to further its claim. If international environmental agreements could be applied in investor-state arbitrations as a 'sword' for investors to compel states to conform to environmental obligations, we might be able to add a layer of 'teeth' to the current international environmental regime that still largely remains voluntary.

Apart from the challenges that this mode of private enforcement faces, renewable energy investor-state arbitration has implications for climate change litigation in Asia and vice versa. With China receiving the largest amount of investment in renewable energy in the world[85] and South Asian countries' projected energy demand growing by around 4.7 per cent annually through 2035,[86] Asia is becoming one of the hottest spots for renewable energy investment.[87] The Association of Southeast Asian Nations targets to increase the component of renewable energy to 23 per cent by 2025 in its energy mix[88] in order to fulfil its commitment under the Paris Agreement, with Indonesia, Malaysia, the Philippines,

[84] *Peter A. Allard* v. *The Government of Barbados*, PCA Case No. 2012-06, Award, 27 June 2016, paras 239–52.

[85] International Energy Agency, 'World Energy Investment 2018 Report' (IEA, 17 July 2018), https://webstore.iea.org/download/direct/1242?fileName=WEI2018.pdf.

[86] International Renewable Energy Agency, 'Renewable Energy Market Analysis: Southeast Asia' (IRENA, 2018), www.irena.org/-/media/Files/IRENA/Agency/Publication/2018/Jan/IRENA_Market_Southeast_Asia_2018.pdf.

[87] International Energy Agency (n 86).

[88] ASEAN Center for Energy, 'Program Area: Renewable Energy' (ACE, 2019), www.aseanenergy.org/programme-area/re/.

Thailand, and Vietnam providing feed-in tariff subsidies for renewable energy.[89] It has been noted that due to the lowering of the cost of renewable energy facilities, feed-in tariff support has also gradually decreased.[90] Renewable energy investor-state arbitrations in Europe could serve as a learning example for Asian countries currently reforming their climate change and energy regulatory frameworks, reminding states that dramatic changes such as the complete pull-out of supportive schemes for renewable energy may be not only a breach of 'voluntary' commitment under the Paris Agreement but also a violation of investment treaties that is subject to compensation. Furthermore, the advancement of climate change litigations in India and Pakistan,[91] where the claimants invoked the public trust doctrine to compel states to take specific actions against climate change, promotes the formation of a global constitutional value to collectively protect the environmental common good. Through these domestic climate change litigations, certain environmental principles such as the precautionary principle may be recognized as customary international law and given priority in international cases concerning GHG emissions.

[89] ASEAN Center for Energy, 'ASEAN Feed-In-Tariff (FIT) Mechanism Report' (ACE, June 2018), www.aseanenergy.org/resources/reports/asean-feed-in-tariff-mechanism-report/.

[90] ASEAN Center for Energy (n 89). For example, China, Malaysia, and Thailand have all decreased their fit-in-tariff support for renewable energy.

[91] *Ridhima Pandey* v. *Union of India* and others, National Green Tribunal, Principal Bench, Original Application __ of 2007. The petition, dated 25 March 2017, is available at http://climatecasechart.com/non-us-case/pandey-v-india/; *Rabab Ali* v. *Federation of Pakistan* and another, Supreme Court of Pakistan, Constitution Petition __ I of 2016. The petition, dated 1 April 2016, is available at http://climatecasechart.com/non-us-case/ali-v-federation-of-pakistan-2/.

PART III

Domestic Law and Domestic Adjudication

7

'Next Generation' Climate Change Litigation in Australia

JACQUELINE PEEL, HARI M. OSOFSKY, AND ANITA FOERSTER

Introduction

> This is an opportunity to be bold spirits rather than timorous souls and provide a lead for the common law world.[1]

Strategic climate change litigation generally involves using the law and court action to advance beneficial outcomes for addressing climate change.[2] Compared to the rest of the Asia Pacific, where climate cases are a more recent development, climate change litigation in Australia has a long and proud history. The first climate change case of *Greenpeace Australia Ltd* v. *Redbank Power Pty Ltd* ('*Redbank Power*') was decided in 1994.[3] That case involved a challenge by Greenpeace to a government decision approving a new coal-fired power station on grounds, including the potential for the power station to emit greenhouse gases (GHG) and contribute to climate change. *Redbank Power* has served as a model for much of the ensuing climate change litigation in Australia over the subsequent twenty years. Like the *Redbank Power* case, this 'first generation' of

[1] Justice Paul L. Stein, 'Are Decision-Makers Too Cautious with the Precautionary Principle?' (2000) 17(1) *Environmental and Planning Law Journal* 3. Justice Stein was discussing judicial innovation to develop understanding and application of the precautionary principle. Other members of the judiciary have argued that a similarly progressive approach is necessary in cases dealing with climate change. See, for example, the US decision of *Juliana* v. *United States of America*, 217 F.Supp.3d 1224 (D. Or. 2016) 1224, 1263, and the Pakistani case of *Leghari* v. *Federation of Pakistan* W.P. No. 25501/2015 Orders of 4 September 2015 and 14 September 2015, both discussed below.

[2] Catherine Corey Barber, 'Tackling the Evaluation Challenge in Human Rights: Assessing the Impact of Strategic Litigation Organisations' (2012) 16(3) *International Journal of Human Rights* 411.

[3] [1994] NSWLEC 178, [1994] 86 LGERA 143.

litigation has largely concerned administrative challenges to government decision-making under planning and environmental legislation, seeking to incorporate climate change within the scope of decision-making on a project. One stream of this litigation has targeted GHG emissions reduction (i.e., mitigation) by challenging coal-fired power and coal mines.[4] A second 'adaptation' stream has focused on climate change impacts for development, such as the risks posed by sea level rise and increased coastal flooding.[5]

The achievements of the first generation of climate change litigation in Australia have been, and continue to be, significant.[6] Over time – in an incremental and iterative fashion – these cases have consolidated the practice of considering climate change in environmental impact assessment for projects with substantial GHG emissions or the potential to be impacted by climate change.[7] More broadly, the cases have raised awareness of climate change in the public, business, professional, and government sectors.[8]

Nonetheless, despite some high-profile challenges,[9] climate change litigation in Australia has not achieved the transformative impact seen

[4] See, for example, Redbank Power (n 3); *Australian Conservation Foundation Inc v. Minister for the Environment* [2016] FCA 1042, (2016) 251 FCR 308.

[5] See, for example, *Wade* v. *Warrnambool City Council* [2009] VCAT 2177; *Tauschke* v. *East Gippsland SC* [2009] VCAT 2231; Chapter 11 (in this volume).

[6] While first-generation climate change cases have been decided by both state and federal courts and tribunals across Australia, many of the cases with the most far-reaching impacts are decisions of the NSW Land and Environment Court. See University of Melbourne, 'Australian Climate Change Litigation (Database)', https://apps.law.unimelb.edu.au/climate-change/index.php, accessed 28 June 2019. Climate change cases before federal courts have not achieved success as a legal matter but have nevertheless had important indirect impacts on public opinion and government behaviour. See Jacqueline Peel and Hari M. Osofsky, *Climate Change Litigation: Regulatory Pathways to Cleaner Energy* (Cambridge University Press 2015).

[7] Jacqueline Peel, 'Environmental Impact Assessments and Climate Change', *Elgar Encyclopedia of Environmental Law* (2016) vol 1, ch I.29; see, especially, 353–5.

[8] These various 'regulatory impacts', direct and indirect, are discussed extensively in Peel and Osofsky (n 6).

[9] The *Rocky Coal Mine* case (*Gloucester Resources Limited* v. *Minister for Planning* [2019] NSWLEC 7) is a notable example of a 'first generation' challenge that has been high-profile and had wide-ranging impact. The NSW Land and Environment Court decision refused a coal mine proposal on various grounds, including its contribution to global climate change. This decision is predicted to have significant implications for future coal mine proposals in Australia, see Justine Bell-James, 'Landmark Rocky Hill *Ruling Could Pave* the *Way* for *More Courts* to *Choose Climate Over Coal*' (*The Conversation*, 11 February 2019), https://theconversation.com/landmark-rocky-hill-ruling-could-pave-the-way-for-more-courts-to-choose-climate-over-coal-111533, accessed 28 June 2019.

in other countries. Australia, for example, has not had a *Massachusetts* v. *EPA* moment equivalent to that of the United States. The US Supreme Court's decision in that case required the Environmental Protection Agency (EPA) either to regulate motor vehicle GHG emissions or better justify its refusal to do so.[10] On the basis of this decision, the Obama administration found that GHG emissions cause pollution that threatens public health and welfare, and introduced regulations to limit such emissions from motor vehicles,[11] and stationary sources, such as power plants.[12] However, the Trump administration has rolled back many of these Obama administration regulations,[13] which has led to legal challenges under *Massachusetts* v. *EPA* and other legal pathways.[14]

Australia also has not seen the kind of common law actions that have been brought in the United States, which allege government or corporate responsibility for likely climate change damage on the basis of actions in nuisance, negligence or under the public trust doctrine.[15] These cases have faced challenges. The US Supreme Court significantly limited federal public nuisance claims on the grounds that such actions are displaced by Congress's grant of authority to the EPA under the *Clean Air Act*.[16] Although that avenue could reopen if the Republican Congress – without

[10] *Massachusetts* v. *Environmental Protection Agency*, 549 U.S. 497 (2007), 127 S. Ct. 1438 (2007).

[11] Endangerment and Cause or Contribute Findings for Greenhouse Gases under Section 202(a) of the Clean Air Act, 40 C.F.R. chapter 1 2009, 74 Fed. Reg. 239 (15 December 2009). See, generally, Peel and Osofsky, (n 6) 65–8.

[12] Standards of Performance for Greenhouse Gas Emissions from New, Modified, and Reconstructed Stationary Sources: Electric Utility Generating Units (Final Rule), 80 C. F.R. Parts 60, 70, 71, and 98 2015, 80 Fed. Reg. 205 (23 October 2015); Carbon Pollution Emission Guidelines for Existing Stationary Sources: Electric Utility Generating Units (Proposed Rule), 40 C.F.R. Part 60 2014, 79 Fed. Reg. 117 (18 June 2014). In addition, the Clean Power Plan has been subject to challenge in industry lawsuits. In February 2016, the US Supreme Court issued a decision staying the EPA's implementation of the Clean Power Plan pending the resolution of these challenges before the District of Columbia Circuit Court. See Order in Pending Case No. 15A773 (S. Ct. 09 February 2016), *West Virginia* v. *EPA*, D.C. Cir No. 15-1363, www.scotusblog.com/wp-content/uploads/2016/02/15A773-Clean-Power-Plan-stay-order.pdf, accessed 28 June 2019.

[13] Repeal of Carbon Pollution Emission Guidelines for Existing Stationary Sources: Electric Utility Generating Units (Proposed Rule), 40 C.F.R. Part 60 2017, 82 Fed. Reg. 198 (16 October 2017).

[14] For a summary of these challenges, see Columbia Law School Sabin Center for Climate Change Law and Arnold & Porter Kaye Scholer LLP, 'US Climate Change Litigation (Climate Change Litigation Databases)', http://climatecasechart.com/us-climate-change-litigation, accessed 28 June 2019 .

[15] Columbia Law School Sabin Center (n 14).

[16] *American Electric Power Co Inc* v. *Connecticut*, 564 U.S. 410, 423 (2011), 131 S. Ct. 2527 (2011), 180 L. Ed. 2d 435 (2011).

the veto constraints under President Trump that President Obama provided – eliminates that authority, such a legislative move appears unlikely at the present time, especially as the Trump administration uses executive authority to unwind Obama administration regulations. Efforts to use the public trust doctrine in the US achieved an important milestone in November 2016, when an Oregon district court held in *Juliana* v. *United States of America* ('*Juliana*') that constitutional due process and public trust claims against the federal government for its failure to address climate change sufficiently had been adequately alleged to survive a motion to dismiss.[17] While the ultimate resolution of the *Juliana* case – and other pending US common law cases – on the merits remains unclear,[18] these cases provide models for how Australian common law cases might be framed.

Courts in other jurisdictions issued ground-breaking decisions around governmental duties to address climate change in the lead-up to the 2015 international climate negotiations in Paris. In June 2015, the Hague District Court in the Netherlands found that the Netherlands government's 2020 GHG emissions reduction target was inadequate in light of international climate science and international climate policy, and ordered the government to increase its target to fulfil a duty of care to its citizens to safeguard them from the effects of climate change.[19] Four months later in September 2015, the Lahore High Court in Pakistan held that the national government violated its citizens' fundamental rights through delays in implementing the country's climate change adaptation policy framework.[20] Greenpeace Southeast Asia, together with local groups and individuals, also filed a petition that same month with the Philippines Commission on Human Rights.[21] The petition claims that major contributors to climate change, including the fifty largest fossil fuel

[17] *Juliana* (n 1).

[18] Sabin Center for Climate Change Law and others (n 14).

[19] *Urgenda Foundation* v. *State of the Netherlands*, ECLI:NL:RBDHA:2015:7196 C/09/456689 / HA ZA 13-1396 (English translation) ('Urgenda'), affd *State of the Netherlands* v. *Urgenda Foundation* ECLI:NL:GHDHA:2018:2610.

[20] *Leghari* (n 1).

[21] Greenpeace South East Asia and others, 'Petition to the Commission on Human Rights (Republic of the Philippines), Requesting for Investigation of the Responsibility of the Carbon Majors for Human Rights Violations or Threats of Violations Resulting from the Impacts of Climate Change' (Greenpeace Southeast Asia [Philippines] 22 September 2015, amended 9 May 2016), https://storage.googleapis.com/planet4-philippines-stateless/2019/05/5a38951a-5a38951a-cc-hr-petition_public-version.pdf, accessed 30 June 2019. See Chapter 3.

companies, are violating Filipinos' fundamental human rights.[22] That December, the international community concluded a decades-long negotiation process to adopt the 2015 Paris Agreement with the central goal of holding global average temperature rises to 'well below 2°C' and pursuing efforts to limit temperature rises to no more than 1.5°C.[23]

In light of these international developments, there has been increasing discussion in the Australian environmental advocacy and legal communities of the potential to emulate recent overseas climate change lawsuits with a 'next generation' of climate change litigation.[24] Yet many questions about what this might involve remain unanswered. What causes of action may be pursued and which might offer the best prospects of success in an Australian legal context? Is there a need for a 'next generation' of novel climate change lawsuits or should efforts be concentrated on building on the strategies and lessons developed through the first generation of climate change cases? This chapter analyses these questions, with the aim of beginning, and informing, further conversations around the future of climate change litigation in Australia and in its neighbouring Asia Pacific region.

After an initial framing of 'next-generation' climate change litigation, Section 7.2 considers the impetus for pursuing these new avenues in Australia. It identifies key drivers, including high-profile international cases, the conclusion of the Paris Agreement, advances in climate change science, and a changing business culture. Section 7.3 then turns to consider how next-generation climate change litigation might be pursued in an Australian context. It canvasses potential pathways for next-generation cases, as well as their relationship to past and ongoing litigation. A critical question that arises is whether next-generation litigation should displace or supplement the first-generation. Section 7.4 concludes with a discussion of competing strategic considerations that are likely to shape Australia's next generation of climate change litigation and its implications for the development of climate cases in the broader Asia Pacific region.

[22] Greenpeace South East Asia (n 21) 3, 8.

[23] United Nations Framework Convention on Climate Change (UNFCCC), 'Report of the Conference of the Parties on its Twenty-first Session, held in Paris from 30 November to 13 December 2015' (29 January 2016) UN Doc FCCC/CP/2015/10/Add.1 Annex ('Paris Agreement') art 2.1(a).

[24] See, generally, Australian Earth Laws Alliance, 'AELA 2016 Conference: The Future of Australian Environmental Law – Politics, Reform and Community Activism' (AELA, 23 February 2016), www.earthlaws.org.au/aela-conference-2016/, accessed 28 June 2019.

7.1 Why a 'Next Generation' of Climate Change Litigation?

Unlike most other countries in the Asia Pacific, Australia already has a significant history of climate change litigation.[25] Therefore, in discussing next-generation Australian climate change litigation, environmental advocates and lawyers are not talking about how to *start* a climate justice movement,[26] but rather whether and how that movement might be revitalised, potentially through bringing new and different sorts of lawsuits. Some of those potential lawsuits might draw on models advanced in court and tribunal decisions elsewhere in the Asia Pacific, whereas others look to developments in the United States and Europe for inspiration.

This part considers how next-generation climate change litigation can be defined. It then discusses some of the drivers that have generated momentum for investigating next-generation lawsuits or, at least, taking a fresh look at climate change litigation in Australia and how its strategic impact might be maximized.

7.1.1 Defining 'Next-Generation' Climate Change Litigation

Climate change litigation itself can be difficult to define.[27] As Peel and Osofsky have discussed in previous work, a useful way of conceptualizing climate change litigation is as a series of concentric circles.[28] At the core are cases that directly engage questions of climate change law and climate science – for example, corporate responsibility for the environmental impacts of GHG emissions. As we move towards the periphery of the circles, climate change tends to feature less in the arguments put before a court, even if addressing the problem of climate change remains one of the key motivators for those bringing the cases. For the most part, 'strategic' climate change litigation – brought with the aim of producing

[25] Meredith Wilensky, *Climate Change in the Courts: An Assessment of Non-US Climate Litigation* (Columbia Law School Sabin Center for Climate Change Law, February 2015). The only country that has had more cases is the United States, see Wilensky (n 25) v.

[26] See International Bar Association Climate Change Justice and Human Rights Task Force, *Achieving Justice and Human Rights in an Era of Climate Disruption* (International Bar Association 2014) 2.

[27] See, for example, David Markell and J. B. Ruhl, 'An Empirical Survey of Climate Change Litigation in the United States' (2010) 40 *Environmental Law Reporter* 10644, 10647; Chris Hilson, 'Climate Change Litigation in the UK: An Explanatory Approach (or Bringing Grievance Back In)' in Fabrizio Fracchia and Massimo Occhiena (eds.), *Climate Change: La Risposta del Diritto* (Editoriale Scientifica 2010) 421, 422.

[28] Peel and Osofsky (n 6) 8.

policy or social change with respect to the issue – involves litigating 'core' climate change cases.

What then is *next-generation* climate change litigation? This necessarily involves some notion of what is encompassed within first-generation climate change jurisprudence and how next-generation cases build upon what has gone before. In Australia, most climate change litigation to date has pursued a standard statutory pathway, albeit with variations depending upon the legislation under which a case is brought.[29] These cases have generally involved challenges to administrative decision-making (either judicial review or merits review) under planning or environmental legislation raising questions of both climate change mitigation and adaptation.[30] There have also been cases brought by the Australian Competition and Consumer Commission (ACCC) relating to misleading 'green' product claims.[31] In addition, in the broader penumbra of climate change litigation, there has been an increasing number of cases focusing on issues such as the use of hydraulic fracturing for coal seam gas exploitation,[32] access to information,[33] and class actions for damage from extreme weather events such as major floods and bushfires.[34] However, the core of first-generation cases is lawsuits that have focused on individual, emissions-intensive *projects*, which have been brought under environmental *statutes*. These cases have generally challenged governmental decision-making, on the basis of a failure to take climate change considerations into account, as a strategy to avoid or condition the approval of these projects.

By contrast, next-generation litigation represents a shift away from this project-level focus and environmental statutory basis. Next-generation cases are founded on an accountability model, whereby legal interventions are designed to hold governments and corporations

[29] ibid 40.

[30] See, generally, University of Melbourne, (n 6).

[31] Brian J. Preston, 'Climate Change Litigation (Part 1)' (2011) 5(1) *Carbon and Climate Law Review* 3, 12–14.

[32] See Environmental Defenders Office New South Wales ('EDO NSW), Before the Courts (EDO NSW, 2019), www.edonsw.org.au/current_cases, accessed 28 June 2019.

[33] See, for example, *Environment Victoria Inc v. Department of Primary Industries* (General) [2013] VCAT 39.

[34] See the New Lawyer, 'Qld Flood Class Action Could Be the Biggest Ever' (*Lawyers Weekly*, 23 March 2012), www.lawyersweekly.com.au/deals/12695-qld-flood-class-action-could-be-biggest-ever, accessed 28 June 2019; Tim Tobin and Andrew Fraatz, 'Bushfire Class Actions' (2012) 109 Precedent 4.

directly to account for their contributions to climate change.[35] Lawsuits in this vein often embrace a broader range of parties with different motivations than those of first-generation litigants. In particular, parties may not be pursuing actions to advance climate change mitigation or adaptation as a primary goal. Even if they are driven by commercial motives, though, the end result is potentially beneficial to addressing climate change where cases foster better consideration of climate change risks in business decision-making and the eventual uptake of clean energy practices. This trend is particularly apparent in lawsuits brought by shareholders and investors against companies and directors over inadequate disclosure of climate change risk. It is also evident in emerging public trust lawsuits (involving youth plaintiffs arguing on behalf of future generations' interests)[36] or human rights cases (drawing links between violation of rights protections and environmental harms, including climate change).[37]

Proposed next-generation cases may also build upon the first-generation administrative law strategies by exploring causes of action found in the common law or other areas of law such as corporate law. This broadening of the scope of legal avenues reflects both concerns with the adequacy of administrative review (particularly judicial review) as a tool for effecting transformative legal change in the climate change arena,[38] as well as a desire to provide stronger foundations for duties of care to address climate change on the part of governments and corporations. It is important to emphasize, however, that the legal avenues being considered as a basis for next-generation climate change litigation are not themselves novel causes of action. Indeed, legal advocates are often looking to the past to shape the litigation of the future. By turning to old legal precedents, well-established mechanisms in other areas of law, and 'ancient' common law doctrines such as the public trust,[39] the architects of next-generation climate change litigation seek to repurpose these existing legal tools for new climate-related ends.

[35] Merits review and judicial review are also a means to hold governments accountable for their decision-making. In first-generation cases, however, such actions are limited to ensuring that governments meet statutory requirements and act within the law. In next-generation cases, the focus is on how government policy, action, or inaction contributes directly to climate change and holding governments to account for those contributions.

[36] See, for example, *Juliana* (n 1).

[37] See John H. Knox, 'Climate Change and Human Rights Law' (2009) 50(1) *Virginia Journal of International Law* 163.

[38] See, for example, Kirsty Ruddock, 'Has Judicial Review Killed ESD?' (2013) 28(6) *Australian Environment Review* 625.

[39] Juliana (n 1) 1262.

7.1.2 *Drivers for Next-Generation Lawsuits*

7.1.2.1 International Legal Developments

Our starting point for this consideration of next-generation cases is the perception – which has been at the forefront of recent discussions of climate change litigation within the Australian environmental advocacy community – that international legal developments have created impetus or opportunities for new thinking about strategic climate change litigation.[40] The *Urgenda* case – which generated significant media attention in Australia as in other countries[41] – is often cited as an important development in this regard.[42] Even though the legal prospects of success in an *Urgenda*-style case in Australia may not be clear-cut,[43] the case undoubtedly inspired and energized the Australian environmental advocacy community regarding the potential for climate change litigation to achieve policy change,[44] with considerable interest from both prospective claimants and funders in pursuing similar style cases.[45] It is evident that *Urgenda* put climate change litigation on the map for a wider range of actors than those usually engaged in first-generation cases, including different constituencies of litigation funders and barristers, encouraging a fresh perspective on possible new litigation avenues.[46]

[40] See, generally, Australian Earth Laws Alliance (n 24).

[41] See, for example, Katherine Lake, 'What Does the Dutch Court Ruling on Climate Targets Mean for Australia?' (*The Conversation*, 26 June 2015), https://theconversation.com/what-does-the-dutch-court-ruling-on-climate-targets-mean-for-australia-43841, accessed 28 June 2019; Don Anton, 'A Dutch Blueprint for Climate Litigation', (*The Sydney Morning Herald* 2 July 2015), www.smh.com.au/opinion/a-dutch-blueprint-for-climate-litigation-20150702-gi3d5d.html, accessed 28 June 2019.

[42] See, for example, Tim Baxter, 'Urgenda-Style Climate Litigation Has Promise in Australia' (2017) 32(3) *Australian Environment Review* 70.

[43] See further discussion in Section 7.3.1.1.

[44] See, for example, The Courier Mail, 'Climate Change: Climate Litigation Specialist Marjan Minnesma to Detail Landmark Legal Challenge at State Library of Queensland' (*The Courier-Mail*, 21 July 2015), www.couriermail.com.au/news/queensland/news-story/211dc09724cea5c870f49038e6635b15, accessed 28 June 2019.

[45] Anita Foerster, Hari Osofsky, and Jacqueline Peel, 'Shaping the Next Generation of Australian Climate Change Litigation, Report on a Melbourne Law School Workshop' (University of Melbourne, 17 November 2016), https://law.unimelb.edu.au/__data/assets/pdf_file/0003/2292285/Workshop-Report-Shaping-the-next-generation-of-climate-litigation.pdf, accessed 28 June 2019.

[46] Felicity Nelson, 'Dutch Climate Champion Brings "Case for Hope" to Australia' (*Lawyers Weekly* 24 July 2015), www.lawyersweekly.com.au/news/16874-dutch-climate-champion-brings-a-case-for-hope-to-australia, accessed 28 June 2019. Cf. Felicity Nelson, 'Dutch Climate Change Case No Roadmap for Aus' (*Lawyers Weekly*, 16 July 2015), www

Another pivotal development that has helped to re-enliven interest in climate change litigation in Australia (and extend it to other countries in the Asia Pacific) is the 2015 conclusion of the Paris Agreement, which will come into effect from 2020.[47] Australia's 2030 emissions reduction pledge under the Agreement – of a 26–8 per cent cut in emissions from 2005 levels – is widely considered inadequate,[48] and there are also serious questions about the capacity of existing federal climate change measures, such as the Emissions Reduction Fund (ERF), to meet even that weak target.[49] Australia's participation in the Paris Agreement is thus likely to increase domestic and international scrutiny of its actions on climate change. That said, President Trump's June 2017 decision to have the United States withdraw from the treaty and abandon domestic federal implementation efforts such as the Clean Power Plan poses a significant challenge to its implementation.[50] US measures were expected to contribute around 20 per cent of pledged global GHG emissions reductions.[51] However, in accordance with article 28 of the treaty, the withdrawal process will not be complete until November 2020, when the next US presidential election is scheduled to occur. Given the divergent views on climate change among US political leaders, that election will likely play a significant role in

.lawyersweekly.com.au/news/16831-can-we-replicate-the-dutch-climate-change-victory, accessed 28 June 2019.

[47] See Paris Agreement (n 23); UNFCCC, 'Paris Agreement: Status of Ratification' (UNFCCC Secretariat, 2019), https://unfccc.int/process/the-paris-agreement/status-of-ratification, accessed 28 June 2019.

[48] David Thorpe, 'Australia's Climate Pledge Leaves Other Countries to Pick up the Slack' (*The Fifth Estate*, 18 August 2015), www.thefifthestate.com.au/urbanism/climate-change-news/australias-climate-pledge-leaves-other-countries-to-pick-up-the-slack, 28 June 2019. See, generally, Australian Government Climate Change Authority, *Comparing Countries' Emissions Targets: A Practical Guide* (Climate Change Authority 2015).

[49] See, for example, Peter Christoff, 'On These Numbers, Australia's Emissions Auction Won't Get the Job Done' (*The Conversation*, 27 April 2015), https://theconversation.com/on-these-numbers-australias-emissions-auction-wont-get-the-job-done-40761, accessed 28 June 2019; Frank Jotzo, 'Australia's 2030 Climate Target Puts Us in the Race, But at the Back' (*The Conversation*, 12 August 2015), https://theconversation.com/australias-2030-climate-target-puts-us-in-the-race-but-at-the-back-45931, accessed 28 June 2019.

[50] See The White House, 'Statement by President Trump on the Paris Climate Accord' (The White House, 1 June 2017), www.whitehouse.gov/briefings-statements/statement-president-trump-paris-climate-accord, accessed 28 June 2018.

[51] Chris Mooney, 'What It Would Really Mean *If* Trump Pulls the US *Out* of the Paris Climate Agreement' (*Washington Post*, 9 November 2016), http://wapo.st/2fD1MoE?, accessed 28 June 2019.

shaping the US future direction.[52] It also remains unclear whether the United States will ultimately stay in the Paris Agreement but seek to 'downgrade' its emissions reduction pledge, as well as how such action or complete withdrawal by the United States might affect the ambition of other state parties.[53]

Even without considering the potential impact of US withdrawal, it is important to note that the Paris Agreement itself offers limited direct prospects for climate change litigation to enforce its requirements,[54] which are mostly directed to states parties' preparation, implementation and review of their 'nationally determined contributions' (NDCs).[55] In particular, the Paris Agreement does not provide specific legal causes of action that could be pursued by individuals or groups to enforce state parties' obligations under the Agreement. Moreover, the Australian government's initial NDC for the period 2020–30 indicates that no new legislation will be enacted to give effect to Australia's obligations, which will instead be achieved relying on existing policy measures such as the ERF.[56]

Despite these limitations, the Paris Agreement does provide a goal for international climate change action and an approach to achieving that goal that is considerably clearer and more transparent than previous agreements, which could help bolster claims in litigation brought using other legal avenues. Two provisions of the Paris Agreement are potentially pertinent in this regard. The first is article 2, which sets out the overarching objective of strengthening the global response to climate change by, inter alia, '[h]olding the increase in the global average temperature to well below 2°C above pre-industrial levels and pursuing efforts to limit the temperature increase to1.5°C above pre-industrial levels, recognizing that this would significantly reduce the risks and impacts of climate change'.[57]

[52] Lavanya Rajamani and Jutta Brunnée, 'The Legality of Downgrading Nationally Determined Contributions under the Paris Agreement: Lessons from the US Disengagement' (2017) 29(3) *Journal of Environmental Law* 537, 539.

[53] ibid.

[54] The Paris Agreement provides for limited dispute settlement and a weak compliance mechanism: see Paris Agreement (n 23) arts 15, 24.

[55] Paris Agreement (n 23) arts 3, 4.

[56] Australian Government Department of Foreign Affairs and Trade, 'Australia's Intended Nationally Determined Contribution to a New Climate Change Agreement' (UNFCCC Secretariat, August 2015), www4.unfccc.int/sites/submissions/INDC/Published%20Documents/Australia/1/Australias%20Intended%20Nationally%20Determined%20Contribution%20to%20a%20new%20Climate%20Change%20Agreement%20-%20August%202015.pdf, accessed 28 June 2019.

[57] Paris Agreement (n 23) art 2.1(a).

This 'long-term temperature goal' provides guidance on the maximum permissible global temperature rise considered acceptable by the international community. Working backwards from the 2°C (or 1.5°C) target, scientists can calculate the remaining global carbon budget to stay within that temperature threshold.[58] Although the Paris Agreement does not specify parties' individual shares of that budget, it does provide for a five-yearly 'global stocktake' to assess the collective progress made in achieving the treaty's goals.[59] These provisions articulate some broad parameters by which courts might judge the adequacy of a government's proposed emissions reduction actions or the environmental significance of a particular emissions-intensive project. While the article 2 objective is not directly enforceable in Australian law, judges may take judicial notice of it as part of their assessment of factual evidence in a case.[60] For instance, an understanding of the long-term temperature goal and how it relates to global carbon budgets could inform judicial evaluation of evidence regarding factual questions such as how much a particular project or a particular entity's activities can contribute to GHG emissions and climate change.[61]

A second key provision of the Paris Agreement is art 4.1, which provides that

> [i]n order to achieve the long-term temperature goal set out in Article 2, Parties aim to reach global peaking of greenhouse gas emissions as soon as possible, recognizing that peaking will take longer for developing country Parties, and to undertake rapid reductions thereafter in accordance with best available science, so as to achieve a balance between anthropogenic

[58] See Malte Meinshausen and others, 'Greenhouse-Gas Emission Targets for Limiting Global Warming to 2°C' (2009) 458 *Nature* 1158; Sivan Kartha, 'Implications for Australia of a 1.5°C Future' (2016), Stockholm Environment Institute Working Paper 2016–09. In its fifth Assessment Report, the Intergovernmental Panel on Climate Change (IPCC) provided its first explicit statements about the available carbon budget for various temperature targets: IPCC, *Climate Change 2014: Synthesis Report* (IPCC 2015) 20, Table 2.2 at 64.

[59] Paris Agreement (n 23) art 14.1.

[60] Rules of evidence concerning judicial notice of matters of common knowledge are a relevant consideration here. Also potentially important is the law regarding the relationship of treaties and domestic law, particularly in situations where the treaty has been ratified by the Australian government, but there is no domestic legislation giving express effect to its substantive goals and objectives, as is the case in relation to the Paris Agreement.

[61] The *Rocky Hill Coal Mine* case provides a good example: see *Rocky Coal Mine* (n 9) [527]. See also Roger Cox, 'A Climate Change Litigation Precedent: *Urgenda Foundation* v. *The State of the Netherlands*' (2015) Centre for International Governance Innovation Papers No. 79.

> emissions by sources and removals by sinks of greenhouse gases in the second half of this century, on the basis of equity, and in the context of sustainable development and efforts to eradicate poverty.

This provision equates to a call for global action to achieve 'net zero emissions' in the second half of the century – a goal attainable only with a phase-out of fossil fuel energy sources.[62] Although article 4.1 does not provide a precise timeline for this phase-out, it does provide added impetus for domestic decision-making to move away from the approval of emissions-intensive projects. Again, article 4.1 does not provide domestic litigants with any direct legal pathway to hold governments or corporate actors accountable for the climate change implications of their activities. However, as with article 2, it may aid plaintiffs in establishing factual points such as the sustainability of continued fossil fuel development.[63]

7.1.2.2 Improvements in Climate Change Science

Another potential impetus for a renewed interest in climate change litigation is the continued development of climate change science. The most recent assessment by the Intergovernmental Panel on Climate Change (IPCC) articulates the strong scientific consensus on the existence and human causes of climate change, as well as the likely nature of its impacts.[64] In *Urgenda*, the Hague District Court extensively referred to IPCC reports to ground its understanding of the GHG emissions reductions required from developed countries in order to prevent dangerous climate change.[65] Australian cases – even in jurisdictions that have previously displayed open scepticism towards climate science – have increasingly embraced the international scientific consensus on the causes and effects of climate change.[66]

What remains more challenging is linking specific projects with specific impacts, or from an adaptation or loss and damage perspective, linking specific weather events with specific harms. However, scientific

[62] Michael B. Gerrard, 'Legal Implications of the Paris Agreement for Fossil Fuels' (*Climate Law Blog*, 19 December 2015), http://blogs.law.columbia.edu/climatechange/2015/12/19/legal-implications-of-the-paris-agreement-for-fossil-fuels, accessed 28 June 2019.

[63] *Urgenda* provides an example: see Cox (n 61) 6–9. The *Rocky Hill Coal Mine* case is another example: see *Rocky Hill Coal Mine* (n 9) [439] and [526]–[527].

[64] IPCC, *Climate Change 2014: Impacts, Adaptation, and Vulnerability*, vol. 1 (Cambridge University Press 2014).

[65] *Urgenda* (n 19) [2.8]–[2.21].

[66] Justine Bell-James and Sean Ryan, 'Climate Change Litigation in Queensland: A Case Study in Incrementalism' (2016) 33(6) *Environmental and Planning Law Journal* 515.

knowledge on 'event attribution' is rapidly improving.[67] While it is still not possible to say definitively that a particular severe weather event was 'caused' by climate change, scientists are increasingly able to 'estimate how much more or less likely the event has become due to human influences on the climate'.[68] For some climate change impacts, such as those related to increased temperatures (e.g., heat waves, coral bleaching, sea-level rise), scientific understanding of causation is far more advanced than for others.[69]

Advances have also been made in quantifying the specific contribution of fossil fuel companies to global GHG emissions and climate change. Richard Heede's pioneering work examining the share of global GHG emissions attributable since industrialization to so-called 'carbon major' companies is one example.[70] This work formed the basis of the previously mentioned 2015 petition to the Philippines Commission on Human Rights alleging the responsibility of carbon majors for climate change impacts on Filipinos' human rights.[71] It was also central to claims in nuisance and negligence brought by various US municipalities in California against fossil fuel companies seeking both compensatory damages for the cost of assessing climate impacts and adaptive civil works and punitive damages for climate change impacts caused by the business activities of these companies.[72]

[67] National Academies of Sciences, Engineering, and Medicine Committee on Extreme Weather Events and Climate Change Attribution and others, *Attribution of Extreme Weather Events in the Context of Climate Change* (National Academies Press, 2016) 1.

[68] Andrew King and David Karoly, 'How We Can Link Some Extreme Weather to Climate Change' (*Pursuit*, 18 March 2016), https://pursuit.unimelb.edu.au/articles/how-we-can-link-some-extreme-weather-to-climate-change, accessed 28 June 2019.

[69] Mitchell T. Black, David J. Karoly, and Andrew D. King, 'The Contribution of Anthropogenic Forcing to the Adelaide and Melbourne, Australia, Heat Waves of January 2014 (Supplement)' (2015) 96(12) *Bulletin of the American Meteorological Society* 145; Matthias Mengel and others, 'Future Sea Level Rise Constrained by Observations and Long-Term Commitment' (2016) 113(10) *Proceedings of the National Academy of Sciences of the United States of America* 2597; Scott F. Heron and others, 'Warming Trends and Bleaching Stress of the World's Coral Reefs 1985–2012' (2016) 6 *Scientific Reports art no.* 38402, www.nature.com/articles/srep38402, accessed 28 June 2019; Ruben van Hooidonk et al., 'Local-Scale Projections of Coral Reef Futures and Implications of the Paris Agreement' (2016) 6 *Scientific Reports* art no. 39666, www.nature.com/articles/srep39666, accessed 28 June 2019.

[70] See Richard Heede, 'Tracing Anthropogenic Carbon Dioxide and Methane Emissions to Fossil Fuel and Cement Producers, 1854–2010' (2014) 122 (1–2) *Climatic Change* 229.

[71] Greenpeace South East Asia and others (n 21).

[72] See, for example, *County of Marin* v. *Chevron Corp and others*, Superior Court of California Case No. CIV 1702586 (filed 17 July 2017, pending hearing).

Another example is the use of research on carbon budgets and climate change impacts. For instance, scientists have given expert evidence in several Australian challenges to coal mining projects regarding the contribution to climate change made by a particular mine proposal – evidence that assists in determining the significance of a project's environmental impacts.[73]

7.1.2.3 Changing Business Culture around Climate Change Risk

The Paris Conference was notable for the constructive engagement of the private sector in a way not previously seen in international climate change negotiations.[74] This engagement points to an ongoing change in business culture as more and more companies and investors recognise the financial risks posed by climate change and begin to take initiatives to transition to clean energy sources and adapt to a changing climate so as to manage these risks and pursue associated opportunities. While some companies, particularly in the fossil fuel sector, remain resistant to this view and may be emboldened by the US Trump administration and its plans to expand coal, gas, and oil production,[75] the broader shift towards treating climate change as a material business risk has gained considerable momentum.[76]

A particularly important driver for this shift has been the Financial Stability Board's Task Force on Climate-Related Financial Disclosures (TCFD), which released its final recommendations for climate risk disclosure in June 2017.[77] The TCFD has greatly increased awareness of the

[73] See, for example, *Xstrata Coal Queensland Pty Ltd v. Friends of the Earth – Brisbane Co-Op Ltd* [2012] QLC 13, (2012) 33 QLCR 79, [552]; *Hancock Coal Pty Ltd v. Kelly* (No. 4) [2014] QLC 12, (2004) 35 QLCR 56, [214]–[216].

[74] Ilario D'Amato, 'Marc Bolland, CEO, M&S: COP21 a "Turning Point" Thanks to Business Engagement and Demand' (*The Climate Group*, 6 December 2015), www.theclimatechangeorganisation.org/what-we-do/news-and-blogs/cop21-a-turning-point-thanks-to-business-engagement-and-demand-marc-bolland-ceo-mands, accessed 28 June 2019.

[75] Mark Barteau, 'What President Trump Means for the Future of Energy and Climate' (*The Conversation*, 10 November 2016), https://theconversation.com/what-president-trump-means-for-the-future-of-energy-and-climate-68045, accessed 28 June 2019.

[76] Sarah Barker and others, 'Climate Change and the Fiduciary Duties of Pension Fund Trustees: Lessons from the Australian Law' (2016) 6(3) *Journal of Sustainable Finance and Investment* 211.

[77] Task Force on Climate-related Financial Disclosures ('TCFD'), 'Final Report: Recommendations of the Task Force on Climate-Related Financial Disclosures' (TCFD, June 2017).

financial implications of climate change, and its final recommendations provide a new benchmark for companies and investors to use to identify and manage climate risks. Other significant early drivers have been investigations launched in the United States by state Attorney Generals and the Securities and Exchange Commission (SEC) into alleged misleading and deceptive disclosure practices of major coal and oil companies regarding climate risks.[78] Similarly, in Australia, leading barristers have issued opinions on the obligations of company directors and pension fund trustees to consider and act on climate change risk,[79] and Australia's financial regulators have foreshadowed increasing attention to climate risk disclosure.[80]

[78] Justin Gillis and Clifford Krauss, 'Inquiry Weighs Whether Exxon Lied on Climate', *The New York Times* (New York, 5 November 2015) A1. Attorney General Eric Schneiderman, 'AG Schneiderman Secures Unprecedented Agreement with Peabody Energy to End Misleading Statements and Disclosure Risks Arising from Climate Change' (New York State Office of the Attorney General, 9 November 2015), https://ag.ny.gov/press-release/ag-schneiderman-secures-unprecedented-agreement-peabody-energy-end-misleading, accessed 28 June 2019. A further investigation is underway in California: Ivan Penn, 'California to Investigate Whether Exxon Mobil Lied About Climate-Change Risks' (*Los Angeles Times*, 20 January 2016), www.latimes.com/business/la-fi-exxon-global-warming-20160120-story.html, 28 June 2019. See also Jackie Wattles, '*SEC Is* Latest Regulator to Investigate Exxon Mobil's Accounting Practices' (*CNN Business*, 20 September 2016), https://money.cnn.com/2016/09/20/news/companies/exxon-mobil-sec-investigation/index.html, accessed 28 June 2019.

[79] Noel Hutley and Sebastian Hartford-Davis, 'Climate Change and Directors' Duties (Memorandum of Opinion)' (Centre for Policy Development and Future Business Council, 7 October 2016), http://cpd.org.au/wp-content/uploads/2016/10/Legal-Opinion-on-Climate-Change-and-Directors-Duties.pdf, accessed 28 June 2019. This opinion was recently updated. Noel Hutley and Sebastian Hartford-Davis, 'Climate Change and Directors' Duties (Supplementary Memorandum of Opinion)' (Centre for Policy Development and Future Business Council, 26 March 2019), https://cpd.org.au/wp-content/uploads/2019/03/Noel-Hutley-SC-and-Sebastian-Hartford-Davis-Opinion-2019-and-2016_pdf.pdf, accessed 28 June 2019. For a similar opinion on the duties of pension fund trustees to consider climate risks, see Noel Hutley and James Mack, 'Superannuation Trustee Fund Duties and Climate Change Risk (Memorandum of Opinion)' (Market Forces, 15 June 2017), www.envirojustice.org.au/sites/default/files/files/20170615%20Superannuation%20Trustee%20Duties%20and%20Climate%20Change%20(Hutley%20%26%20Mack).pdf, accessed 28 June 2019.

[80] Geoff Summerhayes, 'Australia's New Horizon: Climate Change Challenges and Prudential Risk (Speech Transcript)' (Australian Prudential Regulation Authority, 17 February 2017), www.apra.gov.au/media-centre/speeches/australias-new-horizon-climate-change-challenges-and-prudential-risk, accessed 28 June 2019; John Price, 'Climate Change (Keynote Address Transcript)' (Australian Securities and Investments Commission, 18 June 2018), https://asic.gov.au/about-asic/media-centre/speeches/climate-change/, accessed 28 June 2019.

This changing business environment raises possibilities for pursuing a range of new litigation pathways using corporations and other areas of business law.[81] For environmental advocacy groups, these shifts also open up new possibilities both for partnering with investor and shareholder groups or leading companies that wish to further policy development and corporate action, and for identifying laggards who may be the target of litigation.

7.2 Moving Forward Next-Generation Climate Change Litigation

Given the coalescence of factors described previously, this may well be the opportune moment for thinking about a next generation of climate change cases in Australia and its implications for broader climate litigation development in the Asia Pacific region. In the United States, which has led the climate change litigation movement globally and which has inspired many Australian efforts, the actions of President Trump's administration are spurring significant pro-regulatory litigation as environmental advocates, state and local governments, and individuals challenge his regulatory approaches through statutory, constitutional, and common law mechanisms. These cases will provide additional models for Australian advocates.[82] There is also the potential to learn from novel rights-based cases in the Asia Pacific, although the legal avenues for bringing such cases in Australia are more limited than in many neighbouring countries that have constitutional environmental rights.[83]

While there is considerable enthusiasm for new approaches, how this next-generation climate change litigation might be advanced, including what legal causes of action might be used, are issues that have not been systematically explored. Further, there is an ongoing debate in the environmental advocacy community around whether next-generation litigation should be pursued in the alternative to, or alongside, cases that build on strategies or lessons from first-generation cases. This part considers these questions.[84]

[81] See Section 7.3.

[82] See Our Children's Trust, 'Global Legal Actions' (*Our Children's Trust*, 2019) www.ourchildrenstrust.org/global-legal-actions/, accessed 28 June 2019.

[83] Jacqueline Peel and Hari M. Osofsky, 'A Rights Turn in Climate Change Litigation?' (2017) 7(1) *Transnational Environmental Law* 1.

[84] For additional potential international law pathways (including transboundary harm), see Roda Verheyen, 'Climate Change Damage and International Law: Prevention Duties and State Responsibility' (2005) 16(1) *Yearbook of International Environmental Law* 865.

7.2.1 Avenues for Next-Generation Climate Change Litigation

Lawyers and advocacy organizations involved in climate change litigation have generally adopted creative approaches to scoping strategic lawsuits. Nonetheless, unlike the US and some countries elsewhere in the Asia Pacific, Australia has not seen cases pursuing common law, rights-based or constitutional pathways, including actions in negligence, nuisance or public trust, or raising issues of human rights violations. Similarly, beyond the ACCC cases, there have been only limited efforts to date to harness corporate law mechanisms until recently.

In planning a next generation of climate change litigation in Australia, lawyers and advocates have envisaged a suite of lawsuits pursuing different legal avenues or defendants than have been tried in the past and encompassing a broader array of claimants with increasingly diverse interests. There are a range of potential avenues that are currently receiving considerable attention, including

- claims in negligence against government or corporate actors for a breach of duty of care to protect citizens from climate change impacts;[85]
- actions under corporate law, suing companies or their directors, auditors or advisors for failures to disclose adequately or act appropriately on climate change risks to their businesses;[86]
- human rights, indigenous rights, or (environmental) constitutional rights claims asserting that failures of mitigation or adaptation violate rights protections;[87] and

[85] See, for example, Jolene Lin, 'The First Successful Climate Negligence Case: A Comment on *Urgenda Foundation v. The State of the Netherlands*(Ministry of Infrastructure and the Environment)' (2015) 5(1) *Climate Law* 65; Baxter (n 42).

[86] See, for example, Hutley and Hartford-Davis (n 79); Anita Foerster and Jacqueline Peel, 'US Fossil Fuel Companies Facing Legal Action for Misleading Disclosure of Climate Risks: Could It Happen in Australia?' (2017) 32 *Australian Environment Review* 56. Similar avenues are also being pursued in investment law, concerning the obligations of pension fund trustees to disclose and manage climate risks.

[87] See Peel and Osofsky (n83). See also the recent complaint lodged against Australia with the United Nations Human Rights Committee by Torres Strait Islanders who claim the Australian government's climate policies are inadequate to safeguard their human and cultural rights: ClientEarth, 'Climate Threatened Torres Strait Islanders Bring Human Rights Claim against Australia' (ClientEarth, 12 May 2019), www.clientearth.org/press/climate-threatened-torres-strait-islanders-bring-human-rights-claim-against-australia/, accessed 25 June 2019.

- claims based on common law notions of the public trust, perhaps along the lines of *Juliana*,[88] arguing that this doctrine requires the protection of natural resources (coastal wetlands, water resources, the atmosphere) for the benefit of the public.[89]

The following discussion explores the first two avenues, which are arguably the most likely to be pursued in Australia in the near future; indeed, in the case of corporate law avenues, cases have already been initiated. The rights avenue – although promising for many other Asia Pacific countries as well as at an international or regional level – presents significant difficulties in Australia in the absence of a national bill of rights or other constitutional protections for environmental health. In examining new generation possibilities in an Australian context, we focus on identifying significant considerations and developments, rather than engaging in a detailed, substantive assessment of the possibilities of success. We also address how such next-generation cases might potentially interact with first-generation litigation.

7.2.1.1 An Australian Urgenda?

As noted previously, the success of the *Urgenda case* in the Netherlands and its affirmation on appeal have prompted much consideration of the potential to bring a similar action in negligence against government or corporate actors for a breach of duty of care owed to Australians (or to a particular vulnerable group) to safeguard them from harms caused by climate change.[90]

The *Urgenda* case was brought by a Dutch NGO, the Urgenda Foundation ('Urgenda'), which also acted on behalf of 886 Dutch

[88] That case also involves a US constitutional law argument around substantive due process, arguing fundamental rights violations through a failure to regulate climate change, which likely will not be part of an Australian approach. For a review of the potential impact of this case, see Michael C. Blumm and Mary Christine Wood, 'No Ordinary Lawsuit: Climate Change, Due Process, and the Public Trust Doctrine' (2017) 67(1) *American University Law Review* 1.

[89] To date, there has been only limited consideration of the potential applicability of the public trust doctrine to an Australian environmental litigation and policy context and limited opportunity for Australian judges to consider its applicability: see, for example, Tim Bonyhady, 'A Usable Past: The Public Trust in Australia' (1995) 12(5) *Environmental and Planning Law Journal* 329; Jessica Simpson, 'The Public Trust Doctrine and Its Relevance in Australia (Coastal Solutions Forum Conference Paper)' (EDO NSW 2003); Bruce Thom, 'Climate Change, Coastal Hazards and the Public Trust Doctrine' (2012) 8(2) *Macquarie Journal of International and Comparative Environmental Law* 21.

[90] See, for example, Baxter (n 42).

citizens. The case centred on the question of whether the State of the Netherlands had a legal obligation towards Urgenda (and Dutch citizens more broadly) to pursue more ambitious GHG emission reductions. Urgenda argued that the Netherlands' official emissions reduction target at the time (which was likely to result in a 14–17 per cent reduction on 1990 emissions levels by 2020) was unlawful because it was insufficient to prevent foreseeable harm.[91] While Urgenda pursued a number of different lines of argument in the case, the initial District Court's decision in 2015 centred on the general negligence provisions of the Dutch Civil Code.[92] This decision was upheld by the Hague Court of Appeal in 2018, which dismissed all of the defences raised by the state.[93] In contrast to the District Court decision, the Court of Appeal framed the applicable duty of care in terms of the Netherlands' obligations under articles 2 and 8 of the European Convention on Human Rights as it applied in Dutch law.[94]

The reasoning applied by the District and Appeal Courts in finding that the State of the Netherlands owed a duty of care to Urgenda and had indeed breached this duty has been described and analyzed in detail elsewhere.[95] Our focus here is on the potential for a similar claim in negligence to be brought in a common law context, such as Australia. In contemplating an Australian *Urgenda*, local environmental advocacy groups are well aware of the lack of direct correlates between the civil code provisions and human rights applicable under Dutch law and similar doctrines in domestic tort law.[96] Indeed, prior to the *Urgenda* decision, a number of Australian commentators had highlighted the significant doctrinal and practical difficulties of mounting a successful claim in negligence in Australia in relation to climate change harms,

[91] *Urgenda* (n 19) [3.2], [4.26].
[92] ibid [4.52], [4.109].
[93] *State of the Netherlands* v. *Urgenda Foundation*, ECLI:NL:GHDHA:2018:2610 200.178.245/01.
[94] ibid [40]–[43].
[95] On the *Urgenda* District Court decision, see, for example, Lin (n 85); K. J. de Graaf and J. H. Jans, 'The Urgenda Decision: Netherlands Liable for Role in Causing Dangerous Global Climate Change' (2015) 27(3) *Journal of Environmental Law* 517; Cox (n 61). On the Appeal Court decision, see Jonathan Verschuuren, '*The State of the Netherlands v. Urgenda Foundation*: The Hague Court of Appeal Upholds Judgment Requiring the Netherlands to Further Reduce Its Greenhouse Gas Emissions' (2019) 28(1) *RECIEL*, Special Issue 94; Benoit Mayer, '*State of the Netherlands* v. *Urgenda Foundation*, Ruling of the Court of Appeal of the Hague (9 October 2018)' (2019) 8(1) *Transnational Environmental Law* 167.
[96] Nelson, 'Dutch Climate Change Case No Roadmap for Aus' (n 46); Baxter (n 42) 70.

largely dismissing these claims as unworkable.[97] It is useful here to survey these difficulties and reconsider them in light of the line of argument that was successfully taken in *Urgenda*, and the significant recent developments in climate science and climate change law and policy at international and domestic levels.[98]

For these purposes, we refer to the detailed consideration of hypothetical potential actions in tort against corporate entities responsible for GHG emissions, which was undertaken by Abbs, Cashman and Stephens in 2012.[99] In that piece, the authors foreshadowed a range of probable difficulties in establishing a claim. For example, they suggested that Australian courts would be reluctant to recognize a duty of care in situations where there is no direct or specific relationship between a defendant and plaintiff, but rather the defendant's actions in emitting GHG to the atmosphere 'with respect to the world at large' have contributed (together with a multitude of other diverse entities over space and over time) to the harm experienced by the plaintiff.[100] They add that even if a duty of care was recognized, proving a breach would be problematic, as a plaintiff would be required to establish that a reasonable person in the position of the defendant should have anticipated not just the risk of climate change but also the risk of the particular harm to the plaintiff occurring as a result of climate change, and that the defendant should have taken precautions against that risk.[101] Even if it could be successfully argued that the nature of the harm experienced was foreseeable, establishing that the defendant should have taken precautions to avoid that risk (essentially by ceasing to emit GHG) would likely be very difficult given the social utility of the activities which caused the harm (e.g., providing fuel for power generation) and the fact that these very activities have been long sanctioned by society.[102]

[97] See, for example, Nicola Durrant, 'Tortious Liability for Greenhouse Gas Emissions? Climate Change, Causation and Public Policy Considerations' (2007) 7(2) *Queensland University of Technology Law and Justice Journal* 403; Peter Cashman and Ross Abbs, 'Liability in Tort for Damage Arising from Human-Induced Climate Change' in Rosemary Lyster (ed.), *In the Wilds of Climate Law* (Australian Academic Press 2010) 235; Ross Abbs, Peter Cashman, and Tim Stephens, 'Australia' in Richard Lord and others (eds.), *Climate Change Liability: Transnational Law and Practice* (Cambridge University Press, 2012) 67, 85–98 [5.49]–[5.76].

[98] See Section 7.1.2.1.

[99] Abbs, Cashman, and Stephens (n 97).

[100] ibid. [5.55].

[101] ibid. 90 [5.61].

[102] ibid. 90–1 [5.62]–[5.63].

Further, Abbs, Cashman and Stephens argue that establishing factual causation presents near insurmountable barriers for potential tortfeasors due to the multitude and highly dispersed nature of the individual agents responsible for GHG emissions and the consequent difficulty of establishing that the negligence of one particular entity was a precondition to the realization of particular climate change impacts.[103] They consider the limited exceptions to the 'but for' causation test and explore situations where courts have been prepared to consider a material contribution to the loss or damage as being sufficient to establish causation.[104] However, even if some level of material contribution to causation of harm could be successfully established in a climate change context, Abbs, Cashman, and Stephens submit that it is unlikely that an Australian court would conclude that it is 'appropriate' to attribute liability and award damages for the emission of GHG and associated harm.[105]

Abbs, Cashman, and Stephens's consideration was framed in relation to suing a corporate entity for loss or damage experienced as a result of climate change.[106] This focus on compensating harms already experienced by a plaintiff is the traditional path of negligence law in common law jurisdictions. However, in *Urgenda*, the duty of care claim was not directed to compensating loss and damage ex post, but rather to preventing foreseeable future harms. As such, the remedy awarded was not compensation, but rather a court order requiring the State of the Netherlands to take more action to reduce GHG emissions.[107] Baxter argues that a claim in negligence against a governmental defendant

[103] ibid. 94 [5.67].
[104] ibid. 95–6 [5.70]–[5.71].
[105] ibid. 97–8 [5.75]–[5.76].
[106] ibid. 85–6 [5.49]–[5.50]. This is a pathway that has not yet been initiated in an Australian context. However, there have been a number of recent attempts (albeit not yet successful) in the United States to hold corporations accountable in negligence for their contributions to climate change impacts. These claims have relied heavily on the advances in climate science discussed above in Section 7.2.2.2. For example, claims filed in July 2017 by three Californian municipalities against thirty-seven major fossil fuel companies sought compensatory damages for the cost of assessing climate impacts and adaptive civil works and punitive damages for climate change impacts caused by the business activities of these companies. See *County of Marin* (n 72). Another example, pursuing a duty of care style argument, is *Saul Luciano Lliuya* v. *RWE* Az. 5 U 15/17 OLG Hamm (2017), where a Peruvian farmer is seeking to hold Germany energy company, RWE, liable for climate damage stemming from emissions from its energy generation activities.
[107] *Urgenda* (n 19) [5.1].

along these lines is worthy of renewed consideration in an Australian context.[108]

Baxter notes that negligence claims in Anglo-Australian jurisdictions have, until recently, only ever been successful where the primary remedy sought was damages.[109] He argues, however, that seeking a remedy in equity in the form of an injunction to prevent future breach and damage occurring provides a more promising approach that would potentially bypass some of the difficulties in establishing breach and damage that were noted by Abbs, Cashman, and Stephens.[110] Baxter cites a recent decision of the Federal Court of Australia where a claim in negligence in an immigration context was brought on an entirely ex ante basis.[111] In this case, the court was prepared to issue a remedy in equity against the governmental defendant in the form of an injunction to prevent the breach and anticipated damage.[112] Essentially, Baxter argues that taking this novel approach to a negligence claim offers a higher chance of a court being prepared to award a remedy.[113]

However, even pursuing this approach, it would still be necessary to establish that a defendant owed a duty of care, for example, to take action to prevent dangerous climate change, and that the alleged breach of this duty would lead to the anticipated damage.[114] The factual basis upon which such a claim could be brought continues to improve due to a number of factors, such as developments in climate change science, including the ability to attribute climate change impacts to GHG emissions and to calculate comparative contributions to global emissions;[115] the growing body of international and domestic legal and policy instruments acknowledging the extensive threats posed by climate change and the concrete mitigation measures needed to minimise these risks

[108] Baxter (n 42). See also Tim Baxter, 'Can the Commonwealth's Climate Targets *Be* Legally Negligent? An Australian Urgenda (Seminar, Australian-German Climate and Energy College)' (University of Melbourne Climate Energy College, 22 August 2016), http://climatecollege.unimelb.edu.au/seminar/can-commonwealth%E2%80%99s-climate-targets-be-legally-negligent-australian-urgenda, accessed 28 June 2019.

[109] Baxter (n 42) 70, 71.

[110] ibid. Cf. Abbs, Cashman, and Stephens (n 104) 95–6 [5.70]–[5.71].

[111] Baxter (n 42) 71.

[112] *Plaintiff S99/2016* v. *Minister for Immigration and Border Protection* (2016) 243 FCR 17.

[113] Baxter (n 42) 70, 71.

[114] ibid. 72, 73.

[115] See Heede (n 70); Committee on Extreme Weather Events and Climate Change Attribution (n 67).

(including the Paris Agreement); and the fact that the Australian government has consistently participated in and ratified international climate change treaties and has the authority and capacity to implement required mitigation measures.

Nonetheless, the experiences of first-generation litigation in Australia, particularly in arguing causation,[116] underscore the challenges that would-be litigants may face in launching an *Urgenda*-style action. For example, in the context of judicial review of decisions relating to fossil fuel projects, Australian courts have responded only slowly to scientific evidence and arguments put by claimants that the emissions related to a particular fossil fuel project will contribute significantly to cumulative global emissions and climate change impacts, and are therefore relevant when considering the environmental impact of a specific project.[117] While there has been an incremental acceptance of these arguments and associated scientific evidence over time, no Australian court has yet been prepared to refuse a fossil fuel project solely on climate change grounds.[118] Often courts have fallen back on the 'market substitution defence' – that a particular project 'will not have an impact on climate change, because if that proponent does not mine and sell coal, someone else will'.[119] Similar difficulties would likely be encountered in arguing that Australia's GHG emissions were a material contribution to the global problem of climate change sufficient to satisfy tests of causation.[120]

Further, while the Hague District and Appeal Courts came to the conclusion in *Urgenda* that it would not be an intrusion on the separation of powers doctrine for the court to make an order requiring the government to take further action on climate change,[121] Australian courts have tended to take a very restrictive view of their role with regards to 'political

[116] Durrant (n 97) 414–19.

[117] Bell-James and Ryan (n 66) 531–6. This issue was also the subject of the final appeal in the Adani coal mine litigation; see *Australian Conservation Foundation Inc* v. *Minister for the Environment and Energy* [2017] FCAFC 134, 251 FCR 359.

[118] Even in the *Rocky Hill Coal Mine* case that refused a coal mine proposal, climate change was one of many grounds (including environmental issues and amenity concerns) that justified refusal of the proposal in the view of the court: see *Rocky Hill Coal Mine* (n 9) [699].

[119] Bell-James and Ryan (n 66) 535. Notably, the NSW Land and Environment Court did not accept this argument in the *Rocky Hill Coal Mine* case (n 9) [538].

[120] For a discussion of the approach to causation taken in *Urgenda* and set aside traditional causation requirements, see Lin (n 85) 79–80.

[121] Lin (n 85) 80. Lin notes that little justification was given by the court for this approach. See *Urgenda* (n 19) [4.102].

questions' and justiciability.[122] Indeed, it is worth noting that the Court of Appeal's ruling in *Urgenda* is being appealed by the State of the Netherlands on the basis that the court's decision limits the State's freedom of choice in establishing policy on the scope of needed emissions reductions with 'significant consequences' for the government's freedom to make climate policy.[123] It is likely that similar arguments would also be a feature in any Australian litigation attempting to pursue claims against the federal government concerning its weak emissions reduction targets.[124]

7.2.1.2 Suing Companies and Their Directors Using Corporate Law Tools

In other common law jurisdictions, such as the United States and the United Kingdom, both of which have similar, albeit not identical, corporations law regimes to Australia,[125] litigation trends are emerging against corporations and their directors for misleading disclosure of business risks associated with climate change and for related breach of directors' duties arising from failure to disclose and properly manage these risks.[126] These legal interventions are being initiated by regulators, by environmental advocacy groups, and increasingly, by shareholders

[122] See, for example, *Graham Barclay Oysters Pty Ltd* v. *Ryan* [2002] HCA 54, (2002) 211 CLR 540, 553–5, where Gleeson C.J. discusses justiciability in the context of a negligence claim against a governmental authority.

[123] Government of the Netherlands Ministry of Economic Affairs and Climate Policy, 'State to Bring Cassation Proceedings in Urgenda Case (Press Release)' (*Government of Netherlands,* 16 November 2018), www.government.nl/latest/news/2018/11/16/state-to-bring-cassation-proceedings-in-urgenda-case, accessed 28 June 2019.

[124] Arguments of this kind were also raised, but rejected, in the New Zealand case of *Thomson* v. *Minister for Climate Change Issues* [2017] NZHC 733, [2018] 2 NZLR 160.

[125] For example, all three jurisdictions require publicly listed companies to make regular disclosures of their financial position and any material business risks facing the company. The relevant provisions, their similarities and differences, are discussed in Anita Foerster, Jacqueline Peel, Hari M. Osofsky, and Brett McDonnell, 'Keeping Good Company in the Transition to a Low Carbon Economy? An Evaluation of Climate Risk Disclosure Practices in Australia' (2017) 35 *Company and Securities Law Journal* 154, 163, 164, 175.

[126] Sarah Barker and Maged Girgis, 'A New COP on the Beat: Heightened Expectations for Corporate Sustainability Governance and Disclosure (Alert)' (*Minter Ellison*, 2016), www.minterellison.com/-/media/Minter-Ellison/Files/Article-PDFs/corporate-sustainability-governance-and-disclosure.ashx?la=en&hash=952F257C307B0F1854434B29DDFFAD26F61D26E6, accessed 28 June 2019; *Geetanjali* Ganguly, Joana Setzer, and Veerle Heyvaert, 'If at First You Don't Succeed: Suing Corporations for Climate Change' (2018) 38(4) *Oxford Journal of Legal Studies* 841.

claiming compensation for associated financial losses. No similar actions have emerged in other areas of the Asia Pacific, with existing corporate accountability claims, such as the Philippines carbon majors petition, being pursued on a human rights basis.[127]

In the United States, there have been a series of regulatory investigations into the disclosure practices of major fossil fuel companies, including Peabody Energy Corporation[128] and Exxon Mobil.[129] These have been conducted by state Attorney Generals under state laws prohibiting false or misleading conduct in connection with securities transactions,[130] as well as at a national level by the SEC.[131] In general terms, these investigations have alleged that the companies involved have misled shareholders by understating the severe potential impacts of climate change risk to their businesses. In November 2016, a shareholder class action was launched against Exxon Mobil and its directors,[132] alleging that the company made false and/or misleading statements in relation to the value of its oil and gas reserves, leading to a material overstatement of the value of these reserves.[133] Class members are seeking compensation for a drop in share value that occurred following the public reporting of

[127] See Chapter 3.

[128] See New York State Office of the Attorney General (n 78); Attorney General of the State of New York Environmental and Investor Protection Bureaus, 'Assurance of Discontinuance', *In the Matter of Investigation by Eric T Schneiderman, Attorney General of the State of New York, of Peabody Energy Corporation* (Assurance No 15-242, 8 November 2015), https://ag.ny.gov/pdfs/Peabody-Energy-Assurance-signed.pdf.

[129] Gillis and Krauss (n 78); Penn (n 78).

[130] For example, the New York investigation took place under the 1921 Martin Act, now codified in New York General Business Law art 23-A §§ 352-c, 353. Sections 352 and 353 of the Act taken together grant wide powers to the Attorney General to regulate, investigate, and take enforcement action against securities fraud. In October 2018, following their long-running investigation, the NYAG filed a lawsuit against Exxon for defrauding investors regarding financial risk the company faces from climate change regulations. See Steven Mufson, 'New York *Sues* ExxonMobil, *Saying It 'Misled' Investors* about *Climate Change Risks*' (*Washington Post*, 24 October 2018), www.washingtonpost.com/energy-environment/2018/10/24/new-york-sues-exxonmobil-accusing-it-deceiving-investors-about-climate-change-risks, accessed 28 June 2019.

[131] See Bradley Olsen and Aruna Viswanatha, 'SEC Probes Exxon over Accounting for Climate Change' (*The Wall Street Journal*, 20 September 2016), www.wsj.com/articles/sec-investigating-exxon-on-valuing-of-assets-accounting-practices-1474393593, accessed 28 June 2019. This investigation was subsequently closed without enforcement action.

[132] Shareholders Foundation, 'Exxon Mobil Corporation (NYSE:XOM) Investor Securities Class Action Lawsuit 11/07/2016', (*Shareholders Foundation*, 2016), http://shareholdersfoundation.com/case/exxon-mobil-corporation-nyse-xom-investor-securities-class-action-lawsuit-11072016, accessed 28 June 2019.

[133] ibid.

the regulatory investigations into Exxon Mobil's disclosure practices noted previously.[134]

In a similar vein, in the UK, regulatory complaints have been submitted to the Financial Reporting Council (FRC), alleging that major oil and gas companies have failed to disclose climate-related risks to investors.[135] The complaints argued that the lack of any substantive discussion of climate change risks in the annual reports of these companies did not meet statutory requirements including: to provide 'a fair review of the company's business';[136] a proper account of 'the main trends and factors likely to affect the future development, performance and position of the company's business';[137] and a proper 'description of the principal risks and uncertainties facing the company'.[138] As such, the reports therefore prevent shareholders from assessing how the directors have performed their legal duties to promote the success of the company.[139]

There is considerable potential for similar interventions in Australia and some early experimentation with these tools. For example, after considering the statutory provisions governing disclosure and director's duties and the relevant case law, a legal opinion issued by leading barristers concluded that '[i]t is likely to be only a matter of time before we see litigation against a director who has failed to perceive, disclose or take steps in relation to a foreseeable climate-related risk that can be demonstrated to have caused harm to a company'.[140] Specifically, the opinion confirms that Australian company and securities law requires companies to disclose material business risks to shareholders and to the market via annual reports and other continuous disclosure measures.[141]

[134] See Olsen and Viswanatha (n 131). This action remains underway, the defendants' motion to dismiss the lawsuit was denied in 2018.

[135] ClientEarth, 'Referral to the FRC's Conduct Committee SOCO International Plc' (Regulatory Complaint, ClientEarth 18 August 2016), www.documents.clientearth.org /wp-content/uploads/library/2016-08-18-soco-regulatory-complaint-ce-en.pdf, accessed 28 June 2019. ClientEarth, 'Referral to the FRC's Conduct Committee: Cairn Energy plc' (Regulatory Complaint, ClientEarth 18 August 2016), www.documents.clientearth.org /wp-content/uploads/library/2016-08-18-cairn-regulatory-complaint-ce-en.pdf, accessed 28 June 2019.

[136] As required under the Companies Act 2006 (UK) s 414C(2)(a).

[137] Companies Act 2006 (UK) s 414C(7)(a).

[138] Companies Act 2006 (UK) s 414C(2)(b).

[139] Companies Act 2006 (UK) s 172.

[140] Hutley and Hartford-Davis (2016) (n 79) [51].

[141] Corporations Act 2001 (Cth) (Australia) ss 292–301, ss 674–7. See Anita Foerster and others (n 125) 163–4.

It also opines that, increasingly, climate change is recognized as posing significant material risks to Australian businesses across all sectors, but particularly the resource, energy, and finance sectors.[142] Further, company directors under Australian corporations law are bound by legal duties, including to manage the interests of the company with due care and diligence.[143] To fulfil these duties, directors should consider and disclose all material and foreseeable risks posed to their business and the materiality and foreseeability of risks posed by climate change is increasingly acknowledged.[144] In a recent update to this opinion issued in March 2019, the authors strengthened this view, suggesting that the combined effect of coordinated engagement of financial regulators on the issue of climate risk, new reporting frameworks such as that recommended by the TCFD, investor and community pressure, scientific advances such as those discussed above in Section 7.2.2, and associated increased litigation risk has led to an elevation in the standard of care expected by a company director.[145]

The first case to test these arguments in Australia was initiated in August 2017. A shareholder of the Commonwealth Bank of Australia (one of the four major Australian banks) lodged a claim in the Federal Court alleging that the bank had failed to disclose in its 2016 Annual Report the risks associated with climate change that may impact on lending and investment activities, strategies, and prospects. As a consequence, the bank had allegedly failed to present a true and fair view of its position and prospects as required by governing law.[146] The case was subsequently dropped when the bank released its 2017 Annual Report, which included an acknowledgement from directors that climate change posed a significant risk to the bank's operations and a promise to undertake climate change scenario analysis to assess the associated business risks.[147] Another example is the lawsuit

[142] Hutley and Hartford-Davis (2016) (n 79) [14]–[34].

[143] Corporations Act 2001 (Cth) (Australia) s 180(1).

[144] Hutley and Hartford-Davis (2016) (n 79) [14]–[41].

[145] Hutley and Hartford-Davis (2019) (n 79).

[146] Corporations Act 2001 (Cth) (Australia), ss 292(1)(b), 295, 297, 298(1), 298(1AA). See Anita Foerster and Jaqueline Peel, 'Climate Change Is a Financial Risk, According to a Lawsuit against the CBA' (*The Conversation*, 16 August 2017), https://theconversation.com/climate-change-is-a-financial-risk-according-to-a-lawsuit-against-the-cba-82505, accessed 28 June 2019.

[147] Gareth Hutchens, 'Commonwealth Bank shareholders *Drop Suit* over *Nondisclosure* of *Climate Risks*' (*The Guardian*, 21 September 2017), www.theguardian.com/australia-

McVeigh v. *Retail Employees Superannuation Fund*,[148] which was filed against the trustees of a large Australian pension fund. This case raises similar claims of inadequate climate risk disclosure, as well as claiming that the trustee directors are in breach of their duties due to their failure to consider properly the risks climate change poses to the fund's investments.[149]

7.2.2 Relationship between First- and Next-Generation Litigation

While there is much enthusiasm in many parts of the Australian environmental advocacy community about next-generation climate litigation, strategic questions around the relationship between such cases and prior climate change litigation efforts remain unresolved. Some groups – such as the Victorian-based Environmental Justice Australia – have been actively involved in investigating next-generation litigation options as part of their commitment to 'seek[ing] out new and innovative ways to tackle environmental problems'.[150] Thus one vision for next-generation climate change litigation is that it would constitute a break with the past and an opportunity to put litigation resources into new cases seen as more likely to offer prospects for transformative change.

However, equally a next generation of climate change litigation in Australia could coexist with ongoing efforts to build on and expand past and existing first-generation cases. Under this strategy, first generation-style cases would continue. For example, despite the lack of previous success in federal climate change cases, the Australian Conservation Foundation (ACF) decided to appeal the Federal Court decision in the

news/2017/sep/21/commonwealth-bank-shareholders-drop-suit-over-non-disclosure-of-climate-risks, accessed 28 June 2019.

148 [2019] FCA 14.

149 Environmental Justice Australia ('EJA'), 'World First Legal Action to Test Trustee Duties on Climate Risk filed against $A50Bill Fund' (*EJA*, 3 October 2018), www.envirojustice.org.au/projects/world-first-legal-action-to-test-trustee-duties-on-climate-risks-filed-against-50-billion-dollar-fund/, accessed 28 June 2019.

150 EJA, 'Who We Are' (*EJA*, 2019), https://envirojustice.org.au/who-we-are, accessed 25 June 2019. The EJA supported litigants in the Commonwealth Bank case and have launched further novel litigation against a superannuation (pension) fund in respect of non-disclosure of climate risk. See Michael Slezak, 'Super Fund REST Being Sued for Not Having a Plan for Climate Change (ABC)' (*EJA*, 25 July 2018), www.envirojustice.org.au/super-fund-rest-being-sued-for-not-having-a-plan-for-climate-change-abc/, accessed 28 June 2019.

Adani Carmichael mine case[151] – a case based on judicial review under the *Environment Protection and Biodiversity Conservation Act 1999* (Cth)[152] – as far as possible through the appeals process to try to clarify the requirements for consideration of 'scope 3' GHG emissions under federal environmental law.[153] Public interest lawyers at the NSW EDO also foresee an important ongoing role for first-generation climate change cases. The NSW EDO's recent success in stopping a coal mining project in the *Rocky Hill Coal Mine* case in the NSW Land and Environment Court may strengthen this view.[154] This approach has the benefit of building upon a well-established Australian litigation tradition, and so may have a higher rate of success than more innovative approaches. It also offers an important model for many Asia Pacific countries where climate litigation is yet to emerge; lower profile cases based on 'tried and true' legal avenues under existing environmental legislation – the basis of Australian first-generation litigation – may be a more feasible approach for climate litigation in these jurisdictions.[155]

In Australia, a 'middle-way' strategy would involve a combination of both first- and next-generation litigation. Advocates would continue advancing lower risk cases that build from the base of existing litigation while simultaneously attempting novel approaches. If sufficient resources existed, such an approach would have the benefit of allowing for more likely wins paired with high-profile innovation that might capture the public imagination. For example, in the United States, the human rights petition and nuisance cases brought on behalf of Alaska Natives brought a great deal of public attention to climate change and their plight at the same time as statutory cases and challenges to coal-fired power plants achieved more formal success and

151 For the latest decision in this litigation, see *Australian Conservation Foundation Inc* v. *Minister for the Environment and Energy* [2017] FCAFC 134, 251 FCR 359. This was an appeal of an earlier Federal Court finding that the Minister's decision concluding that the scope 3 combustion emissions from the proposed mine would have not relevant impact on the Great Barrier Reef was lawful. The appeal did not succeed.

152 Environment Protection and Biodiversity Conservation Act 1999 (Cth) (Australia).

153 Scope 1 emissions are direct emissions from an activity; scope 2 emissions are indirect emissions from generation of purchased energy; and scope 3 emissions are all other indirect emissions occurring in the reporting entity's value chain: World Business Council for Sustainable Development and World Business Council, *The Greenhouse Gas Protocol: A Corporate Accounting and Reporting Standard* (rev. ed., World Business Council for Sustainable Development and World Resources Institute 2004) 25. See also *Australian Conservation Foundation Inc* (n 4) [136]–[138], [173]–[174].

154 See Mick Daly, 'Cause of Action' *The Saturday Paper* (Melbourne, 18 June 2016); Bell-James and Ryan (n 66).

155 Jacqueline Peel and Jolene Lin, 'Transnational Climate Litigation: The Contribution of the Global South' (2019) 113(3) *American Journal of International Law* 679.

direct regulatory impact.[156] A middle-way strategy also offers the potential for a fruitful division of labour between different organizations with differing missions and experience. Some groups with extensive first-generation litigation experience might continue primarily to pursue these efforts. Others could pursue next-generation options. In the broader Asia Pacific region, a similar mixing of first-generation and next-generation strategies seems likely as litigants seek to adapt climate litigation for their own domestic legal context. As other chapters in this book highlight, next-generation avenues for climate litigation based on human rights claims may have significant appeal in countries with constitutional environmental rights and traditions of judicial activism. In other countries of the Asia Pacific, particularly in the Southeast Asian region, a first-generation litigation strategy that builds consideration of climate change issues into existing environmental laws may be more realistic.

In Australia, how environmental groups ultimately approach next-generation climate change litigation is intimately linked with the question of its relationship to the first generation of cases. If one takes the view that these initial cases have been unsuccessful and unproductive, then next-generation litigation might be designed to displace these cases in favour of new, potentially more productive avenues. However, as indicated in Section 7.1, in our view, the first generation of Australian cases, although not as transformative as many advocates might have wished, still have had a significant impact. This litigation has helped to build practices of consideration of climate change as part of environmental impact assessment, has raised the public profile of the climate change issue, and has made both courts and litigators more accustomed to climate change arguments and climate science.[157] Given these successes, the middle-way strategy of concurrently pioneering new legal causes of action while expanding upon pathways that have already been at least partially successful seems like the most productive approach.

7.3 Shaping the Next Generation of Australian Climate Litigation

Developments around the world create important opportunities for an innovative next generation of Australian climate change litigation. New

[156] See Hari M. Osofsky, 'The Inuit Petition as a Bridge? Beyond Dialectics of Climate Change and Indigenous Peoples' Rights' (2007) 31 *American Indian Law Review* 675.
[157] Bell-James and Ryan 2015 (n 66).

cases in the United States, the Netherlands, Pakistan, and the Philippines help put a human face on climate victims,[158] and provide models for how cases focused on rights, duties, and common law principles might be framed.[159] In addition, evolving efforts to use corporate and other commercial law mechanisms in common law countries such as the United States and United Kingdom, paired with growing attention in Australia to corporate disclosure of climate change risks, suggest that there are interesting new possibilities for litigation. These emerging approaches create an opportunity for Australian advocates to explore new pathways.

As advocates explore these new approaches, however, it will be critical to weigh the prospects of success against possibilities for negative opinions that could undermine further efforts. The more limited US experiments in public nuisance and human rights illustrate the potential for courts to cut off novel pathways. Next-generation climate change litigation will need to be framed in ways that minimize such risks. In addition, because existing approaches have achieved important successes and may represent the greatest likelihood for positive outcomes in the future, they should not be neglected as these new pathways are explored.

In a context in which current efforts are not nearly enough to prevent the worst impacts of climate change,[160] litigation remains an important tool to push and block government action, and to advance mitigation and adaptation efforts. An innovative and effective next generation of climate change litigation is a critical part of that effort, both in Australia and, potentially, in other parts of the Asia Pacific.

[158] David B. Hunter, 'The Implications of Climate Change Litigation: Litigation for International Environmental Law-Making' in William C. G. Burns and Hari M. Osofsky (eds.), *Adjudicating Climate Change: State, National, and International Approaches* (Cambridge University Press 2009) 357, 360.

[159] A case relying in part on a constitutional rights claim is South Africa's first climate change decision: *Earthlife Africa Johannesburg* v. *Minister of Environmental Affairs* [2017] ZAGPPHC 58, [2017] 2 All SA 519 (GP).

[160] See UNFCCC Secretariat, 'Synthesis Report on the Aggregate Effect of the Intended Nationally Determined Contributions' (30 October 2015) UN Doc FCCC/CP/2015/7 11; UNFCCC Secretariat, 'Synthesis Report on the Aggregate Effect of the Intended Nationally Determined Contributions: an Update' (2 May 2016) UN Doc FCCC/CP/2016/2 12. This report assesses countries' current NDCs and concludes that they are not sufficient to limit the estimated temperature rise to below the 'safe' level of 2°C.

8

Climate Change Litigation: A Possibility for Malaysia?

MAIZATUN MUSTAFA

Introduction

Managing climate change impacts is one of the greatest challenges facing the global community at present. The consequences of ongoing human activities that emit anthropogenic greenhouse gases (GHG) are dreadful both in the short and long run as well as on local and international levels.[1] Impacts related to climate change are evident across regions and in various sectors. At the domestic level, climate change–related harm could include impact to human health, agriculture and food security, water supply, or damage to public infrastructure and settlements.[2] The inevitable climate change consequences have raised the question of who should bear the risk of climate harm, is it the industry, the government, or the private individual? A worldwide trend is emerging where governments and entities are blamed for their responsibility in causing the detrimental effects of climate change. Lawsuits have been filed against legislators and policymakers relating to their approach to climate change, in addition to litigations undertaken challenging the validity of a climate change law or seeking to fill any gap within the law. In many situations, climate change policy is shaped when parties continue to turn to the courts in order to protect their interests.[3]

For a developing country such as Malaysia, economic development is often pointed out to be the cause of environmental issues, as well as

[1] M. Mustafa, S. Z. Syed Abdul Kadir, and S. Sufian, "Coping with Climate Change through Air Pollution Control: Some Legal Initiatives from Malaysia" (2012) 33 *International Proceedings of Chemical, Biochemical, and Environmental Engineering* 101, presented at the 2012 International Conference on Environment, Energy and Biotechnology.

[2] Ministry of Natural Resources and Environment, Malaysia, *Malaysia Biennial Update Report to the UNFCCC* (MNRE 2015).

[3] United Nations, *The Status of Climate Change Litigation. A Global Review* (UNEP 2017).

the increase in GHG emissions.[4] International commitment and global pressure have led Malaysia to take some measures, relying on Acts of Parliament and government policies as primary instruments to address climate change.[5] Being a country with strong parliamentary traditions, environmental issues including that pertaining to climate change are governed predominantly by federal law and enforced by related government agencies.[6] In as much as Malaysia is putting serious efforts on combating climate change, litigation has not played a significant role in shaping its climate change policy. As compared to other countries, Malaysia's climate change regulatory instruments have been slower to develop.[7] While litigious culture is not common among Malaysian society, factors such as the state of the judiciary, limited access to justice, limited environmental awareness, and limited recognition of environmental rights have further undermined litigation in the area of environment and climate change.[8] The aims of this chapter are to investigate Malaysia's policy and law relating to climate change and to identify areas of law that can become potential tools directly or indirectly pertinent to climate change litigation. All over the world, litigation has progressively been seen as an effective means in promoting climate change mitigation and adaptation. This chapter is meant to discover whether Malaysia would follow the global trend or whether it is adamant that legal responses to climate change should be based on its local circumstances using different strategies that are not necessarily litigious in nature.

8.1 Malaysia's Climate Change Commitments

The status of Malaysia's environmental quality is very much related to its economic growth. A number of economic activities from various sectors have been identified to be the main sources of environmental pollution. Excessive fossil fuel usage and changes in land use are considered to be

4 Department of Environment Malaysia, *Annual Report* (DOE 2015).

5 Economic Planning Unit Malaysia, *Eleventh Malaysia Plan 2016–2020* (EPU 2016).

6 M. Mustafa, *Environmental Law in Malaysia*, 3rd ed. (Kluwer Law International 2016).

7 United Nations (n 3).

8 A. Harding, *Access to Environmental Justice: A Comparative Study* (Martinus Nijhoff Publishers 2007); C. K. Gan and others, "An Overview on the Public Interest Litigation in Malaysia:Development and Dilemma under Provision of Remedies for Enforcement of Fundamental Rights" (2016) 7(2) *Mediterranean Journal of Social Sciences* 114; G. S. Nijar, *Public Interest Litigation: A Matter of Justice An Asian Perspective* (ASEAN Law Association, 2006), www.aseanlawassociation.org/9GAdocs/Malaysia.pdf, accessed 1 May 2018.

Table 8.1 *GHG emissions by sector in Malaysia*

Sectors	Emissions percentage
Energy	76
Waste	12
Industrial processes	6
Agriculture	5
Land use, land use change, and forestry (LULUCF)	1

Source: Ministry of Natural Resources and Environment[9]

the main reasons for the considerable increase in anthropogenic GHG emissions.[10] Table 8.1 below illustrates sectoral sources' percentages of GHG emissions within the energy sector, such as energy industries, transport, manufacturing, and construction, followed by waste, industrial processes, and agricultural sectors.

With 0.4 percent of the world's population, Malaysia's 31 million people accounted for 0.6 percent of the global carbon emissions. Malaysia's carbon emissions growth is one of the fastest, namely by 221 percent from 1990 to 2004.[11] Rapid transformation from an agricultural to an industrialized economy in the last forty years, apart from expansion in industrial and automotive sectors, the overdependence on fossil fuel, unsustainable waste management, and forest conversion, has contributed to the rapid increases in GHG emissions.[12] The International Energy Agency reported that Malaysia's carbon emission was a total of 220 million tonnes for 2015, which was an increase of nearly 300 percent

9 Ministry of Natural Resources and Environment Malaysia, Malaysia Biennial Update Report to the UNFCCC (n 2).

10 Ministry of Natural Resources and Environment Malaysia, Malaysia Biennial Update Report to the UNFCCC (n 2); S .N. Salahudin, M. M. Abdullah, and N. Ahmad Newaz, "Emissions: Sources, Policies and Development in Malaysia" (2013) 1(7) International Journal of Education and Research 1.

11 United Nations Development Programme, *UNDP Human Development Report 2007/2008 Fighting Climate Change: Human Solidarity in a Divided World* (UNDP 2007), http://hdr.undp.org/sites/default/files/reports/268/hdr_20072008_en_complete.pdf, accessed 24 August 2018.

12 Economic Planning Unit Malaysia, *Eleventh Malaysia Plan* (n 5).

Table 8.2 *Comparison of the carbon dioxide emissions intensity of GDP in 2016*

Country	Population	Annual CO_2 emissions (kt)	GDP (billions of US dollars)	GDP per capita (US dollars)	CO_2 emissions (kg per 1000 US dollars GDP)	CO_2 emissions per capita (mt)
Malaysia	3,11,87,265	2,66,251.50	296.54	9,503	0.33	8.53
Indonesia	26,11,15,456	5,30,035.70	932.45	3,570	0.19	2.03
Philippines	10,33,20,222	1,26,922.70	126.92	2,951	0.17	1.23
Singapore	56,07,283	48,381.80	296.97	52,961	0.11	8.61

Source: World Bank 2016[13]

from 1990 levels.[14] Table 8.2 provides a comparison of carbon emissions intensity of gross domestic product (GDP) between Malaysia and some of its neighboring countries. As a comparison, Malaysia has one of the highest energy uses per GDP, which indicates a lower economic output to carbon emission. As compared to Indonesia, the Philippines, and Singapore, Malaysia's carbon dioxide emission per GDP is the highest.

At the international level, Malaysia's direct involvement in the climate change process began when it ratified the United Nations Framework Convention on Climate Change (UNFCCC)[15] and later the Kyoto Protocol. While the Kyoto Protocol is not legally binding for Malaysia, as one of the Non-Annex 1 parties,[16] Malaysia nevertheless made a pledge to a voluntary reduction of up to 40 percent in terms of emissions intensity per unit of GDP by the year 2020 compared to emission levels in 2005,

[13] The World Bank, CO_2 Emissions (kt), Carbon Dioxide Information Analysis Center, Environmental Sciences Division, Oak Ridge National Laboratory, Tennessee, United States, https://data.worldbank.org/indicator/EN.ATM.CO2E.KT, accessed 1 January 2020.

[14] International Energy Agency, "CO_2 Emissions Malaysia 1990–2016," www.iea.org/statistics/?country=MALAYSIA&year=2016&category=Emissions&indicator=TotCO2&mode=chart&dataTable=INDICATORS, accessed 1 May 2018.

[15] Government of Malaysia, "Intended Nationally Determined Contribution of the Government of Malaysia," www4.unfccc.int/Submissions/INDC/Published%20Documents/Malaysia/1/INDC%20Malaysia%20Final%2027%20November%202015%20Revised%20Final%20UNFCCC.pdf, accessed 1 May 2018.

[16] Ministry of Natural Resources and Environment Malaysia, *Malaysia Second National Communication to the UNFCCC* (MNRE 2011).

conditional on it receiving technology transfer and adequate financing from developed countries.[17] In 2016 when signing the Paris Agreement, Malaysia renewed its pledge to reduce its GHG emissions intensity per unit of GDP by 45 percent by 2030 relative to the emissions intensity in 2005.[18]

At the policy level, serious attention is now given to the energy sector. This is particularly true of power and auto producers, which are the highest GHG contributors from fuel for producing electricity, refining of petroleum, and transformation of natural gas. The electricity sector on the other hand relies heavily on energy generated from power plants that are fired by gas, coal, or oil. Efforts to reduce the heavy reliance on fossil fuel in the energy sector have seen Malaysia taking a fundamental shift in energy policy through the promotion of, among other things, renewable energy (RE), energy efficiency (EE), and green technologies as a major action in carbon reduction efforts.[19] A transition in the energy sector is also meant to benefit the climate change mitigation regime through reducing the demand for energy and increasing the generation of RE in various sectors.[20] During the Seventh Malaysia Plan (1996–2000), the government expressed concern over energy security and started to improve EE and promote non-conventional sources, such as solar and hybrid systems.[21] The government's efforts to mitigate climate change through RE exploitation have been manifested through the National Policy on Climate Change 2012, the National Green Technology Policy 2009, and the National Policy on Renewable Energy & Action Plan 2010, which aim to generate more than 2,000 MW of electricity from RE sources by 2020.[22]

Malaysia's current GHG emission levels, which are mainly produced by nonrenewable sources, means that attaining its carbon emission target is a challenging task. However, triggered by international legal obligations including that of the Paris Agreement,[23] vital measures were subsequently

[17] Ministry of Natural Resources and Environment, "Malaysia National Climate Change Portal," www.nre.gov.my/sites/climatechange/Introduction/Pages/Highlights.aspx, accessed 1 May 2018.

[18] Ministry of International Trade and Industry, "Malaysia and The United Nations Framework on Convention on Climate Change (UNFCCC) – The Paris Agreement," www.miti.gov.my/miti/resources/Article_on_Malaysia_UNFCCC-_Paris_Agreement.pdf?mid=572, accessed 1 May 2018.

[19] Economic Planning Unit Malaysia, *Eleventh Malaysia Plan* (n 5).

[20] International Renewable Energy Agency, *REthinking Energy: Accelerating the Global Energy Transformation* (IRENA 2017).

[21] Economic Planning Unit Malaysia, *Seventh Malaysia Plan (1996–2000)* (EPU 1996).

[22] Association for South East Asian Nations, *ASEAN Renewable Energy Development 2006–2014* (ASEAN Centre for Energy 2016).

[23] Government of Malaysia (n 15).

undertaken, including the revision of domestic policy and adjustment of law, to reflect its increased ambitions. While local policies and measures are already in place, the pursuit of climate change litigation has, however, been very slow to take place. As much as Malaysia is implementing serious efforts to combat climate change, litigation has not played a significant role in shaping its climate change target. In the absence of a specific legislation that responds to climate change, one issue that can be raised is the position of litigation in Malaysia as a climate change strategy. Is there any place for climate change litigation within the existing legal framework? Or can targets be achieved, on the other hand, by other legal means that are not necessarily litigious in nature? As already emphasized, litigation, through the act of suing in court to attain some valued end, has not been a favorable approach in the Malaysian society. While there is a possibility that the tendency toward non-litigation might hinder climate change related cases from being brought to court, current practice has indicated the preference of adopting proactive and targeted approaches to address various environmental problems through the establishment of institutions and enactment of laws.

While Malaysia has a decentralized administrative jurisdiction comprising federal, state, and local governments, strong federalism through the provision of the Federal Constitution means that most matters pertaining to environmental pollution and climate change issues are under the jurisdiction of the federal government. Environmental policies are mostly conducted in a top-down manner from the government to the people. Since the passing of the Environmental Quality Act[24] in 1974, more than thirty environmental laws have subsequently been enacted, applying a clear-cut system of command and control, enforced by various government agencies. The top-down approach has been thoroughly and systematically implemented in Malaysia through policies that showcase consistent goals that are articulated at the top and the enforcement of laws that are aligned with the policy. The establishment of legal and institutional frameworks on the environment, which have existed for more than forty years, can therefore be considered as the main foundation in attaining the country's overall sustainability policy targets.[25]

[24] Environmental Quality Act 1974 (Act 127).

[25] M. Mustafa, "Environmental Quality Act 1974: Development and Reform" [2009] 2 MLJ lv; Mustafa, *Environmental Law in Malaysia* (n 6).

Thus, being a country with strong parliamentary traditions, Malaysia's environmental issues, including those directly or indirectly related to climate change, are governed predominantly by federal law. Like other broad environmental problems, climate change has prompted legal measures, particularly at the federal level, intended to limit, curtail, or reduce its immediate or long-term impact.[26] Malaysia's environmental problems are diverse.[27] The review of climate change–related policies indicates Malaysia's prevailing policy mode today, which is highly focused on provisions within federal legislations that will help this nation reach its climate goals set out in the Paris Agreement.[28] Thus, while litigation may not be the primary option for Malaysia, direct or indirect measures to tackle climate change can be found embedded in legislations and statutory provisions through non-litigious methods. A number of different approaches are being applied to regulate sectors that emit GHG. They include a front-end approach of enforcing a regulatory system through stringent penalty to a back-end, self-regulated economic strategies of setting of emissions standard and allowing polluters to determine how best to meet the standard. Some of these approaches are examined as follows.

8.2 Administrative, Criminal, and Economic Approaches

In its efforts to move toward low emission targets, Malaysia has taken a multifaceted method within the law including that of the imposition of criminal sanctions for any non-compliance. While liability for the violation of environmental regulations can be in the form of criminal, administrative, or civil penalties, the most prevalent method adopted within statutes in Malaysia is the administrative approach. An integral part of the Malaysian system of environmental protection is the requirement for activities that are causing pollution or degradation of natural resources to apply for licenses or permits, which are the central instruments used to ensure compliance with environmental law. The license or permit is granted subject to conditions and can be revoked if conditions are not being fulfilled.[29] A license or permit is generally

[26] Economic Planning Unit Malaysia, *Eleventh Malaysia Plan* (n 5).

[27] Department of Environment Malaysia, *Annual Report* (n 4).

[28] Mustafa, *Environmental Law in Malaysia* (n 6).

[29] See, for example, provisions within statutes such as the Environmental Quality Act (Act 127), National Forestry Act 1984 (Act 313), and Wildlife Conservation Act 2010 (Act 716).

subject to a number of conditions in order to reduce the effects on the environment and to allow enforcement agencies close and continuous control over activities that are causing harm.[30] For example, the Environmental Quality Act 1974, through the Environmental Quality (Clean Air) Regulations 2014, provides for specific parameters that limit emissions by any specific types of gases, particulate matter, dust, and smoke.[31] Generally, these forms of regulations provide some powers to the enforcement agencies to conduct site inspections, as well as to require production of documents and to take samples. Enforcement agencies have a variety of instruments at their disposal to control compliance. Thus, while the law provides for regulatory actions that involve prosecution through the courts, they also contain mechanisms that allow for less severe actions to be taken before recourse to criminal law sanctions is taken through the issuance of a prohibition order to require the activity to stop or to require the polluter to submit a plan for improvement to a process or plant.[32]

The main feature of the administrative system pertinent to emission compliance is the ability of the enforcement agency to take action against a person when conditions of the license are breached. Accordingly, such non-compliance makes the person liable and penalties based on criminal law, such as the payment of fine or imprisonment will be imposed upon him.[33] Acts of Parliament that rely on criminal sanction thus far prevail over other forms of sanction: the majority of environmental cases that have been brought to court were based on criminal prosecution pursuant to statutes instead of private lawsuits.[34] The imposition of criminal liability for environmental harms that can directly or indirectly contribute to climate change has existed since the passing of the Environmental Quality Act in 1974.[35] Continuous amendment of the law to make the penalty more stringent has caused polluters to face heavier fines for activities that would have constituted legitimate practices over a few decades ago. Cases such as *Pendakwa*

[30] Mustafa, *Environmental Law in Malaysia* (n 6)

[31] Environmental Quality (Clean Air) Regulations 2014, PU(A) 151/2014.

[32] M. Mustafa, "Legal Solutions to Air Pollution Control in Malaysia," in Sara Hsu (ed.), *Routledge Handbook of Sustainable Development in Asia* (Routledge 2018).

[33] M. Mustafa and M. Ariffin, "A Review on Environmental Forensics and Environmental Law in the Malaysian Perspective," in A. Z. Aris and others (eds.), *From Sources to Solution* (Springer 2014).

[34] M. Mustafa and N. S. Mohammed, "The Development of Environmental Crime and Sanction in Malaysia" (2015) 11(25) *European Scientific Journal* 29.

[35] Mustafa, "Environmental Quality Act 1974: Development and Reform" (n 25).

Raya v. *NCK Aluminium Extrusion Sdn Bhd*[36] and *Pendakwa Raya* v. *Kotra Pharma (M) Sdn Bhd*[37] are two examples to illustrate the imposition of higher penalties by the courts on environmental offenses.

While climate change offenses through criminal penalties have not been directly regulated by any legislations, the law, however, imposes liability on entities that discharge pollution or emit harmful gases into the environment. In Malaysia, the legislative trend leans toward enforcing accountability for compliance on officers of company for the fault of their companies. Thus, apart from owners and occupiers of premises, the law also imposes criminal liability on company directors, chief executive officers, managers, a partner of the company, and related officers for breaches committed by their companies on environmental related offenses. Such provisions could be found within statutes such as the Environmental Quality Act 1974,[38] the Renewable Energy Act 2011,[39] the Wildlife Conservation Act 2010,[40] and the Access to Biological Resources and Benefit Sharing Act 2017.[41] Specifically, these legislations prescribe that persons holding certain positions within a company would be liable in situations where an offense against the environment has been committed by the company. These statutes, however, provide for defenses such as due diligence, whereby the burden of proof lies with the defendant to prove that the offense was committed without his consent or connivance and that he had exercised all such diligence as to prevent the commission of the offense as he ought to have exercised, having regard to the nature of his functions in that capacity and to all the circumstances.[42] The consequence of having such provision is that, in order to avoid the payment of fine or imprisonment, companies and their officers must ensure that activities conducted did not amount to violation of the law.

A number of cases have already been brought to court against company directors for environmental offenses committed by their company. One example is the case of *Pendakwa Raya* v. *Kotra Pharma (M) Sdn Bhd*,[43] which is an appeal made by the Public Prosecutor against the

[36] [2002] 6 MLJ 96.
[37] [2002] 1 LNS 335
[38] Environmental Quality Act 1974 (Act 127) s 43(1).
[39] Renewable Energy Act 2011 (Act 725) s 55(1).
[40] Wildlife Conservation Act 2010 (Act 716) s 124(1).
[41] Access to Biological Resources and Benefit Sharing Act 2017 (Act 795) s 54.
[42] See, for example, s 43 of the Environmental Quality Act 1974 (Act 127).
[43] *Kotra Pharma* (n 37).

amount of MYR15,000 imposed by the trial court. In this case a director of a company was charged under the Environmental Quality Act 1974 for allowing his company to discharge effluent into an inland water exceeding the permitted limit. The Public Prosecutor, however, made an appeal to the High Court to increase the amount imposed on several grounds, including that of public interest. The court, in accepting the appeal, set aside the MYR15,000 fine and replaced it with a fine of MYR30,000 or six months' imprisonment if the fine is not paid.

The issue of whether a former company director can be charged for environmental offenses committed by his company was raised in the case of *Syed Idrus bin Syed Ahmad* v. *Afandi bin Abdul Manap & Ors.*[44] In this case, the driver of a bus belonging to a company was issued a compound notice under the Environmental Quality Act 1974 when it was found to be emitting excessive smoke. As the compounded fine was not paid, a search was made with the Companies Commission of Malaysia, which found the plaintiff listed as one of its four directors. The plaintiff was subsequently charged with committing the offense under the Act. However, upon realizing that the offense was committed after the plaintiff had ceased to be a director of the company, the charge against him was withdrawn and the case proceeded to completion in the presence of another director who represented the company. The decisions in these two cases provide some outlook on Malaysia's position pertaining to director liability in relation to company activities that have transgressed environmental standards and caused environmental pollution. Making both the company and its directors liable through the payment of monetary penalty and jail sentence is effective to ensure compliance. The risk of heavy penalty, including imprisonment, which is applicable to all industries and sectors, can generate greater accountability and directly help toward control of pollution, emission reduction, and subsequently climate change mitigation.

While criminal sanction is applied to impose financial liability over non-compliance with standards or administrative procedures, preventive strategies through measures based on self-regulation are being adopted to regulate industry activities. One of such measures is environmental audit,[45] which is becoming an important tool in regulating conduct of businesses that might contribute to environmental harm.[46] The governmental decision to impose environmental audits on industry as

[44] [2015] 10 MLJ 390.
[45] Environmental Quality Act 1974 (Act 127), s 33A.
[46] Mustafa, Environmental Law in Malaysia (n 6).

a statutory requirement was partly triggered by a concern over small medium enterprises' (SME) activities. These SMEs represent the majority of all businesses[47] and are considered to be significant contributors of commercial and industrial wastes.[48] SMEs in Malaysia, which are categorized into service, manufacturing, agriculture, mining and quarrying, and construction, are expected to contribute 41 percent to the country's GDP by 2020.[49] The application of environmental audits on the SME which represents about 98 percent of more than 900,000 business establishments[50] was meant to ensure that certain industries with poor compliance records participate in environment improvement plans and improve their environmental performance. Previously, one of the main challenges faced by the government was in ensuring that businesses integrate sustainability policies within their strategies in order to reduce environmental pollution, including carbon emission. The imposition of environmental audits as a statutory requirement would ensure that companies would shift their strategy toward green practices by the effective use of energy and raw materials, thus minimizing the negative impacts and increasing compliance of the law. The concept of 'green SMEs' is still new for Malaysia, while at the same time a number of the SMEs are still striving to fulfil the requirements of environmental law. However, the adoption of green practices is already very well received by a number of sectors, notably manufacturing.[51] It is expected that, through statutory enforcement, environmental audits can play a major role not only in ensuring legal compliance but also toward attaining the policy target of carbon intensity reduction and climate change mitigation.[52]

The increasing use of self-regulation as a legal measure is also evident through the strategy applied to regulate air pollution from stationary

[47] M. Mustafa and others, "Promoting Sustainability through Corporate Social Responsibility: Malaysia Environmental Law Initiative," www.irbnet.de/daten/iconda/CIB_DC26881.pdf.

[48] H. Musa and M. Chinniah, "Malaysian SMEs Development: Future and Challenges on Going Green" (2016) 224 *Procedia – Social and Behavioral Sciences* 254.

[49] Malaysia Investment Development Authority, "SMEs to Contribute 41% GDP by 2020, Says Government," www.mida.gov.my/home/7418/news/smes-to-contribute-41-gdp-by-2020-says-govt/, accessed 28 August 2018.

[50] SME Corporation Malaysia, "SME Statistics," www.smecorp.gov.my/index.php/en/policies/2015-12-21-09-09-49/sme-statistics, accessed 28 August 2018.

[51] Musa and Chinniah (n 48).

[52] Department of Environment Malaysia, *Guidelines for Green Industry Auditor* (DOE 2014).

sources.[53] This form of mandatory control of gaseous emissions through voluntary performance is being applied within the new Environmental Quality (Clean Air) Regulations 2014. Unlike the previous regulations, the current approach on air pollution control is substantially different by focusing on sources reduction and design modifications, taking into account factors such as available technologies and economy. Since air pollutants can be emitted from various sources, any type of premises that are used for burning of wastes or processing air pollutants are required to comply with the regulations. Within the current law, self-regulation means that premises are allowed to adopt various types of suitable abatement technologies in order to reduce their emissions. While the regulations are still at the early stage of implementation, it is nevertheless argued that this type of self-regulation is relevant in supporting current carbon reduction objectives as well as in assisting the present legal framework to address the root causes of climate change. For example, the regulations make it an obligation for the premises to ensure that the control equipment does not cause accumulation of air pollutants so as to threaten public health, safety, or welfare, or the quality of the environment.[54] The obligation that is criminally sanctioned under the law renders the premises liable for the penalty prescribed.

Another form of self-regulation mechanism implemented by the law as a preventive measure against environmental harm is the environmental impact assessment (EIA). Considering the large amount of gaseous emission that can be generated from development, commercial, industrial, energy, and agricultural sectors, EIA therefore has a role to play in carbon reduction and climate change mitigation. In Malaysia, EIAs, which are part of the planning requirements, are made compulsory on activities deemed to have adverse effects on the environment, such as deforestation, residential, commercial and infrastructure development, construction of oil and gas refineries, and waste treatment facilities.[55] As a planning instrument, EIAs must be carried out and approved by both the enforcement agency as well as the relevant project-approving authorities. Compliance with EIAs is regulated by means of self-regulation and enforced through an administrative system and criminal sanctions where criminal penalties are

[53] M. Mustafa and M. H. Rusli, "The Position of Environmental Law in Malaysiain Dealing with Domestic and Regional Air Pollution Problems" (2016) 1(1) *Prosiding Persidangan Antarabangsa Sains Sosial dan Kemanusiaan* 83.

[54] Environmental Quality (Clean Air) Regulations 2014, PU(A) 151/2014, r 20.

[55] Environmental Quality (Prescribed Activities) (Environmental Impact Assessment) Order 2015, PU(A) 195/2014.

involved. EIAs in Malaysia involve a number of self-regulatory steps before approval, including screening, scoping, consultation, and identification of mitigating measures. It is also a requirement for the project proponent to have a proper understanding of policies and legislations relevant to environmental protection for the purpose of the EIA. On the part of the enforcement agency, a decision as to whether a project may be allowed to proceed often rests with the project meeting basic requirements of "international conventions, national policies, local laws, regulations and procedures."[56] Some key policies that play a role in the EIA decisions include the National Policy on the Environment, the National Policy on Biological Diversity, the National Policy on Climate Change, and the National Physical Plan. In this regard, EIAs provide an opportunity to systematically integrate climate change and environmental sustainability measures into a wide range of development projects that can therefore be recognized as the vehicle for the implementation of climate protection within development planning and can be considered the right tool for climate change mitigation.

8.3 New Renewable Energy Law

Increasing the RE share in power generation is an important component of any climate change mitigation policy, and Malaysia has taken decisive steps in this regard.

After RE generation was identified in the National Policy on Climate Change to be one of the main measures to reduce GHG emissions, the Renewable Energy Act 2011[57] was passed to provide for a more comprehensive law on RE. The Act also formed a vital instrument to achieve the objectives of the National Renewable Energy Policy and the National Green Technology Policy, which were introduced to boost the development of green technology and which are expected to assist in mitigating climate issues.[58] Notably, the Act represents the primary regulatory regime to increase RE generation and help enhance low carbon economy. In this vein, the Renewable Energy Act 2011 can be regarded as one of the best measures for Malaysia to combat climate change and to adhere to international

[56] Department of Environment Malaysia, "Environmental Impact Assessment (EIA): Procedure and Requirements in Malaysia," www.doe.gov.my/eia/wp-content/uploads/2013/06/EIA-Procedure-and-Requirements-in-Malaysia.pdf, accessed 28 August 2018.

[57] Renewable Energy Act 2011 (Act 725).

[58] Ministry of Energy, Green Technology and Water Malaysia, *Handbook on the Malaysian Feed-in Tariff for the Promotion of Renewable Energy* (KeTTHA 2011).

environmental accords. Alternative energy and RE sources have a huge potential to supplement the existing energy sources that are mainly based on fossil fuels. The Act applies the feed-in tariff concept on potential RE, which could enable power generation capacity to be increased at the targeted level.[59] Malaysia has been influenced by the success of many developed countries, including Germany, where the feed-in tariff has been the most successful tool in supporting the transition toward RE as a cleaner energy source.[60] Malaysia's feed-in tariff, which provides a mechanism for the selling of electricity generated from RE resources to power utility firms, is currently the main mechanism that incentivizes the generation of renewable projects. It is Malaysia's aim to generate more than 2,000 MW of electricity from RE sources by 2020, with two-thirds from solar and biomass by 2030. Despite some technical barriers, the Renewable Energy Act 2011 is still considered to be the best mechanism in addressing the problem of GHG emission from the energy sector. Since the passing of the Act, there has been a significant increase in non-fossil-fuel energy sources, other than hydro sources, such as biomass, solar, biogas, and natural gas. One positive impact of the Act that provides for a long-term commitment between the government and RE producers is the substantial increase in solar-powered vehicle application and biomass production.[61] The Act, which boosts the supply of new kinds of energy that are renewable, allows for sustainable ways of electricity generation from clean, renewable sources. Although the operation of the Act is still relatively new, the feed-in tariff strategy is expected to provide a speedier transition of RE usage and can help the country to progressively address climate change issue. In addition, reliance on RE is expected to increase when the government starts to gradually remove subsidies for fossil fuels, which is also hoped to have some impact on carbon emission reduction.[62]

8.4 Civil Litigation and the Judiciary

As noted previously, Malaysia's environmental protection relies mainly on conciliatory and punitive styles of securing compliance. Most

[59] F. Ghazali, M. Mustafa, and W. M. Z. Wan Zahari, "Tarif Galakan Bagi Pembangunan Tenaga Boleh Baharu di Malaysia:Suatu Kajian Perundangan Tenaga Baharu" (2018) 30 (2) *Kanun: Jurnal Undang-undang Malaysia.*

[60] Anna Bridel and Lucky Lontoh, *Lessons Learned: Malaysia's 2013 Fuel Subsidy Reform* (IISD 2014), www.iisd.org/gsi/sites/default/files/ffs_malaysia_lessonslearned.pdf, accessed 28 August 2018.

[61] Ministry of Energy, Green Technology and Water (n 58).

[62] ibid.

environmental cases that have been brought to court were by way of an enforcement agency applying criminal sanctions against those who violated the law.[63] However, unlike some other countries such as India, where individual citizens or voluntary organizations can litigate on issues such as public health and nuisance based on statutes,[64] Malaysia has to rely on the common law to allow individual claims to be brought for a wide range of environmental wrongs. There have been a number of civil litigations in respect of environmentally related matters based on tort. One of the earliest decided case was *McGowan & Another* v. *Wong Shee Fun & Another*,[65] where a tort action was taken against the defendants for causing damage to the plaintiff's stream by failing to take all reasonable steps to prevent siltation of that stream. In *Renal Link (KL) Sdn Bhd* v. *Dato' Dr Harman Singh*,[66] an action was taken against the appellant for emitting noxious and toxic fumes and gases to the detriment of respondent's beneficial use of his premises.

One factor pertinent to environmental litigation worth discussing is locus standi. In Malaysia, in order to litigate, a person must go through the procedural hurdle of showing locus standi, which stipulates that if all members of the community suffer equally, none may sue because it is an inconvenience common to everyone.[67] The rationale is to prevent a multiplicity of actions for if one is allowed to sue, others will do the same. Thus only a person who can show peculiar damage suffered by him over and above the ordinary inconvenience faced by the public in general may have the standing to sue. In the past, the courts had adopted a much narrower approach in dealing with the issue of locus standi, as illustrated from the decision of *Government of Malaysia* v. *Lim Kit Siang, United Engineering (M) Berhad* v. *Lim Kit Siang*,[68] where it was held that the defendant had no locus standi, as he had failed to show that his private right had been infringed or that he had

[63] Mustafa and Mohammed (n 34).

[64] S. Deva, "Public Interest Litigation in India:A Critical Review" (2009) 1 *Civil Justice Quarterly* 19.

[65] [1966] 1 MLJ 1 (HC).

[66] [1997] 2 MLJ 373 (CA).

[67] For example, see the judgments in *R* v. *Lloyd* (1802) 4 Esp 200 and *Attorney-General* v. *PYA Quarries* [1957] 2 *QB* 169 (CA).

[68] [1988] 2 MLJ 12 (SC). This judgment has been followed in other cases, such as *Abdul Razak Ahmad* v. *Kerajaan Negeri Johor* [1994] 2 MLJ 297 (HC), *Abdul Razak Ahmad* v. *Majlis Bandaraya Johor Baru* [1995] 2 *AMR* 1174 (HC), *Lee Freddie* v. *Majlis Perbandaran Petaling Jaya* [1994] 3 MLJ 640 (HC), and *Kajing Tubek & Ors.* v. *Ekran Bhd. & Ors.* [1996] 2 MLJ 388 (HC).

suffered a special damage.[69] There is, however, a shift with regard to locus standi when the Federal Court in the case of *Malaysian Trade Union Congress (MTUC)* v. *Menteri Tenaga, Air and Komunikasi*[70] widened the test of locus standi when the facts of the case showed that the case was concerning public interest. The Federal Court, in reviewing the test for locus standi, made a ruling that a person needs at least a genuine interest in an issue but no longer needs to prove that his rights are affected.[71] The Court's decision is considered significant for setting aside the test of locus standi as decided by the Supreme Court in the earlier case of *Government of Malaysia* v. *Lim Kit Siang, United Engineering (M) Berhad* v. *Lim Kit Siang.*[72] By virtue of the Federal Court's decision, the scope of locus standi, which limits the public's access to the court, is now revised by allowing a person to bring his case without the necessity of establishing the infringement of a private right or the suffering of special damage. This decision is being lauded not only for removing the difficult standard of locus standi previously laid down in the *Lim Kit Siang*'s case but also in widening its scope, in that any person who has a genuine interest in an issue may claim without the need to prove special damage. In relation to environmental justice, the Federal Court's decision can pave the way for public interest litigation to be taken up more liberally and provide the opportunity for any individuals or civil society organizations to obtain redress for any activities taking place that are detrimental to public welfare, including those related to climate change.

Malaysia's environmental litigation, or the lack of it, has become a topic of academic discussions for a number of years. The prevailing weaknesses within the legal system and the tendency of Malaysian society not to rely on litigation are among the reasons given for the small number of lawsuits being filed in court.[73] Judicial attitudes toward environmental cases have often been cited as some of the main factors that undermine the implementation of environmental litigation in Malaysia. Judges have long had a central role in enforcing the law for the sake of environmental protection and ensuring access to justice. Thus, when the environmental courts were established in Malaysia in 2012, not only did this have a tremendous

[69] *Lim Kit Siang*, ibid. 20–5 (Salleh Abas LP), 31 (Abdul Hamid Omar CJ [Malaya]), 40 (Hashim Yeop Sani SCJ).

[70] [2014] 3 MLJ 145 (FC).

[71] [2014] 3 MLJ 145 (FC) [53], [57]–[59].

[72] Lim Kit Siang (n 68). This judgment has been followed in other cases such as *Abdul Razak Ahmad v. Kerajaan Negeri Johor* (n 68), *Abdul Razak Ahmad v. Majlis Bandaraya Johor Baru* (n 68), Lee Freddie (n 68), and Kajing Tubek (n 68).

[73] Harding (n 8), Gan and others (n 8), Nijar (n 8).

impact on the environmental attitude of the public, but it also helped improved judges' capacity and awareness on environmental issues.[74]

Table 8.3 *Environmental courts' caseload, 2016, for offenses under the Wildlife Conservation Act 2010 and the International Trade in Endangered Species Act 2008*[75]

State	No. of cases prosecuted
Headquarters	21
Perlis	1
Kedah	3
Penang	0
Perak	4
Selangor	1
Negeri Sembilan	2
Melaka	1
Johor	10
Pahang	10
Terengganu	8
Kelantan	1
Total	62

Source: Department of Wildlife Malaysia[76]

Generally, the main purpose of establishing the environmental courts is for ensuring the uniformity of decision-making on environmental cases, besides improving the administration of justice. Then Chief Justice Tun Arifin Zakaria, in his speech for the Opening of the Legal Year 2017,[77] said that the objective of implementing a nationwide environmental court is to ensure that "access is available to the population at large to lodge grievances or file claims seeking redress for a wide range of complaints."[78] The

[74] M. Mustafa, "Tangani Isu Alam Sekitar Berteras Integriti" (*Berita Harian*, 11 August 2017), www.bharian.com.my/taxonomy/term/10/2017/08/310966/tangani-isu-alam-sekitar-berteras-integriti, accessed 1 May 2018.

[75] Wildlife Conservation Act 2010 (Act 716) and International Trade in Endangered Species Act 2008 (Act 686).

[76] Department of Wildlife and National Parks Peninsular Malaysia, *Annual Report 2016* (Department of Wildlife and National Parks Peninsular Malaysia 2016), www.wildlife.gov.my/images/document/penerbitan/laporantahunan/LP2016%20-%2020022018.pdf, accessed 1 May 2018.

[77] "Chief Justice's Speech for The Opening of The Legal Year 2017," [2017] 1 MLJ i.

[78] [2017] 1 MLJ i [39].

Table 8.4 *Environmental courts' decisions for offenses under the Environmental Quality Act 1974 and its subsidiary legislations (January–March 2018)*

Name of company/ individual	Provisions of the law	Penalty imposed
Desa Kim Long Palm Oil Mills Sdn. Bhd.	Section 16(1) of the Act	MYR25,000 fine for the first charge and MYR20,000 fine for second to fourth charges. (Total fine MYR85,000)
Hompton Development Sdn. Bhd.	Section 34A of the Act	MYR30,000 fine.
Megatrax Plastic Sdn. Bhd.	Sections 18 and 34A of the Act	MYR80,000 fine or 24 months' imprisonment if unpaid, and MYR20,000 fine or 8 months' imprisonment if unpaid, for the violation of the respective sections.
Petronas Dagangan Bhd.	Section 27 of the Act	MYR60,000 fine.
Recron (Malaysia) Sdn. Bhd.	Section 25 of the Act	MYR50,000 fine for the first charge and MYR20,000 fine for the second charge, or 5 months' imprisonment if unpaid.
Agenda Jernih Sdn. Bhd.	Section 29A of the Act	MYR10,000 fine.
Fitri Ariff bin Mohd Afif	Section 22 of the Act	MYR1,000 fine or 1 month's imprisonment if unpaid.
Md. Sharham bin Shariff	Section 22 of the Act	MYR300 fine or 1 week's imprisonment if unpaid.

Table 8.4 (*cont.*)

Name of company/ individual	Provisions of the law	Penalty imposed
Ong Chin Hong	Regulation 10 of the Environmental Quality (Petrol Emissions) Regulations 1996[79]	MYR700 fine or 1 month's imprisonment if unpaid.
PE Plus Industries Sdn. Bhd.	Regulations 11, 12, 7, and 4 of the Environmental Quality (Industrial Effluent) Regulations 2009[80]	MYR20,000 fine or 1 month's imprisonment if unpaid for the first and second charges, respectively.
Sri Ulu Langat Palm Oil Mill Sdn. Bhd.	Sections 16 And 49 of the Act	MYR15,000 fine or 5 months' imprisonment if unpaid for the first and second charges, respectively.
Tex Cycle P2 Sdn. Bhd.	Section 16 of the Act	MYR12,000 fine or 6 months' imprisonment if unpaid for first and second charges, respectively.

Source: Department of Environment Malaysia[81]

timeline set for the disposal of environmental cases is six months from the date of registration. From the date of its establishment in 2012 until 2017, the courts disposed a total of 438 out of 440 cases filed, with the rate of disposal within six months standing at 99.5 percent. Tables 8.3 and 8.4 provide an overview of some decided cases of the environmental courts based on related laws.

[79] Environmental Quality (Petrol Emissions) Regulations 1996, PU(A) 543/1996.
[80] Environmental Quality (Industrial Effluent) Regulations 2009, PU(A) 434/2009.
[81] Department of Environment Malaysia, "Court Case Preview," www.doe.gov.my/portalv1/en/category/info-laporan/paparan-kes-mahkamah, accessed 1 May 2018.

The scope of the Constitution is another concern raised by the then Chief Justice.[82] As the supreme law of the land, the Federal Constitution has a great influence over the nature of environmental jurisdiction and administration in the country, including that concerning environmental rights.[83] While the Federal Constitution does not have any specific provisions relating to environmental rights, it does, however, contain a provision on fundamental liberties under Article 5. Attempts have been made in a number of cases to construct the wording of Article 5 liberally to allow for the right to a healthy environment. One example is the observation of Justice Mahadev Shankar in the case of *Sinuri bin Tubar* v. *Syarikat East Johor Sawmills Sdn Bhd*,[84] when he said that "human calls for nature do not wait for governments to function. Clean water is a birthright of every human being as much as clean air."[85] The decision of *Tan Teck Seng* v. *Suruhanjaya Perkhidmatan Pendidikan & Anor*,[86] which was also based on Article 5, has been noted by the then Chief Justice.[87] According to his Lordship, the Malaysian Constitution has always recognized that the protection on the environment is based on the interpretation of Article 5. The most ideal position, according to him, is for the Constitution to be amended "to expressly include a right to a clean and healthy environment as is found in numerous other modern constitutions."[88]

Previously, the Malaysian judiciary has often been criticized regarding its attitude in relation to environmental protection. Some writers argued that the court was being ultra-conservative[89] and had a tendency to be reluctant, for example, to question the substantive validity of environmental decisions, preferring instead to concentrate on questions of procedural irregularity.[90] The judiciary's lack of seriousness with regard to domestic and international environmental issues can be perceived

[82] "Chief Justice's Speech for the Opening of the Legal Year 2017" (n 77) [30].

[83] M. Mustafa, "Environmental Quality Act 1974: A Tool toward the Implementation and Achievement of Malaysia's Environmental Policy" (2011) 19(1) *IIUM Law Journal* 1.

[84] [1987] 1 MLJ 315 (HC).

[85] [1987] 1 MLJ 315 319.

[86] [1996] 1 MLJ 261 (CA).

[87] "Chief Justice's Speech for the Opening of the Legal Year 2017" (n 77) [30].

[88] ibid [31].

[89] It has been argued, for example, by Wu Min Aun, *The Malaysian Legal System* (Pearson 1990), that the Malaysian court in tradition is rather conservation and disinclined to venture into the area of legislative and executive policies, or in a case of conflict between the individual and state.

[90] Such attitude is reflected in the judgment of *Kajing Tubek* (n 68), where the judge was disinclined to discuss the issue of the constitutionality of the Environmental Quality Act

from the then Chief Justice's annual speech during the Opening of the Legal Year 2017.[91] When the environmental courts were established, steps were taken to improve the courts' efficacy in various areas, including to increase judges' environmental awareness.[92] Until now, the environmental courts have yet to receive any case that is directly concerned with climate change. One civil case so far that indirectly relates to climate change is *Tenaga Nasional Bhd* v. *Jeffry bin Hassan & Ors.*[93] In this case, the court's attention was directed to the importance of a project implemented under various policies such as the Fuel Diversification Policy, the Green Technology Policy, and the Tenth Malaysia Plan for the purpose of encouraging RE to generate electricity to industries.[94] Specifically, the plaintiff, in applying for an injunction against the defendants, had asked the court to consider the importance of a hydroelectric project in relation to the public interest. This is due to the fact that the project has received recognition by the UNFCCC in terms of quality and is beneficial to the public and the environment. It is necessary to highlight that one of the highest penalties ever imposed by the environmental court was in the case of *Public Prosecutor* v. *Azmi Bin Ismail & Din A/L Chilih.*[95] This is a case pertaining to the keeping of parts of totally protected wildlife without special permit under the Wildlife Conservation Act 2010.[96] The court in this case found the accused persons to be liable and imposed a fine of MYR1,200,000 or an imprisonment of 24 months, should the fine not be paid.

Several observations could be made from the decisions in these two cases relating to the courts' attitude in dealing with environmental-related issues. While *Tenaga Nasional Bhd* is not a case that directly concerns climate change, it is pertinent in demonstrating the possible difficulty facing the court in having to decide between conflicting public interest issues which are not uncommon in Malaysia. In this case, a counter-application was filed by the defendants against the plaintiff to claim the rights of native title on a plot of land upon which the plaintiff

1974 (Act 127). The court's attitude in this case toward environmental protection has also been criticized by G. S. Nijar in "The Bakun DamCase, A Critique," [1997] 3 MLJ clxxix.

91 "Chief Justice's Speech for the Opening of the Legal Year 2017" (n 77).

92 Malaysian Judiciary, *The Malaysian Judiciary Yearbook 2012* (Registry of the Federal Court Malaysia 2013), www.kehakiman.gov.my/sites/default/files/WJD000836%20Msian%20judiciady.pdf, accessed 1 May 2018.

93 [2016] MLJU 1376 (HC).

94 [2016] MLJU 1376 (HC) [15].

95 Temerloh Sessions, Court (2017), unpublished.

96 Wildlife Conservation Act 2010 (Act 716).

would be constructing a hydro-electric dam. In this case, the defendants raised the issue of their rights of customary land as indigenous people and asked the court to prioritize such rights. The plaintiff, on the other hand, argued that the project was an environmentally friendly project, was an initiative by the government, was recognized by UNFCCC, and was meant to reduce Malaysia's dependence on fossil fuels. In this case, the court acknowledged the recognition of indigenous rights on customary land. However, since defendants' claim of right to the land was not proven, and since the injunction they sought was on a different hydro-electric project, the court subsequently dismissed the counter-application and allowed the plaintiff to proceed to conduct the downstream impact survey on the land.[97]

In the *Azmi Bin Ismail* case, the penalty imposed, which is one of the highest so far imposed by an environmental court, could be construed as a sign of the courts' increasing willingness to issue strict punishment fines for environmental cases. Previously, fines relating to environmental offenses were very low and failed to make any deterrent effect on offenders. There were also some criticisms that the courts have imposed mainly fines and not imprisonment or meted out a lenient fine not reflecting seriousness of environmental offense. In recent years, Parliament has been constantly raising the maximum monetary penalties and jail terms for environmental offenses under various laws, and this provides a strong support to the judiciary in imposing tougher sentencing. The judge in the *Azmi Bin Ismail* case essentially applied the principle of public interest when imposing the penalty based on the seriousness of the offense and took judicial notice that the wild animal taken by the accused was a totally protected species and almost extinct. In addition, the judge also made a reference to the Hansard to find the policy reasons behind the amendments to the Wildlife Conservation Act 2010, which include to overcome the inadequacy of the punishment imposed by the previous law, taking into account commercial and aesthetic value of the protected species of wildlife. The imposition of such a high penalty in the *Azmi Bin Ismail* case, which was driven by a number of factors, also demonstrates the courts' greater awareness of the impacts of environmental crimes and reflects serious willingness to denounce such conduct. This case may have set a precedent, and the sentence may be found applicable outside the conservation sector and is potentially applicable to other activities that have the potential to damage the environment. On

[97] Tenaga Nasional Bhd (n 93) [56].

the basis that courts have the inherent ability to intervene to safeguard public interest as proven in *Azmi Bin Ismail*, such power can thus create the basis for the court's vital role in the legitimization and mobilization of climate change action.

When the environmental courts were first established, they were intended to be specialist courts aimed at improving the efficiency of the administration of criminal justice. Thus, in the beginning, the court only exercised criminal jurisdiction and dealt with prosecutions of environmental offenses. The court's jurisdiction was subsequently expanded to include civil cases, thereby allowing members of the public to bring actions to remedy or restrain a breach of environmental law. To facilitate the expedited disposal of environment related civil actions, the judiciary, headed by the former Chief Judge of the High Court in Sabah and Sarawak Tan Sri Richard Malanjum, is currently taking the initiative to draft a set of Environmental Rules of Court to facilitate the practice of environmental law.[98] The complexity of environmental law and its enforcement requires proper procedures in order to assist the administration of environmental justice. The proposed procedures are to be part of the Rules of Court 2012 and are meant to provide a proper and solid procedural framework for environmental cases and to facilitate an efficient disposition for such cases. Other aims of the proposed procedures are to facilitate the advancement of constitutional rights to a reasonably healthy and pollution-free environment, to ensure effective enforcement of remedies, apart from providing a simplified, speedy, and inexpensive procedure for the enforcement of environmental laws. These initiatives should be applauded, as they are meant to "statutorize" civil procedure relating to environmental claims, which is lacking in Malaysia at the moment. The proposed reform in Malaysia's civil litigation procedure could therefore allow climate change litigation to take effect with less cost and less intimidation to the potential claimants, who would be more willing to enforce their rights through the court. Since procedural access to justice is a key prerequisite to enable lawsuits, litigation can therefore be effective through the facilitation of lawsuit procedures that allow for easier access to justice in environmental matters, including the issue of climate change. The drafting of a set of Environmental Rules of Court that would support judicial enforcement of environmental law could also help protect the public interest relating to

[98] See the role of Tan Sri Richard Malanjum in spearhead the drafting and introduction of a set of Environmental Rules of Court, as highlighted during the Chief Justice's Speech for the Opening of the Legal Year 2017 (n 77) [89].

climate change issues through public interest litigation, which has been lacking in Malaysia until now.

8.5 Public Participation

Even though public participation is commonly advocated in policy responses to environmental pollution and climate change, mechanisms to support public participation within the Malaysian environmental legal system have been rather weak. Previously, the unavailability of direct provisions on the obligation of prior consultation under environmental or planning laws was considered to be a major obstacle toward active public involvement in environmental matters. The issue of public participation has long been debated as illustrated in the decision of *Kajing Tubek & Ors* v. *Ekran Bhd & Ors*, when the court held that there was no accrued right under the law that a EIA report must be distributed to the public without the public asking for it.[99] Until now, there has yet to be any direct legal provision that provides the public with any opportunity to review any policy decisions or enacted laws on climate change. Nevertheless, it is relevant to highlight the progress made on public participation within the process of EIAs. In order to improve and facilitate greater public participation, the EIA provision was amended through the new Environmental Quality (Prescribed Activities; Environmental Impact Assessment) Order 2015, which contains provisions on public display and public comment for activities identified by the law as prescribed activities.[100] By virtue of this order, public participation is currently legally mandatory for such activities. With the inclusion of these mandatory requirements, there is now a specific structure within the law to involve society in environmental and climate change–related decision-making, and to allow the participation of all affected communities, including indigenous peoples. Considering that the public plays an important role in limiting climate change, the application of EIA and the support of the public to manage emissions from prescribed activities are therefore crucial.[101] The solidification of public participation as a legal requirement is

[99] *Kajing Tubek* (n 68).

[100] Environmental Quality (Prescribed Activities; Environmental Impact Assessment) Order 2015, PU(A) 195/2015, First and Second Schedules.

[101] S. Vong, B. J. Boruff, and A. Morrison-Saunders, "Addressing Climate Change through Environmental Impact Assessment:International Perspectives from a Survey of IAIA Members" (2011) 29(4) *Impact Assessment and Project Appraisal* 317.

considered a positive step toward encouraging public involvement in environmental matters, as well as in becoming a tool to mitigate climate change.

Apart from public participation within the EIA process, another platform available to the general public is the right to make a complaint on environmental issues. Generally, the nature of environmental-related statutes in Malaysia, which relies mainly on administrative and criminal sanctions, means that the power to take action against the polluters remains exclusively with the enforcement agencies. The public, even those who are directly affected by the conduct of the offender, has no rights under the law to bring a case against the wrongdoer. On the other hand, even though the public is not given any rights to prosecute, they are nevertheless provided with an alternative access to environmental justice. This is by way of making a formal pollution complaint to the Department of Environment (DOE) on specific environmental harms, such as open burning, illegal disposal of waste, oil spill, water pollution from industry sources, and air pollution from industries, premises, and vehicles. In response, the DOE will carry out an investigation on the alleged harm.[102] Tracing back the implementation of this process over the years, it is significant to take note of the high number of responses received from the public yearly. For example, during the year 1997, when Malaysia and several neighboring countries were facing a very serious transboundary haze problem, a total number of 4,254 complaints was received. Most were related to air pollution, which makes a total of 3,355 complaints.[103] As a comparison, for the year 2016, the DOE received 5,765 complaints pertaining to environmental pollution.[104] The highest number of complaints made in 2016 was related to air pollution, amounting to 4,580, followed by the rest, which relate to water pollution, noise pollution, illegal dumping of scheduled wastes, oil spillage, and land pollution. The DOE's public complaint platform is therefore an important platform for access to justice in Malaysia and provides strong support for climate change mitigation. First, it allows the public who are either directly or indirectly affected by any environmental harms the right to lodge a complaint straight to the environmental regulatory body for further action. Second, such a process allows the public to become an environmental watchdog for the DOE, especially in

[102] Department of Environment Malaysia, "e-Aduan Jabatan Alam Sekitar," https://eaduan.doe.gov.my/eaduan/index.php?lang=EN.

[103] Department of Environment Malaysia, *Environmental Quality Report 1997* (DOE 1998).

[104] Department of Environment Malaysia, *Annual Report 2016* (DOE 2016).

regard to environmental surveillance and regulation. Third and most importantly, it provides an alternative means to litigation that is not available in any environmental statute.

8.6 Conclusion

While there has been a global trend of litigation even among some developing countries to put pressure on governments and responsible industries to address climate change, this is not currently reflected in Malaysia. This chapter has identified some possible platforms within the environmental legal system pertinent in climate change litigation. The findings, however, suggest that in most situations, heavy reliance is put on the government to solve the country's environmental problems through administrative and criminal measures under environmental law. To date, Malaysia has undertaken numerous responses on climate change that contribute to the objectives of the Paris Agreement. Some of these efforts that have already been highlighted include climate-orientated policies and measures emphasizing RE and promoting self-regulation of development sectors. While Malaysia has yet to enact a specific law on climate change, existing environmental-related laws are already covering a wide range of actions in a number of sectors, and they interact with other policy priorities such as environmental quality, energy, transport, forestry and land use, air quality, and biodiversity. Some promising strategies applied include the front-end approach through enforcement and regulatory systems to a back-end focus of self-regulation to achieve certain emission standards or a sustainability target set. At this juncture, Malaysia's environmental law seems to be moving steadily toward a more effective protection of the environment by removing unnecessary constraints on operators and intensifying the penalties for conduct that actually harm the environment. The need to move away from a carbon-intensive development model requires fundamental policy changes in key sectors of the economy, including the energy sector. Thus the passing of Renewable Energy Act 2011, for example, is meant to achieve the goals of the country's climate change policy through EE and RE. Other measures that directly or indirectly help secure climate change objectives could also be found embedded within multiple approaches, such as planning and self-regulation within the EIA. By nature, EIAs are probably not the most suitable means of tackling climate change, as they are applicable only to future projects to mitigate potential GHG emissions. However, it has been argued in this chapter that EIAs can be effective when action plans involving climate change impacts and mitigation are directly embedded within the EIA procedure as a mandatory requirement for approval.

Climate change continues to present huge challenges for the world, including for Malaysia. In order to make climate change targets achievable through the reliance on legal provisions, a number of fundamental steps need to be taken through a transformation of policy, law, and institutional frameworks. There is a need for measures, such as statutory principles that could provide GHG emitters with some level of certainty regarding climate risks and legal liabilities. A clear-cut policy on sustainable development and GHG emissions reductions needs to be established. In this regard, it is necessary to execute a proper data management on climate change in order to assist the law in setting the right target. The next step is to strengthen regulatory frameworks for the reduction of GHG emissions by adding new features, such as scientifically measured, long-term emissions targets and continual adaptation planning, apart from strengthening the existing mandatory process of monitoring and accountability. From one perspective, the increased strictness in criminal law sanctions and expansion of criminal liability relating to climate change can be regarded as a general acceptance that such activities are serious enough to warrant legal sanctions and the willingness of the enforcement agencies to pursue such cases. In this regard, enforcement agencies have important bearings on environmental protection and pollution control. These agencies are also crucial in providing platforms for public participation as a substitute to civil action. The establishment of the environmental courts and the proposed amendment of civil procedure are breakthroughs for Malaysia, not only in relation to the progress of the environmental legal system, but also toward the development of climate change litigation. This is because the environmental courts could provide a number of potential benefits that were not well established previously, such as promoting greater consistency in the application of the law and increasing awareness of the environment. At this moment, even when climate change has yet to become central to litigation, the judiciary has already increased exposure on environmental cases and climate change arguments. This can be interpreted as a positive indication in the development of environmental litigation in Malaysia. Taking various factors into consideration, it is suggested that the issue of climate change litigation in Malaysia would be best addressed through a nationally consistent, clear regulatory framework to allocate liability for risk of harm. Strictly applied administrative and criminal strategies and eventually civil litigation can help achieve the objectives of the Paris Agreement as part of an integrated approach from the government and other stakeholders.

9

Climate Change Litigation in Indonesia

ANDRI G. WIBISANA AND CONRADO M. CORNELIUS

Introduction

This chapter attempts to examine Indonesia's climate change litigation. In doing so, it first classifies Indonesia's climate change litigation into three different types of lawsuits. The first are lawsuits against the government for failure to meet its obligations related to climate change. The second are lawsuits related to the failure of the existing environmental impact assessment (EIA) documents to take into account the likely impacts of a proposed activity on climate change. The last type are lawsuits related to illegal logging and peatland fires. These lawsuits are brought by the government through the Ministry of Environment (MoE), or currently the Ministry of Environment and Forestry (MoEF), against timber or oil palm plantations for peatland fires or companies allegedly involved in illegal logging.

The third category merits further attention since it is comparable to tort-based climate change litigation. In these lawsuits, the government asks the defendants to pay damages for environmental damage and restoration costs resulting from the defendants' activities or illegal conducts.[1] Nevertheless, similar to other tort-based climate change litigations, successful prosecutions of these claims face the challenge of the notoriously difficult questions about causation.

This chapter argues that the third type of Indonesian climate change litigation is novel and unique in two different senses. First, it addresses climate change not as a primary tort or a tort per se, but rather as a secondary tort. Second, instead of pursuing claims for climate damages

[1] Kevin Haroff and Jacqueline Hartis, 'Climate Change and the Courts: Litigating the Causes and Consequences of Global Warming' (2008) 22(3) *Natural Resources & Environment* 50, 55. See also Michael B. Gerrard, 'What the Law and Lawyers Can and Cannot Do about Global Warming' (2007) 16(1) *Southeastern Environmental Law Journal* 33, 39–40.

only, the government in these cases pursued claims for emission abatement costs.

After this introduction, this chapter will explain the climate change litigation related to the government's failure to take emissions from coal-mining activities and coal-fired power plants into account in EIAs. Afterwards, this chapter describes the Indonesian climate change litigation related to illegal logging and peatland fires. This chapter offers lessons learned from the final category of Indonesian cases. Some concluding remarks are provided at the end of the chapter.

9.1 *Komari et al.* v. *Mayor of Samarinda et al.*: The First Climate Change Litigation in Indonesia

The *Komari et al.* v. *Mayor of Samarinda et al.* ruling came after a citizen lawsuit filed by a group of Samarinda residents in 2013. In this lawsuit, the plaintiffs sued the central and local governments following several environmental degradations due to the mismanagement of and lack of law enforcement with respect to coal mining operations in Samarinda, East Kalimantan. Interestingly, the plaintiffs argued that they were victims of climate change, and their grievances resulted from the failures of the defendants to take into account climate change in issuing permits for coal-mining operations, performing inspections, and conducting effective law enforcement.[2]

The plaintiff contended that the Presidential Regulation Number 61 of 2011 concerning National Action Plan for Reducing Greenhouse Gas Emissions requires the Minister of Energy and Mineral Resources,[3] the Minister of the Environment,[4] and the Governor of East Kalimantan to take actions to reduce greenhouse gases (GHGs) emissions.[5] However, plaintiffs argued that the defendants' lack of commitment to climate-change mitigation resulted in the defendants' failure to evaluate and monitor coal-mining permits.[6]

The plaintiffs asked the Court to declare that the defendants have been negligent for failing to perform their obligations to create a good and

[2] Decision Number 55/Pdt.G/2013/PNSmda, *Komari et al.* v. *Mayor of Samarinda et al.* (District Court of Samarinda, 2013) 3–4.
[3] ibid 13–14.
[4] ibid 19.
[5] ibid 17.
[6] ibid 15, 17, and 20.

healthy environment, which eventually exacerbated the impacts of climate change in the City of Samarinda. The plaintiffs also asked the Court to declare that the defendants' negligence has resulted in material and intangible losses suffered by the residents of Samarinda who are affected by the effects of climate change.[7] All defendants were also demanded to apologise through local and national newspapers, television stations, and radio stations.[8]

In addition, the plaintiffs also asked the Court to order all defendants to:[9]

a. evaluate all mining permits, which should be carried out transparently and in coordination with relevant agencies and Non-Governmental Organisations;
b. immediately require all permit holders to carry out post-mining reclamation works to improve environmental functions;
c. immediately undertake a strategic effort in protecting the agricultural and fishery areas of the community from pollution as a result of mining activities, including in the Makroman, Lempake, and Pampang Subdistrict areas;
d. immediately strengthen child safety policies in mining operations;
e. immediately establish water catchment areas and protect urban forest areas; and
f. immediately develop a climate change adaptation model for the people of Samarinda.

The plaintiffs also asked the Court to give orders to certain defendants. Defendant I, the Mayor of the City of Samarinda, was asked to:

a. provide free health treatment for residents exposed to acute respiratory infection and skin diseases, especially in areas near coal mines in Samarinda;
b. restore clean water sources for everyday life by installing free water facilities and installations in each village that has been the location of coal mining;
c. immediately ask mining companies to stop and prohibit the use of community water sources for mining company operations;
d. immediately make irrigation projects for villages that have an agricultural base; and

[7] ibid 35–6.
[8] ibid 37.
[9] ibid 36.

e. immediately repair public facilities damaged by floods, such as schools, public roads, and houses of worship.[10]

Meanwhile, the Defendant IV, the Minister of Environment, was asked to:

a. immediately restore the green open space of at least 30% of the total area of the city and restore the function of recharge areas in each village or area such as the initial intensity of floods; and
b. immediately make food and agricultural land protection in agricultural areas in Samarinda, limit the operation of mining, and revoke mining permits found to have violated the law.[11]

The District Court of Samarinda ruled in favour of the plaintiffs and declared the defendants had conducted unlawful acts against the plaintiffs by failing to meet their statutory obligations related to mining operations and climate change. The Court consequently asked the government to review existing policies on coal mining, including those related to licenses, inspection, and law enforcement.[12]

9.2 Climate Impact Assessment in Indonesian Courtrooms

There has been an emerging trend in climate change litigation worldwide to focus on the relation between EIA and climate change law. This type of lawsuit might be analogous to the climate change litigation in the United States based on the National Environmental Policy Act.[13]

In Indonesia, one instance of this was in *Ketut Mangku Wijana et al. v. Governor of Bali and another*. This is an administrative law case impugning a permit issued by the Governor of Bali for the development of a coal-fired power plant in Celukan Bawang, Bali.

Referring to a publication from the International Energy Agency, the plaintiffs argued that coal-fired power plant contributes significantly to GHG emissions. The plaintiffs noted that the burning of coal is responsible for 46 per cent of CO_2 emissions from fossil fuels, and

[10] ibid 36–37.
[11] ibid 37.
[12] ibid 141–3.
[13] National Environmental Policy Act, 42 USC § 4321 et seq (US). See, for example, Haroff and Hartis (n 1) 51–3.

72 per cent of CO_2 emissions from the electricity sector.[14] The plaintiffs also argued that the proposed coal-fired power plant is expected to burn almost three million tons of coal per year, or at least seventy-five million tons of coal for the thirty years of the plant's projected operational year.[15] More importantly, the plaintiffs claimed that the projected plant is expected to release two hundred million tons of CO_2 during its thirty years of projected operation.[16] Since these likely emissions were not included in the plant's EIA, the plaintiffs asserted that when issuing the permit for the plant, the Governor failed to consider the likely important impacts of the plant. Accordingly, the permit was in contravention with Law Number 6 of 1994 concerning Ratification of the United Nations Framework Convention on Climate Change and with Law Number 32 of 2009 concerning Environmental Protection and Management (the 2009 EPMA).[17] The plaintiffs also made other claims focusing on the pollution and environmental damage generated by the plant.[18]

The Administrative Court of Denpasar ruled in favour of the defendants, mostly on the ground of the lack of evidence regarding the claimed pollution and environmental damage.[19] The lack of evidence regarding the alleged pollution led the Court to conclude that the plaintiffs had no legal interests to file a lawsuit challenging the permit.[20] Unfortunately, the Court failed to provide meaningful discussions on the question of

[14] Decision Number 2/G/LH/2018/PTUN.DPS, *I Ketut Mangku Wijana et al.* v. *Governor of Bali and another* (Administrative Court of Denpasar, 2018) 17.

[15] ibid 18–19.

[16] ibid 19.

[17] ibid 20. It should be noted that EIAs are required for proposed activities/businesses that are likely to create serious environmental impacts. See the 2009 EPMA, art 22, para 1.

The term 'serious' is defined according to the following criteria: the number of people affected by the proposed activity in question, the extent of the affected area, the intensity and length of the impacts, the number of environmental components likely to be affected, cumulative character of the impacts, and irreversibility of the impacts, and other criteria according to technological and scientific development; see the 2009 EPMA, art 22, para 2.

According to the 2009 EPMA, the approval of the EIA will be used as the basis for the issuance of environmental permits, which then are the prerequisite of an operation permit, see the 2009 EPMA, arts 36–40.

[18] *I Ketut Mangku Wijana et al.* v. *Governor of Bali and another* (Administrative Court of Denpasar, 2018) (n 14) 24–34 and 36.

[19] ibid 148–9.

[20] ibid 151.

whether the issued permit was in contravention with Indonesian laws on climate change. The Court only briefly stated that there is technology available to increase the efficiency of the power plant, which could reduce emissions by 37–38 per cent.[21] However, the Court was silent on the question of whether the EIA for the power plant has taken such a technology into consideration. Moreover, the Court also failed to consider whether the power plant is under the obligation to take into account the likely GHG emission when applying for a licence to operate. The lack of discussions on the link between GHGs emissions and EIA is disappointing, as the plaintiffs have made extensive references to similar cases from in other countries, where the courts considered the importance of including the study of the likely GHG emissions of the project in the EIA.[22] The plaintiff has appealed the Court's decision to the High Administrative Court of Denpasar, and the appeal is currently waiting for decision.

9.3 Litigation on Illegal Logging Activities and Peatland Fires and Climate Change

Lawsuits pertaining illegal logging and peatland fires are brought by the government, through the MoE, or currently the MoEF. According to the 2009 EPMA, the MoEF and local environmental agencies have the authority to file lawsuits against those who has caused environmental damage.[23] The 2009 EPMA defines environmental damage as damage that results from environmental pollution or environmental degradation taking place not in private property.[24] The 2009 EPMA seems to allow the government to file a lawsuit only for damage taking place in an unowned property. Hence, one might wonder whether the government still has the authority to file a lawsuit related to illegal logging and fires taking place in or around concession areas 'owned' by the concession holders-defendants. To answer such a question, it could be argued that the

21 ibid 149.

22 In this regard, the plaintiffs made references to various cases from the United States, Europe, and South Africa. See Plaintiff's Letter of Complaint, in Ketut Mangku Wijana et al. v. Governor of Bali and another (Administrative Court of Denpasar, 2018) (n 14) para 74.

23 The 2009 EPMA (n 17) art 90, para 1.

24 ibid, elucidation of art 90, para 1.

MoEF has the authority to file such lawsuits, seeking compensation for damage to the environment and its ecological functions, because of the provision in the Indonesian Constitution concerning natural resources. Article 33 paragraph 3 of the Indonesian Constitution states that land, water, and all natural resources beneath are controlled by the state for the greatest benefit of the people. Accordingly, it could be argued that a concession to extract or use natural resources only gives the concession holder the right to utilise the resources, but without transferring ownership of the land to the holder. This is especially the case in the forestry and plantation sectors, where permits in these sectors do not change the ownership of the resources from public to private ownership. Since the resources still belong to the Indonesian people as a nation, the state retains the authority to control these resources, and therefore it can file a lawsuit against conducts that damaged the resources.

The first case in which the government sought compensation for the emission of GHGs is *Minister of Environment* v. *PT Selatnasik Indokwarsa and PT Simpang Pesak Indokwarsa.*[25] In 2009, the Minister filed a lawsuit against two mining companies for allegedly conducting illegal activities outside their permitted area. Such illegal activities included the clearing of protected forests for road access to the mining location, conducting open pit mining, building some infrastructure within a natural reserve area, and constructing an illegal port by landfilling the coastal area around 1.7 km seaward.[26] The government requested that the defendants should both be held liable based on their unlawful acts, which is analogous to the negligence rule known in the common law, and strict liability. The government further argued that defendants should jointly pay restoration cost totalling IDR 32.3 billion (around USD 2.3 million).[27] The District Court of North

[25] Decision Number 105/PDT/G/2009/PN.JKT.UT., *Minister of Environment* v. *PT Selatnasik Indokwarsa and PT Simpang Pesak Indokwarsa* (District Court of North Jakarta, 2010).

[26] Decision Number 499 K/PDT/2012, *PT Selatnasik Indokwarsa and PT Simpang Pesak Indokwarsa* v. *Minister of Environment* (Supreme Court Cassation, 2010) 5–6.

[27] ibid 19–20.

It should be mentioned here that the 2009 EPMA recognises two rules as a basis of liability. The first one is liability for unlawful conducts. This is addressed in article 87 of the 2009 EPMA and constitutes a more general rule of civil liability. The second one is strict liability, which is addressed in article 88 of the 2009 EPMA. According to this article, strict liability is more specific liability rule for damage from activities using hazardous substances, or producing hazardous wastes, or posing serious threats to the environment.

For critical comments on the use of strict liability in Indonesia's wildfire litigation, see Andri G. Wibisana, 'The Many Faces of Strict Liability in Indonesia's Wildfire Litigation' (2019) 28(2) *Review of European, Comparative & International Environmental Law* 185-196.

Jakarta ruled in favour of the government and awarded all the government's requests for compensation.[28] The defendants appealed to the High Court of Jakarta, which then upheld the lower Court verdict.[29] The defendants finally filed a cassation to the Supreme Court, which then reversed the lower courts' decisions. According to the Supreme Court, the government failed to prove that the defendants conducted concerted illegal actions. In addition, the Court also argued that the government's lawsuit was premature since there was no complaint filed by the public or the victims of environmental damage. Accordingly, the Court annulled the lower courts' rulings and declared the government's lawsuit inadmissible.[30] As a last effort, the government took an extraordinary review (*peninjauan kembali*). According to Indonesian law, the review is a request for the Supreme Court to re-evaluate its already binding ruling. This extraordinary effort can only be taken if a petitioner has new evidence that had been unavailable and not considered during the earlier proceedings that could have changed the ruling, had the evidence been presented in the earlier proceedings. Other reasons for the request for review include that the previous ruling was based on apparent mistakes by the court, or on fraud or lies. The government argued that the defendants were two companies operating under the same management and hence could undoubtedly be considered to have acted in concert. In addition, the government argued that the defendants conducted unlawful acts, which had clearly resulted in serious environmental damage. The Supreme Court at this review agreed with the government's arguments, and accordingly set aside its previous decision. The Supreme Court review awarded the government all restoration costs it claimed (i.e., IDR 32.3 billion).[31]

Interestingly, the government argued that the defendants' illegal activities had given rise to various environmental impacts, one of which was the release of up to 359 tC (ton of carbon) per hectare of GHGs. For the damaged area of 208 hectares, the defendants' activities had thus released 74,672 tC. The government calculated that the restoration costs was IDR 90,000 per ton, and hence the total restoration cost for the said carbon

[28] *PT Selatnasik Indokwarsa and PT Simpang Pesak Indokwarsa* v. *Minister of Environment* (Supreme Court Cassation, 2010) (n 26) 20.

[29] Decision Number 400/PDT/2010/PT.DKI., *PT Selatnasik Indokwarsa and PT Simpang Pesak Indokwarsa* v. *Minister of Environment* (High Court of Jakarta, 2011).

[30] *PT Selatnasik Indokwarsa and PT Simpang Pesak Indokwarsa* v. *Minister of Environment* (Supreme Court Cassation, 2010) (n 26) 32–3.

[31] Decision Number 109 PK/Pdt/2014, *Minister of Environment* v. *PT Selatnasik Indokwarsa and PT Simpang Pesak Indokwarsa* (Supreme Court Review, 2014) 36–9.

release was IDR 6.7 billion (approximately USD 480,000) – that is, 72,672 tons × IDR 90,000 per ton.[32]

Another illegal logging case that also discussed GHGs emissions is *Ministry of Environment* v. *PT Merbau Pelalawan Lestari*. In this case, the government accused the defendant of conducting illegal logging in the forest areas of 7,463 hectares, of which 5,590 hectares were located outside the defendant's timber concession area and 1,873 hectares were located within the concession area. The government claimed that the illegal logging had caused various environmental damage and economic losses, including those due to the release of carbon. The government asked the court to declare that the defendant had committed unlawful acts of illegal logging and to order the defendant to pay compensation of IDR 16.2 trillion (approximately USD 1.2 billion).[33] The District Court of Pekanbaru ruled in favour of the defendant by stating that the defendant did not undertake the illegal logging it was accused of doing, and hence concluded that no unlawful acts had been committed by the defendant. Consequently, the Court rejected all of the government's claims.[34] The government appealed to the High Court of Pekanbaru, which also ruled in favour of the defendant and upheld the lower court's decision.[35] Dramatically, the Supreme Court overturned the lower court decisions by concluding that the defendant had clearly conducted an unlawful act by conducting illegal logging outside its concession area. The Supreme Court also agreed with the government that the defendant had to pay compensation of IDR 16.2 trillion.[36]

In *Ministry of Environment* v. *PT Merbau Pelalawan Lestari*, the government argued that illegal logging conducted by the defendant had given rise to various types of losses, including those from the release of GHGs. In calculating the appropriate compensation payable for this type

[32] *PT Selatnasik Indokwarsa and PT Simpang Pesak Indokwarsa* v. *Minister of Environment* (Supreme Court Cassation, 2010) (n 26) 12. See also *Minister for Environment* v. *PT Selatnasik Indokwarsa and PT Simpang Pesak Indokwarsa* (Supreme Court Review, 2014) (n 31) 10–11.

[33] Decision Number 157/Pdt.G/2013/PN.Pbr, *Ministry of Environment* v. *PT Merbau Pelalawan Lestari* (District Court of Pekanbaru, 2014) 25–34.

[34] ibid 112–13.

[35] Decision Number 79/PDT/2014/PTR, *Ministry of Environment* v. *PT Merbau Pelalawan Lestari* (High Court of Pekanbaru, 2014).

[36] Decision Number 460 K/Pdt/2016, *Ministry of Environment* v. *PT Merbau Pelalawan Lestari* (Supreme Court Cassation, 2016) 47–8.

of damage, the government argued that the defendant's illegal logging resulted in the release of carbon, which resulted in the need to restore the degraded forest to undo the significant carbon release. The restoration of the forest was thought to cost IDR 32.3 million per hectare or IDR 240 billion (approximately USD 17.2 million) for the total affected area of 7,463 hectares.[37]

In the aftermath of peatland fires, the government has, since 2013, taken several legal actions against companies whose concession areas experienced fires. In *Minister of Environment* v. *PT Kalista Alam*, the government claimed that the oil palm plantation had conducted an intentional unlawful act. In this case, the government argued that for the purpose of land clearing, the defendant had intentionally drained and then burned the peatland in its area. The intention, so the government argued, was indicated not only by the presence of canals to drain the peatland but also by the fact that the logs were piled in such a way so as to facilitate fires.[38] The government also argued that the defendant had also negligently conducted an unlawful act by failing to prevent and control the fires. The government then explained various regulations obliging plantation licence holders to take preventive and control measures, and then indicated that the defendant had negligently violated its legal obligations.[39] In addition, the government briefly mentioned strict liability as the basis for liability.[40]

The government claimed that the fires from the land controlled by the defendant had caused various serious environmental losses. These losses included:

a. ecological damage (e.g., the loss of water reservoir function of the peatland);
b. damage to biodiversity (e.g., the loss of biodiversity);
c. damage due to carbon release; and
d. economic losses due to land degradation.[41]

[37] ibid 20 and 23.
[38] Decision No. 12/ PDT.G/ 2012/ PN.MBO, Minister of Environment v. PT Kalista Alam (District Court of Meulaboh, 2013) 20 and 25.
[39] ibid 26–33.
[40] ibid 25.
[41] ibid 38–48.

Accordingly, the government asked for the defendant to pay a compensation of IDR 115 billion and to conduct restoration costing of no less than IDR 250 billion.[42]

The District Court of Meulaboh concluded that the defendant had conducted land clearing using controlled fires from 2009 until 2012.[43] The Court also observed that fires occurring in several blocks were controlled and planned according to the defendant's objective.[44] Although not clearly stated, the Court holding above implies that the Court was in agreement with the government about the defendant's intentional unlawful conduct. Eventually, the Court declared that the defendant was liable based on the unlawful act rule and ordered the defendant to pay compensation of IDR 115 billion and to conduct restoration works worth at least IDR 250 billion.[45] After the High Court of Banda Aceh affirmed the District Court's ruling,[46] the case went to the Supreme Court, which eventually upheld the lower court rulings.[47]

In calculating its claim for compensation, the government specified two heads of damage related to GHG emission. First, the government argued that the fires released 13,500 tC into the atmosphere. The reduction of the carbon release cost IDR 90,000 per ton. Hence, the total reduction cost for 13,500 tC was IDR 1.2 billion.[48] Second, the government stated that the fires also reduced the ability of the peatland to absorb CO_2. Such a loss of GHG absorption capacity was similar to the emissions of 4,725 tCO_2 (ton of CO_2). A restoration was required to rectify this loss, which cost IDR 425.3 million (i.e. IDR 90,000 per ton × 4,725 tons).[49]

In *Minister of Environment and Forestry* v. *PT Bumi Mekar Hijau*, the government sought compensation and restoration for the 2014 fires covering the defendant's timber plantation of 20,000 hectares. It was argued that the defendant had intentionally set fires to the peatland to support the defendant's land clearing program with the lowest

[42] ibid 51.
[43] ibid 192.
[44] ibid 190.
[45] ibid 231.
[46] Decision Number 50/PDT/2014/PT.BNA, *PT Kalista Alam* v. *Minister of Environment* (High Court of Banda Aceh, 2014).
[47] Decision Number 651 K/Pdt/2015, *PT Kalista Alam* v. *Minister of Environment* (Supreme Court Cassation, 2015).
[48] *Minister of Environment* v. *PT Kalista Alam* (District Court of Meulaboh, 2013) (n 38) 43.
[49] ibid 43–44.

possible cost.[50] The government requested the court to declare that the defendant liable for an intentional unlawful act. The government also claimed that the defendant should pay damages of IDR 2.687 trillion and shoulder restoration costs of affected area, which was at least IDR 5.299 trillion.[51] The government in *Minister of Environment and Forestry* v. *PT Bumi Mekar Hijau* took a similar logic in calculating the damages. In particular, the government argued that fires on the defendant's land had resulted in the release of 135,000 tC and 5,670 tCO_2. Since the cost of carbon reduction was IDR 90,000, the total restoration costs, respectively, were IDR 12.2 billion and IDR 4.3 billion.[52]

The District Court of Palembang rejected the government's claim.[53] The government filed an appeal to the High Court of Palembang, which eventually overruled the District Court. The High Court was of the opinion that the defendant had negligently failed to comply with obligations related to the prevention and control of forest fires.[54] Accordingly, the Court held the defendant liable for committing an unlawful act and ordered the defendant to pay compensation of IDR 78.5 billion.[55] Unfortunately, the Court did not explain the reason why it awarded the government with only roughly 1 per cent of its total claims.

Meanwhile, in *Minister of Environment and Forestry* v. *PT Jatim Jaya Perkasa*, the government sued an oil palm plantation for fires occurring in 1,000 out of 8,000 hectares controlled by the company. The government accused the defendant of committing intentional unlawful acts by setting fires on its land to clear the land for the planting of new oil palms.[56] The government also argued that the defendant negligently conducted an unlawful act by failing to comply with various obligations to prevent and control fires.[57] Lastly, the government also briefly mentioned strict liability as the basis for defendant's liability.

[50] Decision Number 24/Pdt.G/2015/PN.Plg, *Minister of Environment and Forestry* v. *PT Bumi Mekar Hijau* (District Court of Palembang, 2015) 11.
[51] ibid 22.
[52] ibid 17.
[53] ibid 115.
[54] Decision Number 51/PDT/2016/PT.PLG, *Minister of Environment and Forestry* v. *PT Bumi Mekar Hijau* (High Court of Palembang, 2016) 168–9 and 171–2.
[55] ibid 190.
[56] Decision Number 108/Pdt.G/2015/PN.Jkt.Utr., *Minister of Environment and Forestry* v. *PT Jatim Jaya Perkasa* (District Court of North Jakarta, 2016) 18–24.
[57] ibid 24–7.

The government asked the Court to declare that the defendant had conducted an unlawful act related to fires within its controlled area. The government also sought compensation of IDR 119.9 billion and restoration measures costing at least IDR 371.1 billion.[58] Similar to the previous claims on peatland fires, the government also maintained that fires in the defendant's area released 9,000 tC and 3,150 tCO_2. The cost of restoration associated with such an amount of GHGs was IDR 90,000 per ton, and the government claimed that the total restoration costs were, respectively, IDR 810 million and IDR 283.5 million.[59]

The District Court of North Jakarta found that, contrary to the government's claim, the fires only occurred in 120 hectares of defendant's plantation.[60] In addition, the Court determined that fires emanated from areas under the local community's control (and not the defendant's) outside the defendant's plantation.[61] Yet the Court thought that the defendant failed to control the fires, which thus constituted an unlawful act, albeit negligently.[62] Accordingly, the court found the defendant liable. However, liability was limited only to losses resulting from the fires in 201 hectares, for which the defendant had to pay half of these compensation and restoration costs due to the fact that the fires were considered to originate from areas outside its control.[63] For these reasons, the Court ordered the defendant to pay compensation of IDR 7.2 billion, and to conduct rehabilitation measures worth of IDR 22.2 billion.[64]

On appeal, the High Court of Jakarta upheld the lower court decision in concluding that the defendant was liable for fires occurring in its controlled area.[65] However, the High Court annulled the amount of compensation awarded by the lower court. Contrary to the District Court, the High Court was of the opinion that the fires took place in 1,000 hectares of the defendant's concession area.[66]

[58] ibid 38.
[59] ibid 33.
[60] ibid 166.
[61] ibid 164 and 167.
[62] ibid 166. It could, however, be noted that the Court was silent on whether the defendant's unlawful act was conducted intentionally or negligently.
[63] ibid 167.
[64] ibid 170.
[65] Decision Number 727/PDT/2016/PT.DKI, *Minister of Environment and Forestry* v. *PT Jatim Jaya Perkasa* (High Court of Jakarta, 2017) 81.
[66] ibid

Therefore, the High Court awarded the government all its claims (i. e., a compensation of IDR 119.9 billion and restoration works costing at least IDR 371.1 billion).[67]

In *Ministry of Environment and Forestry* v. *PT Waringin Agro Jaya*, the government sued an oil palm company for wildfires covering an area of 1,626 hectares of the company's oil palm plantation. In this case, the government used both the unlawful act rule and strict liability as the grounds of liability. With respect to the unlawful act liability, the government argued that the defendant engaged in intentional unlawful conduct related to the land clearing by burning[68] and negligent unlawful conduct for violating various obligations related to the prevention and control of fires.[69] With respect to strict liability, the government argued that the defendant's activities posed serious threats to the environment, and hence the application of strict liability was justified.[70]

The government claimed that the defendant was liable on the grounds of the unlawful act rule and strict liability, and asked the court to order the defendant to pay compensation of IDR 173.4 billion and conducting restoration measures costing IDR 584.9 billion.[71] In calculating the damages, the government alleged that the fires had resulted in carbon release of as much as 10,979 tons

67 ibid

68 Decision Number 456/Pdt.G-LH/2016/PN Jkt. Sel., *Ministry of Environment and Forestry* v. *PT Waringin Agro Jaya* (District Court of South Jakarta, 2017) 11–23.

69 ibid 23–30.

70 ibid 38–40. One might question the way the Court found oil palm plantation to pose threats to the environment so serious that they justify the use of strict liability. Strict liability is applicable to damage caused by activities that use hazardous substances, produce hazardous wastes, or pose serious threats to the environment. Since plantations arguably do not use hazardous substances nor produce hazardous wastes, the only reason to justify strict liability is that the defendant's activity has posed serious threats to the environment. This is exactly what the Court did. Here, the Court relied its ruling on the ground that the plantation has caused wildfires that have various irreversible impacts to the environment. See ibid 293–94. Wibisana proposes that palm oil plantation might be strictly liable when it is carried out in peatlands. This is because plantation requires the drainage of peatlands. However, draining peatlands might significantly increases the likelihood of fires, and hence it is plausible to ask those who carry out the drainage activities to be liable for the damage resulting from the fires. See Wibisana (n 27).

71 *Ministry of Environment and Forestry* v. *PT Waringin Agro Jaya* (District Court of South Jakarta, 2017) (n 56) 44–5.

and the reduction of carbon absorption capacity by as much as 3,843 tons. Assessing the restoration cost for carbon emissions as costing IDR 90,000 per ton, the total restoration costs were, respectively, IDR 988 million and IDR 345.8 million.[72]

In its ruling, the District Court of South Jakarta found that the defendant's activities related on its oil palm plantation posed serious risks to the environment, and hence strict liability was applicable to this case.[73] In addition, the Court held the defendant strictly liable for the fires occurring in its land.[74] The Court awarded the government with a compensation of IDR 173.4 billion and ordered the defendant to conduct restoration measures worth at least IDR 293 billion.[75]

9.4 The Importance of Indonesia's Tort-Based Climate Change Litigation

The cases in the previous section show that climate change entered Indonesian courtrooms, not through climate change litigation per se. In *Komari et al.* v. *Mayor of Samarinda et al.*, climate change was discussed in a lawsuit which centred around the environmental impacts of coal mining and the government's failures to enforce the law. Meanwhile, in *Ketut Mangku Wijana et al.* v. *Governor of Bali and another*, discussion about climate change came as part of the argument against the current practice of EIAs, which fails to address the GHG emissions of a proposed activity. In litigation concerning illegal logging and peatland fires, climate change was discussed when the government highlighted GHG emissions as a result from the defendants' illegal conduct or damaging activities.

For the purpose of this chapter, the litigation on illegal logging and peatland fires is of a particular interest. This Indonesian experience offers a new and unique approach to climate change litigation. It is new because discussions on climate change, or to be precise, on GHG emissions, came in these nuisance cases primarily focusing on other

[72] ibid 34. The amount of IDR 90,000 per ton is obtained by referring to the Regulation of the Minister of the Environment Number 13 of 2011 concerning Damages as a Result of Environmental Damage and Degradation.
[73] ibid 293–4.
[74] ibid 295–6.
[75] ibid 304.

issues – namely, illegal logging and peatland fires. The defendants were primarily sued because they emitted large volumes of GHG emissions, because they have conducted illegal logging, or because fires occurred in their concession areas. One might call such an approach secondary climate change litigation, in contrast to primary climate change litigation in which a defendant is sued primarily because of its GHG emissions. The Indonesian approach is unique because it offers a solution for tort-based climate lawsuits, by focusing on the cost of emission reduction rather than on climate change damage. The focus allows the plaintiff to avoid a very difficult, if not impossible, task of proving causation between the defendant's conduct and a particular climate-related damage suffered by the plaintiff.

The Indonesian approach is defensible for at least the following two reasons: (1) scientific evidence, and (2) focus on restoration and not monetary compensation.

9.4.1 *Scientific Evidence*

Firstly, science indicates that deforestation and peatland fires could seriously contribute to the increased GHG emissions in the atmosphere.

Forests can be both carbon sinks and sources of GHG emissions. Forests function as sinks because they can absorb and accumulate carbon in wood, leaves, and soil.[76] In this regard, Portela and others estimate that forests have stored more than 280 GtC (gigaton of carbon) in biomass.[77] However, forests can also release GHG emissions whenever they are degraded – for example, through deforestation or fires. According to Greenleaf, forest degradation will also decrease the amount of carbon that forests could otherwise absorb from the atmosphere.[78] Van den Werf and others consider deforestation as the second largest anthropogenic source of CO_2 emissions to the

[76] S. Dresner, 'Forests and Climate Change: Global Understandings and Possible Responses' in Peter H. Freer-Smith, Mark S. J. Broadmeadow, and Jim M. Lynch (eds.), *Forestry and Climate Change* (CABI 2007) 38–39.

[77] Rosimeiry Portela and others, 'The Idea of Market-Based Mechanisms for Forest Conservation and Climate Change', in Charlotte Streck and others (eds.), *Climate Change and Forests: Emerging Policy and Market Opportunities* (Brookings Institution Press 2008) 11.

[78] Maron Greenleaf, 'Using Carbon Rights to Curb Deforestation and Empower Forest Communities' (2010–2011) 18 *N.Y.U. Environmental L.J.* 507, 508. Similarly, see also Dresner (n 78) 39.

atmosphere, estimated to be around 1.2 GtC per year, excluding emissions from peatland degradation.[79]

With respect to fires on peatlands, the relation between GHG emissions and peatland degradation is even clearer. Peatlands are organic soils formed through decomposition of plant materials, accumulated for thousands of years under waterlogged and acidic conditions. Peatlands are typically characterised by their moisture content, hydraulic conductivity, water tension, and water yield.[80] According to Hooijer and others, undisturbed peat consists of plant remains and water, in the proportion of around 10 per cent and 90 per cent, respectively.[81] Tropical peatlands in Indonesia also 'store' a large number of GHGs. They contain at least 30 GtC.[82] Harrison and others argue that the reduction in water table through the construction of drainage is a major trigger for fires. Under natural conditions, undisturbed peatlands are typically waterlogged and flooded for much of the year, making them 'naturally fire resistant'.[83] The environmental impact of degrading peatlands is catastrophic. As Miettinen and Liew put it, logging activities, drainage, fires, conversion to plantations, and expansion of smallholders not only are contributing to the destructive disturbance of ecosystem, but also are affecting gas fluxes between peatland areas and the atmosphere.[84] The natural conditions immediately change after

[79] GR van der Werf and others, 'CO_2 Emissions from Forest Loss' [2009] 2 *Nature Geoscience* 737. Others counted deforestation as responsible for around 18 per cent of the global GHG emissions; see Randall S. Abate, 'REDD, White, and Blue: Is Proposed U.S. Climate Legislation Adequate to Promote a Global Carbon Credits System for Avoided Deforestation in a Post-Kyoto Regime?' (2010–2011) 19 *Tulane J International & Comparative Law* 95, 96.

[80] R. A. Adesiji, P. A. Adeoye, and A. O. Gbadebo, 'Effects of Water Table Fluctuations on Peatland: A Review' (2014) 2(3C) *Scholars Journal of Engineering and Technology* 482, 483.

[81] A. Hooijer and others, 'Current and Future CO_2 Emissions from Drained Peatlands in Southeast Asia' (2000) 7 *Biogeosciences* 1505.

[82] Jukka Miettinen and Soo Chin Liew, 'Status of Peatland Degradation and Development in Sumatra and Kalimantan' (2010) 39 *AMBIO* 394.

[83] Mark E. Harrison, Susan E. Page, and Suwido H. Limin, 'The Global Impact of Indonesian Forest Fires' (2009) 56(3) *Biologist* 156, 158.

[84] Miettinen and Liew (n 82). The authors further point out that peatland deforestation mainly occur in terms of logging activities and large-scale plantation primarily for oil-palm and pulpwood, see Jukka Miettinen, Chenghua Shi, and Soo Chin Liew, 'Two Decades of Destruction in Southeast Asia'sPeat Swamp Forests' (2012) 10(3) *Frontiers in Ecology and the Environment*124, 128.

deforestation and the drainage of peatlands take place. Such drainage enables peat to be oxidised and released as CO_2 emissions, estimated to be around 45–86 tCO_2 per year.[85]

Peatland drainage is also the principal cause of peatland fires. Under natural conditions, fires do not normally spread in the undisturbed peatlands, which are typically moist with a closed-canopy environment.[86] Once fires occur, positive feedbacks can take place, by which the burned peatlands become more susceptible to fires. If fires occur, the impacts are devastating. The 1997 fires, for example, released as much carbon/GHG as 40 per cent of annual global emissions from fossil fuels.[87] The environmental impact of peatlands fires is dramatic. For example, Page and others predict that during the 1997 fires, millions of hectares of peatlands were burned, releasing 810–2,570 MtC (megatons of carbon) into the atmosphere. The amount is equivalent to 13–40 per cent of the mean annual global carbon emissions from fossil fuels.[88] Meanwhile, Harrison and others estimate that peat fires in Kalimantan between 2000 and 2006 produced an average of 74 MtC per year, making Indonesia one of the world's largest CO_2 emitters.[89]

Discussions in this section show a clear picture of GHGs emissions resulting from deforestation and peatland degradation. The Indonesian approach to include CO_2 emissions in calculating environmental damage from illegal logging and peatland fires is thus scientifically sound and correct.

9.4.2 *Focus on Restoration and Not Monetary Compensation*

Focusing on emission reduction costs rather than on climate damage is in line with government-initiated natural resource damage lawsuits in

[85] Arina P. Schrier and others, 'Environmental and Social Impacts of Oil Palm Cultivation on Tropical Peat: A Scientific Review' (2013) *Reports from the Technical Panels of the 2nd Greenhouse Gas Working Group of the Roundtable for Sustainable Palm Oil (RSPO)* 12–13, https://d2ouvy59p0dg6k.cloudfront.net/downloads/the_environemental_and_social_impacts_of_oil_palm_on_peat.pdf.

[86] Harrison, Page, and Limin (n 83) 158.

[87] Peter Aldhous, 'Borneo Is Burning' (2004) 432 *Nature* 144, 145.

[88] Susan E. Page and others, 'The Amount of Carbon Released from Peat and Forest Fires in Indonesiaduring 1997' (2002) 420 *Nature* 61, 64.

[89] Harrison, Page, and Limin (n 83) 157.

many countries, in which the ultimate goal of the lawsuit is environmental restoration rather than monetary compensation.

Generally, nuisance-based climate change litigation can be divided into two categories: those seeking injunctive relief and those seeking monetary damages.[90] The Indonesian experience, however, indicates a third category emerging from the combination between injunction and monetary damages. In particular, one could see that the Indonesian lawsuits on illegal logging and peatland fires contain both elements of restoration, similar to injunctive relief, and some kind of monetary damages. In these lawsuits, in addition to petitioning that the court orders the defendant pay some amount of money to compensate for environmental damage, the government also asks the court to order the defendants to conduct some concrete restoration activities.

Furthermore, it is also important to note that although the government asks for monetary compensation for environmental damage, the way the damages were estimated is apparently similar to the estimation of restoration cost. This is true at least in the calculation of damages due to carbon release. In this case, the government clearly states that the release needs correction through environmental restoration. For example, in *Minister of Environment* v. *PT Kalista Alam*, the government argued that '[*a*]*kibat adanya pembakaran maka terjadi pelepasan karbon sehingga untuk mengembalikannya perlu dilakukan kegiatan pemulihan*' (as a result of fires, there was carbon release which required restoration to return [the carbon]).[91] The restoration cost was then estimated to be IDR 90,000 per ton of carbon. Interviews with Saharjo and Wasis[92] reveal that the amount was estimated by referring to the price of 'carbon credit', which was assumed to be IDR 90,000 per ton of carbon. The interviews also confirmed that the price of carbon credit was considered to reflect the cost required to restore a ton of carbon.[93]

[90] Gerrard (n 1) 39.

[91] *Minister of Environment* v. *PT Kalista Alam* (District Court of Meulaboh, 2013) (n 38) 43. Similar logic was also used in other peatland fire litigations.

[92] Dr. Bambang Hero Saharjo and Dr. Basuki Wasis are professors at the Faculty of Forestry of Bogor Institute of Agriculture. Both have given expert testimonies in all government lawsuits on illegal logging and peatland fires. They are also the ones who estimated monetary valuation to environmental damage in these lawsuits.

[93] Interviews with Dr. Bambang Hero Saharjo and Dr. Basuki Wasis in April and May 2018.

Focusing on restoration rather than monetary damages has been practiced for natural damage claims in other countries. Liu, for example, argues that environmental damage requires restoration more than it needs monetary damages. The more restoration is required, the more government intervention is justified. This is because in many instances, the government is in a better position to determine the extent to which restoration is required.[94] Various other countries also focus on restoration rather than monetary damages.[95]

Despite the hopes that they offer, the Indonesian approach still suffers several problems. In practice, it lacks consistency, especially regarding measurement and concrete restoration. It is, for example, unclear why, when estimating damage due to carbon release, the government in *Ministry of Environment* v. *PT Merbau Pelalawan Lestari* used the restoration cost of IDR 32.3 million per hectare,[96] while in other cases the government preferred to use the restoration cost of IDR 90,000 per ton of carbon.[97]

In addition, although referring to restoration when calculating environmental damage, the government seems to still consider the compensation in monetary terms. It should not be a big surprise that hitherto no real restoration has been conducted by the government, although they have won almost all cases related to illegal logging and peatland fires, in which they asked for compensation based on restoration costs.

The chapter argues that these two problems emerge because the court did not require the government to indicate that the restoration costs are

[94] Liu Jing, 'Compensating Ecological Damage Comparative and Economic Observations' (Dissertation, Maastricht University 2013) 38.

[95] For experience in the United States, see Douglas D. Ofiara, 'Natural Resource Damage Assessments in the United States: Rules and Procedures for Compensation from Spills of Hazardous Substances and Oil in Waterways under US Jurisdiction' (2002) 44 *Marine Pollution Bulletin* 96; Carol Adaire Jones, 'Use of Non-market Valuation Methods in the Courtroom: Recent Affirmative Precedents in Natural Resource Damage Assessments' (1997) 109(1) *Water Resources Update* 10; and Carol Adaire Jones, 'Compensation for Natural Resource Damages from Oil Spills: A Comparison of US Law and International Conventions' (1999) 11(1) *International Journal of Environment and Pollution* 86.

For comparison between the US and European experience, see, for example, Linda B. Burlington, 'Valuing Natural Resource Damages: A Transatlantic Lesson' (2004) 6 *Environmental Law Review* 77.

[96] *Ministry of Environment* v. *PT Merbau Pelalawan Lestari* (Supreme Court Cassation, 2016) (n 36) 20 and 23.

[97] See, for example, *Minister of Environment* v. *PT Kalista Alam* (District Court of Meulaboh, 2013) (n 38) 43.

calculated according to restoration measures already taken or to be taken by the government.[98] The solution is simply for the court to require the government to submit a restoration plan.[99] This restoration plan is important not only to convince the court that the claimed costs are not arbitrarily estimated, but more importantly to ensure that the restoration will be undertaken.

Another important issue is that the Indonesian approach may be vulnerable to criticisms from a fairness perspective because one might question why only certain emitters have to be liable for their emissions while others do not. For example, it is questionable why certain oil palm companies had to pay for emission reduction for the GHGs emissions released from the wildfires occurring in their concessions, while the coal-fired power plant in Celukan Bawang was not required to pay for the emission reduction, although the plant was predicted to release much higher GHG emissions than those released from the wildfires in the plantations. In this context, Heintz and others, for example, argued that nuisance-based climate change litigation is problematic because, with respect to GHG emissions, '[e]very corporation, every government, every human being is a contributor'. In their view, holding GHG emitters liable is similar to holding every human being jointly and severally liable for climate change. Furthermore, holding only a handful of large emitters liable for climate change seems to violate fairness standards.[100] To address this issue, what follows is a brief remark focusing more on the ethical (i.e., fairness) aspects of climate change litigation.

9.5 The Question of Fairness and the Indonesian Experience

The problem of fairness that has constantly loomed behind any attempted climate change litigation is as follows: Why should a person be held responsible for climate change when others are not? Part of the problem pertains to what Adler coined as a 'moral collective action'

[98] Compare, for example, with *Commonwealth of Puerto Rico* v. *The SS Zoe Colocotroni*, in which the court ruled that the claimed restoration costs should be based on a concrete restoration that was already taken or will be taken. See *Commonwealth of Puerto Rico* v. *The SS Zoe Colocotroni*, 628 F 2d 652 (1st Cir, 1980).

[99] For the US practice, see, for example, John S. Applegate and Jan G. Laitos, *Environmental Law: RCRA, CERCLA, and the Management of Hazardous Waste* (Foundation Press 2006) 222–6.

[100] John E Heintz and others, 'Applying Fairness Principles in Climate Change Nuisance Litigation' (2010) 22(2) *Environmental Claims Journal* 91, 103–4.

problem. A moral collective action problem arises when there is a kind of action that, if taken by every or most members of a group, has morally bad consequences, but that each member of the group is morally justified in taking.[101]

Climate change, as Adler argued, poses such moral collective action problem. Even by hypothetically assuming that there is a certain emission threshold, far above the incremental GHGs emission discharge by individuals, in general, through their daily activities, that may likely cause a significant global warming, it is hard to argue that an emission reduction would be morally required from one individual to another, given that his own emission reduction would not change the global temperatures at all.[102] As climate change litigation trends tend to have high emitting industries business actors as the defendants, it thus seems unfair to hold these industries responsible for climate change when the fruits of their labours have benefited people in general, which may even include the plaintiffs themselves.

True, a certain inequality is at play in this problem. Climate change, as Gardiner said, 'involves a serious asymmetry of power, where the possibility of some taking undue advantage of other is pronounced'.[103] One may also refer to Dryzek, Norgaard, and Schlosberg, in saying that those responsible for the happening of climate change might not necessarily be the same people or countries that would be most likely gravely affected by the consequences of climate change. Nor are they also the same people who possess the capability of doing something about it. In this sense, the essence of responsibility in climate justice discussion centres on how the distribution of burdens and benefits of both the action and inaction in facing climate change can be addressed fairly amongst people and countries.[104]

However, it then seems problematic to simply hold high-emitting businesses as defendants liable for their 'unequal' emission volume and the benefits they gain compared to people in general, simply because they

[101] Matthew D. Adler, 'Corrective Justice and Liability for Global Warming' (2007) 155 *University of Pennsylvania L.R.* 1859, 1863.

[102] Alder (n 101).

[103] Stephen M. Gardiner, *A Perfect Moral Storm: The Ethical Tragedy of Climate Change* (Oxford University Press 2011) 7.

[104] John S. Dryzek, Richard B. Norgaard, and David Schlosberg, *Climate-Challenged Society* (Oxford University Press 2013) 75.

are more able to – and, therefore, it is even fairer that they – compensate for climate change induced damage, as well as the costs of its mitigation and adaptation.

To judge such inequality, one must certainly be able to point out the standard whereby equality/inequality can be determined. Therefore, the likeliest solution to the problem of climate justice, according to Caney, is to devise an emission quota and holding everyone under the duty not to emit more than their quota.[105] However, in the absence of such quota, how can the law, especially tort law, guarantee that fairness is served when holding a defendant liable?

From a tort law perspective, there is no liability unless the defendant breaches a duty of care owed to the plaintiff.[106] Such a duty of care is both objective and ordinary.[107] That is, that the law does not impose any specific attributes as a condition of liability, but rather simply asks what a reasonably prudent person would have done under a given circumstances.[108]

Someone can be held liable for climate change only when it can be established that he has, in fact, breached a climate change duty of care owed to a plaintiff. In other words, this is when it can be established that the defendant has emitted unreasonably. How then can such unreasonableness be established? Hunter and Salzman, for instance, have drawn on the development of climate science landscape ranging from 1827 to 2005. They argued that to allege a defendant as to emit tortiously would require a plaintiff to accord the defendant's act to a 'reasonable level' of duty of care to a specific timeline.[109] Even so, it is hard to argue that such a study may somehow establish an objective notion of climate duty of care.

If the courts are willing to hold an emitter liable on the ground of an unreasonable emission, as Maag argues, it is hard to imagine how courts are able to limit the number of potential defendants in climate change litigation since courts would then be tasked to engage with a fact-intensive scientific inquiry. The courts most likely lack the resources

[105] Simon Caney, 'Cosmopolitan Justice, Responsibility, and Global Climate Change' (2005) 18*Leiden J of International Law* 747, 769.

[106] Ernest J. Weinrib, 'The Disintegration of Duty', in M. Stuart Madden (ed.), *Exploring Tort Law* (Cambridge University Press 2005) 143.

[107] John C. P. Goldberg and Benjamin C. Zipursky, *The Oxford Introductions to U.S. Law: Torts* (Oxford University Press 2010) 85

[108] Goldberg and Zipursky (n 107) 86.

[109] David Hunter and James Salzman, 'Negligence in the Air: The Duty of Care in Climate Change Litigation' (2007) 155*University of Pennsylvania LR* 1741, 1770–5.

and ability to do so.[110] To answer this problem, Maag proposes several line-drawing conditions for a successful climate change litigation. In the first place, the litigation should be able to reduce the number of potential defendants. It should also limit liability only to certain categories of emitters. Finally, a climate change litigation should also be able to constrain judicial discretion.[111]

With regards to breach of climate duty of care, as Maag imagined, the liability for unreasonable emission would be apportioned according to the percentage of each defendant's contribution to the atmospheric concentrations of GHGs. The courts would not need to struggle with the problems posed by joint and several liability. Although harm apportionment would be unable to vouch that small emitters may likely be exempted from liability, it would be the case that no party would wish to seek for recovery from their share of the liability, given their small and insignificant part of contribution.[112] Apportionment may be feasible only when the court can find 'a reasonable basis for divisibility of a single harm'.[113]

'Reasonable' in this sense would mean a fair emission quota. What is important about such quota system is that not everyone is subject to the same standard. Rather, what matters is that everyone is subject to a standard that is enough for them to conduct their daily activities.[114] This means that a fair quota would be a quota that treats different classes of emitters with different emission quota standards, since the energy usage varies from one person to another. For example, such quota will not impose the same standard to individual persons compared to, say, power plants, considering the different energy consumption needed for each of them in going through their daily activities.

Another alternative to the above, as Maag suggests, would be that for harm apportionment to work in climate change litigation, the reasonable basis for such divisibility would be contingent to the existence a documented record evincing the defendant's historical emissions of GHGs. Failing to do

[110] Kirk B. Maag, 'Climate Change Litigation: Drawing Lines to Avoid Strict, Joint, and Several Liability' (2009) 98 *Georgetown L.J.* 185, 212.
[111] ibid 198.
[112] ibid
[113] ibid 208.
[114] Harry G. Frankfurt, *On Inequality* (Princeton University Press 2015) 7.

so would result in having significant portions of GHGs being unaccounted in the apportionment analysis.[115]

Harm apportionment according to the unreasonableness of emission not only fulfils Maag's proposed first two criteria of line-drawing mechanism but is also able to limit the court's discretion in determining the reasonable basis for divisibility. Although it may be true that judges may differ over the 'reasonableness' of the basis of divisibility, courts will not be involved with ad hoc factual inquiries that might arbitrarily exempt particular defendants from climate change liability. From Maag's point of view, harm apportionment would limit the number of potential defendants by exempting small emitters from liability because 'the cost of seeking recovery from many defendants may exceed their potential liability, making it inefficient for plaintiffs to seek recovery from them'.[116]

Although harm apportionment would be by far the mechanism that best satisfies the line-drawing conditions for climate change litigation, applying harm apportionment does not at all guarantee that household sector shall be exempted from joint and several liability upon failing to provide a reasonable basis for liability apportionment, since the reason for harm apportionment highly depends on the availability of one's emission historical record documentation. Accordingly, Maag is of the opinion that, at least for the time being, 'climate change litigation expands public nuisance law too far'.[117]

Sharing Maag's scepticism, this chapter is also of the opinion that climate change litigation may have expanded not only public nuisance law in particular, but also tort rules, too far.

Although the Indonesian experience does not at all rise up to Maag's challenge, and this brief chapter will not be attempting to do so, some caveat can be adduced in defence of it. What makes the Indonesian approach defensible is that it is scientifically sound to claim that deforestation contributes to the 'production' of climate change. In that sense, climate change liability imposed on deforestation tortfeasors has met both the factual inquiry as well as harm apportionment by holding defendants liable *only* to the amount of their emission contribution.

[115] Maag (n 110) 209.
[116] ibid 211.
[117] ibid 213.

But, then, the Indonesian experience remains vulnerable from the criticism based on fairness. Why only claim against deforesters defendants and hold them liable? In particular, why only claim against deforesters when other business sectors are being more significant contributors to climate change?[118]

While the Indonesian experience is scientifically defensible, it is nevertheless normatively debatable. It is subject to a further examination, which asks what makes this less significant deforester's emission (more) wrongful compared to other more significant emitters, thus making them liable before tort law. Certainly, an established fact does not necessarily establish a norm. Just because science can establish the factual causal link between deforestation and the production of climate change, it does not equate to saying that the emission from such deforestation is wrongful. The question of how an emission can be wrongful in such instances is nevertheless subject to further examination that relates to the concept of duty of care and its breach in tort law, which this brief chapter will not attempt to provide.

9.6 Concluding Remarks

Several cases in Indonesia can be considered as climate change litigation. These cases are a citizen lawsuit against the government's failure to meet its obligations related to climate change, a lawsuit related to the failure of existing EIA documents to take into account the likely impacts of a proposed activity on climate change, and various government lawsuits on illegal logging and peatland fires. The chapter considers the last type of lawsuits as tort-based climate change litigation in Indonesia.

The Indonesian climate change litigation cases are novel and unique. First, climate change claims are pursued as secondary-tort under some other primary tort claims (i.e., illegal logging and wildfire torts) due to the similar facts that they share. Second, instead of

[118] Based on the Intergovernmental Panel on Climate Change (IPPC) 2014 Synthesis Report, the GHG emission contribution in 2010 from seven different sectors – namely Agriculture, Buildings, Transport, Industry, Electricity and Heat Production, Forestry and Other Land Use, and Other Energy – ranks forestry and other land use (i.e., deforestation) consistently on the bottom four calculated using 100-year and 20-year Global Warming Potential Ranking (GWP) or 100-year Global Temperature change Potential (GTP_{20}). See Rajendra K. Pachauri and others (eds.), *Climate Change 2014: Synthesis Report* (IPCC 2015) 88.

pursuing claims for climate damages, the government, which is the plaintiff in these cases, especially in illegal logging and wildfire cases, pursued claims for emission abatement costs. By going down this road, the Indonesian courts have absolved the plaintiffs from the seemingly impossible task of proving the causal relationship between the defendant's GHGs emissions and the plaintiff's losses due to climate change. The decisions of the Indonesian courts thus suggest that a tort-based climate change litigation is indeed possible. The question is, however, whether such a model of tort-based climate change litigation is fair. This nevertheless remains an important question that should be taken into account when discussing tort-based climate change litigation.

10

From Shehla Zia to Asghar Leghari: Pronouncing Unwritten Rights Is More Complex than a Celebratory Tale

WAQQAS AHMAD MIR

This chapter critically examines the landmark case of *Asghar Leghari* v. *Federation of Pakistan and Others*[1] in the climate litigation docket from the perspective of Pakistani constitutional law. It argues that the *Leghari* case is the result of an evolutionary process, remarkable in its own right, that has seen the Pakistani courts grow increasingly receptive to the adjudication of environmental issues in their constitutional jurisdiction. While this is often lauded as a positive development, this chapter analyses how the story of environmental litigation in Pakistan is much more complex than a celebratory tale. There is a real danger that judicial activity has stultifying effects on the role of the executive in developing, implementing and enforcing environmental laws. While there is good reason to celebrate *Leghari*, there is also a need to be cautious. Each case may not strike the right balance between enforcement of rights and exercising restraint, so as not to interfere with the work of the political branches in a democracy. As such, this chapter also raises some questions about the long-term practical value of cases like *Leghari* and environmental public interest litigation more broadly.

This chapter begins with an introduction to *Leghari*. In Section 10.2, it canvasses a few major cases in Pakistan's environmental law jurisprudence that show how, progressively, various environmental law causes were taken up by these superior courts.[2] Section 10.3 argues that despite high judicial rhetoric from the High Courts and the Supreme Court and

[1] *Leghari* v. *Federation of Pakistan* W.P. No. 25501/2015 ('*Leghari*').

[2] I use the term 'superior courts' to refer collectively to the Supreme Court of Pakistan (the apex court in the country) as well as the five High Courts – there is a High Court for each of Pakistan's four provinces and the Islamabad Capital Territory has its own High Court.

their interpreting the 'right to a clean environment' as part of the 'right to life' under the Constitution of the Islamic Republic of Pakistan 1973 (the Constitution), this judicial activism merits being viewed with caution instead of being celebrated because of unintended consequences. For instance, almost all major environment-related issues in Pakistan end up being litigated before its superior courts (i.e., the High Courts and Supreme Court) instead of being addressed or resolved through discourse that is led by the executive departments tasked with managing these issues. Yet the High Courts as a matter of practice choose not to decide disputed questions of fact, and they have made clear their preference for deciding questions of law (and not fact); nor are they experts when it comes to environmental data or science.[3] The Supreme Court follows a similar tradition in environment-related matters brought before it in its constitutional jurisdiction. To get around this limitation, superior courts in Pakistan rely on court-appointed commissions for fact-finding and expertise in constitutional cases relating to environmental claims. Once commissions submit their findings, courts issue directions to the executive while opining on the scope of rights of citizens. This chapter argues that while the pronouncements of the superior courts might be

High Courts have appellate as well as original jurisdiction, while the Supreme Court has appellate, advisory, and original jurisdiction. For claims raised under Article 199 of the Constitution of Islamic Republic of Pakistan (which is basically the writ jurisdiction) and claims relating to enforcement of Fundamental Rights as enumerated in the Constitution, High Courts have original jurisdiction. The Supreme Court of Pakistan also has original jurisdiction under Article 184(3), Constitution of Islamic Republic of Pakistan, as long as two conditions are met: the matter has to relate to the enforcement of Fundamental Rights provided in the Constitution and has to involve a question of public importance.

[3] For illustration, see Rules and Orders of the Lahore High Court (Revised Edition) 2005 Volume V, Rule 7, Chapter 4-J. As a matter of practice, superior courts in Pakistan will generally not get involved in issues relating to factual controversies. This flows from the basic principles of judicial review that courts will undertake legal, and not factual, review. The case law–generated principle in this regard can be summed up as stating that factual controversy cannot generally be resolved in the constitutional jurisdiction of superior courts. For a well-accepted statement of this principle, please refer to *The Province of East Pakistan* v. *Kshiti Dhar Roy* [1964] 16 DLR (SC) 457, [1964] PLD 636, 647. High Courts follow this principle quite strictly, and the Supreme Court of Pakistan, although ostensibly willing to make pronouncements of fact in high-profile political cases, generally follows this principle when exercising its constitutional jurisdiction in relation to environment related matters. For examples of cases where High Courts did get into questions of disputed facts and evidence while exercising their constitutional jurisdiction, see *Pervaiz Elahi* v.*Province of Punjab* [1993] PLD 595 (Lahore), 655, and *Khawaja Muhammad Sharif* v. *Federation of Pakistan* [1988] PLD 725 (Lahore). For a Supreme Court pronouncement on the issue, see *M Y Khan* v. *M M Aslam* (1974) SCMR 196. None of these cases related to environment-related matters.

good rhetoric in many cases, it is hard to celebrate these cases as bringing about substantive change on the ground. Section 10.4 concludes with some observations about the future of climate change litigation in Pakistan.

10.1 The *Leghari* Case and Lahore High Court's Focus on Climate Justice

Pakistan's Constitution does not contain any provisions dealing with a right, let alone a constitutionally entrenched right, to a clean environment. However, over the years, Pakistan's superior courts (the provincial High Courts and the Supreme Court) have expanded the scope of Fundamental Rights and judicially interpreted the text of Fundamental Rights[4] relating to Article 9, which has been popularly dubbed as 'right to life', and 'dignity of man being inviolable' (Article 14) to include 'the right to a clean and healthy environment'. Article 9 states that no person shall be deprived of life or liberty except in accordance with law. Notwithstanding the negative obligation of the state as per its text, the right has been interpreted broadly to place positive obligations on the state; a process that began in India[5] and has been replicated in Pakistan. This has happened through the creation of a new right (to a clean and healthy environment). For others, this is merely broadening the scope of an existing right (to life). This has been in line with the approach of courts in India where the 'right to life' has been used by courts to derive other rights.[6] Such judicial expansion of the scope of the 'right to life' would not have been possible without the growth of public interest litigation in Pakistan.

10.1.1 Public Interest Litigation

Since the mid-1980s, Pakistan's superior courts – in an ostensible attempt to make the constitution and superior courts more relevant to people's lives – began the process of relaxing traditional rules of 'standing', or locus, to allow citizens challenging state action (or inaction even) to bring

[4] Articles 9 to 28, Constitution of Islamic Republic of Pakistan, comprise Fundamental Rights recognized by the Constitution.

[5] Anuj Bhuwania, *Courting the People: Public Interest Litigation in Post-emergency India* (Cambridge University Press 2017) 26.

[6] James R. May and Erin Daly, *Global Environmental Constitutionalism* (Cambridge University Press 2014), 118.

matters of 'public interest' to court. Taking a cue from India's courts, and expanding their jurisdiction in the process, Pakistani courts recognized a new kind of action titled 'public interest litigation'.[7] Commentators have noted that superior courts underlined the need for looking beyond the Anglo-Saxon model of adversarial litigation[8] – although how far beyond remains unclear even today. The context was a system which promised 'fundamental rights' under the Constitution to millions in a weak state plagued by inefficiency, procedural delays as well as the poverty of the vulnerable. Pakistan's senior judges, while explaining the rationale for PIL, have articulated the importance of enforcement of group rights; as per some of their statements, they were concerned that if a system only recognized grievances when individuals directly aggrieved brought claims before courts, this will deprive a large number of poor and marginalized people of the chance to enforce their rights.[9] If the term 'public interest' sounds uncomfortably vague, and even confusing, take heart from the fact that it is indeed. At the root of recognizing this new form of action was an articulated concern to ensure that those among the vulnerable who cannot approach courts are allowed to benefit from civic activism. This was, and remains, class action without there being the need for a class to come before the court – a single person can file a case on an issue relating to 'public interest' and can point to a class being affected by the issue he or she raises. With rules of standing relaxed, if he or she can persuade the court that state action, or even lack thereof, would adversely affect fundamental rights of the public (or a section thereof), the matter is heard on merits.[10] It was on the back of this jurisprudence that Asghar Leghari approached the Lahore High Court,

[7] For a basic history of public interest litigation, or PIL as it is now generally known, see Mansoor Hassan Khan, *Public Interest Litigation: Growth of the Concept and Its Meaning in Pakistan* (Pakistan Law House 1993). For an excellent and a most thorough analysis of public interest litigation matters decided by the Supreme Court of Pakistan, see Maryam Khan, Genesis and Evolution of Public Interest Litigation in the Supreme Court of Pakistan: Toward a Dynamic Theory of Judicialization (2014) 28(2) *Temple International and Comparative Law Journal* 285.

[8] Ahmed Rafay Alam, 'Public Interest Litigation and the Role of Judiciary' (Supreme Court of Pakistan, 2006, South Asian Association for Regional Cooperation Judicial Conference).

[9] ibid.

[10] A 2010 Lahore High Court ruling written by Justice Mansoor Ali Shah states that 'public interestlitigationis a judicial tool to help resurrect or jump start institutions on the road to healthy democratic values and traditions. Unless substantive democracy takes root, . . . court dockets will continue to be filled with public interest litigation. [C]ourts will continue to redressgrievance with the hope that public institutions will soon come of age.' *Atta Ullah Khan Malik* v. *Federation of Pakistan* [2010] PLD 605 (Lahore).

and he would have been fairly confident that the matter would at least be heard and not immediately dismissed.

The *Leghari* case reached the Lahore High Court at a particularly exciting (and fortuitous) time in Pakistan's constitutional and environmental law jurisprudence. From a time in the early 1990s when there was barely any environment-related constitutional law claims, Pakistan has seen an exponential increase in public interest litigation petitions using the constitution as a basis to raise environment-related claims. In 2015 then, one Asghar Leghari, an agriculturalist and a member of the Lahore High Court Bar Association, approached the Lahore High Court to complain of inaction by the state in fighting climate change. The case was heard and decided by Justice Syed Mansoor Ali Shah, who was then serving as the Chief Justice of the Lahore High Court.[11]

Leghari argued that while Pakistan's Ministry of Climate Change had announced the National Climate Change Policy, 2012 ('the Policy') and the Framework for Implementation of Climate Change Policy (2014–30; 'the Framework'), yet the government had failed to implement them in true letter and spirit. This, Leghari argued, was not just a violation of his Fundamental Rights under the Constitution but also the violation of the rights of members of the public. The rights he invoked were well recognized in Pakistani jurisprudence, thanks to the broad construction of the 'right to life', and hence state inaction was challenged.

While on its face such a claim might sound remarkable to those unfamiliar with Indian and Pakistani case law on public interest litigation, Leghari would have shocked few in Pakistan's courts and newsrooms by lodging this petition. The magnitude of the issue raised and the scope of the petition, however, was and remains remarkable. This was not a claim limited to a particular project or a locality – this was about a global problem that raises questions significant for Pakistan and beyond.

Leghari argued that unless the federal and provincial governments carry out their duties under the Policy and Framework, and unless adaptation measures are taken, he would lose his livelihood. The court dived headlong into the issue and acted out of concern not just for the petitioner but, in its own words, 'for the protection of fundamental rights

[11] Justice Shah has been subsequently elevated to the Supreme Court. In the last twenty years, he has been Pakistan's clearest voice from within the judiciary on environmental law matters. Justice Shah was instrumental in setting up dedicated Green Benches at Lahore High Court, and his legal career as an advocate involved many cases where he argued for expanding constitutional rights to incorporate environmental law protections.

of the citizens of Pakistan, in particular, the vulnerable and weak segments of society who are unable to approach [the] Court'.[12] Recognizing at the very outset that climate change affects everyone, Leghari as an individual petitioner became a representative of the public interest; his individual rights merged with collective rights of all citizens.

From the very beginning of the case, the court acted as a forum of solutions-oriented dialogue between the state and its citizens. After summoning all relevant federal and provincial government departments, and soliciting information about the progress, or lack thereof, in the implementation of the Framework and the Policy, the court set up a Climate Change Commission.[13] This twenty-one member Commission consisted of representatives of the federal and provincial governments, environmental experts and interest groups, as well as petitioner's counsel. And the approach of the court ensured that everyone worked towards the same aim of giving effect to the state's professed aims (i.e., the Framework and the Policy).

Over a period of two years, three months (from September 2015 to January 2018), this case saw the Climate Change Commission acting as, in the court's own words, 'the driving force in sensitizing the [federal and provincial] governments and other stakeholders regarding gravity and importance of climate change'.[14]

The objective of the Commission was immensely broad; it was charged with ensuring 'effective implementation of the Policy and the Framework'.[15] This Commission worked – from September 2015 till January 2018, when it was dissolved – with the relevant government departments to kickstart the process of implementation of the Policy and the Framework. During the pendency of the case, the court received interim and supplemental reports from the Commission, leading the way in fashioning a new approach towards tackling an issue as urgent, and also one as broad, as climate change.

The Commission worked collectively as well as in smaller working groups to kickstart Priority Actions identified under the Framework and the Policy. Over the course of two years, the Commission helped achieve 66 per cent of Priority Actions identified by the Framework.[16] The Commission, among other things, helped develop a framework for

[12] *Leghari* (n 1) [12].
[13] Appointed through *Leghari* (n 1) Orders of 14 September 2015.
[14] *Leghari* (n 1) [19].
[15] *Leghari* (n 1) [13].
[16] *Leghari* (n 1) [19].

design and evaluation of Climate Smart projects.[17] It also helped a provincial government develop a Draft Water Policy, as well as a Draft Climate Change Policy.[18] The work of the Commission also resulted in designation of climate change focal points in all relevant provincial departments and set in place a plan for their capacity building to allow climate change concerns to be incorporated into development plans and growth strategies.[19]

To a South Asian lawyer, a case like *Leghari* is significant but perhaps not for reasons that observers from other jurisdictions (where public interest litigation or complaining of state inaction would be unusual) might imagine. *Leghari* is an important development because, considering the scope of the petition, it represents the latest articulation by Pakistani High Courts that they will treat matters agitating environment-related claims (no matter how broadly framed) as meriting serious indulgence while relating them to fundamental rights under the Constitution; this seriousness is reflected in the detail with which the court guided a petition which sought implementation as well as elaboration of the government's stated policy on an area as wide in scope and reach as climate change. *Leghari* also matters because it tells us that Pakistan's High Courts are now willing to entertain 'a rolling review or a continuing mandamus'[20] in matters relating to environment and fundamental rights related claims. This is significant because in a matter as broad, and indeed as serious as climate change, there is no clear end-point of progress. Yet instead of turning citizens away, the *Leghari* approach gives them another door to knock on while agitating rights-based claims. The case also represents a latest use of courts using a commission as a platform for state actors and citizens to discuss and plan how the country would address the challenges that climate change poses.

The fact that the court treated the petition as 'a rolling review' or a continuing mandamus is, by no means, the norm in Pakistan, even in public interest litigation, which is seen as an inquisitorial rather than adversarial process.[21] *Leghari*, even with the last order in January 2018,

[17] *Leghari* (n 1) [16].
[18] *Leghari* (n 1) [18].
[19] *Leghari* (n 1) [18].
[20] *Leghari* (n 1) [4].
[21] *Sheikh Riaz ul Haq* v. *Federation of Pakistan* [2013] PLD 501 (SC), which reiterated earlier statements of the law made in cases including but not limited to *Watan Party* v. *Federation of Pakistan* [2011] PLD 997 (SC). See also *Alam* (n 7).

was not disposed of but was consigned to the record. As a parting shot, the court established a six-member Standing Committee (composed of members of the Commission) to act as a link between the executive and the court. The Committee can approach the court 'for appropriate orders for enforcement of the fundamental rights of the people in the context of climate change, if and when required'.[22]

Another notable aspect of this case is the fact that Justice Shah further developed the idea of environmental justice (which he had laid down in an earlier case[23]) and took it a step further to articulate what he termed a broader focus on climate justice. To the court, the difference between environmental justice and climate justice was one of scope and reach. In the court's own words, environmental justice as a concept 'was largely localized and limited to our [national] ecosystems and biodiversity'.[24] In distinction to this, climate justice requires acknowledging that we are moving 'from a lineal local environmental issue to a more complex global problem' where 'the identity of the polluter is not clearly ascertainable and by and large falls outside the national jurisdiction'.[25] The court emphasized the importance of achieving 'a human-centred approach safeguarding the rights of the most vulnerable people' and the need for 'equitable stewardship of the world's resources'.[26] The court further noted that the choices available to us are mitigation or adaptation – with the latter being the way forward for Pakistan.[27] By entertaining this petition, Justice Shah gave the clear message that Pakistan's courts are willing to aid the citizens in their quest for adaptation to deal with climate change. Therefore, as a result of *Leghari*, the potential scope of future public interest litigation petitions has been broadened. Also significant is the fact that a mere policy document (including the Framework) was treated as enforceable by a constitutional court – by linking safeguards against climate change to fundamental rights under the Constitution. Petitioners usually cannot claim enforceable rights on the basis of policy documents issued by the executive, and in cases where they make such claims, they need to show clear detrimental reliance to claim enforceable rights. In this case, however, Justice Shah's invocation

22 *Leghari* (n 1) [27].
23 *Imrana Tiwana* v. *Province of Punjab* [2015] PLD 522 (Lahore) ('Imrana Tiwana').
24 *Leghari* (n 1) [20].
25 *Leghari* (n 1) [21].
26 *Leghari* (n 1).
27 *Leghari* (n 1).

of climate justice – and its link with fundamental rights – meant that no detrimental reliance was (or will be) required.

Instead of declaring state (in)action illegal or threatening officials with penal action, the *Leghari* case is a fascinating example of the court working with citizens as well as federal and provincial government departments to acknowledge that grave problems require novel solutions.

The court made no bones about the fact that 'the existing environmental jurisprudence has to be fashioned to meet the needs of something more urgent and overpowering i.e., Climate Change'. The court noted that climate change is not confined to 'local geographic issues'.[28] It emphasized that Pakistan is faced with the threat of serious damage (to its environment, ecology, economy, society) because of climate change. Therefore, instead of focusing merely on 'environmental justice', the court had to view the problem through the lens of 'Climate Justice'. The court, at least in the eyes of those who celebrate this case, did all this without telling the executive what to do. It in fact urged the executive departments to finally do what they had undertaken to all along (i.e., take concrete steps under the Policy and Framework). The decision was not appealed by any party and therefore has attained finality.

There is good reason to celebrate *Leghari* because it did achieve many positives. First, it generated a conversation about the state's responsibilities regarding an issue as urgent and impactful as climate change. Second, in line with the tradition of public interest litigation in Pakistan, it provided a platform, which was not adversarial, for many stakeholders to come together to familiarize themselves with each other's positions, concerns, and limitations. Courts in Pakistan have, in the past, seen themselves as conducting a dialogue between the state and civil society.[29] Even if one can point to rulings that perhaps went too far, there is something to be said for courts ensuring that citizens feel heard and can contribute to public discourse on important issues. Alexandra Lahav has argued that litigation in a democracy is part of self-government and is a manifestation of 'participation on the part of the governed public under the rule of law'.[30] Amartya Sen has reminded us of the importance of John Stuart Mill's argument that a democracy is government by discussion.[31] For those who celebrate public interest litigation, this represents laudable outcomes. *Leghari* has these merits, no doubt,

[28] *Leghari* (n 1) [20].

[29] Paula R. Newberg, *Judging the State* (Cambridge University Press 1995) 13.

[30] Alexandra Lahav, *In Praise of Litigation* (Oxford University Press 2017) 6.

[31] Amartya Sen, *Collective Choice and Social Welfare* (Harvard University Press 2018).

regardless of the broader scepticism about the practical value of public interest litigation. Yet staying with that scepticism is also important, because how far courts go affects other branches of government.

Leghari is the latest step in a process that began in the early 1990s, with the courts of Pakistan using rhetoric as well as substantive law to carve out a new right (i.e., right to a clean environment) that finds no mention in the text of the Constitution. However, can judicially crafting new rights and focusing on outcomes alone be without its problems? In Section 10.2, we look at how Pakistan's courts went about expanding the right to life, and in Section 10.3, we ask some questions about whether what the courts did is worth celebrating in its entirety.

10.2 Unwritten Rights and a Revolution Dressed as Evolution Begins

We now set in context how Pakistani courts' increasing receptiveness over the years to cases relating to the environment set the stage for *Leghari*.

Standard discussions of Pakistani environmental law jurisprudence and public interest litigation will often describe *Shehla Zia and Others* v. *WAPDA*[32] as the case that set the ball rolling for environmental law litigation in Pakistan and articulated a broad definition of the 'right to life'. This is true – except that in September 1992, around seventeen months before *Shehla Zia* was decided, Justice Saleem Akhtar through an order in a *suo moto*[33] proceeding interpreted the constitutionally protected 'right to life' in a manner that would prove to be the harbinger for *Shehla Zia*.

In a human rights case involving environment pollution in Balochistan,[34] Justice Saleem Akhtar, at the Supreme Court of Pakistan, took *suo motu* notice of a news report published on 3 July 1992 in Pakistan's oldest English daily newspaper, *DAWN*,[35] which mentioned that certain business houses were attempting to purchase land around the

[32] *Zia* v. *WAPDA* [1994] PLD 693 (SC) ('*Zia*').

[33] A peculiarity of Supreme Courts of Pakistan and India where judges take notice of an issue themselves and then invite the relevant authorities to explain their position on it. This results in a binding judgment. No one needs to approach the court for the matter to be taken up.

[34] *In re: Human Rights Case (Environmental Pollution in Balochistan)* [1994] PLD 102 (SC) ('*In re: Human Rights Case*').

[35] Pakistan's oldest English daily, www.dawn.com, accessed 29 September 2019.

province of Balochistan's coastal area to convert into a dumping ground for industrial and nuclear waste. On 9 July 1992, Justice Akhtar issued an order expressing reservations that 'if nuclear waste is dumped on the coastal land of Balochistan, it is bound to create environmental hazard and pollution. This act will violate Article 9.' The reference is to Article 9 of the Constitution, which states, 'no person shall be deprived of life or liberty save in accordance with law.' Acting to safeguard this constitutional right, and doing so with a reading that might well have surprised the framers of the Constitution, the Court issued a notice to government officials in the province of Balochistan to enquire whether any land was in fact being allotted for the purpose mentioned in the newspaper story. A letter was also written to DAWN's editor 'requesting him to supply further particulars or give the name and address of the reporter . . . from whom necessary information may be obtained.' Government functionaries appeared and assured the court that no such transaction was taking place. Regardless, the court remained sceptical and, in a flourish of attributing naivety to state officials, said that 'no one will apply for allotment of land for dumping nuclear or industrial waste. This would be a clandestine act in the garb of a legal and proper business activity'.[36] In its order, the court directed the authorities to ensure that a clause be inserted in all future leases/allotments/licenses to prohibit the use of state land for dumping nuclear or industrial waste.[37]

Two things are of immense significance about this order. First, the court interpreted the constitutional 'right to life' as protection from a polluted environment and environmental hazards. It transformed prohibition against deprivation of life or liberty 'save in accordance with law' into a positive obligation for the state. Second, the court broadened the 'right to life' to afford protection against hazardous private action on state owned land. A few months later, in February 1994, Justice Saleem Akhtar – as part of a three-member bench – would interpret the same Article 9 in an equally broad, if not broader, way, and in the process, he would change Pakistan's constitutional litigation history and landscape forever.

In *Shehla Zia,* four residents of a posh Islamabad locality approached the Supreme Court of Pakistan in its original jurisdiction to argue that the construction of a grid station in their locality posed health hazards to residents of the area, including the children and the infirm.[38] The matter

[36] *In re: Human Rights Case* (n 33)104.
[37] *In re: Human Rights Case* (n 33).
[38] *Zia* (n 31) 699–700.

began when a letter was written by a prominent environmentalist to the apex court, requesting that the matter be taken up as a human rights case. The letter argued that a government agency does not have the right to endanger life of an area's residents without their consent and that zoning laws cannot be altered without citizens' consent.[39] Petitioners as well as the respondents submitted materials to the court, arguing for and against the construction of a grid station and whether it posed health and environmental hazards. While the court was clear that Petitioner citizens had the latest research – and that the research materials submitted by the government were dated – it was held that it was 'not possible to give a definite finding on the claims of either side'.[40]

However, the court interpreted this uncertainty in favor of the citizens citing the 'precautionary principle' from the Rio Declaration 1972 to which Pakistan is a signatory.[41] Even though Pakistan had not ratified Rio Declaration 1972 in 1994, and no domestic law existed to this effect, the court said that such international instruments have 'persuasive value and command respect'. Taking on the respondents' argument that this case did not merit indulgence of the Supreme Court in its original jurisdiction[42], the court interpreted the word 'life' broadly enough to mean 'all facets of human existence'. In an oft-quoted paragraph in Pakistani courts, the Supreme Court wrote:

> The word 'life' has not been defined in the Constitution but it does not mean nor can it be restricted only to the vegetative or animal life or mere existence from conception to death. Life includes all such amenities and facilities which a person born in a free country is entitled to enjoy with dignity, legally and constitutionally. For the purposes of present controversy suffice to say that a person is entitled to protection of law from being exposed to hazards of electromagnetic fields or any other such hazards which may be due to installation and construction of any grid station, any factory, power station or such like installations ... Article 184 can be invoked because a large number of citizens throughout the country cannot make such representation and may not make it due to ignorance, poverty and disability. ... In our view the word 'life' is constitutionally so

[39] *Zia* (n 31) 700.

[40] *Zia* (n 31) 709.

[41] *Zia* (n 31) 709.

[42] Under Article 184(3), Constitution of Islamic Republic of Pakistan, the Supreme Court of Pakistan has original jurisdiction to entertain a petition if a two-tiered test is met: the matter relates to Fundamental Rights, as enumerated in the Constitution, and relates to a matter of general public importance.

> wide that the danger and encroachment complained of would impinge fundamental right of a citizen.[43]

The court, in fact, did not stop here and went on to link the constitutional right of 'dignity of man being inviolable' to the 'right to life'. In a particularly consequential instance of rhetorical flourish, the court asked whether a person could be said to have dignity if his right to life could not provide 'food, clothing, shelter, education, health care, clean atmosphere and unpolluted environment'.[44] Realizing that this was an incredibly broad statement, the court in the very next sentence tempered its enthusiasm by saying that such questions will come up for consideration and can be 'dilated upon in more detail in a proper proceeding involving such specific questions'.[45] Although the contours seemed unspecified, if not murky, Justice Saleem Akhtar's broad reading of the 'right to life' ensued in the development of a new judicially crafted right. The court, however, had to sell this new right as only the expansion of the scope of the 'right to life'; otherwise it would have not been able to exercise original jurisdiction over the issue. A prerequisite in this regard is that the matter relates to a Fundamental Right enumerated in the Constitution.

As far as the result of *Shehla Zia* is concerned, the court appointed a commission to examine the scheme and design of the proposed project and report on the likelihood of health hazards. A direction was also issued to WAPDA (the relevant government-owned utility company at the time) to ensure affected members of the public are heard and allowed to raise objections – after newspaper advertisements announcing a project – for all future grid stations or transmission lines. This public hearing requirement was later built into Pakistan Environmental Protection Act 1997 (PEPA 1997) for all projects with an adverse environmental effect. This remains one of *Shehla Zia*'s richest legacies.

Another reason *Shehla Zia* is such a landmark decision is that it made clear that the 'right to life' read with 'dignity of man' now meant a citizen could approach a constitutional court – in fact, the highest court in the land – if a public project had potentially adverse effects on human health and the environment. Claims relating to health and environmental protection could be brought before constitutional courts – even though the text of the Constitution makes no mention of any right to a clean

43 *Zia* (n 31) 712, 713.
44 *Zia* (n 31) 714.
45 *Zia* (n 31) 714.

environment. On one reading, all that Article 9 promises is that you as a citizen will not have your life taken away by the state, except in accordance with law. The fact that the Supreme Court, and in particular Justice Saleem Akhtar, read this with 'dignity of man being inviolable' to mean that citizens could bring claims against environmental and health hazards was and remains nothing less than remarkable.

The door was now open, and a few months later, in July 1994, Justice Saleem Akhtar made an important ruling in *General Secretary, West Pakistan Salt Mines Labor Union, Khewra, Jehlum* v. *The Director, Industries and Mineral Development, Punjab, Lahore*,[46] where he reiterated the link between 'right to life' and 'dignity of man being inviolable' in a case rooted in complaints against pollution of water supply source to the residents and mine workers of salt mines in the hilly area of Khewra. Justice Akhtar wrote that in hilly areas where access to water is 'scarce, difficult or limited, the right to water free from pollution and contamination is a right to life itself'. Just as significant was the court's statement that all persons have the right to unpolluted water.[47] This case resulted in the court holding that Punjab Coal Company (PCC) could not run a mining operation close to the mouth of a water reservoir providing water to residents and miners of Khewra. PCC was directed to relocate, within four months, the mine to maintain a safe distance from the reservoir and stream providing water to the aggrieved parties. A commission was also set up by the Supreme Court to examine whether the mine could actually be moved away from the stream – with a direction to come back to court in case this was not possible.

This case also reiterated that standing or locus standi rules were relaxed for those bringing cases of public importance relating to the Fundamental Rights enumerated in the Constitution.

10.2.1 Right to Life and Planning Permission

The relaxation of the standing requirement by the Supreme Court and the broad reading of the 'right to life' also resulted, in the next few years, of cases challenging building permissions (or lack thereof) being brought to constitutional courts. In *Ardeshir Cowasjee and 10 Others* v. *Karachi Building Control Authority and Others*,[48] the petitioners first went to the

[46] *Salt Miners* v. *Director, Industries and Mineral Development* (1994) SCMR 2061.
[47] ibid 2070.
[48] *Ardeshir Cowasjee* v. *Karachi Building Control Authority* (1999) SCMR 2883.

High Court of Sindh and then appealed to the Supreme Court of Pakistan against the grant of building permission for the construction of a high-rise building on a plot of land that had been earmarked for the construction of a public park. In 1956, a plan for the 132-acre park had initially been approved with an amusement park, recreational facilities, restaurants, shops, skating rink, and so forth all to be situated within its limits. This plan was changed in 1976, and only a revolving restaurant was envisaged in the park; the rest of the land was allotted to an investment firm. Residents of the area where the park had been planned challenged this and were initially turned away by the High Court of Sindh. On appeal, while relying on the relaxed requirements of standing – and saying that all that citizens needed was to show 'sufficient interest' in the performance of a legal duty by a state functionary – the Supreme Court struck down the revised building plan as being without lawful authority since it had not received the relevant approvals. The court also held that when granting permission for the construction of high-rise buildings, the municipal authorities had to keep in view requirements of water, electricity, gas, sewage lines, and other infrastructure.

10.2.2 Parliament Has Its Say in 1997

This was an exciting time for environment-related constitutional law litigation but also one that, quite obviously, raised questions about how far courts should go in the implementation of a judicially crafted constitutional right. It is significant that the proper enforcement of this right required dedication of resources, including finances. Judicial decisions had, even before Parliament acted, created a right with extremely broad contours. Parliament eventually acted and 1997 saw the enactment of the Pakistan Environmental Protection Act (PEPA).[49] The statute set up federal and provincial environmental protection agencies and tasked them with the responsibility and the powers to regulate projects with adverse environmental impact.

However, the state was unable to effectively implement the PEPA. For example, the Act envisaged the promulgation of secondary legislation, including rules and regulations, for various provisions of the PEPA, but these rules and regulations were not immediately made by the executive. This is not entirely surprising because, regardless of judicial rhetoric, the capacity of the state does matter. It is not as if broad pronouncements of

[49] Pakistan Environmental Protection Act 1997.

a right to life by Pakistan's superior courts post-1994 magically altered the state's ability to deal with environmental problems. It was therefore to be expected that problems of implementation and enforcement would remain.

10.2.3 Petitions Filed to Implement the Law

Against this background, petitioners in 2002 approached the Lahore High Court in a public interest petition to seek effective implementation of PEPA.[50] The court wrote an elaborate judgment emphasizing the importance of the governing statute being properly implemented and, after appointing various *amici curiae*, issued 'suggestions' to the government to fight the menace of pollution while also 'directing' the state functionaries to 'implement the provisions of Pakistan Environment Protection Act 1997 in letter and spirit and frame necessary rules and regulations and issue necessary Notifications under the provisions preferably within six months'.[51]

It is noteworthy that despite the promulgation of a comprehensive law in 1997 that creates specific environmental regulatory provisions and tribunals for the settlement of disputes, environmental disputes continue to be framed in constitutional terms (i.e., the right to life). A notable consequence of this trend is that the High Courts continue to play a prominent role in environmental law-making and implementation through its constitutional jurisdiction.

10.2.4 Vehicular Pollution and Air Quality

The judge who decided *Leghari*, Justice Mansoor Ali Shah, in 1997 himself brought a case (as petitioner and lawyer) before the Lahore High Court, which had parallels with *Leghari* in terms of the broad claims made as well as, at least in part, how the court acted to address the petitioners' grievances.

In *Syed Mansoor Ali Shah and 4 Others* v. *Government of Punjab and Three Others* PLD 2007 Lahore 403, the petitioners argued that air pollution in Lahore had become a serious health hazard and required urgent action to safeguard the fundamental rights of the people. The court established a commission by the name of Lahore Clean Air

[50] *Anjum Irfan* v. *Lahore Development Authority* [2002] PLD 555 (Lahore) ('*Anjum Irfan*').

[51] *Anjum Irfan* (n 50) at 586.

Commission (with representation of stakeholders including state, private and civil society actors), which made recommendations to improve air quality and reduce vehicular pollution in Lahore. The terms of reference of this commission were limited to submitting a report on 'feasible and practical solutions' for improving vehicular air pollution in Lahore. The recommendations were not contested by the government, and the case resulted in detailed directions being issued to reduce vehicular pollution. And just like *Leghari*, this case also constituted a Standing Body of the commission to bring, at any appropriate time, applications before the court in case recommendations and directions were not being complied with.[52]

The ruling is fascinating reading because of the open discussion the judicial process facilitated. One of the matters discussed in the ruling was a direction to the government to phase out two-stroke rickshaws by December 2007. This aspect, among others, had important ramifications since rickshaws are driven by a vulnerable segment of the population; these drivers make little money, and a court direction telling the government to phase out these vehicles posed a serious threat to their livelihood. Rickshaw drivers repeatedly made numerous pleas to delay the implementation of the part of the order affecting them. The state, in any case, faces issues of ensuring implementation of existing law. And in August of 2010, the newspaper *The News*[53] reported that the phasing out of existing two-stroke rickshaws and banning of new two-stroke rickshaws remained un-implemented. In 2013, an ADB Report titled *Environmental Laws and Jurisprudence in Pakistan* noted that the High Court order was not enforced.[54] The government did, in theory, order a ban on two-stroke rickshaws, and four-stroke rickshaws were introduced in Lahore to a certain degree. However, there is no detailed study of whether the court or the executive should get the credit for starting the process of phasing out two-stroke rickshaws and even buses beyond a certain age. Questions also remain about the impact on the livelihoods of rickshaw drivers, among others, when a ban and phasing out process was unevenly implemented. And then there are larger questions about

[52] *Syed Mansoor Ali Shah* v. *Government of Punjab* [2007] PLD 403, 422.

[53] *The News* mentioned in *Environmental Rights* (published by LEAD Pakistan), 24 August 2010, available at www.lead.org.pk/hr/attachments/Compandium/04_Environmental_Rights/01_Environmental_Rights-Context.pdf.

[54] Irum Ahsan and Saima Amin Khawaja, Development of Environmental Laws and Jurisprudence in Pakistan (Asian Development Bank 2013), available at https://www.adb.org/sites/default/files/publication/31140/environmental-law-jurisprudence-pakistan.pdf, accessed 10 June 2020.

what this petition achieved – regardless of its good intentions. Yes, it generated a much-needed conversation about air quality in a major city, but it is hard to convincingly argue that it was an all-inclusive conversation where the most vulnerable were heard. It will be hard to argue that air pollution and air quality in the city of Lahore is today a more manageable problem because of this ruling. What is clear is that this case continued to inspire citizens to take issues of pollution and smog in Lahore's air to court. Whether this approach will solve Lahore's air quality problems is not so clear.

10.2.5 Solid Waste Management

In 2002, the Lahore High Court was called upon through a constitutional petition to prohibit City District Government Lahore from using an area close to petitioners' agricultural land from being used for a project meant to produce energy from municipal waste, including waste from hospitals. The basic grievance of the petitioners (residents of locality of Mahmood Booti) was to ensure that solid waste is not dumped in and around their locality in a way that would adversely affect their quality of life. This resulted in Lahore High Court directing the local government to deploy 'all possible resources at their disposal to minimize the effects of the dumping ground'.

In the process, the High Court – while citing an earlier case[55] – termed the issue of pollution 'more dangerous than a hydrogen bomb.'[56] The city government of Lahore assailed the directions given in this case on the basis that petitioners who approached the Lahore High Court should have availed a statutory remedy under the governing law (i.e., Pakistan Environmental Protection Act 1997). In effect, the government was arguing that the petition in which the orders were passed was not maintainable before the High Court. Interestingly enough, a two-member bench of the Lahore High Court refused this prayer by the government in appeal – and held that the matter raised 'issues of general public importance' and fundamental rights of petitioners; therefore the government could not raise objection on the 'maintainability of the petition based on the availability of an alternate remedy'.[57]

[55] *Mrs. Anjum Irfan* v. *Lahore Development Authority* PLD 2002 Lahore 555.

[56] *Muhammad Yousaf* v. *Province of the Punjab* 2003 CLC 576 at 583.

[57] Order dated 11 December 2002 in Intra-Court Appeal No. 798/2002, titled *City District Government* v. *Muhammad Yousaf and Others*, available in Dr. Parvez Hassan, *Resolving Environmental Disputes in Pakistan: The Role of Judicial Commissions* (Pakistan Law House 2018), 150–1.

At the appellate stage, a two-member bench of the Lahore High Court appointed a committee (with its members comprising of government officials, technical experts, elected representatives, lawyers, etc.) to look into the concerns raised by citizens and submit a report.[58] The committee recommended that the area of Mahmood Booti was environmentally suitable for 'safe disposal of solid waste provided there is a proper composting plant, recycling facility and a sanitary landfill'.[59] The committee supported the government's plan of setting up a compost fertilizer plant as feasible to remove the environmental hazard from the area. The court accepted this recommendation and directed the city government to also acquire land at other places for setting up waste-disposal plants. This last bit was on the recommendation of the amicus in the case, Mansoor Ali Shah. This case will be remembered for contributing to public discussion in Lahore about solid waste management – and the executive seems to have continued learning new ways in this area to address people's concerns. Today Lahore manages its waste through a government-owned waste-management company that receives largely positive reviews regarding its performance.

10.2.6 Clean Water

In 2008 in a case before the Supreme Court in *Muhammad Shafiq and Others* v. *Arif Hameed Mehar and Others*,[60] petitioners agitated the issue of supply of clean water to residents of Islamabad. 'Right to life' is not specifically mentioned in the court order, yet this was a petitioner under Article 184(3) requiring a showing that the case relates to the enforcement of Fundamental Rights and is a matter of public importance. Hence there is a strong argument to be made that the court took up this petition while ostensibly relying on the 'right to life'. The case mentions the bench's displeasure at the federal and provincial governments' 'inaction in case of breach of environmental laws', yet the order carries no discussion of whether the relevant environmental protection agencies were first approached by any of the petitioners and how they ruled on any of the

[58] Order dated 25 February 2003 in Intra-Court Appeal No. 798/2002, mentioned in *Report of the Lahore Solid Waste Management Committee on Dumping Ground at Mahmood Booti*, available in Dr. Parvez Hassan, *Resolving Environmental Disputes in Pakistan: The Role of Judicial Commissions* (Pakistan Law House 2018), 158.

[59] Dr. Parvez Hassan, *Resolving Environmental Disputes in Pakistan: The Role of Judicial Commissions* (Pakistan Law House 2018), 165.

[60] *Muhammad Shafiq* v. *Arif Hameed Mehar* [2008] PLD 716 (SC), [2008] CLD 1103.

complaints. The court noted that while it cannot make arrangements for 'removal of filth from public places', it can direct government departments to take 'necessary steps and adopt measures to stop environmental pollution'.[61]

10.2.7 Environment and Suo Motu

Another case relating to an environmental cause that was taken up by the Supreme Court of Pakistan, of its own motion, is the *Suo Motu Case No. 10 of 2005*,[62] where CJ Iftikhar Chaudhry and thirteen other judges took up the case of possible environmental hazards of the New Murree Project.[63] This was the time of the court of CJ Chaudhry, and while issuing notice to the relevant provincial government at the initial stages of the case, one question he posed was whether the provincial government had considered the report of the International Union of Conservation of Natural Resources (IUCN) before approving the project. Another question related to whether any environmental impact survey had been carried out by the government. It is indeed curious, if not unfortunate, that an unelected branch (judiciary) sought to question and second-guess executive discretion and policy-making in this manner – and that too of its own motion (i.e., without any petitioner approaching the court). The case was kept pending for four years – from 2005 to 2009 – and it ended when the provincial government assured the court that the project was not going ahead because the provincial government deemed it unfeasible. The court disposed of the proceedings by noting that the provincial government 'has taken a right decision in disbanding' the project. As far as examples of judicial activism regarding environmental issues go, this is a particularly striking – and unfortunate – case.

In *Suo Motu Case No. 3 of 2006*[64] the Supreme Court under CJ Chaudhry took up the issue of cutting of trees in Jahangir Park, Karachi. Again, despite the executive appearing and submitting that it had decided not to proceed with the project in view of the court's orders and objections by certain NGOs, the court felt that it was necessary to pass an order stating that 'although the project has been abandoned, but [respondent government] is restrained to convert the [relevant land] in future to any other use

[61] *Muhammad Shafiq* v. *Arif Hameed Mehar* [2008] PLD 716 (SC), [2008] CLD 1113.

[62] *Suo Motu Case No.10 of 2005* (2010) SCMR 361.

[63] Murree is a popular hill station in Pakistan, and the New Murree Project envisaged development projects in the vicinity of the existing city.

[64] *Suo Motu Case No. 3 of 2006* [2006] 58 PLD 514 (SC).

save in accordance with the law'.[65] The government was also ordered to restore the status of the pubic park. This case also reads like an example of surprisingly bold use of judicial activism, with the apex court ostensibly making clear its displeasure to the executive and pushing the executive till projects viewed unfavourably by the court are dropped.

10.2.8 Dam Fund

In a particularly striking (some might even say disturbing) example of judicial activism, the Supreme Court of Pakistan (during the tenure of Chief Justice Saqib Nisar), in *Barrister Zafarullah Khan* v. *Federation of Pakistan* 2018 SCMR 2001, while discussing water scarcity, dangers posed by polluted water, and its relation to the constitutional right to life, ordered that the federal government should implement its decisions of constructing various dams that had been approved in principle. The court quoted the words of Justice Saleem Akhtar in *Shehla Zia* that the terms 'life' in the 'right to life' include all amenities and facilities that a person born in a free country is entitled to enjoy. The court's enthusiasm and activism were not tempered, despite the fact that political decision-making process and lack of funds, among other reasons, had resulted in the process of building dams being delayed. The apex court not only set up a fund inviting donations for the dam from the general public but also set up an implementation committee to oversee the construction of dams and the execution of works. Litigants as well as lawyers appearing before the court were regularly told by the court to deposit funds in the dam fund, which caused a fair amount of public controversy.

Soon after Chief Justice Nisar retired, the dam fund stopped being the centre of attention at the Supreme Court. Recently the Supreme Court of Pakistan's website also removed pages with links to the dam fund. The dam fund saga was and remains an instructive lesson in how judicial activism, and an expansionist reading of rights, can raise serious and troubling questions about the court's policy choices as well as its general prestige.

10.2.9 Save Lahore?

A number of major development projects in the capital of Pakistan's largest province, Punjab, have also repeatedly been the subject of litigation before the Supreme Court and the Lahore High Court.

[65] *Suo Motu Case No. 3 of 2006* [2006] 58 PLD 514 (SC) 532.

In 2011, a private organization by the name of 'Lahore Bachao Tehrik' (Save Lahore Movement or LBT) wrote a letter to the Supreme Court,[66] arguing that the provincial government's plan to widen the canal running through the heart of Lahore, and the cutting of trees that would follow, was environmentally hazardous and therefore should be declared illegal. The Supreme Court converted the letter into a *suo motu* case and summoned the provincial government to explain its position. LBT argued that the canal-widening project violated the right to life (Article 9). They also referred to the precautionary principle to bolster their argument that the project be declared illegal. The provincial government's position was that an environmental impact assessment (EIA) had been conducted pursuant to the PEPA and, in the opinion of experts and the provincial environmental agency, the project was environmentally feasible. The petitioners (i.e., LBT) assailed the role of the provincial environmental agency and countered that it was not independent and was essentially under the control of the provincial government. The court, with consent of the parties, set up a Mediation Committee (comprising individuals from the government and those from the private sector with a distinguished public service record). The Committee made recommendations that petitioners almost entirely agreed to, aside from objecting to the size of the widening project. After considering the report of the Committee, the court refused to strike down the EIA report and said that there was no incontrovertible material presented to it that jeopardized the authenticity of the EIA or the discretion exercised by the provincial environmental agency when granting approval to the project. In a move that can be seen as the courts' desire to remain relevant to the lives of citizens, while to a significant extent also having the final word on government's policy choices, the court declared that the canal be protected as a public trust under the public trust doctrine – and held that it would be treated as a Heritage Urban Park forthwith.[67] Without being specific, as is often the case in these matters in Pakistan, the court ordered that 'elaborate steps be taken to ensure that the canal is kept clean and free of pollution. The Chief Secretary shall ensure that a comprehensive action plan is prepared and report is submitted to Registrar of this court within six weeks of this judgment.'[68]

[66] *In The Matter of Cutting of Trees for Canal Road Widening Project*, Lahore (2011) SCMR 1743.
[67] ibid 1801.
[68] ibid 1802.

Another major case regarding a development project in Lahore was the *Imrana Tiwana* case.[69] This case saw a direct challenge before the Lahore High Court to the provincial government's plan to do away with traffic signals (create a signal-free corridor with the aim of facilitating traffic movement) in one of Lahore's most commercially busy and expensive areas. The petitioners challenged the environmental approvals along with the allegedly compromised independence of the provincial environmental agency. This was a reiteration of the earlier argument from 2011 before the Supreme Court that the provincial environmental agency was not independent and hence could not be trusted to fulfil its legal role. Yet another line of attack was that the entire project had been planned under the aegis of the Lahore Development Authority (LDA) – while Article 140A of the Constitution envisaged that control over such planning and municipal matters would be devolved to the local governments in each province. A full bench of the Lahore High Court, headed by Justice Mansoor Ali Shah, declared the project illegal and held that the provincial environmental agency had failed to fulfil its statutory role. The court also held that the provincial agency represented what the court called 'regulatory capture'. Further, in a ground-breaking judgment, the court made clear that an executive controlled development authority (such as LDA) could not act as a substitute for the constitutionally commanded elected local governments. Unfortunately, the Supreme Court of Pakistan set aside this ruling and allowed the project to proceed. The ruling authored by Justice Shah at the Lahore High Court had been celebrated by environmentalists as well as local government activists. It being set aside is likely to adversely impact the development of jurisprudence aimed at empowering elected local governments.

The provided cases present a snap-shot view of the types of cases that have come before the High Courts and Supreme Court of Pakistan under the expanded definition of 'right to life'. As is evident, in a number of cases, the courts have adopted the method of appointing commissions to make recommendations to the court, which then translate into directions for the relevant state functionaries.

In Section 10.3, the analysis turns to the question of whether this exercise of judicial power is worth celebrating and how it affects executive decision-making and policy-making in Pakistan.

[69] *Imrana Tiwana* (n 22). The author served as amicus curiae in this case.

10.3 What Does This Mean for Democracy, and How Far Should Courts Go?

There is indeed a fair bit to celebrate in Pakistan's story of environmental law litigation. However, it can be argued that the story is more complex than what initially appears. One can commend cases like *Leghari* without losing sight of how judicial activism and judicial creation of new constitutional rights can adversely impact executive policy making and implementation. If Pakistan's story has *Shehla Zia* and *Leghari*, then we cannot forget that the same rhetoric was used to set up and celebrate the dam fund by Chief Justice Nisar – a move that raised pressing questions about the court's constitutional role, its prestige, and exposed it to allegations of cherry-picking policy issues it decided to get involved in. There are serious cautionary elements to this tale.

Furthermore, courts in Pakistan must engage with the issue that while public interest litigation receives attention and indulgence, the same treatment does not greet the statutory appeals that come to the High Courts from the environmental tribunals. It should trouble all those concerned with public interest that the treatment your case receives can vary significantly in Pakistan's High Courts and Supreme Court, depending on whether you are a petitioner in a public interest petition or an ordinary appellant under the environmental laws.

It is arguable that courts have to step in because of the executive's failure to ensure sufficient resources for statutory bodies and tribunals charged with administering environmental law legislation. It would be facile to suggest that executive inaction is not a problem. It is, and one must acknowledge that. However, as former UK Supreme Court judge Jonathan Sumption reminds us in the BBC's Reith Lectures 2019, it is worth asking how far should courts go to enforce rights that they think it would be a good idea for people to have.[70] There are cases where courts have acted with admirable restraint when faced with executive inaction. This is illustrated by the case of *SHEHRI C.B.E* v. *Government of Pakistan and Others* 2007 CLD 783, where the Sindh High Court had to take up an environmental law dispute – related to substantive provisions of the PEPA – only because the government had failed to ensure that the Environmental Tribunal (i.e., the body actually charged under the statute with hearing challenges on environmental grounds) was functional. To

[70] Jonathan Sumption, 'The Reith Lectures 2019: Law and the Decline of Politics" (BBC Radio 4, 4 Jun 2019) <http://downloads.bbc.co.uk/radio4/reith2019/Reith_2019_Sumption_lecture_3.pdf> accessed 10 Jun 2020.

its credit, the court acknowledged in this judgment that the technical matters in question were for the relevant environmental protection agency, and not the court, to decide.[71] And yet, as was argued in Section 10.2, Pakistan's courts have not always exercised restraint or exhibited modesty about their role.

The broad elaboration of the 'right to life' has led to some interestingly broad statements by courts over the years; for instance, the High Court of Sindh wrote in 2001 that right to life is linked to necessity of parks, gardens, and open spaces. And there was a consensus between sociologists, judges, and doctors that not providing them '*would create problems of* mental health, rise in crime rate and degradation of moral values of inhabitants'.[72] In 2003, the Lahore High Court was called upon through a constitutional petition to prohibit City District Government Lahore from using an area close to petitioners' agricultural land from being used for a project meant to produce energy from municipal waste. This resulted in Lahore High Court directing the local government to deploy 'all possible resources at their disposal to minimize the effects of the dumping ground'. In the process, the LHC, while citing an earlier case,[73] described the issue of pollution as 'more dangerous than a hydrogen bomb.'[74]

There is no denying that courts exist as a forum of dialogue between the state and its citizens; and it is a good thing if citizens feel confident about approaching courts with their grievances. Furthermore, scholars have noted – and for good reason – that even when courts lack expertise in particular areas, they are particularly good at ensuring that information is furnished by parties participating in the judicial process. But these ostensible positives are not the entire story.

First, when we say that courts exist as a forum of dialogue between the state and its citizens, we should not forget the general state that the Pakistani judicial system is in.[75] And one must not overestimate the faith that ordinary Pakistani citizens have in the judicial system.[76]

71 *Shehri CBE* v. *Govt of Pakistan* [2007] CLD 783, 801.

72 *Shehri* v. *Province of Sindh* [2001] YLR 1139, 1146, and 1147.

73 *Anjum Irfan* (n 49).

74 *Muhammad Yousaf* v. *Province of the Punjab* [2003] CLC 576, 583.

75 For an excellent qualitative as well as quantitative analysis, see Dr. Osama Siddique, Pakistan's Experience with Formal Law: An Alien *Justice* (Cambridge University Press 2014).

76 See Dr. Osama Siddique, 'Law In Practice – The Lahore District Courts Litigants Survey (2010 – 2011)' Development Policy Research Centre Working Paper (2010), www.lprn.org.pk/wp-content/uploads/2015/07/Law-In-Practice-Lahore-District-Courts-Litigants-Survey.pdf, accessed 29 September 2019. One of the many important findings was that very few (8 out of 497) respondents mentioned

Overcrowded dockets, shocking delays, incompetence, and even corruption plague the system and affect an overwhelming number of litigants. Class and finances often determine whether one can even approach a High Court. In his refreshingly nuanced treatment of public interest litigation in India, Anuj Bhuwania reminds us that '[i]t is important to keep in mind that the heroic persona of the Indian judiciary – made possible by PIL – is reserved only for the State High Courts and the Supreme Court' while India's lower judiciary is seen 'as purely pathological – inefficient, corrupt and overly embedded in the Indian social milieu – while the appellate courts of course apparently transcend it'.[77] The same can be said for Pakistan, with significant force. There is hardly any debate on the state of environmental tribunals functioning in Punjab. Their capacity and everyday performance, whether you are a lawyer or litigant, does not inspire confidence. And even though High Courts cite the inability of the poor to approach courts as a justification for greater indulgence given to public interest petitions, it would be naïve to ignore that cases brought by the privileged often involve discourses of the privileged and their positions may not always cater to what would affect, or matter to, a poor citizen. And does this concern for the poor translate into how ordinary cases, including appeals, lodged by the poor and vulnerable are treated?

Pakistan is fast becoming a country where almost every major environmental issue that has made the news ends up before the High Court or the Supreme Court through a petition or is taken up by the Supreme Court of its own volition under its *suo motu* jurisdiction. These are constitutional courts, but they are by no means a sector-specific regulator with the requisite expertise or capacity. Yet, on almost all major environmental issues, instead of first engaging with executive agencies tasked with administering environmental law statutes, citizens prefer to approach the constitutional courts. The interpretation placed on 'right to life' read with 'dignity of man being inviolable', along with the wealth of precedent in this area, ensures that statutory claims are linked to constitutional ones and then brought directly before the High Courts or the Supreme Court. In fact, quite often the more broadly a claim is framed, the easier it has been to convince a constitutional court that the

the positive reason of having 'faith in the fairness of the court system' for choosing the state-provided dispute-resolution system. A majority said they were driven to courts because of a trust deficit with their opposing side.

77 Bhuwania (n 5).

issue should be heard there instead of being sent to the executive agencies. This adds to the already-clogged dockets of overburdened constitutional courts and it is worth having a conversation about whether public interest litigation on every issue is the best way to ensure the much-hyped faith of citizens in courts. When *Shehla Zia* was decided, did the Supreme Court think enough about what it would mean if constitutional courts cannot service all the claims being lodged?

The exercise of *suo motu* powers raises other important questions. When activist Chief Justices like Chaudhry and Saqib Nisar select certain environmental issues without clear indication why some issues are taken up and not others, it can be argued that such cherry-picking of cases opens the judiciary up to charges of being politicized and even biased. In this regard, the approach of the Supreme Court in *suo motu* cases has been far from ideal and merits consistent engagement as well as critique. The judiciary, being an unelected branch of government, should be mindful of intrusive questioning of policy choices made by the elected representatives of the people. Nonetheless, the Supreme Court under CJ Chaudhry and Saqib Nisar showed scant regard over any concerns of judicial over-reach.

Dr. Parvez Hassan, who headed the Climate Change Commission in *Leghari* and has headed more court-appointed commissions in environment matters than any other person in Pakistan, has also recognized some of the limitations of public interest litigation as well as judicial activism. For instance, with specific reference to exercise of *suo motu* powers by the Supreme Court of Pakistan, he notes that *suo motu* notices result in executive bodies like Environmental Protection Agency 'adopt[ing] a "wait-and-see" approach' and that '[t]his results in suffocation of capacity of the [agencies], which would otherwise have gained from the exposure to the issue'.[78] One could argue that not just *suo motu* powers of the Supreme Court but judicial activism generally can hamper the development of executive agencies and can cause them to always look towards the courts.

When we talk about the role of constitutional courts in Pakistan, we must also remember the kind of review that these courts do/can undertake in their constitutional jurisdiction. It is a settled rule of practice[79] that constitutional courts will not decide disputed questions of fact,

[78] Hassan (n 59) 7–8.

[79] For illustration, see Rules and Orders of the Lahore High Court (Revised Edition) 2005 Volume V, Rule 7, Chapter 4-J.

except in very rare cases,[80] or get involved in controversies that require leading and recording of evidence. Hence constitutional courts decide legal questions, not factual disputes; the latter have to be taken to courts of plenary jurisdiction unless matters are, by law, declared to be within jurisdiction of certain sector specific regulators or tribunals. The broad interpretation of 'right to life' and forming of commissions to arrive at recommendations might avoid the need for factual controversies in some cases but this cannot be a recipe for all time. Environmental science can be complex and parties can dispute each other's data or evidence in support of factual claims – yet these are questions that constitutional courts of Pakistan do not cover. Dr. Parvez Hassan argues that the courts' answer to this has been court-appointed commissions that include representation from various stakeholders, including the government, so consensus can be built and recommendations can be implemented.[81] This is a fair point. However, it is hard to argue that presence of court-appointed commissions always results in courts being mindful of their limitations. In issuing directions, courts do exercise discretion, and this can, and indeed often does, result in the line between law and policy becoming murky. Also, once directions in a particular matter are issued and a subsequent policymaker or political administration wants to try a new approach – which is the right of elected branches and executive in a democracy – will they be expected to return to courts which will have a final approving say? This raises important questions of what we can, and should, expect from courts in a democracy. So, this should make us think carefully about the efficacy of using constitutional courts as a forum of first choice for resolving complex disputes or even their efficacy as a platform that facilitates nuanced discourse between state and citizens. Broad framing of rights by courts has often led to broad framing of complaints/issues by petitioners; all of this translates into good rhetoric and uplifting reading material, but little concrete change has happened on the ground. In a recent judgment, the Lahore High Court, while linking the importance of planting and preserving trees and forests in Punjab to the right to life, directed (among other things) that each new house in an approved housing society should have at least two trees planted in the green belt outside it. While such concern for environment is laudable, it is hard to see how such orders can be enforced.

[80] See (n 3).
[81] *Hassan* (n 59) 8.

There is also the issue of courts' own prestige being affected if there is an inflation of orders fuelled by judicial activism with little change on the ground. Judicial orders are more likely to be enforced when they are consistent with what the state can deliver. Judicial rhetoric, even when not enforced, perhaps helps the judiciary build a constituency for itself – since the lack of enforcement is likely to first cast the elected branches in an unflattering light. However, eventually, an inflation of orders is likely to adversely affect the seriousness with which orders and judgments are taken – not just by the executive but also the people and the media; they are an important part of the constituency that judiciaries speak to. Hence even from a strategic, or even selfish, perspective it makes sense for judiciaries to remain sceptical of what activism or public interest litigation can achieve. It can supplement but not substitute democracy. Often times this becomes murky, with little public debate. And this needs to change.

Despite the fact that Pakistan has all this body of case-law on environmental law, and despite being one of the few countries with a dedicated Ministry of Climate Change, it remains a country among the most vulnerable to the dangers posed by climate change[82]. The fact that courts crafted a new right – to a clean environment – and then continued to take on cases related to the environment means that executive agencies (like provincial environmental agencies) are always looking at the courts to first intervene in all major environmental law issues. An inflation of court orders cannot compensate for the state's lack of capacity. And if there is any hope of long-term sustainable solutions, then they will have to come from an executive that can make policy without looking over its shoulder all the time. Even as courts appoint commissions[83] to hand in recommendations, this means that multiple commissions remain in effect for many years. Owing to the slow pace of litigation, this means that the executive remains mired in litigation before the constitutional courts on major environmental issues. This, I submit, acts as a disincentive for the executive agencies to come up with any innovative policies of their own. Even if they want to develop new policies, they have to first run to court to seek approval

[82] Asian Development Bank, *Climate Change Profile of Pakistan* (2017), www.adb.org/sites/default/files/publication/357876/climate-change-profile-pakistan.pdf, accessed 29 September 2019.

[83] For instance, currently you can find on the Lahore High Court website orders establishing the following commissions in various public interest petitions: River Ravi Commission, Wildlife Commission, Fire Safety Commission.

for those policies since, as discussed previously, courts are usually quick to jump on cases involving the environment, and then as long as cases are pending before the constitutional courts, any executive policy has to receive approval of the courts.

It is also worth thinking about how constitutional courts in Pakistan go about concluding matters that come up before them – or in the case of *suo motu*, those that are taken up directly. Vague recommendations are perhaps just as problematic – for being unclear and high on rhetoric than substance – as specific and intrusive directions that essentially frame or reframe executive policy.

Courts, being an unelected branch, should be sceptical when deciding environmental law matters, which quite often relate to policy choices as well as require study of complex information. Executive agencies need to develop their capacity, which is indeed true, but if they are always uncertain of when a court will take up a case and bypass the statutory scheme, then this does not augur well for long term executive agencies' development.

There is no doubt that civil society and courts both learn from each other as a result of environmental law litigation. But this should not mean that executive agencies should miss out on the opportunity to learn from concerned citizens who raise these issues. One cannot ignore that the civil society justifiably complains that the executive agencies are often too slow to react to complaints, but it is also worth considering whether civil society continuously approaching constitutional courts (as a first choice) and bypassing statutory agencies means that civil society is engaging in lazy activism; broad constitutional claims premised on broadly articulated rights by judiciary may not hold in complex matters where data, science, and uncertain choices of remedial steps are involved. The Lahore smog issue is a good example of this where the civil society and the government differed bitterly over the air quality data – there was no initial consensus on why Lahore was witnessing sudden increase in smog or what are the best and most effective steps to protect human health. And the subsequent orders passed by the Lahore High Court mostly remain un-implemented.[84]

Till today the smog remains a serious issue in the winter months, and it is unlikely that a judicial order declaring a health emergency will provide

[84] *Walid Iqbal* v. *Federation of Pakistan* WP No.34789/2016, http://sys.lhc.gov.pk/greenBenchOrders/WritPetition-Miscellanous-Environment-34789-16-17-11-2017.pdf, accessed 29 September 2019.

the solution. The solution will have to come from the executive agencies and their constituents who will need to get together to form a policy document that achieves a consensus on necessary steps and their enforcement. However, we can continue to expect responsible citizens to use constitutional courts to force the executive to listen.

10.4 Looking Ahead While Not Forgetting the Past

In 2019, it is twenty-five years since *Shehla Zia* was decided in 1994. What has Pakistan gained as a result of environmental claims being linked to constitutional rights, and what, then, is the future of climate change litigation in Pakistan?

Looking ahead, It is unlikely that Pakistan will, anytime soon, see a drastic reduction in the number of public interest petitions invoking the right to life to make environment-related claims. Courts are likely to continue entertaining broad readings of constitutional rights, as well as broadly worded claims that allow judicial rhetoric to continue. But we should not expect major environmental law issues to be resolved as a result of this.

It is also interesting to think about how soon Pakistan's courts will receive and react to constitutional claims, linked to the environment, that call for recognition of legal personality for rivers, forests, and other non-human life forms. How will courts wrestle with the text and the need to ensure that climate change litigation continues receiving indulgence and attention? This will be a fascinating challenge for them, and considering Pakistan's jurisprudence, the day may not be far when courts start deciding these questions.

The cautionary note sounded in the previous section is not meant to suggest that one should be despondent about the future. After all, there is something to be said for courts standing up to powerful minorities who adversely affect the environment, just like we expect courts to push back against the tyranny of the majority when it hurts minorities.[85] Pakistan's courts have, in many environmental law cases, managed to strike a balance between enforcing rights and the need to ensure they do not make policy from the bench. But of course questions and problematic elements are also present.

[85] I am grateful to Professor Doug Kysar for reminding me of this point in one of our email conversations.

The toughest question is this: what can courts do in states with bureaucracies that lack training and capacity to tackle climate change? A weak state, even if it is directed by courts or works with courts, will always struggle to achieve real change on the ground. And equally important is the question whether courts are being fair to the political branches in continuously enforcing positive obligations. Do courts do this out of some sense of duty or to build their own constituency among the people? Whether it is the former or the latter, can courts expect meaningful change if public interest petitions are seen as the primary method of ensuring pressing questions are heard and decided?

Environmentally minded jurists do not have an easy job in a state like Pakistan. If they continue building on high rhetoric, they, apart from activism, can be accused of adding to a pile of judicial rulings that do not transform into real change. And if they go beyond rhetoric to substantive steps, there is always the danger of an unelected branch going too far and undermining the legitimate domain of the executive.

One can make a strong argument that *Leghari*, considering the context in which it arose, did an admirable job of striking a balance between competing choices. *Leghari* was essentially about the enforcement of policy and not judge-made policy. It also did not involve questioning of the government's policy choices. There is, however, no guarantee that all judges will be able to negotiate this terrain as skilfully as their colleagues who have both the expertise and a nuanced understanding of all that is at stake in cases like *Leghari*.

Judicial activism is often celebrated in nascent democracies like Pakistan. It makes powerful headlines and often finds support in the argument that because of an allegedly unresponsive executive or even legislature, the courts have to step in. It also gives people hope of a recourse, and that is not without value. Further, it generates conversations and allows people to organize in the hope that if they face hurdles from the executive, they can turn to the courts. As I write this in September 2019, Pakistanis are (in line with a global movement) all set to organize Climate Marches in more than two dozen cities – where the young and old will walk together to resolve to ensure a safer tomorrow. We cannot deny that courts discussing the environment and climate change have contributed to this broader public involvement. And one can say this while also cautioning that pinning hopes on judicial activism is not without its dangers. Will judicial activism in the area of environmental law make the legislature more active (in order to control where the real power lies), or will it make legislators feel helpless?

In scepticism, there may be hope for Pakistan's courts aiding effective progress on climate change without undermining the role of those elected by, and answerable to, the people of Pakistan.

Climate change is an issue that we can only hope to solve after we build a consensus within and across societies. Judiciaries can nudge us in the right direction, but judges cannot play a policing role over the long term. Long-term sustainable change will only come from policy changes, and implementation, by the executive. Courts can play a constructive role in this process by being cognizant of judicial rhetoric and reminding citizens coming before them that while engagement with the state outside the courtroom may not be as glamorous as news reports of judicial activism, it is likely to be more effective in the long run. Encouraging petitioners to be more involved as citizen activists, instead of seeking judicial activism, would potentially set us on a more sustainable and democratically legitimate path of addressing pressing environmental issues like climate change.

11

Climate Change Adaptation Litigation: A View from Southeast Asia

JACQUELINE PEEL AND JOLENE LIN

Introduction

Climate change poses serious challenges for the environment, development and security of countries in Southeast Asia. Threatened impacts include increased exposure to disastrous weather events like cyclones and severe storms, risks to food security and livelihoods from heatwaves and droughts, massive wildfires, and the potential for low-lying areas to be submerged and populations displaced by rising seas.[1] The impacts of climate change on the environment, natural resource management and land-use, and the resulting regulatory responses (termed 'adaptation')[2] are typically managed through planning and environmental law frameworks.[3] For example, environmental law requirements like

1 Yasuaki Hijioka et al., 'Chapter 24: Asia' in Vincente R. Barros et al. (eds.), *Climate Change 2014: Impacts, Adaptation, and Vulnerability. Part B: Regional Aspects. Contribution of Working Group II to the Fifth Assessment Report of the Intergovernmental Panel on Climate Change* (Cambridge University Press 2014) 1327–70.

2 The IPCC defines adaptation as 'the process of adjustment to actual or expected climate and its effects. In human systems, adaptation seeks to moderate or avoid harm or exploit beneficial opportunities'. Katherine J. Mach et al. (eds.), 'Annex II: Glossary' in R. K. Pachauri et al. (eds.), *Climate Change 2014: Synthesis Report. Contribution of Working Groups I, II and III to the Fifth Assessment Report of the Intergovernmental Panel on Climate Change* (Cambridge University Press 2014) 118.

3 Given the extent of greenhouse gases released to the atmosphere by human activities since the beginning of the industrial area, some climate change impacts will not be able to be avoided or ameliorated giving rise to harms known as 'loss and damage'. Cooperative mechanisms for responding to loss and damage in vulnerable developing countries exist under the Paris Agreement (art 8) but expressly do not extend to liability and compensation (UNFCCC, 'Report of the Conference of the Parties on its twenty-first session, held in Paris from 30 November to 13 December 2015, Addendum, Part two: Action taken by the Conference of the Parties at its twenty-first session', FCCC/CP/2015/10/Add. 1 (29 January 2016) para 51). Such claims may still be pursued in domestic litigation and

environmental impact assessment (EIA) may require the consideration of climate change impacts in administrative processes for the assessment and approval of particular projects. Equally, planning laws for urban development, including building codes and spatial planning design standards, may need to take into account potential climate change risks such as extreme heatwaves or increased flooding.[4]

As climate change litigation continues to expand globally,[5] there is the potential that countries in Southeast Asia will also see disputes over their climate change responses come before local courts.[6] However, there is presently a dearth of knowledge, scholarship and practice assessing the potential for, and barriers to, litigation over climate adaptation responses under planning and environmental laws in Southeast Asia. Building a better understanding in this regard is vital for enhancing legal capacity in Southeast Asia to effectively deal with climate change cases where they arise, and to appreciate how court judgments can influence policy responses on adaptation.

The chapter seeks to address this gap in the scholarship by evaluating prospects for adaptation-focused climate change litigation in Southeast Asia. It considers three key Southeast Asian jurisdictions – the Philippines, Malaysia and Singapore[7] – which illustrate differing levels of receptivity to such cases given their existing environmental and planning legal frameworks, and litigation cultures. With climate litigation in general at a nascent stage in these jurisdictions, this chapter attempts to draw lessons for development of this body of case law in Southeast Asia from the more developed climate adaptation jurisprudence in

may have benefits for adaptation – for example, where requested remedies include orders for the defendant to pay relocation costs of affected communities. Our focus in this chapter, however, is on litigation relating to adaptation planning and responses that seek to prevent or ameliorate the worst impacts of climate change on countries' environments.

4 Leslie Hook and Kerin Hope, 'Scorched Earth: The World Battles Extreme Weather' (*Financial Times*, 28 July 2018), www.ft.com/content/fdef0ece-918c-11e8-bb8f-a6a2f7bca546, accessed 28 August 2018.

5 UNEP, *The Status of Climate Change Litigation: A Global Review* (2017).

6 Jolene Lin, 'Climate Change Litigation in Asia and the Pacific' in Geert Van Calster, Wim Vandenberghe and Leonie Reins (eds.), *Research Handbook on Climate Change Mitigation Law* (Edward Elgar2015) 578.

7 These nations were selected as the focus for comparative analysis, given that each has a legal system with a significant common law element that facilitates comparison with Australian laws and jurisprudence; ASEAN Law Association (ALA), *Legal Systems in ASEAN* (2004–), www.aseanlawassociation.org/legal.html, accessed 28 August 2018. The ease of access to case reports, policy documents and secondary literature in the English language was also a factor influencing the choice of case studies.

neighbouring Australia. Australia has considerable exposure to climate change risks and has developed a substantial body of case law assessing the capacity of its environmental and planning frameworks to deal adequately with climate change. The Australian adaptation jurisprudence has led to policy changes, especially to improve the climate change resilience of low-lying coastal areas.[8] This case law offers potential lessons concerning the capacity of similar litigation to shape adaptation planning responses in the Southeast Asian region.

The remainder of this chapter is divided into four parts. Section 11.1 considers the nature of climate change litigation and the characteristics of lawsuits focused on adaptation issues. Section 11.2 surveys the landscape of Australian climate adaptation litigation, with a particular focus on the lessons it offers about the ways case law might be used to highlight and address deficiencies in planning and environmental law frameworks regarding adaptation to climate change. In light of the Australian experience, Section 11.3 then turns to consider the prospects for climate adaptation litigation in the three Southeast Asian case study jurisdictions. We highlight how existing legal frameworks, avenues for access to justice and the receptivity of courts to judicial review challenges has shaped the extent to which climate adaptation litigation has emerged (the Philippines), may emerge (Malaysia) or is unlikely to emerge (Singapore) in the case study jurisdictions. This analysis informs our conclusions in Section 11.4 about the role that climate adaptation litigation is likely to play in climate change governance in these countries and in the Southeast Asian region more broadly.

11.1 Climate Change Adaptation Litigation

In the past decade, litigation concerning climate change has become a globalised phenomenon.[9] The growth of this case law is often viewed as a response to the failures of governments and corporate actors to take adequate action to address the problem of climate change.[10] Under the Paris Agreement, which will come into effect from 2020, state parties are required to prepare and implement 'nationally determined contributions' (NDCs) to the global climate change response that will include

[8] Jacqueline Peel and Hari M. Osofsky, *Climate Change Litigation: Regulatory Pathways to Cleaner Energy* (Cambridge University Press 2015) 108–72.

[9] UNEP (n 5).

[10] Elizabeth Fisher, 'Climate Change Litigation, Obsession and Expertise: Reflecting on the Scholarly Response to *Massachusettsv. EPA*' (2013) 35(3) *Law & Policy* 236–60.

domestic measures for reducing greenhouse gas emissions and for ameliorating the impacts of climate change on their territories and populations.[11] However, the NDCs submitted by state parties to date indicate there will be significant gaps between promised actions and the extent of measures necessary to avoid dangerous global warming and prevent or minimise its impacts.[12] In this context, it is likely that domestic litigation against government and private actors will continue to play a role in efforts to address climate change.[13]

The following sections briefly describe the trajectory of the global development of climate change litigation and the two main categories of climate change cases that have emerged: those focused on greenhouse gas (GHG) emissions reduction ('mitigation litigation') and those focused on responses to climate change impacts ('adaptation litigation').[14] In Southeast Asia, it is anticipated that climate change cases will often raise issues of adaptation, given the vulnerability of these countries to the adverse impacts of climate change and their relatively lower GHG emissions profiles. However, climate adaptation litigation has received far less attention in the literature than generally higher-profile climate change mitigation cases. The final section in this part highlights some of the emerging characteristics of climate adaptation litigation, including its mostly smaller scale, lower profile and focus on climate change impacts in the context of broader environmental protection and natural-resource management issues.

11.1.1 The Global Climate Change Litigation Movement

Lawsuits raising issues of climate change first emerged as a phenomenon in the United States in the early 1990s. Among the earliest US cases was *City of Los Angeles* v. *National Highway Transportation Safety Administration*, decided by the D.C. Circuit Court of Appeals in 1990.[15] That litigation involved a challenge by cities, states and

[11] Paris Agreement (adopted 12 December 2015, entered into force 4 November 2016) (Paris Agreement) art 4.1, 4.2.

[12] UNEP, *Emissions Gap Report* (2017); UNEP, *The Adaptation Gap Report 2017: Towards Global Assessment* (2017).

[13] UNEP (n 5) 40, also noting gaps in international enforcement.

[14] This chapter does not directly canvas cases dealing with unavoidable climate change-related loss and damage, except to the extent that these cases may provide an avenue for addressing adaptation challenges.

[15] *City of Los Angeles* v. *National Highway Traffic Safety Admin.*, 912 F.2d 478 (D.C. Cir. 1990).

environmental groups to the failure of the agency to prepare an environmental impact statement under the National Environmental Policy Act in order to consider the adverse climatic effects of lowering fuel economy standards for motor vehicles. This case – although unsuccessful before the D.C. Circuit – served as a prototype for the vast majority of US climate change litigation brought subsequently.[16] Since that time – and particularly following the US Supreme Court's seminal decision in *Massachusetts* v. *EPA*[17] – climate change litigation in the United States has developed exponentially, now numbering well over seven hundred claims.[18]

In Australia, which also saw early climate change cases from 1994 onwards,[19] the litigation has followed a similar trajectory but not with the same volume of lawsuits.[20] As in the United States, Australian climate change litigation has often involved challenges to administrative decisions on the basis that they inadequately account for GHG emissions or the 'carbon footprint' of proposed projects. However, in Australia, this mitigation-focused litigation challenging carbon-intensive projects such as coal mines and coal-fired power stations has been matched by a substantial body of cases (considered further in Section 11.2) dealing with the implications of future climate change for land use, environmental protection and development planning.

Since the mid-2000s, climate change cases have begun to emerge in a number of other jurisdictions beyond the United States and Australia.[21] Databases tracking climate change litigation globally, such as the climate litigation case charts maintained by Columbia's Sabin Center for Climate Change Law and the LSE Grantham Research Institute's Climate Change Laws of the World, record climate change cases decided in twenty-six

[16] David Markell and J. B. Ruhl, 'An Empirical Assessment of Climate Change in the Courts: A New Jurisprudence or Business as Usual' (2012) 64 *Florida Law Review* 15.

[17] *Massachusetts* v. *Environmental Protection Agency*, 549 US 497 (2007).

[18] Sabin Center for Climate Change Law, 'US Climate Change Litigation Database' (2018), http://climatecasechart.com/us-climate-change-litigation/, accessed 28 August 2018.

[19] The first case of *Greenpeacev. Redbank Power Company* (1994) 86 *LGERA* 143 involved a challenge to a coal-fired power station proposal.

[20] Centre for Resources, Energy and Environmental Law (CREEL) at the University of Melbourne, Australian Climate Change Litigation Database (2018), https://apps.law.unimelb.edu.au/lawapps/climatechange/index.php, accessed 28 August 2018.

[21] Michal Nachmany, Sam Fankhauser, Joana Setzer and Alina Averchenkova, *Global Trends in Climate Change Legislation and Litigation: 2017 Update* (Grantham Research Institute on Climate Change and the Environment 2017) 13. The mid-2000s was also when climate litigation gained significant momentum in both the United States and Australia.

jurisdictions.[22] Excluding the United States, the Grantham Institute reports there were more than 250 cases between 1994 and 2017, in which climate change was a relevant factor.[23] Australia has the largest share of these cases, with more than ninety recorded decisions.[24] The United Kingdom and European Union (EU) also have a significant number of cases, with many EU cases concerning operation of the region's emissions trading scheme.[25] A smaller number of cases are recorded for countries outside the Northern hemisphere, including Brazil, Ecuador, Colombia, New Zealand, India, Pakistan, the Philippines, Nigeria and South Africa.[26] These databases understandably only reference cases for which data are available and hence may not be fully comprehensive, especially for parts of the world such as Southeast Asia, where climate change laws and advocacy have not been as prominent as in jurisdictions like the United States.[27]

By far the majority of cases recorded in global climate litigation databases are mitigation cases. For instance, the Sabin Center's US Climate Change Litigation database classifies only fifty-eight of the several hundred claims it lists as relating to adaptation issues.[28] Likewise, a search of the Grantham Institute's climate change litigation database (which excludes US cases) reveals only sixty cases identified as adaptation litigation, with the lion's share of these decisions (forty-nine out of sixty) coming from Australia.[29] Indeed, case records indicate that Australia has been the epicentre of climate adaptation litigation globally, reflecting – as

[22] Sabin Center for Climate Change Law (n 18) and Grantham Research Institute on Climate Change and the Environment, *Climate Change Laws of the World* (2018), www.lse.ac.uk/GranthamInstitute/climate-change-laws-of-the-world/, accessed 28 August 2018.

[23] Nachmany et al. (n 21).

[24] ibid 14, figure 7. There was a total of ninety-three cases for Australia in Grantham Research Institute on Climate Change and the Environment (n 22) as of 10 August 2018. See also CREEL database (n 20). The exact count depends on how climate litigation is defined.

[25] Sanja Bogojevic, 'EU Climate Change Litigation, the Role of the European Courts and the Importance of Legal Culture' (2013) 35(3) *Law & Policy* 184.

[26] Sabin (n 18) and Grantham Databases (n 22). See also Richard Lord et al. (eds.), *Climate Change Liability: Transnational Law and Practice* (Cambridge University Press 2011).

[27] Lin (n 6).

[28] Sabin Database (n 18), as of 10 August 2018. The database also includes eighty-four cases under the Endangered Species Act, which can be regarded as form of adaptation litigation, as they concern the impacts of climate change on endangered species and habitat protection.

[29] Search done 10 August 2018 filtered for 'Adaptation'. A review of the Australian cases included under adaptation suggests this listing may be overinclusive, with many cases

Section 11.2 discusses in greater depth – its high exposure to climate change risks and the preparedness of its courts to engage with adaptation issues in deciding cases under planning and environmental laws.

11.1.2 Litigation with an Adaptation Focus

Compared with mitigation litigation, adaptation litigation is much more difficult to pigeonhole, which may explain its relative lack of prominence in climate litigation databases and scholarship. In one respect, this is a data-collection problem, as many adaptation-focused cases will not expressly include, or may only incidentally refer to, the term 'climate change' in the case documentation.[30] This may be because the case concentrates on particular environmental risks that are exacerbated by climate change – for instance, fires, heatwaves, flooding, coastal erosion, storm surge, seawater contamination of freshwater resources or water scarcity and drought – but does not directly address climate change as the cause of these heightened risks. Indeed, there may be a deliberate choice made by petitioners or decision makers to focus on environmental and natural resource risks rather than climate change in the case, whether because the former framing is more politically palatable or because these environmental risks can be more readily addressed within the confines of existing legal rules.

Another factor that makes adaptation litigation more likely to go 'under the radar' compared with mitigation litigation is that the former is often concerned with decision-making processes that take place at the local level and are therefore lower profile. While decisions that are relevant to mitigation outcomes can also be small scale and localised (e.g., local government policies promoting less polluting modes of transportation), mitigation cases quite frequently involve high-profile challenges to laws or legal decisions regarding large polluting facilities that have the potential to significantly shape national or regional contributions to GHG emissions.[31] It is this sense of the importance to climate change governance of mitigation cases, such as the seminal US Supreme

included more properly classified as mitigation litigation, given the focus on GHG emissions-intensive projects.

[30] An example is the early Australian adaptation case of *Northcape Properties Pty Ltd* v. *District of Yorke Peninsula* [2007] SAERDC 50, which applied a planning instrument mentioning sea-level rise but made no explicit mention of climate change.

[31] A recent example in South Africa is *EarthLife Africa Johannesburg* v. *Minister of Environmental Affairs and Others* (65662/16) [2017] 2 All SA 519 (GP).

Court decision in *Massachusetts* v. *EPA*,[32] which Elizabeth Fisher identifies as having contributed to a 'scholarly obsession' in the climate change litigation literature.[33]

In addition, policies and measures for GHG emissions reduction are frequently set on a national basis, such as an economy-wide emissions reduction target or a national emissions trading scheme.[34] By contrast, both adaptation planning and the formulation of adaptation measures tend to take place at multiple scales, with a strong preference for localised implementation.[35] This is acknowledged in the Paris Agreement, which sets a 'global goal on adaptation'[36] but recognises that this 'global challenge faced by all' has 'local, subnational, national, regional and international dimensions'.[37] Parties also 'acknowledge that adaptation action should follow a country-driven, gender-responsive, participatory and fully transparent approach, taking into consideration vulnerable groups, communities and ecosystems and should be based on and guided by the best available science and, as appropriate, traditional knowledge, knowledge of indigenous peoples and local knowledge systems'.[38] This more localised, context-based orientation of adaptation actions may mean that legal challenges to the adequacy of such actions are considered to be less high profile, 'run-of-the-mill' cases and thus attract less attention from scholars, practitioners and policymakers. In aggregate, though, these cases may have important incremental effects in improving adaptation planning and measures for ameliorating environmental and natural resource risks likely to be exacerbated by climate change.

This chapter advances the argument that litigation raising questions of adaptation to climate-related environmental and natural resources risks in the context of broader disputes over land use and spatial planning is likely to be a key form of climate change litigation to emerge in the

[32] This case concerned the scope of the federal Clean Air Act to require regulation of greenhouse gas emissions from motor vehicles, with the US Supreme Court finding the definition of a 'pollutant' under the legislation could encompass greenhouse gases.

[33] Fisher (n 10) at 239.

[34] Paris Agreement art 4.4. For examples of emissions trading schemes, see White & Case, 'Greenhouse Gas Emissions Trading Schemes: A Global Perspective' (2018), www.whitecase.com/publications/insight/greenhouse-gas-emissions-trading-schemes-global-perspective, accessed 28 August 2018.

[35] Jan McDonald, 'The Role of Law in Adapting to Climate Change' (2011) 2 *WIRES Climate Change* 283–95, 285.

[36] Paris Agreement art 7.1.

[37] Paris Agreement art 7.2.

[38] Paris Agreement art 7.5.

Southeast Asian region, where adaptation challenges significantly outweigh mitigation ones. This litigation may be lower profile and smaller scale than comparable mitigation case law, given its relationship to localised adaptation concerns (such as site-based flooding risks) and lower scales of decision-making (such as city or local government planning decisions). Experience from the Australian adaptation jurisprudence, as well as the limited adaptation litigation to emerge so far in Southeast Asia (considered further below in Sections 11.2 and 11.3, respectively), indicates that climate change is rarely the sole issue raised in such cases. More commonly in these disputes, adaptation to future climate change is raised as one of a suite of environmental risks pertinent to decision-making on a particular issue of land use or natural resource management.

11.2 Australian Climate Change Litigation and Lessons for Adaptation Planning

Globally, Australia has the most extensive and significant adaptation jurisprudence of any country.[39] The development of this case law has followed rising public concern in Australia over the impacts of climate change to which the island nation is particularly exposed. The following sections explain the factors that contribute to Australia's relatively high climate change risk, and how this has influenced policy developments and spurred the emergence of litigation focused on climate-resilient development and adaptation planning. We survey the types of legal claims that have arisen in Australian adaptation litigation, and discuss their impact on planning and environmental law frameworks. This experience helps illuminate the prospects and preconditions for the emergence of similar litigation in Southeast Asia, as examined in Section 11.3.

11.2.1 Climate Change Risks and Adaptation Planning in Australia

Australia shares with many of its Southeast Asian neighbours a high exposure to hazards associated with climate change.[40] These hazards include

[39] Peel and Osofsky (n 8).

[40] In this section, we adopt the terminology for climate change disaster risk used by the IPCC. Hence *exposure* refers to the inventory of elements in an area in which hazard events may occur. *Hazard* means future occurrence of natural or human-induced physical events that may have adverse effects on vulnerable and exposed elements. *Vulnerability* is the propensity of exposed elements such as human beings, their livelihoods and assets to suffer adverse

slow onset events like sea-level rise, drought and water scarcity, as well as extreme weather events such as heatwaves, cyclones, coastal and inland flooding, and wildfires (known locally as 'bushfires'). This degree of climate change hazard exposure is a function of Australia's geography and environment. A vast arid centre traps heat, whereas ocean waters surrounding the island nation intensify the impacts of sea-level rise, powerful storms and flooding rains. The average annual rainfall across the continent is low but also extremely variable, with rainfall intensity highest in the tropical north and some coastal areas.[41] Australia's hot, dry climate means that bushfires are a frequent occurrence. In addition, the native vegetation, such as eucalyptus, has developed characteristics that promote the spread of fire.[42]

The effects of geography and a naturally harsh climate are amplified by Australia's patterns of settlement. More than 85 per cent of the population of twenty-four million lives within fifty kilometres of the coast and is hence on the front line of climate change hazards such as sea-level rise, coastal inundation and more intense storms, including cyclones.[43] Residential development pushes out from the major urban cities into bushland areas, increasing exposure to wildfire hazards.[44] Inland, agriculture faces a persistent problem of low rainfall, which has led to a reliance on irrigation but also exacerbated problems of soil salinity and acidity.[45]

effects when impacted by hazard events. Low adaptive *capacity* is associated with high vulnerability. Climate change risk is a function of both exposure and vulnerability. Christopher B. Field et al. (eds.), *Managing the Risks of Extreme Events and Disasters to Advance Climate Change Adaptation: A Special Report of Working Groups I and II of the Intergovernmental Panel on Climate Change* (Cambridge University Press 2012).

41 Ross Garnaut, *The Garnaut Climate Change Review: Final Report* (Cambridge University Press 2008) 107–9.

42 Commonwealth Scientific and Industrial Research Organisation (CSIRO), 'Bushfire' (2018), www.csiro.au/en/Research/Environment/Extreme-Events/Bushfire, accessed 28 August 2018.

43 Gaeme F. Clarke and Emma L. Johnston, *Australia State of the Environment 2016: Coasts*, Independent Report to the Australian Government Minister for Environment and Energy, Australian Government Department of the Environment and Energy, Canberra (2017) iv.

44 Michael Buxton et al., 'Vulnerability to Bushfire Risk at Melbourne's Urban Fringe: The Failure of Regulatory Land Use Planning' (2011) 49(1) *Geographical Research* 1. Kevin Hennessy, 'Climate Change Impacts on Fire-Weather in South-East Australia' in *The Joint AFAC/IFCAA Bushfire CRC Conference: 10–13 August 2006: Melbourne Convention Centre Australia: Conference Proceedings* (2006) 536–46.

45 Pichu Rengasamy, 'World Salinization with Emphasis on Australia' (2006) 57(5) *Journal of Experimental Botany* 1017.

As a wealthy developed country, Australia has many economic and other measures at its disposal to reduce the vulnerability of its population to climate change risk, despite high levels of exposure.[46] One such measure is sophisticated legal frameworks for EIA, natural resource management and adaptation planning. For instance, the Intergovernmental Panel on Climate Change has identified that '[l]and use and territorial planning are key factors in risk reduction',[47] as they can reduce exposure and vulnerability to hazards and environmental change.[48]

Nonetheless, before the mid-2000s, climate change was not a matter that received much attention in Australia's planning and environmental laws.[49] When a succession of extreme weather events, including Australia's decade-long 'Millennium Drought', prompted public concern over climate change in the mid-2000s, the government response largely took the form of vulnerability assessments, reports and inquiries.[50] At the national level, this was accompanied by the release of broadly framed policy documents such as the 2007 National Climate Change Adaptation Framework[51] and the 2015 National Climate Resilience and Adaptation Strategy.[52] However, there was and remains no national law specifically dealing with adaptation or associated climate risk management. Instead, adaptation has largely been cast as the responsibility of state and local governments.[53] Control over land use and development planning primarily sits at the state level, with state governments in turn delegating many decision-making powers to local governments. It was these localised decisions under state and local government planning laws that

[46] Socio-economic differences mean there is still high vulnerability in some communities (e.g., the elderly, unemployed, poor, migrant communities and indigenous communities).

[47] Field et al. (eds.) (n 40).

[48] ibid 74.

[49] Australian Government Productivity Commission, *Barriers to Effective Adaptation* (2013) 173.

[50] 2009 Victorian Bushfires Royal Commission and Queensland Floods Commission of Inquiry.

[51] Australia, 'National Climate Change Adaptation Framework' (2007), https://elaw.org/content/australia-national-climate-change-adaptation-framework-2007, accessed 28 August 2018.

[52] Australian Government Department of the Environment and Energy, 'National Climate Resilience and Adaptation Strategy' (2015), www.environment.gov.au/climate-change/adaptation/publications/national-climate-resilience-and-adaptation-strategy, accessed 28 August 2018.

[53] National Climate Change Adaptation Research Facility, 'Roles and Responsibilities for Climate Change Adaptation in Australia' (2012), www.nccarf.edu.au/sites/default/files/18-dccee-2012.pdf, accessed 28 August 2018.

began to be challenged on climate change grounds in courts throughout Australia from the mid-2000s onwards.

11.2.2 Adaptation Litigation in Australia

Prompted by warnings of climate scientists about unavoidable climate change,[54] early adaptation litigation in Australia arose out of a concern on the part of environmental groups and individuals that development approval processes, and planning decisions were not taking sufficient account of future climate change impacts. For this reason, some of the initial cases were supported by Environmental Defender Offices (EDOs) – a national network of public interest community legal centres with a mission to advance environmental law.[55] The New South Wales (NSW) EDO, for instance, assisted local resident, Jill Walker, to challenge a NSW government decision approving a concept plan for a large residential development and aged care facility on flood-prone coastal land at Sandon Point. The decision of the NSW Land and Environment Court (NSWLEC) in *Walker* v. *Minister for Planning* set a benchmark for future adaptation litigation in Australia. The NSWLEC found that planning legislation calling for the encouragement of 'ecologically sustainable development' (ESD) and consideration of the 'public interest' required the NSW Planning Minister to evaluate the impacts of climate change for flooding on the site.[56] On appeal to the NSW Court of Appeal, the Court adopted a narrower construction of the planning legislation and the role of ESD principles in assessing the public interest. However, the NSW Court of Appeal agreed with the primary judge that consideration of ESD principles would 'almost inevitably' have required a consideration of climate change flood risk and commented in *obiter* that in the future it was quite possible that ESD principles would be seen 'as so plainly an element of the public interest' that a failure to consider them would be grounds for declaring a decision invalid.[57] In subsequent cases, these statements by the NSW Court of Appeal were relied on by decision makers to find that ESD principles were a relevant consideration in

[54] Rajendra K. Pachauri et al. (eds.), *Climate Change 2007: Synthesis Report. Contribution of Working Groups I, II and III to the Fourth Assessment Report of the Intergovernmental Panel on Climate Change* (IPCC 2007).

[55] See, e.g., Environmental Defenders Office New South Wales (EDO NSW), 'About EDO NSW' (2018), www.edonsw.org.au/about, accessed 28 August 2018.

[56] *Walker* v. *Minister for Planning* (2007) 157 *LGERA* 124, 191–2.

[57] *Minister for Planning* v. *Walker & Ors* (2008) 161 *LGERA* 423, 454–5.

determining the public interest and for taking account of climate change risks in that context.[58]

The *Walker* case involved judicial review of decision-making under the NSW environmental and planning legislation, which limited the scope of the reviewing court to assess the merits of the proposed development.[59] Many Australian adaptation cases, however, have been decided by courts or tribunals exercising a broader merits review function that has allowed detailed assessment of potential climate change risks.[60] For instance, in another case concerning coastal hazards decided by the Victorian Civil Administrative Tribunal (VCAT) – *Gippsland Coastal Board* v. *South Gippsland Shire Council* – VCAT made its own assessment of the suitability of land for a proposed residential development. The Victorian *Planning and Environment Act 1987*, under which the local council made the challenged decision, did not contain any express reference to climate change or sea-level rise but simply required a consideration of 'any significant effects . . . the environment might have on the use or development'.[61] Nonetheless, the Tribunal found this legislative direction broad enough to encompass the influence of climate change on the proposed development.[62] It specifically relied on the precautionary principle – one of the fundamental principles of ESD – as requiring 'a gauging of the consequences and extent of intergenerational liability arising from a development or proposal and if found to be warranted, appropriate causes of action to be adopted to manage severe or irreversible harm'.[63] The Tribunal's application of the precautionary principle led it to the conclusion that increasing storm severity and rising sea levels due to climate change created 'a reasonably foreseeable risk of inundation of the subject land', strengthening its overall conclusion that the land was unsuitable for development.[64]

While Australian adaptation litigation continues to be dominated by cases concerning coastal climate change hazards, there is also a growing

[58] See, e.g., *Aldous* v. *Greater Taree City Council & Anor* (2009) 167*LGERA* 13, 26–31; *Barrington-Gloucester-Stroud Preservation Alliance* v. *Minister for Planning and Infrastructure* [2012] *NSWLEC* 197 [170].

[59] Following the *Walker* litigation, the NSW government eventually approved the challenged coastal development after taking climate change considerations into account as mandated by the courts.

[60] E.g., *Rainbow Shores Pty Ltd* v. *Gympie Regional Council & Ors* [2013] QPEC 26.

[61] Planning and Environment Act 1987 (Vic) s 60(e).

[62] [2008] VCAT 1545 [37].

[63] [2008] VCAT 1545 [41].

[64] [2008] VCAT 1545 [48].

body of case law focusing on other adaptation issues, particularly flood and fire.[65] Like the cases involving coastal climate change hazards, these lawsuits tend to be focused on smaller scale decision-making (e.g., decisions of local governments or state authorities on project proposals or challenges to local government policies) and involve the interpretation of planning and EIA legislation. Another notable feature of these cases is that the issue of climate change is often not explicitly referenced, although decision-making proceeds on the likelihood of the occurrence of more severe weather events such as greater flooding and extreme bushfires. As a consequence, climate change or the potential for certain environmental risks to be exacerbated by climate change is considered by the court in the context of a broader assessment of land use and planning matters.

A recent example of a case of this kind is the decision of the Western Australian State Administrative Tribunal in *Riggs* v. *Western Australian Planning Commission*.[66] The applicants in the case sought merits review of a decision of the planning commission refusing their application for the subdivision of land bordered by the Leeuwin-Naturaliste National Park. The subject site was located in an area that was densely vegetated and considered to be an extreme bushfire hazard area. One of the relevant planning instruments applicable in decision-making – State Planning Policy 3.7: Planning in Bushfire Prone Area – referred to consideration of 'the potential impacts of climate change' as part of an objective of achieving 'an appropriate balance between bushfire risk management measures and, biodiversity conservation values, environmental protection and biodiversity management and landscape amenity'.[67] No other mention of climate change was made in the case. However, the Tribunal found, relying on expert evidence, that no bushfire management plan could acceptably manage the bushfire risk at the subject site because of inherent risks associated with the extent of density of vegetation at the site, its proximity to the Leeuwin Naturaliste National Park and the lack of adequate publicly available evacuation routes.[68] While bushfire risk

[65] There are many examples recorded in the CREEL database (n 20). For flooding, see *Arora Construction Pty Ltd & Anor* v. *Gold Coast City Council & Anor* [2012] *QPEC* 052 for a prominent illustration. VCAT cases on bushfire risk include *Robertson* v. *Mornington Peninsula SC* [2011] VCAT 1393; Lester v. Yarra Ranges SC [2012] VCAT 9; *Land Management Surveys* v. *Strathbogie SC* [2012] VCAT 1676; *Adamson* v. *Yarra Ranges* SC [2013] VCAT 683; *Carey & Ors* v. *Murrindindi Shire Council* [2011] VCAT 76.

[66] [2017] WASAT 19.

[67] Cl 5.4.

[68] [2017] WASAT 19 (n 66) at [59].

was the principal matter relied upon by the Tribunal in refusing the application for subdivision approval, the decision also considered aspects such as the planning merits of the subdivision proposal and the extent of likely biodiversity impacts. Climate change was, at most, a background factor in the case. However, awareness of this problem has contributed to the increased focus in planning instruments and cases applying those instruments, on environmental risks like bushfire hazard, which climate change exacerbates.

11.2.3 Lessons from the Australian Adaptation Jurisprudence

Since the early cases of the mid-2000s, Australian adaptation case law has continued to grow steadily, far outpacing the higher profile mitigation litigation challenging carbon-intensive projects. Reflecting its lower profile and smaller scale, adaptation litigation in Australia has produced incremental changes in policy and practice, rather than transforming the law in this area. For instance, consideration of future hazards and worst-case scenarios for extreme weather events like massive floods or severe bushfires has become a more routine part of planning and environmental assessment processes.[69] On the issue of coastal hazards, most governments in Australia have introduced policies that support accounting for rising sea levels in designing and approving development in the coastal zone.[70] While partisan divisions have seen pushback against some climate adaptation policies and climate change is not fully acknowledged as a risk driver in all contexts,[71] overall there has been a general improvement in the national adaptation capacity that mirrors the developments in the case law.

What lessons can we learn from this experience about whether, and if so how, adaptation-focused climate litigation might emerge and develop in other parts of the world, like Southeast Asia? One key lesson from the Australian adaptation case law would seem to be the scope for using general environmental and planning law frameworks as a vehicle for

[69] Peel and Osofsky (n 8) 134.

[70] See, e.g., Victorian Coastal Strategy. Summary at CoastAdapt, 'Different Planning Approaches across Jurisdictions' (2 May 2017), https://coastadapt.com.au/different-planning-approaches-across-jurisdictions, accessed 28 August 2018.

[71] For discussion of political backlash against sea-level-rise policies in NSW, see Tayanah O'Donnell and Louise Gates, 'Getting the Balance Right: A Renewed Need for the Public Interest Test in Addressing Coastal Climate Change and Sea Level Rise' (2013) 30 *Environmental and Planning Law Journal* 220.

litigation seeking better integration of adaptation planning in administrative decision-making.[72] Presented with evidence of climate change hazards or increased associated environmental risk, Australian courts and tribunals have relied on broad legal requirements for assessing significant environmental impacts, or taking into consideration sustainable development principles or the public interest, to find that adaptation concerns are a proper matter to be assessed and, in some cases, weighed against approval of a development. In particular, the lack of specific climate change legislative language or climate change legislation has not been a bar to the development of case law that advances adaptation planning.

However, it is clearly not just flexible interpretation of environmental and planning legal frameworks that has boosted the role of Australian courts in climate adaptation governance. Legal structures that enable public participation and access to justice to raise such cases before the courts have been equally important. It is notable, for instance, that most Australian adaptation cases have been determined by specialist environmental courts and tribunals in different Australian states.[73] These courts apply more relaxed standing requirements in planning cases, often have flexible rules regarding the award of costs in litigation, regularly incorporate expert evidence on environmental issues in their proceedings and offer the potential for merits review of decisions (rather than simply narrower judicial review) for many disputes.[74] In comparative analysis of Australian and US courts engaged in deciding adaptation litigation, these features of the former have been found to be a key factor promoting the greater quantity and impact of adaptation cases in Australia as compared to the United States.[75]

[72] Jacqueline Peel and Hari M. Osofsky, 'Sue to Adapt?' (2015) 99(6) *Minnesota Law Review* 2177.

[73] Peel and Osofsky (n 72).

[74] Brian J. Preston, 'Characteristics of Successful Environmental Courts and Tribunals', www.lec.justice.nsw.gov.au/Documents/prestoncj%20characteristics%20of%20successful%20ects.pdf, accessed 28 August 2018; George Pring and Catherine Pring, *Environmental Courts & Tribunals: A Guide for Policy Makers* (UNEP 2016), https://wedocs.unep.org/bitstream/handle/20.500.11822/10001/environmental-courts-tribunals.pdf?sequence=1, accessed 28 August 2018; George Pring and Catherine Pring, 'Greening Justice: Creating and Improving Environmental Courts and Tribunals' (The Access Initiative 2009), www.eufje.org/images/DocDivers/Rapport Pring.pdf, accessed 28 August 2018.

[75] Peel and Osofsky (n 72).

11.3 Climate Litigation in Southeast Asian Nations: Possibilities and Challenges

In this part, we turn to consider the prospects for climate adaptation litigation in the Philippines, Malaysia and Singapore. We find that even taking a broad view of what climate litigation entails, the state of adaptation case law in these case study jurisdictions is at the very early stages of development. In profiling emerging cases, we analyse potential avenues for climate adaptation litigation and identify the likely barriers to the development of a robust climate adaptation case law in these three jurisdictions. Based on the arguments set out in Section 11.1 and lessons drawn from the analysis of Australian adaptation jurisprudence in Section 11.2, we would expect climate adaptation litigation emerging in Southeast Asia to be low profile and small scale. In addition, the term 'climate change' may not feature prominently in the pleadings and other case documentation of lawsuits because climate issues are being packaged together with broader natural resource management and environmental justice claims.

11.3.1 The Philippines

The Philippines is a resource-rich archipelago of thousands of islands. Mining and timber extraction are major economic activities that have caused severe environmental degradation. At the same time, there is a relatively active civil society in the Philippines that plays a key role in raising public awareness of environmental issues and has been active in promoting climate advocacy.[76] It is the only Southeast Asian jurisdiction under study in which climate change litigation has occurred.

11.3.1.1 Case Law Examples

Most notable in the Filipino 'climate change docket' is the Carbon Majors petition, which is the first climate change–related complaint submitted to a national human rights institution.[77] It is also the first to be accepted by a human rights commission and the first to implicate private actors in alleged human rights abuses. The Carbon Majors are forty-seven coal, oil, gas and cement transnational corporations, including Chevron, Exxon,

76 United States Agency for International Development, '2016 CSO Sustainability Index for Asia', 37–46, www.usaid.gov/sites/default/files/documents/1868/2016-Asia-CSOSI-Report.pdf, accessed 28 August 2018.

77 See discussion in Chapter 3

Shell and BHP Billiton. They are among the ninety firms that have been identified as being responsible for nearly two-thirds of global greenhouse gas emissions since the start of the industrial age. The petition calls for the Carbon Majors to account for breaches of the rights to life, food, water, sanitation, adequate housing and self-determination. It also alleges that the Carbon Majors have breached the right of Filipinos to development – particularly of marginalised and disadvantaged groups that are especially vulnerable to the effects of climate change.[78]

Whether this petition ought to be categorised as mitigation-focused or adaptation-focused raises interesting questions that go to the criteria used for classification. It also highlights the point that adaptation litigation is difficult to pigeonhole because of the diverse forms it can take and the multiple scales at which it can occur. On the one hand, it can be argued that the petition is mitigation-focused because the petitioners are seeking to hold the Carbon Majors accountable for their contribution to climate change. On the other hand, the petitioners rely on rights-based arguments to establish responsibility and to recommend the establishment of an accountability mechanism to provide redress for Filipinos whose rights have been adversely affected by the impacts of climate change. Given that the Philippines' Commission on Human Rights does not have the power to compel companies to reduce their GHG emissions or to penalise them for their past and present contribution to climate change, and the nature of the remedies sought by the petitioners, we take the view that the Carbon Majors petition can be viewed as a form of climate adaptation litigation. While this petition has garnered global attention, there are a few other lower-profile cases that raise issues of adaptation to climate risks in the context of local planning and land-use regulatory frameworks.

Global Legal Action on Climate Change v. *the Philippine Government* is a case in point. In this case, an action was brought against a number of government departments, including the Climate Change Commission, the Department of Public Works and Highways and the Department of Interior and Local Government. The case sought to compel the government to perform its duty under Republic Act 6716 to construct rainwater

[78] Zela dT Soriano, Grizelda Mayo-Anda and Hasminah Paudac, 'Human Rights and Climate Change Petition in the *Philippines*' (Bangkok, 13 July 2017; on file with author). For discussion, see Annalisa Savaresi, Iona Cismas and Jacques Hartmann, 'The Philippines Human Rights Commission and the "Carbon Majors" Petition' (EJIL: Talk!, 2 December 2017), www.ejiltalk.org/the-philippines-human-rights-commission-and-the-carbon-majors-petition/, accessed 30 December 2017.

collectors in every *barangay* (village) throughout the country 'in such number as may be needed and feasible'. It was argued that this action was necessary to ensure that the population enjoys a sustained supply of fresh water and is safe from flooding, which occurs frequently because of the absence of a proper rainwater collection system.[79]

Republic Act 6716 went into effect in March 1989 but had never been implemented.[80] The petition was therefore advocating for effective climate change adaptation by seeking enforcement of an existing law. Eventually, a work plan was submitted to the Supreme Court, and the defendant government departments signed a Memorandum of Understanding undertaking to carry out the construction works.[81] The implementation of the work plan was to be subject to monitoring by the Supreme Court, as was the case for the remediation of Manila Bay.[82]

11.3.1.1 Conditions Favouring the Emergence of Climate Adaptation Litigation

In addition to already decided or pending climate cases, the Philippines (in comparison to Malaysia and Singapore, described further below) arguably has more favourable conditions for the emergence of a more developed and robust body of climate-adaptation case law. Among these favourable conditions are key legal innovations that have created mechanisms that enable climate adaptation litigation in the Philippines – notably, the Writ of Kalikasan and the recognition of environmental rights in the national constitution.

Article II (Section 16) of the Philippine Constitution provides that '[t]he State shall protect and advance the right of the people to a balanced and healthful ecology in accordance with the rhythm and harmony of nature'. In 2009, the Philippine Supreme Court crafted a set of innovative

[79] Paras 13.1, 14 of the *Global Legal Action on Climate Change* v. *the Philippine Government Petition* (on file with authors).

[80] Hilario G. Davide Jr., 'The Environment as Life Sources and the Writ of Kalikasan in the Philippines' (2012) 29(2) *Pace Environmental Law Review*, Article 9, 598.

[81] Email correspondence with Antonio A. Oposa Jr. (on file with author).

[82] In *Metro Manila Development Authority* v. *Concerned Citizens of Manila Bay* GR 171947-48 (S.C. Dec 18, 2008), a group of citizens succeeded in compelling the government to clean up Manila Bay after nearly ten years of litigation. The Supreme Court adopted a procedure that has been incorporated in the *Rules of Procedure for Environmental Cases* as the Writ of Mandamus. This Writ is an extensive and continuing order by the court. To ensure that there is implementation of its environmental remediation orders, the court requires the defendant government departments to submit written progress reports every ninety orders till the court is satisfied that its orders have been compiled with.

procedural rules to facilitate protection of the people's constitutionally enshrined rights to life and a healthy environment.[83] The *Rules of Procedure for Environmental Cases* went into effect on 29 April 2010. The Rules govern procedure in civil and criminal cases in the first- and second-level courts that involve alleged violations of environmental laws, rules and regulations. What is particularly notable about these Rules is the introduction of the Writ of Kalikasan or Writ of Nature. Petitioners can apply for a Writ of Kalikasan to be issued when the alleged environmental damage is of such magnitude that it adversely affects life, health or the property of inhabitants in two or more cities or provinces. It is

> a remedy available to a natural or juridical person, entity authorized by law, people's organization, non-governmental organization, or any public interest group accredited by or registered with any government agency, on behalf of persons *whose constitutional right to a balanced and healthful ecology is violated, or threatened with violation* by an unlawful act or omission of a *public official or employee*, or *private individual or entity*. (emphasis added)[84]

Under the Rules, hearings will take place and the court will render judgment within sixty days of the day on which the writ is filed.[85] It was on the basis of this writ that the *Global Legal Action on Climate Change* v. *the Philippine Government* suit was filed, and it is likely that other similar cases will follow.

Another favourable condition is the existence of an EIA system that can provide avenues for litigation against a public authority for allegedly not complying with its obligations under the EIA law, thereby leading to a failure to adapt to climate change. Litigation of this kind would have strong parallels with the Australian adaptation litigation described in Section 11.2. Briefly, the Environmental Impact Statement (EIS) System in the Philippines, like that in Australia, is project-based. It covers environmentally critical projects and projects located in environmentally

[83] This was the result of an initiative led by Chief Justice Puno of the Philippines Supreme Court to promote public interest litigation in the quest for environmental justice. A copy of these Rules can be found at www.lawphil.net/courts/supreme/am/am_09-6-8-sc_2010.html. For discussion, see Gloria Estenzo Ramos, 'Innovative Procedural Rules on Environmental Cases in the Philippines: Ushering In a Golden Era for Environmental Rights Protection' (2010) 1 *IUCN Academy of Environmental Law e-Journal*, www.iucnael.org/en/e-journal/previous-issues/157-issue-20111.html.

[84] Republic of the Philippines Supreme Court, Rules of Procedure for Environmental Cases, Rule 7 Section 1.

[85] ibid, Rule 7 Section 15.

critical areas. Projects are classified into four categories: Category A projects are environmentally critical projects; Category B are those that are considered non-environmentally critical projects but are located in environmentally critical areas, while Category C and D are projects that are not covered by the EIS System. Each category requires different environmental assessment tools and documentation commensurate with the potential impacts of the project in question. The Department of Energy and Natural Resources' Environmental Management Bureau (DENR-EMB) is in charge of implementing the EIS System.[86] The DENR-EMB central office provides policy direction, oversight and overall guidance on EIA matters. It also reviews Category A projects. The DENR-EMB regional offices are responsible for Category B, C and D projects.[87]

The DENR-EMB has promulgated EIA Technical Guidelines Incorporating Disaster Risk Reduction and Climate Change Adaptation Concerns for the conduct of EIA and preparation of EIA reports. The guidelines aim to promote climate change adaptation and disaster risk reduction at the project level.[88] For example, when 'scoping' the parameters of the EIA, the project developer is required to take into consideration natural hazards and climate change risks.[89] The EIA guidelines are unevenly and poorly implemented in the Philippines at present.[90] However, the Australian litigation demonstrates the potential for EIA laws to be used as a vehicle for requiring project proponents to consider future climate change impacts. Similar litigation could be pre-empted in the Philippines if policymakers take action to implement the guidelines' requirements in decision-making.

11.3.2 Malaysia

Malaysia is a federation of thirteen states and three federal territories. Due to historical factors, including British colonial rule and the creation of federal territories, laws do not apply in a uniform fashion across the country. This legal complexity, coupled with a general tradition of

[86] The World Bank Group and Asian Development Bank, *Philippines: The Philippine Environmental Impact Statement System: Framework, Implementation, Performance and Challenges* (2007) 2.
[87] World Bank Group and Asian Development Bank (n 86) 2.
[88] ibid.
[89] ibid. 5.
[90] Interviews on file.

judicial restraint, makes Malaysia an unlikely candidate for the emergence of high profile climate litigation.[91] However, some potential remains for lower-profile adaptation-focused cases, particularly as part of litigation brought to enforce EIA laws.

11.3.2.1 Planning Law

In the area of planning law, there are at least four sources of law that govern land use management and spatial planning in Malaysia. First, the Federal Constitution sets out the distribution of powers in the Federal List, the State List and the Concurrent List. The Federal List sets out those subject matters on which only the national legislature can legislate. Matters that are solely within the states' jurisdictions are set out in the State List. The Concurrent List sets out the subjects on which either the national legislature or the state legislative can make laws. Article 77 states that any matters that are not indicated on the lists are regarded as state matters. Land is included in the State List, while planning is on the Concurrent List. This gives rise to difficult questions of regulatory competence, given that land use and planning are deeply intertwined.[92]

The Town and Country Planning Act 1976 lies at the heart of the planning system in Malaysia. Closely modelled on British planning legislation, the Act provides for a regulatory system based on planning permission.[93] Local governments are the local planning authorities in their respective localities and their role is to, inter alia, 'regulate, control and plan the development and use of all lands and buildings within [their] area'.[94] Section 23 of the Town and Country Planning Act provides for an appeals process to the Appeal Board that has the power to dismiss the appeal, allow the appeal 'by directing the local planning authority to grant planning permission absolutely or subject to such conditions as the Appeal Board thinks fit', set aside any planning

[91] Harding and Sharom make a similar point in the context of environmental decision-making and implementation of environmental laws; Andrew Harding and Azmi Sharom, 'Access to Environmental Justice in Malaysia(Kuala Lumpur)' in Andrew Harding (ed.), *Access to Environmental Justice: A Comparative Study* (Nijhoff 2007) 128.

[92] See, for further discussion, Andrew Harding, 'Planning, Environment and Development: A Comparison of Planning Law in Malaysia and England' (2003) 5(4) *Environmental Law Review* 231.

[93] For discussion of the evolution of planning laws in Malaysia, see Lee Lik Meng, 'Town Planning Law in Malaysia: Politics, Rights and Jealousies' (1991) 15 *Habitat International* 105–14.

[94] Town and Country Planning Act 1976, Section 5(6).

permission granted, or direct the local planning authority to remove or modify any conditions attached to the grant of planning permission.[95]

While this makes the Appeal Board the ultimate authority in the planning process, there is significant ambiguity about the role and scope of powers of the Appeal Board in practice.[96] Further, it should be noted that not all of the states in Malaysia have established appeal boards. In the spirit of federalism, state governments are empowered to choose if they want to bring the Town and Country Planning Act into operation and, if so, which sections.[97] This adds a layer of complexity to land use planning in Malaysia that should be borne in mind. However, it is clear that the local governments play the most significant role in the planning system because they decide on planning applications. Planning authorities in various states have promulgated planning guidelines and standards that are relevant to climate change mitigation and adaptation. For example, the Town and Country Planning Department of the state of Perak has issued guidelines on tree planting and enhancing the green acreage in proposed projects to address the Urban Island Heat (UIH) effect.[98]

Judicial control of the discretionary powers to impose planning conditions has been described as 'relatively undeveloped'.[99] In *Chong & Co. Sdn. Bhd.* v. *Majlis Perbandaran Pulau Pinang*, the court affirmed the right of the local planning authority to impose such conditions as it 'thinks fit'.[100] While there are controls on the exercise of the powers that the planning authorities have – for example, that the powers are not exercised for ulterior purposes that do not accord with their statutory mandate – the Malaysian courts have often refrained from reviewing the decisions of the local planning authorities because such decisions involve policy considerations and 'the courts do not possess knowledge of the policy considerations which underlie such decisions'.[101]

95 Town and Country Planning Act 1976, Section 23.

96 Lee Lik Meng, 'Who's the Ultimate Planning Authority in Malaysia? Reviewing the Powers and Role of the Appeal Board' (2002) *Journal of Malaysian and Comparative Law* 12.

97 Town and Country Planning Act s 1.

98 These guidelines can be found at http://jpbd.perak.gov.my/jpbd/index.php/en/dasar-polisi/garis-panduan-dan-piawaian-perancangan.

99 Ainul Jaria Maidin and Bashiran Begum Mobarak Ali, 'Powers of the Local Authority in Regulating Land Planning and Development Control: Whither Control' (2009) 7 *Journal of the Malaysian Institute of Planners* 133, 142.

100 *Chong & Co. Sdn. Bhd.* v. *Majlis Perbandaran Pulau Pinang* [2000] 5 MLJ 130.

101 *Datuk Bandar Kuala Lumpur z Zain Azahari bin Zainal Abidin* [1997] 2 MLJ 17.

Furthermore, the lack of planning case law is a function of factors such as restrictive standing rules and other procedural barriers. On standing, the Supreme Court decided in *Government of Malaysia* v. *Lim Kit Siang, United Engineers (M) Berhad* v. *Lim Kit Siang* that the applicant did not have sufficient standing on the grounds that he could not distinguish himself from other road users and did not have sufficient interest in the project.[102] According to Harding, this decision has made public interest litigation very difficult, as NGOs are unable to bring lawsuits on behalf of groups of people or communities.[103] This has ramifications for the potential for climate adaptation litigation, which is often advanced as public interest litigation.[104] Additional procedural barriers include a six-week limitation period for anyone wishing to apply to quash a decision.[105] This short limitation period is measured from the time an administrative decision is made, not from the time it was known.

Extra-legal factors for the lack of development of planning law in Malaysia must also be taken into consideration. In their work on access to environmental justice in Kuala Lumpur (Malaysia's capital city), Harding and Sharom explain that, in comparison to most other jurisdictions, developers in Malaysia receive fewer decisions against them.[106] Further, when faced with an adverse decision, developers are far more inclined to pursue two other options instead of judicial review. The first is to apply political pressure for a favourable decision, and the second is to simply find another project, which they describe as being relatively easy in Kuala Lumpur's vibrant economy.[107] Harding and Sharom also suggest that the fact that architects, instead of lawyers, usually handle planning applications may be a contributory factor to the general unwillingness to pursue legal options.[108]

Finally, the reputation of the judiciary has affected the willingness of citizens to resort to the courts to challenge planning decisions. In recent

[102] [1988] 1 MLJ 50; also see Abdull Hamid bin Embong, 'Environmental Justice in Malaysia: Issues and Challenges' (Speech at Second National Seminar on Environmental Justice, 2015), particularly para 7 on standing rules.

[103] Andrew Harding, 'Public Interest Groups, Public Interest Law, and Development in Malaysia' (1992) 11(10) *Third World Legal Studies* 231.

[104] For example, *Asghar Leghari* v. *Federation of Pakistan* (W.P. No. 25501/2015) and the Indian climate cases.

[105] Rules of the High Court 1980, Order 53, r 1A.

[106] Harding and Sharom (n 91) 138.

[107] ibid.

[108] ibid.

years, the judiciary has been the subject of allegations of corruption and executive interference.[109] The judiciary has also been criticised for being ultra-conservative in its views on environmental issues and reluctant to accept new concepts (both substantive and procedural) that have developed in other jurisdictions.[110] However, there might be positive changes to the judicial culture after the unexpected outcome in the 2018 general election.[111] Outrage at rampant corruption tipped the election, ending the rule of the *Barisan Nasional* party, which has dominated Malaysian politics since independence.[112] Shortly after the formation of the new government, a new attorney general, Tommy Thomas, was brought in to replace Mohamed Apandi Ali, who cleared then-Prime Minister Najib Razak of any wrong-doing in the multi-billion-dollar 1MDB scandal.[113] The Chief Justice and Court of Appeal President stepped down from their posts on 31 July 2018, after Najib Razak had appointed them the year before, despite much controversy, because the two judges already exceeded the retirement age.[114]

Against this background, it is not surprising that there is only a modest planning case law in Malaysia, and there have been no cases to date that raise climate change adaptation considerations.[115]

11.3.2.2 EIA Law

In Malaysia, environmental assessment of development projects had been conducted for more than thirty years on a voluntary basis before

[109] See, for example, Hoong Phun Lee, *Constitutional Conflicts in Contemporary Malaysia* 2nd ed. (Oxford University Press 2017); Hoong Phun Lee and Richard Foo, 'The Malaysian Judiciary' in Hoong Phun Lee (ed.), *Asia-Pacific Judiciaries: Independence, Impartiality and Integrity* (Cambridge University Press 2017).

[110] Harding and Sharom (n 91)135.

[111] Amanda Whiting and Renuka Balasubramaniam, 'Malaysia's Remarkable Election Outcome' (Pursuit, 17 May 2018), https://pursuit.unimelb.edu.au/articles/malaysia-s-remarkable-election-outcome, accessed 28 August 2018.

[112] Jaclyn Neo, 'Constitutionalizing Clear Rules for Political Transition: Entrenching the Malaysian Tsunami' (I-CONnect, 16 May 2018), www.iconnectblog.com/2018/05/constitutionalizing-clear-rules-for-political-transition-entrenching-the-malaysian-tsunami-i-connect-column/, accessed 28 August 2018.

[113] Joseph Sipalan, 'Malaysia's Top Two Judges Resign amid Purge of Top Officials' (*Reuters*, 13 June 2018), www.reuters.com/article/us-malaysia-politics-judges/malaysias-top-two-judges-resign-amid-purge-of-top-officials-idUSKBN1J90D6, accessed 28 August 2018.

[114] Sipalan (n 113). For discussion, see Lynette Ong, 'Mahathir Must Not Rebuild Malaysia's Judiciary and Police, Two Institutions He Once Eroded, to Restore People's Faith' (*South China Morning Post*, 1 June 2018), www.scmp.com/comment/insight-opinion/article/2148812/mahathir-must-now-rebuild-malaysias-judiciary-and-police-two, accessed 28 August 2018.

[115] See also the discussion in Chapter 8.

the introduction of EIA legislation in 1988.[116] The Environmental Impact Assessment Order (Prescribed Activities) made the necessary amendments to the Environmental Quality Act 1974 (EQA) to create an EIA legal framework, which was modelled on the US National Environmental Policy Act (NEPA).[117]

Broadly speaking, Malaysia adopted a two-tier system composed of Preliminary EIA and Detailed EIA. All proposed development projects that fall into the 'Prescribed Activities' category set out in the Environmental Quality (Prescribed Activities; EIA) Order 1987 are required to undergo the Preliminary EIA process, while a subset of projects that are envisioned to have significant impacts on the environment are required to undergo a Detailed EIA.[118] It is noteworthy that there are no legal requirements for public participation in the Preliminary EIA process. Detailed EIA reports are subject to modest public display and comment requirements, according to the guidelines issued by the Department of Environment.[119]

The EIA process is beset with a number of problems, including the submission of scoping reports that provide inadequate and vague information, the lack of baseline studies, the late submission of EIA reports (sometimes after the project has already started), and almost non-existent monitoring of the implementation of mitigation measures.[120] In addition, complex state-federal dynamics make the implementation of the EIA law in Malaysia particularly challenging, and the result is often highly detrimental to the environment and local communities.

The Bakun Dam is a case in point. In 2011, after nearly fifty years of delay, the Sarawak government began operation of the Bakun Dam, which is the largest dam in Asia outside China.[121] The project was first proposed in the 1970s but did not really take off till the 1990s, when the

[116] Clive Briffett, Jeff Obbard and Jamie Mackee, 'Environmental Assessment in Malaysia: A Meansto an End or a New Beginning?' (2004) 22(3) *Impact Assessment and Project Appraisal* 221.

[117] Environmental Quality Act 1974 s 34A.

[118] Department of Environment, Ministry of Natural Resources and Environment (DOE), *Environmental Impact Assessment (EIA): Procedure and Requirements in Malaysia* (2007) 11.

[119] DOE (n 118) 11, 13. See also the DOE, *Environmental Requirements: A Guide for Investors*, 11th ed. (2010).

[120] Briffett, Obbard and Mackee (n 116); Nik Norulaini Nik Ab. Rahman, Asyirah Abdul Rahim and Fera Fizani Ahmad Fizri, 'Environmental Management Activities of an Infrastructure Development Project: The Case of Beris Dam, Malaysia' (2006) *Malaysian Journal of Environmental Management* 113.

[121] International Rivers, 'Bakun Dam', www.internationalrivers.org/campaigns/bakun-dam, accessed 28 August 2018.

project was awarded without tender to Ekran Berhad, a company owned by one of Sarawak's richest men, who made his fortune from timber-logging operations and who had close associations with the political elite.[122] The project required more than ten thousand indigenous peoples to be resettled, as the dam construction would require flooding their land. The land included agricultural land, homes of the indigenous peoples and their ancestral lands. The EIA for this mega-project was 'salami sliced' into four EIA reports[123] for separate parts of the project, which would have made it difficult for the relevant departments to assess the cumulative environmental and social impact of the project. In addition, the EIA reports were not made publicly available. The residents of the affected area were therefore not given any information about the proposed project, let alone the opportunity to participate in the EIA process.[124] When they protested, the Minister of Science, Technology and Environment's response was to delegate retrospectively the power of conducting EIA from the DOE to the State Government of Sarawak. This was significant because the State Government EIA requirements are less stringent than those of the DOE and require no public participation.

Subsequently, three indigenous people living in the affected area brought legal proceedings against the relevant agencies.[125] The salient part of their argument, for present purposes, was that they had been denied procedural fairness because they had not been given any opportunity to comment on the EIA for the project. Further, the EIA report was invalid because of its non-compliance with the public notice and comment requirements pursuant to the EQA. Finally, they argued that the transfer of power to the State Government was *ultra vires*. It was held in the High Court that the delegation of power was invalid, and the EQA's EIA requirements had to be followed.[126] The Court of Appeal reversed

[122] Edmund Terence Gomez and Kwame Sundaram Jomo, *Malaysia's Political Economy: Politics, Patronage and Profits* (Cambridge University Press 1999) 110.

[123] European Parliament, 'Written Question by Doeke Eisma (ELDR) to the Commission: BAkun Dam, Malaysia' (28 June 1996), www.europarl.europa.eu/sides/getDoc.do?type=WQ&reference=P-1996-1869&language=EN, accessed 28 August 2018.

[124] The Coalition of Concerned NGOs on Bakun (Gabungan), Malaysia, 'The Resettlement of Indigenous People Affected by the Bakun Hydro-Electric Project, Sarawak, Malaysia' (*World Commission on Dams*, 1999) 8, www.internationalrivers.org/sites/default/files/attached-files/resettlement_of_indigenous_people_at_bakun.pdf, accessed 28 August 2018.

[125] *Kajing Tubek & Ors. v. Ekran Bhd. & Ors.* [1996] 2 *MLJ* 388.

[126] ibid. For discussion, see Raphael Pura, 'Court Decision Poses Hurdle for Malaysia's Bakun Dam' (*The Wall Street Journal*, 1996), www.wsj.com/articles/SB835214167654346500, accessed 28 August 2018.

the High Court's decision, with reasoning that was heavily influenced by considerations about the constitutional allocation of powers between states and the federal government and which lacked appreciation for ecological integrity, sustainable development and the purpose of the EIA process.[127]

As with the planning law regime, the EIA system offers avenues for climate adaptation litigation if it functions well. In particular, better access to information and more open public participation will improve the prospects for climate adaptation litigation to emerge in Malaysia.

11.3.3 Singapore

As a small island city-state, Singapore is vulnerable to climate change risks, particularly those related to sea-level rise. The country's climate adaptation efforts focus on managing climate change risks by enhancing water resource management, coastal protection and flood prevention.[128] The Inter-Ministerial Committee on Climate Change (IMCC), established in 2007, coordinates climate change policies across all ministries and government agencies. While the IMCC and the various working groups determine high-level policy directions, implementation of climate adaptation policies is undertaken by designated government agencies. For example, the Building and Construction Authority is the lead agency tasked with managing Singapore's coastal areas and taking action to enhance the country's coastal resilience.[129]

Climate litigation has not taken off in Singapore, and of the three Southeast Asian study jurisdictions, Singapore would seem to offer the lowest prospects for litigation to play a role in building climate change adaptive capacity. There are three key barriers facing the emergence of

[127] *Ketua Pengarah Jabatan Alam Sekitar* v. *Kajing Tubek* [1997] 3 *MLJ* 23. For broader discussion, see, for example May Tay, 'Development and Environmental Injustice in Malaysia:A Story of Indigenous Resistance in Sarawak' (2017) 1(1) *Justice, Indigeneity, and Development* 7, http://scholarship.claremont.edu/cgi/viewcontent.cgi?article=1006&context=envirolabasia, accessed 28 August 2018.

[128] National Climate Change Secretariat, 'Adapting to Climate Change' (2017), www.nccs.gov.sg/climate-change-and-singapore/adapting-to-climate-change/overview, accessed 28 August 2018; Ministry of the Environment and Water Resources and Ministry of Development, 'Singapore's Climate Action Plan: A Climate-Resilient Singapore for a Sustainable Future' (2016), www.nccs.gov.sg/docs/default-source/publications/a-climate-resilient-singapore-for-a-sustainable-future.pdf, accessed 28 August 2018.

[129] Building and Construction Authority, 'Annual Report 2015/16' (2016), www.bca.gov.sg/AboutUs/BCA_Annual_Report/environmental.html, accessed 28 August 2018.

climate adaptation litigation in Singapore: the lack of an EIA law, limited avenues for administrative review of agency planning decisions and significant hurdles in seeking judicial review of executive/agency decisions. We briefly discuss each of these factors below.

11.3.3.1 No EIA Law in Singapore

Unlike most jurisdictions around the world, Singapore does not have an EIA law. As demonstrated by the earlier discussion of adaptation litigation in Australia, a formal EIA and planning legal regime provides many hooks for lawsuits concerned with flooding in low-lying areas (which is increasingly a concern in Singapore and has been identified as a climate-related risk) and coastal hazards such as sea-level rise. This avenue for adaptation litigation is absent in Singapore.

The practice of EIA in Singapore primarily takes two forms. First, industrial projects are required, pursuant to the Environmental Protection and Management Act, to conduct a Pollution Control Study (PCS). The PCS can be described as a basic environmental permitting process with a fairly circumscribed scope. It is intended to assess the operating impacts of the proposed industrial facility such as emissions of air and water pollutants, land contamination, the proper handling and storage of hazardous chemicals and noise pollution. Second, voluntary EIAs have been conducted by government agencies and companies for major projects such as rail infrastructure and desalination plants.[130] It has been argued that these voluntary EIAs are more of an attempt at due diligence to incorporate environmental best practices into the planning and construction phases of the proposed project, but are not likely to exercise any real influence on higher-level decisions such as the design of the project and choice of technologies.[131] As there is no EIA legal framework in place, project developers do not face any legal requirements to disclose EIA studies to the public or to consult the public. Reports and monitoring results are therefore kept confidential and are not available in the public domain. This makes it nearly impossible for civil society and other interested parties to participate in the deliberation processes related

130 For example, the Land Transport Authority has conducted a number of internal EIAs for its rail planning and construction projects. The Public Utilities Board and the National Environment Agency have also conducted EIAs for major projects concerning the siting and development of municipal infrastructure and waste incineration plants.

131 Deng Mao and Rick Reidinger, 'Evaluating EIAFollow-Ups in Chinaand Singapore' in Lin-Heng Lye et al. (eds.), *Sustainability Matters: Environmental Management in the Anthropocene* (World Scientific 2018) 253.

to development and land use in Singapore, let alone to challenge the viability of proposed projects from a climate adaptation perspective through litigation.

11.3.3.2 Limited Avenues for Review of Planning Decisions

The origins of urban planning in Singapore can be traced to the British town planning policies that were introduced during the colonial period. The British colonial government introduced comprehensive planning by way of a 'master plan', development control and planning legislation. Today, the Planning Act provides the legal framework governing land use planning and urban development in Singapore. The 'Master Plan' is defined in Section 6 of the Planning Act to refer to the plan that was 'submitted and approved by the Governor in Council on 5th August 1958' and which has been amended every five years since. The Master Plan is a country-wide land-use plan that designates different land uses, including infrastructure, recreational spaces and residential zones.

Planning permission is required before any form of development can proceed (Section 13 of the Planning Act), and the authority can impose conditions on the grant of any planning permission. Pursuant to Section 22 of the Planning Act, a person aggrieved by a planning decision may appeal to the minister. It should be noted, however, that '[t]he decision of the Minister shall be final and shall not be challenged or questioned in any court'.[132] In *Borissik Svetlana* v. *Urban Redevelopment Authority*, the presiding judge held that it was improper for the applicant to seek judicial review of an administrative planning decision in that case as the legislature had clearly intended that the courts should not become involved with issues of planning permission, as these issues involved considerations of fact, law and policy, which are better dealt with through an appeals procedure to the minister.[133]

While in recent years the planning process in Singapore has become more open to public consultation with various stakeholders in society, it is still a highly centralised process and the courts have a circumscribed role to play. As such, there are limited prospects for planning litigation to emerge as a vehicle for introducing climate adaptation governance in Singapore, unlike the case in Australia.

[132] Planning Act s 22(7).
[133] [2009] 4 SLR 92 (HC) [25]–[30].

11.3.3.3 Hurdles to Seeking Judicial Review

Looking beyond the planning legal framework, there are other regulatory agencies that are responsible for land use management, water supply and environmental protection, and therefore contribute towards climate change adaptation goals within the remit of their regulatory responsibilities. For example, the functions and duties of the Public Utilities Board include providing an adequate supply of water at reasonable prices, maintaining and managing stormwater drainage systems, and promoting water conservation.[134] Another example is the Building and Construction Authority, which is responsible for Singapore's coastal areas and increasing the city's resilience to climate-related coastal risks.[135] In Australia, administrative decisions of regulatory agencies are subject to the Administrative Decisions Judicial Review Act 1977 at the federal level and similar judicial review laws at the state level.[136] Furthermore, various planning and environmental laws often contain provisions for public consultation on new regulations and rights to object to and/or appeal particular decisions on development proposals.[137] There are, therefore, opportunities for interested parties to participate in the development of climate adaptation policies and regulatory initiatives, as well as opportunities to challenge the decision-making processes of regulatory agencies on procedural grounds. These opportunities are absent in Singapore because there is no legislation similar to the Administrative Decisions Judicial Review Act in place.

It is also important to note that there are significant doctrinal hurdles to overcome when one seeks to bring judicial review proceedings in Singapore. The first issue to consider is that of standing. In Singapore, there is an absence of specific statutory or procedural guidance on standing. It has, therefore, been open to the courts in Singapore to determine the level of interest needed by an applicant to access the remedy of judicial review. The issue of standing is not problematic when the applicant is an individual against whom a decision has been made by a government department (for example, a decision by the immigration authority to

134 Public Utilities Act (Cap. 261, 2002 Rev. Ed.) art 6(c), 6(e), 6(f)(iii).

135 National Climate Change Secretariat, 'Coastal Protection', www.nccs.gov.sg/climate-change-and-singapore/adapting-to-climate-change/coastal-protection, accessed on 29 August 2018.

136 See, generally, Mark A. Robinson, *Judicial Review: The Laws of Australia* (Thompson Reuters 2014).

137 Stephen Willey, 'Planning Appeals: Are Third Party Rights Legitimate? The Case Study of Victoria, Australia' (2006) 24(3) *Urban Policy and Research* 369–89.

deny renewal of a visa permit to be in Singapore). More problematic are cases where individuals are challenging general policies or legislation of general application or where groups or associations commence judicial review proceedings to represent a public interest. Climate adaptation cases are most likely to fall into the latter category – hence the salience of this discussion of standing rules in Singapore.

In general, the rules on standing in Singapore have traditionally only permitted applicants directly and individually affected by either a legislative provision or executive action to commence judicial review proceedings. As such, there has been highly restricted scope for public interest litigation (in its various forms).[138] The restrictive approach to the rules on standing is largely driven by concern that expanding standing rules beyond individuals with a concrete interest would involve the courts in politically motivated litigation and that judicial review may end up being a surrogate political process.[139] Jhaveri argues that while the courts in Singapore have, in recent cases, been prepared to expand standing rules to permit judicial review in novel situations, they have still anchored such expansion of the rules to some personal connection of the applicant to the case. Such connection could take the form of a violation of a personal right or special damage suffered by the applicant.[140] While this is similar to the common law position in Australia, many environmental and planning laws under which climate change adaptation cases have been brought have more relaxed or 'open' standing rules.[141]

Second, Singapore has followed the UK approach (also adopted in Australia) in administrative review, whereby decisions by regulatory agencies and the executive can be subject to review by the courts only on the basis of illegality, irrationality and procedural impropriety. In a review based on illegality, the allegation is that the statutory body in question has exceeded its express authority or that its powers have been used for

[138] For a general discussion of public interest litigation in Singapore, see Tsun Hang Tey, 'Limitations on Public Interest Litigation in Singapore: Internalizing Political Ideology and Institutionalizing Judicial Self-Restraint' in Po Jen Yap and Holning Lau (eds.), *Public Interest Litigation in Asia* (Routledge 2011).

[139] Swati Jhaveri, 'Advancing Constitutional Justice in Singapore: Enhancing Access and Standing in Judicial Review Cases' (2017) *SJLS* 53, 56.

[140] ibid 61.

[141] For example, the New South Wales Land and Environment Court has open standing rules and a merits review jurisdiction that has facilitated environmental and climate litigation in NSW: see generally EDO NSW, 'EDO NSW Report: Merits Review in Planning in NSW' (Report, July 2016), www.edonsw.org.au/merits_review_in_plannin g_in_nsw, archived at https://perma.cc/6JGA-JC7Q, accessed on 29 August 2018.

improper purposes that are contrary to the policy and objectives of its governing statute. This is a very high threshold to meet. Most statutory provisions that set out the functions and obligations of the agency confer powers in fairly broad terms. Further, statutory purposes can be express, implied from the wording of the statute, or implied from parliamentary debates. Adopting a facilitative rather than adversarial role in administrative review, the Singapore courts are likely to find that the exercise of the authority's power incidental to the statute's purpose is valid.[142] It should also be noted that in Singapore, there is a strong assumption that administrative decisions are unlikely to be *ultra vires* because of a long-standing practice whereby ministries and regulatory agencies usually seek the advice of the Attorney General on the legality of their proposed actions and policies.[143] As for irrationality, this is an extremely high threshold to meet. It would be difficult to make the argument that in failing to take climate change considerations into account, the planning authority or environmental protection agency made a decision 'which is so outrageous in its defiance of logic that no sensible person who had applied his mind to it could have arrived at it'.[144] Further, it is worth noting that in determining irrationality, the court will limit itself to the decision-making process and not review the merits of the decision itself.[145] As discussed in another chapter in this book, there is also a record of failure in the Australian judicial review cases focused on climate change mitigation because of the difficulties of discerning these grounds of illegality and irrationality.[146]

11.4 Conclusion

This chapter sought to evaluate the prospects for adaptation-focused climate change litigation in Southeast Asia and to consider the conditions

[142] *Public Prosecutor* v. *MM Pillay* [1977] 1 *MLJ* 228. Means adopted to achieve the desired purpose were considered exercise of power incidental to the statute's purpose; Chan Sek Keong, 'Judicial Review – From Angst to Empathy' (2010) 22 *SAcLJ* 469.

[143] This was noted in an extrajudicial writing by Chan Sek Keong, the former Chief Justice of Singapore (n 142). He observed that the prevalence of this practice meant that fewer decisions are vulnerable to judicial review.

[144] Stated by Lord Diplock in *Council of Civil Service Unions* v. *Minister for the Civil Service* [1984] *UKHL* 9 (the *GCHQ* case) 410 and reaffirmed in *Tan Seet Eng* v. *Attorney-General and another matter* [2016] 1*SLR* 779 (CA).

[145] *Chee Siok Chin* v. *Minister for Home Affairs* [2006] 1 *SLR* 582 (HC) at [93]: 'Judicial review is, however, limited to the decision-making process and does not extend to a review of the merits of the decision itself'.

[146] See Chapter 7.

that need to be in place for development of this body of case law. Presently, adaptation litigation in the case study jurisdictions is best described as being at a nascent stage. Accordingly, in assessing the potential for litigation growth in Southeast Asia, we drew lessons from the more developed climate adaptation jurisprudence in neighbouring Australia.

In our analysis, we found that the factors that are particularly important include a functioning planning law system, an EIA system that works effectively (and is not simply regarded as an exercise in checking boxes on a list), and more flexible locus standi and other procedural requirements to enable bringing legal proceedings. Prevailing social attitudes towards litigation and the judiciary are also salient considerations. While one might say that these findings state the obvious, there is no legal scholarship to the best of our knowledge that offers a systematic study of how these factors come into play to determine the prospects for climate adaptation litigation in Southeast Asia. As such, this chapter offers novel insights and fills a gap in the climate change litigation scholarship, which tends to be heavily focused on jurisdictions in the Global North. It also serves to highlight the need for capacity building in many jurisdictions – to develop environmental governance, access to justice and, indeed, adherence to the rule of law in development-related decision-making – as a precursor to the emergence of climate litigation.

Based on the survey in Section 11.2, we conclude that litigation currently plays a modest role in the Philippines' response to climate change, and a negligible role in Malaysia and Singapore, although the prospects are more favourable in Malaysia if other access to justice barriers can be overcome. This points to a wider question of how the climate change governance landscape in certain countries, particularly those in Southeast Asia and the Global South more broadly, will look quite different from the Global North, reflecting the prevailing legal, socio-economic and political conditions. When litigation is an expensive option that is not available to the majority of the population, and particularly out of reach for those vulnerable communities that are most likely to suffer the brunt of climate change impacts, it could well become a source of environmental injustice instead of a regulatory pathway towards greater climate change resilience. This invites us to reconsider the prevailing notions about climate litigation in theory and in practice – a larger and more ambitious research agenda to be canvassed in the future.

PART IV

China, Courts and Climate Change

12

Climate Change Litigation: A Promising Pathway to Climate Justice in China?

JIANGFENG LI

Introduction

There is a body of sound scientific evidence on the serious threats that climate change poses to the Earth's systems and humanity.[1] According to the Intergovernmental Panel on Climate Change's Fifth Assessment Report, we know with more than 95 per cent certainty that human activity is responsible.[2] Against this background, the world has witnessed numerous instances of climate change litigation filed in domestic courts and international tribunals. Specifically, climate change litigation has been brought in the European Union and twenty-seven other countries.[3] These cases share the common trait of applying public or private law to the problem of climate change, making courts an important forum for debate or discussion regarding transnational climate change regulation.[4] Notably, China, the world's largest greenhouse gas

[1] S. Vijayavenkataraman, S. Iniyan, and R Goic, 'A Review of Climate Change, Mitigation and Adaptation' (2012) 16*Renewable and Sustainable Energy Reviews* 878, 878–85; Environment and Ecology, 'Climate Change Threats and Solutions: What Can We Do to Make a Difference?', http://environment-ecology.com/climate-change/785-climate-change-threats-and-solutions.html, accessed 1 June 2019.

[2] T. F. Stocker and others, *IPCC, 2013: Summary for Policymakers in Climate Change 2013: The Physical Science Basis. Contribution of Working Group I to the Fifth Assessment Report of the Intergovernmental Panel on Climate Change* (Cambridge University Press 2013), 15.

[3] The numbers are based on the data provided by Columbia Law School Sabin Center for Climate Change Law (led by Professor Michael Gerrard), which made two charts in collaboration with Arnold and Porter LLP: 'U.S. Climate Change Litigation' and 'Non-U.S. Climate Change Litigation'; Sabin Center for Climate Change Law, 'Climate Change Litigation Databases', www.climatecasechart.com, accessed 1 June 2019.

[4] Hari M. Osofsky, 'The Continuing Importance of Climate Change Litigation' (2010) 1(1) *Climate Law* 3, 4.

emitter,[5] is missing from this trend, as it has not employed litigation as a means of climate change regulation.

Nevertheless, recent legal developments in China show that the country is opening its doors to climate change litigation. For example, China included the 'Climate Change Response Law' as a 'Research Project' in its 2016 national legislative agenda.[6] The first draft of the Climate Change Response Law released in 2015 for public comment included a general provision for public participation, which would have served to encourage corporate entities or individuals to report non-compliance to regulatory authorities or bring enforcement lawsuits.[7] Though the draft law did not provide details of the specific requirements for bringing lawsuits over climate change, it signalled the Chinese government's changing attitude towards climate change litigation. It can be argued that China's position with respect to this recent legal development is consistent with its continuing climate mitigation efforts, which have largely been driven by domestic concerns (energy demand and security, environmental deterioration, and economic transformation) and the need to maintain a responsible international image.[8] In addition, the enabling of public interest litigation by NGOs was one of the major reforms to the Environmental Protection Law ('EPL') introduced in 2014.[9] A pilot program launched in July 2015 has seen public procuratorates bring proceedings against ministries and sub-national governments to enforce environmental laws.[10]

[5] United States Environmental Protection Agency (EPA), 'Global Greenhouse Gas Emissions Data – Emissions by Country', www.epa.gov/ghgemissions/global-greenhouse-gas-emissions-data#Country, accessed 1 June 2019.

[6] PRC National Development and Reform Commission Climate Change Division, 'China's 2017 Annual Report on Policies and Actions to Address Climate Change [中国应对气候变化的政策与行动2017年度报告]' (31 October 2017), www.ndrc.gov.cn/gzdt/201710/t20171031_866090.html, accessed 1 June 2019.

[7] China Hubei Emission Exchange, 'Zhong Hua Ren Min Gong He Guo Ying Dui Qi Hou Bian Hua Fa (Chu Gao) [PRC Climate Change Response Law (First Draft for Comments)] (中国人民共和国应对气候变化法(初稿))' (16 September 2017), www.hbets.cn/index.php/index-view-aid-705.html, accessed 1 June 2019.

[8] Lisa Williams, 'China's Climate Change Policies – Actors and Drivers' (2014), The Lowy Institute for International Policy, www.files.ethz.ch/isn/182715/chinas-climate-change-policies.pdf, accessed 1 June 2019.

[9] See Environmental Protection Law of the People's Republic of China (2014 Revision; (24 April 2014) [Effective on 1 January 2015] (中华人民共和国环境保护法 (2014修订)) (Promulgated by Standing Committee of the National People's Congress), http://en.pkulaw.cn/display.aspx?cgid=223979&lib=law, accessed 1 June 2019 ('the EPL').

[10] See the Supreme People's Procuratorate of the People's Republic of China, 'Jian Cha Ji Guan Ti Qi Gong Yi Su Song Shi Dian Fang An [Pilot Program for Procuratorial Organs

Against this background, this chapter will engage in a theoretical analysis of the prospects for climate change litigation in China. Section 12.1 defines the concept of 'climate change litigation' in the context of China, since this term can have either a broad or narrow meaning. Section 12.2 undertakes a theoretical prognosis of the potentially available forms and types of claims for climate change litigation in China, with analysis focusing on China's current legal framework as well as utilizing empirical evidence from other countries' climate change litigation experience and China's progress in other types of environmental litigation. Section 12.3 analyses the various factors that are either obstacles or impetuses for promoting climate change litigation in China, and provides an overall assessment of the prospects for climate change litigation in China. Section 12.4 makes some proposals for China to further its legal initiatives and reforms to advance climate change litigation. Finally, some concluding observations are provided.

12.1 Defining Climate Change Litigation in the Chinese Context

In order to understand how climate change litigation in China might look like, it is necessary to first resolve the threshold question of what the term climate change litigation means. Climate change litigation, if understood in its broadest sense, can encompass a variety of litigation types, because climate change is the accumulated effect of an enormous number of human activities from daily life to commercial dealings and industrial production. Thus virtually all litigation can be regarded as having climate change implication if one looks hard enough.[11] In particular, as China's economy largely depends on coal usage, which is not only the major contributor to China's air pollution but also the main source of China's greenhouse gas (GHG) emissions, any litigation over the control of coal usage will inevitably have an impact on climate change by indirectly reducing GHG emissions. It can therefore be argued that looking to the consequences of a lawsuit does not help one to understand climate change litigation as a separate category.

To Initiate Public Interest Litigation] (检察机关提起公益诉讼试点方案)' (3 July 2015), www.spp.gov.cn/zdgz/201507/t20150703_100706.shtml, accessed 1 June 2019.

[11] Chris Hilson, 'Climate Change Litigation in the UK: An Explanatory Approach (Or Bringing Grievance Back In)' in F. Fracchia and M. Occhiena (eds.), *Climate Change: La riposta del diritto* (Editoriale Scientifica 2010), 421–36, www.reading.ac.uk/web/files/law/Milan_Climate_Change_Litigation_in_the_UK_v2.pdf, accessed 1 June 2019.

Therefore, when we talk about climate change litigation as a separate and identifiable category, it makes better sense to require some common features to narrow down and identify this group of lawsuits. Markell and Ruhl define climate change litigation as '[a]ny piece of federal, state, tribal, or local administrative or judicial litigation in which the tribunal decisions directly and expressly raise an issue of fact or law regarding the substance or policy of climate change causes and impacts'.[12] This definition is widely accepted by other scholars.[13] This definition avoids the mechanical difficulty of exploring the inner motivations behind the litigation, and instead looks to the visible judgments issued by tribunals or courts to determine whether the litigation falls within the scope of climate change litigation. However, this definition excludes litigation that does not reach the stage of judicial decisions or litigation that raises climate change issues of fact or law at some point during proceedings, where the tribunals or courts involved do not endorse or address these issues in their final judgments.

This narrow definition, though a good approach for the purpose of engaging in an empirical study, is unsuitable for the discussion relating to China. First, the Chinese legal system does not abide by the common law precept of stare decisis, and Chinese courts do not regularly publish their decisions.[14] As such, the number of reported cases available in China is very limited. Also, Chinese courts do not engage in the same sort of detailed, thorough, and lengthy reasoning in their judgments as common law courts do, so it is difficult to classify Chinese litigation based on court decisions. In addition, since the purpose of this chapter is to evaluate the prospects of developing climate change litigation in China, it is more appropriate to define climate change litigation at the stage of initiation or filing of a lawsuit.

Accordingly, this chapter will adopt a definition of climate change litigation that is broader than that of Markell and Ruhl. It borrows Hilson's definition of climate change litigation as including any administrative or judicial case in which the claimants or defendants included

[12] David Markell and J. B. Ruhl, 'An Empirical Assessment of Climate Change In The Courts: A New Jurisprudence Or Business As Usual?' (2012) 64 *Florida Law Review* 15, 26.

[13] See Michael Byers, Kelsey Franks, and Andrew Gage, 'The Internationalization of Climate Damages Litigation' (2017) 7(2) *Washington Journal of Environmental Law & Policy* 265, 270; Meredith Wilensky, 'Climate Change in the Courts: An Assessment Of Non-U.S. Climate Litigation' (2015) 26 *Duke Environmental Law & Policy Forum* 131, 134.

[14] Mark Jia, 'Chinese Common Law? Guiding Cases and Judicial Reform' (2016) 129 *Harvard Law Review* 2213, 2215–16.

climate change elements (facts, laws, or arguments) in the framing of their claims or defences – these elements may be the causes or impacts of climate change, or correlation with climate change.[15] This definition does not include cases that are initiated for the purpose of achieving GHG reductions, but the parties do not frame their claims with reference to any climate change elements. As mentioned previously, the exclusion of such cases makes sense because unless the parties explicitly reveal their underlying intentions, it is impossible to know the real motives and drivers behind each case. This definition also does not include cases that are not initiated with climate change elements but have the result of achieving GHG reductions, either directly or indirectly. It can be argued that this exclusion is warranted because the definitional scope would otherwise be too broad to effectively assess the impacts of litigation on climate change regulation. Therefore, the definition only addresses those cases with obvious consideration of climate change elements.

Using this definition, there are currently no cases in China that qualify as climate change litigation. This chapter therefore seeks to evaluate the prospects for the emergence of climate change litigation in China.

12.2 Theoretical Prognosis of Potential Climate Change Litigation in China

As the world's most populous country and fast-growing economy, China has surpassed the United States as the world's largest GHG emitter.[16] Therefore, it has a significant role to play in global efforts to address climate change.[17] Recognizing the important role that litigation can potentially play in the climate change regulatory landscape, this section will engage in a theoretical analysis of the various avenues for pursuing

[15] Chris Hilson (n 11).

[16] See Union of Concerned Scientists, 'Each Country's Share of CO2 Emissions' (20 November 2017), www.ucsusa.org/global-warming/science-and-impacts/science/each-countrys-share-of-co2.html#.Wsw3XE3Vw5t, accessed 1 June 2019; John Vidal and David Adam, 'China Overtakes US as World's Biggest CO_2 Emitter' *The Guardian* (19 June 2007), www.theguardian.com/environment/2007/jun/19/china.usnews, accessed 1 June 2019.

[17] Guoyi Han, Marie Olsson, Karl Hallding, and David Lunsford, 'China's Carbon Emission Trading: An Overview of Current Development' (2012) 1 FORES Study, https://fores.se/wp-content/uploads/2013/04/WEB-FORES-China.pdf, accessed 1 June 2019, xiii; International Energy Agency, 'World Energy Outlook 2017 – Executive Summary' (14 November 2017), www.iea.org/Textbase/npsum/weo2017SUM.pdf, accessed 1 June 2019, 3.

climate change litigation and the potential types of claims available to plaintiffs in China.

12.2.1 Potential Forms of Climate Change Litigation in China

Climate change litigation can be categorized according to factors such as the type of plaintiff, type of defendant, objectives of the litigation, or the laws supporting the claims.[18] Since China has not had any climate change litigation, it is more meaningful to discuss potential avenues for litigation on the basis of the type of plaintiff, as this is closely linked to the question of standing (i.e., who is allowed to bring a lawsuit in front of the court or tribunal).[19] Assessing the potential avenues for climate change litigation through the 'type of plaintiff' lens can shed light on the practical viability of developing each of these legal avenues in China.

This section discusses three key avenues for climate change litigation: (1) public interest litigation (PIL), which refers to lawsuits brought by environmental groups or other social group entities; (2) government enforcement litigation, which refers to lawsuits brought by government entities against other government entities, corporate entities or individual citizens;[20] and (3) private rights of action, which refers to lawsuits brought by private actors (individual, corporations or other private entities)[21] against government defendants, other corporate entities, or individuals for the infringement of certain rights.[22] Although China has not had climate change litigation, there has been litigation in these three forms in other areas of environmental law. As China is a civil law system with a strong emphasis on the application of statutory law, and courts will usually resort to statutes to determine whether to hear specific claims. The following analysis, while drawing experience from other environmental law litigations in China, will

[18] Meredith Wilensky, 'Climate Change in the Courts: An Assessment of Non-U.S. Climate Litigation' (*Sabin Center for Climate Change Law [Columbia Law School]*, February 2015), http://columbiaclimatelaw.com/files/2016/06/Wilensky-2015-02-Climate-Change-in-the-Courts.pdf, accessed 1 June 2019, i.

[19] Giulio Corsi, 'A Bottom-Up Approach to Climate Governance: The New Waveof Climate Change Litigation' (2017) *ICCG Reflection No.* 57, 2–3.

[20] Wilensky (n 18) iii.

[21] Broadly speaking, environmental groups are also private actors, but considering that public interest litigations have become a notable standalone type of lawsuits and there are usually different procedural rules for public interest litigations, this paper singles out private interest litigation as a separate form of litigation distinct from the private right of actions.

[22] Wilensky (n 18) iii.

provide a realistic evaluation of the feasibility of developing each form of climate change litigation in China.

12.2.1.1 Public Interest Litigation

PIL refers to a lawsuit which is filed to advance the cause of a minority, disadvantaged group or individuals, or which uses the law to raise issues of broader public concern.[23] PIL is different from ordinary litigation in that the intention of PIL is to protect the interests of the public at large or a large group of people beyond those bringing or defending the lawsuit.[24] Usually, public interest lawsuits are brought by environmental non-governmental organizations (NGOs). Public interest lawsuits have also been employed for climate change. In the United States, the plaintiffs in the majority of associated lawsuits are environmental NGOs targeting government agencies in connection with permits, rules, or impact assessments.[25] Environmental groups in non-US jurisdictions have also brought lawsuits to challenge permissions for an emissions source or to require new governmental action to reduce GHG emissions.[26] For example, a Ukrainian environmental group successfully brought an action against the environmental ministry for its failure to act on climate change, which thereby breaches Ukraine's international obligations.[27]

In China, though there has been no public interest lawsuit focusing on climate change, there have been a number of public interest lawsuits addressing other environmental issues. China saw its first real public interest lawsuit in 2009, which was brought by an environmental group against a private company for pollution.[28] However, the number of cases has grown rapidly since the revised version of the Environmental Protection Law (EPL) came into force in January 2015.[29] Since the new EPL took effect, Chinese courts at all levels have tried more than fifty cases of environmental public interest litigation.[30] This was largely due to

[23] The PILS Project, 'About Public Interest Litigation', www.pilsni.org/about-public-interest-litigation, accessed 1 June 2019.

[24] Action 4 Justice, 'What Is Public Interest Litigation?', https://action4justice.org/q_and_a/public-interest-litigation/, accessed 1 June 2019.

[25] Markell and Ruhl (n 12) 74.

[26] Wilensky (n 18) ii, 26–7, 34.

[27] ibid.

[28] Richard Zhang and Benoit Mayer, 'Public Interest Environmental Litigation in China' (2017) 1 *Chinese Journal of Environmental Law* 202.

[29] ibid.

[30] Bo Zhang and others, 'China's New Environmental Protection Regulatory Regime: Effects and Gaps' (2017) 187 *Journal of Environmental Management* 464, 466.

the stronger legal basis laid out in the new EPL for public interest lawsuits. The new EPL grants environmental NGOs that have been registered and engaged in environmental protection activities for over five years, standing to file environmental public interest lawsuits.[31] This was further supported by a detailed judicial interpretation on civil environmental public interest litigation, issued by China's Supreme People's Court in January 2015.[32]

It can be argued that the EPL does not preclude lawsuits on climate change. Article 58 of the EPL states that qualified environmental NGOs can bring lawsuits against 'acts of polluting the environment or destroying ecology, which undermine the public interest'.[33] Since there is strong scientific evidence that climate change has adverse impacts on the ecological system and human well-being (i.e., undermine the public interest), there is scope for courts to interpret Article 58 to include climate change claims raised by qualified environmental NGOs. However, there is a potential conflict between the EPL and PRC Civil Procedure Law as revised in 2017, since the latter only states that the environmental NGO may bring lawsuits in connection with acts that 'pollute the environment . . . or otherwise damage the public interest', and the language 'destroy ecology' is missing.[34] There is thus some uncertainty regarding how the court would interpret this provision when presented with a climate change claim.

Nonetheless, the public interest litigation mechanism provided under the EPL does provide what appears to be a feasible hook for environmental NGOs to bring climate change lawsuits. More importantly, this mechanism solves the question of standing, which is the common obstacle to climate change lawsuits. According to the PRC Civil Procedure Law, a plaintiff has to hold a direct interest in the lawsuit it files and has to satisfy the burden of proof for its claims[35] such as causation and injury-in

[31] The EPL (n 9) Art 58.

[32] Interpretation of the Supreme People's Court on Several Issues Concerning the Application of Law in the Conduct of Environmental Civil Public Interest Litigations (6 January 2015) [Effective on 7 January 2015] (最高人民法院关于审理环境民事公益诉讼案件适用法律若干问题的解释) (Issued by the Supreme People's Court), http://en.pkulaw.cn/display.aspx?cgid=f81c55e05ed7c7f6bdfb&lib=law, accessed 1 June 2019.

[33] The EPL (n 9) Art 58.

[34] The Civil Procedure Law of the People's Republic of China (2017 Revision) (27 June 2017) [Effective on 1 July 2017] (中华人民共和国民事诉讼法) (Promulgated by the Standing Committee of the Twelfth National People's Congress), http://en.pkulaw.cn/display.aspx?id=6d9ce94e57cee7afbdfb&lib=law, accessed 1 June 2019, Art 55 ('the CPL').

[35] Interpretation of the Supreme People's Court on the Application of the Civil Procedure Law of the People's Republic of China (30 January 2015) [Effective on 4 February 2015] (最高人民法院关于适用《中华人民共和国民事诉讼法》的解释) (Promulgated by

-fact, which are usually difficult to establish in climate change claims.[36] But in public interest litigation, environmental NGOs are given de jure standing when pursuing public interest goals. Therefore, this chapter argues that PIL is a viable avenue for advancing climate change litigation in China.

12.2.1.2 Government Enforcement Litigation

Government enforcement litigation refers to lawsuits brought by the government against other government agencies, corporate entities or other social entities. There is climate change litigation in the form of government enforcement lawsuits in other jurisdictions, but the total number of cases is relatively small compared to other forms of litigation.[37] The few existing precedents include government-initiated lawsuits against national governments for failure to fulfil obligations under international treaties such as the Kyoto Protocol,[38] against corporate entities for providing false information when applying for renewable energy credits,[39] and against individuals for violating laws in relation to the EU emissions trading system.[40]

In China, government enforcement litigation is a viable avenue for climate change litigation, as China has successfully experimented with it in other areas of environmental protection. Specifically, China launched a pilot program to authorize the People's Procuratorate to initiate public interest lawsuits in areas including environmental and ecological protection.[41] This pilot program was subsequently turned into a formal mechanism when it was codified into the revised 2017 PRC Civil

the Supreme People's Court on 18 December 2014), http://en.pkulaw.cn/display.aspx?cgid=82f91c0394dcdc28bdfb&lib=law, accessed 1 June 2019, Art 91 ('SPC's interpretation on the Application of CPL').

[36] Corsi (n 19) 2–3.

[37] Wilensky (n 18) 13. (According to Wilensky, there were only six enforcement cases filed by government agencies for violation of a climate change regulation or statute.)

[38] *Case C-107/05 Commission* v. *Finland* [2006] ECR I-00010; *Case C-122/05 Commission* v. *Italy* [2006] ECR I-00065; Case CC-2007-1/Greece/ EB Compliance Procedure of Greece Under the Kyoto Protocol [2008].

[39] *Clean Energy Regulator* v. *MT Solar Pty Ltd* [2013] FCA 205 (Federal Court of Australia). (Imposing penalties for providing false information in relation to the installation of solar panels and Renewable Energy Certificates.)

[40] *Regina* v. *Dosanjh* [2013] EWCA 2366 (England and Wales Court of Appeal [Criminal Division]).

[41] Decision of the Standing Committee of the National People's Congress on Authorizing the Supreme People's Procuratorate to Launch the Pilot Program of Initiating Public Interest Actions in Certain Areas (1 July 2015) [Effective on 1 July 2015] (全国人民代表大会常务委员会关于授权最高人民检察院在部分地区开展公益诉讼试点工作的决

Procedure Law, which specifies that the People's Procuratorate can initiate public interest lawsuits in situations where it identifies acts of endangerment to the ecological environment or protection of natural resources.[42]

According to an implementation guideline issued by the PRC Supreme People's Court, government enforcement litigation is divided into civil action and administrative action depending on whether the defendants are government or non-government entities: (1) civil actions are those filed against private citizens, corporate entities (legal persons), or other entities that commit acts that harm social and public interests;[43] and (2) administrative actions are those cases filed against a government entity that has the administrative power to implement the laws governing ecological protection and protection of natural resources, but illegally exercises its authority or fails to perform its statutory duties, thereby harming the state's interests or public interests.[44]

Though China uses the term 'public interest litigation' to refer to government enforcement lawsuits, these actions resemble government enforcement actions in other jurisdictions. These enforcement actions usually address very serious environmental pollution or matters affecting the public interest, and the remedy sought is usually governmental action to restore the public good in question. Hence, monetary damages, which are usually available in other types of public interest litigation, are generally not available for the government enforcement actions. For example, in a 2017 case in Jilin province (which is located in northeast China), the local People's Procuratorate, in collaboration with the local government, initiated 266 proposals for the administrative organs to halt serious air pollution and improve the environmental quality in the Changbai Mountain area. After the relevant agencies acted on 199 of the proposals, the Procuratorate initiated 42 lawsuits that were aimed at getting the agencies and private actors to carry out environmental remediation.[45] To

定) (Promulgated by the Standing Committee of the National People's Congress), http://en.pkulaw.cn/display.aspx?cgid=1494267aa72b2d42bdfb&lib=law, accessed 1 June 2019.

42 The CPL (n 34) Art 55.

43 Notice of the Supreme People's Court on Issuing the Measures for the Implementation of the Pilot Program of Trial by People's Courts of Public Interest Litigation Cases Instituted by People's Procuratorates (25 February 2016) [Effective on 1 March 2016] (最高人民法院关于印发《人民法院审理人民检察院提起公益诉讼案件试点工作实施办法》的通知) (Promulgated by the Supreme People's Court), http://en.pkulaw.cn/display.aspx?cgid=c220eb7b873b2485bdfb&lib=law, accessed 1 June 2019, Art 1.

44 Notice of the Supreme People's Court (n 44) Art 11.

45 See cases relating to Jinlin Changbai Mountain Ecological Environment and Resource Protection Public Interest Litigation, in 'The Supreme People's Procuratorate Published

avoid confusion, this chapter considers such enforcement litigation as a stand-alone category rather than a subset of public interest litigation.

Government enforcement litigation is viewed as a possible form of climate change litigation in China, as the relevant laws are open to the possibility of courts broadly interpreting them to cover climate change claims. As stated previously, both the PRC Civil Procedure Law and the Supreme People's Court's guidelines state that the People's Procuratorate can pursue lawsuits against acts of endangerment to the ecological environment or protection of natural resources or illegal performance or non-performance of government duties in these areas. Since it is possible to establish linkage between acts contributing to climate change problems and adverse impacts on the ecological environment and natural resources, there is scope for the People's Procuratorate to pursue lawsuits in this field.

12.2.1.3 Litigation by Private Actors

Lawsuits brought by private actors (i.e., individual citizens or other private social entities like corporate entities) have been the dominant form of climate change litigation in other jurisdictions. Private actors usually seek redress from government agencies, companies, or other private actors for infringement of their rights based on human rights treaties, domestic statutory provisions (like tort law), and constitutional rights provisions.[46] According to Wilensky, nearly 80 per cent of all non-US climate change litigation was brought by individuals (not including environmental organizations) and industries, and more than 90 per cent of the cases were brought against governments.[47] This is in contrast with the situation in the United States, where the majority of cases have been public interest lawsuits brought by environment NGOs against the government.[48]

In China, private actors have brought the following types of lawsuits. (1) Lawsuits have been raised against government agencies for failure to act or inadequately performing their duties relating to environmental protection. For example, an individual sued his local environmental protection bureau for not taking action to address an environmental hazard caused by his

26 Typical Cases of Public Prosecution Trials Initiated by Procuratorial Organs', case No. 2 (2017年6月30日) (June 30, 2017).

[46] Jacqueline Peel and Hari M. Osofsky, 'A Rights Turn in Climate Change Litigation?' (2018) 7(1) *Transnational Environmental Law* 37, 40.

[47] Wilensky (n 18) 33–4.

[48] Markell and Ruhl (n 12) 71.

neighbour in a 2016 case,[49] and a private company sued a local environmental protection bureau to vacate its administrative order punishing the company for emitting air pollution while burning coal.[50] (2) Lawsuits have been raised against other individuals or private entities for harm caused by environmental pollution[51] or breach of contract for misrepresenting the status of conformance with compulsory environmental standards for transacted products.[52]

The issue of standing may pose challenges for private actors who wish to bring climate change lawsuits. As mentioned earlier, the PRC Civil Procedure Law requires a plaintiff to have a direct interest in the lawsuit it files and to satisfy the burden of proof for all aspects of the claim,[53] such as causation or injury-in-fact.[54] For example, in an environmental lawsuit, a group of individuals sued an owner of a hog farm for creating a stench in the neighbourhood. The first instance court dismissed the claim on the basis that the plaintiffs' claim should be pursued via the public interest litigation route, but the plaintiffs are not qualified environmental organizations and therefore do not have standing to bring a public interest lawsuit.[55] Though the appellate court reversed and held that the individuals had standing because they were directly affected by the smell from the hog farm, this case illustrates the strict approach Chinese courts can take on the standing question. In a climate change lawsuit, it is even more difficult for the plaintiff to establish that it has been directly affected by a particular defendant's GHG emissions or a government agencies' inaction or improper action. This chapter is therefore of the view that the difficulties of establishing standing may hinder private climate change lawsuits in China.

[49] *Yang Shibing* v. *the Environmental Protection Bureau of Xinhuang Dong Autonomous County* [杨仕炳与新晃侗族自治县环境保护局不履行法定职责案] Xiang 1227 Xingchu No. 5 (People's Court of Xinhuang Dong Autonomous County, Hunan Province 2016).

[50] *Hanchuan Baiyun International Hotel Management Co Ltd.* v. *Hanchuan Environmental Protection Bureau* [汉川市白云国际大酒店管理有限公司诉汉川市环境保护局处罚案] E 0984 Xingchu No. 1 (People's Court of Hanchuan City, Hubei Province 2017).

[51] See, e.g., *Yue Zhenqi* v. *Wang Baohua* [原告岳振岐诉被告王宝华环境污染责任纠纷一案] Liao 1481 Minchu No. 1968 (People's Court of Xing Cheng City, 2016).

[52] See e.g., *Gansu Haitian Dingsheng Automobile Trading Group Co Ltd.* v. *Zhang Chunqing* [甘肃海天鼎盛汽车贸易集团有限公司与张春清买卖合同纠纷案] Gan 04 Minzhong No. 149 (Baiyin City Intermediate People's Court, 2016).

[53] The CPL (n 34) Art 119; SPC's interpretation on the Application of CPL (n 35) Art 91.

[54] Corsi (n 19) 2–3.

[55] *Li Taiping etc.* v. *Yang Xiaowei* [李太平等诉杨小伟] Jin 04 Minzhong No. 53 (Shanxi Changzhi Intermediate People's Court, 2016).

In summary, this chapter argues that public interest lawsuits and government enforcement lawsuits are possible forms of climate change litigation in China, despite the uncertainty of whether courts will take the necessarily expansive approach in interpreting the relevant laws. However, litigation by private actors offers less potential, as Chinese courts can be quite strict on the issue of standing.

12.2.2 Potential Typology of Climate Change Litigation Claims

After assessing the potential forms of climate change litigation in China, it is worthwhile to explore the types of claims that a plaintiff could bring. In other jurisdictions, climate change lawsuits have involved different types of claims, which mainly include (1) tort-based claims, using traditional theories of nuisance, negligence, or civil conspiracy; (2) claims based on fraud or misrepresentation as to the environmental attributes of goods and services in contracts or trade practices; (3) claims based on administrative law to institute judicial and merit review proceedings challenging government agency's decisions or conduct relating to climate change issues; and (4) rights-based claims brought under constitutional law or human rights law.[56] China is a civil law country; its legal system is different from other jurisdictions like the United States and Australia where most climate change lawsuits have occurred. Some grounds of action available in other jurisdictions, such as constitutional-based claims, are not available in China.

12.2.2.1 Statutory Claims

Following the continental civil law tradition, China's legal rules are all codified and promulgated by the legislature or government bodies that have been given law-making functions.[57] The codified legal rules are the basis for judicial decisions.[58] In order to file a claim concerning climate change, an applicant has to rely on specific legislation, which provides for

[56] See Brian J. Preston, 'Climate Change Litigation: A Conspectus' (LAWASIA 23rd Conference, 11–14 November 2010), www.lec.justice.nsw.gov.au/Documents/preston_climate%20change%20litigation%20-%20a%20conspectus.pdf, accessed 1 June 2019.

[57] Wang Chenguang, 'Law-Making Functions of the Chinese Courts: Judicial Activism in a County of Rapid Social Changes' (2006) 1 *Frontiers of Law in China* 524.

[58] The CPL (n 34) Art 7; The Administrative Procedure Law of the People's Republic of China (4 April 1989) [Effective on 1 October 1990], www.cecc.gov/resources/legal-provisions/administrative-procedure-law-chinese-and-english-text, accessed 1 June 2019, Art 5. ('When trying civil cases, the people's courts must base on facts and according to the laws.')

litigation as a means of resolving the dispute in question. For climate change litigation, the alleged violation of climate change laws would constitute the most direct pathway for adjudication. However, China currently does not have a specific climate change statute. It is noteworthy that this situation might change as China has embarked on an initiative to enact a specific climate change law. China included a 'Climate Change Response Law' as a 'Research Project' in its 2016 national legislative agenda.[59] The Climate Change Department under the National Development and Reform Commission ('NDRC') had circulated a first draft of the 'Climate Change Response Law' in 2015 for public comment.[60]

The draft Climate Change Response Law reflects a top-down regulatory mindset, as it mainly emphasizes the government's responsibilities with respect to climate change mitigation and adaptation. For example, it stipulates that (1) China's central and local governments should set up a GHG emission accounting system and a climate change control responsibility evaluation system, conduct on-site inspection of GHG emitting enterprises, and establish a disclosure system for climate change information;[61] (2) the central and local governments should take adaptation measures to prevent or reduce climate change impacts;[62] and (3) the government should establish a GHG reporting system to track the GHG emissions of important institutions or enterprises and a GHG emission verification system to verify the GHG emission reporting from institutions or enterprises.[63] The draft Climate Change Response Law includes a general provision for public participation, which encourages corporate entities or individuals to report climate change violations to the regulatory administrative authorities, or bring a lawsuit through the courts.[64] This provision suggests that climate change litigation will be an option available to the public.

Though the draft law does not specify the forms of lawsuits available under the 'public participation' provision, it seems that the most likely form of lawsuits will be public interest lawsuits against government

[59] China's 2017 Annual Report on Policies and Actions to Address Climate Change (n 6).

[60] NDRC Department of Climate Change, 'The Climate Division Sought Comments from Business Community and NGOs on "Climate Change Law (Initial Draft)" (气候司就《应对气候变化法（初稿）》征求企业界和非政府组织意见)' (23 September 2015), www.ndrc.gov.cn/fzgggz/flfg/gzdtn/201509/t20150923_751878.html, accessed 1 June 2019.

[61] PRC Climate Change Response Law (First Draft for Comments) (n 7) ch 2.

[62] ibid. ch 3.

[63] ibid. Art 18, 21.

[64] ibid.

agencies for inaction or improper performance of their regulatory duties or private litigation brought by institutions or enterprises against government agencies for harm caused by those agencies' wrongful decisions. According to the draft Climate Change Response Law, government agencies and officials will be subject to administrative penalties (and criminal prosecution for serious violations) for failure to perform their administrative and supervisory duties specified in Climate Change Response Law, and will also be liable for any harm caused to the institutions or enterprises within their regulatory scope.[65] Though the draft law includes provisions to impose administrative penalties on GHG emitters for emission over permitted quotas, or for failure to report or making fraudulent or misleading reports with respect to GHG emissions, the draft law does not grant the public access to lawsuits against private actors.

Currently, since China's draft Climate Change Response Law is still on the legislative agenda, it is unclear whether China will eventually adopt a specific climate change law, and if adopted, how the law will actually address the issue of climate change litigation. Without a specific climate change statute in place, there is the possibility of bringing climate change claims under other climate change related statutes, such as the 2015 Environmental Protection Law and the 2015 Atmospheric Pollution Prevent and Control Law.[66]

The PRC Environmental Protection Law, first adopted in 1989 ('1989 EPL') and then revised in 2014 ('2014 EPL'),[67] states that environmental protection encompasses all factors affecting human existence, including air, water, the sea, land, forests, grasslands, and so on.[68] As mentioned earlier, the 2014 EPL allows environmental NGOs to bring lawsuits for acts that pollute the environment or cause ecological damage, and these may potentially cover climate change. Also, the latest revision in the 2015 Atmospheric Pollution Prevention and Control Law, included regulation of GHG emissions within its ambit by requiring 'coordinated control' of

[65] PRC Climate Change Response Law (First Draft for Comments) (n 7) Art 33.

[66] Atmospheric Pollution Prevention and Control Law of the People's Republic of China (2015 Revision) (29 August 2015) [Effective on 1 January 2016] (中华人民共和国大气污染防治法 (2015修订)) (Promulgated by Standing Committee of the National People's Congress), www.pkulaw.cn/fulltext_form.aspx?db=chl&gid=256292, accessed 1 June 2019 ('PRC Law on the Prevention and Control of Atmospheric Pollution').

[67] See the EPL (n 9) Art 58.

[68] Environmental Protection Law of the People's Republic of China (1989 Edition), www.ilo.org/dyn/natlex/docs/ELECTRONIC/92655/108043/F315004188/CHN92655%20Eng.pdf, accessed 1 June 2019, Art 2; the EPL (n 9) Art 2.

air pollutants and GHGs.[69] This provides potential bases for claims against the government for its failure to effectively control GHG emissions. However, GHGs control only appears in this one general and declaratory provision of the 2015 Atmospheric Pollution Prevention and Control Law. Also, when requiring coordinated control of air pollutants and GHGs, the law makes it clear that GHGs are not regarded as pollutants under the statutes. Enforcement measures enumerated in the law are also mainly targeted at air pollutants, without any reference to GHGs, so it is unclear how a Chinese court will interpret the meaning of 'coordinated control' of air pollutants and GHGs. It is very likely that courts will adopt a narrow and restrictive approach when interpreting and applying these statutes, thus excluding application to climate change issues.

12.2.2.2 Tort-Based Claims

Tort-based claims have been brought with respect to climate change in other jurisdictions like the United States.[70] These claims have evolved from being 'derided as frivolous long shots that would be shot down quickly' to being more frequently relied on by private actors seeking damages from GHG emitters.[71] In China, bringing tort-based claims have become a common practice in other environmental lawsuits. Under the PRC Tort Liability Law, there is a separate chapter on 'Liability for Environmental Pollution'. The rules have been designed to be favourable towards plaintiffs by adopting the principle of causation presumption (i.e., the burden of proof of causation is reversed and the defendant bears the burden of proving that it should not be held liable or that there is no causality between the alleged act and the harmful result).[72] In addition, strict liability applies to environmental torts, which means that the party causing cognizable harm will be held liable without the need to establish fault.[73]

[69] PRC Law on the Prevention and Control of Atmospheric Pollution (n 66) Art 2.

[70] Robert F. Blomquist, 'Comparative Climate Change Torts' (2012) 46(4) *Valparaiso University Law Review* 1053, 1053.

[71] Luciano Butti, 'The Tortuous Road to Liability: A Critical Survey on Climate Change Litigation in Europeand North America' (2011) 11(2) *Sustainable Development Law & Policy* 32, 33.

[72] Tort Law of the People's Republic of China (26 December 2009) [Effective 1 July 2010] (中华人民共和国侵权责法) (Promulgated by Standing Committee of the National People's Congress), http://en.pkulaw.cn/display.aspx?cgid=125300&lib=law, accessed 1 June 2019, ch VIII, Art 66 ('PRC Tort Liability Law').

[73] ibid., Art 65. ('Where any harm is caused by environmental pollution, the polluter shall assume the tort liability.')

The 2014 revised EPL, which is regarded as the most progressive and stringent environmental protection law in China,[74] states that a violator can be held liable for tort liability under the PRC Tort Liability Law for any harm caused by its environment pollution or ecological acts, and the statute of limitation is three years.[75] Also, the 2015 Atmospheric Pollution Prevention and Control Law gives individuals a private right of action under the PRC Tort Liability Law, to sue polluters for harm caused by air pollution.[76] The laws do not explicitly provide for tortious liability as a remedy for climate change. As a result, some observers hold the view that since Chinese law does not provide for private law liability for harm directly caused by climate change, tort liability is not available for climate change lawsuits in China.[77] However, this chapter takes a more liberal view. It argues that the 2014 revised EPL, as well as the 2015 Atmospheric Pollution Prevention and Control Law, provide possibilities for bringing tort-based claims, as both statutes have general provisions encompassing ecological destruction or GHG control.

However, since GHG control only appears in the general and declaratory provision of the laws, and since both laws are mainly targeted at environmental pollution while GHG control is not yet regarded as a pollutant, it is uncertain whether the courts will take a proactive approach to expand tort liability to GHG emissions. Also, the provisions on reversing the burden of proof and applying strict liability are available for claims based on environmental pollution, but may not apply to climate change claims since they are not formally classified as environmental pollution. Therefore, bringing tort-based claims in China will face the same obstacles that plaintiffs face in other jurisdictions – plaintiffs will have to establish standing[78] and causation.[79] Though public interest lawsuits can overcome the hurdle of standing because the law grants de jure standing to the plaintiffs, plaintiffs in such lawsuits still face the problem of establishing causation. As climate change is caused by a multiplicity of human actions and is accumulated across different

74 Zhang and others (n 30) 464.

75 The EPL (n 9) Art 64, 66.

76 PRC Law on the Prevention and Control of Atmospheric Pollution (n 66) Art 125.

77 Blomquist (n 70) 1066.

78 Butti (n 71) 33.

79 David A. Grossman, 'Tort-Based Climate Litigation' in William C. G. Burns and Hari M. Osofsky (eds.), *Adjudicating Climate Change: State, National, and International Approaches* (Cambridge University Press 2009), 217.

generations, it is difficult to identify specific harms that may be attributed to a particular defendant.[80]

Currently, the draft Climate Change Response Law proposed by the Chinese government does not include tort liability as it adopts a top-down regulatory approach to climate change issues. It is unclear whether the final Climate Change Response Law, if enacted, will accept this approach or take a different approach to include bottom-up regulation – that is, allowing litigation for any climate change violations by government agencies as well as private actors and allowing private lawsuits under tort law. If so, then tort-based claims will be made available under the Climate Change Response Law. Otherwise, the absence of tort liability in the final Climate Change Response Law will be a factor discouraging the courts from ruling on tort-based claims, as the legislation will have intentionally left out this option by not including provisions analogous to those currently in both 2014 EPL and the 2015 Atmospheric Pollution Prevention and Control Law.

12.2.2.3 Rights-Based Claims

There is a growing trend of raising rights-based claims in climate change lawsuits in other jurisdictions, especially after the landmark case of *Ashgar Leghari* v. *Federation of Pakistan* in September 2015.[81] In that case, the Pakistani court ruled in favour of the plaintiff in a public interest lawsuit, holding that the national government's inadequate implementation of the country's National Climate Change Policy 2012 violated the citizen's fundamental rights safeguarded by Pakistan's 1973 Constitution, including the right to life, the right to dignity of person and privacy of home, and the right to property.[82] While there are good prospects for the growth of rights-based litigation in some jurisdictions (including Pakistan, South Africa, and the Philippines),[83] this chapter argues that rights-based litigation is an unlikely prospect in China. First, constitutional rights are not enforceable rights in China and therefore the public cannot bring lawsuits on constitutional grounds. China's Constitution Law, though silent on climate change, has a general provision (Article 26) that includes the duty of the state to protect the environment (i.e., it

[80] Butti (n 71) 33.

[81] *Ashgar Leghari* v. *Federation of Pakistan* (W.P. No. 25501/2015), Lahore High Court Green Bench, Orders of 4 September 2015 and 14 September 2015, https://elaw.org/PK_AshgarLeghari_v_Pakistan_2015, accessed 1 June 2019.

[82] Peel and Osofsky (n 46) 62–3.

[83] Peel and Osofsky (n 46) 66.

recognizes citizen rights with respect to the environment): 'The State protects and improves the environment in which people live and the ecological environment. It prevents and controls pollution and other public hazards. The State organizes and encourages afforestation and the protection of forests.'

In theory, the Chinese Constitution, enacted by the National People's Congress, which is in principle the supreme body of state power, sets out the fundamental guiding principles under which China is governed and its laws are enacted.[84] However, in practice, the Chinese Constitution has generally been viewed as a static and primarily hortatory and nominal political document, and the provisions are largely empty promises instead of legally binding norms.[85] Scholars have critiqued that its 'theoretical supremacy' does not have much meaning to the public, since the judicial branch is not allowed to directly rely on constitutional provisions to decide cases, and although the courts can apply ordinary statutes, the courts do not have the power to conduct judicial review with regard to the constitutionality of these statutes.[86] Though the Constitution plays an important role in China's governance and regulation, especially through influencing the legislative process under its guiding principles,[87] it cannot be used as a legal basis for a climate change lawsuit in a Chinese court.

Second, it would seem difficult to directly enforce the human rights provisions in international treaties to which China is a signatory. China's constitution is silent on the issue of whether Chinese courts can directly apply international treaties. Some key statutes such as the PRC General Principles of the Civil Law and PRC Civil Procedure Law have provisions stipulating that a court should apply the provisions of an international treaty concluded or acceded to by China, where there is a conflict between the treaty and China's domestic laws, but these provisions only

[84] Constitution of the People's Republic of China (Revised 11 March 2018) [Effective on 4 December 1982] (中华人民共和国宪法) (Promulgated by National People's Congress), www.npc.gov.cn/npc/xinwen/2018-03/22/content_2052489.htm, accessed 1 June 2019, Preamble.

[85] Thomas E. Kellogg, 'Constitutionalism with Chinese Characteristics? Constitutional Development and Civil Litigation in China' (2009) 7 *International Journal of Constitutional Law* 215, 216–17.

[86] Albert Chen, 'An Introduction to the Legal System of the People's Republic of China' in Yash P. Chai (ed.), *Hong Kong's New Constitutional Order – The Resumption of Chinese Sovereignty and the Basic Law*, 2nd ed. (Hong Kong University Press 1999).

[87] Yan Lin and Tom Ginsburg, 'Constitutional Interpretation in Lawmaking: China's Invisible Constitutional Enforcement Mechanism' (2015) 63(2) *The American Journal of Comparative Law* 467, 467.

apply to situations where the dispute involves foreign elements.[88] The term 'foreign elements' means civil relations and cases in which (1) one or both parties are foreign nationals or entities; (2) the habitual residence of one or both parties is located in a foreign territory; (3) the legal facts that establish, change, or terminate the legal relations arise in foreign territories; or (4) the subject matter of the dispute is located in a foreign territory.[89] However, there is no definitive answer as to whether a Chinese court can directly apply international treaties in domestic disputes (i.e., without foreign elements), especially when there is a potential conflict between the treaty and domestic law.[90] Although, in theory, international treaties are treated as a source of law in China, and thus a Chinese court can justify their application, in practice, it is unlikely that a court will directly apply an international treaty if it contradicts Chinese constitutional law or a key statute enacted by the Standing Committee of People's Congress.[91] What a court may do is to decline to apply domestic law which conflicts with an international treaty.[92] Though it is conceivable for a plaintiff to argue that the failure of the government to implement certain measures to address climate change violates his/her human rights as enshrined in the international human rights treaties that China has ratified, it is unlikely that such arguments will be accepted by the court, especially when considered against the political backdrop of the Chinese government denying allegations about its human rights record.[93]

[88] See General Principles of the Civil Law of the People's Republic of China (2009 Amendment) (27 August 2009) [Effective 27 August 2009] (中华人民共和国民法通则(2009修正)) (Revised by the Standing Committee of the National People's Congress), http://en.pkulaw.cn/display.aspx?cgid=27f092abe1cd5ab4bdfb&lib=law, accessed 1 June 2019, Art 142; the CPL (n 34) Art 260.

[89] Interpretation of the Supreme People's Court on the Application of the Civil Procedure Law of the People's Republic of China (Interpretation No. 5 [2015] of the Supreme People's Court) [Effective on 4 February 2015] (最高人民法院关于适用《中华人民共和国民事诉讼法》的解释), http://en.pkulaw.cn/display.aspx?cgid=82f91c0394dcdc28bdfb&lib=law, accessed 1 June 2019, Art 522.

[90] Xue Hanqin and Jin Qian, 'International Treaties in the Chinese Domestic Legal System' (2009) 8(2) *Chinese Journal of International Law* 299, http://danielturpqc.org/upload/2015findoc/XUE_et_JIN-_International_Treaties_in_China.pdf, accessed 1 June 2019, 302 and 305; Chen Xinxin, 'Application of International Human Right Treaties in China' (China Law Network), www.iolaw.org.cn/showNews.aspx?id=1036, accessed 1 June 2019.

[91] Ibid.

[92] Ibid.

[93] See, for example, Lily Kuo, 'China SaysUN Criticism of Human Rights Record Is "Politically Driven"' *The Guardian* (China, 6 November 2018), www.theguardian.com/world/2018/nov/06/china-un-criticism-human-rights-record, accessed 1 June 2019.

Therefore, it seems that the prospect of bringing rights-based claims in China, whether based on constitutional law or international human rights treaties, is not promising. Again, the most likely avenues for climate change litigation in China are premised on enforcement of specific climate change laws. This is because the Chinese legal system is a code-based one, and the courts are most comfortable with carrying out its role of applying and interpreting the codes and auxiliary statutes.[94]

12.3 Assessment of the Prospects of Climate Change Litigation in China

Having considered various pathways for climate litigation to emerge in China in the preceding discussion, this section then considers a variety of factors that are likely to obstruct or facilitate the emergence of climate litigation in China. These factors have to be considered in light of the fact that the legal culture in China is not as strong as that in the United States or Australia. Furthermore, apart from the law on the books, there are socio-economic and political factors that are salient considerations when one discusses the potential for climate change litigation in China. This section begins with a discussion of the hurdles that stand in the way of climate change litigation's emergence in China. These factors include the lack of judicial independence and the absence of specific climate change legislation. The next part then examines the factors that are likely to encourage the emergence of climate litigation in China – namely, the growing concern among the citizenry of the impacts of climate change and the government's awareness of the importance of addressing climate change.

12.3.1 Obstacles against Climate Change Litigation in China

While the world is witnessing a growing trend in favour of climate change litigation, one may wonder why this type of litigation has not taken root in China. There are many factors contributing to this situation: first and foremost, China's economic model – the 'carbon economy' – hinders China's adoption of climate change litigation; second, China does not have a specific statute granting Chinese citizens the option to pursue climate change litigation; third, China lacks an independent court system to take on a regulatory

[94] Wang (n 57).

role through its climate change adjudications; and fourth, China lacks a litigating culture that might have pushed forward the emergence and development of climate change litigation.

12.3.1.1 The 'Carbon Economy' in China

China has become the world's second-largest economy in terms of gross domestic product (GDP) since 2010,[95] and its economy has largely depended on consumption of fossil fuels (principally coal, natural gas, and oil). During the years of 1985–2014, more than 95 per cent of China's energy consumption came from coal, oil, and natural gas.[96] The total amount of consumption of the three types of fossil fuels for the year 2014 was also seven times more than that of 1980.[97] In particular, coal accounted for more than 70 per cent of the total energy consumption every year during that period, which in turn accounted for more than half of the world's total coal consumption.[98] With its economic development heavily dependent on fossil fuel consumption, China's economy is essentially a 'carbon economy', which has contributed nearly one-third of global energy-related carbon dioxide emissions.[99]

The predominance of the carbon economy significantly contributes to the current lack of climate change litigation in China. Given that more than 95 per cent of China's energy comes from the burning of fossil fuels, the majority of China's enterprises are responsible for the country's emissions, including state-owned enterprises and large private companies. If China opens its door to climate change litigation, these enterprises are likely defendants in lawsuits. This is an outcome that the Chinese government would like to avoid as these enterprises play a vital role in China's economic growth. From the Chinese government's perspective, allowing climate litigation to occur might open a Pandora's box and force the shift to a low-carbon economy at a speed that the government is uncomfortable with. This lack of control sits uneasily with

[95] See International Monetary Fund, 'World Economic Outlook Database' (24 October 2017), www.imf.org/external/pubs/ft/weo/2017/02/weodata/index.aspx, accessed 1 June 2019; Ryan Avent, 'Second in Line: China Passes AnotherGDP Milestone' *The Economist* (Washington, 16 August 2010), www.economist.com/blogs/freeexchange/2010/08/china_0, accessed 1 June 2019.

[96] Lawrence Berkeley National Laboratory's China Energy Group, 'Key China Energy Statistics 2016', https://china.lbl.gov/sites/default/files/ced-9-2017-final.pdf, accessed 1 June 2019, 18.

[97] ibid.

[98] ibid.

[99] ibid.

the Chinese government's traditional style of governance, which would almost certainly seek to retain control of the speed and direction of the transition.

12.3.1.2 Lack of Specific Climate Change Legislation

As discussed in the earlier part of the chapter, China has not enacted a specific law that would allow the public to directly bring claims to address climate change issues. Although several existing laws could be interpreted to apply to climate change issues, their specific meaning or scope of application is still vague. Most importantly, GHGs have not been listed as pollutants under PRC law, as mentioned earlier. The latest revision in the 2015 Atmospheric Pollution Prevention and Control Law included regulation of GHG emissions within its ambit by requiring 'coordinated control' of air pollutants and GHGs.[100] The language of this law makes it clear that GHGs are not regarded as pollutants under the statutes. As such, existing laws may not be applicable to the control of GHG emissions.[101] Therefore, there is a lot of uncertainty as to whether climate change lawsuits could be brought under these existing statutes.

12.3.1.3 Lack of Independent Courts

The extent to which courts could effectively play a regulatory role in climate change litigation is largely affected by the ability of courts to independently make judicial rulings, through which the judges can freely undertake reasoning and consider the climate change issues in their applicable legal framework. However, Chinese courts are highly politicized and lack independence.[102] Their work is subject to Communist Party monitoring and control through political-legal committees at each level.[103] Also, in China, courts need to perform their adjudicative function in a highly hierarchical structure, which demands their loyalty and deference to higher policies and directives whereby they are subjected to

[100] PRC Law on the Prevention and Control of Atmospheric Pollution (n 66) Art 2.

[101] Deng Haifeng, 'China' in Richard Lord, Silke Goldberg, Lavanya Rajamani, and Jutta Brunnee (eds.), *Climate Change Liability: Transnational Law and Practice* (Cambridge University Press 2012), 133.

[102] See Li Rongzhen, 'The Administrative Trend of Our Country's Judicial Work and Proposals for Reform [我国司法工作的行政化趋势及改革建议]' (1999) 4 *Chinese Lawyer* 8.

[103] Phyllis L. Chang, 'Deciding Disputes: Factors That Guide Chinese Courts in the Adjudication of Rural Responsibility Contract Disputes' (1989) 52 *Law and Contemporary Problems* 101, 115.

vertical control.[104] It is unlikely that a Chinese court would take a proactive or innovative approach in accepting climate change claims or issuing rulings based on climate change concerns, unless guided by the Chinese government that climate change litigation is allowed or encouraged.

12.3.1.4 General Cultural Resistance to Litigation

Generally speaking, China is not a litigious country. The non-litigious nature of Chinese society is due to deep-rooted historical and social factors. Historically, Chinese society and state governance were predominantly influenced by the philosophy of Confucianism, which put a great emphasis on social roles, clan ethics, and *lǐ* (ritual propriety).[105] Confucianism posed that social order was best preserved through maintenance and coordination of social relationships under the guidance of moral principles, and laws and punishment only served an ancillary and secondary role.[106] Following this theoretical belief, the Chinese society developed a well-established social practice of resorting to *guanxi* (social connections) to resolve disputes.[107] Though some scholars argue that the role of *guanxi* in contemporary China is decreasing due to the establishment of stronger and more formal legal structures and a market economy,[108] and it has become more risky and difficult to circumvent legal requirements by using one's social connections, it is undeniable that longstanding cultural resistance to litigation embedded in the *guanxi* ideology still influences the Chinese general public.[109]

In addition, Chinese society's perception of the government is still influenced by the historical ideology of rejecting western notions of

[104] Yedan Li, Joris Kocken, and Benjamin van Rooij, 'Understanding China's Court Mediation Surge: Insights from a Local Court' (2018) 43 *Law & Social Inquiry* 58, 60.

[105] John W. Head and Xing Lijuan, *Legal Transparency in Dynastic China: The Legalist-Confucianist Debate and Good Governance in Chinese Tradition* (Carolina Academic Press 2013), 465. (*lǐ* means 'proper behavior generally, based on the place or status of a person within the family or the social and political system'.); Ambrose Yeo-chi King, 'Kuan-his and Network Building: A Sociological Interpretation' (1991) 120 *Daedalus: Journal of the American Academy of Arts and Sciences* 63, 73–5.

[106] Yujun Feng, 'Legal Culture in China:A Comparison to Western Law' (2010) 16 *Revue Juridique Polynesienne* 115, 116.

[107] Carol Jones, 'Capitalism, Globalization and Rule of Law: An Alternative Trajectory of Legal Change in China' (1994) 3 *Social and Legal Studies* 195, 195–220.

[108] See Douglas Guthrie, 'The Declining Significance of Guanxi in China's Economic Transition' (1998) 154 *The China Quarterly* 254.

[109] Randall Peerenboom, 'Globalization, Path Dependency and the Limits of Law: Administrative Law Reform and Rule of Law in the People's Republic of China' (2001) 19 *Berkeley Journal of International Law* 161, 222–23.

a limited and neutral government and favouring a paternalist state which has superior authority to determine moral standards.[110] The people have cultivated a strong reliance on the government's decisions and usually demonstrate willing deference to government authority. When individuals or the public feel that their interests are infringed, they tend to first think of bringing the issue to the attention of government officials to seek government assistance in resolving the issue.[111]

Together, these factors largely explain why China has not developed climate change litigation. Some of these factors, such as the lack of specific climate change law and cultural resistance to litigation, have been evolving, and thus their hindering effect seems to be decreasing. But other factors, such as the lack of an independent court system and the dominance of the carbon economy, will continue to affect the prospects of climate change litigation in China into the foreseeable future.

12.3.2 Impetus for Climate Change Litigation in China

Though there have been notable obstacles hindering China's adoption of climate change litigation in the past, contributing to a non-climate-change-litigation status quo, it should be noted that China's stance in this regard has been changing, especially in recent years. There are a number of factors that may contribute to the nation's evolving sentiment towards climate change litigation. Understanding these evolving factors, especially the government's stance towards climate change, will shed light on a more realistic prediction or analysis of climate change litigation development in China.

12.3.2.1 China's Domestic Concerns Relating to Climate Change

As Lisa Williams has pointed out, China has its own domestic concerns relating to climate change, which in turn drives the Chinese government to take a stance on controlling GHG emissions. First, China is vulnerable to

110 ibid 186, 220–1.

111 For example, the lay people would seek the government's help in order to get their unpaid salary from their employers. See, for example, 'Seeking Payment of 160 Million Yuan for Migrant Worker (为农民工讨薪1.6亿元)' *Renmin Daily* (19 January 2018), http://paper.people.com.cn/rmrb/html/2018-01/19/nw.D110000renmrb_20180119_3-13.htm, accessed 1 June 2019.

the adverse impacts of climate change, and the Chinese government regards China as one of the countries most vulnerable to those impacts.[112] Second, as the world's largest energy consumer,[113] China's increasing demand for energy cannot be satisfied with China's domestic supply alone. Energy security has become a concern for the Chinese government because it is 'an important strategic issue concerning China's economic growth, social stability, and national security'.[114] Third, China has an urgent need for economic transformation, which will involve adopting green-development policies that will indirectly reduce GHG emissions. The green growth path provides an opportunity for China to rebalance economic growth and environmental protection.[115] Fourth, China views its international image, namely how the international community regards China's role on the world stage, as an important factor for its success in economic growth.[116] The Chinese government has always emphasized that it is a responsible government, and has taken a series of actions to address climate change.[117]

Under the impetus of these domestic concerns, the Chinese government has intrinsic incentives to overcome the obstacles listed earlier, and to adopt a more pro-regulatory stance against climate change and employ climate change litigation as a means of climate change regulation. Also, as China undertakes to change its carbon-dominated economic model, the obstacle created by hydrocarbon reliance will also decrease.

12.3.2.2 Chinese Government's Growing Climate-Sensitive Stance on Climate Change

China has been accused in the past of not fulfilling its responsibilities to reduce GHG emissions, and of acting obstructively against international

112 The Central People's Government of the People's Republic of China, 'China's Policies and Actions for Addressing Climate Change (中国应对气候变化的政策与行动)' (29 October 2008) www.ccchina.org.cn/Detail.aspx?newsId=28091&TId=60 accessed 1 June 2019.

113 David Shambaugh, *China's Future* (Cambridge: Polity Press 2016), 93.

114 Oystein Tunsjo, Security and Profit in China's Energy Policy: Hedging Against Risk (Columbia University Press 2013), 118.

115 OECD, 'China in Focus: Lessons and Challenges' (2012) www.oecd.org/china/50011051.pdf accessed 1 June 2019, at X.

116 ibid.

117 'Response to Climate Change: China Is A Responsible Country (应对全球气候变化，中国是负责任国家)' *China Daily* (16 November 2017) www.ccchina.org.cn/Detail.aspx?newsId=8720&TId=57 accessed 1 June 2019; The Central People's Government of the People's Republic of China, 'China's Policies and Actions for Addressing Climate Change (中国应对气候变化的政策与行动)' (29 October 2008) www.ccchina.org.cn/Detail.aspx?newsId=28091&TId=60 accessed 1 June 2019.

efforts to control climate change.[118] However, China has undertaken substantial efforts to improve and enhance its climate change regulation and has demonstrated an increasingly climate-sensitive stance. First, China has incorporated climate change into the country's strategic goals for economic and social development. In 2007, China included 'emphasis on GHG control', for the first time in its national 11th FYP (2006-2010)[119] for economic and social development.[120] Subsequently, the 12th FYP (2011-2015) released in March 2011 named green and low-carbon development as an important guiding policy, and for the first time set a binding target of reducing CO_2 emissions per unit of GDP – i.e., by 17 per cent.[121] The 13th FYP promulgated in March 2016 includes a separate chapter regarding 'actively responding to global climate change', which aims to achieve GHG control in the key industries of electricity, steel, construction, and chemicals, and to promote low-hydrocarbon reliance in industrial, energy, construction, transportation, and other important areas.[122] In June 2007, China issued its first national plan addressing climate change – China's National Climate Change Program ('2007 National Program'),[123] which was also the first national plan on climate change issued by a developing country.[124]

Second, the Chinese government has paid great attention to institutional development for the administration of climate change. As early as

[118] ibid.

[119] 'List of China's Five Year Plans' (*People.com*) http://dangshi.people.com.cn/GB/151935/204121/ accessed 1 June 2019. The FYPs are shaped by the China's Communist Party through the plenary sessions of the Central Committee and approved by National People's Congress, and are regarded the most authoritative national guidelines for the whole country's economic and social development.

[120] 'The People's Republic of China's 11th Five-Year Plan for the Development of National Economy and Social Development' (*People.com*, 19 October 2005) http://theory.people.com.cn/GB/41038/3781986.html accessed 1 June 2019, Article 19.

[121] 'The People's Republic of China's 12th Five-Year Plan for the Development of National Economy and Social Development' (*People.com*, 28 October 2010) http://cpc.people.com.cn/GB/64093/64094/13066322.html accessed 1 June 2019.

[122] 'The People's Republic of China's 13th Five-Year Plan for the Development of National Economy and Social Development (Approved by the Fourth Session of the Twelfth National People's Congress on 16 March 2016)' (8 July 2016) www.npc.gov.cn/wxzl/gongbao/2016-07/08/content_1993756.htm accessed 4 May 2018, ch 46.

[123] 'Notice of the State Council on Printing and Distributing China's National Plan on Climate Change (国务院关于印发中国应对气候变化国家方案的通知): Guofa (国法) [2007] No. 17' (28 March 2008) www.gov.cn/zhengce/content/2008-03/28/content_5743.htm accessed 1 June 2019; See English Version, 'China's National Climate Change Program (June 2007)' (China-UN, 30 June 2007) www.china-un.org/eng/chinaandun/economicdevelopment/climatechange/t626117.htm accessed 1 June 2019.

[124] Deng (n 101) 116.

1990, China set up a National Coordination Group on Climate Change, which was then restructured in 1998 as the National Coordination Group on Climate Change Response Strategies.[125] In June 2007, China established a National Leading Committee on Climate Change (the 'Leading Committee'), which has been led by the Prime Minister and involves heads of twenty ministries and government departments.[126] In 2008, the Department of Climate Change was created, which undertakes the major responsibilities of analyzing the impacts of climate change, as well as developing and coordinating important strategies, plans, or systems on climate change etc.[127]

Third, China has continuously undertaken reforms to improve or perfect the country's policy and legal frameworks in relation to climate change.[128] China has demonstrated active efforts to enact black-letter laws and policies, and through this process, China has established an extensive set of top-down laws and policies relating to environmental protection.[129] Certainly, China currently does not have a statute specifically and directly addressing climate change. However, in recent years, China has made attempts to enact such laws. China included 'Climate Change Response Law' as a 'Research Project' in its 2016 national legislation agenda, and it released the first draft of a 'Climate Change Response Law in 2015 for public comment. The draft climate change law, by including a provision to allow the public to bring lawsuits on climate change issues, signals the government's changing attitude toward climate change litigation.

These efforts undertaken by the Chinese government to enhance climate change controls parallel the growing trend toward climate change litigation in other parts of the world. This development can be viewed as an impetus for climate change litigation in China as it shows that the Chinese government is open to tightening climate change

[125] The People's Republic of China, 'Second National Communication on Climate Change of The People's Republic of China' (*UNFCCC*, 14 November 2012), 46.

[126] 'Notice of the State Council on Establishing A National Leading Committee on Climate Change, Energy Saving and Emission Reduction (国务院关于成立国家应对气候变化及节能减排工作领导小组的通知): Guofa (国法) [2007] No. 18' (12 June 2007) http://fgcx.bjcourt.gov.cn:4601/law?fn=chl357s249.txt accessed 1 June 2019.

[127] NDRC Official Website, 'Department of Climate Change' http://en.ndrc.gov.cn/mfod/200812/t20081218_252201.html accessed 1 June 2019.

[128] Deng (n 101) 113.

[129] Alex Wang, 'Green Litigation in China today&' (*China Dialogue*, 18 July 2011) www.chinadialogue.net/article/show/single/en/4413-Green-litigation-in-China-today accessed 1 June 2019.

regulation. In particular, its legislative initiative on the specific climate change law shows that climate change litigation will at least not be restricted or prohibited *per se* in China.

It should be pointed out, however, that these regulatory efforts by the Chinese government demonstrate that the Chinese government focuses on top-down climate change regulation, as the national plans, policies and legislative initiatives are all top-down regulatory means. Since the government agencies will be the key players for top-down regulation, it is unsurprising that the Chinese government is open to these regulatory approaches. Nevertheless, since climate change litigation involves bottom-up regulation, which will be mainly driven by private actors, it is more uncertain whether the Chinese government will be willing to open its door for climate change litigation over which it will be more difficult for the government to maintain control.

12.3.2.3 China's Evolving Social-Cultural-Legal Context

As mentioned earlier, China does not have a litigious culture, and the public generally does not view litigation as the most effective way to achieve satisfying results for the resolution of grievances. Therefore, this factor is an obstacle to developing climate change litigation in China. However, despite the fact that the Chinese public still favours non-adversarial means of dispute settlement (such as mediation or conciliation), there is a recent trend showing that traditional attitudes toward law and the courts are changing and lawsuits brought by Chinese plaintiffs are on the rise.[130] Therefore, even though the Chinese public does not regard instituting climate change litigation as the most effective means of resolving climate change disputes, it should not be regarded as an odd or unfavourable thing to do. Also, although China only saw its first public interest environmental lawsuit in 2009, it has witnessed fast growth in public interest litigation since then. For example, Chinese courts at all levels have tried more than 50 cases of environmental public interest litigation since the new EPL entered into force in 2015.[131] This shows that the Chinese society is more receptive to environmental litigation.

[130] Bee Chen Goh, Law without Lawyers, Justice without Courts: On Traditional Chinese Mediation (1st edn, Routledge 2002), ch 6.

[131] Zhang and others (n 30) 466.

12.3.3 An Overall Assessment: Mixed Prospects

Generally speaking, there are notable obstacles hindering the development of climate change litigation in China. The fact that China's economy is carbon-dominated and cannot be changed in the short term may continue to discourage the Chinese government from allowing or encouraging bottom-up regulation through climate change litigation. In addition, without a specific climate change statute and independent courts, there will be foreseeable difficulties for the Chinese public to have the courts hear and pass judgment on climate change claims. Also, since China's climate change regulation has mainly focused on top-down regulation from central and local governments, it is reasonable to predict that this status quo will be maintained for several years to come.

Nevertheless, under the pressing need for the Chinese government to address domestic climate change concerns, especially the need to mitigate and adjust to the increasingly adverse impacts of extreme weather and the intrinsic desire to transform its economic model, having climate change regulation only through top-down regulation without bottom-up regulation will be insufficient. In the meantime, with increasing public awareness on the seriousness and urgency of addressing climate change and the continuing flow-on influence from other jurisdictions' developments in climate change litigation, there will be increasing calls or pushes for bottom-up regulation. Without a specific climate change statute granting the public direct access to the courts for climate change lawsuits, the chances of succeeding in attempts to file climate change lawsuits will be quite low. However, even unsuccessful attempts may have the positive flow-on effect of pushing forward the development of climate change litigation, such as the enactment of a pro-litigation specific climate change statute. As China has witnessed the blossoming of public interest litigation in other types of environmental litigation because of the encouragement under the new EPL for environmental NGOs to bring environmental lawsuits, the country may well have a promising future for climate change litigation if it finally adopts a pro-litigation climate change statute.

12.4 Proposals for Paving the Way for China's Climate Change Litigation

Climate change litigation, as a bottom-up approach to climate change regulation, is an important means of regulation, which can effectively test and provide feedback on the top-down government regulation. Though China does not currently have climate change litigation, theoretical analysis shows that the current legal framework does not preclude its development, and potential forms and claims seem to exist under current legal structures. However, due to continuing obstacles that impede potential climate change lawsuits in China, this paper proposes that China should at least undertake the following reforms to encourage and facilitate the development of climate change litigation so that China can fill the gap of bottom-up climate change regulation in its overall regulatory landscape.

12.4.1 Enact a Pro-litigation Specific Climate Change Law

Though China has undertaken legislative groundwork for a specific climate change statute, the current draft released by the Chinese government does not seem to be pro-climate-change litigation. Though the draft includes a provision seemingly encouraging the public to file lawsuits in connection with climate change issues, this litigation-relevant provision has a very narrow application – the draft law only outlines lawsuits against government agency administrative action, and does not seem to allow targeting of private actors. Unlike the EPL and the Atmospheric Pollution Prevent and Control Law, the draft law does not provide environmental NGOs with locus standi to bring public interest claims, nor does it provide access to tort claims. This may be due to the underlying mindset of the government that climate change is not as urgent or serious as pollution, and therefore should not enjoy the same favourable rules relaxing the requirement for standing and burdens of proof. However, climate change is indeed a serious problem, which needs effective regulation. Therefore, this paper proposes that China should adopt a pro-litigation specific climate change law, which should allow the public to initiate climate change lawsuits against government agencies or private actors. Furthermore, the law should expressly allow tort liability in climate change lawsuits, though the plaintiffs should still need to overcome the obstacle of burdens of proof. A specific climate change statute would be the most direct impetus for encouraging the public to undertake climate change litigation. It is true that international and top-down national efforts are critical to tackling climate change,[132] but

[132] Brian J. Preston, 'Climate Change Litigation (Part 1)' (2011) 5 *Carbon & Climate Law Review* 3.

climate change litigation can also play an important role in the multi-dimensional climate change governance regime and should not be neglected. Climate change litigation brought by the public can serve as a bottom-up driving force for climate change regulation.[133] The public, through non-government entities or individuals, can resort to the assistance of courts by initiating climate change lawsuits, which urge the court to apply or interpret climate change-related laws, regulations or rules, and pass judgment on rights and duties with respect to fact-specific climate change issues.

12.4.2 Extend Government Enforcement Litigation to Climate Change Violations

Government enforcement litigation (i.e., lawsuits brought by people's procuratorates for environmental violations) has been adopted by the Chinese government as a special means of public interest environmental litigation. Though the rules include some general language, which could potentially cover climate change issues, there is still great uncertainty on whether the courts would actually adopt the broad interpretation required. Considering that government enforcement lawsuits play an increasingly important role in challenging other government agencies' regulatory behaviour and private actors' environmental violations, it is necessary to expressly extend government enforcement lawsuits to climate change violations at the policy level, so that climate change lawsuits brought by government agencies can also enjoy the same favourable rules on standing and burdens of proof.

12.4.3 Enhance Public Participation in Climate Change Regulation

As mentioned earlier, public participation in climate change regulation, either through bringing climate change litigation or undertaking social advocacy, can serve as a driving force for bottom-up climate change regulation. Though the current legal framework presents notable obstacles for climate change litigation in China, China's experience with the development of other types of environmental litigation indicates that as the public becomes more environmentally sensitive and well equipped with access to the courts, the public will gradually become more willing to

[133] Amelia Thorpe, 'Tort-Based Climate Change Litigation and the Political Question Doctrine' (2008) 24 *Journal of Land Use & Environmental Law* 79, 88.

resort to litigation to resolve their environment-related concerns. Currently, though the Chinese public seems to have an increasing awareness of climate change, the idea of suing GHG emitters may still seem novel or unusual. Therefore, China should first enhance publicity and increase access to information concerning other country's developments in climate change litigation, supporting the public's social activities or movements in advocating for climate change controls. With increasing awareness of the climate change issue and the potential regulatory role climate change litigation can play, China will have fertile soil for developing climate change litigation.

12.5 Conclusion

Currently, China does not have climate change litigation, which refers to any administrative adjudication or judicial action in which the claimants or defendants include climate change elements (facts, laws, or arguments) in the framing of their legal claims. However, this chapter advances the argument that China should develop climate change litigation because climate change is a serious problem that requires effective regulation. This, in turn, requires a multidimensional governance regime, which includes both top-down regulation from government agencies and bottom-up regulation from public participation in judicial or non-judicial activities.

Litigation can be a driving force for an effective response to climate change through the process of the courts applying and interpreting statutes, prods and pleas, and the flow-on regulatory effects of the litigation process. Considering the potential regulatory role climate change litigation can play, this chapter has offered a theoretical prognosis of potential pathways for the emergence of climate change litigation in China. It also discussed the economic, social, historical, and cultural factors that will impede the development of climate change litigation in China. However, considering that China has its domestic concerns about the risks and impacts of climate change, and China's legal framework and social sentiments regarding climate change and environmental litigation are evolving in pro-regulation and pro-litigation directions, it is possible for climate change litigation to develop in China. In light of these factors, this chapter proposed that China should enact a pro-litigation climate change statute, extend government enforcement litigation to climate change, and enhance public participation and education with respect to climate change regulation. Though there is still considerable uncertainty regarding the future prospects of climate change litigation in China, this chapter holds an optimistic view that China will gradually become receptive to climate change litigation, as it has been for other types of environmental litigation.

13

The Subordinate and Passive Position of Chinese Courts in Environmental Governance

ZHU YAN

As the name suggests, climate change litigation (CCL) attempts to proactively address the causes of climate change and to facilitate adaptation to climate change impacts such as sea-level rise. CCL is initiated by public interest groups against transnational corporations and certain government departments, but often fails for a number of reasons – among them an inability to prove causation in tort. Notwithstanding the lack of successful CCL claims, such efforts have advanced the protection of the global ecological environment through judicial means. As the world's largest carbon-emitting country, it behoves China to actively meet its international obligations. A condition precedent to discussions about whether there exists a possibility of introducing CCL[1] in China is an in-depth understanding of the role played by its courts in environmental pollution and ecological harm over the past decades. Thus this chapter is not focused on examining the feasibility of CCL in Chinese courts, but on the efforts, role and inadequacies of such bodies in environmental and ecological protection. Such an exploration will undoubtedly be invaluable in determining the future possibility of Chinese courts as drivers of CCL.

In this chapter, I will attempt to sketch out, in Section 13.1, Chinese courts' efforts at environmental protection over the past decades. Guided by an empirical approach, Section 13.1 draws upon the *Work Report of the People's Court (Fayuan Gongzuo Baogao)* published by the Supreme People's Court (SPC) and its Report to National People's Congress (NPC), and analysis of relevant cases

[1] It is rather unlikely that CCL will see the light of day in China anytime soon, although the environment and ecological protection has received hitherto unprecedented protection.

from *China Judgments Online Data Bank (Caipan Wenshuwang)* and the *China Environment Yearbook (Zhongguo Huanjing Nianjian)* to reveal the dominance of administrative punishment. It also notes the inability of Chinese courts to provide victims with effective or meaningful relief, given that, in litigation, the number of criminal cases far eclipses their civil counterparts. Section 13.2 endeavours to demonstrate that, in China's executive-led society, the judiciary only serves a secondary supporting role. China's unique political ecology explains this result, with the absolute leadership core of the Chinese Communist Party (CCP) placing the executive in the driving seat of formulating and enforcing specific environmental protection policies. The executive at all levels is the absolute centre of environmental governance, whether from the perspective of power allocation, administrative resources or coping capacity. Section 13.3 introduces the establishment of special environmental resources tribunals within Chinese courts, reflecting efforts to actively promote judicial protection of the environment. Yet, whether one looks at the matter from the point of view of personnel allocations or the trying of cases, environmental litigation in China has not achieved the function of judicially driven changes in environmental policy. In other words, the judiciary does not have policy-making functions in China. Section 13.4 offers an in-depth look at environmental public interest litigation (EPIL) and concludes that, whether from the limited number of organizations competent to bring a case or the procedural system itself, EPIL faces significant challenges.

13.1 Basic Facts of Environmental Cases in Mainland China-Basic Data on Environmental Litigation

13.1.1 From the Report of the SPC

A highly authoritative document delivered by the President of the SPC at annual sessions of the NPC, the *Work Report of the People's Courts* (hereinafter '*Work Report*') contains data on environmental cases which reflects the efforts of Chinese courts in environmental protection over the past decades. The earliest mention of the environment made in the *Work Report* came at the Second Meeting of the Sixth NPC on 26 May 1984.[2] However, since the 1987 *Work*

[2] The 1984 *Work Report of the SPC* reads: 'From now on, people's courts at all levels must continue to strictly enforce . . . the *Environmental Protection Law*, the *Marine Environment Protection Law*'.

Report proposed to strengthen law enforcement in respect of environmental resources in cooperation with administrative authorities,[3] successive versions referred to 'protection of the marine environment'[4] in maritime judgments or 'environmental protection' in administrative judgments, mostly as a reference to the type of case or the parties involved.[5] 'Environmental pollution' was mentioned for the first time in the 1998 *Work Report.*[6] In setting out work arrangements for that year, the 2001 *Work Report* mentioned that it is necessary to 'strengthen the scope of striking against crimes that damage ecological and environmental resources, and promote protection for ecological construction and the environment', in order to create a rule-of-law environment conducive to the development of the Western regions. Thereafter, environment-related issues received no mention in the 2002, 2003 and 2005 *Work Reports.* In setting out work arrangements for that year, the 2004 *Work Report* mentioned the need to 'be highly attentive to and tactfully handle litigation arising from infringement of

[3] The 1987 *Work Report* reads: 'We suggest strengthening publicity around relevant laws and regulations such as the *Forestry Law*, the *Mineral Resources Law*, the *Plains Law*, **the *Environmental Protection Law (trial)* and the *Administrative Measures for Forests* and *Wild Animal Natural Reserves*.** Common observance and enforcement thereof is relevant to the long-term interests of our country's ecological environment and people.'

[4] The 1989 *Work Report* reads: 'In four years, maritime trial work has achieved a certain degree of success, exerting a positive effect on maintaining navigational order, **protecting the marine environment**, promoting shipping and the development of foreign economics and trade.'

[5] For example, the 1990 *Work Report* reads: 'In 1989, people's courts across the country have concluded 9742 administrative cases at first-instance, involving many administrative agencies such as public security, land, industry and commerce, tax, **environmental protection** and customs'; the 1991 *Work Report* reads: 'Apart from administrative cases concerning security and land, which still account for 65% of the total cases accepted by the people's courts, administrative cases also involve industry and commerce, forestry, **environmental protection**, customs, tax, urban planning, medicine and health-care and sanitation' ; the 1993 *Work Report* reads: 'in the work of trying administrative cases, the people's courts must ... strengthen the trial of such cases as land, industry and commerce, tax and **environmental protection**'; the 1996 *Work Report* reads: 'Trying administrative cases in accordance with the law ... administrative cases heard by the people's courts involve some 40 administrative agencies such as land, public security, urban planning, industry and commerce, sanitation, customs and **environmental protection.**'

[6] In chapter 2, entitled 'Proper Resolution of Civil Disputes', the 1998 *Work Report* states: 'in recent years, new circumstances have arisen in these two types of case: one, the gradual proliferation of disputes over private loans ... ; there is also a marked increase in disputes involving **environmental pollution.**'

workers' rights, delayed payment of wages and environmental pollution as a result of demolishing and relocating urban and rural housing, the expropriation of rural land or restructuring of rural enterprises. Petitioning due to improper case-handling should be prevented'. Statistical data from the 2006 *Work Report* was the first to include environmental trials.[7]

In the 2007 *Work Reports*, environment litigation did not appear separately in statistics of the previous year's trial work, nor was it even mentioned in civil judgments. In fact, references to environmental litigation were limited to such formulations as 'the trial of such administrative cases as natural resources and environmental protection' and 'important judicial interpretations were formulated for such specific questions of legal application as environmental pollution cases'. Yet, in the chapter entitled '2007 Work Arrangements', content related to environmental law appeared in work surrounding civil and administrative trials, as well as judicial interpretations. The 2008 *Work Report* made no mention at all of the previous year's environmental trial work. In the entire text of the report, only the chapter entitled '2008 Work Arrangements' mentioned 'trying environmental tort cases in accordance with the law'. The 2009 *Work Report* followed its predecessor in failing to mention the previous year's environmental trial work, and only mentioned the need to 'try cases related to resource and environmental protection, and promote the construction of ecological civilization'.

Not until the beginning of 2010, when the SPC began issuing annual reports on the work of People's Courts,[8] did statistics surrounding environmental cases first appear.

Based on the data collected from the annual Reports on the Work of the People's Courts by SPC and its Work Report to NPC, I have set Table 13.1, comparing the yearly case numbers regarding environmental cases in these two Reports.

[7] The 2006 *Work Report* states: 'The SPC concluded the trial of 62 major administrative and state compensation cases involving such matters as urban planning, housing demolition and relocation, labor and social security, **environmental protection** and industrial and commercial management.'

[8] Weiquan Yang and Fei Chen, 'The SPC Publishes Its First Annual Report on the Work' (*Legal Daily*, 2010) (Z1): 84. Each annual report reports statistical figures for the preceding year. The SPC issued Legal Document No. 55 of 2009 (*Opinions on Further Strengthening Judicial Statistical Work*), signalling the entry of judicial statistics gathering into formal territory.

Table 13.1 *Number of environmental cases on annual basis*

Source / year	Annual Report on the Work of the People's Courts by SPC[9]	Work Report to NPC[10]	Notes
2009	1,783 civil damages cases for environmental pollution, and 10,767 new environmental resources-related offences heard by courts at all levels.[11]	Not mentioned.	A 1:6 ratio of civil to criminal cases.
2010	Not mentioned.	Courts at all levels concluded trials in 12,018 damages cases for environmental pollution, up 2.83% from the previous year.[12]	In the *annual Report on the Work of the People's Courts* and *Work Report to NPC* for 2009–2012, mention of environmental judgments has
2011	1,883 civil cases for damages arising	Not mentioned.	

[9] From 2010, the Supreme People's Court will publish the previous year's work in the subsequent year. See Weihan Yang and Fei Chen, 'Supreme People's Court Publishes Initial Annual Work Reports on the Work' (*Legal System Information*, 2010) (Z1): 84. Each annual report contains figures for the previous year. On a related note, the Supreme People's Court issued the 'Opinion on Further Strengthening Judicial Statistics' (*Fa Fa*, 2009) Document No. 55. This signalled the progressive regularization of judicial statistics.

[10] The Report to NPC, unlike the annual Report on the Work of the People's Courts(White Paper), is exclusively submitted to the Representatives of NPC for review. Although both are quite similar in terms of basic information, there are still many substantial differences related to the data.

[11] See Supreme People's Court of the People's Republic of China, *Work Report of the People's Courts (White Paper)* (2009), www.court.gov.cn/qwfb/sfsj/201007/P020100716295433349727.doc, accessed 6 May 2019.

[12] The figures may include criminal and administrative litigations that involve the environment.

Table 13.1 (*cont.*)

Source / year	Annual Report on the Work of the People's Courts by SPC	Work Report to NPC	Notes
	out of environmental pollution, down 7.38% from the previous year.[13]		always been missing from one of the two. From this, it would seem that environmental trials have yet to become a core caseload for the country's supreme judicial organ.
2012	2,306 civil cases for damages arising out of environmental pollution, up 22.46% from the previous year.[14]	No figures provided. Only a very brief mention of work arrangements for the next year in regard to environmental trials.[15]	
2013	1,906 cases of damages arising from environmental pollution, down	19,000 environmental pollution and resource destruction cases heard and	Significant fluctuations in figures for all cases except criminal ones, due perhaps to

[13] In this work report, cases of marine ecological pollution may be folded into maritime judgments. See Supreme People's Court of the People's Republic of China, *Report on the Work of the People's Courts (White Paper)* (2011), www.court.gov.cn/zixun-xiangqing-4106.html, accessed 6 May 2019.

[14] Similar to the previous year, maritime pollution cases may have been folded into maritime judgments. See Supreme People's Court of the People's Republic of China, *Report on the Work of the People's Courts (White Paper)* (2012), www.pkulaw.cn/CLI.WP.6599, accessed 6 May 2019.

[15] In the work report delivered by then-President of the Supreme People's Court *Shengjun WANG* during the first meeting of the 12th National People's Congress on 10 March 2013, arrangements for environmental resources trial work for 2014 were neatly summed up in twenty-seven characters under the theme 'provide effective judicial guarantees for socio-economic development': 'try cases involving environmental protection and resource exploitation in accordance with the law, and advance construction of a beautiful China'. However, environmental resources trial work for the previous year was conspicuously absent. See www.court.gov.cn/zixun-xiangqing-82552.html, accessed 6 May 2019.

Table 13.1 (*cont.*)

Source / year	Annual Report on the Work of the People's Courts by SPC	Work Report to NPC	Notes
	17.35% from the previous year.[16]	concluded, up 18.8% from the previous year. 78,000 civil cases involving environmental protection.[17]	differences in statistical method. Cases of marine ecological pollution have not been included, as they are based on estimates. Civil environmental protection
2014	3,331 cases of ownership rights to environmental resources and infringements thereupon.[18]	16,000 cases of environmental pollution and destroying environmental resources.	

[16] Similar to the previous year, marine ecological pollution cases may have been folded into maritime trials. See Supreme People's Court of the People's Republic of China, *Report on the Work of the People's Courts (White Paper)* (2013), www.pkulaw.cn/CLI.WP.6606, accessed 6 May 2019.

[17] That this figure differs from the annual work report is perhaps due to the inclusion of cases, such as those involving contractual disputes over environmental resources. For different statistical numbers to appear in two official documents within the space of one year suggests either intent or indifference on the part of the supreme judicial organ as to this kind of statistic. In other words, all that matters are for environment-related cases to appear in publicly-available figures, and issues such as how to refine the numbers or resolve the issue are of lesser importance.

[18] According to the 'Regulations on Civil Causes of Action' issued by the Supreme People's Court, contractual disputes involving the supply of water, power, gas and heating (items 84–87), contractual disputes involving agriculture, forestry, fisheries and animal husbandry (items 115–118), disputes over the right to mineral extraction and prospecting (items 50–51) and disputes over the right to draw water (item 52) also belong to civil environmental resources cases. These cases far outnumber those for compensation arising out of damage caused by environmental pollution. Published in the *China Environmental Resources Trials White Paper*, figures for July 2016 to June 2017 show a total of 62,457 cases involving contractual disputes for the supply of water, power, gas and heating. These account for the vast majority of civil environmental resources cases. A total of 10,096 cases involved contractual disputes involving agriculture, forestry, fisheries and animal husbandry. Over the same period, there were only a measly 1,737 cases for compensation due to environmental pollution, almost 41 times less.

Table 13.1 (*cont.*)

Source / year	Annual Report on the Work of the People's Courts by SPC	Work Report to NPC	Notes
2015	18,656 criminal cases concerning destruction of environmental resources; 2007 cases of compensation for environmental pollution, down 30.34% from the previous year.[19]	Trial concluded in 19,000 criminal cases of, among others, environmental pollution and destruction of environmental resources. Hearing concluded in 78,000 civil cases involving environmental protection.	cases alone have many statistical methods, thus resulting in significant fluctuation.[20] Repeated changes in statistical method seem to hint at the fact that, during this period at least, the supreme judicial organ does not have a great appetite

[19] This figure includes resources-type cases such as those involving mineral or forestry rights. See Supreme People's Court of the People's Republic of China, *Report on the Work of the People's Courts (White Paper)* (2014), www.court.gov.cn/fabu-xiangqing-13848.html, accessed 6 May 2019.

[20] In Fa Fa Document No. 55 of 2009, entitled 'Opinions on Further Strengthening Judicial Statistics', the Supreme People's Court noted that 'judicial statistics are an important way for the people's courts to grasp the reality of trial work, evaluate trial trends and summarize trial experience. They are also indispensable for the realization of scientific decision-making and management by the people's courts. Strengthening judicial statistics is of huge importance to enhancing the overall grasp of trial work, promoting court business and advancing scientific development of the people's courts.' Yet significant differences in statistical scope in publicly available figures for environmental resources cases, coupled with the randomness inherent in publicly available figures, points to an overall lack of categorization and structure. The root cause may be the supreme judicial organ's lack of top-level design with respect to this area, and is only passively (perhaps even in a perfunctory manner) rather than actively advancing work in this area.

Table 13.1 *(cont.)*

Source / year	Annual Report on the Work of the People's Courts by SPC	Work Report to NPC	Notes
2016	–[21]	13,300 first-instance cases concerning environmental resources.	for advancing environmental resources trials.[22]
2017	–	88,000 criminal cases related to environmental pollution. Trial concluded in 487,000 civil environmental cases, 11,000 cases for compensation due to ecological destruction, 1,383 instances of environmental public interest litigation brought by prosecutorial agencies, 252 cases of environmental public interest litigation brought by social organizations.	Changes in statistical method have been observed even for criminal cases. This year's figures have spiked sharply due to inclusion of the two offences: destruction of natural resources and environmental pollution.

[21] See Supreme People's Court of the People's Republic of China, *Report on the Work of the People's Courts (White Paper)* (2015) in Law Press (2016) 9, 29.

[22] After publishing the 'Report on the Work of the People's Courts (2015)' in 2016, the SPC suspended the report without clarification.

Figures from the SPC show significant fluctuations in the number of criminal prosecutions for environmental pollution. Note the sharp spike following the 2014 amendment of China's *Environmental Protection Law*.[23]

As the provided statistics show, environmental pollution in China steadily worsened for two decades since the 1990s, with the Chinese courts omitting to protect the environment under the guise of judicial activism. Rather, it was only with the CPC Central Committee's and the State Council's introduction of policies strengthening environmental protection that the level of environmental protection began to increase. Related cases are dominated by criminal prosecutions for environmental pollution, with small numbers of tort cases emphasizing victim compensation growing slowly due to the following reasons. First, under the contemporary focus on economic development, local governments across the country have prioritized GDP growth. As a result, environmental pollution, as an acceptable cost in the quest to attain this goal, failed to garner sufficient attention. Second, owing to the Chinese courts' position in the overall power structure, it would be unthinkable for courts to pre-empt explicit central policy by overstepping into political roles. Third, environmental pollution cases often involve a glut of victims. Once the floodgates are opened, problems of social stability will emerge, in direct opposition to China's goals of social security governance. Thus, prioritizing criminal environmental cases will not only deter and warn potential suspects but mollify the anger of victims. It can also, to a certain degree, lay the ground work for compensation. Since 2011, the number of environmental torts heard by the people's courts have increased, reflecting China's strengthening of environmental governance. This shows that justice must follow the CPC Central Committee's macro-policies and underlines the strengthening of environmental protection by judicial means.

[23] Haisong Yu, 'From 32 cases to 1691 cases' (*China Environmental News*, 6 April 2016) 5. The text is largely concordant with the Interpretation of the SPC and Supreme People's Procuratorate on Questions of Applicable Law in Trying Criminal Cases of Environmental Pollution – A Practical Analysis, with the sole difference being that the Analysis uses figures no later than October 2014. It is therefore reasonable to surmise that the figures originate from within the SPC and are therefore authoritative. The Analysis is edited by Xi Xiaoming and published from page 182 onwards of the *Guidance for Environmental Resources Trials*, vol. 1 (People's Court Press 2015).

13.1.2 Litigation Figures on China Judgments Online Data Bank[24]

This figure is an important initiative of the SPC to promote publication of trial information and judicial justice.[25] Thus, the collection and sorting of cases concerning the environment allows for reflection of the current state of judicial environmental protection.

I used the following three search methods. First, a search for first-instance judgments using the terms 'civil cause of action-dispute over tortious liability-dispute over liability for environmental pollution' yielded 568 results for 2014, 367 results for 2015, 1,443 results for 2016 and 545 results for 2017. Second, a search for first-instance judgments using the terms 'criminal cause of action-offense of obstructing social management and order-environmental pollution' yielded 846 results for 2014, 713 results for 2015, 1,499 results for 2016 and 1,539 results for 2017. Third, a search for first-instance judgments using the terms 'administrative cause of action-scope of environmental protection' yielded 369 results for 2014, 301 results for 2015, 592 results for 2016 and 739 results for 2017. A total of 764 results were given for the year 1 July 2016 to 30 June 2017.

The provided data confirms what has already been noted in the annual *Report on the Work of the People's Courts by SPC* – namely that the courts have not actively conducted trial work in relation to the environment for the same reasons discussed herein.

13.1.3 Data from Reports and Yearbooks of Environmental Protection Bureaus (EPB)

Unlike judicial organs, EPBs in China occupy the central role in environmental protection. I organized relevant figures[26] for the years 1997–2015 from the *China Environment Yearbook*[27] as shown in Table 13.2.

[24] 中国裁判文书网 [China Judgements Online], http://wenshu.court.gov.cn, accessed 10 Jun 2020.

[25] On 2 July 2013, the *Provisional Measures for the Online Publication of Judgments of the SPC*, the first such specialized document that regulates online publication of the SPC's judgments, was released. The *Provisional Measures* state that, excepting special circumstances otherwise provided by law, judgments, consultation and decisions of the SPC that have become effective should be published on the internet. This is especially so for cases closely followed by society.

[26] Figures from the *China Environment Yearbook*, published by the China Environment Yearbook Press in each year shown.

[27] Figures from pages 173, 174 and 628 of the 1998 *China Environment Yearbook* (China Environment Yearbook Press 1998). The most recent available edition of the *Yearbook* is 2016, recording data for the previous year.

Table 13.2 *Enforcement actions by environmental protection bureaus*[28,29]

Year	Cases involving compensation for environmental pollution	Environmental protection criminal cases	Environmental pollution criminal cases	Administrative litigation	Administrative punishment	Administrative petition
1997			–	64	29,523	30,000
1998			<10	621	39,754	36,000
1999			<10	427	53,101	36,000
2000			<10	580	55,209	61,000
2001			<10	696	71,089	75,000
2002			<10	993	100,103	74,000
2003			<10	579	92,818	73,000
2004			<10	616	80,079	71,000
2005			<10	399	93,265	69,000
2006			<10	353	92,404	62,000
2007			≈20	199	101,325	43,000
2008			≈20	146	89,820	41,000
2009	1,783	10,767	≈20	249	73,710	41,000
2010	2,033		≈20	168	112,025	33,000
2011	1,883		≈20		119,333	54,000
2012	2,306		≈20		117,308	54,000
2013	1,906	19,000	104		139,059	46,000
2014	2,881	16,000	988	429	97,084	51,000
2015	2,007	18,656	1,691	350	102,084	48,000
2016	1,700	15,000		690		
2017	2,764			860		

28 Before 2006, the number of environmental pollution criminal cases was no more than 10. Between 2007 and 2012, the number remains at approximately 20. In 2013, the number increases to 104. In 2014, it jumps to 988, and in 2015 it reaches 1691 (see n 23). The reason for this increase can be explained by the relaxation of requirements for the crime in the 'Interpretation of Environmental Pollution' issued by SPC in 2013. It has therefore been much easier since 2013 for the Courts to find actors guilty.

29 **Figures on cases involving compensation for environmental pollution:** the 2010 figures are deduced from data for 2011 ('1,883 civil cases of compensation for environmental pollution were tried and concluded, down 7.38% from the previous year'). Similarly, 2014 figures are deduced from data for 2015 ('2,007 cases of compensation for environmental pollution, down 30.34% from the previous year'). According to deductions on cross-year data from *China Environmental Resources Cases*, the number of cases in 2016 should be less than

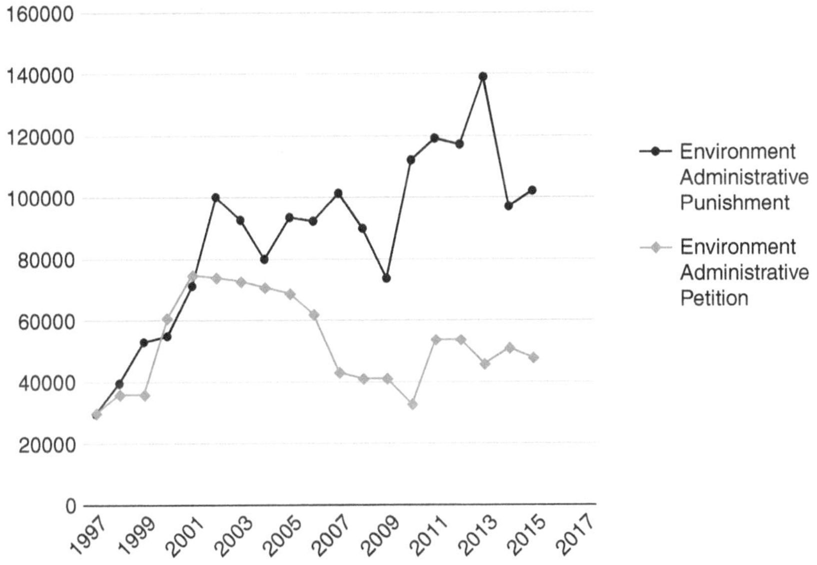

Figure 13.1 Number of administrative environmental cases and petitions

Figure 13.1 shows administrative and judicial data. In this figure, the round line represents administrative environmental cases, while the diamond line represents the number of petitions related thereto. If we consider the increase in administrative law enforcement over time, the graph can show a certain similarity in trends of the two sets of data (i.e., the number of visits related to admin-

1,737 (as the year-long figures for 2017 manifestly exceeded 1,737). 1,700 is thus entered as a rough guide. Figures for 2017 are an estimate of 2017 data rather than actual figures.

Data on environmental protection criminal cases: the 2009 figures show the number of cases accepted and not the number of cases resolved. The unit for 2014 and 2015 is '10,000 cases', meaning that the table shows only estimates. According to cross-year data from *China Environmental Resources Cases*, the number of criminal cases in 2016 should also be around 15,000, a downward trend compared to previous years and cohering with the courts' cautious approach to case conclusion before the promulgation of Judicial Interpretations. Relevant figures sky-rocketed in 2017, which may be related to the release of the *Interpretation on Issues of Applicable Law in Trying Criminal Cases of Environmental Pollution* by the SPC and Supreme People's Procuratorate on 23 December 2016.

Figures on administrative cases: the data for 1997–2010 come from the *China Environment Yearbook*, with the publication ceasing to provide relevant data thereafter. Figures for 2014–2017 are deduced from cross-year figures in *China Environmental Resources Cases* and the number of online judgments for the same period. Blanks in the table indicate a lack of publicly available data.

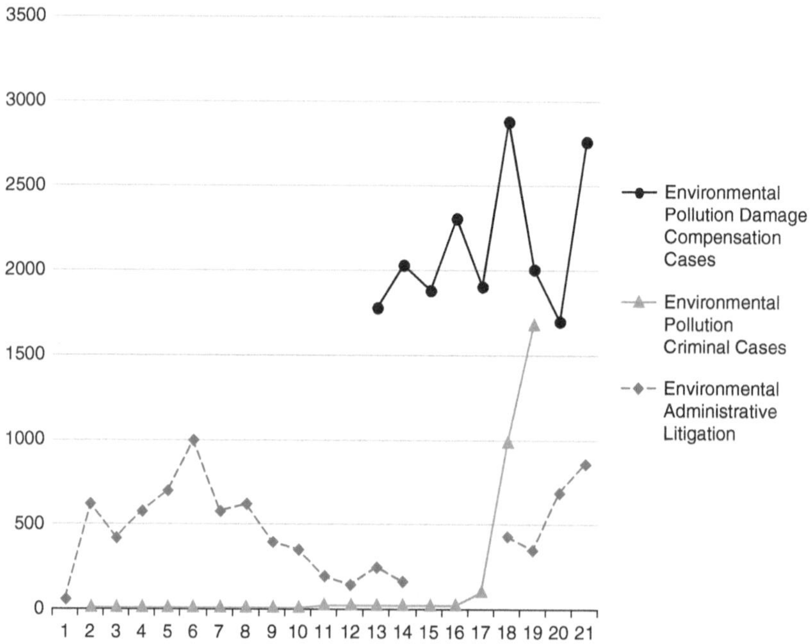

Figure 13.2 Environmental litigation statistics (statistics and estimated judicial data were shown previously[30])

istrative environmental cases should, to a certain extent, reflect the needs of environmental law enforcement for that year). In Figure 13.2, round represents the number of cases involving compensation for environmental pollution, diamond represents the number of environmental administrative litigation and triangle represents the number of criminal cases of environmental pollution.

[30] Figures in the original graph having included enormous amounts of statistical data on offenses related to the destruction of natural resources; only figures pertaining to criminal cases of environmental pollution were used to make the graph. Pre-2016 figures come from the above-cited work of Haisong Yu (n 23), with 2016 figures from the *China News* article, 'The courts accepted more than 20,000 criminal cases concerning environmental resources' (22 June 2017). This notes a total of 20,394 cases, of which 18,874 have been concluded, and 23,727 persons involved in judgments that have already entered into effect. The number of cases involving destruction of natural resources sits at 18,322, of which 17,027 have been concluded and 20,783 persons were involved in judgments that have already entered into effect. See the article at www.chinanews.com/sh/2017/06-22/8257974.shtml, accessed 3 May 2018.

13.1.4 Remarks

The provided statistical figures clearly show that administrative punishment make up the vast majority of cases of environmental protection. In the relatively small number of judicial decisions, criminal cases take up a large proportion, attesting to the priority of using the criminal law in judicial proceedings to deter enterprises from destroying the environment and its resources (see Table 13.2). Punishing the offender has become the first order of judicial business, with the above figures showing that the majority of victims did not obtain adequate compensation.

Other Chinese environmental law scholars have also drawn the same conclusion from empirical studies and data analysis. For example, in analyzing 954 environmental decisions gathered across China for the decade 1999–2008, 75.4 per cent of civil litigation was undertaken by sole plaintiffs, 17 per cent was by more than two plaintiffs (excluding representative action) and 7.6 per cent was representative action; 83.9 per cent of cases were brought by natural persons and 16.1 per cent were by legal persons and other organizations; plaintiffs aged more than 40 years accounted for 67.6 per cent of litigants; 49.5 per cent of plaintiffs were farmers, 17.5 per cent were workers and 33 per cent others.[31] Hence, the authors concluded that the typical plaintiff in civil environmental litigation was the lone middle-aged farmer or worker, most of whom were from vulnerable and disadvantaged groups.[32] The ratio of lone plaintiffs may reflect weak organizational strength, and it may be more apt to describe such persons accordingly. Moreover, both the rate of appeals and re-examination in environmental cases far exceeded other types of cases for the comparable period (567 per cent and 404 per cent, respectively),[33] implying that judicial organs have been unable to adequately resolve environmental disputes. Finally, the authors view judicial remedies for environmental torts in the 1999–2008 decade as lethargic, noting that

> precious few cases make it into the administrative process, and still fewer are admitted into the judicial one . . . the majority of environmental torts

[31] See Zhongmei Lv et al., 'Ideals and Reality: the Current State of Affairs in Environmental Torts in China and the Construction of a System of Remedies' (*China Law Press*, August 2011) 19–20.

[32] ibid 22.

[33] The rate of re-examination for environmental cases was 2.87 per cent, compared to figures for the same period (2003–7) of 0.71 per cent for the overall national rate; the rate of appeals in environmental cases was 56.6 per cent, compared to 9.99 per cent for the entire country in 2003–7. ibid 34.

> are resolved outside the system; hardships encountered by judicial remedies are belied by such factors as difficulty in adducing evidence, imperfect legal rules and lengthy periods for enforcement; judicial remedies are lacking and have been unable to coordinate the environmental and private interests; the lack of administrative remedies; public interest litigation and environmental protection courts have been similarly unable to play their respective roles.[34]

The primacy enjoyed by criminal cases over their civil counterparts in judicial trials is another Chinese characteristic. Environmental pollution events are usually required to reach a certain threshold of severity before they can be regarded as crimes. As such, most environmental criminal cases usually involve mass torts such as the illegal dumping of hazardous waste that causes widespread poisoning among the local population.[35] However, there exist two inherent procedural and substantive weaknesses in judicial intervention in mass environmental torts through criminal cases. Procedurally speaking, the courts have always been in a passive position in criminal litigation. Unlike certain civil law jurisdictions, prosecutorial agencies in China have the power to approve compulsory measures in the investigative stage, completely shutting out courts during this process. Therefore, the courts' authority to judge criminal cases is contingent upon and restricted by the initiation and exercise of investigative powers by public security organs (*Gongan*). If we consider that the latter are closely attached to administrative departments, and the natural affinity between party/government and administrative departments, judicial intervention on the criminal level is wholly incapable of carrying the load of mass environmental torts. Moreover, the priority accorded to criminal cases over civil ones means that civil cases are relatively dependent on evidence obtained during investigations of the former. Some scholars go further in pointing out the 'high degree of reliance on scientific evidence';[36] as a result, the subordination of criminal trials to politics even filters through to the civil arena via evidence.

[34] ibid 44–7.

[35] This was affirmed by the 2016 *Interpretation on Issues of Applicable Law in Trying Criminal Cases of Environmental Pollution*. Although the *Interpretation* came into effect on 1 January 2017, it was formulated on the basis of practical trial experience of the SPC and Supreme People's Procuratorate. Thus, the qualifying threshold for criminal environmental pollution from 1 May 2011 (when *Amendment VIII to the Criminal Law* changed the crime of severe environmental pollution to environmental pollution) to 31 December 2016 should not differ too much.

[36] Lv (n 31) 24.

In environmental administrative cases, the plaintiff is typically a person who has been found guilty of causing pollution and files a suit against the EPB to challenge the decision. As such, it is not a remedy for mass environmental torts, but arguably a form of self-help for the suspected polluter facing administrative punishment. In fact, it constitutes judicial supervision of administrative punishment. Some scholars have classified cases on China Judgments Online for the five years 2012–2016, revealing a total of 499 first-instance judgments for environmental administrative litigation. Of these, 297 cases involved dissatisfaction with punishment meted out by EPBs, accounting for 60 per cent of the total.[37] Viewed from the macro-perspective, therefore, environmental administrative litigation mostly appears as a supplementary judicial measure under administrative guidance. It serves to rectify maladministration and provides a legal pathway for resolving disputes between officials and the people. Some scholars go further in pointing out the high failure rate faced by plaintiffs in administrative cases,[38] which is in fact relatively low when compared with the overall national levels of failure in administrative litigation.[39] In this sense, and compared with other types of administrative litigation, environmental administrative litigation has already played a greater role of assistance and supervision.

Compared with the administrative and criminal fields, civil adjudication occupies a relatively independent position in dispute resolution. As it intervenes between subjects of equal status – tortfeasor and victim – and is directly related to the latter's remedies, civil adjudication plays more than a supporting role in environmental cases. Since neither criminal nor administrative litigation is capable of directly compensating the victim, and given the non-existence of a system of liability insurance for environmental pollution,[40] civil cases have an

[37] See Jiangang Qi, Kai Huang and Meiling Tang, *Supply and Demand in the Law of Environmental Administrative Cases*. See also Lv (n 31) 89.

[38] Qi, Huang and Tang (n 37) 106.

[39] According to figures provided by the SPC, for the years 2010–15, administrative organs lost 59,000 cases for a rate of 9.1 per cent. See Mengyao Wang, '9.1% Failure Rate for Administrative Organs over the Past Five Years' (*Beijing News*, 3 November 2011) A05. The national failure rate for administrative organs in relevant cases for 2016 was 14.62 per cent, an increase of 0.84 per cent on the previous year. See '14.62% Failure Rate for Administrative Organs in the Past Year' (*Beijing Evening News*, 13 June 2017) A11.

[40] The *Environmental Protection Law* only contains the principle of 'State Encouragement of Purchasing Liability Insurance for Environmental Pollution', with pilot areas falling into limbo since their implementation in 2007. Xiao Zhu, 'On the Construction of a System of Liability Insurance for Environmental Pollution' 2015 33(1) *Law Review* 160–3.

irreplaceable role to play. Currently, more than one-third of specialized environmental trial organizations established by the high courts still specialize in civil trials,[41] with the evident intent of improving judicial remedies for victims.

The number of civil environmental tort cases has remained relatively stable at around 2,000 per year.[42] Despite breakthroughs in the figures for 2014 and 2017, this trend is set to continue for the short term. Generally speaking, the number of petitions will always be fewer than the number of environmental disputes, and the number of civil environmental tort cases pales in comparison to the amount of visits (1 out of 20) and the number of petitions (1 out of 50).[43] In the seven years following the entry into force of the Tort Liability Law, there were 2,765 first-instance cases of environmental torts, 885 second-instance cases, 43 cases of re-examination, an average appeal rate of 32 per cent, an average appeal rate for civil cases over the same period of 14.8 per cent and an average appeal rate across all cases of 15.15 per cent. Environmental tort cases were 2.16 times more likely to be appealed than general civil cases, reflecting more intense antagonisms between the parties and the increased difficulty of harmonizing their interests.[44] In addition, large-scale litigation conflicts with the governance value of social stability and goes against the prioritization

[41] With the SPC pushing for the unified trial of environmental resources case, environmental resources trial organs established by the high courts in Shandong, Guangxi, Jiangxi, Guangdong, Hunan, Jilin and Gansu (among others) are still only trying civil cases at July 2017. See *China Environmental Resources Trials White Paper* (n 18) 32.

[42] Similar conclusions have been drawn by scholars on the basis of figures for the years 2010–16, gathered from publicly available channels. Bao Zhang and Haiyang Dou, *Environmental Tort Cases: Logic and Experience*. Lv (n 31) 54.

[43] Vice President Yang Chaofei of the Chinese Society for Environmental Sciences stated in 2014: 'investigations reveal that less than 1% of environmental disputes are resolved through judicial litigation'. Chaofei Yang, 'The Predicament for Environmental Rule of Law and Solutions' (2014) 5 *Current Events* 32–3. In China's mainland, 'Visit' refers to the action of citizens, legal persons or other organizations in communicating inadequacies, offer suggestions and opinions or to lay complaints with government at all levels or government agencies at county-level and above. It may take the form of letters, emails, facsimiles, telephone calls and in-person visits, and concerns wrongful or unfair treatment, popular opinion or official (police) shortcomings. 'Petition' refers to the action of complaining to superior organs, especially central organs, when one feels aggrieved by administrative actions or judicial decisions. When enterprises and individuals feel aggrieved, they will often lodge a case with the bureaux of letters and visits (a non-specific judicial process). The actual number of cases thus resolved is quite low, due to factors such as the lack of legitimacy in the visitors' plea and a back-log of cases caused by the sheer impossibility of dealing with each and every visit.

[44] Zhang and Dou (n 42) 57.

of economic development.[45] This deprives judicial forces of the authority and resources necessary for independently resolving environmental disputes.

13.2 The Status of the People's Courts in China

At the 19th CPC National Congress in 2017, General Secretary Xi Jinping delivered an important speech which emphasized the importance of 'maintaining the Party leadership in all work. The Party leads all'.[46] The judiciary is also a key aspect of the CPC's leadership, and an important link in the 'comprehensive governance of the country in accordance with the law' of the 'Four Comprehensives'. In accordance with this logic, and wholly unlike the concept of judicial independence under the Western separation of powers model, Chinese courts are deemed to be organs of the state under the CPC's leadership.

Articles 131 and 136 of the Chinese Constitution provide that 'the People's Courts independently exercise adjudicative authority in accordance with the law, without interference from administrative organs, social groups or individuals' and 'the People's Procuratorates independently exercise supervisory authority in accordance with the law, without interference from administrative organs, social groups and individuals'. However, care must be taken not to confuse the independent adjudicative authority conferred on Chinese courts with the concept of an independent judiciary in the Western model. During a meeting of national High Court presidents convened on 14 January 2017,[47] President Zhou Qiang of the SPC stressed that erroneous Western thinking of 'constitutional democracy', 'the separation of powers' and 'judicial independence' must be vigorously resisted, and the path of the socialist rule of law with Chinese characteristics must be kept with ardent resolve. He explained

[45] 'Even while environmental issues rose in prominence, however, economic growth and stability remained paramount priorities'. Rachel E. Stern, 'The Political Logic of China's New Environmental Courts' (2014) 72 *The ChinaJournal* 61.

[46] Report delivered at the Nineteenth National People's Congress of the Communist Party of China by Xi Jinping: 'the first of 14 basic tenets enunciated under the title of "Socialist thought with Chinese characteristics in a new era and basic general plan": 1) resolutely uphold the leadership of the party in all work. All people are to follow the party, and its leadership is supreme'. See http://cpc.people.com.cn/n1/2017/1028/c64094-29613660-5.html.

[47] Lei Wang and Baoli Qiao, 'Implementing Legally Independent Judicial Powers Is Not Equivalent to Western Judicial Independence' (*China Court*, 15 January 2017), www.chinacourt.org/article/detail/2017/01/id/2512854.shtml, accessed 7 May 2019.

that China's government differed from the Western 'separation of powers' concept in four respects: the national organization of power, the political party system, the legal system and system of selection of judicial personnel.

The Report of the 19th CPC National Congress made one sole mention of courts, in referring to 'the Party's leading position in national political life. Strengthening the Party's centralized leadership, as well as supporting the NPC, government and the CPPCC are wholly consistent with the lawful exercise of their roles and performance of their functions by the courts and procuratorates'.

It is clear to see that people's courts in China enjoy independent adjudicative authority under Party leadership, meaning that they do not occupy the status of balancing the legislative and executive branches, as in the West. Here, the courts can remedy legislative shortcomings and promote executive reform through trying cases. In short, western courts can play a 'policy-making' role. In the past, Chinese courts did flirt with the idea of 'active justice (*Nengdong Sifa*)',[48] which, as the name suggests, advocates for judges to take an active approach in trying cases according to social needs, uphold certain legal values, obey certain legal rules, creatively apply the law and make rational decisions. Such a campaign was meant to constantly promote reform and development of such areas as politics, the economy, the law and culture. But, this experiment is subordinate to obedience of Party leadership and overall policy. It would simply be unthinkable for Chinese courts to attempt far-reaching social change without the macro-arrangements of the Party. As for environmental protection, protection of the ecological environment can supersede crude economic growth only after relevant pronouncement of macro-policy, such as the 16th,[49], 17th,[50] 18th[51] and 19th[52] CPC

[48] Jiang Bixin (Vice-President of the SPC), 'Active Justice: Basis, Scope and Limits' (*Guangming News*, 4 February 2010) 9.

[49] The Report of the 16th CPC National Congress consecrated 'harmony between man and nature, and setting the entire country on a civilized path of development consisting of production, a prosperous life and a sound ecological environment' as one of the four goals for comprehensively building a society of moderate wealth.

[50] General Secretary Hu Jintao noted in the Report of the 17th CPC National Congress that 'with the construction of an ecological civilization and markedly higher portions of renewable energy, the concept of ecological civilization has firmly taken hold throughout all of society'.

[51] The Report of the 18th CPC National Congress made the strategic decision to 'vigorously pursue the construction of ecological civilization'.

[52] See Part IX of the Report of the 19th CPC National Congress, entitled 'Accelerating Reform of the System of Ecological Civilization and Building a Beautiful China'.

National Congresses. Prior to this, courts at all levels across China found it difficult to stop local government in pushing for regional economic growth by sacrificing the environment, a conundrum aggravated by the fact that courts are funded by local governments.

Until the end of 2015, which saw the publication of the *Pilot Program for Reforming the System of Compensation for Harm to the Ecological Environment*, civil adjudication had not been made a tool in the arsenal of measures governing mass environmental torts. Following publication of the *Pilot Program*, administrative measures still took precedence over civil litigation, with authorized local governments actively guiding their institutional development.

13.3 The Establishment and Shortcomings of Environmental Tribunals

13.3.1 The Establishment of Environmental Resources Tribunals within People's Courts

As early as 1982, scholars recommended the creation of environmental tribunals.[53] The earliest such example traces back to 1989,[54] with general consensus ascribing the honour to the Environmental Protection Tribunal of the Qingzhen People's Court in Guiyang City, set up in November 2007. As of 2010, there were thirty-nine environmental protection tribunals of various descriptions across China, almost all of which were set up through individual trial by the provincial High People's Courts (*Sheng Gaoji Renmin Fayuan*).[55] In June 2010, the SPC issued the *Opinions on Providing Judicial Guarantees and Services for Accelerating Transformation of the Mode of Economic Development*, and supported the establishment of environmental protection tribunals across the country. By the end of 2014, there were more than 150 such bodies established, with the Hainan and Fujian High People's Courts still

[53] Such bodies would have been set up within the SPC as well as the higher, intermediate and basic-level people's courts in cities of all sizes. Dianrong Luo and Jianxu Deng, 'The Establishment of Environmental Tribunals Is Only a Matter of Time' (1982) 1 *Environmental Protection* 3–4.

[54] In 1989, the Dunkou District People's Court in Wuhan established an environmental tribunal in conjunction with the Environmental Protection Bureau. After the Hubei High People's Court sought guidance from the SPC, the establishment of environmental protection tribunals at the grass-roots level was found to lack a legal basis, and the effort halted. Yili Zhang, 'Are Environmental Tribunals Exceeding Their Quota?' (2008) 7 *Environment* 68–9.

[55] Lv (n 31) 12–13.

promoting such efforts within their respective provinces. On 26 June 2014, the Environmental Resources Tribunal of the SPC was established.[56] As of June 2017, 976 environmental resources tribunals (344), collegial panels (589) and circuit courts (43) had been established within people's courts at all levels across the country. Twenty-one high people's courts, including those in Guizhou, Fujian, Hainan, Jiangsu and Hebei, established environmental resources tribunals, with other high people's courts designating specialist organizations or establishing specialized collegial panels to perform equivalent tasks; a three-tier environmental resources trial system was established by courts in, inter alia, Fujian, Henan, Guizhou, Jiangsu, Hainan and Chongqing; 162 intermediate people's courts and 160 basic-level people's courts established specialized environmental resources tribunals.[57]

13.3.2 Shortcomings in Professional Environmental Resources Courts and Tribunals

The establishment of professional courts and tribunals has unquestionably improved professional standards in environmental litigation, and responds to the huge significance of environmental civil cases in adjudication. However, the subordinate status of the people's courts in Chinese environmental protection remains unchanged.

First, figures show that the majority of cases handled by such bodies are, in fact, not civil torts whereby the victims are directly compensated. Trial work can be separated into the two categories of environment and natural resources, with the latter quantitatively exceeding the former. In criminal cases, only a very small percentage of cases involve environmental pollution, with perhaps 10 per cent of environmental resources crimes being concerned with pollution. In recent years, the number of civil cases involving the environment and resources has exceeded 100,000. For example, the amount of cases tried and concluded for the July 2016–June 2017 year was 151,152. The *Work Report* presented at the 2018 NPC revealed 487,000 instances of civil litigation involving the environment in 2017, of which a paltry 2,000 or so touched on liability for environmental pollution;[58] the majority of administrative

[56] ibid 13.

[57] *China Environmental Resources Trials White Paper* (n 18) at 17.

[58] According to the *China Environmental Resources Trials White Paper* (n 18), the majority of civil environmental resources cases (62,457) involved contractual disputes for the supply of water, electricity, gas and heating. This was followed by contracts for

cases, nearly ten times the amount of administrative environmental protection cases, involved resources management (land, forestry, plains, minerals, energy and others). Of these, land and forestry cases account for the absolute majority.[59]

Second, the number of personnel allocated to environmental resources tribunals is usually significantly less than the number available to ordinary civil courts. Taking the Environmental & Natural Resources Tribunal of the SPC as an example, its ten members (composed of the president, vice-president and judges) are the fewest in all of the tribunals of the SPC.[60] It should be noted that the SPC is not only responsible for adjudicating appellate cases but is also the first-instance court for a significant number of cases. As such, these judges face a formidable workload, which arguably renders it unrealistic to expect them to actively promote environmental protection.

In addition, as described previously, environmental pollution events are transformed into mass torts litigation when there are many victims involved. There is the concern that mass torts litigation will open the floodgates and threaten social stability in China. In addition, it is assumed that the executive ought to play a leading role in victim compensation as it has the power and social resources to do so. For example, on 3 July 2010, in a case of severe pollution involving Zijin Quarry, the copper mine on Mt Zijin in Fujian's Shanghang County discharged a certain volume of acidic waste-water (containing copper) into the River Ding. This caused parts of the river to become polluted and massive fish die-offs in the lower flows thereof. The local government in Fujian actively intervened in and treated this incident as a public incident, moving quickly to come up with an action plan to alleviate fishermen's losses and temporarily mollify popular anger. Moreover, some of the dead fish were quickly caught, buried and otherwise treated to render them harmless. In order to prevent dead fish from entering the market, the county in question reinforced supervision and checks on local fish and marine produce markets, in addition to setting up inspection stations at crucial road junctions to prevent the external spread of dead fish. The series of measures were relatively effective in preventing the situation from degrading and protecting the victims'

agriculture, forestry, fisheries, and animal husbandry, totalling 10,096 cases. Other causes include disputes over liability for environmental, maritime and waterways pollution, disputes over easements and disputes over mineral and water rights.

59 Figures from Lv (n 31) 89–90.

60 See the organizational structure of the SPC at www.court.gov.cn/jigou-fayuanbumen.html, accessed 3 May 2018.

interests. But almost no damages were paid directly to the victims based on a government intervention.

In the even more severe Bohai Oil-Spill Case, ConocoPhillips China, China National Offshore Oil Corporation (CNOOC) and China's Ministry of Agriculture reached an agreement on 24 January 2012. This provided that ConocoPhillips China and CNOOC will pay, respectively, RMB 100 million and RMB 250 million towards restoring and maintaining natural fisheries resources. On 27 April 2012, ConocoPhillips China and China's State Oceanic Administration reached a second compensation agreement, whereby it agreed to pay RMB 1.203 billion and CNOOC RMB 4.8 billion. It is singularly regrettable that fishermen in the affected Bohai Bay area did not receive timely and effective civil compensation, for despite the court having accepted some litigation in this respect, the court as a whole was unable to provide effective judicial remedies.[61] The two classic cases above show that Chinese courts are unable to provide adequate judicial remedies for the majority of victims in civil compensation cases for mass environmental torts. As Stern has argued, 'environmental courts play a role between administration and law and serve multiple functions, including policy advocacy, education and social control' in China.[62]

13.4 The Dilemma of Environmental Public Interest Litigation (EPIL)

Since environmental interests are by their very nature public, and victims are often limited to seeking compensation for harm to their person or property, the need for a litigation system that maintains environmental public interest (EPI) becomes especially apparent. A feature newly introduced by the 2013 Civil Procedure Law,[63] EPIL was substantively

[61] In some cases, the plaintiffs lost because they were unable to adduce the necessary evidence, such as Case No. 263: *He Yecai et al* v. *ConocoPhillips China and China National Offshore Oil Corporation*, dismissed by the court in Qingdao. Others were not accepted. The only case currently being heard in China is the case involving twenty-one fish farmers in Leting, Hebei. Hearings officially commenced on 9 December 2014 at the Tianjin Maritime Court, while the case had been brought in December 2011. In addition, a lot of Chinese fishermen attempted to file compensation claims with the Court for the Southern District of Texas, where ConocoPhillips is headquartered. See 'The War Drags on in the Bohai Oil Spill Compensation Case-Farmers Left without Recourse' (*Caijing Magazine*, 16 December 2014).

[62] Stern (n 44) 61.

[63] Article 55: 'Where acts harming the social public interest such as environmental pollution and infringement of the legitimate rights and interests of a multitude of consumers are

consecrated by the Environmental Protection Law in 2015.[64] But the number of cases remains relatively low, with 208 cases heard across China in both 2015 and 2016.[65] Some scholars view this situation as 'hardly ideal for fulfilling the needs of protecting environmental public interest'. This is related to the fact that the system is still in its early days, and local governments often tolerate environmental pollution or ecological destruction in the pursuit of economic growth.[66] In the few instances of EPIL that exist, the rate of mediation is also relatively high.[67]

It is worth noting that China places strict limits on the subject of public interest litigation. Taking 2015/16 cases as an example, and deducting ninety-four cases where prosecutorial organs were the plaintiffs,[68] the rest were largely initiated or managed by government departments under the guise of 'civil organizations'.[69] According to rough estimates, of the 208 EPIL cases brought in two years, only twenty-eight were initiated by civil organizations without government oversight. Of the twenty-eight, the majority were initiated by Friends of Nature.[70]

committed, agencies and relevant organizations recognized by the law may initiate litigation with the people's courts'.

64 Prior to the enactment of the *Environmental Protection Law*, courts at all levels across the country accepted 72 EPIL cases. This has led some to view the *Environmental Protection Law* as giving substance to the EPIL system. Lv (n 31) 169.

65 For details, see Annex 4 on page 47 of Lv (n 31), Table of Environmental Public Interest Litigation Statistics.

66 Zhongshun Huang, 'Annual Survey Report on the System of Civil Public Interest Litigation in China' (2017) 31(6) *Contemporary Law Review* 130.

67 'Mediation can alleviate the antagonism of parties to the litigation, promote cooperation during the process of enforcement and solve problems of real concern more flexibly and pragmatically.' Gu Gong, 'Empirical Analysis of Environmental Public Interest Litigation in Chinafor 2015' (2016) 9 *Law Science* 22.

68 On the role of public prosecutors, they are reluctant to do certain things because their most important task is to bring criminal actions.

69 'There are four types of civil environmental organizations in China, including those established through government initiatives, those established by civil society itself, student bodies and international organizations in China.' All-China Environment Federation (ACEF), *Report on the Development of Civil Environmental Organizations in China* (2006) 61.

70 The estimates are rough because twenty-eight cases, such as the 2015 case of *Friends of Nature (Chaoyang) and the Green Home of Fujian* v. *Xie Zhijin et al*, are jointly brought by governmental and non-governmental civil groups. Established in 1994, Friends of Nature is China's earliest NGO dedicated to environmental protection. As such, it has helped advanced the cause of EPIL in China. Friends of Nature has initiated thirty-seven EPIL cases, with thirty-one being filed and nine concluded. Of these, the majority of cases were dismissed for want of sufficient funds to prove causation.

In practice, the initiating subject and procedural connectivity are especially problematic for EPIL.[71] Problems with the initiating subject are difficult for both political reasons and those related to civil groups themselves.

First, NGO entitlement to EPIL has undergone a tortuous history that arguably reflects hesitation on the part of the state to the participation of social organizations in EPIL. These include the types of organization who had standing to bring EPIL cases before the courts, as well as the requirement for there to be some connection between the case and the NGO's mandate.[72] The latter would suggest that an NGO dedicated to protection of the marine environment. For example, during the amendment process for the Environmental Protection Law, whether the EPIL provisions should stay or go was hotly debated. The draft amendment had also severely restricted subjects of EPIL.[73] However, the state has also at times relaxed such control,[74] but the reality of public interest litigation from 2015 to 2016 shows that with increasingly strict filters, the only organizations capable of bringing such suits in practice are government-administered NGOs.

[71] Xiaohua Ye and Yanyang Liu, 'On Practical Difficulties of Environmental Public Interest Litigation in China-Based on Field Studies in Zhejiang' (2018) 46(2) *Environmental Protection* 64. The text also mentions such problems as difficulties in collecting evidence and the lack of detailed rules on their use. However, these are excluded since they do not appear to be unique to environmental public interest litigation.

[72] Article 58 of the Environmental Protection Law, expanded upon in Article 2 of the SPC Interpretation on Issues Concerning the Application of Law in Trying Environmental Public Interest Cases (Fa Shi, 2015, No. 1). Article 4(2) of the SPC Interpretation embodies the mandate restriction.

[73] 'Article 55 of the *Amendment to the Civil Procedure Law* added the provision on environmental public interest litigation, which was singularly absent from the *Amendment to the Environmental Protection Law*, introduced in August 2012. . . . [I]n June 2013, the *Amendment to the Environmental Protection Law*, submitted to the NPC Standing Committee for a second reading, restricted standing for EPIL to the All-China Environment Federation and its branches in provinces, autonomous regions and municipalities.' Zhongmei Lv, 'Environmental Judicial Rationality Cannot Stop at Astronomical Compensation: Case Analysis of the *Taizhou* Environmental Public Interest Litigation' (2016) 3 *China Law Science* 247.

[74] 'In the beginning of 2012, the Beijing Civil Affairs Bureau announced that it would explore promoting the transformation of the competent units of social organizations to business guidance units. When registering in Beijing, industrial and commercial organizations, public charitable organizations, social welfare organizations and social services organizations may do so directly with the civil affairs departments.' Qingzhi Huan, 'The Environmental Movement in Chinaand Its Strategic Choices under the Political Opportunity Structure' (2012) 11(4) *Journal of Nanjing University of Technology* (Social Sciences Edition) 31.

Second, China is extremely strict in managing foreign NGOs, especially those involved in sensitive areas. Foreign or international NGOs can partner with their Chinese counterparts in the environmental field but will be subject to severe budgetary restrictions. The Foreign NGO Management Law, which entered into force on 1 January 2017, stipulates strict regulatory oversight of foreign NGOs' sources of funding, bank accounts and management. The law requires foreign NGOs to make their audited financial and accounting records available to the public. Foreign NGOs are also not permitted to 'recruit or purport to recruit members in China'.

Third, civil society in the sphere of environmental protection advocacy in China faces considerable limitations. Generally speaking, civil society groups are latecomers in China, grew rapidly but unevenly, and lack core personnel. Government-initiated civil environmental groups are numerous, well-organized, highly capable but insufficiently independent, and some organizations below provincial level do not hold activities with sufficient regularity. Student environmental groups are numerous, highly enthusiastic but lack stability with the governance structure frequently changing. Grassroots environmental groups are comparatively active, few in number, structurally loose and imperfect, as well as arbitrary in carrying out their work. International environmental organizations on the Chinese mainland are few in number and have good work processes, but are generally not registered.[75] Currently, environmental organizations still face problems such as difficulty in fundraising, insufficient policy support from the government, low levels of professionalism and the tendency of some civil environmental groups to publicize small things, monopolize big ones and impose a blockade on core information.[76] In sum, civil environmental groups have voluntarily chosen to play a comparatively more negative role in EPIL, regardless of the causes. 'Environmental civil groups have elected not to actively join or lead popular social mobilization or "mass environmental protests", instead adopting a stand-offish approach'.[77]

Procedural connectivity is another obvious problem in public interest litigation. EPIL has inherent problems such as internal conflict and functional overlap with existing systems.[78] Through the previous procedure, procedural connectivity serves to limit civil public interest litigation

75 ACEF (n 69) 64.

76 Guojun Ding, 'Exploring the Path of Development of Civil Environmental Groups in China' (2015) 43(21) *Environmental Protection* 53.

77 Huan (n 74) 34.

78 Li Luo, 'Structural Problems in China's Environmental Public Interest Litigation System and Their Solution' (2017) 3 *ChinaLaw Science* 244–66.

initiated by prosecutorial organs and also reflects the supervisory function of prosecutorial organs in respect of social organizations.[79]

In terms of the specific mode of litigation, Chinese law also faces significant challenges. The Civil Procedure Law provides for representative litigation, which is similar to the class action in US law. However, these provisions have fallen into abeyance,[80] see extremely little use[81] and have long since disappeared.[82] In addition, the SPC appeared at one time very hostile to the idea of representative action, with the *Notice of the SPC on Relevant Issues Concerning the Acceptance of Cases of Disputes over Civil Torts Arising from False Statement in the Securities Market*, issued on 15 January 2002, providing that 'civil compensation cases arising from fictitious statements shall be tried through individual or joint actions, rather than group actions'. The subsequent 2005 *Notice on Accepting Joint Action Cases by the People's Courts* provided that 'joint actions with a large number of persons in one or both parties shall be accepted by people's courts at the grassroots-level. Where the accepting court thinks such cases inappropriate for a joint hearing, they may accept them separately'.[83]

In light of the above, parties to mass litigation are unlikely to choose litigation as the sole vehicle for resolving their disputes. In fact, even before the case gets to court, parties have already transformed the issue into a social one through petitions and the media. Thus, even though party and administrative forces may have had nothing to do with the dispute in the first place, they are forced to step in out of consideration for political and social stability. The competition between a multitude of forces is just one of the elements that influence adjudication of disputes.

[79] Article 55(2) of the *Civil Procedure Law* permits the people's procuratorates to supervise, advise and support civil organizations prior to public interest litigation. Jun Lu and Xuefei Uamg, 'Reviewing the Practice of Prosecutorial Organs Prior to Civil Public Interest Litigation' (2017) 25(6) *Journal of the National Prosecutors' College* 67–82, 170–1.

[80] Wei Jiang, 'Future Directions of the Representative Action and the Resolution of Mass Disputes' (2016) 35(5) *New Heights* 117.

[81] 'Precious few cases of mass environmental torts in China actually use the representative action.' Cuimin Wang, *Study on Mass Litigation* (Intellectual Property Press 2017) 105.

[82] 'In some developed areas and central cities, the representative action has essentially disappeared.' Wushen Zhang and Yanyan Yang, 'Legislative and Judicial Practice of China's Mass Litigation' 2007(2) *Chinese Journal of Law* 115.

[83] For a critique of this view, see Zhang and Yang (n 82) 117–18, where the authors describe successive interpretations as dealing 'body blows' to the representative action, being limited to Article 54 of the *Civil Procedure Law*.

13.5 Conclusion

Data analysis in this article highlights the dominant position of administrative punishment in cases involving environmental pollution. In litigation, the number of criminal cases far eclipses civil ones (see Table 13.2), suggesting that Chinese courts have been unable to directly provide effective judicial remedies to the victims.[84] On the contrary, China's current political ecology obliges the people's courts to uphold the leadership of the CPC, thus preventing them from unbridled judicial promotion of environmental protection and flinging open their doors to masses of victims.

From a professional perspective, specialized environmental tribunals are a means for Chinese courts to actively respond to environmental and ecological protection. However, viewed pragmatically, environmental tribunals are still subject to the passive role of Chinese courts in general and cannot be an independent force for advancing environmental protection. On this basis alone, expecting Chinese courts to accept CCL, as it is international custom, would be unrealistic.

In mainland China, it is still more unrealistic to pin the hopes for advancing environmental protection on NGOs independent of the government. Political considerations deprive such bodies of the necessary environment for growth in China, relegating them to the roles of increasing awareness of environmental protection and keeping polluting enterprises on their toes. It would be impossible for NGOs to nip environmental pollution and ecological destruction in the bud, through specialized channels of litigation. Furthermore, NGOs cannot independently moot the idea of CCL in China, and foreign ones face a hostile environment here too.

Protecting the ecological environment is the common mission of mankind, who is paying a heavy price for climate change as a result of their destruction and degradation. As a responsible big power, let us wait for China – especially the courts – to play a more active role in the future, and to provide Chinese judicial experience in the globalized mission of preventing climate change.

[84] An empirical survey also demonstrates the similar conclusion: 'Despite occasional successes, civil environmental litigation remains a weak tool for environmental protection.' See Rachel E. Stern, 'From Dispute to Decision: Suing Polluters in China' (2011) 206 *The ChinaQuarterly* 310.

14

Tort-Based Public Interest Litigation on Air Pollution in China: A Promising Pathway for Chinese Climate Change Litigation?

YUE ZHAO, WEI LIU AND SHUANG LYU

Public interest litigation (PIL) to address air pollution has been a novel judicial phenomenon in China since 2016. The modification of the *Civil Procedure Law* in 2012 and the *Environmental Protection Law* in 2014 has conferred standing on environmental NGOs (ENGOs) and public prosecutors to bring environmental PIL cases. Since the introduction of these reforms, the total number of environmental PIL cases has been increasing rapidly.[1] In the early days, water pollution attracted much attention, while PIL on air pollution was rare. This is arguably due to the diffusive and cumulative nature of air pollutant emissions, and the conceivable difficulties of assessing damages as a result. In 2016, the final judicial decision for China's first tort-based air pollution PIL case was pronounced in Shandong, representing a break-through for litigants who seek to promote the regulatory control of air pollution through courts. In contrast, climate change litigation (CCL) based on tort law has not been successful globally. Given the similarities shared by climate change and air pollution, this chapter seeks to shed light on how tort-based air pollution PIL has advanced in China and considers whether it presents a potential avenue for the emergence of CCL in China.

This chapter is divided into four sections. Section 14.1 introduces the Chinese legal context for CCL. Section 14.2 analyzes the relevance of air pollution PIL to CCL. It will show that the current PIL on air pollution may not only indirectly prepare legal preconditions for CCL, but may

[1] See 颜运秋 [Yan Yunqiu], '我国环境公益诉讼的发展趋势 – 对新《环境保护法》实施以来209件案件的统计分析 [Development Trend of Environmental Public Interest Litigation in China – Statistical Analysis of 209 Cases since the Implementation of New *Environmental Protection Law*]' (2017) 10求索 [*Seeker*] 117.

also directly become the pathway for CCL. Section 14.3 will discuss the characteristics of tort-based air pollution PIL, through the empirical analysis of relevant cases. Section 14.4 will consider the potential applicability of tort-based air pollution PIL for Chinese CCL in the future. Based on the analysis of two variables – namely, whether regulatory measures over air pollutants and greenhouse gas emissions (GHGs) are coordinated and whether the judicial remedy concerns an injunctive relief to stop or reduce emissions – we conclude that the implications of tort-based PIL for climate change vary from case to case. We argue that air pollution PIL could not only become a direct channel for CCL, but also indirectly provide the rule to support or to partially achieve the same ends.

14.1 CCL in the Background of China

Peel and Osofsky proposed a broad definition of CCL, including 'litigation with climate change as central issue' (core cases), 'litigation with climate change as peripheral issue', 'litigation with climate change as one motivation but not raised as an issue', and 'litigation with no specific climate change framing but implications for mitigation or adaptation'.[2] In 2016, the Chinese Supreme People's Court (SPC) issued the *Opinion on the Enhancement of Judicial Functions in Promoting the Construction of Ecological Civilization and Green Development (the Opinion)*[3] and the *Report on the Environment and Resources related to Chinese Judicial Practices (the Report).*[4] Under the category of 'civil litigations of environment and natural resources', both documents included certain 'litigation as response to climate change'. This constitutes the only formal statements of CCL in Chinese official judicial documents. However, our empirical analysis shows that these so-called Chinese CCLs are mostly contractual disputes between or relevant to

[2] Jacqueline Peel and Hari M. Osofsky, *Climate Change Litigation: Regulatory Pathways to Cleaner Energy* (Cambridge University Press 2015), 9.

[3] '关于充分发挥审判职能作用为推进生态文明建设与绿色发展提供司法服务和保障的意见 [Opinions on Giving Full Play to the Role of Judicial Functions to Provide Judicial Services and Guarantees for Promoting Ecological Civilization Construction and Green Development]' (中华人民共和国最高人民法院 [The Supreme People's Court of the People's Republic of China], 2 June 2016) www.court.gov.cn/fabu-xiangqing-21651.html, accessed 12 April 2019.

[4] '中国环境资源审判（白皮书）[China Environmental Resources Trial (White Paper)]' (中华人民共和国最高人民法院 [The Supreme People's Court of the People's Republic of China], 27 July 2016), 24.

energy enterprises.[5] If core cases with the 'deliberate framing of the arguments or judgment in climate change terms' have not emerged in China, 'litigation with no specific climate change framing but implications for mitigation or adaptation' may have already appeared considering the growing judicial practices of air pollution PILs in Chinese courts. What are the legal hurdles faced by 'core CCL' in the context of China? Could Chinese current air pollution PILs provide potential avenues for 'core CCL' cases to emerge in China? To answer these questions, an analysis of the Chinese legal context is first needed.

In global practices of CCL, holding the governments responsible for their misfeasance or nonfeasance in climate change is generally regarded as a convenient way to claim the climate-related damage. However, in China's context, where the authoritarian regime has been assured by law, the scenario obviously changes, mainly due to the following causes.

14.1.1 Governmental Climate-Related Duties Specified by Policy Documents Are Not Actionable

China is more willing to promulgate policies in response to climate change than drafting laws. Hence, the government's duties directly related to responding to climate change are all specified in government policy documents. Since 1992, China began to take measures on energy conservation and green development, especially by promoting the development of clean energy, the so-called low-carbon economy. From 1992 to 2002, China participated in several international climate change negotiations. As the Chinese government believed that the implementation of strict measures would be at the expense of the country's economic development, the country held a suspicious and cautious attitude when it came to establishing the corresponding climate change mechanisms.[6]

In 2007, the National Development and Reform Commission (NDRC) formulated the *National Climate Change Program* to address the importance of green technology, clean production and promoting environmental awareness among people. Ever since the *2009 United Nations Climate Change Conference* in Copenhagen, China has started to publish

[5] The team has conducted an empirical study based on keyword searching in China Judgements Online. See Yue Zhao et al., 'Prospects for Climate Change Litigation in China' (2019) 8(2)*Transnational Environmental Law* 349–377.

[6] See 肖兰兰 [Xiao Lanlan], '中国在国际气候谈判中的身份定位及其对国际气候制度的建构 [Changes of Identity of Chinain the International Climate Talks and Its Role in Constructing Climate Regime]' (2013) 2太平洋学报 [*Pacific Journal*] 69.

its *Annual Report on Policies and Actions to Combat Climate Change*. This report mainly focuses on China's move towards a low carbon economy. According to the *13th Five-Year Plan of Ecological Environmental Protection of China*, by 2020, the target unit of carbon dioxide emissions from GDP will fall by 18 per cent compared to 2015, and the total amount of carbon emissions will be effectively managed. These policy documents, which are binding on the government, clearly defined and distributed the climate change–related administrative duties and competencies. However, these policy documents can hardly be the basis of administrative CCL according to Chinese law. In keeping with the Administrative Procedure Law, the jurisdiction of administrative proceedings in China is limited to 'specific administrative acts', which are not aimed at a certain person and can be applied repeatedly.[7] However, 'abstract administrative acts', which comprise governmental policy-making, its general implementation, and so forth, are usually not actionable.[8] In fact, instead of judges, it is the government per se that enjoys the power to review the lawfulness of these policies and supervise their proper implementation.

14.1.2 Subordinate Role of Chinese Courts to the Government

Another critical legal precondition for the emergence of administrative CCL in the United States is the independence of courts and judges. Lawsuits brought in countries where governments have given express priority to development, such as Pakistan and in countries where governments are actively addressing climate change, such as the Netherlands, Sweden, and Switzerland, demonstrated that this sometimes means using the courts to push for concrete action. In these countries, the judges are actually partaking in judicial activism when invoking people's environmental rights as fundamental rights or ordering the administrative agencies to include carbon dioxide into the list of pollutants.

In China, a certain degree of judicial activism does exist. However, the definition of such activism is very different. In the United States, for example, judicial activism is based on its judicial independence that is safeguarded by the separation of powers. It often represents a legitimate

[7] See 郝明金 [Hao Mingjin], '论可诉性是行政行为的本质属性 [Suability Is an Essential Characteristic of the Administrative Act]' (2006) 3, 法学论坛 [*Legal Forum*] 77.

[8] Article 13 of the Administrative Procedure Law specifies that 'decisions and orders with general binding force formulated and announced by administrative organs' are not judiciable.

form of judicial review of the executive and legislative actions of the government. In China, where judges always refrain from judging creatively, lest they are seen as legislating, judicial activism is usually understood as a way to help realize state policy goals, which is a form of assuming the 'judicial administrative competence' of People's Courts.[9] Judges are deemed responsible for adjudicating according to the public policy addressing climate change.

Important institutional arrangements exist behind this relatively weak role of judiciaries. As stronger judicial power would contradict the People's Congress system of the Chinese Constitution, judicial power is under strict restriction in China.[10] This explains the reasons underlying the rejection by the courts of direct application of international law, as well as the absence of judicial review systems over the so-called abstract administrative acts. If the courts could directly apply all treaty provisions that are binding upon China or review the legality of governmental policies formulated based on relevant legislation, the courts would be conferred a stronger position in relation to the Peoples' Congress.[11] In this context, it would be unrealistic to count on the courts to adjudicate against the government when the law has not prescribed its duties in reducing the GHG emission. As Rachel Stern has correctly pointed out, Chinese judges are 'rule-interpreting bureaucrats' other than 'values-driven lawmakers'.[12]

14.2 PIL on Air Pollution and Climate Change Litigation

Despite the limited power of Chinese courts and hence, limited feasibility of CCL holding the government responsible for climate change, tort-based CCL directly targeting carbon emitters is, however, more promising in China's context. It can be argued that tort-based PIL offers the most strategic approach to halt environmental damage caused by air

[9] See 李清伟 [Li Qingwen], '司法克制抑或司法能动 – 兼论公共政策导向下的中国司法能动 [Judicial Restraint or Judicial Initiative – On China's Judicial Initiative under the Guidance of Public Policy]' (2012) 3法商研究 [*Studies in Law and Business*] 85.

[10] See 顾培东 [Gu Peidong], '能动司法若干问题研究 [Research on Several Issues of Judicial Activism]' (2010) 4 中国法学 [*China Legal Science*] 5.

[11] See 余军, 张文 [Yu Jun and Zhang Wen], '行政规范性文件司法审查权的时效性考察 [Timeliness of Judicial Review Right of Administrative Normative Documents]' (2016) 2, 法学研究 [*Chinese Journal of Law*] 42.

[12] Rachel E. Stern, *Environmental Litigation in China: A Study in Political Ambivalence* (New York: Cambridge University Press, 2013) 2.

pollution and climate change, as well as obtain damages for pollution victims.

Conventional air pollutants and GHGs may directly cause damage to public interests and indirectly do harm to human health and property. More specifically, although carbon dioxide is non-toxic and harmless, excessive emissions of carbon dioxide into the atmosphere contribute to the greenhouse effect, leading to climate change and related extreme climate disasters, such as sea-level rise and ocean acidification. Consequently, human lives and personal/public properties will be jeopardized. Similarly in the case of air pollution, injuries to human health and damage to personal/public properties are the indirect effects of air pollution. Yet damage to the atmosphere could be taken as the direct impact of air pollution and GHGs. As far as indirect damage is concerned, establishing causation between the emissions and the harm represents a big challenge. However, when it comes to the direct impact, the establishment of the causal link might be much easier. In this regard, instead of using tort law to advance claims, public nuisance may be a more tactical approach for litigation involving large-scale environmental damage.

Since the atmospheric environment represents a common good, direct damage due to air pollutants and GHGs should fall within the scope of environmental PIL. How would current Chinese tort-based air pollution PIL benefit potential CCL in the legal context of China? To answer this question, the regulatory context should first be clarified before analyzing the complex relationship between air pollution and GHGs.

14.2.1 GHGs and Air Pollutants Are Regulated Under Different Frameworks

Chinese environmental legislations and jurisdictions mainly focus on 'pollution control'. In the field of protection of the atmospheric environment, the Chinese environmental administrative authority (formerly Ministry of Environmental Protection [MEP]) controls the emission of air pollutants under a relatively well-developed legal framework.[13] Chapter 8 of China's Tort Liability Law, titled 'Tort Liability of Environmental Pollution', stipulates, 'Polluters should bear tort liability

13 The *Law of the People's Republic of China on the Prevention and Control of Atmospheric Pollution* (29 August 1995) has stipulated the management duties of the related environmental protection administrations, such as establishing the central and local environmental standards and discharging standards.

for damage caused by environmental pollution.' It thus limits the cause of environmental tort litigations to pollutions. According to the Law on the prevention and control of air pollution (revised in 2015), 'in order to prevent and control the air pollution . . .the synergistic control of particulate matter, sulfur dioxide, nitrogen oxides, volatile organic compounds, ammonia and other atmospheric pollutants and GHGs should be carried out' (article 2). Curiously, instead of giving a broad definition, Chinese legislation chose to follow the 'list method', which is less flexible, but clearer and more enforceable. Therefore, GHGs are explicitly excluded from the list of pollutants. In this context, while PIL cases on air pollution are emerging in China, the emission of GHGs and the emission of other air pollutants are nonetheless regulated differently. This hinders the immediate emergence of PIL on climate change.

14.2.2 Interactions between the Air and Climate Pollutants

Air pollutants and GHGs are both mainly the by-products of fossil fuel combustion. The burning of coal and other fossil fuels discharges both air pollutants (such as fine particles, sulfur dioxide, and nitrogen oxide) and 'climate pollutants' (such as carbon dioxide and black carbon). Air pollutants and climate pollutants are closely related and may interreact under certain circumstances. On one hand, global warming will affect air pollution and aggravate the impacts of air pollution on human health and ecological systems. On the other hand, air pollution could also contribute to global warming effects. For instance, in the case of high radiation intensity and high temperatures, nitrogen oxide and volatile organic compounds in the air will generate ozone, methanol, acetaldehyde, and other secondary pollutants through a series of photochemical reactions. Ozone is the major cause of air pollution in China, especially during the summer, and a short-lived climate pollutant that contributes to global warming.[14]

Because of the homologous relationship between air and climate pollutants, regulatory control over air pollutant emissions often leads to GHG emission reductions. Likewise, regulatory measures to reduce GHG emissions will also limit the release of air pollutants. From this perspective, pollutant emission reduction driven by tort-based air pollution PIL will also reduce carbon emissions to some extent. Therefore, the

[14] Both black carbon and methane are dangerous air and climate pollutants, with various detrimental impacts on human health, agriculture, and ecosystems.

current tort-based air pollution PIL may pursue the same objectives as that of CCL, and meaningfully involve the courts in China's transition towards low-carbon development. If carbon dioxide could be defined as an air pollutant and even brought into the track of coordinated control of air pollutants, PIL on air pollution may even become the direct path for CCL in China.

GHGs are not defined as air pollutants in the *Law on Air Pollution Prevention and Control*. However, Article 2 explicitly states, 'air pollutants and greenhouse gases shall be controlled in a coordinated way'. Unfortunately, China has yet to officially plan for such coordinated control of greenhouse gases and air pollutants to date.

The reasons for this regulatory inaction are strongly related to China's institutional arrangements for the regulation of environmental pollution and climate change. For a long time, the control of industrial discharge of pollutants was the main competence of the former Ministry of Environmental Protection (MEP), while the regulation of GHGs emission reduction and overall planning of response measures involving climate change were under the administration of the National Development and Reform Commission (NDRC).[15] The main functions of NDRC include the formulation of comprehensive economic and social development policies and the implementation of economic reform policies. As the 'designated national authorities' of China to address climate change, NDRC's main function was to authorize Clean Development Mechanism (CDM) projects, which generate certified emission reductions (CERs) that could be traded in emission transactions. Therefore, NDRC is more of a carbon economic-oriented department than a GHG emissions regulator when compared with MEP. In this context, there was no reason for the NDRC to include carbon dioxide on the list of air pollutants that were under the control of the former MEP and represented the environmental public interest instead of the economic growth goals of the country. It is thus clear that, in China, GHG emission reduction has been regarded as an economic development issue but not as an environmental issue.[16]

[15] Before that, the response to climate change was merely considered as a scientific question, as the main competent administrative authority related to climate change was the Ministry of Science and Technology. See Pu Wang, Lei Liu, and Tong Wu, 'A Review of China's Climate Governance: State, Market and Civil Society' (2018) 18(5) *Climate Policy* 664.

[16] In the Chinese environmental political terms, 'low-carbon economy' and 'energy saving and emission reduction' appears repeatedly. 'Low-carbon economy': through the

Due to this disadvantageous arrangement for the effective and coordinated control of GHGs and air pollutants, the economic interests represented by NDRC have been often more easily embodied in Chinese environmental legislation, while the environmental interests to reduce GHG emissions were usually neglected.

However, this situation may change following a major institutional reform of the Chinese central government in 2018. According to the *Program for Institutional Reform of the State Council* adopted on the first meeting of the Thirteenth National People's Congress, the Ministry of Ecology and Environment (MEE) was established to integrate the competence of the former MEP and the relevant functions of other six ministries.[17] As a result, the new MEE has achieved 'five coordinations', including the coordination of the 'carbon monoxide and carbon dioxide'.[18] Therefore, the government has overcome one of the major institutional obstacles of coordinating control of air pollutants and GHG emission reductions.

14.2.3 Counteractions between the Reduction of Conventional Air Pollutants and GHG Emissions

The synchronization effect of air pollution and GHGs control is not absolute. First, studies have shown that air pollution may reduce the direct amount of sunlight that reaches the ground. The pollutants discharged by mineral fuel combustion, such as black carbon aerosol and other atmospheric aerosols, are a type of short-lived climate pollutant. These pollutants may directly affect the radiation from the earth-atmosphere system

guidance of the system and technical innovation, under the premise that no economic growth is impaired, the input of high carbon energy in the production is decreased. Therefore, the direct consequence of 'low-carbon economy' is the reduction of pollutant emissions. However, the carbon dioxide emission reduction is only a by-product of Chinese 'low-carbon economy', and not the direct goal positively pursued by the 'low-carbon economy' in the practices. For a long time, the Chinese pollutant control policy and the policies and measures coping with climate change have not been arranged in general.

[17] See 环境保护'杂志编辑部 [*Environmental Protection* Magazine Editorial Department], '组建生态环境部：'大部制'带来'大环保' [Establishment of the Ministry of Ecology and Environment: "Big Ministry System" Brings "Big Environmental Protection"]'(2018)3 环境保护 [*Environmental Protection*] 2.

[18] '环保部部长：生态环境部将实现'五个打通' [Minister of the Ministry of Environmental Protection: The Ministry of Ecology and Environment Will Realize "Five Breakthroughs"]' 中国新闻网 [*China News*] (China, 17 March 2018), www.chinanews.com/gn/2018/03-17/8470030.shtml, accessed 12 April 2019.

by scattering or absorbing solar radiation, and by absorbing and emitting infrared radiation. At the same time, aerosol plays the role of a cloud condensation nucleus. So, the density of the cloud droplet increases, while the average radius of the cloud droplet decreases and the sun reflection of the cloud increases. As the cloud life is extended, the impact of climate warming might be alleviated. In this regard, the emission reduction of air pollutants does not necessarily slow down global climate warming; on the contrary, it may even accelerate climate change.

Second, from the regulatory perspective, as mentioned previously, since the coordinated control of GHGs and air pollutants has not been planned, some measures aimed at improving air quality are in fact unfavourable for coping with climate change. For example, the Chinese government promotes limestone-gypsum wet desulphurization and seawater desulfurization as important air pollution reduction measures. However, more carbon dioxide will be released when flue gas sulphur dioxide is purified and absorbed. Besides, flue gas desulfurization consumes energy, which will undoubtedly increase GHG emissions.[19] Therefore, the air pollutant emission reduction and GHG emission reduction are not positively correlated. Thus the emission reduction promoted by air pollution PIL does not necessarily limit GHG emissions. To this respect, it is difficult for air pollution PIL to directly become the path for CCL.

14.2.4 Overview of Potential Applicability of PIL on Air Pollution for Climate Change Litigation

Despite the counteractions between air and climate pollutants, air pollution PIL arguably provides certain experience and even creates certain legal preconditions for future CCL in China. Being 'diffuse and disparate in origin, lagged and latticed in effect',[20] the emissions of both air and climate pollutants may not be easily accepted by courts as a reasonable cause of harmful activity. Whether it concerns CCL or PIL on air pollution, legal hurdles including proving causation, injury, and determining remedies are all important challenges for the claimants. Undoubtedly, the

[19] See 王金南，宁淼，严刚等 [Wang Jinnan, Ning Miao, Yan Gang, et al.], '实施气候友好的大气污染防治战略 [Implementing Climate-Friendly Strategy for Air Pollution Prevention and Control]' (2010) 10中国软科学 [*China Soft Science*] 28.

[20] Douglas A. Kysar, 'What Climate Change Can Do about Tort Law' (2010) 41(1) *Environmental Law* 42, 4.

successful settlement of this problem by tort-based PIL on air pollution will provide an important template for future Chinese CCL.

First, establishing causal relationship is a big challenge for both CCL and PIL on air pollution. In terms of the space dimension, atmospheric pollutants diffuse in nature are usually discharged by stationary emissions. Yet, along with the flowing air, the impacts could spread to surrounding areas, and in the case of climate pollutants, even to a biblical magnitude across the globe. Then, in terms of the time dimension, air pollution and climate change both result from the accumulation of minor, diffuse activities into a regional or global environmental problem. It is important to note that this accumulative impact could lie dormant for years. Since air has certain self-cleaning capacities, the short-time and unorganized discharge will not immediately cause damage to the atmospheric environment or indirectly to human health. Only large-scale and long-time discharge will finally cause air pollution. This 'dormant effect' may be more radical with GHG emissions. The 'long-lived climate pollutants' headed by carbon dioxide may survive for a hundred years in the atmosphere.[21] Such a long latent period means that the accumulation of a particular discharge may show effects even after the emitter has already disappeared. Lastly, in terms of the substance dimension, single pollutants neither cause air pollution nor climate change. Six major GHGs regulated by the Kyoto Protocol are carbon dioxide, methane, nitrous oxide, hydrofluorocarbon, perfluorocarbon, and sulfur hexafluoride. Yet this list is far from being exhaustive since vapor and ozone, for example, are also recognized as GHGs. It is the same with air pollutants. Thus, since the causal link is hard to establish, it is difficult to identify any actor or actors as particularly responsible for the damage in tort-based PIL on air pollution and CCL. However, current tort-based air pollution PIL cases may provide important experiences for future CCL.

Second, due to the same diffusive, latent, and complex nature of the damage arising from air pollutants and GHG emissions, the spatial scale and the extent of damage caused by air pollution and climate change are difficult to identify. Another challenging question that judges face is deciding what an appropriate remedy would be, given that it is extremely difficult and costly to reinstate the environment to the conditions it would have been in had the air pollution or climate change not occurred.

[21] See 黄婧 [Huang Jing], '国际温室气体减排责任分担机制研究 [Research on Responsibility Sharing Mechanism for International Greenhouse Gas Emission Reduction]' (北京：中国政法大学出版社，2014 [Bing Jing: China University of Political Science and Law Press, 2014]) 137.

Traditional civil remedies for environmental infringement include the cessation of infringement, eliminating the hazard, remediation, or recovery to the original state and monetary compensation. In practice, several remedies are usually applied in a combined way. Cessation of infringement or eliminating the hazard in question often means injunctive relief to stop or reduce the discharge of pollutants. Yet neither remedy could compensate the damage that has already been caused by the relevant emissions. Contrastingly, ordering the defendant to take measures to achieve 'recovery' to the original state and the award of monetary compensation could fill the gap by ordering the polluters to pay for the damage or even repair it, whenever possible. Therefore, how Chinese courts determine the damage of air pollution and corresponding remedies in tort-based air pollution PIL provides important insights into the future of potential CCL in China.

14.3 Empirical Analysis of Tort-Based Air Pollution PIL

Based on keyword searches for tort-based air pollution PIL cases from September 2015 to May 2018 in the database *China Judgments Online*, we collected ten total judicial cases heard by the Chinese courts at all levels.[22]

14.3.1 Overview

With regard to outcomes, the courts dismissed two out of ten cases (one filed by an enterprise and another by an individual) for failing to meet standing requirements. The other eight cases were all filed by eligible plaintiffs. In one case, the defendant had corrected its behaviour, under the supervision of the environmental protection authority, causing the plaintiff to withdraw the lawsuit. Three cases involved the determination of the jurisdiction of courts, while two other cases concerned the court's recognition of reconciliation agreements reached by the plaintiffs and the defendants. In the last two cases, the courts decided in favour of the plaintiff.

In summary, in five cases, the plaintiffs achieved their objectives due to the defendant's rectification, the reconciliation agreement, or the

[22] '中国裁判文书网 [China Judgements Online]', http://wenshu.court.gov.cn/, accessed 12 April 2019.

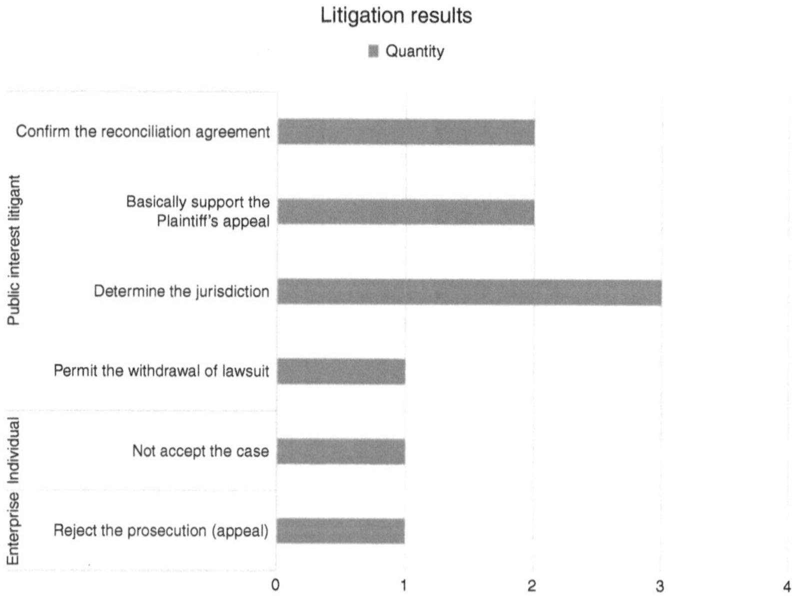

Figure 14.1 Tort-based air pollution PIL cases (September 2015–May 2018)

explicit support by the courts. In the other five cases, the claimant's petitions were rejected, challenged mainly by procedural hurdles including the threshold requirement of standing and a jurisdiction problem.

14.3.2 The Plaintiff and the Defendant

In 2012, modifications to the *Civil Procedure Law* (CPL) led to a breakthrough for tort-based PIL in China. Two years later, the *Environmental Protection Law* (EPL) clarified the standing of Chinese ENGOs to bring cases.[23] In 2015, Chinese prosecutors became the only

[23] *Environmental Protection Law of the People's Republic of China, art. 58 (24 April 2014),* states that 'with regard to the environmental pollution, ecological destruction and damage of social public interests, the social organization which meets the following conditions may lodge a lawsuit to the people's court: (1) it is registered in the civil affairs department of the people's government at the level of city divided into districts and above according to the law; (2) it has been specialized in the environmental protection public interest activities for more than five years consecutively, without any law-breaking record. If the social organization meeting the foregoing regulations lodges a lawsuit to the people's court, the people's court shall accept the case pursuant to the law. The social

other eligible plaintiffs for tort-based PIL as a result of the pilot project initiated by the Standing Committee of the National People's Congress of China in nine provinces.[24] Two years later, amendments to the CPL finally crystallized the standing of both ENGOs and public prosecutors in tort-based PIL:[25] public prosecutors can bring a lawsuit in the absence of the petition of eligible ENGOs. The CPL also specifies that public prosecutors can support the ENGOs, while the lawsuit is filed by the ENGOs. In other words, although both public prosecutors and ENGOs have legal standing to bring tort-based PIL, ENGOs are prioritized.

Our empirical study reveals that ENGOs are the foremost claimant in bringing tort-based air pollution PIL. Among eight cases, six of them were filed by ENGOs and only two of them were filed by Chinese procuratorates. It is thus clear that ENGOs play a very important role in filing PIL cases. Two cases in which the procuratorate acted as the Plaintiff were filed in December 2016 (pilot period) and December 2017 (after the CPL was modified).

In eight out of ten cases, enterprises were the defendants, including two petrochemical companies, one motor vehicle parts producer and seller, and five traditional manufacturers of electrical products, building materials, parts of means of transportation, environmental protection equipment, and glass. In addition, one case was filed against an individual who incinerates hazardous materials and one case was filed against a cultivation cooperative, an individual, and a state-owned forestry station. It is thus clear that in the judicial practices of tort-based PIL on air pollution, enterprises, especially petrochemical industrial enterprises and

organization that lodges the lawsuit shall not seek any economic benefits through the lawsuit.'

24 The Standing Committee of the Twelfth National People's Congress, 'The Decision on Authorizing the Supreme People's Procuratorate to Carry out the Pilot Work of Public Interest Litigation in Some Regions', 1 July 2015.

25 This is subject to *Civil Procedure Law of the People's Republic of China, art. 55 paragraph 2 (9 April 1991)*, which states that 'during the performance of responsibilities, if the people's procuratorate discovers the destruction of ecological environment and resources protection, infringement on the lawful rights and interests of many consumers in the food and drug field, and other behaviors which impair the social public interests, the people's procuratorate may lodge a lawsuit to the people's court, provided that there is no organ or organization specified in the foregoing paragraph, or the organ and organization specified in the foregoing paragraph do not lodge any lawsuit. If the organ or organization specified in the foregoing paragraph lodges a lawsuit, the people's procuratorate may support the prosecution.'

traditional manufacturing enterprises, have a higher risk of prosecution compared to individuals.

Moreover, in these tort-based air pollution PIL cases, the targeted polluters are usually enterprises that failed to take corrective actions after being repeatedly punished for excessive discharge or discharges without permits.

14.3.3 Targeted Pollution Activities

Apart from two cases where the specific pollution activities were not mentioned, the other eight cases focused on various pollution activities. First, the most common pollution activity is the industrial discharge of air pollutants. Among five relevant cases, three of them involved the 'excessive discharge' of industrial pollutants (i.e., discharge in levels exceeding environmental standards), while for the other two cases, no mention has been made of whether or not it concerned an 'excessive discharge'. Second, the discharge of pollutants without emission permits could also be subject to judicial proceedings. One case concerned an individual's direct incineration of hazardous wastes without handling the environmental protection approval formalities and another one involved a livestock farm's illegal pollutant discharge generating odorous gas. In one particular case, the defendant did not directly discharge any air pollutant, but since it's illegal production and sale of an 'annual inspection device' for cars helped the car owners circumvent environmental inspection, the enterprise was also sued.

14.3.4 Causal Relationship

To establish the causal relationship between the alleged damage and a particular emission, the application of the 'burden-shifting' doctrine has been ensured by the judicial interpretation of the Chinese Supreme Court. The Supreme People's Court issued the *Interpretation on Several Questions Concerning Applicable Law in the Adjudication of Environmental Tort Liability Dispute Cases* (Environmental Tort Interpretation-ETI) on 1 June 2015. According to Article 7, to prove that there is no causal relationship between the emission and the claimed damage, the polluter (as defendant) shall provide evidence to prove one of the following circumstances: (1) the discharged pollutant could not cause such damage; (2) the discharged pollutant which may cause such damage did not arrive at the place of occurrence of such damage; (3) such damage has occurred before the pollutant discharge; (4) other circumstances which may establish that there is no causal relationship between the pollution behaviour and the damage. It explicitly clarifies the defendant's burden of proof on causation. In other words, if the defendant can prove that the allegation concerns 'impossible substance', 'impossible space', or 'impossible time', then a causal relationship may not be established. However, if the defendant fails to demonstrate that there is no causal relationship between its pollutant discharging behaviour and the resulting damage, under the circumstance of no liability mitigation or exemption, the defendant should bear the corresponding civil liability.

The polluter, instead of the claimant, should provide evidence to testify that there is no causal relationship between the emission and the damage. However, is this rule applicable in affirming the causal relationship of tort-based PIL? According to our empirical study of relevant cases, the court also applied this 'burden-shifting' rule, which is often applied in private interest litigation on environmental infringement, to the tort-based PIL on air pollution.

For example, in *All-China Environment Federation* v. *Dezhou Jinghua Group Zhenhua Co., Ltd* and *Public Interest Litigant Fuzhou People's Procuratorate* v. *Shi Jun and Huang Rensheng*, the court invoked the 'burden-shifting' rule in Article 66 of the Tort Liability Law[26] and Article 7 of the ETI. As both defendants failed to prove non-existence of a causal relationship, the court decided in favour of the plaintiffs.

14.3.5 Types of Harm

In tort-based air pollution PIL, although the burden of proof for causation has shifted, the claimant still has to provide 'initial' evidence to prove that the public interest is damaged or has a major risk of being damaged in order to be treated by courts as an acceptable cause of action. To win the case, the plaintiffs should evaluate the extent of damage. Yet, different from the private tort-based litigation, where the claimant should prove that the polluter has conducted certain pollution activities and that the claimant has suffered the damage that could be traced back to the defendants' activities, in Chinese tort-based PIL on air pollution, the public interest litigant only has to prove the non-compliance of the defendant with

[26] *Tort Liability Law of the People's Republic of China, art. 66 (26 December 2009)* states that in case of any dispute due to the environmental pollution, the polluter shall bear the burden of proof for not bearing the liability or for mitigation of liability and for no causal relationship between its behaviour and damage subject to the legal provisions.

environmental regulations, whether it concerns a pollutant discharge without permission or excessive pollutant emissions. The standard of proof required to establish such existence of harmful activities differs according to different circumstances. In the latter case, the court would generally recognize the existence of harm or a major risk of harm if the plaintiff can prove that the defendant discharged pollutants without completing any environmental protection approval formalities.[27] In the case of excessive pollutant discharge, the fact that the defendant's discharge of air pollutants has exceeded relevant environmental standards represents the premise for damage caused by the defendant.[28]

Furthermore, the plaintiff's burden of proof is significantly relieved. First, the defendant, at the request of the plaintiff, is under the obligation to provide relevant information about its emission activities.[29] Second, the environmental protection authorities would usually join the case by providing the evidence to support the plaintiff, including historical administrative penalty decisions issued by the environmental protection authorities and monitoring reports provided by the environmental monitoring centre.

14.3.6 Remedies

Civil remedies for infringement of environmental laws include cessation, eliminating the hazard in question, recovery to the original state, fixing damages, and providing an apology.[30] Among the ten cases, only four have had specific remedies awarded.[31] First, when the 'cessation of

[27] Case of Civil PIL on Environmental Pollution in the lawsuit lodged by Public Interest Litigant, *Public Interest Litigant Fuzhou People's Procuratorate* v. *Shi Jun and Huang Rensheng* [2017] Gan 10 Min Chu No. 142.

[28] Case of Dispute over Environmental Pollution Liability, *All-China Environment Federation* v. *Dezhou Jinghua Group Zhenhua Co. Ltd* [2015] De Zhong Huan Gong Min Chu Zi No. 1.

[29] The Supreme People's Court Interpretation on Several Issues on Applicable Laws in the Hearing of Case of Dispute over Environmental Infringement Liability, art. 13.

[30] Interpretations of Several Issues on Applicable Laws in the Hearing of Case of Environmental Civil Public Interest Litigation of the Supreme People's Court, art. 18.

[31] In All-China Environment Federation (n 28), the remedies include 'damages', 'apology', and 'recovery to the original state'. In Fuzhou People's Procuratorate (n 27), 'damages', 'recovery to the original state', and 'elimination of hazard' were applied by the court. *All-China Environment Federation* v. *Dezhou Jinghua Group Zhenhua Co. Ltd* [2015] De Zhong Huan Gong Min Chu Zi No. 1. Remedies such as 'damages', 'recovery to the original state', 'elimination of hazard', and 'cessation of infringement' are applied in both *China Environmental Protection Foundation* v. *Sinopec Nanjing Chemical Industries Co. Ltd* [2016] Su 01 Min Chu No. 2048 and

infringement' is applied, the court will usually order the polluter to stop emitting once for all, that is to say, the complete shutdown of factories and the stop in production of pollutant-emitting devices. Otherwise, the court will require the defendant to correct its emission activities. Second, the 'elimination of hazard' mainly includes activities such as the reconstruction of environmental protection control projects, the re-establishment of a project on environmental protection and control and the harmless treatment of hazardous wastes. Third, the scope of 'monetary compensation' covers the property damage directly caused by the air pollutant discharge, as well as necessary expenses for taking reasonable measures to eliminate the pollution, prevent the deterioration and repair the ecological environment. Yet the compensation for personal damage is not included. According to our empirical studies, the ecological environmental repair expenses, the litigation fees, the environmental damage appraisal and assessment fees, the attorney fees, and all other reasonable expenses are all borne by the defendant who lost the case.

Lastly, 'recovery to the original state' refers to repairing the ecological environment to its original state and function before the damage was caused. When the damage is irreversible, which is usually the case, the court will then order the defendant to take effective measures to realize an 'alternative ecological restoration'.[32] In three out of four cases, the defendants were asked to conduct an 'alternative restoration', and in one case, the defendant was ordered by the court to restore the forestation and pay the ecological environmental repair expenses at the same time. In one case, the defendant could either repair the damage by itself or choose to pay the cost to a third party that was entrusted to do so; in two other cases, the defendant was only required to pay the ecological environmental repair expenses.

14.4 Assessing the Potential Applicability of Tort-Based Air Pollution PIL for CCL

Based on the provided analysis, current Chinese tort-based PILs on air pollution are mainly cases filed by the ENGOs or the public prosecutors against air polluters for the damage or the major risk of damage caused

China Environmental Protection Foundation v. *Dalian Petrochemical Branch of PetroChina Co. Ltd* [2016] Liao 02 Min Chu No. 267.

[32] Interpretations of the Supreme People's Court (n 30) art. 20, para 1.

by the excessive pollutant discharges or by discharges without permits. In these cases, the litigant usually requests judicial remedies such as the 'cessation of infringement', the 'elimination of hazard', the 'recovery to the original state', and the 'monetary compensation'. According to our empirical analysis, the courts have found in favour of the plaintiff in most cases.

In the following section, we consider how successful tort-based air pollution PIL offers valuable insights into the potential emergence of CCL in China. We argue that CCL is likely to follow the trajectory that air pollution PIL has taken and, in particular, tort-based air pollution PIL offers a promising pathway for addressing climate change through the Chinese courts.

14.4.1 Defendants and Targeted Activities

In terms of the types of defendants and pollution activities involved, similarities do exist between current Chinese PIL on air pollution and CCL. The defendants in tort-based PIL on air pollution (i.e., the petrochemical enterprises, the traditional manufacturing, as well as the motor vehicle producers) will also generate tremendous GHGs while generating air pollutants. Moreover, another targeted emitter, the livestock farm, will also produce much methane gas while generating odorous gas. Therefore, the 'pollutant majors' are also 'carbon majors'.

14.4.2 Damage and Causal Relationship

With regard to the causal relationship and the resulting damage, tort-based PIL on air pollution is also of significant importance for Chinese future CCL. As for the damage, although its extent still needs to be proved by the claimants, the mere existence of damage is 'self-evident', as long as it involves an excessive emission. In terms of establishing causal relationship, the 'burden-shifting' doctrine is adopted. Both rules, when applied to CCL, will significantly relieve the burden of proof on the claimant. Yet whether these rules could be applied to Chinese future CCL still depends on the development and gradual improvement of relevant environmental policies and legal systems. Thus far, no legislation in China has specifically addressed climate change.

In 2010, under the aegis of the NDRC and the MEP, a draft of the *Law on the Response to the Climate Change* was drawn up by a group of environmental jurists.[33] It clarified the duty of the government to take actions against climate change. However, thus far, it merely remains a draft that has not been the subject of serious discussion among the Chinese legislators. As a non–Annex I country with no legally binding obligation to reduce carbon emissions under the Kyoto Protocol, China's GHG emission reductions are voluntary. Therefore, in international climate negotiations, China usually refers to the principle of 'common but differentiated responsibility' under the UNFCCC to reject the proposal of a new legal agreement which distributes binding emission reduction objectives to both Annex I and non–Annex I countries under the UNFCCC.[34] This governmental reluctance to be bound by the international legal duties to reduce GHG emissions could partly explain the absence of specific climate legislation in China.[35] Since no mandatory administrative regulation framework has been carried out, the industrial reduction of GHG emissions in China still depends on the voluntary participation of carbon emitters. Therefore, any claim regarding the existence of 'excessive emission' of greenhouse gases will likely be found to be groundless. However, following the recent creation of MEE, which gives rise to the possibility to coordinate control over air and climate pollutants, the application of the aforementioned judicial rules in potential CCL could still be expected.

14.4.3 *Possible Remedies*

If tort-based claims holding emitters responsible for causing climate change are unlikely to be supported by Chinese courts in the short term, could current tort-based PIL on air pollution serve as a convenient channel to indirectly achieve the same results of CCL? Supposing the answer is yes, the remedy that will be chosen will be a decisive factor

[33] '中华人民共和国气候变化应对法 [People's Republic of China Climate Change Response Law]'.

[34] See Jin Hong et al., 'Distribution Characteristics and Prospects for CDM Projects in China' (2011), https://pdfs.semanticscholar.org/a8af/ad6b8b13105043e5f313607ff80435411lab.pdf, accessed 12 April 2019. See also Z. Chen, and H. Gong et al., 'Overview on LFG Projects in China' (2010) 30(6) *Waste Management* 1006.

[35] This absence of legal clarification makes it difficult to claim that the government has failed to fulfil their climate-related legal duties.

that affects the synergetic effect of relevant reduction triggered by litigation on air pollution. Considering that China has yet to realise the collaborative control of air pollutants and GHG emissions, some measures aimed at reducing air pollutant discharges may increase GHG emissions. Therefore, 'corrective reliefs' adopted in PIL on air pollution may not necessarily lead to the GHG emission reduction. The most effective remedy among four options is injunctive relief to stop the emission once and for all, such as the complete shutdown of factories or halting the production of pollutant-emitting devices.

14.4.4 Summary

Based on the provided analysis, the applicability of tort-based PIL on air pollution for climate change litigation may be summarized as follows.The coordinated control over GHG emissions and air pollutant discharges have not yet been realized. As a result, in cases where injunctive relief is ordered, especially where orders are given for emissions to be stopped once and for all, tort-based PIL on air pollution can serve as a convenient channel to achieve the same goal as that of CCL. However, if corrective relief is ordered, it is then difficult to evaluate whether the tort-based PIL on air pollution can become the indirect path for CCL.

If the synergy between the emission reduction of air and climate pollutants is ensured by coordinated strategies, especially by including GHGs into the list of air pollutants, tort-based PIL on air pollution can become the direct path for CCL, regardless of whether it concerns an injunctive relief or a corrective one. Therefore, climate petitioners could possibly directly initiate tort-based PIL on air pollution to vindicate climate public interests table 14.1

Table 14.1 *Tort-based air pollution PIL as a pathway for CCL*

Remedy options Coordinated control	Application of injunctive reliefs	Application of corrective reliefs
Without coordinated control of air pollutant and greenhouse gas	Indirectly applicable	Unknown applicability
With Coordinated control of air pollutant and greenhouse gas	Directly applicable	

14.5 Conclusion

CCL is an important judicial approach to promote climate change regulation the world over. Presently, although real CCL has yet been recorded in China, PIL cases on air pollution are emerging as a new judicial phenomenon. Through empirical research, this article reveals that tort-based PILs on air pollution in China are mainly filed by ENGOs or public prosecutors against the air polluters for damage or the major risk of damage caused by excessive pollutant discharges or discharges without permits. In these cases, courts usually order the following judicial remedies: 'cessation of infringement', 'elimination of hazard', 'recovery to the original state', and 'monetary compensation'.

Generated from similar sources, air and climate pollutants are both diffuse, latent, and complex in nature. Tort-based PIL on air pollution could therefore provide a possible channel to realize the same goal as that of CCL, despite being brought to the courts. However, the synergetic effect between the emission reduction of air and climate pollutants is not absolute, especially considering that the coordinated strategy is not yet in place. Nevertheless, how PIL cases on air pollution manage to overcome important legal hurdles faced both by air pollution claimants and climate petitioners could lend important insights into future Chinese CCL, whether it concerns the standing of eligible plaintiffs and the targeted potential defendants, the establishment of the causal relationship between a particular emission and the claimed damage, or the remedy options. It is also important to note that the synergetic control of air and climate pollutants is not the only factor in determining the potential applicability of tort-based PIL for climate concerns. Whether the judicial remedy concerns an injunctive relief or a corrective one is another variable to consider.

In conclusion, tort-based PIL on air pollution not only may offer a convenient avenue to achieve the ends of CCL, but may also become the direct path for climate change litigation in the future, when coordinated control of air pollutants and GHGs, in addition to injunctive remedies, are implemented.

INDEX